Space and Spatialization in Contemporary Music: History and Analysis, Ideas and Implementations

By Maria Anna Harley

Ph.D. Dissertation
McGill University, School of Music
1994, Montreal, Quebec, Canada

Space and Spatialization in Contemporary Music: History and Analysis, Ideas and Implementations

By Maria Anna Harley

Ph.D. Dissertation
McGill University, School of Music
1994, Montreal, Quebec, Canada

© 1994 by Maria Anna Harley
Copyright renewed © 2011 by Maja Trochimczyk

*Space and Spatialization in Contemporary Music:
History and Analysis, Ideas and Implementations*
By Maria Anna Harley

Ph.D. Dissertation McGill University, School of Music
1994, Montreal, Quebec, Canada

© 1994 by Maria Anna Harley. Copyright renewed © 2011 by Maja Trochimczyk
This volume is a publication of Moonrise Press
P.O. Box 4288, Los Angeles – Sunland, CA 91041-4288
info@moonrisepress.com | www.moonrisepress.com | moonrisepress.blogspot.com

© Copyright 2011 by Moonrise Press and the author,
Maria Anna Harley (Maja Trochimczyk)

All Rights Reserved
No part of this book may be reproduced or utilized in any form or by any means, electronic or mechanical, including photocopying and recording, or by any information storage and retrieval system, without permission in writing from the publisher.

Book design and layout by Maja Trochimczyk. Cover design by Maja Trochimczyk.

MANUFACTURED IN THE UNITED STATES OF AMERICA

LIBRARY OF CONGRESS CATALOGING DATA

TITLE: *Space and Spatialization in Contemporary Music: History and Analysis, Ideas and Implementations*
AUTOR: By Maria Anna Harley (b. 1957-), since 2001 Maja Trochimczyk

FORMAT: 21.59 cm X 27.94cm. (8.5 in. X 11 in.) P 465 pp. consisting of xvii pp. of preliminary matters + 391 pp. of text + 52 pp. of music examples, as well as 5 pp. of additional information; charts, diagrams, bibliography and index.

ISBN 978-0-9963981-6-9 (paperback)
ISBN 978-0-9963981-7-6 (eBook – PDF format)

1 2 3 4 5 6 7 8 9 10

References and Citations

Maria Anna Harley's Ph.D. Dissertation

*Space and Spatialization in Contemporary Music:
History and Analysis, Ideas and Implementations*

Bibliographical Citation Format:

Harley, Maria Anna (Maja Trochimczyk). 1994. *Space and Spatialization in Contemporary Music: History and Analysis, Ideas and Implementations.* Ph. D. Dissertation. Montreal, Quebec, Canada: McGill University, Faculty of Music. PDF Reprint. Los Angeles, California: Moonrise Press, 2011.

Publications Based on Dissertation Research

Forthcoming Books and Book Chapters:

Trochimczyk, Maja. *Henry Brant On His Music: Interviews*. Collection of conversations with the composer, 1992-2004. With essays about his music; list of works, calendarium of life, index. Forthcoming, Moonrise Press.

Trochimczyk, Maja, ed. *Górecki in Context: Essays on Music*. Essays about Henryk Mikołaj Górecki and his contemporaries; with a list of works, calendar of life, and index. Forthcoming, Moonrise Press.

Trochimczyk, Maja. "Witold Lutosławski's Concept of the Sound Plane and its Sources in French *musique concrète*," forthcoming in Maja Trochimczyk, ed., *Górecki in Context,* Moonrise Press.

Books and Book Chapters:

Trochimczyk, Maja, ed. *The Music of Louis Andriessen*. Studies and interviews with the composer, with additional texts by his Dutch collaborators: Elmer Schönberger, Frits van der Waa, and Reinbert de Leeuw. New York: Routledge, 2002.

Trochimczyk, Maja. "*Dans la Nuit:* The Themes of Night and Death in Lutosławski's Oeuvre," in *Lutosławski Studies*, Zbigniew Skowron, ed. London: Oxford University Press, 2001, 96-124.

Trochimczyk, Maja: "Dans la nuit" - motywy śmierci i nocy w twórczości Lutosławskiego" ["Dans la nuit:" The motives of night and death in the music of

Lutosławski"] in Zbigniew Skowron, ed., *Estetyka i styl twórczości Lutosławskiego"* [Aesthetics and Style in the Music of Lutosławski]. Kraków: Musica Iagellonica, 2000, 117-150. Polish translation by Zbigniew Skowron.

Harley, Maria Anna. "Canadian Identity, Deep Ecology and R. Murray Schafer's *The Princess of the Stars.*" Chapter of *Soundscape Yearbook,* vol 1. Helmi Jarviluoma and R. Murray Schafer, eds. Tampere, Finland: University of Tampere, 1998, 119-142.

Harley, Maria Anna. "The Polish School of Sonorism and its European Context," in *Crosscurrents and Counterpoints: Offerings in Honor of Bengt Hambraeus at 70,* ed. Per Broman, Nora A. Engebretsen, and Bo Alphonce. Gothenburg: University of Gothenburg, Sweden, 1998: 62-77. Reprinted in Polish as "Polski sonoryzm i jego europejski kontekst" [Polish sonorism and its European context], in *Dysonanse - Pismo muzyki współczesnej,* no. 0 (Fall 1997).

Harley, Maria Anna. "Music as Text, Musical Movement and Spatio-Temporal Features of the Musical Work," in *Musik als Text*, vol. 2. , *Proceedings of the Internationaler Kongress der Gesellschaft fur Musikforschung "Musik als Text,"* (Freiburg im Breisgau, Germany, September 1993), ed. Hermann Danuser, Berlin: Barenreiter, 1998.

Peer-reviewed Journal Articles:

Trochimczyk, Maja. "Ultra? Alter? Kontra? minimalizm Louisa Andriessena," in Polish translation in *Glissando,* no. 7 (2005).

Trochimczyk, Maja. "From Circles to Nets: on the Signification of Spatial Sound Imagery in New Music." *Computer Music Journal* 25, no. 4 (2001): 37-54. Special issue on sound in space.

Trochimczyk, Maja. "At Home with Phenomenology: Roman Ingarden's Work of Music Revisited." Chapter of Maja Trochimczyk, ed., *After Chopin: Essays in Polish Music*, Los Angeles: Polish Music Center, 2000, 91-110.

Harley, Maria Anna. "Composing in Color: Marta Ptaszynska's *Liquid Light*" in Martina Homma, ed., *Frau Musica (nova). Komponieren heute/ Composing today.* German transl. by Martina Homma. Sinzig: Studio Verlag, 2000, 307-330.

Harley, Maria Anna. "Spatiality of Sound and Stream Segregation in 20th-Century Instrumental Music." *Organized Sound* 3, no. 2 (1998): 147-166. Special issue on sound and space.

Harley, Maria Anna. "A Mystic in the Cathedral: Music, Image and Symbol in Andriessen's *Hadewijch.*" *The American Journal of Semiotics* 13, no. 1-4, (Fall 1996 [1998]): 249-275. Special issue, "Signs in Musical Hermeneutics," ed. Siglind Bruhn.

ACKNOWLEDGMENTS

This dissertation presents the results of doctoral research conducted at the Faculty of Music, McGill University (1988-1994; under the supervision of Prof. Bo Alphonce and Prof. Susan McClary). The research was begun at the Institute of Musicology, University of Warsaw, Poland (1986-1988; with Prof. Zofia Helman). This project, spanning two continents and lasting for eight years, has involved interactions with many people to whom I owe debts of gratitude. First and foremost, I would like to thank the composers whose music is the subject of my study and with whom I have discussed various issues of musical spatiality: Pierre Boulez, Henry Brant, Andrzej Dobrowolski, James Harley, Zygmunt Krauze, Cort Lippe, R. Murray Schafer, Marco Stroppa, Judith Weir, Iannis Xenakis. I am particularly grateful for the permission to use unpublished sketches and other material given by Pierre Boulez, Andrzej Dobrowolski, Zygmunt Krauze and Iannis Xenakis.

Since in the word "musicology," *music* is followed by *logos*, I would like to follow my expression of gratefulness to the composers with thanks for those who have assisted me in finding words for my thoughts and who have helped me to think in the first place: my advisers. My interest in spatial topics took shape under the guidance of Prof. Zofia Helman (my M.A. adviser, the director of the Institute of Musicology, University of Warsaw) whose wide knowledge of musicological literature (e.g. Kurth, Zuckerkandl) and friendly encouragement influenced my early efforts. However, most of the research has been conducted and the dissertation written in Montreal, under the supervision of two distinguished scholars. Prof. Bo Alphonce agreed to share in my explorations of vast realms of "space" and music; he allowed me to set up my own objectives and follow an individual schedule. Yet, he made sure that the scope of the project remained comprehensive and that I would not bypass important figures (e.g. Clifton, Varèse). As the Chair of the Department of Theory, he supported my grant applications without which my work (including travels to Paris, Toronto, and New York) would not have been possible. Finally, Prof. Alphonce discovered many factual and logical mistakes in the first draft of the text and suggested ways of correcting them. For all this, but especially for his wisdom and tolerance, I am truly grateful. Prof. Susan McClary entered the project in 1993 and guided me towards its completion with gentleness and efficiency. Her invaluable insights have helped me to produce a readable and balanced text (its weaknesses, though, are mine; advisers are not responsible for what I have missed or misrepresented). The assistance of Prof. McClary enabled me to find a way through the overabundance of the research material, as well as to focus on important issues, and to complete the dissertation on time. She suggested consultations with professors at the Faculty of Philosophy (for Chapter I) and supported my scholarly endeavours with constant encouragement and wise criticism. I hope that all students are as happy with their advisers as I am with mine.

In addition, I would like to thank the professors from outside the Faculty of Music who offered comments on the first chapter of the dissertation: Prof. Philip Buckley and Prof. Alison Laywine at the Faculty of Philosophy, McGill University, as well as Prof. Jeff Mitscherling at the Faculty of Philosophy, Guelph University. I am also grateful for the clarification of various issues offered by other professors at McGill University: Bengt Hambraeus (Faculty of Music, graduate seminar), Bruce Minorgan (Faculty of Music, Doctoral Colloquium), Steven Huebner (Faculty of Music), and Albert Bregman (Faculty of Psychology).

Dr. Martina Homma shared with me her knowledge of the German musicological and philosophical literature (e.g. Gosztonyi, Sacher); in addition, she presented me with copies of material unavailable elsewhere as well as with a package of A4 paper on which this dissertation was to have been written at the time of drastic paper shortages in Poland. Dr. Heimar Lehnert (Bochum, Germany) explained the principles of his virtual environment project while Judith Weir (England) provided me with information about British composers of spatialized music (Ferneyhough, Bryars, Musgrave, Tavener). Lise Viens graciously translated the abstract into French and, as a fellow doctoral student at McGill, shared my predicaments and preoccupations. Here, I would also like to express my appreciation to the staff of Marvin Duchow Music Library and to the staff at Interlibrary Loans at MacLennan Library, McGill University.

I gathered insights into the psychoacoustic and electroacoustic aspects of spatialization during my studies at the Faculty of Sound Recording, F. Chopin Academy of Music, Warsaw, Poland (with Prof. Krzysztof Szlifirski, my M.A. adviser, and Profs. Andrzej Rakowski, Nikodem Wolk-Laniewski, and Lech Dudzik). My awareness of, and interest in, Ingarden's aesthetics (Chapter IV) dates back to my studies with Prof. Zofia Lissa and Prof. Zofia Helman at the Institute of Musicology of the University of Warsaw (1976-1986), to whom I am thankful for stimulating my intellectual curiosity which led me to become a musicologist rather than a sound recording engineer.

Next, I would like to express my appreciation for the financial support without which this dissertation could not have been written. In 1990-1992 I was the recipient of a Doctoral Fellowship of the Social Sciences and Humanities Research Council of Canada. (Recently, the same Council awarded me a Postdoctoral Fellowship to be carried out at McGill from July 1994 to June 1996). At McGill University, I also received the Sarah Berlind Memorial Scholarship from the Faculty of Music (1988--1990), a Travel Grant from the Faculty of Graduate Studies and Research (1992), and a Travel Grant from McGill Alumni Funds, Faculty of Music (1993). However, my research trip to Paris in August 1992 could not have been possible without the assistance of Cort Lippe who arranged my stay at IRCAM and provided me with lodgings in his own home (Cort and Lena's hospitality is much appreciated).

The greatest debts of gratitude cannot be expressed in words. I owe a lot to my husband, James Harley, who has actively supported my project from the beginning and has participated in its realization through supplying me with research material (scores, recordings, books, computer maintenance), editing and proofreading drafts of the text, and disputing my "half-baked" ideas. I could rely on his love, patience and willingness to help whenever a need arose. I am thankful for Jim's loving presence by my side through all the "student" years; this text could not have been written without him. However, the dissertation is offered to two people who have witnessed my scholarly efforts from afar: my parents, Henryka and Aleksy Trochimczyk.

Copyright permissions

The dissertation contains numerous musical examples and diagrams, reproduced by permission of the copyright holders. This permission, in many cases, does not extend to include the right to microfilm the dissertation and sell its copies (for this a separate permission must be sought and appropriate fees must be paid). Chapters IV, V, VI and VII contain excerpts from my article "From point to sphere: spatial organization of sound in contemporary music (after 1950)" published in *Canadian University Music Review* 13 (© 1993), used by permission. The following list presents the sources of cited material with appropriate acknowledgements.

Chapter III

Excerpts from the following four compositions are used by permission of European American Music Distributors Corporation, sole U.S. and Canadian agent for Universal Editions, London, and Universal Editions, Vienna: Gustav Mahler *Symphony No. 2* (© 1971 Universal Edition, Vienna--London), Karlheinz Stockhausen *Gruppen für Drei Orchester* (© 1963 Universal Edition, London), Pierre Boulez *Rituel in memoriam Maderna* (© 1975 Universal Edition, London); diagrams for the spherical pavilion at the EXPO 1970 in Osaka, reproduced from Karlheinz Stockhausen's *Spiral* (© 1973 Universal Edition, London). Sketches for *Muzyka na smyczki i 4 grupy instrumentów dętych* by Andrzej Dobrowolski (1964) used by permission of the composer. Excerpt of Charles Ives's *Symphony No. 4* (© 1965 Associated Music Publishers Inc., New York) used by permission. Diagram of sound paths for Varèse's *Poème électronique* (© Fondation Le Corbusier, Paris) used by permission. Edgard Varèse's sketch for sound trajectories, reproduced by permission (from Wehmeyer's *Edgar Varèse*, © 1977 Gustav Bosse Verlag, Regensburg). Diagram from Pierre Schaeffer's *Traité des objets musicaux* used by permission: "*Traité des objets musicaux*, de Pierre Schaeffer, coll. *Pierres vives*,© Éditions du Seuil, 1966."

Chapter V

Excerpts from the following four compositions are used by permission of European American Music Distributors Corporation, sole U.S. and Canadian agent for Universal Editions, London and Universal Editions, Vienna: Béla Bartók, *Music for Strings, Percussion and Celeste* (© 1937 Universal Edition, Vienna; copyright renewed),

Luciano Berio, *Circles* (© 1961 Universal Edition, London), Karlheinz Stockhausen, *Carré* (© 1964 Universal Edition, London), Pierre Boulez, *Répons* (© 1988 Universal Edition, London).

Excerpt from Louis Andriessen's *Hoketus* (© 1991 Donemus, Amsterdam) used by permission of copyright holder, Boosey & Hawkes Ltd., London. David Schiff's diagram for Carter's *Double Concerto* (© 1983 Eulenburg Books, London) reprinted by permission. John Chowning's diagram (© 1970 John Chowning) used by permission of the author. Excerpts from *Ultimos Ritos* by John Tavener (©1972 J. & W. Chester Ltd., London) Reprinted by Permission of Chester Music New York, Inc. (ASCAP). Excerpts from *Folk Music* by Zygmunt Krauze (© 1974 PWM Edition, Kraków). Used By Permission Of The Publisher, Sole Representative U.S.A. Theodore Presser Company. Diagram from Zygmunt Krauze's *La Rivière Souterraine* (1987) used by permission of the composer. Diagrams by Jacques Lejeune from *L'Espace du Son II* (© 1991 Musiques et Recherches, Ohain, Belgium) used by permission.

Chapter VI

Excerpts from Henry Brant's *Antiphony I* (© 1968), *Millennium II* (© 1978), *Western Springs* (© 1984), *Meteor Farm* (© 1982), *Voyage Four* (© 1964), *Bran(d)t aan de Amstel* (© 1984), *500: Hidden Hemisphere* (© 1992) used by permission of the publisher, Carl Fischer Inc., New York.

Chapter VII

Excerpts from Iannis Xenakis's *Pithoprakta* (© 1967) and *Eonta* (© 1967) used by permission from the publisher, Boosey & Hawkes, London. Sketches for *Pithoprakta, Terretektorh, Nomos Gamma* reproduced by permission of Iannis Xenakis. Excerpts from Xenakis's *Terretektorh* (© 1969), *Nomos Gamma* (© 1968), *Persephassa* (© 1970), *Alax* (© 1987) used by permission from the publisher, Editions Salabert, Paris. An abridged and revised version of the text of this chapter is forthcoming as "Spatial sound movement in the instrumental music of Iannis Xenakis" in *Interface, Journal of New Music Research* vol. 23 no. 3 (August 1994). The copyright for this material has been transferred to the publisher, Swets and Zeitlinger bv, Lisse (Holland).

Chapter VIII

Excerpts from R. Murray Schafer's *North/White* (© 1980 Universal Edition [Canada], Ltd., Toronto) used by permission. Excerpts from R. Murray Schafer's *Music for Wilderness Lake* (© 1981 Arcana Editions), *Patria. The Prologue: The Princess of the Stars* (© 1986), *Third String Quartet* (© 1983), *Apocalypsis Part One: John's Vision* (© 1981), *Apocalypsis Part Two: Credo* (© 1986) used by permission of Arcana Editions, Bancroft, Ont.

LIST OF TABLES

Table		Page
I-1.	Meanings of "space" in *the Oxford English Dictionary*	21
II-1.	Boulez's taxonomy of musical spaces	93
V-1.	Classification of spatial designs	210
V-2.	Spatialization in *Répons*	237
VI-1.	Formal units in *Western Springs*	269
VIII-1.	Invocations in *Credo*	311
VIII-2.	Spatial patterns of Responses in *Credo*	312

LIST OF MUSICAL EXAMPLES AND ILLUSTRATIONS[1]

Example		Inserted after page
III-1:	"The Last Trump" in Mahler's *Symphony No. 2*; movement V, mm. 448-471.	125
III-2:	Division of the instruments into two orchestras in Ives's *Symphony No. 4*, movement II, p. 26.	128
III-3:	Sound paths for Varèse's *Poème électronique* at the Philips Pavilion at EXPO 1958, Brussels.	144
III-4:	Varèse's design of sound trajectories in space for *Poème électronique*.	144
III-5:	Poullin's diagram of four-channel system for spatial projection of sound (1955).	147
III-6:	Three-dimensional image of the sound object from Pierre Schaeffer's *Traité des objets musicaux* (1966).	147
III-7:	Spatial intervals and scale of directions on the circle in Stockhausen's "Musik in space" (1959/1961: 82).	157
III-8:	Placement of the 3 orchestras in Stockhausen's *Gruppen für drei Orchester*.	157
III-9:	Illusion of sound movement in Stockhausen's *Gruppen*, group 119.	157
III-10:	Plans for the German Pavilion (spherical) at EXPO 1970, Osaka; from Stockhausen's *Spiral* (1973).	161
III-11:	Disjunct and conjunct intervals in Boulez's *Musikdenken heute* (1963).	161

---

[1]This dissertation contains 62 pages with 93 illustrations (musical examples, diagrams, copies of compositional sketches, etc.). These pages are not numbered and are not included in the pagination of the text (chapters III, V, VI, VII, and VIII).

Example	Inserted after page
III-12: Seating plan in Boulez's *Rituel in memoriam Maderna* (1975).	161
V-1: Positions of the performers in Béla Bartók's *Music for Strings, Percussion and Celeste* (1937).	216
V-2: Antiphonal dialogue in Bartók's *Music for Strings, Percussion and Celeste*, movement IV, mm. 184-193.	216
V-3: Textural transformation in Bartók's *Music for Strings, Percussion and Celeste*, movement IV, mm. 224-232.	216
V-4: Three positions of the singer in Luciano Berio's *Circles* for female voice, harp and two percussionists (1960).	222
V-5: Seating plan in Elliott Carter's *Double Concerto* (1961) for harpsichord and piano with two chamber orchestras (from Schiff 1983).	222
V-6: Excerpt from Louis Andriessen's *Hoketus* for two groups of five instrumentalists (1975-1977), p. 5.	224
V-7: Placement of 21 instrumental groups in Zygmunt Krauze's *Folk Music* for orchestra (1972).	224
V-8: Excerpt from Krauze's *Folk Music* (1972), p. 7.	224
V-9: Placement of musicians and the public in Karlheinz Stockhausen's *Carré* for four orchestras and four mixed choirs (1959-60).	227
V-10: Fragment of Stockhausen's sketches for *Carré*.	227
V-11: Spatial patterns in *Muzyka na smyczki i 4 grupy instrumentów dętych* by Andrzej Dobrowolski (1964).	227
V-12: Extent and dimensions of virtual sound images in stereophonic sound projection systems: (a) standard image, (b) image enhanced with the spatializer.	230
V-13: Virtual sound movement in quadrophonic space (Chowning 1970).	230
V-14: Dependence of the apparent size of sound images on signal coherence and reverberation (Blauert 1983).	230

Example	Inserted after page
V-15: Two arrangements of multiple loudspeakers for Jacques Lejeune's *Messe aux oiseaux* (Lejeune 1991).	232
V-16: Projection space in Zygmunt Krauze's *La rivière souterraine* (1987)	232
V-17: Placement of performers, orchestra and loudspeakers in Pierre Boulez's *Répons* (1981-1988) for six instrumental soloists, instrumental ensemble and live electronics.	236
V-18: Excerpt from the "audio" score of *Répons*, with changes of attenuation levels for different soloists, no. 42, p. 58.	240
V-19: Excerpt from the "computer" score of *Répons* with hand-written details of frequency shifts and delay times, no. 95, p. 187.	240
V-20: Renaissance woodcut, the inspiration for Brian Ferneyhough's *Transit* for six solo voices and chamber orchestra (1975).	245
V-21: Positions of the performers in *Ultimos Ritos* by John Tavener (1972)	245
V-22: Fragment of "The descent of the Eucharist" in the second movement of *Ultimos Ritos*, p. 67.	245
VI-1: Five layers in the climax of Henry Brant's *Antiphony I* (1953/1968).	252
VI-2: Polytonal imitation in *Antiphony I*, p. 31.	252
VI-3: Arrangement of the instruments in Brant's *Millennium II* (1954).	256
VI-4: Entries of Trumpets 1-5 in *Millennium II*, p. 1-2.	256
VI-5: Sound axes in *Millennium II*, p. 54.	256
VI-6: Directional sound patterns in *Millennium II* (only in the parts of the trumpets and the trombones).	259
VI-7: Canons in horns and tubas, and in timpani in *Millennium II*, p. 28	259
VI-8: Placement of musicians in Brant's *Voyage Four* (1964).	259
VI-9: "Gamelan 6" and tuba solo in Brant's *Voyage Four* (1964), p. 10.	261

Example		Inserted after page
VI-10:	Order of events in Section 17 of Brant's *Meteor Farm* (1982)	264
VI-11:	Song No. 12 of Chorus I in *Meteor Farm*	264
VI-12:	Flute parts of Brant's *Bran(d)t aan de Amstel* (1984): (a) part for boat IV, p. 1; (b) part for boat I, p. 20	266
VI-13:	Tutti in Brant's *Western Springs* (1984), p. 96	268
VI-14:	Placement of the bands in Brant's *500: Hidden Hemisphere* (1992); (a) according to the score; (b) during the first performance.	270
VI-15:	Steel drums in *500: Hidden Hemisphere*, p. 1	270
VI-16:	Clash of different styles in *Bazaar II* from *500: Hidden Hemisphere* p. 117 (SD--ostinato, BI--waltz, BII--march, BIII--tango)	274
VI-17:	Spatial canon between 3 bands in *Trinities I*, from *500: Hidden Hemisphere*, p. 35-36	274
VII-1:	Sketch for mm. 239-250 of *Pithoprakta* by Iannis Xenakis	281
VII-2:	Mm. 238-247 of Xenakis's *Pithoprakta* (1955-56)	281
VII-3:	Placement of performers in Xenakis's *Eonta* (1963-64)	285
VII-4:	Alteration of brass timbre by movement and dynamics in mm. 72-74 of *Eonta*.	285
VII-5:	Hypothetical positions of brass instruments in m. 74 of *Eonta;* (a) if each motion spans 90°; (b) if II and III Trombone move by 120° to 180°	285
VII-6:	Resonances of brass sounds in the piano in *Eonta*: (a) Brass players seated at the right, bells directed at the ceiling, piano with 3rd pedal, mm. 143-153; (b) Brass players standing next to the piano, bells in the piano, mm. 317-318.	285
VII-7:	Excerpt from the "promenade" in *Eonta* (mm. 356-359).	285

Example	Inserted after page
VII-8: Seating plan for *Terretektorh:* (a) Xenakis's sketch of 1965; (b) final version in the score (1969), with the location of high woodwinds participating in sound rotations in mm. 125-195.	285
VII-9: Diagram of mm. 1-75 of *Terretektorh*.	285
VII-10: Xenakis's sketch of rotations in mm. 125-195.	288
VII-11: Two rotations in the woodwinds in mm. 125-146 of *Terretektorh*.	288
VII-12: Mathematical functions for logarithmic, Archimedean and hyperbolical spirals.	290
VII-13: Seating plan of Xenakis's *Nomos Gamma* (1967-68).	290
VII-14: Xenakis's sketches for Nomos Gamma: (a) table of sound material (set X); (b) sketch of alternating spatial textures in the strings.	290
VII-15: Shifting textures in the strings in mm. 296-299 of *Nomos Gamma*.	290
VII-16: Sound rotations in *Nomos Gamma,* mm. 511-513.	293
VII-17: Placement of instruments in Xenakis's *Persephassa* (1969).	293
VII-18: Semicircular movement in mm. 38-41 of *Persephassa*.	293
VII-19: Mm. 1-5 of *Persephassa*, percussions A-F in unison.	293
VII-20: Entries of 4 layers of rotations in mm. 352-362 of *Persephassa*.	293
VII-21: Diagram of all rotations, mm. 352-420 of *Persephassa*	293
VII-22: Sound planes in mm. 94-96 of Xenakis's *Alax* (1985)	298
VII-23: Twelve-part spatial canon in *Alax*, mm. 44-46.	298
VII-24: Three-part canon of brass glissandi in *Alax*, mm. 17-18.	298
VII-25: Evolution of pitch and timbre,(violins, clarinets and flutes) in m. 52 of *Alax*.	298

Example		Inserted after page
VIII-1:	Spatial sound movement in *North/White* by R. Murray Schafer (1979)	305
VIII-2:	Sounds of Masonite sheets and a quarter-tone cluster in *North/White*	305
VIII-3:	Performer movement in Schafer's *Third String Quartet* (1981), I.	305
VIII-4:	Conclusion of Schafer's *Third String Quartet* (1981), III, p. 26	305
VIII-5:	Ideal and actual performance space for Schafer's *Apocalypsis Part One: John's Vision* (1977), (a) ideal, p. ii; (b) actual, p. B.	307
VIII-6:	12 choirs in Schafer's *Apocalypsis Part Two: Credo* (1976).	307
VIII-7:	Sound rotation and spatial texture in Response VI from *Credo*	311
VIII-8:	Spatial patterns in Bass parts in Response IV from *Credo*.	314
VIII-9:	"Lapping water" in *Dawn*, from Schafer's *Music for Wilderness Lake* (1979), p. 16-17.	314
VIII-10:	Axial rotations of performers in *Dusk, Music for Wilderness Lake*.	318
VIII-11:	Chords and echoes in *Dawn, Music for Wilderness Lake*, p. 20	318
VIII-12:	Position of performers and recording crew during the first performance of *Music for Wilderness Lake*.	318
VIII-13:	Placement of the audience and peformers in Schafer's *Patria: The Prologue. The Princess of the Stars* (1981-1984); (a) Editing Unit 2: "The Dawn Light Breaks;" (b) Editing Unit 4: "Wolf's Arrival".	318
VIII-14:	Editing Unit 8: "Arrival of Dawn Birds," *The Princess of the Stars*.	318
VIII-15:	Excerpts from instrumental parts for the "Dawn Birds" sections of *The Princess of the Stars* (Editing Units 8 and 9); (a) flute, p. 37; (b) percussion, p. 42.	318
VIII-16:	Vocal echoes in Editing Unit 2 from *The Princess of the Stars*.	321
VIII-17:	Sound rotations around the lake in the conclusion of *The Princess of the Stars*, p. 83.	321

TABLE OF CONTENTS

ABSTRACTS	ii
ACKNOWLEDGEMENTS	iii
LIST OF TABLES	vii
LIST OF MUSICAL EXAMPLES AND ILLUSTRATIONS	ix

INTRODUCTION 1

    Space and time 1
    Space and spatialization 3
    The dissertation: Premises and objectives 4
    Space and music: The literature on the subject 7
    The dissertation: Summary and significance 12

PART ONE: CONCEPTS OF SPACE 17

CHAPTER I: The meaning of "space" 18

    1.1. "Space" in language 18
    1.2. Selected philosophical concepts of space 23
    1.3. Notions of space in mathematics 28
    1.4. Space-time theories in modern philosophy of science 33
    1.5. Human experience and perception of space: philosophy of life
          and phenomenology 38

CHAPTER II: A history of concepts of space in music 53

    2.1. Space without space: A history of the notion of "musical space"
          in music theory and aesthetics 55
    2.2. Space as stasis: Spatialization of time as a compositional paradigm 76
    2.3. Space as pitch: Analytical and compositional theory 90
    2.4. Change of perspective: The "musical space" of performance 108

PART TWO: SPATIALIZATION IN THEORY AND PRACTICE 116

CHAPTER III: Music in space and the idea of spatialization 117

    3.1. Music in space: a historical background 118
    3.2. Spatial simultaneity of layers: Mahler, Ives and Brant 123
    3.3. Musical objects in space: from Satie and Varèse to electroacoustics 135
    3.4. Theories of spatialization in Darmstadt: Stockhausen and Boulez 151
    3.5. Conceptual experimentation: Cage, Lucier and Schafer 169

CHAPTER IV: Spatialization and the musical work 180

    4.1. Introduction: Listening to "B-A-C-H" 180
    4.2. Listening to music in space: A psychoacoustic account 184
    4.3. Roman Ingarden's "work of music" revisited 190
    4.4. Towards a definition of spatialization 201

CHAPTER V: Spatial designs in contemporary music 207

    5.1. Classification of spatial designs 207
    5.2. Categories of mobility: Performers and audiences 215
    5.3. Spatial designs in real sound-space 222
    5.4. Selected designs in virtual sound-space 228
    5.5. Mixed designs: *Répons* by Pierre Boulez 235
    5.6. Spatial imagery and symbols 243

PART THREE: IMPLEMENTATIONS (THREE COMPOSERS) 249

CHAPTER VI: Experimental tradition in the "spatial music" of Henry Brant 250

    6.1. *Antiphony I* and the American experimental tradition 253
    6.2. New spatial effects in *Millennium II* 257
    6.3. Stylistic contrasts and collages: *Voyage Four, Meteor Farm, and Bran(d)t aan de Amstel* 260
    6.4. Symmetry and improvisation in *Western Springs* 267
    6.5. Tradition and innovation in *500: Hidden Hemisphere* 270

CHAPTER VII: Spatial sound movement in the instrumental music of Iannis Xenakis ... 279

7.1. Real and virtual motion of sound in *Pithoprakta* and *Eonta* ... 281
7.2. Spirals and circles in *Terretektorh* ... 285
7.3. Spatialization and group theory in *Nomos Gamma* ... 290
7.4. Sound rotations in *Persephassa* ... 293
7.5. Spatial canons and sound planes in *Alax* ... 296

CHAPTER VIII: Soundscapes and rituals in the music of R. Murray Schafer ... 301

8.1. Canadian soundscape in *North/White* ... 303
8.2. Movement to unity: *Third String Quartet* ... 306
8.3. Mysticism and virtual space in *Apocalypsis Part Two: Credo* ... 308
8.4. *Music for Wilderness Lake* and its soundscape ... 315
8.5. An outdoor ritual: *The Princess of the Stars* ... 319

SUMMARY AND CONCLUSIONS ... 325

BIBLIOGRAPHY ... 346

BIBLIOGRAPHY A: Space ... 347
BIBLIOGRAPHY B: Sound and Music ... 353

INTRODUCTION

Space and time

Space is experienced in time, time in space: in human experience there is no absolute space existing without time nor time without space.[1] As Alexander Gosztonyi writes in the introduction to his history of the notion of space in Western philosophy and science, space and time are interrelated, together forming the basic framework of knowing and being:

> Als psycho-somatisches Wesen ist der Mensch dem Raum und der Zeit ausgeliefert, sein Leben vollzieht sich in Dimensionen, sein Denken--vorwiegend--in Kategorien, die von Raum und Zeit bestimmt sind. Er ist gewohnt, die beiden fundamentalen Gegebenheiten seines Daseins nebeneinanderzustellen, ohne abzuklären, ob sie tatsächlich zusammengehören. Sie hängen insofern zusammen, als sie gemeinsam die quantitative Struktur der Welt bedingen. (Gosztonyi 1976: 29)

Yet both entities, space and time, are often construed as being mutually exclusive.[2] This critical dichotomy permeates much of the philosophical reflection about art, underlying for instance the classification of the arts as spatial (painting, sculpture, architecture) and temporal (music, theatre). As Johann Gottfried von Herder writes, "space cannot be time and time--space, the visible cannot be heard, the audible visualized. . . It is precisely because the arts exclude each other from the point of view of their medium, that they acquire their own domains, their own

---

[1] These words, although formulated independently, mirror Hermann Minkowski's statement from his epoch-making lecture of 1905 in which he introduced the idea of space-time: "No-one has yet observed a place except at a time, nor yet a time except at a place" (Minkowski 1905 cited in Gray 1979: 171).

[2] The diametric opposition of time and space is particularly prominent in the philosophies of Newton and Bergson. For a brief discussion of the Newtonian concepts of "absolute time" and "absolute space" existing independently of each other see Chapter I. Clear explanations of these ideas are given by Gosztonyi (1976) and van Fraassen (1985). For a discussion of absolute and relational theories of space see Grünbaum (1977).

kingdoms."[3]

The existence of this polar opposition allows for a hierarchical ordering of the two contrasted notions. As Kevin Korsyn writes (in reference to the polarity of history and theory), the oppositional structure "fosters the illusion that one side of the dichotomy might dominate, marginalize or even exclude the other" (Korsyn 1993: 469). This domination has not been illusory in critical reflection about music; time has often been assigned an unquestionable primacy. For Susanne Langer, for instance, "music makes time audible and its form and continuity sensible" (Langer 1953: 110). Similarly, Jonathan Kramer insists on defining music as a purely temporal art:

> Music unfolds in time. Time unfolds in music. . . . Music becomes meaningful in and through time. . . . If we believe in the time that exists uniquely in music, then we begin to glimpse the power of music to create, alter, distort, or even destroy time itself, not simply our experience of it.
> (Kramer 1988: 1, 5)

While Kramer believes in "the time of music," Igor Stravinsky writes that "the phenomenon of music is given to us with the sole purpose of establishing order in things, including, and particularly, the coordination between man and time" (Stravinsky 1962: 54). Not between man and space: this is the domain of the visual arts. The common assumption is that time, the domain of events and processes, is audible, while space, the realm of objects, is visible; time is the equivalent of Becoming, space--of Being.[4]

---

[3]This quote from Herder's *Kalligone. Gesammelte Werke* (vol. 22, Dresden: 1916, 18) is adopted from Lissa's article (1965). In this text, Lissa discusses Hegel's thesis (from his *Ästhetik*) that time-- not space--constitutes the most essential element of music, because the temporality of sound is co-extensive with the temporality of the listening subject and, therefore, sound may "permeate" the consciousness of the "I."

[4]The opposition of Being and Becoming is identified with the opposition of space and time by George Rochberg (Rochberg 1963: 10). According to Jonathan Kramer, Being and Becoming correspond to the two aspects of time: "I identify becoming with temporal linearity. Nonlinearity is more like being. . . . Linearity and nonlinearity are complementary forces in *all* music, although they appear in vastly different ways" (Kramer 1988: 19).

Yet, the suppressed and the marginalized are bound to return with a vengeance; a virtual explosion of interest in the spatial aspects of music took place in the 1950s and 1960s. This occurrence was contemporaneous with the proposition that the "spatialization of time" provided a basic compositional paradigm for new music (cf. Chapter II). Since that time, the interest in space has been growing steadily; a variety of concepts of musical, tonal, auditory and perceptual spaces has emerged in musicological, theoretical and compositional discourses (cf. Chapters II and III). Many composers and scholars began to construe music as inherently spatial; discussions of the true nature of this musical spatiality frequented the pages of scholarly journals.[5] Simultaneously, musical compositions themselves commenced "the conquest of space"--through spatialization.

Space and spatialization

The bi-polarity of the relationship of music and space is frequently captured by the juxtaposition of two concepts: "musical space" and "spatial music" or "music in space."[6] In order to avoid the limitations implied by such a conceptual opposition (i.e. the assumption that these terms and their designates are in an inverse or complementary relationship) a less confrontational pairing of "space" and "spatialization" is proposed in this dissertation. As I intend to demonstrate, "space" in music is, of necessity, ambiguous--denoting a multitude of often incompatible entities (cf. Chapters I-II). The semantic field of "spatialization" is narrower, relating to the

---

[5] E.g. Anthony Gilbert's response to Robert Morgan's proposal of a new notion of "musical space" (Gilbert 1981).

[6] Krzysztof Szwajgier (1973) juxtaposes "muzyka przestrzenna" (spatial music) with "przestrzen muzyczna" (musical space); Stephen Gryc (1976) writes about "musical space" and "music in space;" Marcel Bacic (1980) opposes "Klangraum" (sounding space) and "Raumklang" (spatial sound); Pierre Louet (1991) considers the dichotomy of "espace de la musique" (space of music) and "musique de l'espace" (music of space). In each case, however, the meaning of "space" is somewhat different.

musical utilization of the physical-acoustical-perceptual spatiality of sound (cf. Chapters III-VIII).

The presence of spatialization can be recognized in every situation in which spatial extensions, positions (directions and distances) of the sound sources as well as the acoustic quality of the performance space are given compositional significance. Such "spatialization" accompanies "space" as its derivative and subordinate, yet--to paraphrase Langer's dictum quoted earlier-- it is through spatialization that "space" becomes audible. Thus, the "spatial" and the "spatialized" often have identical senses. These notions may also be placed in opposition or belong to altogether different realms of reflection and experience, e.g. when "spatial" is identified with the "static" or the "visual" (mostly in reference to pitch) and "spatialized" refers to physical-technological-perceptual aspects of sound projection (as in electroacoustic music).

In this dissertation, the ramifications of the concepts of space in 20th-century music will be explored in considerable detail. The subject will not be exhausted, because its scope, that is, the abundance of "spaces" existing in current musicological, aesthetic, theoretical, psychoacoustic and musical literature, makes their full review virtually impossible. Nonetheless, main conceptual fields will be identified, their interrelationships revealed, their history traced.

The dissertation: Premises and objectives

As stated above, one of the main theses of this dissertation is the existence of a manifold of different spaces in music; an investigation of this plurality of "spaces" constitutes an important aspect of the inquiry. Moreover, the various notions of space (and spatialization) are intertwined; they form a complex network of ideas, rather than a single line of development. Different authors use the same terms (e. g. "musical space") to denote widely divergent entities; others seek recourse to an array of notions to name one phenomenon (e.g. the extrinsic, acoustic, perceptual, auditory, or sound space). The dissertation seeks to clarify this terminological confusion caused, in part, by the multiplicity of the term's meanings outside the musical domain. To this purpose, the text includes a survey of selected philosophical, psychological, physical and mathematical conceptions of space. A particular importance is attributed to the difference between the human experience of space (e.g. a natural space-consciousness, action space, lived space), and various theoretical constructs of space (e.g. absolute space, vector space, space as a set), as having vital consequences for the discourse on space in music. Finally, in reference to "spatialization," the dissertation presents a thesis that the commonly accepted opposition of "space and time" is fallacious in music if the sonorous (rather than notational) dimension is taken into account; musical sound material is essentially spatio-temporal. This thesis, grounded in phenomenological conceptions of space (Merleau-Ponty) and art (Ingarden), provides a foundation for the study of selected, distinct compositional approaches to "spatialization" in the analytical portion of the dissertation (Chapters V-VIII).

The conceptual aspects of this dissertation situate it in the domain of the history of ideas, that is, ideology, according to one of the word's senses.[7] "Space" is one of the central notions of modern music; in this paradigmatic function it resembles the idea of "absolute music"--the paradigm of the 19th century according to Carl Dahlhaus (1978/1989). "Paradigm"--a term borrowed by Dahlhaus from Thomas Kuhn's *The Structure of Scientific Revolutions*--means, for Kuhn, "universally recognized scientific achievements that for a time provide model problems and solutions to a community of practitioners" (Kuhn 1970: viii). For Dahlhaus, paradigms are "basic concepts that guide musical perception and musical thought" (Dahlhaus 1978/1989: 2). The two types of paradigms differ in that, in art, the omnipresence of an idea does not guarantee its unequivocal meaning neither does it ascertain its normative status. Hence, the universal appeal of "space" in music has not been accompanied by the development of a consensus about what exactly this term

---

[7] S.v. "ideology" in *The Oxford English Dictionary* (1989). The term refers to (sense 1a) "the science of ideas; that department of philosophy or psychology which deals with the origin and nature of ideas" or to (sense 1c) "the study of the way in which ideas are expressed in language." I hope that this dissertation will not be classified as belonging to the domain of ideology in sense 2: "ideal or abstract speculation; in a depreciatory sense, unpractical or visionary theorizing or speculation."

means.

The dissertation relies on yet another "paradigm" in the Dahlhausian sense--the notion of "the musical work." This crucial conception is borrowed from Roman Ingarden's phenomenological aesthetics of art (Ingarden 1958/1986).[8] In Ingarden's formulation, the "work of music" is a single-layered, intersubjective and intentional object with an ontological basis in the score--the work's schema which is differently complemented in each performance.[9] According to the philosopher, the musical work differs both from the score, that is the work's abstract, notational schema, and from the performance, that is its sonorous, spatio-temporal realization. The work's internal structure consists of a single stratum of sound; music in itself has no meaning, no content. Such a conception is applicable (if at all) only to "absolute," instrumental music of the Western high-art tradition, the domain of self-contained, unique musical works.[10] Therefore, Ingarden's understanding of music does not embrace all possible 'musics.'[11] This mode of thinking of music in terms of individual, separate and original compositions, significantly differs from conceiving music in terms of a process of sound-making, or as orally transmitted and variable repertory, or as a

---

[8] My use of the phenomenological method differs from that of Clifton (1983), Smith (1979), and Ferrara (1991). Clifton and Smith borrow the idea of *epoché* from Husserl's *Ideas I* (1913) and focus on descriptions of the listener's experience in "lived time" (in addition, Clifton draws from Merleau-Ponty, Smith--from Heidegger). Ferrara, critical of their work, attempts to create a form of a comprehensive "hermeneutic phenomenology of music" based on ideas from Husserl and Heidegger. None of the three authors considers consequences of Husserl's later work (ideas of *Leib, Lebenswelt*) and Ingarden's phenomenology of art.

[9] Roman Ingarden's *The Work of Music and the Problem of Its Identity*, written in 1928-1957, was published in Polish in 1958 and in English translation in 1986.

[10] For the notion of "absolute music" see Dahlhaus's *Die Idee der absoluten Musik* (1978; English translation 1989). Recently, Lydia Goehr studied the concept of the work, its genesis, and reception in *The Imaginary Museum of Musical Works. An Essay in the Philosophy of Music* (1992).

[11] Zofia Lissa criticized the social, spatial (geographic) and temporal (historical) limitations of Ingarden's phenomenological aesthetics from a Marxist perspective (Lissa 1966/1975, 1968/1975).

process of sound-making, or as orally transmitted and variable repertory, or as a social activity, or as an element in a culture.[12]

In this dissertation, "the musical work" is treated as an object that we perceive, rather than a text that we read; this emphasis on the perceptual features of music is most apparent in the study of spatialization.[13] Yet, references to the semantic and symbolic aspects of musical spatiality cannot be completely absent from a dissertation written in an era of "semiosis," "narrative" and "intertextuality."[14] For many composers, "spatialization" is a means of expression, an element in the symbolic or discursive design of their works. In these cases, the placement and movement of sound is not simply structural, it is structured to relate to various symbolic, cosmic, social and religious spaces. These aspects of space and spatialization frequently appear in the historical and analytical parts of the dissertation (cf. Chapters V-VIII).

Space and music: The literature on the subject

As a comprehensive history and detailed analysis of ideas of space in music, supported by a review of extra-musical notions of space, and based on a broad survey of musicological literature as well as my interviews with several contemporary composers and analyses of numerous spatialized compositions, this dissertation does not have a predecessor. Yet, the literature of the subject is quite extensive--as it

---

[12] For a recent vision of music as a socially conditioned art see *Music and Society. The Politics of Composition, Performance and Reception*, eds. Richard Leppert and Susan McClary (1987).

[13] Chapter IV contains a section on spatial sound perception (a brief review of the current state of knowledge); various aspects of spatialization are explored in Chapters III-VIII.

[14] The notion of "intertextuality," borrowed from the domain of literary criticism, provided a key concept for many authors presenting their work at the International Conference of the Gesellschaft für Musikforschung, *Musik als Text*, Freiburg im Breisgau, September/October 1993 (Proceedings are forthcoming).

can be seen in the bibliography of about 400 items.[15] However, many of these contributions examine one particular, and often quite narrow, aspect of the spatiality of music.[16] Papers of a larger scope range from analytical investigations of various spatial aspects of the music by one composer (e.g. Serocki studied by Davies, 1983; Carter analyzed by Bernard, 1983; Reynolds discussed by Vérin, 1991) to thorough and insightful examinations of chosen aspects of space or spatialization.[17] Many smaller articles contain either information about individual projects[18] or reflections on the new "musicalisation of space" (term from Brelet, 1967) in contemporary music. Papers of the latter category are rather general, with the scope and nature of a manifesto rather than of an in-depth study (e.g. Brelet 1967; Schnebel 1976; de la Motte-Haber 1986; Dhomont 1988).

Several collections of articles on space and music include both types of brief contributions (*Die Reihe* no. 7: "Form--Raum," 1960/1965; *Musik und Raum* ed. Thurig Bräm, 1986; *L'Espace du Son* I-II, ed. Francis Dhomont, 1988, 1991).[19]

---

[15]The bibliography is subdivided into sections: general writings on space (part A), writings on sound and music (part B). Bibliography B includes references to compositions studied (including compositions and writings by Brant, Schafer and Xenakis), as well as entries from the areas of music aesthetics, history, theory, musicology, music technology (e.g. Lehnert and Blauert 1991, Bloch et al. 1992, Schroeder 1984) and music perception (e.g. Bregman 1990, Deliège 1989, Sheeline 1982, Wenzel 1992).

[16]For instance, Kagel's "Translation-Rotation" (1960) presents an idiosyncratic approach to the spatialization of time; Purce's "La spirale dans la musique de Stockhausen" (1974) analyzes one issue in the output of one composer.

[17]To name just a few articles of considerable merit: Blaukopf's "Space in electronic music" of 1971; Kunze's "Raumvorstellungen in der Musik" of 1974; Duchez's "La représentation spatio-verticale. . ." of 1979; Bush's "On the horizontal and vertical presentation. . ." of 1985/1986; Begault's "Spatial manipulation and computers" of 1986.

[18]For instance, Chowning's discussion of his computer program for the simulation of sound movement (1970), or Clozier's description of the "Gmebaphone" sound projection system (1988).

These collections contain papers of varied scope and quality, gathered together in order to highlight the multi-faceted reality of space in contemporary music--linked to considerations of form and structure, from music notation to architecture in the 1960's (*Die Reihe*) to reflections on sound projection and perception in electro-acoustic music as well as to comments about avant-garde experiments in the 1980's (*L'Espace du Son, Musik und Raum*). In addition to articles on contemporary music, *Musik und Raum* includes a number of studies of various historical aspects of "space as the carrier of musical sound" (Binkley on medieval drama, Meyer on Haydn's concert halls, etc.).

The contributions to the general history of the 20th-century "music in space," tracing the evolution of spatialization, are few and far between: articles by Winckel (1970, 1971), Szwajgier (1973), Angerman and Barthelmes (1984), Vande Gorne (1988); books by Sacher (1985),[20] Przybylski (1984),[21] and Bayer (1987).[22] The subject of spatialization may be encountered also in general histories of 20th-century music (Watkins 1988), histories of music after 1945 (Schwartz and Godfrey 1993, Nyman 1974) or studies of the music by one composer (e.g. Stockhausen: Harvey 1975, Maconie 1976/1990). So far, only the music of Henry Brant has been thoroughly investigated from the spatial point of view (Drennan 1975); the contributions of other composers to the development of spatialization still await full review. Perhaps not surprisingly, entries on "space" and "spatialization" are conspicuously absent from major reference works, including *The New Grove's*

---

[20]In his doctoral dissertation, entitled *Musik als Theater,* Sacher puts forward the thesis that all spatialization is primarily theatrical; this supposition is disputed in Chapter IV (also in Harley 1993).

[21]This is a study of the spatialized compositions performed at the Warsaw Autumn Festival in Poland.

[22]Bayer's enigmatic notion of "espace sonore," which is, for him, the paradigm of all modern music, refers simultaneously to pitch space and acoustic space used by contemporary composers, from Schoenberg to Cage. Thus, it embraces both "musical space" and "spatial music."

contributions of other composers to the development of spatialization still await full review. Perhaps not surprisingly, entries on "space" and "spatialization" are conspicuously absent from major reference works, including *The New Grove's Dictionary of Music and Musicians* and *Musik in Geschichte und Gegenwart*.[23]

Numerous writings about space in music present one, particular conception of a "musical space," and therefore belong to the subject of this dissertation, rather than the "literature on the subject" (cf. Chapter II). Such is the case with North American doctoral dissertations in musicology that refer to "space" in their titles: by Lippman (1952--"space"), McDermott (1966--"musical space"), Judkins (1988--"virtual space") and Stofft (1975--"space"). The most comprehensive of these studies, and the most valuable as a scholarly text, source of data and inspiration for further research, is the earliest one--by Edward Lippman (cf. Chapter II). "Space" or "musical space" is also the concern of doctoral students in other disciplines (e.g. in experimental psychology, Monahan 1984).

Among many concepts of a phenomenal musical space (discussed in Chapter II), Thomas Clifton's (1983) is best known in North America, while Ernst Kurth's (1930) has been the most influential in Europe.[24] The identification of space with stasis or with pitch has been a common phenomenon in contemporary musical-theoretical thinking.[25] Compositional discussions of space and spatialization range from comprehensive studies (e.g. Boulez 1963/1971), to brief reflections (e.g. Boulez and Nattiez 1991). Stockhausen's "Musik im Raum" (Stockhausen 1959/1961) best exemplifies the former category, including a survey (and an ultimate rejection) of all

---

[23]Jonathan Kramer has noticed a similar deficiency in respect to the notion of time, deploring that "musical time has not been widely recognized as an independent field of study" (Kramer 1988: 1).

[24]However, its reception has been limited to the community of musicologists and philosophers, not composers.

[25]For "stasis" see Chapter II, section 2 (e.g. Adorno 1948, Ligeti 1960, Rochberg 1963, McDermott 1966); for "pitch" see section 3 of the same Chapter (e.g. Boulez 1963, Morris 1987).

previous explorations of musical spatiality, from Gabrieli to Mahler, and a postulate of the serialization of spatial direction--envisioned as a new solution to the problem of music in space. I discuss Stockhausen's article in Chapter III.

In addition, the dissertation presents (in Chapter IV) and the bibliography includes chosen investigations into spatial sound perception[26] and spatial representations of sound.[27] The interest in spatial sound perception is particularly strong in the electroacoustic community, which is, perhaps, due to the nature of the medium (composing directly in sound). In these writings, topics of technology, psychoacoustics and aesthetics are intertwined, from the early studies of sound projection (Poullin 1955, Meyer-Eppler 1955) through general discussions of the nature of space in electroacoustic music (Kaegi 1967, Blaukopf 1971, Stroppa 1991), to compositional considerations of individual issues or projects (e.g. Rzewski 1968, Chowning 1971; Stockhausen 1963-1989; Reynolds 1978; Leitner 1986; Kupper 1988).

At this point, it is important to add that some results of my doctoral research have already been published in an article, "From point to sphere: spatial organization of sound in contemporary music (after 1950)" in *Canadian University Music Review* (vol. 13, 1993, pp. 123-144). Four other publications are forthcoming: (1) "Into the city, onto the lake: site-specific music of Henry Brant and R. Murray Schafer" in *Contemporary Music Review*, vol. "Site-specific music," ed. Lawrence Casserley; (2) "Spatial sound movement in the instrumental music of Iannis Xenakis" in *Interface. Journal of New Music Research* (vol. 23 no. 3, August 1994); (3) "Music as text, musical movement and spatio-temporal features of the musical work" in the

---

[26]Blauert's study of spatial hearing (Blauert 1974/1983) and Bregman's theory of auditory scene analysis (Bregman 1990) are chosen here as basic references in the domain of psychoacoustics.

[27]For instance, the three-dimensional image of the "sound object" in Pierre Schaeffer's *Traité des objects musicaux* (1966), the multi-dimensional models of pitch designed by Roger Shephard (1982) or the two-dimensional "timbre space" by David Wessel (1979).

May 1992)," in *Circuit. Revue Nord-Americaine de Musique du XXe Siècle*, special issue about Iannis Xenakis, 1994.[28]

The dissertation: Summary and significance

The dissertation is divided into three parts, examining the history and analysis of the concepts of space (Part I), the history and analysis of "music in space," that is, of "spatialization" (Part II), and three distinct compositional approaches to spatialized music (of Henry Brant, Iannis Xenakis and R. Murray Schafer; Part III).

The presentation of the multiplicity of meanings of the term "space" is contained in the first chapter of the dissertation, commencing with a survey of chosen classical philosophical conceptions of space. A brief examination of the plurality of spaces in mathematics is followed by an inquiry into the term's current ambivalence in the philosophy of physics--the debate between absolutists believing in the objective existence of space as such, and relationalists considering the relational structure between objects as the only existing aspect of "space." The subsequent section of the first chapter contains an investigation into selected aspects of human experience and the perception of space. The emphasis is placed on the phenomenologically crucial

---

[28]I have also presented papers relating to the dissertation at national and international conferences: (1) "The 'work of music' revisited: Roman Ingarden's phenomenological aesthetics" at the Annual Conference of the Canadian University Music Society (Calgary, June 1994); (2) "American experimental tradition re-examined: Henry Brant's 'spatial music'" at the 1994 Conference of the Sonneck Society for American Music (Worcester, Massachusetts, April 1994); (3) "On reality, unreality, and virtual reality in music: two dialogues with a commentary" at the International Conference on Acoustic Ecology, *The Tuning of the World* (Banff, Alberta, August 1993); (4) "On the use(ful/less)ness of analysis for the performance of 20th-century music (Xenakis, Bartók, Stravinsky)" at the 1993 Conference of the Canadian University Music Society (Ottawa, May/June 1993); (5) "The technique of spatial sound movement in the instrumental music of Iannis Xenakis" at the Fall Meeting of the New York State--St. Lawrence Chapter of the AMS (Albany, October 1992); (6) "The concept of 'musical space' in music theory and aesthetics (1930s-1980s)" at the 12th Congress of the International Association for Empirical Aesthetics (Berlin, July 1992).

difference between the perception and the models of space. Here, the notions of "Lebenswelt" (Husserl) and "incarnate subjectivity" (Merleau-Ponty") are of particular importance.

An outline history of the concept of "space" in musicological literature constitutes Chapter II.[29] Firstly, I examine different theories of the 'internal' musical or tonal space which manifests itself in the perceptual experience of music. The second section of Chapter III is devoted to the concept of musical spatiality postulated as a paradigm for the new music of the 1960's (space as stasis, spatialization of time). The identification of space with pitch is the subject of section 2.3. Here, I also present chosen mathematical concepts of space used in the research and creation of contemporary music. Finally (in section 2.4), I discuss and examplify the shift in the meaning of "musical space" towards the physical-acoustic-perceptual space. This chapter, a comprehensive historical survey of the idea of space in music, addresses issues of dimensions, attributes and structure of space, as well as problems of internal consistency and area of applicability of the various theories and models of space. These conceptions are placed in their appropriate philosophical and historical contexts. For example, the conceptual dependence of various "musical spaces" on the paradigmatic concept of an absolute, three-dimensional, physical space is revealed and the futility of comparisons between the "logical spaces" of music and the perceived qualities of the physical space is pointed out.

The third chapter of the dissertation presents the idea of "spatialization" in contemporary music. A brief examination of the intricate relationships between various types of space associated with music (e.g. pitch-space, represented space, performance space) is followed by a survey of compositional concepts of spatialization, from Ives and Varèse, through Stockhausen, Boulez and Brant, to Smalley and Dhomont.

Chapter IV contains a new definition of spatialization preceded with a review

---

[29]Here, I use the term "musicology" broadly, in reference to all writings about music, including music theory, aesthetics, musicology, texts by composers, etc.

of Ingarden's phenomenological model of the "musical work." I develop certain aspects of Ingarden's theory (e.g. "quasi-spatial structure") and demonstrate that compositional use of spatial features of sound does not breach the integrity of the work-concept. The definition of spatialization is supported with considerations of issues pertinent to this topic, e.g. the relationships of spatialization to instrumentation, texture, polychorality and the "theatralization" of music.

In Chapter V, I put forward a proposal for a general classification scheme of spatial designs in music, illustrated with numerous examples of spatialized compositions. Here, references to isolated examples from the earlier musical repertoire accompany a richly illustrated survey of 20th-century compositions which treat spatial sound quality, localization and movement as musical characteristics of primary importance. This survey highlights significant developments in the areas of vocal-instrumental and electroacoustic music after 1950.

The subsequent three chapters, constituting Part III of the dissertation, present the oeuvre of several composers central to the idea of spatialized music (Brant, Xenakis, Schafer). The selection of compositions for closer scrutiny serves to reveal the similarities and differences between the approaches of individual composers. The music of Henry Brant, discussed in chapter VI continues the American tradition of experimentation and benefits from the composer's pioneering explorations into the spatial perception and performance of music. Iannis Xenakis's concern with the structuring of musical architectures of exceptional novelty, cohesion and strength, is reflected in his application of mathematical concepts to spatialization (especially to spatial sound movement). In the dissertation, however, these ideas are discussed only in reference to Xenakis's instrumental music. R. Murray Schafer's explorations of soundscapes and performance rituals (Chapter VIII) take music beyond the space of the concert hall, overcome the separation of the roles of performers and listeners, and transgress the traditional boundaries of "the work of music."

The analytical emphasis on spatio-temporal features of music reflects my conviction that space in music, as everywhere else, is structured and experienced in time, in its two basic relationships of succession and simultaneity. The analyses, highlighting perceptual aspects of spatialization, reflect my "auditory insights" acquired during rehearsals and concerts of spatialized works.[30] The discussion of the music is based, in part, on the composers' unpublished sketches; it is also supported with their opinions expressed in a series of interviews that I conducted in 1992.[31]

In conclusion, the main objectives of this dissertation may be summarized as follows:

1. To present the plurality of the meaning of space;

2. To trace the history of the idea of "space" in the musical thought of the 20th-century;

3. To clarify the conceptual contexts and interrelationships of the various theoretical constructs of space in music;

4. To outline the historical development of the idea of "spatialization" in the theory and practice of contemporary music (after 1950);

5. To propose a new definition of spatialization and a new classification scheme for spatialized compositions;

6. To present, in detail, three different approaches to spatialization (Brant, Xenakis, Schafer);

7. To highlight the unity of time and space in contemporary music by an analytical focus on the perceptual and temporal aspects of musical spatiality;

8. To document contemporary music "in statu nascendi" by expanding the knowledge of the music (analyses) and of the views of the composers (interviews).

---

[30] I listened to numerous spatialized works at the concerts of the International Festivals of Contemporary Music "Warsaw Autumn" in Warsaw, Poland (1976-1987). During the research phase for this dissertation, I attended concerts of music by Henry Brant (New York, August 1992), R. Murray Schafer (Toronto, October 1992; and Montreal, June 1992) and participated in rehearsals of Pierre Boulez's *Répons* at IRCAM, Paris (3-7 August 1992).

[31] Besides interviewing Henry Brant, Pierre Boulez, R. Murray Schafer and Iannis Xenakis, I discussed issues of musical spatiality with the following composers: Andrzej Dobrowolski and Zygmunt Krauze (Poland), Cort Lippe and Marc Stroppa (France), as well as with my husband, James Harley (Canada).

The dissertation realizes all these objectives and captures in vivid detail one of the main musical preoccupations of our times. This contemporaneous validity highlights its merits as an original contribution to knowledge. The history of the concepts of "musical space," and "spatialization" includes important discoveries and reevaluations. The text emphasizes the interrelationships of ideas and articulates main conceptual trends. The dissertation contains numerous analytical examples from a repertory of spatialized works which has not previously attracted much critical attention. Moreover, even well-known compositions (e.g. Bartók's *Music for Strings, Percussion and Celeste*) reveal spatial aspects unnoticed in earlier theoretical scrutiny. Thus, the dissertation establishes a new ground for musicological research, bringing together issues vital to composition and perception of music in space, topics pertaining to asthetics and philosophy of music, themes of current interest and future importance.

PART ONE

CONCEPTS OF SPACE

CHAPTER I

THE MEANING OF "SPACE"

1.1.

"Space" in language

A survey of definitions of space included in *The Oxford English Dictionary* (1989) brings forth the surprising conclusion that the predominant meaning of space is time.[1] The earliest citation, dating back to the year 1300, reads: "faith lasted littel space."[2] Here, "space" denotes a duration, a "lapse or extent of time between two definite points, events, etc." (sense **1.a** in the *OED*; cf. Table I-1).[3] In relation to time, space has other, similar meanings: "the amount or extent of time comprised or contained in a specified period" as well as "a period or interval of time," that is *a space of time*. These senses appear in many literary sources. For instance, Jonathan Swift writes about the "space of ten hours," John Keats about "a moments's space" and Harriet Beecher Stowe about "a space to say something."[4]

---

[1]The following summary includes senses of "space" chosen because of their possible relevance for music; numerous denotations have been omitted as obsolete or rare.

[2]*The Oxford English Dictionary*, 2nd ed., vol. 16, 1989, p. 87-89. In subsequent citations, I will use the abbreviation to OED.

[3]The Table I-1 (at the end of section 1.1) contains a selection from the meanings of "space" listed in the entry in the *OED*. Here, I include some of the infrequently encountered meanings of "space" to illustrate the polysemous character of this term.

[4]Swift's citaiton comes from *Gulliver's Travels* (1726), Keats's from *St. Agnes* (1820), and Stowe's from *Uncle Tom's Cabin* (1852); all from the *OED*.

The temporal senses of "space" associate this term with the ideas of "measurement" and "distance." This conceptual link underlies the philosophical idea of the "spatialization of time" (Bergson 1913; see section 1.5 of this Chapter). Indeed, the expression "the space **of** time" is as common as "the space **and** time"--the former denoting the measurement of time, the latter the totality of existence.[5] Here, the problematic nature of the notion of space becomes apparent.[6] The two meanings of space as the complement and the attribute of time are diametrically opposed, yet frequently intertwined; this "entanglement" has consequences for the meaning of space in music (cf. Chapter II).

Another large group of the senses of space refers to area and extension. "Spatial" is what co-exists simultaneously, what is present at the same temporal instant. Again, as in the group of "temporal" senses, the relation of space to measurement is of primary importance. The 17th-century poet, John Milton writes: "Twixt Host and Host but narrow space was left. A dreadful interval" (Milton 1667; in the *OED*: 87). Here, space means "linear distance; interval between two or more points or objects." In this sense, space has one, measurable dimension.[7]

"Space" may also mean "superficial area, extent in three dimensions." Thus, all three-dimensional objects, including musical instruments and bodies of the musicians "occupy a certain space." If so, space may be sufficient or insufficient for

---

[5]This conclusion may be reached on the basis of citations listed in the *OED*; these quotes are gathered to document linguistic practice, rather than delimit the range of possibilities (i.e. the Dictionary is descriptive, not prescriptive).

[6]"Space" is equally polysemous in other Indo-European languages; to the extent that these languages express the experience and heritage of a common, Western-European culture, the main areas of denotation remain the same (time, area, extension, interval, void, etc.).

[7]A specific application of the general notion of space as interval appears in the rudiments of Western musical notation: notes are written on lines or in the spaces "between the lines of a staff." The same general meaning underlies a specific typographic sense of space as "an interval or blank between words, or lines, in printed or written matter."

a purpose (synonym to "room"): "there is no space!" writes Chaucer (1374; OED: 87). Finally, space may mean "continuous, unbounded, or unlimited extension in every direction." It is a common notion in astronomy where it denotes "the immeasurable expanse in which the solar and stellar systems, nebulae, etc., are situated; the stellar depths." This definition recalls the Newtonian conception of "absolute space" (cf. section 1.2), a "cosmic" space which is usually coupled with time and associated with "emptiness" and "immensity."

In summary, space may be understood as "an interval, a length of way, a distance," or as "a period of time," or as "a void or empty place," or as "the dimensional extent occupied by a body."[8] This plurality of linguistic spaces reflects the richness of human experience of space; space is lived in, travelled through, measured, shaped and contemplated. The complexity of human relations to space increases because of the continuous development of new conceptions of space in art, philosophy and science. In mathematics, for instance, the meaning of space differs from the ones encountered in everyday language. Here, space is "usually regarded as a set of points having some specified structure."[9]

The multiplicity and diversity of associations evoked by this one term opens up a vast realm of potential significations of "space" in music. Not surprisingly, as we shall see in Chapter II, the meaning of "musical space" differs depending on whether "space" signifies an interval or a definite extension, if one means by "space" a vast, unlimited expanse, or a slot, a place for something, if one refers to a set of elements or to a cosmic void. All these "spaces" are constructs, yet all are superimposed upon a reality of human experience of and existence in space. The clarification of the various meanings of space will help to see these conceptual knots untangled.

---

[8] For a fuller list of senses of "space" see Table I-1.

[9] E.g. *metric space, topological space, vector space*. The mathematical notions of space are discussed in Section 1.3.

Table I-1: Meanings of "space" in *The Oxford English Dictionary*

I. Denoting time or duration.

- 1.a. Without article: Lapse or extent of time between two definite points, events, etc.

- 2. (*Obsolete*): Time, leisure, or opportunity for doing something.

- 3. With *the (that*, etc.):
- 3.a. The amount or extent of time comprised or contained in a specified period.
  - b. The amount of time already specified or indicated, or otherwise determined.

- 4.a. With *a*: A period or interval of time.
  - b. With *of* (Frequently *a space of time*).

II. Denoting area or extension.

Without article, in generalized sense.

- 5.a. Linear distance; interval between two or more points or objects.

- 6.a. Superficial extent or area; also, extent in three dimensions.
  - b. Extent or area sufficient for some purpose; room.
  - c. Extent or room in a letter, periodical, book, etc., available for, occupied by, written or printed matter.

- 7. (*Metaphorical*): Continuous, unbounded, or unlimited extension in every direction, regarded as void of matter, or without reference to this. Frequently coupled with *time*.

- 8.a. (*Astronomy*): The immeasurable expanse in which the solar and stellar systems, nebulae, etc., are situated; the stellar depths.

Table I-1: Meanings of "space," continued.

8.c. In more limited sense: Extension in all directions, esp. from a given point.

**In particularized or limited senses.*

9. A certain stretch, extent, or area of ground, surface, sky, etc.; an expanse.

10. a. A more or less limited area or extent; a small portion of space (in sense 6 a).
    b. A part or portion marked off in some way; a division, section.
    c. A void or empty place or part.

11. a. An interval; a length of way; a distance.

12. (*Obsolete, rare*): Course, custom, procedure.

13. The dimensional extent occupied by a body or lying within certain limits.

14. (*Music*): One or other of the degrees of intervals between the lines of a staff.

15.a. An interval or blank between words, or lines, in printed or written matter.

16. In specific uses (quotations from medicine, etc.).

17. (*Mathematics*): an instance of any of various mathematical concepts, usually regarded as a set of points having some specified structure; cf. *metric space, topological space, vector space*.

1.2.

Selected philosophical concepts of space

The conceptual "thickness" of space in modern English is paralleled in the term's complicated historical evolution, of which only the briefest of accounts can be given here (again, considering only the notions of space which have a potential relevance for music). According to the venerated Western-European tradition, history begins with ancient Greeks, and the history of the concept of space is not an exception: Alexander Gosztonyi's monumental study of the notion of space in philosophy and science (Gosztonyi 1976) opens up with Hesiod's "chaos."[10] In classical (Greek to pre-Kantian) philosophies of space its physical, cosmological, metaphysical and existential dimensions are intertwined; only the advent of modern science separates these domains, with important consequences for the modern opposition of positivist ("objective") and phenomenological ("subject"-oriented) views of space.

For **Aristotle** (Gosztonyi 1976: 90-110; Jammer 1954: 15-21), space is inseparably associated with "place" (this connection is reflected in the linguistic senses II.1-3 and III.1-4, above). "Topos" is a quantity; it is continuous, infinitely divisible, exactly definable, and three-dimensional. However, Aristotle uses six rather than three dimensions--thus reflecting human-centred orientation of the "place:" up--down--left--right--before--behind (Gosztonyi 1976: 94). While emphasizing this existential focus, the "Aristotelian school tried to get along without the concept of independent (absolute) space" (Einstein 1954/1976: xv).

This concept is an artifact of classical science, usually referred to as Cartesian, Euclidean, or Newtonian space. For **René Descartes** (1596-1650), space exists

---

[10] The title of Gosztonyi's book (*Der Raum. Geschichte seiner Probleme in Philosophie und Wissenschaften*) does not specify its limitation to the domain of Western-European culture. Although the book contains references to Arabic philosophy of the Middle Ages, it does so only because of the reception of this philosophy in medieval Europe (Gosztonyi 1976: 164-167).

materially; it is a continuous, homogeneous, static mass (Gosztonyi 1976: 245). Moreover, he ascribes to it a geometric structure expressible in a three-axial coordinate system (with notions from Euclidean geometry, e.g. point, line, plane). In the account of Maurice Merleau-Ponty:

> It was necessary first to idealize space, to conceive of that being--perfect in its genus, clear, manageable and homogeneous--which our thinking glides over without a vantage point of its own: a being which thought reports entirely in terms of three rectangular dimensions. . . Descartes was right in setting space free. His mistake was to erect it into a positive being, outside all points of view, beyond all latency.
> (Merleau-Ponty 1964/1972: 69)

The opposition underlying the Aristotelian and Cartesian conceptions (space made manifest in and through objects, and space in itself) has been formulated by Albert Einstein who contrasts two basic understandings of "space:"

> (a) space as positional quality of the world of material objects; (b) space as container of all material objects. In case (a), space without a material object is inconceivable. In case (b), a material object can only be conceived as existing in space; space then appears as a reality which in a certain sense is superior to the material world. Both space concepts are free creations of the human imagination, means devised for easier comprehension of our sense experience.
> (Einstein 1954/1976: xiv)

Space of Einstein's type (b), that is, the absolute space described by Descartes, plays a very important role in the philosophy of **Isaac Newton** (1643-1727). As Michael Friedman puts it: "Newtonian physics pictures material objects or bodies as embedded or contained in an infinite, three-dimensional Euclidean space" (Friedman 1983: 12). For Newton and his followers, as for Descartes, "space is very much like a material body, of a very ethereal kind, but not entirely" (van Fraassen 1985: 109). In his *Philosophiae naturalis principia mathematica*, the basis of classical physics, Newton writes: "Absolute space in its own nature, without relation to anything external, remains always similar and immovable."[11] This space is then associated with

---

[11] Quoted from Jammer (1954: 97). Source of this quotation: F. Cajori, ed., *Sir Isaac Newton's Mathematical Principles of Natural Philosophy and His System of the World. A Revision of Mott's Translation*, (Berkeley: University of California Press,

God's "boundless uniform Sensorium," i.e. God's way of perceiving and creating things (Jammer 1954: 110-112, Gosztonyi 1976: 338-344).[12] The Newtonian identification of the omnipresence of space with the omnipresence of God, used later as a proof for the Divine existence,[13] forms the basic contradiction within his conception of space: the location of a metaphysical Being at the centre of a hypothetical-deductive system of mechanical physics.

The universal acceptance of Newtonian physics led to the adoption of the notion of absolute space as a basic, scientific truth, not an artifact of limited scope and applicability. An awareness of the paradigmatic status of this notion ("paradigmatic" in the sense introduced by Kuhn in 1962) arose only with the renewed interest in the nature of space spurred by the development of relativity theory in the 20th century (discussed in Section 4, below). Meanwhile, one philosopher who adopted a Newtonian world-view, **Immanuel Kant** (1724-1804), formulated a new notion of space that influenced philosophical discourse on space for several generations.

As Patrick Heelan writes, "so persuaded . . . was Immanuel Kant of the apodicticity of Newtonian physics, that he proposed as a self-evident truth that the space of empirical objects and intuitive experience is Euclidean" (Heelan 1983: 250). Heelan has criticized Kant's limitations from the position of a phenomenologist; Michael Friedman points out that for the positivist as well, Kant's conception of space suffers from "its too intimate connection with outmoded mathematics and physics" (Friedman 1983: 7). Nonetheless, Kant's theory continues to influence research into

---

1934, 6). The notion of absolute space is contrasted by Newton with that of the relative spaces, which are, in contemporary language, different frames of reference (cf. van Fraassen 1985: 115).

[12] As Newton writes about God: "He is not eternity and infinity, but eternal and infinite; He is not duration or space, but He endures and is present. He endures for ever, and is everywhere present; and by existing always and everywhere, He constitutes duration and space" (Newton/Cajori 1934: 544; quoted by Jammer 1954: 110-111).

[13] For instance by Samuel Clarke, cf. Gosztonyi (1976: 346-348) and Jammer (1954: 127).

issues of space in different domains, e.g. in psychology (cf. Eliot 1987).

But what is space for Kant? According to Alexander Gosztonyi (Gosztonyi 1976: 400-456), Kant's ideas of space differ greatly in the pre-critical and critical periods of his philosophy. For the sake of brevity, only the final, "critical" formulation will be discussed here.[14] For Kant, space is by no means "absolute." In the *Critique of Pure Reason* (1781) he posits that space is, along with time, a form of "pure intuition" (reine Anschauungsform) which is a precondition for all perception (Gosztonyi 1976: 429-432; Heelan 1983: 41). Max Jammer explains that, according to Kant,

> Not itself arising out of sensations, the concept of space is a pure intuition, neither objective nor real, but subjective and ideal. . . Space is a form of intuition, instrumental in the process of cognition as an ideal organizer of the contents of sensations.
>
> (Jammer 1954: 132-133)

In Kantian philosophy, space is synthetic a priori. It is a pure form of sensibility (*reine Anschauungsform*): pure--because antecedent to all experience, and universal--because independent of the particular data of our sensations (Jammer 1954: 134-135). Contemporary philosophers of science often disagree with the Kantian "a-prioricity" of space which implies its unrevisability and necessity. As Michael Friedman points out, "if the developments in post-Kantian mathematics and physics show anything, they show that one central Kantian formal component--the Euclidean-Newtonian picture of space and time--is clearly not *a priori* or unrevisable" (Friedman 1983: 18). Patrick Heelan (whose phenomenological philosophy of science is discussed in Section 5 of this Chapter), agrees with Friedman only partly, for he does not share the "anti-a-priori" conviction:

> In summary, while all philosophy today is pursued in the light of the Kantian heritage, and philosophers accept the view that what we find in experience is prefigured in intentionality, and that the empirical object as known is actively constructed according to a priori rules, still it is evident that the undisputed

---

[14]Kant's critical writings dealing with the topic of space include: *Critique of Pure Reason* (1781), *Critique of Practical Reason* (1787) and *Prolegomena* (1783).

content of that legacy is unclear. This is particularly so as regards the uniqueness of the geometrical rules active at the transcendental level, and their origin in the subject, or possibly in ways in which subject and World collaborate to construct space--visual, perceptual (in the broader sense), physical (of our local environment, or cosmological).

(Heelan 1983: 42)

Finally, Alexander Gosztonyi notices that the Kantian postulate of the transcendental ideality of space does not provide solutions to the ontology of the physical space in itself (Gosztonyi 1976: 455). In the light of Gosztonyi's critique, Kant's most important contribution to the development of the idea of space lies in his analysis of the spaces of intuition (Anschauungraumes) conducted from a phenomenological point of view. Here, Kant notices the importance of the temporal moment of spatial perception (i.e. the connection of space and time in human experience) and opens up the way to phenomenological studies of space by Husserl, Heidegger and Merleau-Ponty (Gosztonyi 1976: 456).[15]

---

[15]In the domain of musical thought, the Kantian legacy has particular significance for the German theorists of "musical space" (cf. Chapter II, section 1).

1.3.
Notions of space in mathematics

What Kant could not have known, that space is not necessarily Euclidean, has slowly come to be understood over the course of the 19th century--the time of the development of various non-Euclidean geometries.[16] Their emergence has heralded the birth of mathematical notions of space which have little to do with the experience of the human (bodily and environmental) spatiality. In mathematics, space is "usually regarded as a set of points having some specified structure" (linguistic sense III.9 listed in Section 1).[17] The main stages in the evolution of such counter-intuitive concepts of space are outlined below.

According to the classical formulation of **Euclidean geometry** (that of the *Elements* by Euclid), spatial relations between elementary entities (point, line, plane) are supposed to fulfil five postulates, of which the fifth one, the so-called parallelism postulate is the most questionable. Bas van Fraassen formulates these postulates in the following manner:

> (I) If x and y are distinct points, there is a straight line incident with both.
> (II) Any finite straight line (segment) is part of a unique infinite straight line.
> (III) If x is a point and r a finite distance, there is a unique circle with x and radius r.
> (IV) Any two right angles are equal.
> (V) If a straight line falling on two straight lines makes the interior angles on the same side less than two right angles, the two straight lines, if produced indefinitely, meet on that side on which the angles are less than two right angles.
>
> (van Fraassen 1985: 117-118)

---

[16]For an overview of these developments see van Fraassen (1985); a detailed history is given by Gray (1979).

[17]Whether any particular mathematical spaces can be coordinated with entities from the physical reality (i.e. discovered) or whether their existence is purely ideal (i.e. invented or construed) is a matter of contention. Some philosophers assert that the geometry of space has little to do with spatial intuition or experience (cf. Gosztonyi 1976: 467-473).

Numerous attempts to prove the truthfulness of the fifth postulate have ultimately led to the discovery of new, **non-Euclidean geometries** (hyperbolic, spherical and elliptical geometries were the first to be studied).[18] Other non-Euclidean geometries developed in the 19th century are more basic than Euclidean geometry because they involve fewer primitive (i.e. undefinable) concepts. According to van Fraassen, "in *affine geometry* the notions of distance and perpendicularity do not appear, in *projective geometry* neither these nor parallelism appears, and in *topology (analysis situs)* even the notion of line does not appear" (van Fraassen 1985: 122). As Jeremy Gray explains, "before, roughly, 1800, mathematicians hoped to show that Euclidean geometry was the only possible geometry of space, whereas afterwards they sought to establish the possible validity of other geometries" (Gray 1979: 155). In the course of this development, the basic tenet of Kantian epistemology, that of the a-prioricity of Euclidean geometry of space, was abandoned. According to Hans Reichenbach,

> We must therefore reject the arguments for the priority of Euclidean geometry within mathematics. The geometrical axioms are not asserted to be true within mathematics, and mathematical geometry deals exclusively with implications; it is a pure deductive system. . . . Mathematical geometry is not a science of space insofar as we understand by space a visual structure that can be filled with objects--it is a pure theory of manifolds. . . . The visual elements of space are an unnecessary addition.
> (Reichenbach 1927/1958: 92, 100)

For Reichenbach, geometry is a theory of relations, and all geometrical

---

[18]By denying postulate (V), Euclidean geometry is transformed into hyperbolic geometry (Karl Friedrich Gauss, János Bolyai, and Nikolai Lobachevsky). By replacing postulate (V) with (V*) "there is no line parallel to any other line" and changing postulate (II) into (II*) "any two lines have two distinct points in common" spherical geometry is developed (Bernhard Riemann). If postulate (V*) is supplemented with (II**) "any two lines have a unique intersection" elliptical geometry is introduced (van Fraassen 1985: 120-121). For a popular explanation of spherical geometry see Einstein's "Geometry and Experience" (1921/1976); for a discussion of the nature of geometry as a theory of relations and the problem of the visualisation in Euclidean and non-Euclidean geometries see Reichenbach (1927/1958: 37-90); for a detailed history of non-Euclidean geometries see Gray (1979).

concepts can be expressed as functions of basic, purely logical concepts, such as *"element, relation, one-to-one correspondence, implication*, etc." (Reichenbach 1927/1958: 93-94). And, if space is a visual container of objects, geometry has nothing to do with space. But what if "space" means a "manifold"? This notion was introduced in Bernhard Riemann's habilitation dissertation of 1854.[19] As van Fraassen writes,

> In this work, Riemann presented the general concept of a manifold: the spectrum of color hues is a one-dimensional manifold, and space, as ordinarily conceived is a three-dimensional manifold. The term 'manifold' is not much in use any more; today we speak of spaces instead of manifolds. Riemann defined a n-dimensional space to be one in which each position can be characterized by a set of n coordinates. Thus, he envisaged space of more than three dimensions.
>
> (van Fraassen 1985: 126)

Riemann's study of discrete and continuous manifolds as well as his trigonometric descriptions of various geometries have led to "the reformulation of geometry in local terms, rather than global ones: 'line' and 'plane' were defined in terms of geodesics and curvatures" (Gray 1979: 158). His discovery of the notion of the metrically amorphous manifold "allows us to see all the different kinds of geometrical structures--Euclidean and non-Euclidean; constant curvature and variable curvature; two-, three-, and higher dimensional spaces--as particular instances of the very general ideal of an n-dimensional manifold" (Friedman 1983: 10). These mathematical developments proved invaluable for the introduction of new theories of space-time and for the formulation of relativity theory by Albert Einstein.

In special branches of mathematics, such as general topology, various types and properties of space are identified, defined and refined, e.g. the concepts of topological space, distance and metric space. The definition of the **topological space** (the most basic and least structured space) reads:

---

[19]The significance of Riemann's dissertation, *On the hypotheses which lie at the foundations of geometry* is discussed by Gosztonyi (1976: 493-500), and van Fraassen (1985: 126-129).

Let X be a non-empty set. A class T of subsets of X is a *topology* on X iff T satisfies the following axioms.

[O_1] X and ϕ belong to T.
[O_2] The union of any number of sets in T belongs to T.
[O_3] The intersection of any two sets in T belongs to T.

The members of T are then called *T-open sets*, or simply *open sets*, and X together with T, i.e. the pair (X,T), is called a *topological space*.
(Lipschutz 1965: 66)

In order to proceed from a topological space to a **metric space**, the notion of distance needs to be introduced. In general terms, distance is defined as a real-valued function satisfying several axioms (that a distance from any point to another is never negative, that a distance from a point to itself is zero, etc.; cf. Lipschutz 1965: 111). After defining distance, the establishment of the conception of a metric space is possible, with "point" and "distance" as basic notions. Therefore, a metric space is simply "a collection of points with as metric a distance function on that collection" (van Fraassen 1985: 127). Moreover, each of the Euclidean and non-Euclidean geometries mentioned earlier is a particular type of metric space and can be axiomatized by articulating exact conditions for the concept of distance.

Finally, one related notion of space should be mentioned: the **logical space**--first introduced by **Ludwig Wittgenstein** in his *Tractatus Logico-Philosophicus* of 1922. For Wittgenstein, "logical space" is (proposition 2.11) "the existence and non-existence of atomic facts" whereas (proposition 1.13) "the facts in logical space are the world" (Wittgenstein 1922/1988: 39, 31). Therefore, as the philosopher explains (proposition 2.0131), "a speck in a visual field need not be red, but it must have a colour; it has, so to speak, a colour space round it. A tone must have a pitch, the object of the sense of touch a hardness, etc." In Wittgenstein's definition, the musical notion of "pitch" is a logical space.[20]

---

[20]Nonetheless, the musical implications of this "state of affairs," to use Wittgenstein's term, have not been consciously explored. The applications of mathematical concepts of space in music theory and composition appear only in the

Bas van Fraassen explains that a logical space is "a mathematical construct used to represent conceptual interconnections among a family of properties and relations" (van Fraassen 1985: 102-104; cf. also Reichenbach 1927/1958: 132). This logical space may be used to represent physical space. If each event receives three space coordinates (real numbers), "the logical space in which . . . all spatial relationships are represented, is the set of all triples of real numbers" (p. 167). If, on the other hand, events are considered in a four-dimensional space-time, "the logical space, in which, for us, all spatio-temporal relationships are represented is the set of all quadruples of real numbers" (p. 167).[21] In addition, van Fraassen argues that time is a logical space, and "furthermore, that this logical space (time) is the real line being used to represent all possible temporal relations among events and the conceptual interconnections among these relations" (van Fraassen 1985: 102). So much for absolute, independent time and space! Having begun this survey of concepts of space from an intuitive conception of "the space of time" (cf. linguistic senses I.1--I.3 in Section 1), we reach one philosopher's conclusion that time is a logical space.

---

writings of those composers or theoreticians who have studied mathematics, and have sought to transplant mathematical ideas into music (cf. Boulez, Xenakis and Morris in Chapter II).

[21]The logical space exemplified by van Fraassen resembles very closely Riemannian notion of an n-dimensional discrete manifold.

1.4.
Space-time theories in modern philosophy of science

As Hans Reichenbach states lucidly, "mathematical space is a *conceptual structure*, and as such ideal. Physics has the task of coordinating one of these mathematical structures to reality" (Reichenbach 1927/1958: 287).[22] This opinion of a prominent representative of logical positivism,[23] reflects the state of affairs in mathematical physics, in which competing views on space and space-time are constantly being proposed, tested and rejected.

The breakthrough came with **Albert Einstein**'s relativity theory supported by the Minkowskian model of space-time as a four-dimensional manifold (Einstein 1934/1976, 1954/1976; Friedman 1983; Gray 1979). The significance of Einstein's theory is, partly, due to the fact that "it exhibits such an intimate interdependence of temporal and spatial relations that time and space can no longer be treated as essentially independent subjects" (van Fraassen 1985: 140). Thus, as Minkowski triumphantly proclaimed, "three-dimensional geometry becomes a chapter in four-dimensional physics. . . . Space and Time are to fade away into the shadows and only a world in itself will subsist."[24] Hermann Weyl explains this unification of the two formerly independent entities in the following manner:

> The scene of action of reality is not a three-dimensional Euclidean space but rather **a four-dimensional world, in which space and time are linked together indissolubly**. . . . It is a four-dimensional continuum, which is neither 'time' nor 'space.' Only the consciousness that passes on in one portion of this world experiences the detached piece which comes to meet it

---

[22]Albert Einstein expresses a similar view in his lecture of 1921, "Geometry and Experience," (published in English translation in *Ideas and Opinions*, in 1976: 227-239).

[23]As Reichenbach announces in the introduction to *The Philosophy of Space and Time* this work is meant "to give an example of the superiority of a philosophical method closely connected with the results of empirical science" (Reichenbach 1927/1958: xv).

[24]Minkowski's statement from a lecture of 1905, cited by Gray (1979: 171).

and passes behind it as **history** that is as a process which is going forward in time and takes place in space.

(Weyl 1918/1952: 217)

There is an essential difference between the four-dimensional space-time of special relativity and the space-time of the classical physics in which every event is also given four coordinates (three spatial ones and a time coordinate) and in which the totality of physical events is also "embedded in a four-dimensional continuous manifold" (Einstein 1954/1976: 350-366). As Einstein explains, in classical physics, unlike special relativity, this continuum can be separated into a one-dimensional time and a three-dimensional space of simultaneous events.[25] By introducing the relativity of simultaneity, "the four-dimensional continuum is now no longer resolvable objectively into sections, which contain all simultaneous events; 'now' loses for the spatially extended world its objective meaning" (Einstein 1954/1976: 360). In other words, "there is no physical basis for the relation of simultaneity between events that are spatially separate" and therefore "one and the same pair of events may be simultaneous in one frame of reference . . . and not in some other frame of reference" (van Fraassen 1985: 155).[26]

This dissolution of the independence of time and space by the relativity of simultaneity implies a radical transformation of the scientific world-view, because from now on, as Einstein writes, it is "more natural to think of physical reality as a four-dimensional existence, instead of, as hitherto, the *evolution* of a three-dimensional existence" (Einstein 1954/1976: 361). Distant echoes of this Einsteinian

---

[25]The connection of space and time into space-time is by no means intuitively obvious, for as Hermann Weyl notices: "it is remarkable that the three-dimensional geometry of the statical world that was put into a complete axiomatic system by Euclid has such a translucent character, whereas we have been able to assume command over the four-dimensional geometry only after a prolonged struggle" (Weyl 1921/1976: 217). Hans Reichenbach disagrees with this dissolution of space and time into a continuous space-time and emphasizes the differences between the two notions as "a fundamental fact of the objective world" (Reichenbach 1927/1958: 109-112, 279).

[26]"A frame of reference is simply an assignment of time and space coordinates to all events" (van Fraassen 1985: 157).

revolution may be perceived in Merleau-Ponty's phenomenological philosophy of existence (cf. section 1.5).

The transition from the Newtonian notions of absolute, separated space and time to their alliance in the four-dimensional space-time continuum of Einstein's special theory of relativity (1905) was hardly final.[27] According to Michael Friedman, in special relativity "there is indeed no three-dimensional, Euclidean embedding space, but there is a four-dimensional, semi-Euclidean space-time in which all physical events are embedded" (Friedman 1983: 16). The introduction of general relativity in 1916 was partly motivated by Einstein's desire to get rid of that rigid, embedding four-dimensional space-time.[28] Einstein believed that general relativity solved the problem of the existence or non-existence of absolute space and he maintained that "there is no such thing as an empty space, i.e. a space without field. Space-time does not claim existence on its own, but only as a structural quality of the field" (Einstein 1954/1976: 365). Nevertheless, contemporary physicists and philosophers of science are still greatly divided on this issue, and the existence of space-time as well as its structure are the matter of an on-going debate. As Lawrence Sklar reminds his colleagues, "in considering formalization of the spacetime theory of general relativity, we must remember that this one theory allows at least the lawlike possibility, relative to its

---

[27]Hans Reichenbach opposes the view advocated here and emphasizes the distinction between space and time: "Calling time the fourth dimension gives it an air of mystery. One might think that time can now be conceived as a kind of space and try in vain to add visually a fourth dimension to the three dimensions of space. It is essential to guard against such a misunderstanding of mathematical concepts. If we add time to space as a fourth dimension, it does not lose in any way its peculiar character as time. Through the combination of space and time into a four-dimensional manifold we merely express the fact that it takes four numbers to determine a world event, namely three numbers for the spatial location and one for time." (Reichenbach 1927/1958: 110). These reservations have been shared by Henri Bergson (Bergson 1922/1965; cf. below, section 1.5).

[28]Michael Friedman defines general relativity as "a theory of gravitation formulated in the context of the conceptions of space and time due to special relativity" (Friedman 1983: 17).

laws, of many distinct spacetime worlds" (Sklar 1985: 127). Hence, there is "a wide variety of spacetimes compatible with the theory," because in general relativity "spacetime is itself a variable dynamic element in the theory" (ibidem).

For **Michael Friedman**, the general principle of relativity is neither as revolutionary as, nor analogous to, the special principle of relativity for "it merely replaces a flat affine-metrical structure (of space-time) with a nonflat one" (Friedman 1983: 29). In general relativity, space-time is variably curved and "endowed with a perfectly definite metric . . . which is related in a definite way to the distribution of mass-energy by Einstein's field equations. . . . There is no sense in which this metric is determined by arbitrary choice or convention" (Friedman 1983: 26). Friedman emphasizes the distinction of intrinsic and extrinsic features of a space-time: intrinsic features of a space-time reflect those aspects of geometrical structure that objectively characterize the space-time while extrinsic features vary from one coordinate representation to another (Friedman 1983: 339). In particular, that the space-time is a four-dimensional manifold is only a local assertion, for, as Friedman writes, "space-time in the large can be finite or infinite, closed like a sphere or open like a plane, connected (no holes or missing pieces) or disconnected (with arbitrary deletions) and so on" (Friedman 1983: 33).

If space-time is "the set of all places-at-a-time or all actual and possible events," theories of space-time picture the material universe (i.e. "the set of all actual events") as embedded in a space-time which possesses a specific type of geometric structure. Where the various theories disagree is what this structure really is. According to Friedman's view, the basic or primitive elements of space-time theories are of two kinds: "space-time and its geometrical structure; and matter fields--distributions of mass, charge, and so on--which represent the physical processes and events occurring within space-time" (Friedman 1983: 32). Friedman's critique is directed against relationalism, which does not require the existence of space-time independently of matter and energy. As Hartry Field puts it:

> According to the relational theory of space-time, the physical world contains spatio-temporal aggregates of matter (spatio-temporally extended physical

objects, spatio-temporal parts of such objects and aggregates consisting of spatio-temporal parts of different objects); these aggregates of matter are interrelated in various ways by various geometric (and also non-geometric) relations, but the physical world does not contain a space-time over and above these aggregates of matter and their interrelations.

(Field 1989: 171)

Einstein himself (1954/1976), Reichenbach (1927/1958), Grünbaum (1963/1973, 1977) and van Fraassen (1985) have all subscribed to the relational view on space-time which defines this entity merely as an attribute of matter or field.[29] The opposite, substantival view, represented by Friedman, is equally possible in the light of general relativity. In the words of Hartry Field:

According to the substantival view of space-time, the physical world contains not only aggregates of matter (physical objects, their spatio-temporal parts etc.) but also (over and above these, i.e., not logically constructed from them) space-time and its spatio-temporal parts.

(Field 1989: 171)

It is quite natural to identify an object with the part of space-time that it occupies--hence, for instance, the absence of absolute space in Aristotelian thought. The debate, whether space-time theories describe only spatio-temporal relations or independent entities of space-time, and whether spatio-temporal relations and properties can be reduced to or defined by other relations and properties is far from being solved (Friedman 1983: 62; Sklar 1985: 8-9).[30]

These discussions about space-time in contemporary philosophy of science

---

[29]Friedman distinguishes two types of relationalism: (1) Leibnizean--limiting applicability of space-time concepts, and (2) Reichenbachian--limiting vocabulary of space-time theories to relations defined in a proper way (Friedman 1983: 63). Elsewhere, Friedman labels Reichenbach's position "conventionalism" rather than "relationalism" (Friedman 1983: 264-339).

[30]Lawrence Sklar, one of the participants in the debate between substantivism and relationism describes the kinship of relationism to other "doctrines regarding theories, doctrines which attribute genuine reference only to the names and predicates of the theory which aim to denote observable entities and properties, and which treat the apparently denoting terms which allegedly refer to nonobservable entities and properties as not really referring in nature at all" (Sklar 1985: 11).

concentrate on spatio-temporal properties and relations, objects, processes and events. What is excluded is human consciousness and the lived experience and perception of space-time on an intermediary scale, neither macro- nor microcosmic. These aspects are the subjects of philosophical reflection in phenomenology.

1.5.
Human experience and perception of space: philosophy of life and phenomenology

One of Minkowski's arguments for the validity of his theory of a unified four-dimensional continuum of space-time refers to human perceptual experience: "No-one has yet observed a place except at a time, nor yet a time except at a place."[31] Here, space and time do not have independent existences. As Jeremy Gray comments (alluding to Newtonian metaphysics): "Put like that it is unarguable, but it dethrones God from his Sensorium of space in which time passes" (Gray 1979: 171).

Henri Bergson (1859-1941) apparently did not intend to "dethrone God," because his existential philosophy emphasizes a complete opposition of time (duration, *durée*) and space (*espace*) in human experience (Gosztonyi 1976: 869-872).[32] For Bergson, space is the sworn enemy of duration while spatial representations rule tyrannically over human cognition and language. As humans think in spatial terms, they confuse duration with extension, quality with quantity, real succession with

---

[31]Hermann Minkowski's statement is here quoted from Gray (1979: 171). Minkowski, the German scientist, should not be confused with Eugène Minkowski, a French psychiatrist and philosopher of a phenomenological orientation (cf. Kockelmans and Kisiel, eds. 1970: 235).

[32]This review of Bergson's philosophy of time is based on *Essai sur les données immédiates de la conscience* (1883-1887, published in 1889, 6th ed. of the English translation published in 1950) and *Durée et Simultanéité* (published in 1922, in English translation in 1965).

simultaneity. False, spatial representation of time, based on "homogeneous time" has nothing to do with duration which is experienced in the flow of consciousness, but makes time a "phantom of space" instead. Bergson explains: "pure duration is wholly qualitative. It cannot be measured unless symbolically represented in space" (Bergson 1889/1950: 105). Homogeneous time, emptied of its experiential content, may be measured and co-opted to space as its fourth dimension; it may be **spatialized**. According to Bergson, we spatialize time "as soon as we measure it" and, thus, we produce "a time dried up as space" (Bergson 1922/1965: 60).[33] The association of spatiality with stasis and with the quality of being measurable, the idea of spatialized time, and the antinomy of space and time so forcefully argued in Bergsonian philosophy have had a tremendous significance for the development of the idea of musical spatiality (cf. Chapter III, section 2). Interestingly, Bergson himself used a musical example to prove that measured time is spatial. When listening to a series of strokes of a distant bell people "range the successive sounds in an ideal space and then fancy that they are counting them in pure duration" (Bergson 1889/1950: 86). This is not the case, argues Bergson: if the bell sounds are counted and arranged in a rhythmic pattern, this operation takes place "in space"--the space of time (p. 87).[34]

Following the emergence of Einstein's theory of relativity, with its central notion of "space-time," Bergson attempted to argue the superiority of his dualistic

---

[33]Bergson's philosophy of pure duration may be seen as a reaction against the traditional, spatial image of time in which it is modelled as a line with a moving point representing the present moment (temporal intervals can be measured as distances on this line). This spatial image of time may be found, for instance, in the pre-critical writings of Kant (e.g. his *Inaugural Dissertation*, according to Prof. Alison Laywine; private communication). Incidentally, Martin's Heidegger's theory of the ontological primacy of time which led him towards grounding space in time (*Being and Time*) is also based on the negation of the temporal spatialization. According to Prof. Philip Buckley (private communication), Heidegger's criticism of Bergson's philosophy relates to its dualist nature which is manifest in the opposition of lived and spatialized time.

[34]"If the sounds are separated, they must leave empty intervals between them. If we count them, the intervals must remain though the sounds disappear: how could these intervals remain, if they were pure duration and not space?" (Bergson 1889/1950: 87).

theory of time and space over a unified model of a four-dimensional space-time continuum (Bergson 1922/1965). He criticized treating time as "the fourth dimension of space" (p. 140) and claimed that space and time "remain what they were, separate from one another, incapable of mingling except as the result of a mathematical fiction intended to symbolize a truth in physics" (p. 155).

In seeking to formulate a general philosophy of life, Bergson explores dualities: concrete and abstract, intuition and intellect, time and space. Intuition, associated with a pure temporality, has an absolute primacy over the intellect which is linked to spatial abstractions. Curiously, as Gosztonyi notices, Bergson is aware of two different types or aspects of space: homogeneous (i.e. abstract, construed or imagined) and heterogeneous (i.e. concrete, encountered in experience). Contrary to what might have been expected, the philosopher gives priority to the homogeneous space, which is singularly detached from the physical reality. This space is static, immovable and unchangeable. Here, the familiar, absolute space of Newton and Descartes makes an unexpected reappearance (compare especially Merleau-Ponty's critique of Descartes in Section 2 above). Bergson contrasts his innovative conception of duration, that is, "time-as-experienced," with "space-as-conceived-of" (the homogeneous space resembling absolute space from earlier accounts) rather than with the duration's natural counterpart, that is "space-as-experienced" (the heterogeneous space encountered in human life). When both time and space are taken in their experiential immediacy their opposition is bound to disappear and what is left is a lived "space-time." Despite this logical and conceptual weakness, the virtue of Bergsonian philosophy is the renewed focus on the human, subjective experience of time (and space).

The interest in "space" in **phenomenology and existential philosophy** has been far less pronounced than the interest in "time." This is apparent in the titles of the main phenomenological writings, for instance Husserl's *The Phenomenology of Internal Time-Consciousness*, not "Space-Consciousness," or Heidegger's *Being and*

Time, not "Being and Space".³⁵ The balance here is completely different than in the philosophy of science, which has examined the problems of time to a much lesser extent than those of space.³⁶ The difference in treatment of time and space is a result of a difference in purpose: the connection of human life and consciousness with time is more obvious than with space, and these are the central domains of phenomenological and existential philosophies.

The belief that consciousness is purely temporal and non-spatial has been quite wide-spread, for it has been associated with a disembodiment of human identity in its purely "spiritual" rather than the "psycho-somatic" interpretation.³⁷ This disembodiment has constituted a basic tenet of Western-European thought since antiquity, and has been challenged only in the 20th century (e.g. by Merleau-Ponty's phenomenology of perception). Even Hans Reichenbach, a logical positivist, writes that "time order is possible in a realm which has no spatial order, namely in the world of the psychic experiences of an individual human being." The philosopher continues:

> This is the reason why the experience of time is allotted a primary position among conscious experiences, and is felt as more immediate than the experience of space. There is indeed no direct experience of space in the direct sense in which we feel the flow of time during our life. The experience of time appears to be closely connected with the experience of the ego. 'I am' is always equivalent to 'I am now,' but I am in an 'eternal now' and feel myself remaining the same in the elusive current of time.
> (Reichenbach 1927/1958: 110)

In the phenomenological philosophy of **Maurice Merleau-Ponty** (1900-1961)

---

³⁵For a discussion of the problem of space in the constitutive phenomenology of Edmund Husserl see Gosztonyi (1976: 844-861); the connections of space and time and the metaphysics of lived space in the existential philosophy of Martin Heidegger are presented by the same author (Gosztonyi 1976: 885-895).

³⁶In science, "some philosophers have believed that a philosophical clarification of space also provided a solution of the problem of time . . . [which] has none of the difficulties resulting from multidimensionality" (Reichenbach 1927/1958: 109).

³⁷For many philosophers, though, the disembodiment of human consciousness is linked to its supra-temporality; "I" exist above time, in the perennial present.

"I am" means "I am **here** and now" because "I" is understood as an "incarnate subject," that is a spatio-temporal, psycho-somatic being (Merleau-Ponty 1945/1981, 1964/1972).[38] Body and soul are not separate entities, which may exist independently: in the actual world, "we are the compound of soul and body."[39] As the philosopher writes, the body that the soul animates,

> is not, for it, an object among objects, and it does not derive from the body all the rest of space as an implied premise. The soul thinks with reference to the body, not with reference to itself; and space, or exterior distance, is stipulated as well within the natural pact that unites them. . . . For the soul, the body is both natal space and matrix of every other existing space.
> (Merleau-Ponty 1964/1972: 71)

Therefore, the notion of space is dramatically changed:

> Space is no longer . . . a network of relations between objects such as would be seen by a witness or my vision or by a geometer looking over it and reconstructing it from outside. It is, rather, a space reckoned starting from me as the zero point or degree zero of spatiality. I do not see it according to its exterior envelope, I live in it from the inside; I am immersed in it. After all the world is all around me, not in front of me.
> (Merleau-Ponty 1964/1972: 73)

Body and soul are not separated, and neither are space and time:

> We must therefore avoid saying that our body is *in* space, or *in* time. It *inhabits* space and time. . . . Just as it is necessarily 'here,' the body necessarily exists 'now' . . . In so far as I have a body through which I act in the world, space and time are not, for me, a collection of adjacent points nor are they a limitless number of relations synthesized by any consciousness, and into which it draws my body. I am not in space and time, nor do I conceive space and time; I belong to them, my body combines with them and includes them.
> (Merleau-Ponty 1945/1962: 138)

---

[38] My account of Merleau-Ponty's philosophy of space does not include some of his important concepts (e.g. "spatial level" and "field of presence") which are discussed in detail by Gosztonyi (1976: 919-925) and Kockelmans (1970: 274-316). These ideas are omitted because they are not fundamental for this dissertation.

[39] According to Prof. Philip Buckley (private communication, 17 February 1994), Merleau-Ponty developed the notion of the "incarnate subject" or "body-subject" on the basis of Husserl's concept of the "lived-body" (*Leib*) which was introduced in the second part of *Ideas* (Merleau-Ponty studied this work in manuscript).

This connection of human, lived spatiality and temporality is of great significance in the "spatio-temporal" context of the modern philosophy of science. Paradoxically, it is in phenomenology, a philosophy first formulated as a critique of the impersonal, objectivist quality of science (embodied in empirical and logical positivism),[40] that the junction of space and time posited by science is considered a central characteristic of human existence.[41] Positivism (e.g. Reichenbach) still assumes the existence of a transcendental ego, in the eternal "now"--thus adopting uncritically a notion from outmoded anthropology. In the *Crisis of European Sciences*, Edmund Husserl, Merleau-Ponty's mentor and predecessor, writes:

> The world is a spatiotemporal world; spatiotemporality (as 'living,' not as logico-mathematical) belongs to its own ontic meaning as life-world. . . All objects in the world are in essence 'embodied'; and for that very reason all take part in the space-time of bodies. . . The human spirit, after all, is grounded on the human physis; each individual human psychic life is founded upon corporeity.
>
> (Husserl 1937/1970: 168, 216, 271)

How do humans experience time and space? In movement, for it encompasses simultaneously position, temporality and identity (Langer 1989: 85). Merleau-Ponty considers corporeal spatiality in association with human "motility," that is, the potentiality of the exploration of space in time (chapter 3 of Part I in the *Phenomenology of Perception*, 1945/1981).[42] "Movement is not thought about

---

[40] Husserl, Ingarden and Merleau-Ponty all consider positivism, empiricism and materialism as epistemologically deficient. A brief discussion of Husserl's critical attitude towards modern science and empirical or logical positivism is contained in Patrick Heelan's phenomenological philosophy of science (Heelan 1983). *Phenomenology and the Natural Sciences*, a collection of essays and translations (eds. Kockelmans and Kisiel; 1970) includes three in-depth studies of Husserl's attitude towards science. I thank Prof. Jeff Mitscherling of Guelph University for information about this book.

[41] According to Joseph Kockelmans, Merleau-Ponty excludes the possibility of considering spatial relations of co-existence outside of time: "the coexistence defining space is not alien to time; this coexistence is the 'appertaining' of two phenomena to the same temporal wave" (Kockelmans 1970: 294).

[42] Merleau-Ponty's *Phenomenology of Perception* commences with a study of the body (Part I), and the perceived world (Part II), to conclude with an analysis of being-

movement and bodily space is not space thought of or represented" (Merleau-Ponty 1945/1962: 137). The capabilities to and experience of movement are the potential and actual sources of knowledge; movement provides us with access to the world and to the objects situated within this world. Motility elucidates spatial existence; human spatiality, inherently dynamic, is the pre-condition, not only for the perception but also for the creation of a meaningful world (Langer 1989: 47).[43]

One of Merleau-Ponty's examples of this grounding of meaning in the spatial situation of incarnate subjects is drawn from music--that is, from performance. An experienced organist is capable of performing a piece of music on a new instrument, with a different arrangement of manuals and stops, than the one he usually plays, only after a short rehearsal during which,

> he does not learn objective spatial positions for each stop and pedal, nor does he commit them to 'memory'. . . Between the musical essence of the piece as it is shown in the score and the notes which actually sound round the organ, so direct a relation is established that the organist's body and his instrument are merely the medium of this relationship. . . The whole problem of habit here is one of knowing how the musical significance of an action can be concentrated in a certain place to the extent that, in giving himself entirely to the music, the organist reaches for precisely those stops and pedals which are to bring it into being.
>
> (Merleau-Ponty 1945/1962: 146)

In this case, the body of the organist articulates an expressive space, constituted and possessed in and through movement (action). The world of human perception is inseparable from human awareness of the body in its placement, orientation and motility. For Merleau-Ponty, the human being is not a pure thinker but a body-subject situated in a world; this ontological change towards incarnate

---

for-itself and being-in-the-world (Part III).

[43]This association of space or spatiality with movement in human existential experience had been articulated earlier in the philosophy of Max Scheler, especially in his *Idealismus--Realismus* of 1927-1928 (Gosztonyi 1976: 873-879).

subjectivity redefines epistemology.[44] As Monika Langer writes,

> Merleau-Ponty points out that all knowledge takes place within the horizons opened up by perception, that the primordial structures of perception pervade the entire range of reflective and scientific experience, and that all forms of human co-existence are based on perception. . . . Ideas are never absolutely pure thought, but rather cultural objects necessarily linked to acts of expression whose source is the phenomenal body itself as already primordially expressive.
> (Langer 1989: xiv-xv)

Merleau-Ponty's philosophy of incarnate subjectivity implies a crucial shift in the notion of space (chapter 2, Part II of *Phenomenology of Perception*), for he seeks to overturn the antinomy of "objective-subjective" space. In descriptive phenomenology, the subject of experience is the phenomenal body inseparably bound up with the world in which a human being lives and moves, is situated and orientated. The human body is the vehicle of one's "being-in-the-world." As Joseph Kockelmans writes, "body and world constitute a unity of mutual implication. . . We are in the world through our body and perceive it with our body" (Kockelmans 1970: 278, 280). The "body-subject" is inescapably located in space. This anchoring of the body in the world opens up a possibility for the creation of a "human space" encompassing the world of emotions, dreams, myths and madness, as well as the world of reflection (Langer 1989: 87).[45]

The notion of the world used by Merleau-Ponty differs from the physical "totality of all actual events" and is inseparably bound with incarnate subjectivity. The world is known, created and encountered in human experience. In the phenomenological philosophy of **Patrick Heelan**, a World is "the preexisting structure

---

[44]According to Monika Langer, Merleau-Ponty rejects Husserl's idea of the transcendental ego, an important element in Husserlian transcendental idealism (Langer 1989: xiv). Incidentally, Roman Ingarden, was critical of the same element in the thought of his teacher (Rieser 1971/1986: 161).

[45]Kockelmans calls these spaces of myths, hallucinations, and dreams "anthropological spaces" and discusses the tension between living in any of these spaces co-constituted by our intentionality and the physical belonging to a geometric, "nonhuman" space (Kockelmans 1970: 304).

of actual and possible objects of our experience" which include "the space and time of our perceptions" extended and influenced by technology and science (Heelan 1983: 10).[46]

> A World, though singular in that it applies exclusively to a particular community at a particular place and period, is not the only World: Worlds are historical and anthropological, differentiated by peoples, times, places, and perhaps professions. A World is always intersubjective, the shared space of a historical community with a particular culture that uses a common language and a common description of reality.
> (Heelan 1983: 10)

The "World" is not only a particular space at a particular time, a spatio-temporal region. It is a *Lebenswelt*[47] created and inhabited by human beings who are simultaneously the World's objects (physical and material) and subjects (nonphysical and immaterial, i.e. exercising responsibility and rationality). The individual human subject, a *being-in-the-World*, is "not just a piece of irritable organic material, a "third-person process," nor just a disembodied Cartesian spirit, but a Body" (Heelan 1983: 12). For Heelan, as for Merleau-Ponty, the human subject is an embodied subject "connoting physicalities as well as intentionalities" and "neither science nor unaided perception give us anything other than a world-to-and-for-human-embodied-

---

[46]Heelan's notion of the "World" draws from the concept of the *Lebenswelt*, introduced in the late writings of Edmund Husserl and defined briefly as "the world of common experience" (Gurwitsch 1972: 350). The *Lebenswelt* has two main senses: (1) the pre-cognitive world of experience, common to all human beings, (2) the world created by humans, including science, art, culture, etc. Heelan discusses both meanings and reveals how the primordial World (*Lebenswelt I*) is obscured and blurred by cultural conditioning. I owe the clarification of this issue to Prof. Philip Buckley.

[47]The lived world presents itself to human consciousness directly and in an immediate experience; its opposition is the world of science, "a theoretico-logical superstructure which, in the thinking of modern Western man, passes for reality" (Gurwitsch 1972: 352). In the second sense, *Lebenswelt* has a historico-social connotation and "is relative to a certain society at a given moment of its history" (ibidem).

subjects" (Heelan 1983: 13, 279).[48] Hence, the principle of the "ontological primacy of perception" which, together with the methodology of hermeneutics and "horizonal realism" constitutes the conceptual basis for Heelan's philosophy of science and his study of the nature of the visual space. In horizonal epistemology,

> there is no identity of reference between individual objects of a manifest image (e.g. this patch of sensed-color) and individual objects of the relevant scientific image (e.g. this spectral mix of wave lengths), only many-to-one and one-to-many mappings of perceptual objects contextually defined within mutually incompatible but complementary contexts.
> (Heelan 1983: 270)

Objects and events in the World are perceived through the mediacy of a multitude of "horizons"--each being "a structured domain of reality" with "a particular descriptive language and a corresponding context for its correct use" (Heelan 1983: 177-178). The contexts may be compatible and cumulative, or incompatible and non-additive, or even mutually exclusive.[49]

In particular, according to Heelan, human visual space is structured into a hyperbolic space of variable curvature (and of different near and far zones), but under the influence of modern science and the human "carpentered" environment, becomes organized in a Cartesian-Euclidean way (straight lines, uniformity, perpendicularity). The Euclidean visual space is a "cultural artifact" and represents a new horizon of reality made accessible to perception by the mediacy of science (Heelan 1983: 53). Mathematics provides a source of possible models of the structure of perception (i.e. Riemannian hyperbolic geometry) and an important influence on the content of perception itself (Euclidean geometry with the Cartesian coordinate system).[50]

---

[48]According to Heelan, "all intentionality, even that operative in perception, is essentially hermeneutical, since it is concerned with making sense of our experience" (Heelan 1983: 12).

[49]This is true of writings about music; the plurality of "meta-musical" languages has been disscussed by Eggebrecht (1955, 1974), Bengtsson (1973), Nattiez (1987/1990).

[50]Heelan's hermeneutical phenomenology investigates "the way mathematical models, scientific theories, and technological instrumentation can influence, transform,

Nonetheless, Heelan claims that the hyperbolic nature of visual perception is pre-reflective and independent of the perceiver's act of choice (Heelan 1983: 158-160).

Heelan's phenomenology of vision is influenced by the writings of Husserl, Heidegger and Merleau-Ponty, and strives to incorporate or validate the first-person account in a disciplined and scholarly context. The same sources of inspiration, and a similar methodology, though with a stronger reliance on introspection, are utilized by **Don Ihde** in his *Listening and Voice: A Phenomenology of Sound* (1976).

One of Ihde's main premises is the difference between aural and visual perception, both providing different data about the spatio-temporal environment in which human beings are inescapably situated. Silence is the horizon of sound, while invisibility is the horizon of objects (Ihde 1976: 50), but "listening makes the invisible present" (p. 51). Thus, auditory and visual fields have overlapping and non-overlapping regions (p. 54); they differ, particularly in shape: sounds are omnidirectional so that the human subject is at the centre of the auditory space (and at the edge of the visual space). As Ihde writes,

> Were it to be modelled spatially, the auditory field would have to be conceived of as a sphere within which I am positioned, but whose 'extent' remains indefinite as it reaches outward towards a horizon.
> (Ihde 1976: 74)

Ihde points out that this spherical field is shaped and transformed by the human voluntary focus of attention on auditory events from a certain direction (p. 74). However, the most important aspects of auditory fields are, in this theory of perception, the twin dimensions of "directionality" and "surroundability." In Ihde's opinion, the essential ambiguity of auditory perception stems from the fact that

> the global encompassing surroundability of sound, which is most dramatic and fully present in overwhelming sounds and the often quite precise and definite directionality of sound presence which is noted in our daily 'location' of sounds, are both *constantly co-present*.
> (Ihde 1976: 76)

---

and enrich the content of perception" (Heelan 1983: 8).

Ihde claims that directional hearing is a matter of everyday experience, while the awareness of the "surroundability of sound" is an attribute of a purely "musical" mode of listening:

> If I put myself in the 'musical attitude' and listen to the sound as if it were music, I may suddenly find that its ordinary and strong sense of directionality, while not disappearing, recedes to such a degree that I can concentrate upon its surrounding presence.
>
> (Ihde 1976: 76-77)

Ihde's introspective analysis of an experience of listening to a symphony in a concert hall clarifies what he means by the "surrounding presence of sound." This experience arises while the listener, immobile in his or her location, faces the orchestra on the stage and hears sounds from all directions (directly from the orchestra and reflections from all the walls). Enveloped in the spatially rich and evolving sonorities, the listeners bracket out the physical reality of sound and their own corporeality in order to perceive a disembodied music of pure temporality, a music that sounds from nowhere (cf. Chapter II). This kind of "musical" listening belongs to a particular historical and social context, i.e. it is an element of one World (in Heelan's sense). Ihde's mistake is to assume the universal validity of what is culturally circumscribed; this limitation results, partly, from his reliance on the first-person account (this is a characteristics of the phenomenological method).[51]

Whereas Don Ihde points out the difference between the aural and visual modes of spatial perception, Patrick Heelan focuses on the nature of visual perception of space, which is--in his theory--primarily hyperbolic and only secondarily (through cultural conditioning) Euclidean. Finally, in Merleau-Ponty's phenomenology of perception a particular importance is ascribed to the tactile-kinaesthetic aspects of the

---

[51]Cognitive acts of perception or belief, can be studied from an objective, third-person perspective or from a subjective, first-person standpoint. The latter stance, according to Heelan, "supposes that the inquirer is also a perceiving subject, has direct access to perceptual acts of the kind that is being studied, and can use this evidence in the inquiry. A first-person study then asks the question: what is it for one like me to perceive a state of the World?" (Heelan 1983: 6). The problem, of course, is to decide what it means to be "one like me."

spatial experience.[52] This variety of modes of spatial perception indicates the richness of the human existence in space.[53]

This existence can be divided and systematized in **spatial spheres** ordered according to their increasing magnitude or growing distance from the self.[54] Therefore, starting from Merleau-Ponty's "zero degree of spatiality" that is the awareness of one's own bodily space, various personal spaces may be distinguished: a space of intuition and perception (extended through technology), a space of bodily action.[55] There are, then, the communal spaces of increasing size, from the inhabited space of the home, through various spaces and places of social life, to spaces constructed in art.[56] All these "spaces" are centred upon human corporeality and constitute various aspects of the experience of human "spatial life." In this, they differ completely from the "spaces" of physics and mathematics, spaces conceived of *in abstracto*, as ideas existing beyond the subjective experience of space (Gosztonyi 1976: 1004-1028).

One of these abstract notions of space, the timeless, "absolute space" of classical physics has become a tenet of modern culture, as the assumed scene of reality

---

[52]Notions of bodily-kinaesthetic intelligence and spatial intelligence appear in Howard Gardner's theory (Gardner 1985).

[53]For an overview of the various types of spatial perception (visual, aural and tactile), as well as their dependence on time and the connection with movement, see Gosztonyi (1976: 794-823).

[54]Cf. the discussion of spatial spheres of existence in Gosztonyi (1976), or a systematization of these spheres by Whiteman (1967).

[55]Cf. Whiteman (1967). Psychological development of concepts of personal space (of increasing magnitude) in children has been outlined in an influential study by Piaget and Inhelder (1956).

[56]Cassirer (1931), Porebski (1978), and Heelan (1983) talk about the plurality of spaces in culture; Genette ((1966-1969), Bachelard (1967), Glowinski (1978), and Mitchell (1980) deal with various issues of space and literature; Norberg-Schultz (1971) focusses on existential dimensions of space in architecture; writings on issues of space in other arts (sculpture, painting) are too numerous to be quoted.

contemplated by the detached and disembodied Cartesian Minds.[57] This conceptual framework falsifies the spatio-temporal nature of the human, personal and incarnate existence--the source, medium and purpose of the spatio-temporality of arts. As Patrick Heelan reminds us, "persons, however, are not Minds: they are natural entities with a special power, that of constructing worlds and horizons to live in." (Heelan 1983: 257).

Heelan distinguishes two basic types of "Worlds" in which space is construed in a diametrically opposed manner. In modern naturalistic Worlds, "there is no part of space, no matter how distant, that is not like local space, and that is not metrically continuous with local space, and consequently, that is not in principle profane" (Heelan 1983: 256). This infinite, continuous, and homogeneous space without local irregularities bears a close resemblance to "absolute space."

On the contrary, in premodern, primitive and religious Worlds, space is discontinuous and non-homogeneous: it is divided into the spheres of the Sacred and the Profane. Both spheres are experienced in time. The reality of the non-scientific Worlds is organized by religious myths that project "the space and time of human life against the background of mythological events occurring in sacred Space and Time" (Heelan 1983: 254). The profane space is well known and well structured, it is the inhabitable space of everyday life. The sacred spaces are mysterious and unknowable; these meeting places with deities, these locations of the re-enactment of sacred rituals create discontinuities in the Profane and allow for the Sacred, the eternally present, to invade the ordinary spatiality and temporality of life.[58] The sacred Temples, Labyrinths or Mountains, the revered places of rituals and encounters with the

---

[57]As Heelan writes: "Mind for the new scientific culture was the disembodied spectator of an infinite physical universe spatially integrated with the laws of classical physics and Euclidean geometry" (Heelan 1983: 257).

[58]However, in some religious cultures all life, all time and all space are considered sacred, because the transcendental Sacred is simultaneously immanent. The Deity is manifest and encountered "in and through" the world, not "over and above" the world (c.f. Pierre Teilhard de Chardin's *Le Milieu Divin*, 1957/1960).

transcendental mystery, are visited in a sacred Time which is set aside from ordinary living (cf. Cassirer 1931, Porebski 1978).[59]

Conclusion

The multitude of meanings of space presented in this Chapter, along with their historical evolution, casts light on the conceptual difficulties with defining space in music. From ordinary language we learn that space may mean an interval, distance, expanse, or, for instance, a three-dimensional infinite void. From classical philosophy we learn that the notions of space evolve and are historically limited. From modern physics we learn that there is no space independent of time, but only a space-time. However, we do not learn that with the reassuring certainty of absolute Truth: is there a space-time? What is a space-time? The philosophical-scientific debate continues. From phenomenological analysis of the human condition, we learn that "to be is to be situated" in a World (Merleau-Ponty), and that this World is a construct of the human creativity and imagination. In the spatio-temporal experience of human life, as analyzed by phenomenology, and as in modern science after the Einsteinian revolution, space and time are inseparably intertwined. This unity has important consequences for the re-definition of music as a "spatio-temporal" art.

---

[59]In an analogous way, the Concert Hall is the temple of Music, a purely temporal and disembodied art (cf. Chapter II).

CHAPTER II

A HISTORY OF CONCEPTS OF SPACE IN MUSIC

Introduction

> In the overwhelming presence of music which fills space and penetrates my awareness, not only am I momentarily taken out of myself in what is often described as a loss of self-awareness which is akin to ecstatic states, but there is a distance from things. The purity of music in its ecstatic surrounding presence overwhelms my ordinary connection with things so that I do not even primarily hear the symphony as the sounds of the instruments.
>
> (Ihde 1976: 77-78)

Don Ihde's phenomenological description of listening to music in the concert hall articulates certain features of this perceptual experience. The experience is, as the philosopher observes, often accompanied with "the temptation toward the notion of a pure or disembodied sound" (p. 78).[1] This disembodiment of music accompanies its transformation into a domain co-extensive with human inner life, a profound realm inaccessible to cognitive analysis and verbal description. One may say that the history of the notion of "space" in music, outlined in this chapter, is a history of yielding to and overcoming this "spiritualizing" temptation. Many authors sought to discover an internal "musical space" perceived while listening to music without noticing the physical spatiality of the musical sound. A history of these endeavours is presented in section 2.1. Other theoreticians and composers considered "space" the epitomy of "stasis" and claimed that "spatialization of time" is an important feature of

---

[1] As Susan McClary writes, "a very strong tradition of Western musical thought has been devoted to defining music as the sound itself, to erasing the physicality involved in both the making and the reception of music" (McClary 1991: 136).

contemporary music, a feature which distinguishes new music from the art of the past. This type of musical spatiality is discussed in section 2.2. Another large area of compositional research and theoretical reflection links space to pitch. In addition to the traditional concepts of intervals, scales, etc., mathematical notions of space have been introduced in the research and creation of contemporary music. Here, the tendency to "disembody" musical materials reaches its apex (section 2.3). Finally, the "musical space" becomes what it has always been--the space of performance and perception (section 2.4).

Various perceptual and cognitive types of space appearing in the conceptions discussed here differ in many of their essential attributes including the number of dimensions. A phenomenal musical space, for instance (section 2.1), has been defined as being three-dimensional (Kurth, Clifton), one-dimensional (Brelet) or completely non-dimensional (Zuckerkandl). Such space, originally related to pitch and/or time and often labelled "musical," is placed in opposition (as superior) to "auditory" or "acoustic" space. The relationship of space to time is particularly equivocal: for some authors musical space is the opposite of musical time (e.g. Cogan, Morris), for others time is included in the concept of space as one of its dimensions (Kurth). Further confusion arises from the usage of the same terms (such as musical, auditory or sonic space) in altogether different meanings.

2.1.
Space without space: A history of the notion of "musical space" in music theory and aesthetics

The origins of "musical space" can be traced back to the writings of German theoreticians, for whom space was an important, new subject of research. This novelty was a result of a change in focus, and not a consequence of the non-existence of "spatial" topics in earlier writings about music. The "spatio-vertical" representation of pitch, for instance, has been one of the fundamental characteristics of Western music since the 9th century (Duchez 1979).[2] In the 19th century, **Hermann von Helmholtz** emphasized "the characteristic resemblance between the relations of the musical scale and of space" (Helmholtz 1863/1954: 370). Helmholtz, an eminent scientist with important contributions to the philosophy of space to his credit,[3] wrote:

> It is an essential character of space that at every position within it like bodies can be placed, and like motions can occur. Everything that is possible to happen in one part of space is equally possible in every other part of space and is perceived by us in precisely the same way. This is the case also with the musical scale. Every melodic phrase, every chord, which can be executed at any pitch, can be also executed at any other pitch in such a way that we immediately perceive the characteristic marks of their similarity. . . Such a close analogy consequently exists in all essential relations between the musical scale and space, that even alteration of pitch has a readily recognised and unmistakable resemblance to motion in space, and is often metaphorically termed the ascending or descending *motion* or *progression* of a part. Hence, again, it becomes possible for motion in music to imitate the peculiar characteristics of motive forces in space, that is, to form an image of the various impulses and forces which lie at the root of motion.
> (Helmholtz 1863/1954: 370)

Helmholtz's analogy between space and scale is based on the idea of the

---

[2] Various aspects of spatial representation of pitch are included in most theories of musical space; these issues are discussed in section 2.3 of this chapter.

[3] The introduction to the reprint of Helmholtz's *On the Sensations of Tone* (1954) contains an overview of his scientific output including a list of main publications. Reichenbach (1927) and Gray (1979) discuss Helmholtz's *Axioms of geometry* (1868).

"absoluteness" of static, homogeneous and isotropic space which contains all objects and events.⁴ This is a Newtonian concept of space (see Chapter I). Pitch space, in Helmholtz's account, has similar features: melodies and chords can be transposed to "any other pitch" without being affected by this change. The parallel between the two domains is underscored by the phenomenon of motion which is common to both, occurring in the space of "pitch" (ascending or descending) or "in space."

While pointing out the analogy between the two domains Helmholtz does not use the term "musical space." The emergence of this notion was simultaneous with the introduction of new paradigms of space and time in the modern philosophy of science. This development was stimulated by **Ernst Cassirer** who proposed the theme of "space-time" for the Fourth Congress of the Society for Aesthetics held in 1930 in Hamburg.⁵ Amongst four papers on music presented at this Congress, Hans Mersmann's discussion of the two-dimensionality of musical time (cf. below in this Section), and Walter Riezler's comparison of spatiality in "static" music by Debussy and in painting, were the most notable (Wellek 1931).⁶ In a comment on the results of the Congress, Siegfried Nadel regretted that too little attention had been given to

---

⁴Robert Morris's arguments for the parallels between pitch and space resemble Helmholtz's (cf. section 2.3).

⁵*Der Raum-Zeit-Kongress der Gesellschaft für Ästhetik und allgemeine Kunstwissenschaft* took place on 7-9 October 1930. Proceedings of the Congress and a detailed report by Albert Wellek were published in 1931. Cassirer, a philosopher with comprehensive scientific interests, sought to bring aesthetics up to date with new developments in 20th-century science, such as Einstein's relativity theory (Cassirer 1921; 1931). At the Congress, Cassirer discussed the idea of plurality of spaces (i.e. mythical, aesthetic and theoretical notions of space).

⁶For Riezler, in Debussy's music "all tectonic articulations are destroyed, the tones are melodically of equal value and equally important, various 'directions' in space can no longer be spoken of--the clearly dimensioned tonal space no longer exists" (Riezler 1930: 194; quoted in Lippman 1952: 404). Interestingly, Riezler's study predates Schoenberg's well-known description of a 'unified' space in which separate dimensions can not be distinguished (Schoenberg 1941/1975). The article also antecedes Adorno's critique of stasis in Debussy's music (Adorno 1948/1973).

defining "musical space" (Nadel 1931).[7] Attempting to fill in this apparent gap, Nadel emphasized the distinction between the auditory space of sound localization (*der phänomenale Raum*) and the specifically musical sonic space (*der spezifische Tonraum*). This important opposition of the "auditory" and the "musical" recurs in other musicological writings (Kurth, Wellek, Zuckerkandl, cf. this section, below). In all these texts, a rigorous distinction is maintained between musical and non-musical sounds, *Töne* and *Klänge*.[8] Nadel's "musical space" has a cognitive rather than a phenomenal character; it is related to pitch height and analogous to geometric space (similarly to Helmholtz's musical scale). In contrast to Helmholtz, Nadel emphasizes the complexity of sonic space (*Tonraum*) which results from considering timbre and harmony as independent musical dimensions, as well as from the intricacy of pitch itself--which is, as Nadel notices, best represented by a spiral, not a straight line.[9]

Several issues discussed in the texts mentioned so far recur throughout the history of the notion of "musical space:" (1) separation of "musical" from "auditory" space, (2) comparison of such musical space to the three-dimensional space known from experience and geometry, (3) static character of space, (4) spatial character of pitch and pitch relationships, (5) spatial representations of pitch, (6) spatial features of musical time.

---

[7] It is likely that Nadel introduced the term "musical space" (*musikalischer Raum*); I have not found instances of its earlier usage. Nadel used the terms "musical space" and "sonic space" (*Tonraum*) as synonymous.

[8] In Ihde's phenomenology of sound, a similar distinction provides a basic characteristic of human mode of listening which is divided into musical and non-musical types (Ihde 1976, cf. Chapter I, 1.5). A translation of the terminological distinction of "Ton" and "Klang" into modern English poses considerable difficulties, especially because of the lack of an appropriate term for "Ton." If "tone" were used, one would need to speak of "tonal" spaces (e.g. Morgan, 1980) but "tonal" already appears in musical contexts in a well-established sense.

[9] Nadel's brief article seems to have inspired Wellek's theory (1934/1963).

Hans Mersmann

Hans Mersmann's contribution to the Space-Time Congress touched upon the spatial character of pitch and time as it focused on the vertical and horizontal dimensions of music.[10] For Mersmann, both dimensions are complex, both include pitch and time: the temporal succession of tones is "horizontal," their simultaneity, "vertical." Thus, the horizontal dimension of music refers to melody, the vertical--to harmony (Mersmann 1926: 11). While the musical dimensions are temporal and complement each other as twin relationships of simultaneity and succession, Mersmann's space (*Raum*) is not dimensional at all. This notion, the second "spatial" aspect of his concept of music presented in the *Angewandte Musikästhetik* (1926), is not paired with time but with "force" (*Kraft*). Mersmann sees music as a projection of energy or force in space, and considers "force" to be masculine, developmental and dynamic, while "space" is feminine, non-developmental and static (Mersmann 1926: 87).[11] Moreover, only force can be described; space is essentially ambiguous and evasive--only when divided does it acquire a degree of clarity. This "force--space" antinomy is, then, used to explain various analytical concepts, e.g. the opposed ideas of dynamic development and static juxtaposition. For Mersmann, space and force provide a double perspective in which musical forms can be perceived. The ambiguity of "space" in Mersmann's theory of music is increased by the fact that space is, simultaneously, the background for force and its complement. It is not, however, related to the physical spatiality of music (e.g. to phenomena of distance,

---

[10]Mersmann introduced this theory in *Angewandte Musikästhetik* [Applied Musical Aesthetics] in 1926.

[11]The association of space with stasis has distinct Bergsonian overtones. Moreover, Mersmann's equation of the polar opposition "force-space" with the gender difference "male-female" draws from an archetype of Western culture. Teresa de Lauretis, for instance, describes this opposition as underlying the traditional Western narrative in which a male hero is "the active principle of culture" while the female is "an element of plot-space, a topos, a resistance, matrix and matter" (De Lauretis 1984: 119). I cite De Lauretis ("Desire in narrative," in *Alice Doesn't*, Bloomington: Indiana University Press, 1984) from Susan McClary's *Feminine Endings* (McClary 1991: 14).

echoes, etc.); neither is it modelled on three-dimensional, physical space.

Various aspects of Mersmann's theory frequently re-emerged in subsequent discourse about music, especially within the Germanic tradition. The association of musical space with staticity reappeared in the writings of Adorno (1948), and was embraced by those avant-garde composers who proposed a spatial image of music, based on the "spatialization" of time, as a new compositional paradigm for the 1960s (see section 2.2). The introduction of geometric terms to label the two dimensions of simultaneity and succession (the vertical and the horizontal) is echoed in Schoenberg's idea of musical space (1941).[12] An a-dimensional and--as it were--"non-spatial" space constitutes an important aspect of Victor Zuckerkandl's philosophy of music (1957). Finally, the dualism of space and force, characteristic of Mersmann's "tectonic-energetic" conception of music, forms one of the primary elements in Ernst Kurth's philosophy of music, presented in the second part of *Musikpsychologie* (1931), entitled "Kraft, Raum, Materie."

Ernst Kurth

For Ernst Kurth, "space and material are manifestations of a stratum between deep subconscious events and the actual world of sound" (Kurth 1931; quoted in Lippman 1952: 116). Here, the essence of music lies not in sound but in inner psychic processes, which reveal their characteristics in sound.[13] The primal sense of "movement," one of the fundamental features of music, requires the intuition of space for its existence: space is **where** the musical motion is taking place. This version of the "container" space (see Chapter I, 1.2) draws from Mersmann's opposition of force (here replaced by movement) and space.

According to Kurth, musical space, belonging to the world of inner, psychic

---

[12]Schoenberg's concept, in contrast to Mersmann's, aims at transcending the separation of the opposed dimensions.

[13]Kurth's notions of energy, matter, and spatiality of music reappear in Leopold Conrad's philosophy of music (1958).

processes, is also essentially ambiguous. It is distinct from visual space, but it includes similar dimensions: pitch as the musical analogue of height and time of width (here Kurth differs from Mersmann). Kurth is aware of limitations in the representation of the one-directional temporal flow of music by the reversible spatial dimension of width. At the same time, he cannot conceive of space otherwise than in terms of a physical, three-dimensional entity: a space simply must have depth!

After rejecting earlier proposals of equating this third dimension of music with dynamics, harmony or actual spatial location (various distances of the instruments from the audience), Kurth points to the unclear feeling of fullness of the inner space as its source; however ambiguous, depth still constitutes a real component of the musical experience.[14] One obvious reason for the ambiguity of the dimension of depth (a reason not discussed by Kurth) is its absence from the geometry of musical notation, in which the vertical orientation on the staff denotes pitch height, while the horizontal placement of notes from left to right signifies their placement in time.[15]

The most important feature of Kurth's musical space is its manifestation in and through movement.[16] Inner musical geometry is similar to, but not identical with, the geometry of the external space; it is linked to the structure of the intervals, chords, and forms of melodic motion (Kurth 1931: 121). Echoing the observations made earlier by Helmholtz, Kurth notices the spatial qualities of pitch, melodic line, contrary and oblique motion, as well as the distance of notes in an interval (*Zwischenraum*). However, cautious of drawing the analogy too far, Kurth considers

---

[14] A three-dimensional model of musical space (with the axes of pitch, time, dynamics) has been proposed by Hans-Joachim Moser (1953). This model includes four beats in common time as units on the time axis, and standard dynamic levels (p, mf, f) as units on the dynamics axis.

[15] However, the musical notation is not entirely "geometric," because it uses a rich array of symbols, in addition to the vertical and horizontal orientations, to indicate relations of pitch and time.

[16] Kurth's idea of a close connection between space and motion influenced writings on musical space by Ingarden (1958) and Lippman (1952)--both discussed in this chapter.

the limitations of a three-dimensional geometric model of music. If melody were linear, polyphony of several melodic lines would have to be called planar (two-dimensional), but chords would make polyphony voluminous (three-dimensional), due to the impression of matter that they convey (Kurth 1931: 125). Since polyphony and harmony coexist in music, it would be simultaneously two- and three-dimensional, which is, obviously, a contradiction.[17] Kurth's argument is devised to demonstrate the absurdity of a one-to-one transition from musical to geometric space, and the complexity of the former. Nonetheless, it is based on an unexplained change of the coordinates of the musical dimensions. In the discussion of the three-dimensionality of music, "linear" melody is one-dimensional; yet, melody includes aspects of pitch and time (analogues of "height" and "width" in Kurth's theory) and is, as such, two-dimensional.

Kurth's study of perceptual aspects of *das musikalische Raumphänomen* includes spatial percepts of different rank and scope. Thus, various meanings of "space" co-exist in his text: space as distance, interval, volume, expanse to be filled, measured time, etc. At the same time, the search for a musical equivalent of the spatial dimension of depth reveals a partiality for the idea of three-dimensionality of space. It is not easy to establish whether this preference originated from convictions acquired in ordinary living experience, was gleaned from classical science or borrowed from Kant's philosophy. However, a certain affinity exists between Kurth's idea of a pre-reflective, inner experience of musical spatiality, and Kant's "pure intuition" of space, which precedes all experience.

---

[17]Here, it may be of importance to recall Anton von Webern's description of monophonic music as linear (horizontal) and his account of how the transition into polyphony by the addition of voices creates an impression of depth (Webern 1933). "Depth" in music may also signify a "spiritual" dimension of profundity, completely unrelated to any physical phenomena (Savage 1989: 70).

Albert Wellek

Distinctions between various types of space in music are refined in the thought of Albert Wellek who distinguishes between auditory space (*Gehörraum*) and the unclear three-dimensional space of musical sounds, the sonic space (*Tonraum*; Wellek 1934/1963). Equally important is the additional, new distinction between *Tonraum* and *Musikraum*, a unique "musical space" of the total perceptual experience in which all spatial aspects of music interact to create a complex overall effect. While acknowledging the four-dimensionality of auditory space (with three spatial dimensions and time), and mentioning examples of its use in music (e.g. in polychorality), Wellek ascribes to this space the status of being external to music and, apparently, inferior to *Tonraum*.

Wellek's definitions of the three dimensions of sonic space (*Tonraum*) resemble those of Kurth, and take into account the ambiguity and non-linear character of pitch (the first dimension), the irreversibility of time (the second dimension), and the contentious character of musical depth, which is there--one could say--only because space has to be three-dimensional. The vertical dimension of music, described as a system of relationships, includes two aspects of pitch--one which changes monotonically with frequency and one rotating in a cycle of octave repetitions. This distinction is captured in modern psychoacoustic terminology as the dualism of "pitch height" (linear dimension) and "pitch chroma" (circular dimension).[18] Similarly to Kurth, Wellek refers to the distance between pitches in an interval as a "Zwischen-raum." He also considers the spatial, two-dimensional quality of musical notation as a proof of the existence of sonic space (*Tonraum*), the basis for musical space. Nevertheless, the emphasis is placed on a separation of the psychological experience of the spatiality of music from the objective spatial features of the musical material. Musical space, the result of a complex interaction of auditory space, sonic space and

---

[18]This terminology, introduced by Bachem (1950) has been recently used by Shephard (1982), Ueda and Ohgushi (1987), Semal and Demany (1990). The difference between the rectilinearity and circularity of pitch is discussed by Brelet (1949) and underlies Morris's differentiation between p-space and pc-space (1987).

emotional space (*Gefühlraum*), evades a clear definition, remaining, for Wellek as for Kurth, ambiguous.

The relegation of the physical spatiality of music outside the domain of the proper "musical" space while considering its consequences (i.e. the notions of texture, volume, distance) is a conceptual drawback shared by Kurth, Wellek, and later writers about music (e.g. Clifton 1983). Another difficulty in formulating such general theories of musical space results from the simultaneous consideration of spatial phenomena of different orders. Wellek discusses, for instance, the perceived spatiality of a pause ("empty space") along with the spatial quality of harmony, apparent in the existence of tonal and chordal "regions"--analogies of "places." These phenomena have little in common, and the notion of a "musical space"--by embracing both and much more--becomes necessarily opaque. Despite these shortcomings, Wellek's three-fold distinction of the **auditory - sonic - musical space** has the merit of revealing the complexity and multi-dimensionality of the spatial aspects of music.

The significance of Mersmann, Kurth or Wellek in German musicology ensured the inclusion of "space" among topics requiring consideration in theoretical discourse about music. A reflection of this can be found in **Heinrich Schenker's** *Der Freie Satz* (1935). For Schenker, tonal or sonic space (*Tonraum*) is an aspect of *Urlinie*: "Unter dem Begriff *Tonraum* verstehe ich den Raum der horizontalen Urlinie-Erfüllung, erst durch diese ist ein Tonraum gegeben und beglaubigt" (Schenker 1935/1956: 43). This space is one-dimensional, purely horizontal; it also effectively duplicates the notion of the *Urlinie* which is supposed to be embedded in sonic space. The concept of *Tonraum* seems superfluous in Schenker's theory, but its presence here may be explained by the currency of spatial topics in German musicological literature.[19]

---

[19]Schenker's notion of space has influenced Robert Morgan's theory (1980).

Brelet, Langer and Ingarden

The phenomenological writings of two philosophers of music, Gisèle Brelet and Roman Ingarden deal with musical space in the manner of Kurth (Brelet 1949; Ingarden 1958/1986). An echo of the Germanic style of discourse on space in music can also be found in the symbolic philosophy of Susanne Langer (1953).

According to **Gisèle Brelet** (1949), a French philosopher of music, sonic space is not three-dimensional: "l'espace sonore est unidimensionnel comme le temps" (Brelet 1949, 93).[20] Reflections on musical space, which is termed alternately *l'espace sonore* or *l'espace musical*, are a subordinate part of Brelet's extensive study of musical time.[21] For Brelet, as for Kurth, physical direction and distance of sounds are irrelevant for music. Brelet rejects also the Bergsonian identification of spatiality with measurement.[22] Yet her elucidations of what is and is not spatial in music are not particularly clear. Brelet writes, for instance, that "harmony unites in succession what space separates, just as it separates what space unites. . . . Spatial and harmonic relations are the inverse of each other" (Brelet 1949: 106; quoted from Lippman 1992: 444-445). This statement becomes more comprehensible in its context: Brelet introduces the dual notions of "harmony" and "space" in her explanation of a spatial image of pitch as a rising spiral, a spiral on which the shortest harmonic interval is the fifth, and the shortest spatial interval, the second. The distinction between the terms "spatial" and "harmonic" in Brelet's idiosyncratic usage is somewhat similar to the differentiation between "pitch height" and "pitch chroma" in psychoacoustics, or

---

[20] I choose to translate Brelet's *l'espace sonore*, which describes a phenomenal entity, as "sonic space" to indicate the similarity of her term to Wellek's *Tonraum*. The translation of *sonore* by "sonorous" appears in Lippman's history of aesthetics (1992).

[21] Spatial topics are dealt with in the first volume of *Le Temps Musical* (devoted to sonic form in music) and include: the ambiguity of sonic space, the difference from visual space, spatial terms in language about music (pitch height, volume, form, melodic line), the spatial quality of the interval (*espace intermédiaire*), the irreversibility of time, the questions of depth and the three-dimensionality of music.

[22] Cf. Chapter I, section 1.5.

"pitch" and "pitch-class" in music theory.

For Brelet, the main function of space in music is to express the dynamism of the musical form, which is particularly apparent in romantic music, which she considers the opposite of classical music. Like Mersmann, Brelet describes the dualism of the romantic and the classical in terms of the antithesis of the dynamic and the static. She claims, for instance, that "la forme générale de l'oeuvre romantique est mouvement dans l'espace dynamique, croissance ou décroissance" (Brelet 1949, vol. 2: 627). As her emphasis is placed on the one-dimensionality of space "as time," a question arises as to the difference in Brelet's theory between time and space. If none, if "space" signifies merely the measurable aspect of time, then this term is expendable. And indeed, Brelet later uses the term "musical space" in a different context, as relating solely to performance space (Brelet 1967).

The notion of space as "a reflection" of musical time is invoked also in *Feeling and Form* by **Susanne Langer** (1953). For Langer, music is "the image of time" whereas "virtual space" is the domain, or "primary illusion," of the fine arts. The philosopher expresses this in her celebrated statement, "music makes time audible and its form and continuity sensible" (Langer 1953: 110). While doing so, it relies on, or creates, a "secondary illusion" of "tonal space" which is defined by Langer, rather opaquely, as "a genuine semblance of distance and scope" (Langer 1953: 117). Langer is aware of several different conceptions of musical spatiality, but does not support any single one, emphasizing that space "arises from the way virtual time unfolds" (a similarity to Ingarden's conception is noticeable). Moreover, as she writes, "space, in music, is a secondary illusion. But, primary or secondary, it is thoroughly 'virtual' i.e. unrelated to the space of actual experience" (Langer 1953: 117). In conclusion, Langer considers the existence of spatial aspects of music as a proof of the interrelatedness of the arts. A "secondary illusion" of space exists in primarily *temporal* music, a "secondary illusion" of time in essentially *spatial* painting.

In **Roman Ingarden**'s phenomenological ontology of music, the musical work has the status of an intentional, intersubjective entity (Ingarden 1958/1986). The ontological basis for the work's existence is found in the score (the schema for performance) brought to life in a multitude of realizations which complete and interpret the notation (Ingarden 1958/1986: 34-40). The work of music contains sonic and non-sonic components;[23] quasi-temporal structure, form, movement and musical space are included in the latter group (p. 88-93). For Ingarden, as for Kurth and Wellek, "musical space" is related neither to the real space of performance nor to any imagined form of space associated with music. This space constitutes itself in the multiplicity of movements of the sonorities; it is--so to say--heard in motion. As such, it is superimposed on the internal time of the musical work.[24] As Ingarden writes:

> The space that constitutes itself in the work in the multiplicity of motions of the sound-constructs is strictly bound up with the shape of those motions; it is designated by them as the specific medium in which they occur.
> (Ingarden 1958/1986: 91)

The Polish philosopher makes a clear distinction between this "peculiar musical space" and the visual space imagined while listening to the music, when the music is programmatic and designed to evoke definite spatial images. Such associative space is not a part of the work, but merely an addition warranted by the presence of "representational elements of the work" (p. 91).

Edward Lippman

Edward Lippman's doctoral dissertation constitutes a new and important stage in the development of the idea of "musical space" in the philosophy of music (Lippman 1952). The three parts of his dissertation deal respectively with (I) music and the space of performance, (II) the question of an intrinsic musical space (its types,

---

[23] Adam Czerniawski translates Ingarden's "dzwiękowe i nie-dzwiekowe skladniki" (Ingarden 1958: 235) as "sounding and nonsounding elements" of the musical work. My translation of "sonic and non-sonic" is more precise. In Polish, "dzwiekowy" refers to "sound" in itself, not to the physical actuality of the action of "sound-ing" which is expressed by the word "dzwieczacy."

[24] Here Ingarden agrees with Brelet and Langer.

dimensions, the high and low in pitch, volume, distance), (III) the relation of music to various non-musical spatial conceptions (synaesthesia, harmony of spheres, dance, symbolism). In the first part of his work, Lippman quotes a large number of psychoacoustic studies in order to emphasize the multi-faceted quality of spatial perceptions in music. This significant aspect of his study will be discussed in more detail in Chapter IV. In the present context of a review of theories of a phenomenal musical space, Lippman's insight into "sound-ideals" of various historical periods is particularly enlightening. As he points out,

> The sound-ideal of romanticism in general seems based, essentially on the lack of localization of the source. It is as though to enter this newly idealized and mystical world of sound we had to abandon our whole clear perception--visual *and* auditory--of the material world of humdrum existence.
> (Lippman 1952: 87)

In other words, romantic music "exists in a world apart--in an internal world of imagination and emotive experience. . . but by no means in the empirical world of sense perception" (p. 87). This is the source of the romantic penchant for the sonority of the French horn (which is difficult to localize), and for the blending of instrumental timbres. The sound-ideal of the 20th century--continues Lippman--"discards the veil placed over music by reverberation" and favours a perceptual separation of the different sound sources clearly localized in space. The romantic idealization of music and musical sound is reflected in the "auditory-versus-musical" opposition common in most theories of musical space including Lippman's own.

In the second part of the dissertation, Lippman emphasizes the difference between auditory space and the intrinsic musical space which he sets out to define in a new way, after reviewing several conceptions of musical spatiality (Kurth, Wellek, Brelet). For Lippman, in music we are dealing with a double spatial experience: "there is the experience of the intrinsic space of music, and there is the experience of auditory perceptual space" (p. 254). "Tonal space" is treated as synonymous with "musical space" and antonymous to "empirical," "sensational," or "perceptual space" throughout his text. Lippman--like Kurth and Ingarden--notices the junction between musical space and motion and writes that "it is possible to regard motion in music as even more basic than space, and to derive space from it as the somewhere in which the motion transpires" (Lippman 1952: 225). However, motion is simultaneously defined as "a temporal change of spatial position" (in pitch space)--which implies a precedence of space.

According to Lippman, the relationship of music to space is analogous to the relationship of mathematics to "empirical and physical" space (p. 231); both express formal properties of space. As he notices, "the concepts of 'order' and 'relation' and 'structure' and 'interval' are not merely acclimated, they are indigenous to music" (p. 231; here Lippman parallels the argumentation by Helmholtz). Music becomes connected with empirical space by virtue of its "formal similarity" to space; it is spatial as "mathematics of space is spatial" (ibidem).[25]

For Lippman, and for him only, pitch and volume (both dependent on the frequency and intensity of sounds) are the two basic dimensions of musical space, dimensions from which "we can derive distance and motion, and largeness and smallness--characterizations basic to musical experience" (Lippman 1952: 237). In the "intrinsic musical space" pitch cannot be represented by height, duration by width or loudness by depth, and the complex spatial dimensions are difficult to conceive of. However, simultaneously, Lippman identifies musical space with "a spatial continuum of sensations in a direction which we call by preference 'low-high'" (p. 236)--that is with pitch.

The difficulty with envisioning spatial dimensions of music in unequivocal terms may be a consequence of the fact that Lippman's definitions of the perceptual attributes of sounds differ from those commonly accepted. According to Lippman, these features include pitch, loudness, volume and density for simple tones, and the same attributes, with added brightness, fullness and roughness, for complex sounds (p. 216). The eighth feature, "richness," is left undefined, though it is also considered

---

[25]For a phenomenological analysis of the "spatial" nature of mathematics, and of the ontological status of mathematical spaces see Becker (1923/1970). I present mathematical aspects of musical spatiality in section 2.3. of this chapter.

spatial. Here, Lippman attempts to describe music "as heard"--in a phenomenological manner, yet without the complex terminological apparatus of phenomenology. At the same time, he grapples with the complexity of issues resulting from his attempt to embrace all aspects of musical spatiality in one theory.[26]

Lippman expresses a conviction that "the striking similarity of music and space can be nothing but an outcome of intrinsic spatiality in music" (p. 235). Having said that, he devotes the third part of the dissertation to the relations of music to other types of space (in visual arts, physical sciences, etc.). While pointing out the multiplicity of phenomena requiring consideration in this respect, Lippman touches upon various spatial and symbolic aspects of music (ranging from instrument sizes, through dance, to cosmic harmony).[27] Nonetheless, the importance of Lippman's work in the development of the idea of space in music, lies primarily in pointing out the spatial features of sound as potential musical material, just at the time when contemporary music was on the verge of spatialization.

Victor Zuckerkandl

In contrast to Lippman, Zuckerkandl ignores the physical spatiality of sound (Zuckerkandl 1957). The basic premise of his theory is that music belongs to the "external" world, a world placed beyond the physical and beyond the psyche.[28] This world "stands to the two others in the relation of the general to the particular, of the

---

[26] In an article based on the dissertation, Lippman limits himself to reviewing perceptual and physical aspects of space as factors in music and avoids the complicated and confusing issue of the intrinsic musical space (Lippman 1963).

[27] He emphasizes the absence of one simple explanation for all these relationships, and proposes a theory of the synaesthetic foundation for the relations of music and the visual arts.

[28] Zuckerkandl's metaphysical idea of space and Brelet's writings inspired Paul William Stofft's "structuralist approach to music and painting" (Ph.D. dissertation of 1975). Stofft's "musical space" is alternatively termed "tonal space" and depicted with a three-dimensional graphic representation.

primary to the derivative" (Zuckerkandl 1957: 145).[29] For Zuckerkandl, tones possess dynamic qualities which "can only be understood as manifestations of an orderly action of forces within a given system" (p. 35). The system in question is the tonality of Western music, with different keys, seven-note scales, tonics and dominants, and so forth. Here, Zuckerkandl asks his readers to make a "leap of faith:" he posits an existence, in a realm beyond, of certain metaphysical forces which can be revealed (i.e. made audible) solely by Western tonal music. To agree with Zuckerkandl that space is "placeless and flowing" seems to be quite easy if we can accept that!

According to Zuckerkandl, auditory space differs from visual space (defined as an aggregate of all places) for it is completely indivisible: "the ear knows space only as an undivided whole . . . the space we hear is a space without places" (p. 276). More importantly, a fundamental significance is ascribed to the distinction between hearing tones and noises:

> it is the meaning of the noise to draw our attention to the particular locality in space where it is generated, whereas it is part of the meaning of tone to divert us from any distinguishing of localities in space.
> (Zuckerkandl 1957: 279)

Noises belong with other sensations in the visual-tactile space, only tones alone are purely "auditory."[30] Despite a difference in terminology, this dichotomy mirrors the persistent separation of the auditory space (Zuckerkandl's noises) from the musical space (Zuckerkandl's tones) in writings of Kurth, Nadel, Wellek and others. This clear-cut opposition also reflects the romantic idealization of music (discussed by Lippman) and prefigures a dichotomy of modes of listening distinguished in Ihde's phenomenology of sound (Chapter I, 1.5).

In Zuckerkandl's description, "the placeless, flowing space of tones" entirely lacks three-dimensionality, yet it surrounds the hearer by "moving toward him, from

---

[29]Here, Zuckerkandl's theory resembles romantic philosophies of the spiritual essence of absolute music, e.g. Schopenhauer's (Dahlhaus 1978/1989).

[30]Clifton found Zuckerkandl's distinction between tone and noise particularly unwarranted (Clifton 1983: 138).

all about" (p. 290). Tones fill the space, but their spatiality cannot be measured--in Zuckerkandl's auditory space all boundaries, parts, locations are absent.[31] Yet depth exists. It "refers not to the distance between my ear and the location in space where a tone is produced . . . it refers to the space I encounter in tones, to the 'from' element of the encounter" (p. 289). Finally,

> space . . . is not only that whence something encounters me, space is also that in which what encounters me is mutually related. Space is the whence of the encounter and the where of the relation.
>
> (Zuckerkandl 1957: 302)

Interestingly, Zuckerkandl's definition of space as "the whence of the encounter and the where of the relation" could be easily applied to the physical spatiality of musical sound.[32] The "dynamic" quality of space revealing itself in motion places Zuckerkandl's theory in opposition to many other concepts of musical space, in particular to those who identify space with stasis (cf. Section 2.2). I share his conviction that space in music is dynamic (for me, music is "spatio-temporal"), but I disagree with his description of space as "placeless." Zuckerkandl's notions of "auditory space" and the "external world" are unique to this author; his spiritual conception of musical spatiality belongs to the realm of the romantic metaphysics of music.

Thomas Clifton

Clifton's phenomenologically oriented study of "music as heard" touches upon various aspects of the perceptual experience including musical space, examined in compositions ranging from chant to works by Mahler and Ligeti (Clifton 1983: 137-204). The concept of musical space plays a major role in Clifton's philosophy; space belongs to the four constitutive elements of music (together with "time," "play" and

---

[31] Ihde's notion of the *surroundability* as the main characteristic of the *musical* mode of listening resembles this "placeless, flowing" space of tones (Ihde 1979; cf. Chapter I).

[32] "Encounters" of listeners with spatio-temporal sounds; "relations" of sounds originating from various positions in space.

"feeling"). Musical space is construed in the context of a rigorous separation of the two worlds, the acoustic and the musical. For Clifton, as for Kurth, Ingarden and Zuckerkandl, "musical space and musical movement are inseparable, each defines the other" while "space is not frozen, immobile and antithetical to time" (p. 153). He does not link spatiality to stasis.

In *Music as Heard*, the notion of space embraces diverse aspects of the perceptual experience of music, such as the awareness of source distance or the apparent thickness of melodic lines.[33] Clifton juxtaposes descriptions of aspects of abstract pitch/time space with observations of chosen features of spatio-temporal musical performances. What makes his characterization of musical space more elusive is, according to Edward Lippman, "the inclusion of the contribution of the experiencing subject as well as the musical object" in the analysis (Lippman 1992: 461). This is a consequence of his methodology of phenomenological orientation.[34] Clifton suggests that

> the distinction between being physically located in acoustical space and phenomenally located in musical space must be constantly kept in mind. . . . We hear tones as occupying certain positions of a purely phenomenal, non-physical nature.
> (Clifton 1983: 142-143)

---

[33] The ideas of "line" and its perceptual "thickness" have appeared earlier in the doctoral dissertation by Victor McDermott (1966) and his article about "a conceptual musical space" based on the dissertation (1972); cf. Section 2.2.

[34] Clifton's study is based on Husserl's *Ideas I* and *The Phenomenology of Internal Time-Consciousness* complemented with Merleau-Ponty's *Phenomenology of Perception*. Lawrence Ferrara criticizes Clifton for his reluctance to deal with the hermeneutical aspects of Heidegger's philosophy as well as for his misreading of Merleau-Ponty's phenomenology (Ferrara 1991: 152-154). This critique, as any other, reveals Ferrara's own agenda; hermeneutics constitutes an important aspect of his eclectic analytical method. I think that Clifton's omission of Husserl's late writings (*Ideas II*, and especially *The Crisis of European Sciences*) which introduce the concepts of "lived body" and "life-world" is more significant. In addition, the weakness of Clifton's and Ferrara's studies lies in their bypassing of the phenomenological aesthetic of Roman Ingarden, Husserl's disciple, in favour of drawing directly from Husserl or Heidegger, whose "transcendental" and "constitutive" (Husserl) or "ontological" (Heidegger) studies are of limited applicability in music.

In Clifton's theory, musical space is neither an analog of visual space nor a counterpart of the physical space of performance. However, its existence depends on the perceptual experience of texture to the extent that Clifton uses a quasi-Husserlian expression of "texture-as-space" (p. 69) to indicate what type of musical spatiality he sets about to define. This space includes lines, flat surfaces, surfaces revealing varying degrees of relief, and masses with different degrees of solidity (and, at times, with "holes" in them). As Clifton writes, "masses themselves can dissolve back into tangled webs of lines in three dimensions of musical space" (p. 69). Here, the various types of space are described in the order of increasing complexity and with a rising number of dimensions.

"The narrowest, if not the simplest form of musical space is the single line" (Clifton 1983: 143). Lines may be thin or thick, or may fluctuate along certain dimensions while remaining constant along others. According to Clifton's phenomenological analysis of the experience of listening to Gregorian chant, the line comprises "at least five parameters: contour, width, distance, timbre, rhythmic level" (p. 151). This is a surprising statement: can a line have composite dimensions and remain a "line"--that is a one-dimensional entity? Clifton's description becomes clearer when he explains that while listening to chant in the reverberant space of a church "both spaces, the phenomenal and the physical collaborate in the production of a line" (p. 151).[35] The "line" is, then, a complex perceptual construct wedding together various features of sound heard by a listener who is located in the space of performance. What about the performers, though? Is their experience of singing the chant, a liturgical form of music, not a part of this chant's "musical space"? Are features of the "line" the same for the singer and the listener? Clifton's theory ignores this issue. Instead, he presents spatial constructs in a "geometric" order from

---

[35]The diagrams of "width" and "distance" do not represent the physical-spatial features of chant heard during a performance in a reverberant church. Clifton claims that "purely by means of changes in vowel sound, the width of the line varies in thickness" (Clifton 1983: 145). The alternation of soloistic and choral passages also increases the thickness and thinness of the line.

line, through surface, to volume.

A thick line changes into a surface. This type of texture, in turn, exists in several varieties: (1) undifferentiated surface (without movement, contrasts or timbral complexity); (2) surface with low relief (with a line adhering to it, with a slight fluctuation of timbre, etc.); (3) surface with middle relief (with temporal transformations of contours and timbres); (4) surface with high relief (constituting a ground from which a figure is projected). "High relief introduces more pronounced experiences of line and depth" (p. 173). When lines, surfaces and volumes create a truly three-dimensional space, the notion of depth comes to the foreground (p. 178).

Clifton explains how musical, phenomenal depth differs from the one known from sensory experience, pointing out that in music apparent size and magnitude are not correlated with distance and depend, instead, on "dynamic level, tone color, and the kind of texture involved" (p. 179). He considers four different ways in which depth may be present in music: distance, penetration, multidimensional linear forms and faceting. While the phenomenon of distance in the physical space is overtly excluded from Clifton's theory, it is, nevertheless, considered in abstracto.[36]

According to Clifton, "the description of the way in which musical space is transformed from line to surface seems, in retrospect, to have only begun" (p. 202). The morphology of the surface is the most convincing part of the whole discussion, probably because the examples are often taken from works conceived in textural and spatial terms (e.g. Ligeti). Clifton generalizes individual and vividly imaginary experiences of hearing musical textures into the phenomenal essences of these textures, interconnecting what Nattiez calls "the esthesic" and "the neutral" levels of music (Nattiez 1990). The comprehensive scope of Clifton's theory of musical space,

---

[36]The first mode of articulation of depth in music, that is "penetration," means that the space "is filled with a reverberation of lines and surfaces just previously experienced" (p. 189). Depth exists also in "multidimensional linear form" (p. 194) and in "faceting" which is defined as "a kind of space not created exclusively by up or down, receding or projecting, or revolving motions, but perhaps, by an unnamable combination of all three motions at once" (p. 202). "Unnamable" is a crucial word in this highly enigmatic text.

not limited by stylistic prejudices against new or early music, seems particularly laudable in comparison with other writings on the "phenomenal" musical space.

Conclusion

The various theories of musical space presented here have a certain number of common features. All highlight the spatial quality of pitch (from Helmholtz onwards) and make a clear separation between the musical and the auditory types of space. The "musical space" also called "sonic" (Brelet's *espace sonore*) or "tonal" (Wellek's *Tonraum*), is diametrically opposed to the "auditory" or "empirical" (Lippman) space. The opposition of internal--external, vividly articulated in Zuckerkandl's contrast of "the space of tones versus the space of noises," is a valuative, not purely aesthetic category. This value judgement, excluding mundane noises from the elevated, spiritual realm of music, results from a romantic idealization of music. An important characteristic of the "intrinsic musical space" is the inclusion of time as one of its dimensions. Space is perceived in the experience of music "as heard" in temporal motion, not "as composed, performed, or analyzed." The connection of musical space to motion--space as the "where" this motion is taking place--is an important aspect of all phenomenologically oriented texts (Kurth, Ingarden, Brelet, Clifton). Motion manifests the interrelationship of space and time, both on a grand scale of modern physics and in human experience. If one considers the original inspiration for studies of space and time in the arts (Cassirer, Space-Time Congress and the philosophy of science) the existence of the connection between space and time here is not surprising.

Nevertheless, the perception of musical spatiality in "lived" time, but outside or beyond "lived space" is necessarily ambiguous. This is apparent in the problematic nature of the sensation of distance which is simultaneously excluded (on principle, as an element of auditory space) and included (e.g. by Kurth and Clifton). Difficulties encountered by the various writers in dealing with issues characteristic of orchestral music (dynamics, texture, volume, spatial distances) in the context of a "phenomenal musical space" reveal the limitations of concepts of space based on the exclusion of the actual spatiality of sound.

2.2.

Space as stasis: spatialization of time as a compositional paradigm

The understanding of space as stasis which is seldom encountered in the history of the "phenomenal" variety of musical space (exceptions: Mersmann, Brelet) underlies an important aspect of compositional thought in the 1960s. The postulate that new music may be as spatial as painting appeared in the context of a conceptual and constructivist renewal of musical forms and materials which characterized much post-war compositional thinking (e.g. serialism, aleatorism).[37] The idea of the two-dimensional spatiality of music required a modification of the meaning of music's dimensions from the temporal (simultaneity and succession) to the geometric (vertical pitch and horizontal time). This transformation coincided with the abolishment of "melody" (the horizontal) and "harmony" (the vertical) from the music, now organized exclusively according to serial principles.

Here, a parallel to the Bergsonian opposition of time and space should be pointed out. In his philosophy of time, Bergson associates the condition of being measurable and/or divisible with being spatial. He also emphasizes the opposition between a continuous time flow and a spatialized time of measurement (Bergson 1910/1950).[38] The notion of "spatialized time" in new music displays a marked similarity to Bergson's terminology.

It is impossible to attribute the "invention" of the idea of the static spatiality of new music to one particular author. As every history needs its protagonists, this

---

[37] A comparison of music and painting has been undertaken by Riezler (1930), Bergmann (1938), Adorno (1948, 1966), Haftmann (1959), Bertola (1972), Krellmann (1970), Stofft (1975), among many others.

[38] The spatial conception of time (i.e. time is a sequence of points placed on an imaginary line directed from the past to the future) is a classic notion of Western philosophy. Bergson's importance lies in contrasting it with the notion of "lived" time of human experience (cf. Chapter I).

narrative places emphasis on writers who attracted international attention (Schoenberg, Adorno, Ligeti, Kagel) or who were instrumental in the generalization of the idea of the spatial temporality of music to a paradigmatic level (Rochberg, McDermott).

Arnold Schoenberg

Schoenberg's well-known statement that "the two-or-more dimensional space in which musical ideas are presented is a unit" (Schoenberg, 1941/1975: 220) has stimulated considerable interest among music theorists (e.g. Bush, 1985/86). Researchers, however, have usually focused on the set-theoretical consequences of Schoenberg's theory, not on its historical context and conceptual antecedents. Schoenberg does not explicitly discuss the staticity of musical space. He is preoccupied with the interrelationships between music's two dimensions:

> The elements of a musical idea are partly incorporated in the horizontal plane as successive sounds, and partly in the vertical plane as simultaneous sounds. The mutual relation of tones regulates the succession of intervals as well as their association into harmonies; the rhythm regulates the succession of tones as well as the succession of harmonies and organizes phrasing. And this explains why . . . a basic set of twelve tones can be used in either dimension, as a whole or in parts.
> (Schoenberg 1941/1975: 220)

It is clear that "the vertical" refers to the simultaneity of sounds, that is to harmony not to pitch, while "the horizontal" indicates successive sounds--not time. Thus, Schoenberg's concept of space draws from terminology used in Mersmann's designation of the two musical dimensions (Mersmann 1926, see above). The composer's uncertainty about the number of dimensions ("two-or-more"?) is best understood in the light of the difficulties with defining depth in music, as discussed by Kurth (1931) and Wellek (1934/1963). Yet, Schoenberg is concerned with the abolition of dimensions of the musical space, not their clarification:

> the unity of musical space demands an absolute and unitary perception. In this space . . . there is no absolute down, no right, or left, forward or backward. Every musical configuration, every movement of tones has to be comprehended primarily as a mutual relation of sounds, of oscillatory vibrations, appearing at different places and times.
> (Schoenberg 1941/1975: 223)

These far-reaching relationships cancel out the opposition of the two temporal dimensions of music (simultaneity and succession). In the twelve-tone universe, sets of pitch-classes may be envisioned in any position, "regardless of their directions, regardless of the way in which a mirror might show the mutual relations, which remain a given quality" (Schoenberg 1941/1975: 223). According to the composer, this musical space resembles the "directionless" heaven of Swedenborg (described in Balzac, Schoenberg 1941/1975: 223). Thus--writes Schoenberg--tone rows are similar to physical objects which remain recognizable whatever their position in physical space. As an analogue to physical space, musical space is an absolute, empty space containing objects; the abolition of directions leads to isotropy and homogeneity of this space. It is also connected with the "objectivity" of musical time: here, movement is perceived in terms of relations between sounds (quasi-objects) appearing at "different places and times."[39]

In addition to its negative affinity to Mersmann's theory, Schoenberg's text evokes associations with Riezler's statement that in Debussy's music "various 'directions' in space can no longer be spoken of--the clearly dimensioned tonal space no longer exists" (Riezler 1930; quoted in Lippman 1952: 404). Is Schoenberg's vision of a "unified" musical space indebted to or inspired by Riezler's? A positive answer is not impossible, if only for reasons of temporal and geographic proximity.[40] Regardless of its sources and context, Schoenberg's theory heralds the transformation of the notion of "musical space" from a perceptual model to a compositional construct.

Theodor W. Adorno

Adorno's identification of space with stasis in *Philosophy of Modern Music* and

---

[39]The coupling of "place" and "time" in Schoenberg's description of musical space implies an identification of "pitch" with "space" or "place"--which recurs in Morris's theory (1987).

[40]However, atonality was, for Riezler, non-spatial.

in a separate article on music and painting (Adorno 1948/1973; 1966) had precedents in the work of Mersmann and Riezler. Yet, the philosopher's pervading influence ensured a wide circulation of his ideas which led to their subsequent assimilation by the musical avant-garde. In a chapter of the *Philosophy of Modern Music* entitled "Music--A Pseudomorphism to Painting," Adorno criticizes the seeming conversion of temporal relations into spatial ones in Stravinsky's music as a regressive trait, one amongst what he sees as that music's many faults (i.e. depersonalization, infantilism, hebephrenia, catatonia and denaturation--to name only a few). According to Adorno, a non-developmental treatment of form results in a timelessness of music, in which "there is no 'end,' the composition ceases as does the picture, upon which the viewer turns his back" (Adorno 1948/1973: 186). This type of form was introduced by Debussy, in musical impressionism where the teleological process, a characteristic of tonal music, has been replaced by a "juxtaposition of colors and surfaces" (p. 187).[41] For Adorno, this is, ultimately, "the abdication of music . . . [for] all painting--even abstract--has pathos in that which is; all music purports a becoming" (p. 191).

Even though such a regrettable deprivation of music's innermost essence happened in France, Adorno claims that it had its roots in Germany: "In Wagner's work progression is, in many places, actually mere displacement. Debussy's motivic technique is derived from this source; it consists of an undeveloped repetition of the simple tonal successions" (p. 189).[42] The philosopher continues:

> Stravinsky directly adopted the conception of music involving spaciousness and surface expanse from Debussy . . . The partial spatial complexes stand in harsh contrast to one another. The polemic negation of the gentle reverberation is fashioned into the proof of force, and the disconnected end product of dynamics is stratified like blocks of marble. . . The spatial dimension becomes absolute . . .
>
> (Adorno 1948/1973: 192)

---

[41]A spatial interpretation of Debussy's music as an analogue to painting was proposed by Riezler (1930, cf. Section 2.1 above).

[42]Thus, Debussy and Stravinsky lose their originality; this interpretation enhances the strength of Adorno's arguments in favour of Schoenberg.

This suspension of truly musical time "corresponds to the total consciousness of a bourgeoisie which . . . denies the time process itself and finds its utopia in the withdrawal of time into space." Obviously, in Adorno's view, the "spatialization" of music by Debussy and Stravinsky is not a phenomenon to be praised.[43] Nonetheless, composers of the younger generation intentionally embraced the static, non-developmental concept of time that Adorno had exposed as Stravinsky's fault. Not only have they defied his critique: paradoxically, they linked stasis with serialism-- Schoenberg's discovery and kingdom!

György Ligeti

The idea of a new spatiality of time found a particular currency in the serialism of the Darmstadt school and frequently reappeared on the pages of early issues of *Die Reihe*. Herbert Eimert, for instance, described the "moulded acoustic space" of the music of Anton Webern in terms of groupings of intervals which "open up the time-continuum as space" (Eimert 1955/1958: 35). In this structured spatial dimension-- here Eimert paraphrases Schoenberg--"the antithesis of vertical and horizontal no longer exists" (p. 32). A similar (mis)reading of Webern's compositional technique as essentially spatial in nature was perpetuated by others, including Pierre Boulez and György Ligeti.[44]

Ligeti's article, "Metamorphoses of musical form," introduces the idea of the spatialization of time ("die Verräumlichung des Zeit") as one of the consequences of

---

[43]In addition to musical spatiality associated with Stravinsky and Debussy, Adorno describes a type of "musical space" which relates to harmony: "But like painting, music does not simply abolish space; rather it replaces the illusion, the pretence of it, with an, as it were, expanded, peculiarly musical space" (Adorno 1981: 161). This space is an offspring of tonal harmony, which "creates the illusion of spatial depth" (ibidem). Schoenberg's music is non-spatial because "the twelve-tone rows do not describe a musical space within which the work unfolds" (p. 167).

[44]Boulez writes about Webern's crucial role in overcoming the "contradiction that formerly existed between the horizontal and vertical phenomena of tonal music" by creating music of "points, or blocs, or figures no longer on the flat space, but in the sound-space" (Boulez 1966/1968: 383).

serialization.[45] The term itself mimics Bergson's "spatialized time" (Bergson 1889/1950; 1922/1965). Nonetheless, unlike Bergson for whom the bond between spatiality and measurement was decisive, Ligeti underscores the connection of "spatialization" to "stasis." He supports his thesis with quotes from Adorno and--after discussing pointillistic and statistical textures in modern music--proceeds to characterize Webern's compositions as the true beginning of the spatialization of time in music (Ligeti 1960/1965). According to Ligeti, Webern's music brought about

> the projection of the time-flow into an imaginary space by means of the interchangeability of the temporal directions, provoked by the constant reciprocity of the motivic shapes and their retrogrades.
> (Ligeti 1960/1965: 16)

Webern's structures are not entirely static, though, for they seem to "circle continuously in their illusory space, driven by the strength of the intervallic tensions and shifting accents" (p. 16). Therefore, in Webern's music "time is after all still time, although at the same time it is also pseudo-space" (p. 17). The latter phrase mirrors Bergson's notion of time as a "phantom of space" expressed, for instance, in his colourful description of "time dried up as space" (Bergson 1922/1965: 60). Interestingly, the paradoxical wedding of Stravinsky (through Adorno) and Schoenberg (through a misreading of Webern) in the genesis of a new, "spatial image" of music articulates a transcendence of contrasts into a higher-level synthesis--a truly Hegelian process.

Ligeti appears to be ambivalent in his evaluation of the role of this temporal spatialization in new music. Although spatialization of time is, for Ligeti, a vital element of the new compositional practice, he notices that the renunciation of time-flow causes perceptual difficulties. Perhaps for that reason, soon after the commencement of the "spatialization of time" the composers reintroduced a dynamic continuity of time in music.

One idea from Ligeti's article needs to be emphasized as bearing consequences

---

[45]The article, written in 1958, appeared in German in 1960, in English in 1965.

for the study of spatialized music: the relationship of the "spatialization of time" to the actual spatialization of music by Cage, Stockhausen, and others. Ligeti is aware of a dissimilarity between two types of spatiality, one relating to "time" and the other to the "physical" space. Despite this divergence, caused primarily by the irreversibility of the direction of time-flow, composers have transferred "the imaginary space of formal matters into a real space, by distributing instrumental groups or loudspeakers around the concert hall" (note 41 on p. 17). The connection between spatialization of time (i.e. the static, spatial character of musical material) and the technique of spatialization of sound in performance space is also articulated by Stockhausen in "Music in space" (1959/1961). According to Stockhausen, the expansion of music into space is a consequence of the fact that musical ideas themselves are "becoming increasingly spatial" (Stockhausen 1959/1961: 70).[46]

Mauricio Kagel

While Ligeti considers the spatialization of time in its relationship to serialism, Kagel, in his contribution to the same issue of *Die Reihe* ("Translation--Rotation"), envisions an application of geometrical transformations to the two-dimensional musical space of pitch and time (Kagel 1960/1965). For this purpose, time needs to become non-temporal, that is to lose its directional quality represented by the irreversibility of the orientation from left to right in musical notation. Kagel's musical "geometry in two dimensions" obliterates the incongruity between time and pitch and includes the procedures of translation, that is, the source of transposition in pitch and repetition in time, and rotation which leads to inversion and to the modification of pitch relationships into temporal ones. The interchangeability of pitch and time engenders "a multi-dimensional variability" of music (Kagel 1960/1965: 36-37). As the

---

[46]Cf. chapter III. A thesis that spatialization is a consequence of serial techniques is also supported by Roger Savage (Savage 1989: 61) and Francis Bayer (1987). Bayer claims that spatialization in *Terretektorh* by Xenakis, or *Carrè* by Stockhausen, results from a "purely musical" spatiality that relates to sonic clouds in the first case and moment form in the second (Bayer 1987: 15).

composer writes,

> in the matter of rotating note-dots, the vertical and horizontal can only be materialized in fixed positions; the inclusion of circular shifts resolves both dimensions into moments of a rotation: simultaneous becomes successive and vice versa.
>
> (Kagel 1960/1965: 37)

The equation of the two-dimensional plane of a page of music paper with the two-dimensional space of pitch and time advocated in Europe by Kagel was explored in North America by John Cage and his associates. Cage's *Music for Carillon No. 1* (1952), for instance, was composed by plotting points on a graph score to indicate pitches and attack times of bell sounds; each point was then "interpreted as a musical event" (Pritchett 1993: 92). In *Music for Piano* (1952-1956), the points were generated by marking minute imperfections in the paper and drawing lines of the staff to accomodate them. Indeterminate works by other American experimentalists, such as Earle Brown's *December 1952* for any number of instruments and Christian Wolff's *For Prepared Piano* (1952), also explored the invertibility of two-dimensional graphic images representing sound events in the dimensions of pitch and time (Pritchett 1993: 106). One could, indeed, say that the whole field of graphic music is spatial because it relies on the visual representation of time and pitch.[47]

In the ensuing development, the notion of "space as temporal stasis" was taken beyond narrow compositional concerns and transformed into a "paradigm" of modern music. Much of this development took place in North America, as George Rochberg's speculative concept of a "new image" of Western art music based on the idea of static, spatial time (Rochberg 1963) was expanded by Vincent McDermott into a general theory of "musical space" (McDermott 1966).

---

[47]A study of experiments with such "visible" or "visual" music (terms from Schnebel 1972 and Bräm 1986) associated with indeterminacy of notation, open forms and other concerns of the avant-garde should be left for a different occasion.

George Rochberg

According to Rochberg, a new "spatial image" has emerged in contemporary music, an image comparable with the many-faceted and complex cubist paintings (Rochberg 1963: 1). This "image" constitutes the end-point of the main musical developments of this century, embodied in works of Ives, Schoenberg, Webern and Varèse (p. 7). As examples of these developments, Rochberg names the liberation of sound from harmonic functions, the suppression of beat and pulsation and the resultant unpredictability and discontinuity. All these phenomena found their fulfilment in the new "spatialization of music" (p. 8-9). Here, the temporal aspect of music is at the service of the sounding forms:

> Whether these forms are differentiated by timbre alone, by reflective symmetry, or by the geometric analogue of the figure-ground relationship, they take on the characteristics of spatial projections and configurations, self-sufficient entities, sonorous bodies with mass and density moving in time.
> (Rochberg 1963: 7)

Rochberg's spatial images of music resemble those used by Edgar Varèse; for instance, the concepts of "shifting sound-masses" and "sound-projection in space" (Varèse 1966). A similar grandiosity of vision links these two writers. Rochberg explains that

> in the new music, time as duration becomes a dimension of musical space. The new spatial image of music seeks to project the permanence of the world as cosmos, the cosmos as the eternal present. It is an image of music which aspires to Being not Becoming.
> (Rochberg 1963: 10)

Here, Rochberg's allusion to Heidegger's "Being" with a capital "B" (Heidegger 1929/1967) unwittingly (?) inverts Adorno's statement that "all music purports becoming" (Adorno 1948/1973: 191). For Rochberg, the emergence of music's "spatial image" does not imply the "abdication of music" (Adorno), but its objectified "permanence." His final distinction, between music dominated by the temporal image (i.e. "Becoming") and music dominated by the spatial image (i.e. "Being") draws from the classical separation of space and time into distinct, non-interpenetrable realms (Descartes, Newton, Kant; cf. Chapter I, section 1.2.).

Simultaneously, it provides a basic premise for the theory of musical space proposed in a doctoral dissertation by Rochberg's student, Vincent McDermott (1966).

Vincent McDermott

Unlike Rochberg, who does not consider the question of the dimensionality of the "spatial image" of music and who describes music in terms of the "spatialized time" and "sonorous forms" with particular timbral or pitch-related qualities, McDermott suggests that the primal dimension of musical space is pitch (McDermott 1966). In most Western music, pitches do not exist in themselves but as elements of lines which with "the interrelationships between lines are the primary formative elements of the spatial grouping process" (McDermott 1966: 37). Lines emerge from pitches spaced out in time. Pitch and time are, therefore, the two basic musical dimensions used by McDermott in diagrams of a wide array of compositions.[48]

Here, McDermott formulates a general theory of the development of Western art music, emphasizing the distinction between a temporally dominated style of music (*time-space*) and a spatially dominated style of music (*space-time*). This terminological symmetry may pose difficulties for the reader: "time-space" and "space-time" differ only in the order of the elements and may be easily confused.[49] The transition from the one style to another has a definite historical location, and corresponds to the change from the romantic to the modern (p. 107). The key distinction is the treatment of duration. If "a goal-directed time flow predominates" the spatial parameter is subordinate. "Where temporal continuity disintegrates under a disruptive durational articulation" *space-time* emerges (p. 55). A list of composers, who are thought to have contributed to the development of *space-time* includes Liszt, Mahler, Debussy, Schoenberg, Ives, Bartók, Webern, and Varèse.

---

[48]The diagrams capture only "the pitch-registral and durational aspects of pieces" and are, according to McDermott's self-critique, "inherently weak" (p. 246).

[49]The first term is reminiscent of Schnebel's category of "time space" contrasted with "time flow" (Schnebel 1958).

For McDermott, the modern "space-time" is based on two general principles: "objectification of the sound material and the disassociation of spatial articulation from a compelling temporal progression" (p. 183). The main idea, though, is that a musical work--in its entirety--is conceived of as a spatial whole by "our mind's eye." This is best realized in 20th-century music, in which "the 'statue' of an entire work . . . begins to take a more concrete form in a series of smaller 'statues' or note-complexes which are thrust out as individual objects ." (McDermott 1966: 168).

Among modes of spatiality, the dualism of spatial and temporal relations is particularly significant. For McDermott, space and time concisely define the boundary between modern and traditional music, as well as "summarize the delineation between static objects and dynamic motions" (p. 296). Here, he reiterates the main thesis of Rochberg's article. The opposition of static (spatial) and dynamic (temporal) is also reminiscent of Mersmann's polarity of *Raum--Kraft* discussed in Section 2.1. (Mersmann 1926). These notions are rooted in the classic philosophical division of space and time (cf. Chapter I).

In contrast with Rochberg, for whom the "spatial image of music" emerges through "spatialization," McDermott emphasizes the difference between musical space and spatialization. The first term is cognitive and relates to the spatial character of pitch (first pointed out by Helmholtz 1863/1954, cf. Section 2.1). "Spatialization," on the other hand, is described as "a tense emotional response, actually intuitively felt" when listening to certain works, particularly, but not exclusively, of contemporary music (McDermott 1966: 299). This identification of features of the perceptual experience with attributes of musical compositions resembles that encountered in *Music as Heard* by Thomas Clifton (Clifton 1983; cf. Section 2.1). The kinship of the two conceptions stems from a similar concern with the description of a phenomenal musical spatiality experienced while listening to the music.[50]

In the dissertation, McDermott uses the term space in several different

---

[50]Among the parallels are McDermott's idea of the line, and his conception of the apparent "thickness" or "thinness" of a composite spatial image (p. 136).

meanings: "(1) pitch relations alone, (2) pitch changes intermixed with duration forming 'lines,' and (3) lines conjoined with still other non-pitch elements" (p. 52). In fact, these meanings reflect different aspects of musical spatiality and cannot be welded into one, coherent "musical space."[51] Ideas from McDermott's dissertation and his article on "a conceptual musical space" (McDermott 1972) have found continuation in subsequent essays in music theory. The article provided a direct inspiration for yet another conception of "musical space" by Stephen Gryc (1976). The representation of music in a non-traditional notation has been developed in graphic music analyses.[52] For instance, the two-dimensional image of music--that is plotting of registral and durational components of compositions from various historical periods in pitch/time diagrams--constitutes a basic premise for the theory of "sonic design" by Robert Cogan and Pozzi Escot (1976). The assumption that "space" (*l'espace sonore*) is a key to explaining the evolution of contemporary music as a whole, from Schoenberg to Cage, has been made by Francis Bayer (1987).[53] Finally, the idea of space as stasis has resurfaced in writings by Robert P. Morgan.

Robert P. Morgan

Morgan shares McDermott's conviction about the spatial character of the form of the musical work; this idea appears in "Spatial form in Ives" (Morgan 1974). In an

---

[51] The illusion that such an amalgamation is possible, as well as the representation of the evolution of Western art music governed in its totality by two basic form-bearing categories (of "time-space" and "space-time") are McDermott's main weaknesses.

[52] This is not to say that McDermott "invented" graphic representation of music in pitch/time space.

[53] Bayer examines a wide range of topics: the transition from tonality to "metatonality," the relationship of space and time (in Stockhausen's music), the formalization of sonic space by Xenakis, microtonality, spatial continuity (glissandi, clusters, sonic clouds), open form, indeterminism and chance, the dichotomy between constructed and lived spaces (Bayer 1987). The unifying principle for this wealth of different phenomena is provided by the notion of "sonic space" (*espace sonore*) identified with pitch and distinct from the acoustic space of performance (*espace acoustique*).

essay on "Musical time/musical space," he claims that static "musical space" is a sole domain of contemporary music (Morgan 1980). He reiterates the main points introduced by Adorno and expanded by Rochberg and McDermott: in new music structure is "frozen," the music produces spatial effects by cutting back and forth among essentially static blocks of sound.

In Morgan's account, "modern music is spatial only on the surface" which accounts for its "somewhat shallow quality" (p. 534-535). Contemporary music makes use of two kinds of superficial spatial effects: the actual physical space of performance and the notational space of the score.[54] Morgan shares the traditional bias against the "external" space of performance and perception. He laments its "commonplace" use in contemporary music (Morgan 1980: 537) and proposes a theory of musical space that articulates this negative judgement of compositions of his time. Contemporary music, "deficient in a system of substructural coordinates," reveals how "a weakening of one kind of musical space was countered by a strengthening of another, more literal one" (p. 537). If one could agree with the second part of Morgan's statement, his diagnose of a "deficiency" of contemporary music as a whole is more questionable. Perhaps, "substructural coordinates" in new music differ from the ones found in compositions of earlier times? Clearly, Morgan's musical ideal resembles that of many of his predecessors, including Zuckerkandl: tonal music of the 18th and 19th centuries.[55]

According to Morgan, tonality delineates a highly structured musical space which is best represented by the Schenkerian method of analysis.[56] This approach, in

---

[54]Here, Morgan alludes to the double "spatialization" of music discussed by Ligeti: "spatialization of time" and "spatialization of music" in performance space (Ligeti 1960; cf. Section 2.2). The total "spatialization" of compositional thinking (e.g. by Xenakis) is completely ignored.

[55]For a critique of Morgan's thesis from the composer's vantage point see the response by Gilbert (1981).

[56]The idea that the tonal system is a "space" with distinct regions of the various keys separated from each other by uneven, though not specific, distances has been earlier

his words "might be said to define the 'logical space' of a musical composition" as it describes this space "in terms of a conventionalized unchanging vertical background that is rendered linear through a set of equally fixed operations" (p. 532). The introduction of this notion of space, which--incidentally--diverges from Schenker's own, is an unexpected outcome of Morgan's review of various spatial features of music (e.g. texture, pitch). After defining a tonal space as "an abstract indication of the range of humanly perceptible pitches" (p. 528), Morgan proceeds to discuss the "more generalized musical space" which incorporates "all the elements of compositional structure" and is equivalent to "a total set of relationships" of a composition (p. 529).[57] Unfortunately, these relationships are limited not only to those of pitch, and pitch-class, but solely to the embodiment of a Schenkerian *Ursatz*. Although Morgan agrees with his predecessors that new music is intrinsically spatial, his value judgement differs from theirs. He considers the static spatiality of new music as the music's essential weakness.

Conclusion

The identification of musical space with stasis which is examined in this section, is based on a radical conceptual opposition of space and time, staticity and development, Being and Becoming. These binary pairs are useful within their immediate contexts, even though they simplify a complex network of relationships which interconnect such "polarized" entities. The "static" spatialization of music, postulated and described by various authors, takes place in the context of the disembodiment of musical material. This limitation of music to a skeleton of pitch and time underlying the doctrines of spatial stasis also provides a foundation for the identification of musical space with pitch, frequent in compositional and analytical theories which are described in the subsequent section of this chapter.

---

advocated by Riezler (1930), Conrad (1958) and Stofft (1975). The introduction of the notion of a tonal "region" is customarily ascribed to Schoenberg (*Harmonielehre*, 1911). However, Helmholtz implies this notion in his analogy of space and musical scale discussed at the beginning of section 2.1 of this chapter (Helmholtz 1863/1954).

[57]Here, Morgan uses a mathematical notion of space as a set (Cf. Chapter I, 1.3).

2.3.

Space as pitch: analytical and compositional theory

The recognition of the spatial quality of pitch relationships is common to most theories of musical space mentioned so far, from Helmholtz onwards. However, this awareness is not always coupled with the identification of the notion of "musical space" with "pitch space." In theories discussed in this chapter, pitch is considered to be inherently spatial either because it is an analogue to the spatial dimension of height (e.g. Bernard) or because it is a mathematical concept per se (e.g. Boulez, Morris).

Mathematical notions of space defined broadly as a set of points with some specified structure (Lipschutz 1965) appear in many areas of contemporary music theory and composition.[58] This "mathematicization" of space in music has taken place almost exclusively in the context of serial or atonal thinking, in marked contrast to the theories of musical space discussed in section 2.1. The different modality of the discourse is also noticeable: while the "phenomenal" notions of musical space frequently relate to the perception of music of the past, "abstract" spaces delineate realms of musical material of contemporary (Xenakis) or future (Boulez, Morris) compositional significance. These generalized or formalized theories of space have appeared simultaneously with the "spatialization of time" in new music (section 2.2).

The use of the term "musical space" exclusively to denote the domain of pitch height is problematic when it is accompanied by a negation of the physical spatiality of music. Although pitch height is a spatial concept, musical spatiality does not exhaust itself in pitch relationships. However, these relationships are spatial in an abstract sense and may be formalized and generalized with the aid of mathematical notions of space (e.g. continuum, metric space, vector space).

---

[58] E.g. Xenakis (1971), Alphonce (1974), Wessel (1979), Lewin (1987), and Morris (1987).

In the words of **Iannis Xenakis**,

> The dimension of pitch resembles, in principle, points on a line--any kind of line that can be mapped onto a straight line, like a curve which can stretched, but not looped, without intersections. The principle, that is, the mental structure, is the same in the case of this line and in the case of pitches.
> (Xenakis 1992: 3)

This statement recalls **Hermann von Helmholtz**'s remark about "the characteristic resemblance between the relations of the musical scale and of space" (Helmholtz 1863/1954: 370).[59] Helmholtz points out the similarity of spatial motion in the domains of pitch height and of the Euclidean, physical space (ascending and descending motions). At the same time, he emphasizes the role of "measurement" (a concept traditionally associated with spatiality) in the establishment of the spatial features of music:

> The musical scale is as it were the divided rod, by which we measure progression in pitch, as rhythm measures progression in time. Hence the analogy between the scale of tones and rhythm naturally occurred to musical theoreticians of ancient as well as modern times.
> (Helmholtz 1863/1954: 252-253)

This analogy based on the existence of common principles of measurement for the domains of pitch and time has been explored in serialism.[60] If Helmholtz may compare musical scale to a "divided rod" of measurement, Pierre Boulez arranges a full taxonomy of such potential "divisions" into a speculative theory of musical space.

Pierre Boulez

In 1961, Pierre Boulez wrote a series of essays on the current potential of

---

[59] I discuss Helmholtz's text in Section 2.1. Edward Lippman points out the analogy between the relationship of music to space and the relationship of mathematics to "empirical and physical" space: both express formal properties of space (Lippman 1952: 231).

[60] The postulate of isomorphisms between musical dimensions of pitch and time does not require comparisons with the physical space-as-experienced: the domains of pitch and time are both "logical spaces" (cf. Chapter I).

serialist compositional technique. These essays, written "in Darmstadt for Darmstadt," include an enumeration of possible pitch spaces (section on "musical space") and an expansion of the list of available musical parameters which now embrace the spatial distribution of sound (Boulez 1963/1971).

According to Boulez, one of the "most urgent objectives of present-day musical thought is the conception and realization of a *relativity* of the various musical spaces in use" (Boulez 1963/1971: 83). The composer envisions an exploration of "variable spaces, spaces of mobile definition capable of evolving (by mutation or progressive transformation) during the course of a work" (p. 84). These spaces are exemplified with pitch spaces, but due to the very generality of notions invoked, an application to other domains (duration, dynamics, timbre) is also possible.

Boulez states that the concept of series may be used in the context of "any tempered space, according to any temperament and to any non-tempered space, according to any module, whether it be the octave or some other interval" (p. 83). Then, he proceeds to enumerate all those possibilities in a detailed taxonomy (p. 87-88). For Boulez, the continuum of available pitch space may be partitioned in a regular and irregular way. Temperament, a choice of standard measure, "will 'striate' the surface, the musical space, and will provide our perception . . . with useful points of reference" (p. 85). Irregular partitions, on the other hand, are characteristic of smooth spaces. The key opposition between smooth and striated spaces is not very clear: "The properties of the partition determine the micro-structural properties of the smooth or striated space, and the way it is perceived; in extreme cases smooth and striated space fuse into a continuous line" (Boulez 1963: 85).

This perceptual ambiguity is caused by the distinction between a space and its actual realization through a choice of intervals from those available in this particular space. Meanwhile, pitch continuum can not be defined as a straight line, or as an integrated whole. Boulez discusses the "macro-structural properties of space" (p. 86), such as the existence of a module (usually the octave) which causes spaces to be straight (with a constant module) or curved (with a changing module). The defining module, a reference point for all other divisions, is called the focus and may be placed in the centre or at one edge of the space. Focuses define the curvature of space. Table II-1 presents Boulez's list of all available spaces (pp. 87-88).

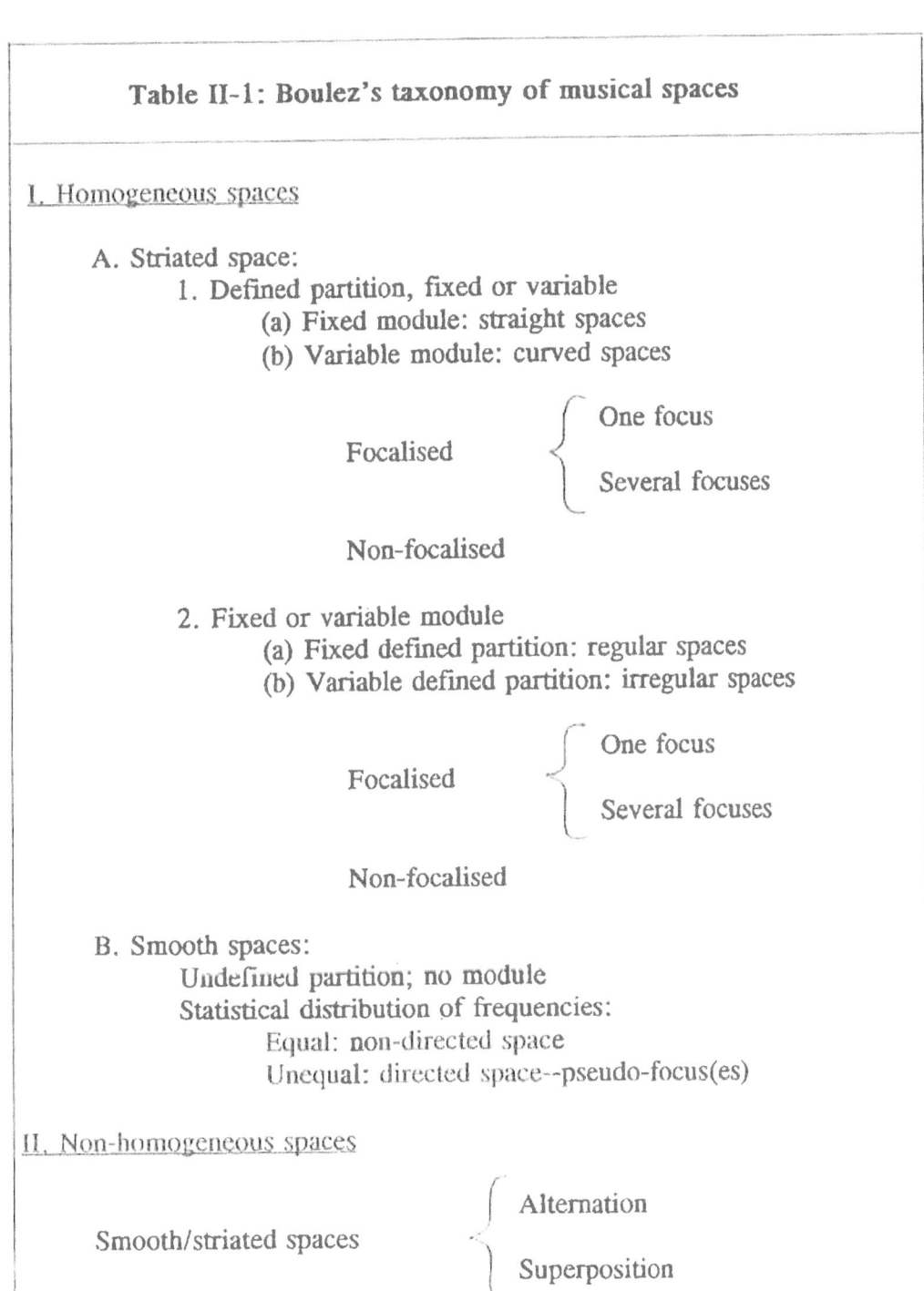

In the domain of pitch, these spaces may be realized by the "construction of instruments whose temperament could be precisely varied, according to prepared and ordered combinations" (p. 89). Electronic instruments are preferable, for they "will provide all these musical spaces, which seem of prime importance, both at the present time and for the future" (p. 91). Thirty years later, Boulez's prophetic urgency has all but disappeared and the conquest of non-tempered, non-octaviating spaces is no longer a central concern for composers. For Boulez, the meaning of "space" in music shifted to the space of performance, the space of sound placements, distances, volumes and motions (Boulez and Nattiez 1991; Boulez 1992; cf. Chapter III).

Spatial models of pitch

The issue of the spatiality of pitch is, indeed, a perplexing one. The vertical dimension of music, described as a system of relationships, includes two aspects of pitch--one which changes monotonically with frequency and one rotating in a cycle of octave repetitions. This distinction is captured in modern psychoacoustic terminology as the dualism of "pitch height" (linear dimension) and "pitch chroma" (circular dimension).[61] The combined representation of the two requires the use of a geometric model of a cylindrical spiral (helix).[62] This two-dimensional image embedded in a three-dimensional space is not the only possible image of pitch. Theoretically, as Roger Shepard has demonstrated, the musical domain of pitch may be represented with one- to five-dimensional structural models (Shepard 1982). His "structural representations" of pitch use torus-type surfaces made of spirals embedded in spirals to portray the complexity of pitch relationships in tonal music.

According to **Marie-Elizabeth Duchez**, the rationalization and geometric

---

[61]This terminology, introduced by Bachem (1950) has been recently used by Shepard (1982), Ueda and Ohgushi (1987), Semal and Demany (1990), and others.

[62]The significance of this image for the dimensionality of musical space has been mentioned by: Nadel (1931), Wellek (1934), Révész (1937, 1946), Brelet (1949) and Stofft (1975). The difference between the rectilinearity and circularity of pitch underlies the distinction of pitch space and pitch class space (Morris 1987).

representation of the sensation of pitch result in the emergence of a "conceptual perception" ("perception conceptuelle," Duchez 1979). Duchez concentrates on the history of the notion of "pitch height" ("la hauteur de son") from the 9th to the 19th century. Its spatial representation, motivated by various factors, is a rational construct superimposed on the perception of a quality of sound called in French "grave-aigu" (in English "low-high"). Once established, the cognitive construct of "pitch height" influences perception, so that listeners trained in Western music hear pitches as high and low, pitch sequences as ascending and descending. Musical symbolism is based on this principle and many musicians have difficulties with conceiving of pitch in non-spatial terms.[63] Yet, as Duchez writes, "cette construction rationelle, bien que très répandue, n'est ni générale, ni, sans, doute, définitive" (Duchez 1979: 56).

Duchez's conviction about cultural origins of the spatial representation of pitch is shared by Iannis Xenakis for whom

> it is not necessary to have pitch represented by the dimension of height, with the standard directions of 'up' and 'down.' This representation is, indeed, a connection between music and space, but this connection is completely artificial and arbitrary.
>
> (Xenakis 1992: 2)

Xenakis supports his argument about pitch height as a "borrowing from physical space into music" with an anecdote about his young daughter's perception of "small" rather than "high" sounds (p. 2).[64] An additional example relates to ancient Greek opposition of "acute" and "heavy" sounds-- also pointed out by Duchez (Duchez 1979: 58). According to Xenakis, the musical meaning of spatial representation of pitch is a consequence of "the invention of notating music in a

---

[63]For instance, Henry Brant considers the association of high pitches with spatial elevation as self-evident (cf. Chapter VI).

[64]"I remember that when my daughter was six or seven, I was trying to teach her about sounds. I said that certain pitches are very high, pointing upwards with my hand. Afterwards I asked her what were high pitches and she said 'small' and pointed down. Why? Because children, who are small, also have small, high-pitched voices whereas adults are big and have big, low-pitched voices" (Xenakis 1992: 2).

graphic way" (Xenakis 1992: 2).⁶⁵ The spatial definitions and representations of sound become widely accepted for pragmatic reasons, "because it makes it easier to imagine and remember music. We know what is up and what is down from our existential experience, so when the dimension of height is ascribed to pitches we can manipulate them better" (Xenakis 1992: 3).⁶⁶

Thus, the vertical representation of pitch, introduced to facilitate the manipulation of sounds, has become a characteristics of pitch itself and, as such, a condition for the creation and perception of music as well as the theoretical reflection about both. Incidentally, this development parallels the relationship between science and life-experience described in Patrick Heelan's phenomenological philosophy of science (Heelan 1983; cf. Chapter I, 1.5). Scientific artifacts, initially separated from the "pre-reflective" world of everyday experience, in the final analysis form a part of the intersubjective lived World, defined as "the shared space of a historical community with a particular culture that uses a common language and a common description of reality" (Heelan 1983: 10). In particular, as Heelan suggests, the "cultural artifact" of the Euclidean visual space, at first constituting only a mode of description, eventually becomes the content of perception itself.

Similarly, the domain of pitch, represented and construed in spatial terms, becomes "spatial" in perception. This spatiality is more general than the vertical quality of pitch height (although its importance for the emergence of "spatial" notion of music should not be underestimated). It relates to the profusion of abstract notions and relations: the awareness that musical interval is a form of measurement, the belief that shifts of positions in pitch space are possible without affecting the moving

---

⁶⁵The composer explains: "When you say, for instance, that you are able to distinguish high and low pitch you are using spatial terms and a spatial way of discriminating between them, resembling that of physical space. But this is, in fact, only a borrowing from physical space into music." (Xenakis 1992: 2).

⁶⁶Incidentally, Henry Brant, when asked about the reality of a musical space (pitch/time) responded: "I do not think that this deals with things that actually exist. It is on a metaphysical level and it does not interest me even slightly." (Brant 1992: 1).

"objects" (true within a limited area), etc.

As Edward Lippman observes, "the concepts of 'order' and 'relation' and 'structure' and 'interval' are not merely acclimated, they are indigenous to music" (Lippman 1952: 231). If so, music is a form of geometry--assuming, with Hans Reichenbach, that mathematical geometry is a pure theory of relations (Reichenbach 1927/1958). For Reichenbach, all geometrical concepts can be expressed as functions of basic, purely logical notions, such as "element, relation, one-to-one correspondence, implication, etc... The visual elements of space are an unnecessary addition." (Reichenbach 1927/1958: 93, 100). Thus, geometry transcends itself when it breaches its original connection to the visualization and measurement of objects in space. Analogically, the music of pure pitch relations (i.e. mathematical modelling of pitch) transcends its foundation in sound as it abandons its basis in a lived experience of perception and performance.

The domain of pitch may be represented as a space of zero-dimensionality (set of points), one-dimensional, topological continuum (i.e. the total range of audible pitches), one-dimensional, discrete, metric space (e.g. all pitches of the piano, a mode), two-dimensional space embedded in three-dimensions (pitch height and pitch chroma together) and other models of higher dimensions. These are all logico-mathematical concepts; it is not a coincidence that Ludwig Wittgenstein used pitch as the example of a "logical space" (Wittgenstein 1922/1988; cf. Chapter I). It is also not accidental that a mathematician (Helmholtz) first noticed the parallels between "musical scale and space" (Helmholtz 1863/1954; cf. sections 2.1 and 2.3 above). The basic notion of interval, i.e. distance, is crucial for the musical structuring of pitch, and the mathematical structuring of space (metric space).

A one-dimensional model of pitch (an element in a two-dimensional space) appears in *Sonic Design* by **Robert Cogan** and **Pozzi Escot**; a book that includes "musical space" and "spatial motion" among its basic concepts (Cogan and Escot

1976).[67] Musical space, seems, at first, to be equated with pitch range and register: music is thought to be unfolding "in space and time." Cogan and Escot delimit space to its linear, vertical aspect "from lower to higher frequencies" (Cogan and Escot 1976: 43).[68] While describing numerous examples from different epochs of Western music, the authors transform the notion of musical space into a two-dimensional entity. This change of the meaning of space is perceptible, for instance, in discussions of "a single melodic line as a shape in space" (p. 40) or "the interaction of voices forming directed, unified linear flows in musical space" (p. 24). Space permitting shapes and linear motion is not one-dimensional as line; it requires time as its second dimension.[69]

The representation of pitch in one dimension recurs in **Jonathan Bernard's** analytical method (Bernard 1983). Here, music is analyzed in a "truly spatial context, with criteria of absolute size and distance" (Bernard 1987a: 41). These criteria belong to the realm of pitch, i.e. neither pitch-class space nor the "external" space of performance. Bernard emphasizes the primacy of the vertical dimension in Varèse's music, using the word "space" as synonymous with "pitch" and analyzing works, also by other composers, with pitch/time diagrams (Bernard 1983, 1986, 1987a, 1987b). The use of pitch and time as dimensions in these diagrams is not equivalent to the use of the same dimensions by McDermott (1966) or Cogan and Escot (1976). In contrast

---

[67] Cogan and Escot represent music with two-dimensional graphs (pitch/time space) which resemble the graphs used by McDermott; (compare p. 20 of *Sonic Design* and p. 66 in Mcdermott's text).

[68] Cogan and Escot call the humanly audible frequency range "acoustical space" and interchange this term with "musical space."

[69] Cogan preserves the identification of musical space with pitch while replacing schematic diagrams with spectral photographs in *New Images of Musical Sound* (Cogan 1984). Musical space still has "different regions, lower and higher, and different directions, ascending and descending" (p. 7). The spectral pictures are supposed to "transmute time and its musical spectral formations into visible space: they make visible what was initially invisible" (Cogan 1984: 14). Here, the postulate of the "spatialization of time" is realized in the domain in music analysis, not composition.

to his predecessors, whose diagrams simply translate musical notation into a graphic mode of representation, Bernard introduces a rigorous, reductive method of music analysis. Nevertheless, the context of "spatialization of time" (cf. Section 2.2) well illuminates his, and other, attempts at visualization of pitch relationships.

Robert Morris's theory of compositional designs presents "an account of contemporary pitch resources available to composers who are willing to work within the constraints of the (now standard) equal-temperament chromatic scale" (Morris 1987: 2).[70] His taxonomy of pitch spaces begins with a detailed discussion of the most general variety, contour space (c-space). In c-spaces the sizes of intervals are ignored while contours are defined as "the elements of c-space ordered in time" (p. 23), in particular, as they relate to various pitch regions (i.e. all pitches in-between two selected pitches). When exact distances between pitches are considered,

> we can classify pitch-spaces as either *u-spaces*, having different intervals between their successive adjacent pitches, or *p-spaces*, having equal intervals between adjacent pitches. As an example of each, the total chromatic compass of the piano forms a p-space while the strings of the harp form a u-space.
> (Morris 1987: 23)

This differentiation of p- and u-spaces emphasizes the same opposition that Boulez has pointed out in the distinction of regular and irregular striated spaces (Boulez 1963: 83-88). Nevertheless, the role of a "modular interval" in defining pc-space in Morris's theory (p. 23-24) differs from that of Boulez. This interval is, for Morris, the basis for the idea of pitch-class, described as a set of equivalent pitches (p. 24). Hence,

> Modular pitch-spaces consist of classes of equivalent pitches (pitch-classes) arranged in a circular or cyclic pattern. . . In general, any modular space of pitch-classes is a 'collapsed' version of some u- or p-space; m-spaces are collapsed u-spaces, and pc-spaces are collapsed p-spaces.
> (Morris 1987: 24)

---

[70]The rationale for this constraint is that most Western musicians, conditioned by equal temperament "tend to hear music in unfamiliar p-spaces as 'out-of-tune' and/or as being structured only in c-space" (p. 35).

The diagram of four basic pitch-space categories includes linear (u-, p-) and cyclic (m-, pc-) spaces; it also indicates the presence of equal steps (p- and pc-space) or unequal steps (u- and m-space) in these spaces. The distinction between pitch and pitch class, cardinal for Morris's taxonomy, is all but ignored by Boulez who treats the general opposition between smooth and striated spaces as more significant.

Morris's system is designed to be comprehensive and to generalize pitch systems of Western classical music (pythagorean, just and mean-tone intonation) by means of an interaction of u-and m-spaces. Simultaneously, the p- and pc-space "model two different ways in which we hear more recent music" (that is twelve-tone and atonal music based on equal temperament).

In the seventh chapter of Morris's book, "Toward a unity of musical time and space" (p. 306-307) the term "musical space" makes an unexpected appearance.[71] In an attempt to justify an isomorphism between times and spaces of the same order, Morris discusses the correspondence of this isomorphism to "some of our ordinary perceptions and experiences of time and space," that is to concepts of a "place" within space and a "now" in time (p. 306). In experience--as Morris argues--the multi-dimensional aspect of space (height, length and depth) is paired with the one-dimensional quality of time. This ontological contrast of space and time "matches the constraint of many nontemporal musical sequential dimensions to one s-time" (p. 306).[72]

Morris's explication of the nature of time and space as experienced confuses perception with its cognitive model, based--in his case--on the classical opposition of an absolute three-dimensional space and an absolute one-dimensional time. This distinction, paradigmatic for Newtonian physics, has widely influenced the 'common-

---

[71]The usage of the term "musical space" in reference to pitch space and pitch-class space is common in David Lewin's theory of generalized musical intervals (1987).

[72]If musical space is identified with the domain of "pitch," what is "timbre"--a complex variety of contour space? The issue of projecting many pitch spaces onto one dimension of sequential (linear) time is also a matter of contention: the linearity of musical time itself is at question (Kramer 1988; Pressing 1993).

sense' notion of space, but is blurred in the actual, spatio-temporal experience (cf. Chapter I). In human, subjective encounter with reality (that Morris seems to be referring to) it is not possible to "match many places with one time." *Here* is always *now*--that is what descriptive phenomenology points out (Merleau-Ponty, cf. Chapter I, 1.5). The notions of time and space are also interconnected in various "space-times" in modern philosophy of science (cf. Chapter I, 1.4). The relativity of simultaneity, for instance, precludes assumptions about the absolute independence of three-dimensional space and linear time.

The equivocality of the analogy between "musical time and space" and the "time and space" is increased by Morris's references to different spatial phenomena in music: the idea that performers have various spaces "under the hand" or "in a register or tessitura," as well as the idea that temporal form perceived in its entirety (through notation and memory) is spatial (cf. also McDermott 1966; discussed in section 2.2). The bodily space of performance corresponds to the space of intuition and action (the domain of lived experience); the cognitively integrated spatial form of time is a conceptual construct (the domain of music cognition). These are two different spaces, not various manifestations of a one, total "musical" space that is, somehow, opposed to and plotted onto one, linear "musical" time.

Multidimensional spatial models of music

At the time when Pierre Boulez grappled with a taxonomy of potential pitch spaces and Mauricio Kagel studied planar geometry (Kagel 1960, cf. section 2.2), **Emilio Carapezza** posited the emergence of a "new constitution of music" in avant-garde compositional practice prefigured in the music of Anton Webern (Carapezza 1961). Carapezza shared the objective of creating a general model for all of new music with the authors of the conceptions of the "spatial image" of modern music (Rochberg 1963 and McDermott 1966; cf. Section 2.2). At the same time, his model of space anteceded Iannis Xenakis's compositional use of vector spaces (Xenakis 1963/1971/1990, cf. below).

The spatial nature of Carapezza's "constitution" of music is captured in a stereometric, three-dimensional image. Here, composing means moving points in a three-dimensional space delineated by a Cartesian system of co-ordinates including frequency, amplitude, and time.[73] However, Carapezza's selection of the physical (i.e. frequency) rather than perceptual (i.e. pitch) attributes as musical dimensions, as well as the introduction of Cartesian (geometric) co-ordinates, reflects a "scientific" vision of music, characteristic of the post-war musical avant-garde. The three-dimensional image of musical space in which configurations of points may be constructed, juxtaposed and transformed is an explicit duplication of the Cartesian-Euclidean model of space in which space is static, homogeneous and isotropic. Carapezza's use of this "mathematical" imagery, however, closely resembles other descriptions of musical spatiality in Webern's music by Eimert (1958), Ligeti (1960) or Boulez (1966/1968).

Spatial thinking about musical materials, based on a differentiation of perceptual features of sound into distinct parameters, which can be quantified into separate dimensions of a musical space, was an important element in the aesthetics of the post-war European avant-garde.[74] This notion of space occurs also in **John Cage**'s writings--as a concept of a multidimensional "total sound-space," the realm for compositional exploration in "experimental music" (Cage 1961).[75] The position of a sound in this five-dimensional space

---

[73]The dimensions of Carapezza's space resemble those suggested by Kurth and used by Hans-Joachim Moser: pitch, time, dynamics (Moser 1953). This model is designed for classical, orchestral music, not for compositions consisting of "pitch points."

[74]In this context, an interesting question arises pertaining to the origin of ideas: have spatial models of music been influenced by the habitual physical description of sound in three dimensions (frequency, amplitude, duration)? These characteristics provide the dimensions for Pierre Schaeffer's description of sound objects in *Traité des objects musicaux* (1966). The perceptual characteristics of sound are correlated to the three physical dimensions, yet this correlation is not straightforward (cf. Deutsch 1982).

[75]Cage uses this term in "Experimental music," a lecture presented in the winter of 1957 in Chicago and published in *Silence* (Cage 1957/1961: 9). James Pritchett equates the notion of space with "a totality of possibilities" mentioned by Cage in "Experimental music: doctrine" (Cage 1955/1961: 15).

is the result of five determinants: frequency or pitch, amplitude or loudness, overtone structure or timbre, duration and morphology (how the sound begins, goes on and dies away).... Any sound at any point in this total sound space can move to become a sound at any other point.

(Cage 1961: 9)

Cage adds that these possibilities may be realized in electroacoustic music, "only if one is willing to change one's musical habits radically" (p. 9), that is, to abandon the discrete steps of traditional musical scales for the sake of a multidimensional continuum. Some of the dimensions of this continuum reveal Cage's equation of physical and perceptual features of sound (e.g. the identification of timbre with overtone structure). Others belong to incongruous levels of sound-description; for example, morphology, denoting transient characteristics of sounds, is a composite dimension built on the basis of frequency, amplitude and duration.

The idea of a total sound-space with the dimensions of physical, analytical parameters of sound (frequency, time, duration, spectrum, etc.) as a domain for composition was common in the early years of electronic music and *musique concrète* (Meyer-Eppler 1955; Schaeffer 1952, 1966; Kaegi 1967). However, the realization of continuous transformations of sound in the specified dimensions proved more difficult than Cage and others had envisioned. The "reification" of physical factors as the true dimensions of music constitutes an aspect of the great revision undertaken by the avant-garde in an effort to rupture the continuity of musical tradition and achieve a new "objectivity" in the music. Despite claims of many authors that the existence of a "spatial image" is an exclusive characteristic of modern music, spatial representation of musical structures is possible regardless of musical style. This thesis was defended by **Gerard Zielinski** in a doctoral dissertation at the Institute of Mathematics of Warsaw Polytechnical University (Zielinski 1970). Zielinski put forward a rigorous, mathematical model of a three-dimensional discrete sound-space in which traditional compositional techniques (pre-dodecaphonic) may be simulated. This sound space, with dimensions delineated by three perpendicular axes (pitch, duration, loudness) is embedded in one segment of the three-dimensional, continuous Euclidean space. The structure of a composition is represented by point structures placed in the discrete space.[76] Here, the spatial representation of musical structures is not coupled with the "modern" characteristics of these structures.

Iannis Xenakis

Xenakis's compositional theory presented in *Formalized Music* makes use of two-, three- and multidimensional spaces, including vector spaces (Xenakis 1963/1971/1991).[77] His description of the compositional process for stochastic music subdivides the work's creation into eight phases.[78] The definition of sonic entities, the second phase of this process, may require the use of the concept of multi-dimensional vector space. Xenakis writes:

> The sonic entities of the classical orchestra can be represented in a first approximation by vectors of four usually independent variables, E_r (c, h, g, u):
>
> c_a = timbre or instrumental family
> h_i = pitch of the sound
> g_j = intensity of the sound, or dynamic form
> u_k = duration of the sound.
>
> The vector E_r defines a point M in the *multidimensional space* provided by a *base (c, h, g, u)*. This point M will have as *coordinates* the numbers c_a, h_i, g_j, u_k.
>
> (Xenakis 1971: 23)

If these points are plotted on an axis E_r, another axis, t, perpendicular to it,

---

[76]There is a one-to-one correlation between elements of the model (i.e. a vertical dimension of the space) and its designates (i.e. dimension of pitch height). Sets of possible pitches, possible durations, and possible dynamic levels are pre-determined.

[77]Xenakis's compositional theory, first published in *Musiques Formelles* (1963), is fully articulated in *Formalized Music* (1971) of which the first six chapters are a translation of the previous book. The second, revised edition of *Formalized Music* (1991) contains important enlargements and additions, but does not change the basic notions discussed here. For this reason the subsequent references will be to the 1971 edition.

[78](1) initial conceptions, (2) definition of the sonic entities, (3) definition of the transformations, (4) microcomposition, including algebra outside-time and algebra in-time, (5) sequential programming, preparing the entire schema of the work, (6) implementation of calculations, (7) final symbolic result (traditional notation, numerical expressions, graphs), (8) sonic realization (adopted from Xenakis 1971: 22).

may represent "lexicographic" time in which the points M are presented in succession. Thus, a two-dimensional space (E_r, t) may be conveniently defined, represented, and implemented in the compositional process. Here, one type of space (four-dimensional vector space) is embedded in another (two-dimensional space of events in time). Moreover, both pitch and time are modelled geometrically. Time is described as a straight line subdivided into line segments representing durations (Xenakis 1971: 12).

Chapter VI of *Formalized Music* presents a stricter formulation of vector space (p. 161-170). Here, its definition requires the existence of set H (melodic intervals), set G (intensity intervals), set U (time intervals) and set T (intervals of time separating the sonic events). The dimensions of the vector space are built from the basic entities of the first three sets. As all these sets are isomorphic with set R of the real numbers, the composer may proceed to utilize specific mathematical functions and operations. Here, Xenakis takes the notion of vector space as a starting point and explores various aspects of mathematical group theory.[79]

Xenakis puts forward another, simpler variant of spatial representation of sound in Chapter II of *Formalized Music*, where it is linked to the idea that "all sound is an integration of grains . . ., of sonic quanta. Each of these elementary grains has a threefold nature: duration, frequency and intensity" (p. 43). This analytical notion of sound underlies Xenakis's definition of the *screen*, the audible two-dimensional area (with the axes of frequency and intensity) fixed by a grid of elemental cells in which clouds of sonic grains are located (p. 51). These cells may be constructed with points or with elemental vectors (p. 55). Varied density and topography of grains and cells may be achieved through the application of ataxy (order or disorder). The "entropy table" of the screens contains a classification of possible designs (p. 66).

This conception appears in the context of Xenakis's definition of an *algebra outside-time* (for sonic events), a *temporal algebra* (for temporal intervals) and "one-to-one correspondences" between both types of algebraic functions, that is, an *algebra*

---

[79]Implemented in *Nomos Gamma* for orchestra and *Nomos Alpha* for cello solo (cf. studies of *Nomos Alpha* by DeLio 1980; Vriend 1981).

in-time (p. 160). According to Xenakis, most musical analysis and construction may be based on (1) the study of the sonic event characterized in pitch, intensity and duration, captured by a structure outside-time, (2) the study of temporal structure, (3) the correspondence between both (p. 160-161). While discussing "algebra in-time," Xenakis uses the term "musical space" to denote various spaces of two dimensions, "e.g. pitch-time, pitch-intensity, pressure-time, etc." (p. 169). This usage indicates that, for him, "musical space" refers to any "space" in music, and is not limited to one phenomenal entity, neither to pitch, nor to the plane of musical notation.

Xenakis's description of the three-dimensional space has common features with other three-dimensional models of music; his two-dimensional "screens" superficially resemble Kagel's planar geometry. Yet, their application is to stochastic music with large number of sonic quanta organized in unusual large-scale patterns. The presence of geometric representations of sounds, clouds of sonic grains, screens and vector spaces, etc. in Xenakis's conception may be interpreted as indicating the existence of a "spatialization of time" in this music, that is, its staticity (cf. section 2.2). The composer clarifies this matter:

> Music develops in time and when you write in space, using the two-dimensional space of your paper, you are, in fact, representing lengths of time as segments of space . . . In music, time does not mean chronometric time . . . . Music, even when it uses bars, and pulses, exists on a level above these divisions. . . . The content of time is important, not absolute duration. The content means the possibility of using time simultaneously and independently by various musical events.
>
> (Xenakis 1992: 5)

Of particular interest is Xenakis's statement that in music "one thinks in different types of dimensions than those of the physical space, or the space of human experience" (Xenakis 1992: 1). Here, the composer subscribes to the idea of the existence of a "musical space" independent of and contrasted to the "physical space." Nevertheless, Xenakis's definition of a "musical space" is thoroughly "modern" in that it refers to various mathematical notions of space, including multidimensional vector space, that are implemented in the creative process. However "spatial" Xenakis's screens and sonic clouds may be, especially in their graphic representation, their "spatial projection" in the physical space of performance is still necessary. Xenakis envisions "protocols of screens attached to a particular point in space" as his option for "the spatialization of sound" (p. 109). The use of "space" as a compositional tool enables Xenakis to structure actual spatial placements and movements of sound with mathematical means (e.g. Archimedean spirals, group theory). His music is, therefore, spatial on several levels at once.

Xenakis's theory of a two-fold, nested nature of space in music constitutes an important contribution to the study of musical spatiality. Nonetheless, his implementation of mathematical notions of space in compositional practice is neither systematic nor consistent. Yet, his vision of formalized methods of composition is supported with an impressive body of musical works created with the aid of these methods (cf. Chapter VII). Such practical realization of theoretical speculations is absent, for instance, in Boulez's investigation into the spatial nature of pitch.

2.4.

Change of perspective: The "musical space" of performance

In the domain of music, as elsewhere, objects and events are known through the mediacy of "a particular descriptive language and a corresponding context for its correct use" (Heelan 1983: 177-178). The discussions of musical spatiality are not exempted from the influence of such compatible, cumulative or mutually exclusive contexts. Theoretical and aesthetic studies of the idea of space in music have often had different objectives and have attempted to answer different questions: is there a musical space? what is it? what are its features? how is it experienced? how can it be constructed or explored? To unravel the web of relationships connecting the various notions of musical spatiality is, therefore, an extraordinarily complicated task. The fact that authors of these concepts use different meanings of space interchangeably and that they often refer to several aspects of music at once does not make it any easier. If the history of this concept could be represented by a simple spatial model, a "line" should not be chosen but rather a "network," suggesting a complexity of interrelationships instead of a simple, linear progression.

The review of different concepts of musical spatiality in the three sections of this Chapter presents a variety of notions of "musical space" revealing a range of disparate conceptions of music. The choice of a quasi-introspective mode of description (Kurth), phenomenological-metaphysical speculation (Zuckerkandl), or mathematical formalizations (Xenakis) reflects the author's belief in what music is or should be. Some theoretical applications seek universality; yet even in these supposedly general models of space idealizations and simplifications are still present. For Morgan, for instance, only music with a deep structure which is analyzable in Schenkerian terms is fully spatial. He considers contemporary music *en masse* to be spatially deficient (lacking a deep structure)--an evaluation that Boulez or Xenakis would probably not agree with. Morgan articulates a common distinction between "music" of the classical and romantic eras and "modern music" of the serialists and avant-garde experimentators. The conceptions of musical space may be divided along similar lines: earlier concepts of dynamic, phenomenal spaces (section 2.1) and theories of static or abstract spaces (sections 2.2 and 2.3). The notion of "musical space" has appeared in the context of the romantic idealization of music conceived of as a purely temporal art. When music is a domain of disembodied, immaterial sounds, its actual spatial aspects of performance and perception are dismissed as irrelevant. Roman Ingarden expresses this view succinctly:

> Sounds as processes or objects persisting and taking place here and now in real time and constituting the elements of specific peformances do not belong to the musical work itself. . . A musical work, given as an aesthetic object on the basis of a particular performance, is not a real event lasting during the performance.
> (Ingarden 1958/1986: 42-43, 55)

This idealization of music and its detachement from the reality of acoustic space, together with the frequent assumption that space necessarily has three dimensions, has caused difficulties in defining "musical space." If pitch is one of its dimensions, this space can no longer be described in terms known from "lived" experience which is--and this needs to be reiterated--highly influenced by concepts from classical physics and geometry (Heelan 1983). Geometric models of "musical space" often use three dimensions of pitch, time, dynamics (or frequency, duration, amplitude), represented by the Cartesian system of coordinates. This graphic image of three perpendicular axes intersecting at one point is taken to denote "space"--the Euclidean space, to be exact--a metric space that is static, empty, homogeneous and isotropic. Musical space visualized through such an unchangeable, "absolute" entity loses its vital characteristics, such as the irreversibility of time-flow and the incongruity between the various dimensions.

The meaning of space in music depends on the notions of "space" adopted for each inquiry. If space means the "container" of all things including motion (absolute space), musical space is a phantom of musical time (e.g. Ingarden, Langer, partly Kurth and Mersmann). Here, the argumentation is as follows: (1) music occurs in motion, (2) motion has to happen somewhere, (3) musical space is the "where" in which motion is taking place. The contention that the existence of spatial relationships in music (motion) requires the existence of a musical space in which those relationships are actualized is not necessarily true, especially in light of the disputes about the relativity or "absoluteness" of space in contemporary philosophy of science (van Fraassen 1985, Friedman 1983; cf. Chapter I). Therefore, if musical space refers exclusively to a vague spatial impression heard in all music as a "shadow" of time (a synaesthetic phenomenon), this concept becomes expendable.

When a rigorous separation between space and time is maintained (as in the pre-modern paradigm of science) musical space becomes the antipode or complement of musical time. Thus, the term "spatial" is used in music theory as a synonym of "registral" in reference to pitch (Cogan, Bernard). Simultaneously, because the pair of "space and time" usually denotes a totality of existence, the usage of the phrase "musical space and time"--frequent in this context--endows a particular theory with the aura of authoritative generality.

Duchez (1979) points out the dependence of the spatial representation of pitch, and the concept of the vertical pitch-height on conventions of musical anotation. The graphic representation of music also affects time. One characteristic of notated time is its "spatialization." Here, the condition of being spatial is associated with being measurable and static (Bergson) and musical spatiality is considered to be identical with temporal stasis. According to Mersmann and Brelet, "spatial stasis" is a characteristic of all formal divisions and symmetries. Therefore, classical music is spatial while romantic is not. For Adorno however, it is music which lacks development and direction (Debussy and Stravinsky) that should be considered spatial (cf. section 2.2). Such music, constructed from static blocks of sounds (without motion and teleological orientation) is an analogue to painting. Adorno's description of "withdrawal of time into space" prefigures later conceptions of temporal stasis which articulate the absence of goal-oriented development in the music, e.g. "temporal space" of Denis Smalley (1991) and "vertical time" of Jonathan Kramer (1988).[80]

---

[80]Smalley writes: "Temporal space is an impression of space . . . created through relative stability and continuity in time. This occurs where evolution and forward motion

An important aspect of "spatialization of time" has been pointed out by Eimert, Ligeti, Boulez and others in reference to the music of Anton von Webern. These writers construed Webern's compositions as consisting of configurations of points and blocks of sound in a "pseudo-space" (Eimert 1958), which is either flat as a surface (pitch/time) or three-dimensional. The various musical "objects" are envisioned with a solidity of physical entities or an immateriality of geometric abstractions. They may rotate, shift and reappear in different points of the space which is continuous, homogeneous and unified by a coherent geometric structure. This musical space abandons the traditional melodic/harmonic structuring in two separate dimensions for the sake of a "directionless" unity (Schoenberg).

Here, the "objectivity" of elements of musical texture indicates a more general idea of the "objectivity" of the musical work; as a form which is constructed of segments, layers and sections, a composition is perceivable in its entirety as an object fixed in time (Brelet, McDermott). The "outside-of-time" permanence of musical compositions, guaranteed by notation, allows for the simultaneous co-existence of different types of spatiality. In particular, the compositional design may be based on mathematical notions of space which are not immediately perceivable as spatial in a conventional sense (Xenakis, Morris).

As it has been stated earlier, the sense of "musical space" depends on the notion of space that is considered "musical." Therefore, if space means "space," that is a segment of the physical three-dimensional expanse in which the performance of music is taking place, musical space is synonymous with the space of performance and perception. This sense of the expression "musical space" is rare (exceptions are discussed below); the terminology of "spatial music" (Varèse) or "spatialization" (Boulez) is far more common in this respect (cf. Chapter III). Here, the focus shifts from the question of "how can space be musical?" to "how can music be spatial?"

---

are slow or seem static, and the listener's attention is not focussed on lower level activity. In other words, continuing existence can approach a quasi-permanence analogous to the contemplation of the visual permanence of a landscape." (Smalley 1991: 123).

However, this distinction is, in part, illusory: most theories of "musical space" have been put forward in order to reveal the nature of musical spatiality, i.e. to define what is "spatial" in music.

Nonetheless, the use of "musical space" in reference to the space of performance indicates a shift in signification resulting from the emergence of new modes of perception and cognition. In contemporary music, literal space, previously considered "external" to music, has become--to paraphrase the title of Henry Brant's important article--an "essential aspect of musical composition" (Brant 1967). In this article, **Henry Brant**, whose expertise with spatial aspects of musical sound has been verified in an impressive oeuvre of "spatial music" (cf. Chapter VI), warns about the danger of conceiving "visual aspects of musical space" on paper, without practical tests in the performance space. Brant presents an "essentially rectangular view of musical space"--meaning by the "view" the standard shape of the concert hall (Brant 1967: 242). The composer deplores that "this view is limited to a one-room concept of musical space--even the most elaborate and complex events in Western musical culture still take place in single four-walled, all-enclosed halls." (Brant 1967: 242). In an effort to overcome this limitation, Brant takes his music outdoors, into city squares and streets (cf. Chapter VI). Thus, the space of urban life is made "musical."

The meaning of "musical space" as the space in which music is performed appears also in essays included in a collection *Musik und Raum*, edited by **Thuring Bräm** (Bräm 1986). The editor describes the content of this volume as touching upon three thematic realms: "(1) musical space in historical perspective, (2) visual music, and (3) musical space in contemporary perspective of composers and interpreters" (Bräm 1986: 8). As specified in the book's subtitle, "musical space" is considered here primarily as the carrier of sound ("Klangträger für die Musik"). This sense seems to imply a focus on the acoustic, not aesthetic aspects of musical spatiality.

However, according to **Dagmar Hoffman-Axthelm**'s study of the "metamorphosis of musical space exemplified by Church and Chamber" (Hoffman-Axthelm 1986: 17), the choice of spaces in which music may be performed endows the music with definite meanings. Music belonging to the sacred space of the Church is spiritual and immaterial, unlike "concrete" music of the profane, lived space of a Chamber (room). According to Hoffman-Axthelm, this distinction has been neutralized in the Concert Hall--designed to free music from its social confinement and abolish its functional involvement in favour of an aesthetic autonomy.

Even in the Concert Hall, though, the meaning of "musical space" as the space of performance reflects an intersubjective, social situation: the presence of performers and listeners in a space that unites them and brings them together. According to **Ludwik Bielawski**, a musical anthropologist, one of the important functions of music is to provide connections and ensure communication between participants in a musical situation, performers and listeners. This is achieved mainly through their co-presence in a "musical space shaped acoustically and psychologically" (Bielawski 1976: 220). The limitation of space with the walls of a room or a concert hall is not a condition for creation of "psychologically closed musical space" (p. 221). Such a space may be created outdoors and in any type of architectural setting because, as Bielawski observes: "spatial situation of music is created by people who directly participate in this space (in an active or a passive manner); they delineate the boundaries of this space" (p. 221).

This understanding of musical space locates music in the realm of spatio-temporal arts. But was it not there before? All music (composed to be performed and heard) is spatio-temporal, because all sounds are spatio-temporal, all the instruments are spatio-temporal, all the performers are spatio-temporal and so are the listeners. As Ludwik Bielawski writes, the connection between space and music is originally established in the spatial character of musical instruments (Bielawski 1976: 219). Performance implies an action in space: a conscious filling it in with music (p. 220).[81]

---

[81]It may be of interest here to recall that one of the main arguments in Maurice Merleau-Ponty's philosophy of embodied subjectivity, is a description of the motility of an organist, whose spatial memory and intuition allow for an unconscious, yet perfect use of the space of the instrument in performance. The conscious willing to do things would imply a separation of body and mind, its unconscious skilled use indicates the existence of a profound, psychosomatic union (Merleau-Ponty 1945/1962).

"Pianistic" sounds and textures, for example, are only possible because there are "pianos" (spatio-temporal objects) with their characteristic sounds made by spatio-temporal "pianists." In the words of Edgard Varèse, "not until the air between the listener's ear and the instrument has been disturbed does music occur. . . Music must live in sound." (Varèse 1939/1967: 199).

If musical sounds are spatio-temporal in themselves, if they have extensions, boundaries and localizations, if relationships of sound distance and direction, as well as patterns of distribution and movement may be musically significant, "musical space" completely changes its meaning. The "external" space in which performance takes place now becomes vital for the constitution of music. Various aspects of this "realistic" meaning of "musical space" are discussed in the remaining part of the dissertation.

Reflections about spatial qualities of sound (not pitch) as material for music have arisen quite recently. The genesis of this topic in metamusical discourse parallels the emergence of a new musical genre, in which spatial relationships need to be composed in their entirety, that is electroacoustic music (cf. Chapter III). The consideration of spatial aspects of electroacoustic, "invisible" music makes one feature of "musical space" immediately obvious. **Denis Smalley** writes:

> Musical space is not empty and cannot be separated from its sounding content. The elastic continuum of composed and superimposed space is expressed through its sound materials and sound-behaviours. Therefore a full understanding of the nature of musical space requires a discussion of musical language.
>
> (Smalley 1991: 123)

There is a necessity for the connection between space and sounds that reveal its existence and characteristics: spatial texture and continuity, dimensions and density, "spatio-morphology" (Smalley's term). Musical, spatial experience "depends on all aspects of content and context, it is the product of a collaboration of factors which cannot be conveniently packaged or easily discussed as an independent 'parameter'" (p. 124). Therefore, the optimal compositional approach is not through systematization and formalization, but through experience.

Here, Smalley shares Ernst Kurth's conviction about the complexity of the musical-spatial phenomenon, though the musical space that he writes about is diametrically different from Kurth's (cf. section 2.1). In the view of Kurth and his other, distinguished colleagues, the notion of "musical space" has been dissociated from the spatial actuality of music in the "external" world. Why? Perhaps because music, usually included among spiritual creations of the human mind, had to be considered outside of space when human identity was represented with an image of a purely temporal consciousness imprisoned in a material body (an element of the spatial world). Hermann Weyl thus articulates this gap between the consciousness and the world, the unbreachable rift between time and space:

> On the one side, our spaceless consciousness which continuously changes in the form of the enduring now, and, on the other side, the spatially extended but timeless reality of which consciousness contains merely a continually changing phenomenon.
> (Weyl 1918/1970: 99)

This image, as Weyl himself admits, is a falsification. According to Edmund Husserl, the scientific construct of Nature, "is an idea that has arisen out of idealization and has been hypothetically substituted for actually intuited nature" (Husserl 1937/1970: 265). An analogical process of substitution takes place in music. Theories of a phenomenal or intrinsic musical space, which is heard during the performance but does not include the physical-spatial features of sound (cf. section 2.1) impose "geometric" images of musical spatiality on the perceptual experience. Thuse, the "musical space" arises out of idealization, and replaces the "actually intuited space" in which listeners, performers and sounds are located, the space in which music "lives in sound" (phrase from Varèse 1939/1967: 199).

CHAPTER III

MUSIC IN SPACE AND THE IDEA OF SPATIALIZATION

Introduction

C'est seulement à l'époque moderne que le compositeur devient pleinement conscient de la nécessité de s'approprier l'espace et de l'organiser pour en faire une dimension intrinsèque de la composition. . . Par l'integration de l'espace, la musique n'a pas conquis seulement une dimension nouvelle et une nouvelle mobilité, mais une neuve et fascinante magie, aux inépuisables pouvoirs.
(Brelet 1967: 496, 500)

Gisèle Brelet attributes the compositional discovery of the spatiality of sound to "modern" times (after 1950s). Yet, there are ways in which music has always been spatial: in respect to the acoustic environment of its performance, the type and location of sound sources within this space, and the "lived" bodily-spatial experience of the listeners and performers. I discuss these aspects of "music in space" in the first section of this chapter. The main portion of the text presents main developments within the compositional theory and practice of "spatialization" in the 20th-century.[1] The domain of spatialization may be subdivided into four large conceptual areas: (a) spatial simultaneity of different musical layers, from Mahler and Ives to Brant (section 3.2); (b) "objectivity" of musical material projected into space, from Satie and Varèse to electroacoustic music (section 3.3); (c) speculative theories of spatialization in Darmstadt (Stockhausen and Boulez, section 3.4); (d) conceptual experimentation (Cage and his followers, section 3.5). These areas are ordered chronologically, according to the time of the emergence of the principal concept in each domain.

---

[1] Although the emphasis is on the composers' explicit statements about space and spatialization, I also take into account their ideals expressed through the music. Here, "spatialization" denotes the expansion of musical resources to include spatial features of sound, such as the direction and distance from the listeners, movement in space, etc.

Nonetheless, the various approaches to spatialization are interrelated and intertwined. This fact renders the division into sections somewhat arbitrary: for instance, Cage (section 3.5) was inspired by Ives and Varèse (sections 3.2 and 3.3) and wrote, in part, for Darmstadt (section 3.4). Moreover, composers change their views on spatialization through the years (e.g. Boulez, cf. section 3.4).

3.1.
Music in space: a historical background

The history of the notion of "musical space" presented in Chapter II concludes with an account of the shift in the meaning of this expression from the domain of pitch to the area of the architectural space of performance (Brant, Bräm and Hoffman-Axthelm; cf. section 2.4). However, when Barbara Hoffman-Axthelm pointed out the contrasts in musical style associated with the distinct "musical" spaces of the Church and the Chamber, she did not venture into new ground. Attempts at establishing a causal connection between space and style have been quite numerous since the 1920s. H. Bagenal, for instance, claimed that the reverberation time of a performance space was a decisive factor in the evolution of polyphony (Bagenal 1930).[2] Edward Lippman quotes a number of authors asserting that acoustic environment and performer placement have exercised significant influences on the development of musical style (Lippman 1952). The main difficulty with confirming the existence of such a spatio-musical causality arises from the question of historical precedence: was the music shaped and transformed by space or was the space chosen (built and shaped) for the music? There is no simple solution to this dilemma.

Nonetheless, it is difficult not to agree with Lippman that enclosures, by excluding external noise, make possible music of a greater intricacy of detail and

---

[2]Cf. also Lowinsky's discussion of physical and musical space in the renaissance (Lowinsky 1941). Interestingly, the idea of the dependence of musical style on the conditions of performance finds a modern advocate in R. Murray Schafer (Schafer 1981).

dynamic nuance--especially if reverberation time is not excessively long (Lippman 1952: 99). There is also an intimate connection between type of performance space and instrumentation, because the spatial setting influences the "sound-ideal of a time" (p. 100). Hubert Le Blanc's diatribe against the violin in defense of the viola da gamba (1740) corroborates Lippman's observation:

> The violin, to be sure, could not compete with the viol in delicacy of moving sound or in chordal playing, so refined in its resonance when heard in the proper place for appreciating its attributes at close range. So to allow themselves to make an impression, the trio moved the setting to an immense hall, where there would be many effects which were as prejudicial to the viol as they would be favourable to the violin.
> (Le Blanc 1740/1984: 206)

The contrast between the refined and subtle effects of the viola da gamba, which are best appreciated in smaller halls, and the louder, "piercing" sonorities of the violin, which are appropriate for larger spaces, prefigures the differentiation between chamber and symphonic music established much later. This distinction implies musical differences relating to the number of performers and the nature of the interactions of instrumental sounds with the acoustic properties of the concert hall. Even in atonal music, often considered only in abstract terms, the size and type of the hall may be a part of the compositional design. Anton von Webern wrote to Schoenberg on 6 July 1910 about his *Pieces for Orchestra op. 10:*

> There will be a number of short pieces that I shall call chamber pieces for orchestra in order to indicate that they should not be played in a large hall. Until now the instrumentation has been very small--a fact that gave me this idea (...) In a large hall one would hardly be able to hear anything of the music.
> (Moldenhauer 1978: 194-195)

Thus, space relates to music in the most general sense: music is spatial because a certain sound quality (influenced by the size of performance space) is associated with different genres and types of instrumentation. This relationship is one of the three basic aspects of musical spatiality. The second category refers to the location of sound sources within the space of performance (here, musicians are treated as "objects" dispersed in space and producing sounds). Finally, spatiality of music relates to the nature of performing and listening. If the musicians (and the listeners) are not "minds" but "body-subjects" (Merleau-Ponty 1945, Heelan 1983) their active involvement in the production and perception of sounds endows music with a full, bodily spatiality. However, music seen through the lenses of such phenomenological anthropology cannot be identified with abstract, timeless entities--the "musical works."[3]

Music becomes spatial when the location of the performers in a space as well as their spatial disposition within this space acquires a special meaning (the second aspect of musical spatiality). In Edward Lippman's words "space really interpenetrates the music" in the antiphonal style through the ages and in the music of the Baroque, with its ideals of the concerto and polychorality (Lippman 1952: 103-5). Polychorality is often seen as the beginning of spatial thinking in composition; Stockhausen, among others, has cited the use of divided choirs at San Marco in Venice as proof of the dependence of musical style on architecture (Stockhausen 1960). Nonetheless, according to Carver, who has traced the history of *cori spezzati* from the beginning of this technique in the 16th century to its climax in the work of Gabrieli and Schütz,

> a polychoral work or passage is one in which the ensemble is consistently split into two or more groups, each retaining its own identity, which sing separately and together within a through-composed framework in which antiphony is a fundamental compositional resource. . .
>
> (Carver 1988: xvi)

Carver's definition linking polychorality to antiphonal singing does not mention the exact localisation of performers within the performance space. This is because, for him, as for the theoreticians and composers of polychoral music who did not include diagrams of performer placement in their texts and scores, the basic characterization of the polychoral style relates to the *division* of the performers into groups. It suffices to disperse the groups of musicians, each playing different

---

[3] I discuss the notion of the musical work as defined by Roman Ingarden (1958) and criticized by Zofia Lissa (1968) and Lydia Goehr (1992) in Chapter IV.

material, in the performance space without specifying their exact positions for the perception of "polychorality" to be established. The division of music into spatially separated layers is one of the main categories of musical spatialization (cf. section 3.2).

Carver associates the origins of polychorality with antiphonal singing in the Church. The spatial division of performers into two groups in the responsories and antiphons of the Gregorian chant allows for the realization of the musical structures of a dialogue between a soloist and choir or between two choirs. This is, however, just one spatial aspect of the chant, which, as the music of a religious ceremony, implies participation. Chant belongs to the spatio-temporal schema of the liturgy, a schema superimposed on (and realized in) the particular space-time of "performance." Music, as part of the ritual, helps to create an existential experience for the listener-performers who are physically immersed in musical sounds and involved in their concrete, spatio-temporal interactions. Here, the anthropological meaning of a "musical space," a space delimited by the presence of participants, needs to be recalled (Bielawski 1976; cf. Chapter II, section 2.4). This type of spatiality emerges in the context of musical actions.

A beautiful, ancient example of such "spatial" music is described in the Book of Nehemiah.[4] The prophet describes an immense spatio-temporal ritual "with songs of thanksgiving, with cymbal, lute and lyre" celebrating the dedication of the wall of Jerusalem which was rebuilt after the return of the Israelites from Babylonian captivity (Nehemiah 12:27). As Nehemiah writes:

> I then made the leaders of Judah come on to the top of the wall, and organized two great choirs. The first made its way along the top of the wall, right-handed . . . The second choir made its way left-handed; I followed it, with half the leaders of the people, along the top of the wall . . . The two choirs then took their places in the Temple of God.
>
> (Nehemiah 12: 31, 38, 40)

---

[4]Quoted from the *Jerusalem Bible. Popular Edition.* London: Darton, Longman & Todd, 1974: 520.

The great choirs included singers and men carrying trumpets and "the musical instruments of David, the man of God" (Nehemiah 12:36). Although neither the act of playing music while walking around the wall, nor the instrumental performance at the Temple were specifically mentioned, it is possible to assume that this great processional did include continuous singing and playing. The music constituted a part of the liturgical celebration which was designed to sanctify a unique, architectural space. Consequently, not the music, but the space of sacred action as well as the actions of the participants, including the exact routes of each choir, were described in detail.[5]

The three ways of rendering music "spatial" recur throughout music history. Space as the most general condition for the performance of music influences the sound ideal associated with different instruments and ensembles. The spatial separation of groups of musicians allows for clear distinctions of the layers of sound and creates conditions for their lively interactions. Finally, the experience of participation in a musical-spatial ritual brings out the fullness of human existence in "incarnate subjectivity" (Merleau-Ponty's term).

---

[5]Music which is deeply involved in a ritual may not be easily subdivided into individualized musical works worthy of particular attention. It would be quite ridiculous to extend the meaning of a phenomenal "musical space" in the sense used by Kurth or Clifton (cf. Chapter II) to the music used for the dedication of the wall of Jerusalem. This music does not belong to the context of the "work-concept" (Goehr 1992).

3.2.
Spatial simultaneity of layers: Mahler, Ives, and Brant

The idea of the separation of performers into groups, known in music "since time immemorial," preceded other notions of musical spatialization, especially those advocated by the Darmstadt avant-garde. Karlheinz Stockhausen claimed that his "serialization of direction" was the first real (i.e. non-theatrical and non-programmatic) attempt at composing music in space (cf. Stockhausen 1959/1961).[6] I subscribe to a vision of "spatialization" which differs from his; I think that the 20th-century history of spatialized music began with the juxtaposition of simultaneously developing "streams" of sound material in the works of Mahler and Ives.

Gustav Mahler

The frequent use of off-stage instruments in Mahler's symphonies has attracted the attention of many commentators (Gottwald and Ligeti 1974, Mitchell 1975, Sine 1983, McCoy 1993). What has not been sufficiently pointed out is the mobility of the sonorities juxtaposed in the simultaneous layers of the music, such as in the Finale of *Symphony No. 2* (1893-1894). Off-stage instruments (4 trumpets, 4 horns, triangle, cymbal and bass drum) appear in the development (m. 343-379) of this movement and in the section preceding the Resurrection chorus (mm. 448-471). During the off-stage band's first appearance, its military fanfares are superimposed on a layer of music in the strings. According to Donald Mitchell,

> Mahler goes out of his way to spell out the character differences between the two kinds of music involved (the passionately lyrical and the quasi-military) and the two types of instrumental sonority involved, by making a clear rhythmic differentiation as well as a spatial separation.
> (Mitchell 1975: note 23 to p. 337)

---

[6]Stockhausen made his claim after dismissing the works of earlier earlier composers such as Gabrieli, Berlioz or Mahler as architecturally or theatrically motivated; cf. Section 3.3 below.

At first, the band sounds in the furthest distance (m. 343); during its subsequent entries (m. 355, 376) the fanfares become gradually louder, i.e. closer. The image of a distant, approaching brass-and-percussion band, the music of which is superimposed on the layer of orchestral sonorities, is further explored in the section called "The Last Trump" by Mitchell (mm. 448-471, cf. Ex. III-1). Here, sounds from "a far distance" (trumpets, horns, timpani) are juxtaposed with those of the orchestra (drum, flute and piccolo). The horns are consistently distant, beginning with an echo which disappears into the silence (m. 448), and concluding with long-held notes gradually "dying away" (m. 470-471).

Although the score does not include a placement scheme for the instrumentalists, a note for the conductor indicates that "the four trumpets must sound from different directions." At first, the trumpets alternate, then are heard together-- from all directions at once. In addition to being contrasted in direction, with two of the trumpets placed at the right (1, 3) and two at the left (2, 4), the sounds of the trumpets are mobile. Their successive entries are gradually nearer and louder, especially in the 4-measure fanfare (mm. 455-458; the order of entries: trumpets 2, 4 from the left, and 1, 3 from the right). At the end, the off-stage music gradually dies away, sounding (especially trumpet 1) "more and more distant," and joined by the "dying away" sounds of the flutes--which have been evoking birdsong throughout this section. According to a draft program of this Symphony (dating from 1901), the distant, approaching brass sounds have a definite, apocalyptic meaning. In Mahler's words: "The *'great summons'* is heard; the trumpets from the Apocalypse call; in the midst of the awful silence we think we hear in the farthest distance a nightingale like a last quivering echo of earthly life." (Mahler 1901; transl. Mitchell 1975: 183-184).

The "earthly" nightingale (of the flute) is located in the orchestra, while the "supernatural" trumpets are heard from the distance, with their sounds approaching from all sides and fading away at the end. Thus, Mahler's use of spatial movement is both dramatic and symbolic. It is also quite sophisticated, with superimposed contrasting and changing acoustic plans, varied depths and directions. Sound placement and movement in Mahler's *Second Symphony* are interesting in their own right, not only as carriers of meaning--which is, however, their primary function.

According to Mitchell, Mahler's inclination to create such multi-layered, spatially stratified textures was influenced by his interest in the music of Hector Berlioz as well as a fascination with the "random, everyday, open-air polyphony" of the world of everyday experience (Mitchell 1975: 336, 342). Natalie Bauer-Lechner described Mahler's delight at hearing the chaotic music of a fête with the simultaneous sounds of "innumerable barrel-organs blaring out." Hearing this, the composer exclaimed:

> That's polyphony and that is where I get it from! For it's all the same whether it resounds in a din like this or in a thousandfold bird song, in the howling of the storm, the lapping of the waves, or the crackling of the fire. Just so--from quite different directions--the themes must enter; and they must be just as different from each other in rhythm and melodic character. Everything else is merely many-voiced writing, homophony in disguise. The only difference is that the artist orders and unites them all into one concordant and harmonious whole.
>
> (Bauer-Lechner; quoted from Mitchell 1975: 342)

Mitchell considers Mahler's awareness of the spatiality of environmental sounds as a decisive factor in the development of the composer's "original concept of acoustic space in which there is even an idea of directional sound involved" (Mitchell 1975: 215). Interestingly, the same natural phenomena that Mahler took as models for true polyphony (storm, wind, waves, fire) inspired Iannis Xenakis's "stochastic music," which is built from dense masses of sound in which individual elements cannot be distinguished (Xenakis 1971; cf. Chapter VII).

Nonetheless, Mahler's use of spatial sound has more in common with that of Charles Ives than with Xenakis's. Both Mahler and Ives used the spatial separation of groups of instruments (on-stage and off-stage, at a distance) for the purpose of establishing clear perceptual differentiations between at least two simultaneous layers of sound, contrasted by timbre and musical material.[7] There are differences, though.

---

[7] The examination of Mahler's use of space, and of his relationship to Ives and other composers are topics which would require an expanded discussion in a different context. The influence of Mahler's ideas of musical spatiality on the post-war avant-

Ex. III-1: "The Last Trump" in Mahler's *Symphony No. 2*; movement V, mm. 448-471.
© 1897, 1925 by Universal Edition A.G., Vienna. Assigned 1952 to Universal Edition (London) Ltd., London. This revised edition ©copyright 1971 by Universal Edition Vienna-London. Used by permission of European American Music Distributors Corporation, sole U.S. and Canadian agent for Universal Edition Vienna-London.

Because of Mahler's practical involvement in the performances of his music, he was concerned with providing precise guidelines for the conductor, e.g. specifying the directions from which the individual trumpets should play in the Finale of the *Second Symphony*. Ives's lack of such experience resulted in the absence of exact indications, even in works which require the distribution of performers in space.[8]

Charles Ives

In 1933 Henry Cowell observed that the music of Charles Ives is often subdivided into independent layers (Cowell 1933). He also noticed that in dense, Ivesian polyphony, performers are frequently independent, both melodically and rhythmically, "yet the whole synchronizes into a rich unity of sound" (p. 134).[9] Cowell suggested that the idea of this "layering technique" (term from Morgan 1974) came from Ives's live experience of "hearing two bands passing each other on the march, each playing a different piece" (p. 134-135). When these bands marched by each other (music in spatial movement), the dynamic proportions of the two strands of music gradually changed.[10]

The idea of musical independence of simultaneous layers may be realized by means of two orchestras which perform musical material differing in its characteristic

---

garde, for instance, was more pervasive than the title of this section might suggest (cf. Gottwald and Ligeti 1974). Mahler's interest in distant sonorities inspired aspects of the compositional thinking of György Ligeti (cf. Dadelsen 1976) and R. Murray Schafer (cf. Chapter VIII).

[8]Moreover, the composers differed in their attitudes towards musical quotations and stylizations. For Mahler, "the distance between music and the aural experiences from life, even when they were of a directly musical character, represented a very significant and clearly defined gap" (Mitchell 1975: 170). For Ives, this chasm was of considerably smaller dimensions.

[9]This idea inspired Brant's approach to spatial polyphony (cf. Chapter VI). Nicholls describes simultaneity of lines as "massed voices" (Nicholls 1991: 16).

[10]The effect of the approach and disappearance of the music from and into the distance may be imitated with dynamics, as in Mahler's *Second Symphony*.

harmonic, melodic and rhythmic features. Ives writes in the *Conductor's Note* to the second movement of the *Fourth Symphony*:

> The instruments are divided here [i.e. on p. 26 of the score] into two separate orchestras, the lower continuing the proceeding adagio, while the upper, including woodwind, brass, tympani and both pianos, breaks suddenly in, cancelling the sounds of the lower orchestra unless its players can be placed near enough to the majority of listeners or the upper orchestra removed sufficiently so that it may, in a way, be heard through the lower.
> (Ives 1929/1965: 12)

The two orchestras perform in different tempi, and the upper accelerates while "the lower orchestra in no way increases its tempo or intensity" (ibidem). The slow, contemplative layer of sound is symbolic of Pilgrims' hymns which are "constantly crowded out and overwhelmed"[11] by snatches of a "worldly," noisy din with rapidly increasing density. The continuous layer of quiet music may be heard before and after these interpolations, thus providing a background canvas on which the louder, foreground elements are presented. Nicholls considers this separation into "musical foreground and background" an idea of exceptional importance for Ives's use of space (Nicholls 1990).[12] According to J. Peter Burkholder, the separation into layers is a convention used by Ives in his pieces "about life experiences:"[13]

---

[11]Expression from a program note by Henry Bellman quoted from the preface to Ives's *Fourth Symphony* by John Kirkpatrick (Ives 1927/1965: viii).

[12]This idea is realized, for instance, in "In the night" from the *Set for Theatre or Chamber Orchestra* (1906) which includes offstage instruments, and *The Housatonic at Stockbridge* (1908) with the sounds of bells tolling in the distance (Nicholls 1991: 42). In "Music and its Future" Ives writes about an experience of listening to an outdoor performance of music in which: "the players were arranged in two or three groups around the town square. The main group in the bandstand at the center usually played the main themes, while the others, from the neighboring roofs and verandas, played the variations, refrains and so forth. . . A man, living nearer the variations, insisted that they were the real music and it was more beautiful to hear the hymn come sifting through them than the other way around." (Ives 1933: 192).

[13]Quoted from Chapter Ten ("Quodlibet and Collage") of J. Peter Burkholder's forthcoming book *All made of tunes: Charles Ives and the uses of musical borrowing*.

Ex. III-2: The division of the instruments into two orchestras in Ives's *Symphony No. 4*, movement II, p. 26.

> The foreground represents the events themselves, and the background, often in many layers of varying audibility, evokes the noises of the environment that one may notice or ignore but are always there nonetheless. . . In a piece about remembered events, there also is a background hum, but it is not the hum of traffic or natural noises: it is the cloud of memory, as each remembered event, person, or thing recalls others aroused involuntarily by their association with or resemblance to the first.
>
> (Burkholder 1993: 11)

Thus, the division of the music into simultaneous strata has programmatic significance. It may not, however, require a spatial differentiation through the placement of the musicians. The two orchestras in the second movement of the *Fourth Symphony* are not separated in the space of performance. Instead, their division is articulated in pitch, which clarifies the distinctions of their timbre, meter and tempo (cf. Ex. III-2).[14]

The division of performers into groups according to their register is well-known as a technique of polychorality.[15] Ives's reference to the stratification of music in pitch space was not unique to the *Fourth Symphony*. As the composer wrote in his *Memos* (1932/1972), in the fall of 1915 he had envisioned a composition of two layers, the upper symbolizing Heaven and the lower representing the Earth. This piece would need to be played twice, with the listener first focusing on one stratum then on the other (Ives 1932/1972: 106). The planned portrayal of the earthly space made abundant use of pitch-related imagery in,

> a kind of uneven and overlapping counterpoint sometimes reaching nine or ten different lines representing the ledges, rocks, woods, and land formations--lines of trees and forest, meadows, roads, rivers, etc.--and undulating lines of mountains in the distance. . .
>
> (Ives 1932/1972: 106-107)

---

[14] Notice that the vertical alignment of the music performed by the two orchestras is approximate because of the difference in tempo. The flow of the music is falsified in the notation, because of the visual image of the barlines.

[15] For instance, in the third part of Praetorius's *Syntagma Musicum* (1619) polychorality is discussed in terms of registral divisions into higher and lower choirs (cf. Carver 1988: 147).

Both the "body of the earth" and the Heaven were planned to be represented by chords, though of different kinds.[16] Of more importance, though, is the fact that Ives envisioned a separation of the lower and the upper groups by "a vacant space of 4 whole tones" (p. 107). This gap in the pitch space would allow for a sufficient perceptual differentiation of the two layers without their separation in space, had the piece been composed.[17]

Ives explored contrasts of a static background and an evolving foreground in the second movement of the *Fourth Symphony* and, much earlier, in *The Unanswered Question* (1906), where he also introduced differences in the spatial placements of the instruments (off-stage strings).[18] If the co-presence of contrasting elements is an important aspect of the music, these contrasts may be amplified by spatial location. In "Music and its Future" Ives wrote:[19]

> Experiments, even on a limited scale, as when a conductor separates a chorus from the orchestra or places a choir off the stage or in a remote part in the hall, seem to indicate that there are possibilities in this matter that may benefit the presentation of the music, not only from the standpoint of clarifying the harmonic, rhythmic, thematic material, etc., but of bringing the inner content to a deeper realization (assuming, for argument's sake, that there is an inner content).
>
> (Ives 1933: 191)

---

[16]All musical material of various scales, including microtonal divisions, and chords of different structure, was to relate to one, fundamental pitch.

[17]This planned *Universe Symphony* was to consist of three sections representing the Past (creation), Present (Earth, "evolution in nature and humanity") and Future ("Heaven, the rise of all to the spiritual"). Thus, the Ivesian "Universe" was all-embracing, joining space and time together (Ives 1932/1972: 106).

[18]This composition played a formative role in the development of Henry Brant's ideals of spatial music. It has also been performed in a variety of spatial arrangements, different from those planned by Ives and including, for instance, variable positions for the trumpet, which causes each "question" to sound from a different point in space.

[19]This article is a slightly altered version of a lengthy footnote to the *Conductor's Note* for the second movement of the *Fourth Symphony*, first published in 1929, reprinted in 1965.

Ives's view on the use of spatial separation to "clarify" the musical material found confirmation in the words of Henry Brant and Pierre Boulez.[20] According to Henry Brant, the main function of space in music is "to make complexity intelligible" (Brant 1992: 1). For Pierre Boulez, the purpose of spatial organization in music is "to clarify the situation of polyphony" (Boulez 1992: 1). Moreover, Ives's preoccupation with spatial matters, as expressed in "Music and its Future," has proven to be prophetic in respect to the ubiquity of spatialization in post-war music. According to Ives, any combination of more than two players has the potential for the "distribution of instruments or groups of instruments or an arrangement of them at varying distances from the audience" (Ives 1933: 191). Chapter V of this dissertation presents a survey of designs used for such "ensemble dispersion" (term from Drennan 1975) in contemporary music.

The co-existence of spatially separated layers stimulates a change in perception, by giving the audience the option to focus on individually selected musical strata. When two strands of music emanate from two points in space,

> the listener may choose which of these two rhythms he wishes to hold in his mind as primal. . . . As the eye, in looking at a view, may focus on the sky, clouds, or distant outlines, yet sense the color and form of the foreground, and then by observing the foreground, may sense the distant outlines and color, so, in some similar way, the listener can choose to arrange in his mind the relation of the rhythmic, harmonic and other material.
>
> (Ives 1933: 193)

Here Ives confirms his interest in the perceptual organization of music into a foreground and a background, a division articulated by the voluntary focus of attention. As he writes, in music based on more than two different "rhythmic, melodic, harmonic schemes, the hearer has a rather active part to play" (Ives 1933: 196). Elsewhere in the article, Ives notices that the mobility of the listeners may enrich their experience of the music; for example, a shift in aural perspective brings about interesting changes in the perception of music heard while walking (p. 192).

---

[20] I interviewed both composers in 1992.

The composer concludes that "music seems too often all foreground," so it needs to be enriched by perspective and distance (p. 194). Ives's awareness of the role of distance for the quality of sound is quite striking; he notices that

> it is difficult to reproduce the sounds and feeling that distance gives to sound wholly by reducing or increasing the number of instruments or by varying their intensities. A brass band playing *pianissimo* across the street is a different-sounding thing from the same band, playing the same piece *forte*, a block or so away.
>
> (Ives 1933: 191)

This difference is caused by the absence of transients (onset and offset characteristics) in the sounds, and by the change of timbre with distance (attenuation of higher partials by the air). Therefore, as Ives remarks, "a horn over a lake gives a quality of sound and feeling that it is hard to produce in any other way" (p. 192). R. Murray Schafer may well have read these words before composing music to be performed specifically over a cold Canadian lake (cf. Chapter VIII). This is just one example of the continuing significance of Ives's ideas of musical spatiality which have also inspired such well-known composers as John Cage and Henry Brant.[21]

Henry Brant

According to Henry Brant, whose interest in musical spatiality has largely been influenced by Ives (Brant 1967, 1992), *The Unanswered Question* "presents, with extraordinary economy and concentration, the entire twentieth-century spatial spectrum in music, and offers guidelines for solving all the practical problems involved" (Brant 1967: 225). This may seem an overstatement, but it does clearly articulate Brant's compositional concerns. The elevated opinion of Ives's work indicates its importance for Brant's own spatial music, which is, like *The Unanswered Question*, characterized

---

[21]In this context, it is difficult to agree with Robert P. Morgan's conclusion that "Ives's concern with physical space is only a symptom . . . of a more fundamental spatial orientation within the music itself" (p. 147). Morgan cites harmonic stasis as one of these "fundamental" spatial aspects of Ives's music. Perhaps, this stasis was only a symptom of a more fundamental concern with the spatiality of the music itself?

by a complete musical contrast of widely separated layers of sound (in regards to timbre, tempo, meter, range, as well as harmonic, melodic and contrapuntal material) as well as the lack of rhythmic co-ordination between these independent layers.[22]

As Brant wrote in 1967, his earliest contacts with the spatial aspects of Ives's music predated 1951: he conducted a version of *The Unanswered Question* with strings backstage, "flutes in a 'box' halfway down the hall and the trumpet solo at the very back of a high balcony" (Brant 1967: 223). He also experimented with performances of polychoral and polyphonic compositions from the Renaissance and the Baroque (Tallis, Gabrieli) and heard a performance of Berlioz's *Requiem op. 5* (with brass ensembles separated in space).

Brant's concern with the spatialization of music (Brant himself did not use this term) was first expressed in print in 1955, in a brief article published in the *American Composer's Alliance Bulletin* ("The Uses of Antiphonal Distribution and Polyphony of Tempi in Composing"). In 1967, the composer summarized the main observations from this article in four points (Brant 1967: 224):[23]

> **1. spatial separation clarifies the texture**: if the music consists of several layers "each with its own distinctive sonority scheme, over the same octave range," the presence of casually-occurring unisons should be avoided by distributing the performers into widely separated positions in the hall.
>
> **2. separated groups are difficult to coordinate**: exact rhythmic simultaneities are impossible because of the distances between the musicians.
>
> **3. spatial separation is equivalent to the separation of textures in pitch space (if performers are together on stage)**: separation allows for the differentiation of musical strands "with no collision or crossing of textures" and permits a greater complexity in the music.
>
> **4. spatial arrangements must be planned exactly, but allow adjustments of details**: there is no one optimum position of the listeners or the performers in the hall, each situation is different.

---

[22]Brant's spatial music and issues arising from its features are the subject matter of Chapter VI of this dissertation.

[23]I summarize Brant's points, but leave their order intact.

This text, written in 1954, and published a year later, may have been known to John Cage and Karlheinz Stockhausen, as it predates writings on space and spatialized compositions by both composers. I refer here to *Silence*, a collection of Cage's lectures and articles published in 1961, and to Stockhausen's spatial music manifesto *Musik im Raum*, published in 1959 following the composition of *Gesang der Jünglinge* of 1956 and *Gruppen für drei Orchester* of 1955-1957. There is a marked similarity of certain ideas expressed by Brant and Cage, especially the notion of the co-existence of independent layers in what Brant calls "a total antiphony" and Cage describes as the "co-existence of dissimilars" (in "Experimental music," 1957/1961: 12; cf. section 3.5). The clarification of distinct elements in a complex texture by spatial separation of performers, proposed by Brant, was realized in Stockhausen's *Gruppen für drei Orchester* (cf. section 3.4).

During the subsequent decade, Brant expressed his interest in spatial features of sound primarily in his music (cf. Chapter VI). However, because his approach to composition was a practical one, he performed numerous experiments with the placement and movement of the musicians in space; he proceeded through methods of "trial-and-error" and evaluated the effects aurally. Brant documented the new discoveries resulting from his experimentation in the article on "Space as an Essential Aspect of Musical Composition" (Brant 1967). The composer found out, for instance, that the effect of distance depends on the size of the hall, and that this affects horizontal distances more than vertical ones. He was also convinced that vertical height creates an impression of higher pitch (but that register is more important than absolute pitch; p. 229).[24] Moreover, two distant groups on the stage or in the hall with independent material and instrumentation give a clear impression of separateness. This observation is of great importance for Brant's conception of spatial music. During an interview in 1992, he criticized Stockhausen's *Gruppen für Drei Orchester*

---

[24]In 1930 C.C. Pratt published a study proving the thesis that rising pitch is associated with vertical elevation in space; this study has been discussed by Lippman (1952).

as a piece which is not really spatial, because "all of the orchestras have brass, woodwinds and percussion, so the direction and the tone quality cannot indicate the source of the material" (Brant 1992: 12). Then, the composer declared that

> one of the essential realities of space music, as I have come to understand it, is that direction and tone quality should work together to identify certain kinds of music, and if this cannot be done, or if it is not done, then the space does not do anything at all, except create confusion.
> (Brant 1992: 12)

Spatial separation in conjunction with timbre may give rise to interesting new effects such as *a wall of sound* (created by the strings placed vertically, by the wall of the hall and arranged from the lowest to the highest), *spill* (when the similarity of timbre and musical material causes a fusion of sounds which are performed by widely spaced musicians but seem to extend and cover the whole area in-between), and *filling up* (when stationary performers placed around the walls of the hall begin to play one after another and gradually increase the spatial extension and the volume of sound). In all three cases, musical sounds tangibly occupy segments of physical space (their temporal character may be either static or dynamic). The apparent extension of the sounds depends on the similarity of the timbre of the instruments and the correspondences in the musical material of the distant groups.

Wide distances between groups of musicians are beneficial for textural differentiation, but they cause a deterioration in rhythmic coordination and are detrimental to a perception of harmony. The absence of exact rhythmic correspondence,

> permits simultaneous contrasted meters and tempi, easily controlled either by assistant conductors, soloists, or section leaders. Extreme overall rhythmic intricacy and a sense of great rhythmic freedom are attainable by this kind of procedure; at the same time, maximum control within well-defined limits, as well as ease and naturalness in playing, is retained.
> (Brant 1967: 234)

In thinking about music in space, Brant is not concerned with analytically isolated characteristics of sound (the approach of Stockhausen and Boulez, cf. section 3.4), but with the total perceptual experience. While his approach to spatialization is pragmatic, his musical material is often traditional (cf. Chapter VI). Brant does not share the European interest in a systematic search for new means of unifying musical structures. Instead, he continues the tradition of Mahler and Ives, the tradition of spatial simultaneity of contrasting musical layers.

3.3.
Musical objects in space:
From Satie and Varèse to electroacoustics

In contrast to the dynamic, multi-layered spatiality of music envisioned by Brant and Ives, the idea of spatialization through "reification" of musical material implies a certain staticity in the music or its elements. Satie's *musique d'ameublement*, Stravinsky's idea of a work of music as a "musical object," and Varèse's conceptions of sound-masses projected in space display this trait to different extents. Moreover, the reification of pre-recorded sound objects which may be projected into space during performance acquired a new meaning in *musique concrète*, the source of inspiration for Stockhausen's idea of spatialization (cf. section 3.4).

Eric Satie

Although Eric Satie did not formulate a theory of spatial music or spatialization, he introduced an idea of consequence for the "objectivity" of music discussed in this section. Satie's invention, called *musique d'ameublement*, that is furniture or furnishing music, was designed to "fill up the awkward silences in conversation" and "neutralize the street noises" (Gillmor 1992: 231-232). Such music would be present in various everyday situations and not consciously listened to. Thus, wryly comments Gillmor, Satie "officially invented Muzak in 1920" (p. 232).

Satie composed several pieces of *musique d'ameublement*, two of them, with Darius Milhaud, for the intermissions during a concert at the Galerie Barbazange on 8 March 1920 (*Chez un Bistrot* and *Un Salon*; Gillmor 1992: 339). The composers wanted the music to come from all sides at once, so they "posted the clarinets in three different corners of the theater, the pianist in the fourth, and the trombone in a box on the balcony floor" (Milhaud 1953: 123). The musicians performed

> fragments of well-known pieces such as Saint-Saëns's *Dance macabre* and Thomas's *Mignon*, together with simple ostinato patterns repeated endlessly while Satie circulated through the audience exhorting people to talk, walk about, drink, to carry on as if nothing was happening.
> (Gillmor 1992: 232)

Despite Satie's admonitions not to pay attention to the musical wallpaper, however, everyone listened without speaking and "the whole effect was spoiled" (Milhaud 1953: 123). However, as Milhaud observed 30 years later, the intermittent listening made possible by the ubiquity of recorded and broadcast music, soon became a habit; in private and public spaces people are "drenched in an unending flood of music" to which they do not pay conscious attention (p. 123).

Musique d'ameublement was designed to blend with the environmental noises in various situations in the office, the restaurant and the home, for instance, during the arrival of guests. Satie's composition, entitled *Tapisserie en fer forgé*, provides a musical background for the latter spatio-temporal, social event. The piece is scored for flute, clarinet, trumpet and strings and consists of four measures repeated at libitum. As the music is supposed to be heard, but not listened to (the attention is turned towards the act of greeting the guests), it has a spatial presence, extension and timbre, but no developmental form.[25] Here, "spatial" does, indeed, mean "static." *Musique d'ameublement* aspires to the mode of being of objects, which persist in time, have physical dimensions and a definite location in space.

Igor Stravinsky

The idea of the transformation of compositions into "musical objects" found a forceful expression in Igor Stravinsky's famous neoclassical manifesto:[26]

---

[25]Satie used a similar idea of endless repetition in his famous *Vexations* for piano.

[26]Stravinsky's text, "Some ideas about my *Octuor*" was published in 1924 in *The Arts* (5 no.1, January 1924, 5-6) and reprinted by E. W. White (1979: 574-577).

> My *Octuor* is a musical object. This object has a form and that form is influenced by the musical matter with which it is composed. The differences of matter determine the differences of form. . . [The] play of movements and volumes that puts into action the musical text constitutes the impelling force of the composition and determines its form.
>
> (Stravinsky 1924/1979: 574-575)

Stravinsky designed this reification of music to counter the emotional excesses of romanticism, the main target of his polemics at that time. He used wind instruments to achieve a "certain rigidity of form" associated with an emotional detachment and the elimination of nuances (p. 574). In this music, expression and interpretation were expendable.[27] Yet, for Stravinsky, the objectivity of music did not mean its "spatialization." The composer subscribed to the vision of music as a temporal art. As he wrote in *An Autobiography*, "the phenomenon of music is given to us with the sole purpose of establishing order in things, including, and particularly, the coordination between man and time" (Stravinsky 1936/1962: 54).

Nonetheless, Stravinsky's conception of "objective" music with the weight and solidity of material things has played a role in the development of spatialization. According to Olivia Mattis's recent paper, Stravinsky's manifesto was a source for Varèse's spatial ideas (Mattis 1993). She has documented the contacts between the two artists and has revealed the relationships between their concepts, concluding that "Stravinsky was a catalyst for Varèse, providing him with a vocabulary with which to articulate concepts that were Varèse's own" (Mattis 1993: 7).

---

[27] For Stravinsky, "all music suffers, in time, a deformation through its execution" (Stravinsky 1924/1979: 575). His objective of removing the variability and distortion caused by performance found full realization in electroacoustic music "for tape" (or other carriers of sound) in which a composition is fixed in respect to most of its essential elements.

Edgard Varèse

In an article of 1925, "Edgar Varèse and the geometry of sound," Massimo Zanotti-Bianco wrote:

> If we project an imaginary sound-mass into space, we find that it appears as constantly changing volumes and combinations of planes, that these are animated by the rhythm, and that the substance of which they are composed is the sonority. The sound-mass whose weight, whose substance is given by the intensity of sound, would derive its movement from the rhythm which transports it into time.
>
> (Zanotti-Bianco 1925: 35)

According to Olivia Mattis, Varèse co-authored this article which included concepts that he used to the end of his life, e.g. "sound-geometry" and "sound-mass" (Mattis 1993: 3). The idea of "musical objectivation" was of particular importance, for it established a connection between a "musical object" (Stravinsky) and a "sound-mass" (Varèse). Mattis defines the latter notion as "a composite sound that has a recognizable timbre, rhythmic profile and articulation, but whose components can be altered one by one to highlight different aspects of the sonic gesture" (Mattis 1993: 2). The projection of sound-masses into space is a fundamental feature of Varèse's vision of spatial music--given a vivid description in his lecture in Santa Fe, in 1936.[28]

Varèse hoped that in the future, new instrumental means would make possible a creation of music with "the movement of sound-masses, of shifting planes" which would replace linear counterpoint (Varèse 1936/1967: 197). He expressed his "prophecy" in an intense, though somewhat nebulous text:

> When these sound-masses collide, the phenomena of penetration or repulsion will seem to occur. Certain transmutations taking place on certain planes will seem to be projected onto other planes, moving at different speeds and at

---

[28]Only a certain portion of this lecture has been published, under the title "New Instruments and New Music" in a collection of fragments of Varèse's texts edited by Chou Wen-chung and entitled "The liberation of sound," in *Contemporary Composers on Contemporary Music*, ed. Elliott Schwartz and Barney Childs (New York: Holt, Rinehart, and Winston, 1967), 195-208. An abridged version was published in 1966 in *Perspectives of New Music*. According to Olivia Mattis, the original title of this lecture is "Music and the Times" (Mattis 1992: 582 n. 65).

different angles. There will no longer be the old conception of melody or interplay of melodies. The entire work will be a melodic totality. The entire work will flow as a river flows.

(Varèse 1936/1967: 197)

In music which is as fluid "as a river" and in which sound-masses move at different speeds, collide and interpenetrate each other, time is not static. The "spatialization" of musical materials (sound-masses) is not identical with the absence of directed motion and development. Musical objects (sound-masses) flow, change, expand and contract, yet they have a certain tangibility, a concreteness established by clearly defined boundaries.[29] These boundaries between what Varèse also calls "zones of intensities" are created by differentiation in timbre and dynamics. Thus, the distinct zones have various colours and magnitude, and they appear "in different perspectives for our perception" (Varèse 1936/1967: 198). When a "non-blending" of distinct zones is possible, tone colour becomes an "integral part of form" (ibidem).[30]

The idea of the separation of distinct sound-masses, articulated by timbre and dynamics as well as by spatial location is not completely dissimilar to the spatial simultaneities of musical layers as envisioned by Ives and Brant. The three approaches share the presence of a conceptual relationship to linear counterpoint.[31] Only in Varèse, though, are the "sound masses" in a process of transformation-- through motion, interpenetration, collision, etc. His "zones of intensities" are in flux; the layers of Ives and Brant need to retain their stable, separate identity.

In Varèse's spatio-temporal notion of music sound objects are projected and

---

[29]Here, Varèse's image of spatial music diverges from the material solidity of Stravinsky's musical objects. For Varèse, individual elements of a composition (sound-masses) possess the concreteness of objects, not the work as a whole.

[30]The separation of the "zones of intensities" by timbre reflects the perceptual organization of auditory sensations into auditory streams; this theory of auditory scene analysis has been put forward by Albert Bregman (1990).

[31]However, Ives and Brant seek an expansion of counterpoint into space, while Varèse postulates its replacement with a new compositional technique.

moved about in aural space as physical objects are moved about in physical space.[32] Here, music has an added dimension of "projection." As the composer writes:

> We have actually three dimensions in music: horizontal, vertical, and dynamic swelling or decreasing. I shall add a fourth, sound projection--that feeling that sound is leaving us with no hope of being reflected back, a feeling akin to that aroused by a beam of light sent forth by a powerful searchlight--for the ear as for the eye, that sense of projection, of a journey into space.
> (Varèse 1936/1967: 197)

Following in Varèse's footsteps, post-war avant-garde composers appended "location (topography)" (Stockhausen) or "spatial distribution" (Boulez) to their lists of musical characteristics (cf. section 3.4). Interestingly, Varèse's three dimensions of music include a "dynamic," not a "diagonal" dimension. He does not attempt to reconcile the third dimension of music with the other two in a coherent, three-dimensional musical space, the search for which preoccupied many theoreticians (cf. Chapter II, section 2.1). Elsewhere, Varèse calls sound projection the third--not the fourth--dimension of music; thus, he connects dynamic and spatial aspects of the musical sound (Charbonnier 1970: 74).[33] Obviously, the notion of "sound projection," is very ambiguous. As "a journey into space" it seems to imply that the sound disappears into a fathomless distance ("with no hope" to return). This description would be appropriate even for Mahler's sonorities "dying away" in the distance--an effect realized through dynamics.

The lack of clarity in Varèse's pronouncements about sound projection encouraged Jonathan Bernard to shift the meaning of this term entirely into the domain of pitch. Bernard defines projection as a "transference of structure to a new pitch/registral level" in pitch space (Bernard 1987: 48). The vertically conceived pitch space (different from the pitch-class space of set theory) is called internal and

---

[32]Varèse's emphasis on the "objective" solidity of the sonorous entities that are moved about in space is another distinctive feature of his approach to spatial music.

[33]The "vertical" and "horizontal" dimensions of music clearly refer to the simultaneity and succession of pitch in time. Varèse's usage of these expressions is similar to Schoenberg's (cf. Chapter II, section 2.2).

opposed to the "external" space of performance.³⁴

In a lecture of 1939, given at the University of Southern California ("Music as an Art-Science") Varèse defined sound projection in less ambiguous terms (Varèse 1939/1967: 200). While reminding composers that the "raw material of music is sound," he unfolded a vision for the future, with new machines for sound production making possible novel harmonies, new scales, timbres, a full range of dynamics and rhythm, as well as "a sense of sound-projection in space by means of the emission of sound in any part, or in many parts of the hall, as may be required by the score" (Varèse 1939/1967: 201). This definition of sound projection has remained current in the domain of electroacoustic music, where Varèse is considered a "founding father."³⁵

Varèse did not fully realize his conception of a spatial music of sound-masses, planes and volumes in his own works until the composition of *Déserts* (1952-1954) and *Poème électronique* (1957-1958). The final phase of the preparation of the tape part for *Déserts* took place at the studio of the Groupe de Recherches de Musique Concrète in 1954 in Paris (Mattis 1992: 559). At that time, Varèse worked with Pierre Schaeffer, the founder of *musique concrète* who introduced the idea of sound movement in space along *trajectoires sonores* ("sonic trajectories;" cf. Poullin 1955: 126). The movement of sound in *Poème électronique* in the Philips Pavilion was a large-scale realization of this concept (cf. below). During the performance of this piece, Varèse, for the first time, heard his music "literally projected into space" (Varèse 1959/1967: 207)--as he indicated in a lecture at Sarah Lawrence College in

---

³⁴Consequently, if Varèse makes a reference to spatialization, Bernard diminishes its importance. For instance, he writes about the planning stage of *Espace* that it "suggests an intent to *externalize* spatial considerations beyond their existence within the score itself" (Bernard 1987: 7; italics added). In this context, it is interesting to notice that Bernard analyzes examples only from Varèse's instrumental works, avoiding electroacoustic compositions and relating unpitched percussion sounds of, e.g. *Ionisations* to their approximate pitch-height (through an implied one-dimensional scaling of timbre).

³⁵His prophecies and pronouncements are often quoted in the writings from this area, e.g. in two recent collections of texts on sound space in electroacoustic music, edited by Francis Dhomont (*L'Espace du Son I, II*; 1988, 1991).

1959 ("Spatial music").

In this lecture, occasioned by a presentation of the recording of the *Poème*, Varèse attributed the emergence of his conception of musical spatiality to an inspiration by Joseph Hoëne-Wronsky's definition of music, which made him think of "bodies of intelligent sounds moving freely in space" (Varèse 1959/1967: 204).[36] He described the spatiality of his earlier, instrumental music, composed with sound-masses, as "a *trompe l'oreille*, an aural illusion" (p. 205) and discussed the real, spatial aspects of this piece, the musical counterpart to Le Corbusier's *Poème électronique*, a slide and light show performed at the Philips Pavilion during the EXPO 1958 in Brussels, was recorded on a three-track magnetic tape. Four hundred twenty five loudspeakers were mounted in groups which formed different 'sound routes' around the Pavilion, allowing for the creation of different spatial effects, e.g. echoes, sound movement along the various paths and dispersion in many points of space at once (Varèse 1959/1967: 207) A diagram of the set-up for the different sound paths in the Philips Pavilion is given in Ex. III-3. The sound routes mirror the outline of the Pavilion, both in the horizontal plane and along the complex shape of the roof, which was structured from two intersecting conoids with three peaks (marked on the diagram as A, B, C).[37]

Varèse's sketch of sound trajectories planned for the *Poème électronique* abounds in dynamic markings; crescendi to fortissimo prevail (Wehmeyer 1977: 169; cf. Ex. III-4). This may reflect yet another meaning of sound projection habitually

---

[36] Hoëne-Wronsky's definition is quite mysterious: "Music is the corporealization of the intelligence that is in sound" (quoted from Wehmeyer 1977: 30).

[37] For a discussion of the architecture of the Philips Pavilion see Xenakis (1958 and 1971: 6-11). The design of the Pavilion, originally attributed to Le Corbusier who received a commission for it, was actually created by Xenakis, Le Corbusier's assistant at the time. Reluctantly, Le Corbusier admitted Xenakis's share in the project and co-signed the work (Matossian 1986). Xenakis remained embittered and continued to claim full ownership of the design, maintaining, for instance, that there was a causal chain of ideas that led him to "formulate the architecture of the Philips Pavilion from the score of *Metastasis*"--a work premiered in 1955 (Xenakis 1971: 10).

used by the composer. Here, the projection of sound refers to "immense crescendi of single chords" (Bernard 1987: 252 n. 30). These crescendi are usually followed by an abrupt pause, allowing for the reverberation of the sonority in the performance space and in the memory of the listeners.[38]

The sketch reveals Varèse's involvement in the spatialization of his composition; "spatialization"--that is--in the current, electroacoustic sense of the term. Since the original recording of Varèse's *Poème électronique* (which no longer exists) consisted only of three tracks, the dynamic profiles of the various sonorities and their exact localization in space were not unequivocally defined. The recorded composition needed a "spatialization" in performance, that is the articulation of concrete dynamic proportions between various segments of the music (projected simultaneously or successively from different locations in space) and the realization of sound movements along pre-designed paths.[39]

Besides this affinity to *musique concrète*, Varèse's ideas of "spatial music" display a certain, formal similarity to those of Ives. Both composers made bold pronouncements about the future of music, both worked on plans for monumental compositions "about space" to be performed "in space." A counterpart to Ives's *Universe Symphony* is Varèse's "amorphous magnum opus" (term from Mattis 1992: 575), *Espace*, a work that remained incomplete because it could never have been

---

[38] According to Varèse's statements (from about 1955) published in 1970 in a book of interviews with Georges Charbonnier, this idea of sound projection was inspired by an aural experience of listening to a performance of Beethoven's Seventh Symphony in Salle Pleyel in Paris (Charbonnier 1970: 74). During the performance the sounds seemed to be virtually projected into space; the reverberation played a role in establishing this impression.

[39] This type of "spatialization" has remained current in electracoustic music for multi-loudspeaker sound projection systems, the so-called "orchestras of loudspeakers" used in Paris, Bourges, Montreal, etc. (for a description of several of such systems see *L'Espace du Son I, II*; 1988, 1991).

completed.[40] Olivia Mattis comments that, "we can suppose that the title *Espace* represents not only astronomical space... but also the unbroken terrestrial expanse of the southwest, as well as the spaces, what Varèse called the 'deserts' of the mind." (Mattis 1992: 576).

"Space" is, for Varèse, simultaneously "a literal representation and a psychological symbol" (Mattis 1992: 576). This interconnection of the various meanings of space--experienced, visualized and filled with sound is a characteristic feature of many spatialized compositions, such as, for instance Francis Dhomont's electroacoustic work, *Espace/Escape* (1989).

Varèse's prophetic importance is not limited to the field of electroacoustics. His influence can also be discerned in the compositional ideas of **Iannis Xenakis** (cf. Chapter II, section 2.5, and Chapter VII). Xenakis, who (as the assistant to Le Corbusier) was responsible for the design of the Philips Pavilion for the EXPO 1958, composed a short *musique concrète* piece, *Concret PH*, to precede the projections of Varèse's *Poème électronique*. He also participated in designing the sound projection system for the Pavilion. As he recalled in 1992, he "went with Le Corbusier to Einhoven and studied the distances at which the loudspeakers should be placed in order to obtain the effect of continuous sound movement" (Xenakis 1992: 12). At the same time, he admitted that Varèse's visionary ideas of spatial music, sound projection, sound-mass, etc. have influenced his own interest in spatialization. Xenakis's music often features "various trajectories" of sound motion, realized by means of multi-channel sound projection systems (electroacoustic works) or by small groups of musicians placed at different points of the space of performance (instrumental compositions).

---

[40]In 1947, a selection from the material for *Espace* was given the title *Etude pour Espace* and performed in New York (Bernard 1987: 237-238).

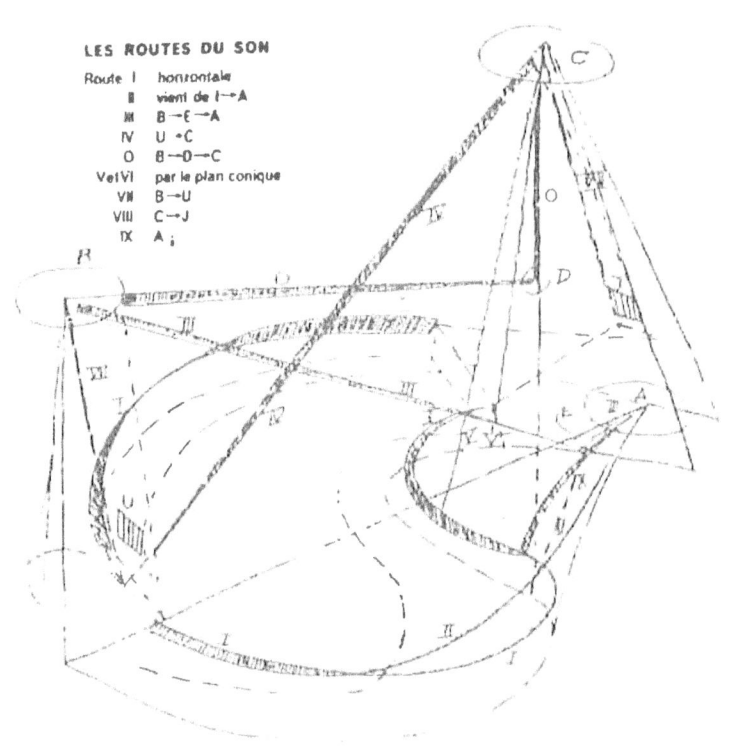

Ex. III-3: Sound paths for Varèse's *Poème électronique* at the Philips Pavilion at EXPO 1958. Brussels.

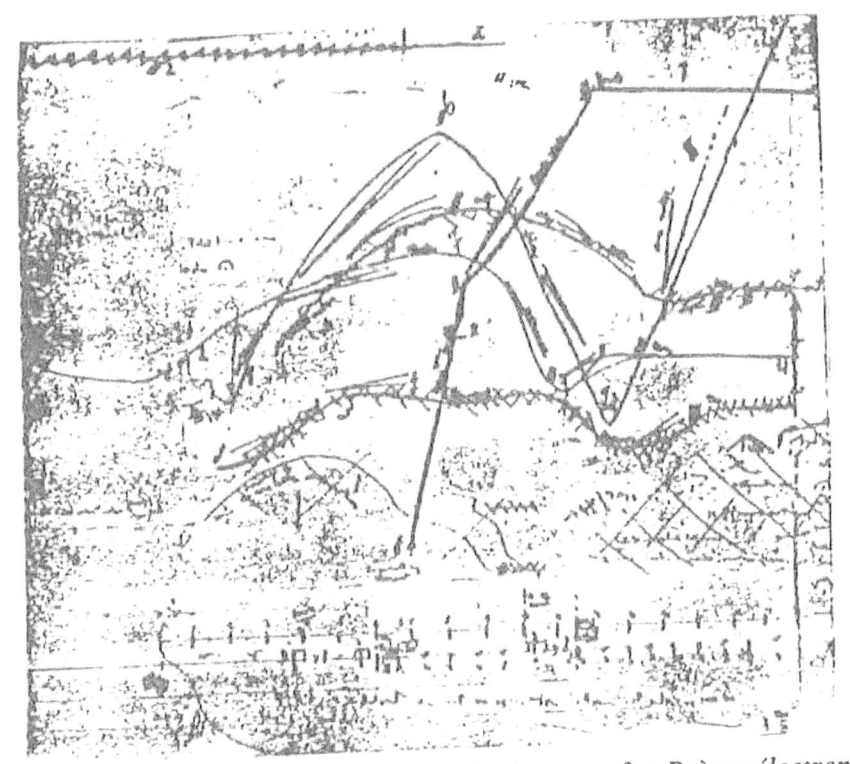

Ex. III-4: Varèse's design of sound trajectories in space for *Poème électronique* (Wehmeyer 1977: 169).

Sound objects and sound projection in *musique concrète*

In 1959, Varèse envisioned his music to be performed in "spatial relief" (Varèse 1959/1967: 204). This expression, also applied by the composer to his *Intégrales* (Strawn 1975: 142), was actually lifted from the parlance of *musique concrète*.[41] **Jacques Poullin** used similar expressions in 1955, in a description of two basic types of sound projection, static relief and kinematic relief (Poullin 1955).

Poullin was one of the three founding members (with Pierre Henry and Pierre Schaeffer) of the Groupe de Recherches de Musique Concrète and the director of the first studio of electroacoustic music which was opened in Paris in 1951. In his contribution to *Klangstruktur der Musik*, a collection of articles designed to support the humble beginnings of electronic music with the authority of science (Winckel 1955),[42] Poullin summarizes the main conceptual and technological aspects of *musique concrète*, including composition with "sound objects" ("Tonobjekte" and "Klangobjekte") and "sound projection" ("Klang-Projektion," Poullin 1955).

In his article, Poullin describes two varieties of sound projection possible with loudspeakers. The first type, *static relief* ("statisches Relief"), refers to the projection of distinct, simultaneous parts of a composition from different points in space, made possible by multi-track recordings and multi-channel sound projection systems (Poullin 1955: 125). This type of sound projection, though essentially static, involves the use of stereophony to create virtual sound images localized in-between the loudspeakers. Poullin describes a system of four loudspeakers surrounding the listener and projecting a theoretically unlimited number of sound sources from the various locations in space

---

[41] Varèse's contacts with composers of *musique concréte* (especially with Pierre Schaeffer) at the time of composing *Déserts* and *Poème électronique* are well documented (e.g. by Mattis 1992). The French term "relief spatial" was used in reference to concerts of Henry and Schaeffer of 1951 (Vande Gorne 1988).

[42] The title page of this book is adorned with an impressive series of "Prof. Dr."--a rarity even among scholarly publications. Interestingly, a contribution on electronic music by Werner Meyer-Eppler does not discuss sound projection at all, focussing entirely on new structures and materials (Meyer-Eppler 1955b). This is one of the differences between electronic music and *musique concrète*.

(cf. Ex. III-5).

The second type of sound projection, *kinematic relief* ("kinematisches Relief"), is more peculiar to *musique concrète*. It was introduced during the concerts of Pierre Henry and Pierre Schaeffer in 1951-1952 in Paris (Poullin 1955: 126). Kinematic relief, envisioned by **Pierre Schaeffer**, was realized in live performance in two ways. The first involved the aid of the *potentiomètre d'espace*, "a device for controlling the trajectory of sounds between four loudspeakers" invented by Poullin (Palombini 1993: 17).[43] The second type of spatial sound projection (with the same number of loudspeakers) was based on the idea of controlling the movement of sound by the gestures of the operator.[44]

The historical importance of the second invention, which soon became technologically obsolete, lies in the consequences of its use. The experience of hearing spectacular movements of sound images in space during the concerts of *musique concrète* in the early 1950s played a formative role in the development of Stockhausen's and Boulez's theories of spatialization.[45]

The second spatial aspect of *musique concrète*, that is, the choice of "sound objects" as compositional material, has remained an important feature of electroacoustic music. This music, no longer restricted to sounds of a clear and stable pitch but embracing all sonorous phenomena that can be recorded and manipulated,

---

[43]This way of creating "spatial relief" in music was heard for the first time during a concert of Schaeffer and Henry on 6 July 1951 in Paris, when *Symphonie pour un homme seul* and *Orphée 51* were performed (Vande Gorne 1988: 9). Here, music acquired a spatial form which could be either static or kinematic ("statique ou cinématique"), with sounds presented on various planes or outlining different trajectories. This was, according to the program notes for this concert, the first attempt at sound projection in three dimensions ("la hauteur, la largeur et la profondeur").

[44]This system, also designed by Poullin, was publicly presented for the first time on 23 May 1952, during the performance of Pierre Henry's *Antiphonie* (Vande Gorne 1988: 9).

[45]Both composers worked in the Paris studio in 1952-53. Stockhausen's preoccupation with sound movement in space is expressed in many compositions (cf. Harvey 1975; Purce 1974).

required a change in the visualization and notation of music (Schaeffer 1952). To this purpose, Schaeffer introduced a new, three-dimensional representation of sound objects (Ex. III-6).

In this notational system, the axes of frequency, time and intensity delimit three planes representing different aspects of a complex sound: the melodic plane (frequency and time), the spectral--or later, harmonic[46]--plane (frequency and intensity) and the dynamic plane (intensity and time). Such detailed notation of the internal structure of sound is somewhat redundant in these areas of electroacoustic music which explore solely the manipulation of recorded sounds.[47] Only sound synthesis in electronic and computer music requires precise descriptions and representations of musical materials. Here, new versions of "spatial" images of auditory phenomena are constantly being developed (cf. De Poli et al. 1991).

A full discussion of the intricacies of Schaeffer's "musical objects" would entail a venture into the phenomenological aspects of this philosophy of the creation of music directly in sound (Schaeffer 1966). In the context of the present study, however, it suffices to point out its two most important aspects, (1) the dichotomy of object and structure, and (2) the distinction between *objet sonore* and *objet musical*. According to Schaeffer, in creating a "morphology" of sound objects the scale of description is crucial; what is an "object" at one level becomes a "structure" at another (Schaeffer 1967: 36). Complex sounds always entail a temporal evolution; minute changes in their spectral and dynamic envelopes may either be ignored (higher level of description, macro-scale) or be highlighted (lower level, micro-scale). The differentiation between sound objects and musical objects, on the other hand, takes

---

[46]Poullin uses the term "spectral" is used in his description of Schaeffer's notational system (Poullin 1955: 116); the term "harmonic" appears in Schaeffer's *Traité des objets musicaux* (Schaeffer 1966: 415).

[47]However, composers need a form of musical notation of electro-acoustic works for copyright purposes. The notation may also serve various functions in the compositional process (prescriptive, descriptive) without being "interpreted" in repeated performances.

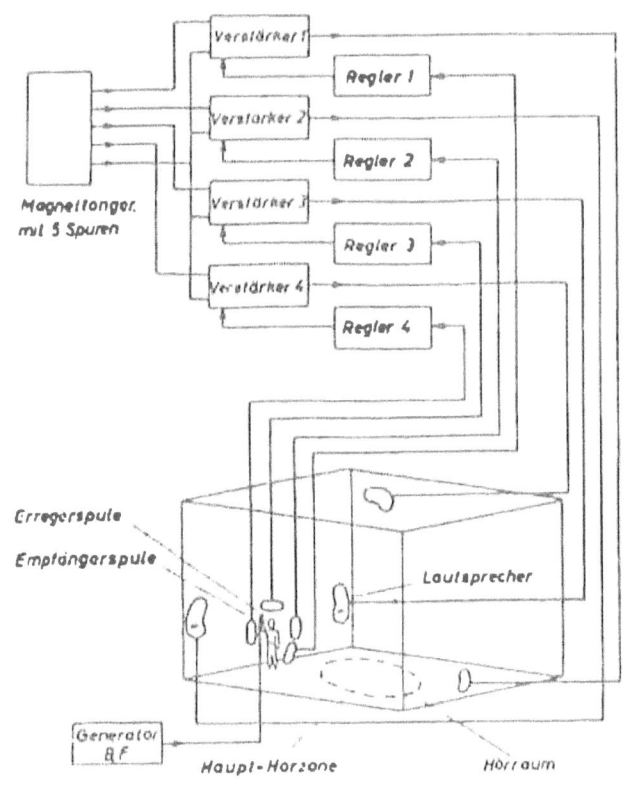

Ex. III-5: Poullin's diagram of four-channel system for spatial projection of sound (Poullin 1955: 126).

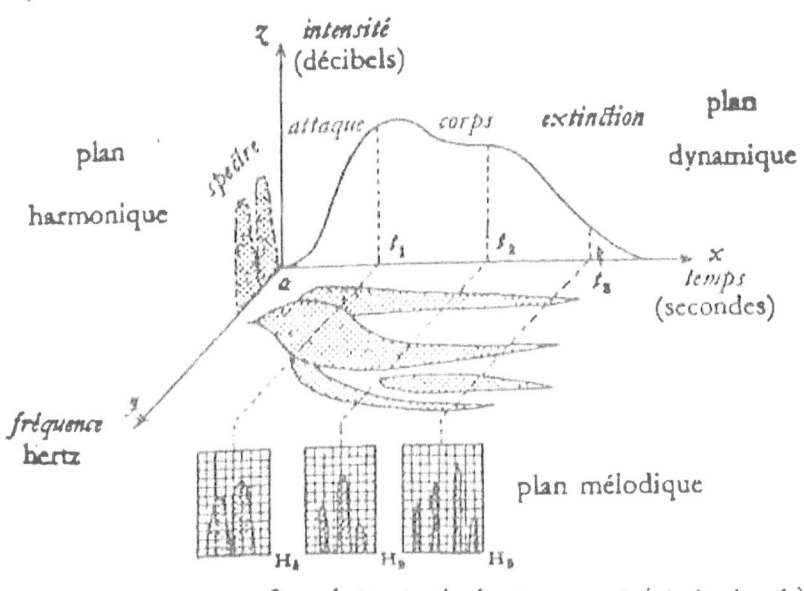

Ex. III-6: Three-dimensional image of the sound object from *Traité des objets musicaux* (Schaeffer 1966: 415).

their compositional potential into account; sounds become musical when they are freed from their concrete associations and when they are appreciated solely as sounds.[48]

Schaeffer's morphology of musical objects, inspired by Gestalt psychology, deals with the perceptual aspects of sound images, that is, subjective experiences arising in those listening to sounds which exist in the objective, physically fixed form of recordings. Due to the infinite multitude of such potential "sound objects" their full classification is impossible. This is one reason why "space" has replaced "sound object" as the paradigmatic concept in the domain of electroacoustics (cf. *L'Espace du Son I, II*, 1988, 1991; Stroppa 1992). The invention and exploration of new spaces in electroacoustic music is often linked to the reflection on the music's inherent spatiality. According to Léo Kupper, creator of several multi-channel sound cupolas,[49] electroacoustic music presented in his installations is "a new three-dimensional art" (Kupper 1991: 97). Kupper claims that "space is not an effect of the pitch dimension, but a parameter more important than pitch or rhythm and timbre articulations in music" (Kupper 1988: 61). Few composers share this radical view; its emergence, though, is symptomatic of the increasing importance of spatial organization in music.

Spatialization in electroacoustic music

A review of recent writings in this area reveals that the conceptual and terminological framework of "space and spatialization" is not clearly defined. According to Michel Chion, the first of the two types of space used in musique

---

[48]I.e. all sounds, without exception, may become musical. However, the separation of sounds from the context of their production is often unsuccessful. In recent electroacoustic music, the recognition of sound sources (e.g. the flapping of wings) plays a significant role in the poetic network of meanings evoked by (and belonging to) a given composition.

[49]A sound cupola or a "sound dome" consists of a large number of loudspeakers located on a semi-spherical surface above the listeners heads. If the distances between the loudspeakers are equal this system is called a "tempered sound dome;" its design resembles Stockhausen's Osaka sphere (Stockhausen 1971). Kupper's domes have been installed in art galleries, churches, or auditoria of appropriate size and dimensions.

concrète is *internal space.* It embraces all the spatial aspects of music which are compositionally predetermined in a recording, e.g. reverberations, locations, planes and distances (Chion 1988). The second variety, the *external space*, is articulated during the work's performance. Chion posits the necessity for an interrelationship between these two, and lists several synonymous terms describing the performance of electroacoustic music ("diffusion, spatialisation, projection sonore") in which spatial relationships inherent in the work itself are amplified and clarified during its presentation to the audience (Chion 1988: 32). He uses the term "spatialization" in reference to the music's performance, not its composition; spatialization means making music physically and audibly spatial (i.e. not static).

A dichotomy between the spaces of composition and performance has also been noticed by Jean Claude Risset who writes about the fragility of the "illusory space" (composed and recorded) which is superimposed on the "real space" of the performance (Risset 1988). This composer observes that only in electroacoustic music are sounds freed from their spatial constraints. Here, sounds may be "spatialized," i.e. dispersed in space in a variety of patterns and moved in space along different paths.[50]

Finally, Denis Smalley lists a whole array of different spaces that need to be considered in electroacoustic music, from the *composed space*, i.e. the spatial imaging considered by the composer (the equivalent of Chion's internal space), to the *listening space* which is either personal or public and "lies outside the composer's control" (Smalley 1991: 121). What a listener perceives during a concert is a *superimposed space*, "a nesting of the composed spaces within a listening space" (ibidem). Of primary importance here, is the relationship of the dimensions of the *musical space* to features of space known from non-musical experience (such as the opposition of intimacy and immensity). Moreover, musical space cannot be grasped without its

---

[50]To "spatialize" means, for Risset, "de jouer sur la localisation sonore aussi sur son déplacement, sa cinétique" (Risset 1988: 21). As the primary example of virtual sound movement, the composer quotes John Chowning's program for simulation of moving sound sources in a quadrophonic sound projection system (Chowning 1971).

sonorous content; here, a variety of topics needs to be taken into account, such as:

> whether sounds are realistic or not, whether we detect human content either through sounding gesture or utterance, the energy and motion of sounds, how sounds 'behave' among themselves (conflict, coexistence, cause and effect, etc.), whether we regard sounds as things or objects, whether we are reminded of visual or environmental phenomena--in other words all the interpretative mechanisms involved in how we relate spectro-morphologies and musical contexts to our experience outside music.
>
> (Smalley 1991: 123)

From Satie and Varèse to Dhomont and Risset, spatialization of music means either sound projection, or one of the forms of the reification of sounds into "musical objects" (e.g. compositional design, recording, perception and cognition). Both meanings intersect in the domain of electroacoustic music. A full study of the spatial aspects of this 20th-century art form must be left for a different occasion.[51] The importance of electroacoustic music, especially *musique concrète,* for this study of space and spatialization is due to the influence exerted by electroacoustic theory and practice on composers of instrumental music, especially the early "avant-gardists" from Darmstadt.

---

[51]The bibliography lists many writings from this area: Barrière (1991), Begault (1986), Berkhout (1988), Blaukopf (1971), Chowning (1970), Dhomont (1988, 1991), Federkov et al. (1978), Gelhaar (1991), Hunstinger (1982), Keane (1984), Kendall (1992), Kupper (1988, 1991), Lakatos (1991), Lehnert and Blauert (1991), Leitner (1986), Montague (1991), Reynolds (1978), Risset (1991), Schlemm (1972), Sheeline (1982), Stroppa (1991, 1992), Winckel (1973).

3.4.

Theories of spatialization in Darmstadt: Stockhausen and Boulez

The discussion of the "spatialization of time" in Chapter II (section 2.2) included references to the association of the spatiality of musical material with the distribution of such static sound matter in the space of performance (Stockhausen 1959/1961; Ligeti 1960/1965; Bayer 1987). This connection was pointed out by composers affiliated with the Darmstadt Courses for New Music who attributed the conquest of "physical" space to the "temporal" staticity of new music (Stockhausen, Boulez, Ligeti). As Stockhausen expressed it, music ventured into space, because musical ideas were "becoming increasingly spatial" (Stockhausen 1959/1961: 70).[52]

The ideas of post-war avant-garde music are spatial in two ways: (1) in a geometric sense, because music is often conceived of as consisting of points, blocks, and shapes presented in a space of two or three dimensions (e.g. Webern's music interpreted by Ligeti and Eimert); (2) in a general, mathematical sense, because features of sound are separated into "musical parameters" and manipulated by spatial means (e.g. the use of vector space by Xenakis). Music composed of spatial sound matter which is characterized by a solidity of physical objects or a staticity of geometric figures is not designed to be expressive and does not leave much room for freedom of interpretation.[53]

Two compositional theories of spatialization discussed in this section (Stockhausen and Boulez) exemplify the strengths and weaknesses of highly

---

[52]Xenakis shared this view and considered the possibility of an expansion of his compositional technique into space: "We can, for example, imagine protocols of screens attached to a particular point in space. . ." (Xenakis 1971: 109).

[53]Here, a similarity to Stravinsky's notion of "musical objects" is immediately apparent. In addition, the concept of the static spatialization of musical material may be seen as the summit of formalist aesthetics (cf. Hanslick 1854/1986) as well as the fulfilment of the idea of "absolute" music, deprived, however, of its spiritual dimension and limited to its purely structural aspects (cf. Dahlhaus 1978/1989; Goehr 1992).

speculative approaches to the subject of musical spatiality. For both composers, spatial location (or distribution) is yet another "parameter" of musical sound.[54] They focus on isolated features of sound material, giving no attention to the experiential, expressive or symbolic functions of spatialization.

Karlheinz Stockhausen

While studying in Paris (in 1951-1952) Stockhausen had ample occasion to witness the very earliest experiments with three-dimensional movement of sound at the *musique concrète* concerts (cf. section 3.3). Soon afterwards, he composed his first spatialized pieces: for orchestra (*Gruppen für Drei Orchester*, 1955-1957), and for electroacoustic sound projection (*Gesang der Jünglinge* for five loudspeakers, 1956).[55]

Stockhausen presented his notion of spatialization which he developed on the basis of these experiences in an influential article, "Music in space," written after the premiere of *Gruppen* in 1958.[56] In this text, as a true "avant-gardist," Stockhausen dismisses earlier examples of "spatial" music as irrelevant to the future of compositional technique. Thus, he considers Gabrieli's polychorality as a mere expansion of the principle of dialogue into space, and he criticizes Mozart's Serenades for their exclusive use of the baroque echo principle, and Berlioz's dramatic use of spatial effects as too theatrical to be relevant to the "structural" concerns of contemporary music.[57] According to Stockhausen, these three "antiquated" ways of making music spatial must be replaced by a new spatiality associated with

---

[54]Leigh Landy writes about "the 'parameter' space" in a separate chapter of his status report about the state of experimental music in the 1980s (Landy 1991: 105-116).

[55]The latter work was recorded on two tapes, one with four channels and an additional one with the remaining, fifth channel. The number of channels indicates that the loudspeakers worked as independent point sources not as stereo pairs.

[56]This article was prepared as a lecture for Darmstadt (Stockhausen 1959/1961).

[57] Mozart's *Serenata notturna* K. 239 and *Nocturne* K. 286. Stockhausen does not mention Mahler, Ives, Varèse, nor Brant.

serialization.[58]

Stockhausen's argument for the necessity of spatialization links it with a need to clarify the constantly varying surface of serialized music, which can evolve so rapidly that it gives the impression of not changing at all:

> The music finally becomes static: it changes extremely quickly, one is constantly traversing the entire realm of experience in a very short time, and thus one finds oneself in a state of suspended animation, the music 'stands still'.
> (Stockhausen 1959/1961: 69)

The "standstill" of the music results from the equalization of all the parameters of sound: if one sound characteristic predominated, it would act to articulate the music but, simultaneously, would destroy the work's balanced structure. Therefore, in order to make the music more interesting for the listeners, various long time-phases of homogeneous sound structures may be distributed in space, among different groups of loudspeakers or instruments. Thus, spatialization heals the dissolution of polyphony into monody (a characteristic of serialized music); it is "possible to articulate longer pointillistic structures by having them wander in space, by moving them from one place to another" (Stockhausen 1959/1961: 70). With a separation in space, "one easily perceives two layers of one and the same sound pattern" (ibidem).

This statement resembles Brant's main argument in favour of the use of space in music: spatial separation clarifies musical texture, especially if this texture consists of many layers confined to the same register (Brant 1955; cf. section 3.2 of this chapter). However, unlike Brant, Stockhausen is (at that time) primarily preoccupied with isolated "musical parameters." Thus, he presents a general hierarchy of tone-characteristics in Western art music, ranked from the most important down (p. 72):

1. pitch (harmony-melody)
2. duration (metre-rhythm)

---

[58]According to Henry Brant, Stockhausen used Brant's article of 1955 while composing *Gruppen* (Brant 1992: 14). In order to substantiate his claim, Brant cites a biography of Boulez which contains "eye-witness" accounts by people who saw Brant's article on Stockhausen's desk in the mid-1950s (Peyser 1976).

3. timbre (phonetics)

4. loudness (dynamics)

5. location (topography)

Stockhausen rejects distance as a possible "musical parameter," on the grounds that the perception of distance is a combined impression of changes in the intensity and timbre of the sound in open space, depending, in addition, on the proportion of direct to reverberated sound in enclosures. As he rightly observes, loudness is a spatial characteristic of sound (the greater the distance the weaker the sound).[59] Moreover, the perception of the "near--far" dimension is based on the change in the spectral content of the sound (including temporally defined characteristics, such as transients). As the serialist's objective is to apply the same means of structuring to all the different features of sound, these characteristics should be clearly isolated from each other and manipulated separately. Therefore, according to Stockhausen, distance cannot be a compositional parameter: it lacks independence from the remaining characteristics of sound. Instead, the composer postulates the adoption of spatial direction, easily serialized, as the new parameter in music.

The composer considers several variants of linking the organization of other, isolated parameters to spatial position, beginning with a one-dimensional arrangement of sound sources. If, for example, 48 musicians are placed on a straight line, in front of the listeners, from left to right, and if each musician performs one chromatic pitch from the four-octave compass (48 pitches), it is possible to create a kind of "*space--melody*" which evolves in pitch and in space simultaneously.[60] Therefore, one can "relate proportions of pitch, duration, timbre and loudness with those of tone-locality" (p. 79). However, more interesting effects may be created when the performers are

---

[59]The perception of distance depends also on other cues (cf. Chapter IV).

[60]This effect enables the audience to experience aural images similar to those heard by musicians performing on large keyboard instruments, such as the piano and the organ: music is physically extended in space in front of the listeners.

placed on a circle surrounding the listeners. Here, spatial direction differs from the remaining features of sound in that it is circular. According to Stockhausen, "all parameters mentioned so far are one-dimensional: pitches between low and high, durations between long and short, timbres between dark and bright, loudness between soft and loud." (Stockhausen 1959/1961: 79).

By establishing exact proportions, analogous to durational ratios, between various positions on the circle it is possible to create "the scale of localities corresponding to the scales of pitch, duration, timbre and loudness" (p. 82; cf. Ex. III-7). Stockausen thinks that it would be necessary, however, to ascertain by experiments the smallest unit that can be perceived and used as an element in the scale of spatial locations. He concludes that it is also possible to use continuous sound motion along the circumference of the circle. He had already demonstrated this possibility in *Gesang der Jünglinge*, his first musical attempt to make "the direction and movement of sound in space" accessible as a "new dimension for musical experience" (p. 68).

Stockhausen's image of a circle, evenly subdivided into equal segments, represents a scale of directions which, while theoretically possible, is, in reality, perceptual nonsense. The acuity of the perception of sound direction differs depending on the orientation of the listener; human beings distinguish sounds from the front, side, and back with different degree of exactness (Blauert 1983: 37-50). Moreover, the so-called "localization blur" depends on the familiarity of the sound and on its detailed characteristics, including pitch and spectrum. Therefore, Stockhausen's metric scale of directions (measured as intervals on the circle or as angles) is a theoretical construct without a perceptual basis. However, this idea is inherent in total-serialist thinking: all aspects or parameters of sound should be treated equally and all should be readily available for manipulation.

The composer attempted to serialize direction in this manner in *Gesang der Jünglinge*; in the orchestral *Gruppen für Drei Orchester* (1955-57), though, he used spatial separation mostly to clarify dense and complex textures. This work, one of the most influential compositions in the history of spatialized music, calls for a massive force of 109 musicians.[61] These are split into 3 orchestras (each with its own conductor) arranged in a horseshoe position on platforms semi-surrounding the audience in a large hall (cf. Ex. III-8). In Stockhausen's words:

> The similarity of the scoring of the three orchestras resulted from the requirement that sound-groups should be made to wander in space from one sounding body to another and at the same time split up similar sound-structures: each orchestra was supposed to call to the others and to give answer or echo.
>
> (Stockhausen 1959/1961: 70)

For the composer, it is important "to be able to experience the simultaneity of various time-spaces and movements" in this work (Stockhausen 1959/1961: 71). An instance of sound movement is presented at group 119 in the score with the rotation of three successive hexachords in the brass. The illusion of movement is constructed by the temporal overlapping and dynamic shaping of the sounds (Ex. III-9). The chords swell dynamically in the third, the second, and finally in the first orchestral group, creating an impression of the continuation of the sound essential for the perception of its movement. The simulation of motion through stationary sources is not entirely successful: there are too few instrumental groups which are too distant in space and which play chords with the dynamic peaks too widely spaced in time. This, and the fact that brass timbres are quite difficult to match exactly, hampers the perception of a single auditory stream, that is, the image of one rotating sound.[62] The perception of movement requires the establishment of the identity of a moving object (brass hexachord), and the existence of a time-space that this object travels through. Obviously, changes in the pitch domain are unwarranted--they would destroy the identity of the rotating "musical object." Nonetheless, moments of sound movement in *Gruppen* are quite rare (they are limited to interludes). The predominant, dense texture of this work results from a simultaneous performance of the three orchestras.

---

[61]Among composers who admit being influenced by *Gruppen* are Andrzej Dobrowolski, Kazimierz Serocki, Elliott Carter and Marco Stroppa.

[62]The term "auditory stream" is taken from Bregman (1990).

"Music in space," written predominantly in the future tense, contains, in addition to the speculative theory of spatialization and the discussions of Stockhausen's compositions, a proposal for a new, ideal concert hall:

> My idea would be to have a spherical chamber, fitted all round with loudspeakers. In the middle of this spherical chamber, a platform, transparent to both light and sound would be hung for the listeners. They could hear music, composed for such adapted halls coming from above, from below and from all directions.
>
> (Stockhausen 1959/1961: 69)

The spherical pavilion would be a musical equivalent to an art gallery, featuring continuous programmes of electronic music, that one could hear "at any time of day" (p. 69).[63] This idea was realized in the German Pavilion at EXPO 1970, in Osaka (Ex. III-10). The Pavilion housed Stockhausen's own compositions exclusively, including *Spiral* for solo performer (the source of description of this set-up; Stockhausen 1973). A special multi-channel system for sound rotation in space was designed, allowing for circular (on a plane) and spiral (ascending to the top of the construction) motions of sound. The rotations of sound were controlled manually in a live performance by means of two "soundmills" with moving joysticks (Stockhausen 1971/1989: 103).[64] This idea of transforming the spatial gesture of a performer into a trajectory of sound movement resembles the principle of "kinematic relief" in *musique concrète* (Poullin and Schaeffer, cf. section 3.3).[65]

---

[63] Recall Franz Liszt's vision of a museum of musical masterpieces, in which performances of the greatest compositions are scheduled daily (cf. Liszt's "On the position of artists and their place in society" of 1835, quoted by Walker, 1987: 160).

[64] As Stockhausen said in a lecture of 1971 ("Four criteria of electronic music"), the two soundmills connected one input with ten outputs each and allowed a speed of rotations up to 5 revolutions per second. Three trajectories could be explored at once, and the music could be either improvised or predetermined. Thus, "a free spatial composition" was possible (Stockhausen 1971/1989: 103-105).

[65] Stockhausen's vision of a new, versatile performance space was not an absolute novelty. The spherical concert hall had a predecessor in the form of a spherical theatre, proposed in 1924, but never realized, by Andreas Weininger, who wanted to have the audience seated at the internal side of the sphere (Braun 1982: 221). The platforms,

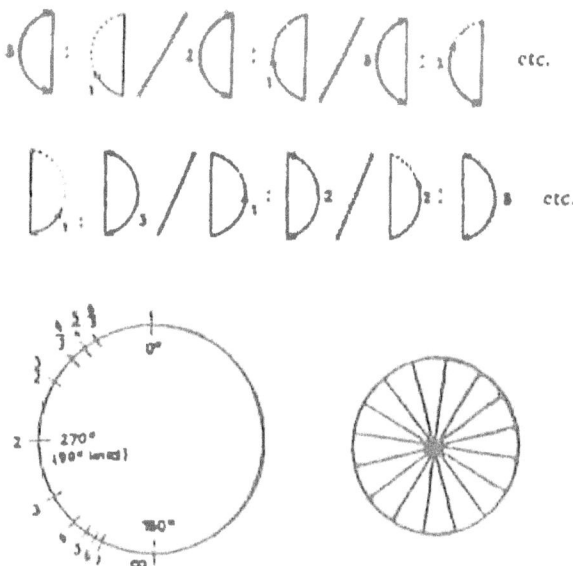

Ex. III-7: Spatial intervals and scale of directions on the circle in Stockhausen's "Musik in space" (1959/1961: 82).

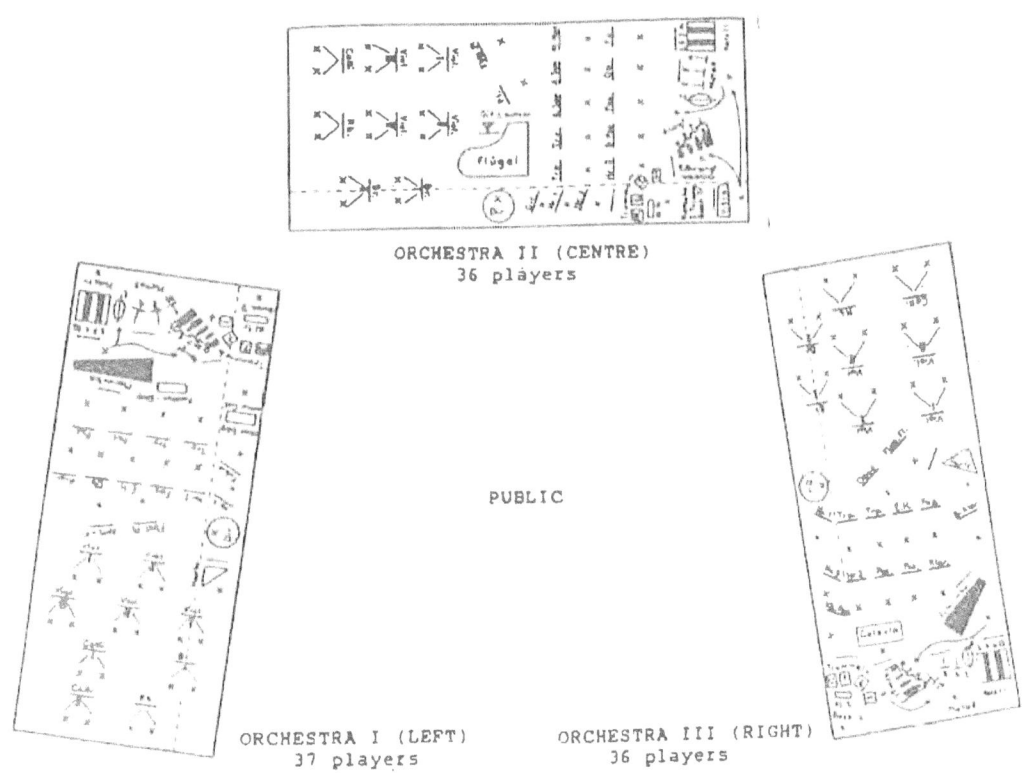

Ex. III-8: Placement of the 3 orchestras in Stockhausen's *Gruppen für Drei Orchester*.
© Copyright 1963 by Universal Edition (London) Ltd., London. © Copyright renewed. All Rights Reserved. Used by permission of European American Music Distributors Corporation, sole U.S. and Canadian agent for Universal Edition (London) Ltd., London.

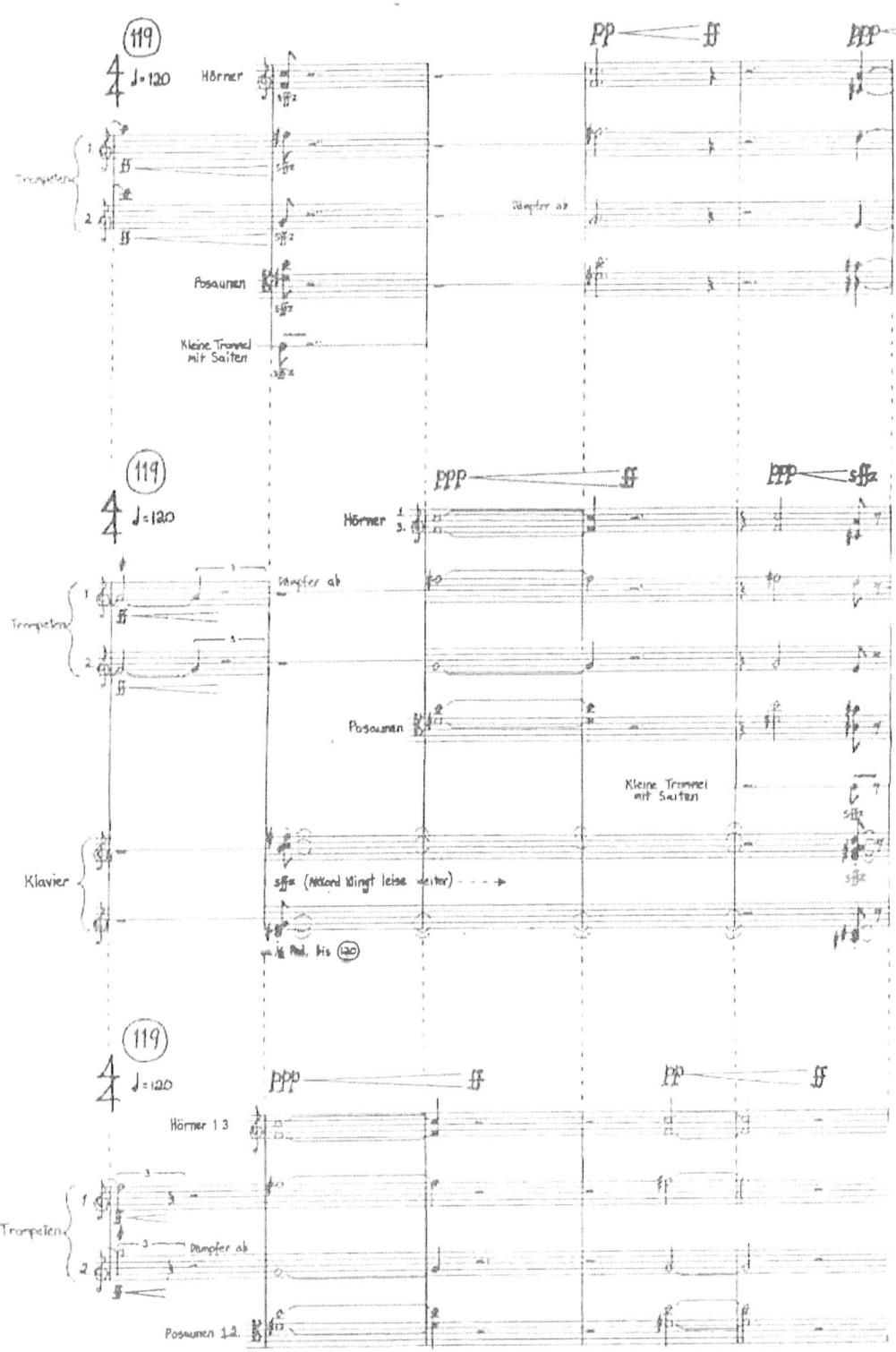

Ex. III-9: Illusion of sound movement in Stockhausen's *Gruppen*, group 119.

© Copyright 1963 by Universal Edition (London) Ltd., London. © Copyright renewed. All Rights Reserved. Used by permission of European American Music Distributors Corporation, sole U.S. and Canadian agent for Universal Edition (London) Ltd., London.

Carré (1959-1960), *Kontakte* (1960) and many other instrumental and electroacoustic compositions by Stockhausen reveal his continuous preoccupation with sound movement (Harvey 1974: 88). Nonetheless, his awareness of musical spatiality has been transformed by years of practical experience, especially with electroacoustics. In a lecture of 1971, the composer considered "the multi-layered spatial composition" as one of the "four criteria for electronic music." The composer explained:

> Multi-layered spatial composition means the following: that not only does the sound move around the listener at a constant distance, but it can also move as far away as we can imagine, and also come extremely close. These characteristics are distinctly different. . . Building spatial depth by superimposition of layers enables us to compose perspectives in sound from close up to far away, analogous to the way we compose layers of melody and harmony in the two-dimensional plane of traditional music.
> (Stockhausen 1971/1989: 105-106)

This statement contradicts the earlier theory (put forward in "Music in space") in which distance is superseded by direction, the only "parameter" of sound localization allowing for its serialized treatment. With a growing awareness of the qualities of the virtual sound space in electroacoustic music, Stockhausen's interest in the serialization of direction recedes, as it were, into an infinite distance. Finally, spatialization means a polyphony of musical layers presented simultaneously or structured in time; the music, no longer serialized, ceases to be static.[66] Thus, the evolution of Stockhausen's conception of musical spatiality has led towards the "mainstream" type of spatialization: the co-existence of distinct layers (Ives and Brant; cf. Section 3.2).

---

balconies, gangways would create a multi-level three-dimensional theatrical space filling the inside of this sphere. The difference between the two spherical spaces (listeners surrounded by music and spectators around theatrical actions) reflects the distinction between auditory and visual perception, the auditory being omnidirectional, the visual limited to the frontal area.

[66]However, Stockhausen's vision of the interpenetration of sonorities presented at various planes, at different distances from the listener, bears a resemblance to Varèse's notion of "zones of intensities" (cf. above, section 3.3).

Pierre Boulez

Boulez's formative experiences in the domain of spatialization resemble those of Stockhausen. As a student, he had participated in the early experiments of *musique concrète* in Paris (1951-52).[67] Later, he prepared the premiere of *Gruppen* in 1958 (as one of the three conductors, with Stockhausen and Maderna). Finally, he was actively involved in the foundation of the Darmstadt Courses. These activities of the composer, conductor, thinker and lecturer shaped Boulez's awareness of musical spatiality which he expressed in a series of essays "written in Darmstadt for Darmstadt" and published under a German title, *Musikdenken heute* (Boulez 1963/1971).[68]

In a text from this collection, "Musical Technique," Boulez discusses the ramifications of serialism, and general compositional resources available at the time, including spatialization and "musical space."[69] Similarly to Stockhausen, Boulez considers different "parameters" of sound in isolation (pitch, durations, timbre, dynamics, and spatial characteristics).[70]

Space, however, is not "an intrinsic function of the sound phenomenon, but rather its index of distribution" (Boulez 1963/1971: 66). Boulez deplores the apparent mistakes committed in the use of space in the past (in the vein of Stockhausen), maintaining that spatialization "was almost always reduced to altogether anecdotal or

---

[67] For a recent discussion of the composer's early interest in spatialization and the role of space in Boulez's music see Boulez and Nattiez (1991).

[68] This book is also known under its French title, *Penser la musique aujourd'hui* (Paris: Gonthier, 1963); English translation, entitled *Boulez on Music Today* appeared in 1971. Here, I will refer to this translation.

[69] Boulez's concept of "musical space" is discussed in Chapter II, section 2.3.

[70] In the overall schema of "musical syntax" (p. 115) spatial distribution constitutes the final element. The schema includes: pitch (absolute pitch and relative tessitura), time (durations/proportions, tessituras and tempo), dynamics (absolute dynamics, i.e. ratios; relative dynamics, i.e. values; dynamic profiles), timbres, and spatial distributions (Boulez 1963/1971: 115). The universal concepts of fixity and mobility can be applied in all these areas.

decorative proportions, which have largely falsified its use and distorted its true functions." He dislikes the superficial use of spatial effects, both in the distant past (Berlioz and the Venetians) and in more recent times (the mannerism of clockwise or anticlockwise motion, and the abuse of *space-glissandi*, linked to an "immoderation" in the use of clusters).[71] For Boulez, *spatial distribution* merits a sophisticated compositional treatment, "just as refined as the other sorts of distribution already encountered" (p. 67):

> It ought not only to distribute spaced-out ensembles according to simple geometric figures, which after all always turn out to be contained in a circle or an ellipse: equally--and in fact even more so--it must order the microstructure of these ensembles. While speed of displacement has always been stressed above all, little attention, amounting almost to total neglect, has been paid to the properties of statistically distributed objects linked in a circuit, or of mobile objects.
>
> (Boulez 1963/1971: 67)

Spatial distribution is primarily related to temporal simultaneity and succession, but relationships to pitch, dynamics and timbre are also possible. For Boulez, spatialization involves the articulation of textural details in complex sonorities: "the real interest in distribution lies in the creation of 'Brownian movements' within a mass, or volume of sound" (p. 67). Moreover, the position of the listeners "outside or inside the area within which the sound events occur" is crucial for their involvement in the music; either they observe the sound from outside, or they are "observed by the sound, surrounded by it" (p. 68).

Boulez distinguishes two types of distribution of structures: *static distribution* and *mobile distribution*, also called *static relief* and *dynamic relief*" (p. 68). This distinction and terminology closely resembles that of *musique concrète* (Poullin 1955; cf section 3.3). The composer proposes that mobile distribution should be realized by *conjunct and disjunct movements* which are not dependent on distance, but on the

---

[71] According to Luciano Berio, Boulez called these "space-glissandi," that is the rotational movement of sound "car racing" (Berio 1981/1985: 154). Berio himself also expressed a lack of interest in these easy tricks of "moving the sound round and round the hall" (ibidem).

temporal overlapping of sounds with common features in the domain of pitch, timbre, dynamics and duration). Boulez explains this theory with an example. If two chords are performed, and if

> the first chord is played at a given point in space, the second at some distance from this point; if the first is still sounding at the moment of entry of the second, and dies away to reveal it the result is what I call a *conjunct interval*.
> (Boulez 1963/1971: 68)

Disjunct interval occurs when a pause separates the two chords; this pause should be sufficiently short to allow for the impression of the displacement--if the pause is too long the perception will be of two distinct events (cf. Ex. III-11).

By using the two types of spatial intervals, it is possible to create "continuous displacements of lines or discontinuous leaps between points" at various levels of structure (p. 69). Nevertheless, Boulez has reservations about such mobility of musical gestures, because movement brings out theatrical aspects of performance, with negative consequences for the music. Therefore, he prefers a *fixed spatial lay-out* in which the conjunct and disjunct intervals are fixed. This type of distribution "represents in the arrested state what a spatial lay-out offers kinematically" (p. 69). The intervals observe the "elementary laws of regular or irregular symmetry, of asymmetry, and of the combination of these two forms." Here, Boulez takes into consideration all possible combinations of groups of instruments in space. As he explains,

> two groups will be symmetrical if they are situated at an equal distance from an axis of some kind; if they possess homogeneous or non-homogeneous timbres, identical in quality and density, they can be considered as *regularly symmetrical*; they are *irregularly symmetrical* if their homogeneity is not of the same nature (a group of brass against a group of strings, for example) or if their non-homogeneity differs in quality and density; they will otherwise be *asymmetrical*.
> (Boulez 1963/1971: 70)

Here, the typology of spatial relationships between instrumental groups includes timbre as an important criterion for symmetry. The remainder of the article is devoted to other matters; nonetheless, the composer returns to the idea of

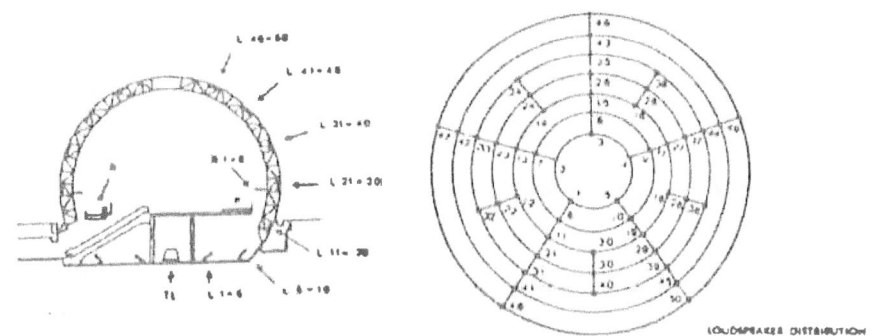

Ex. III-10: Plans for the German Pavilion at EXPO 1970 Osaka (from Stockhausen's *Spiral* 1973).

Ex. III-11: Disjunct and conjunct intervals described by Boulez in *Musikdenken heute* (1963).

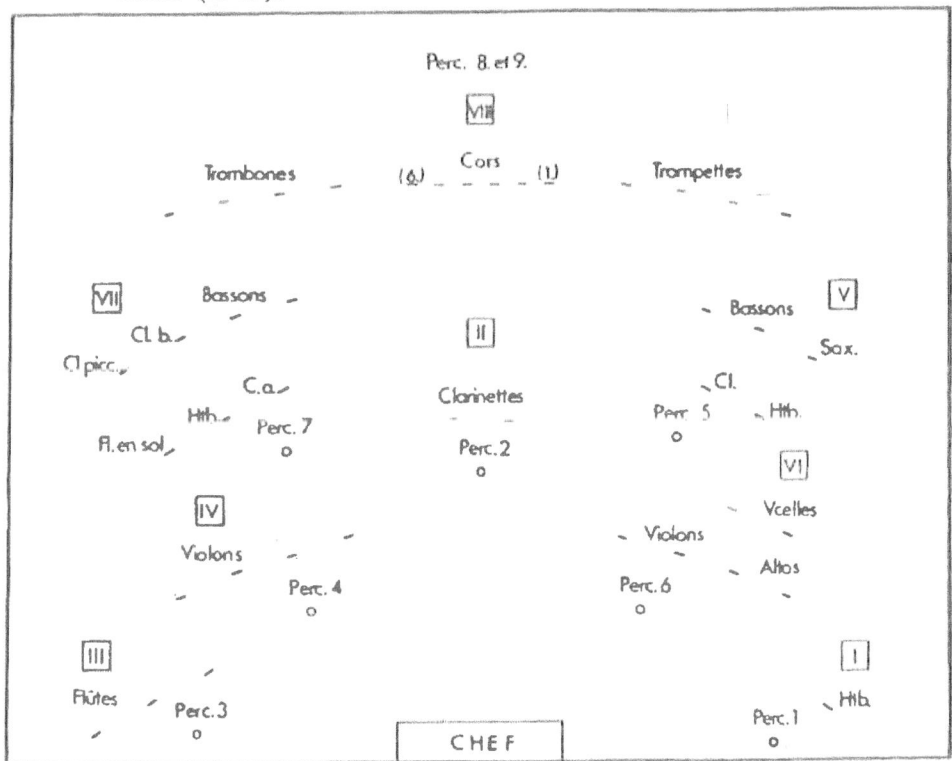

Ex. III-12: The seating plan for Boulez's *Rituel in memoriam Maderna* (1975).

© 1975 by Universal Edition (London) Ltd., London. All Rights Reserved. Used by permission of European American Music Distributors Corporation, sole U.S. and Canadian agent for Universal Edition (London) Ltd., London..

spatialization, that is "the distribution of structures" in order to consider the choice of compositional procedures applicable in this domain (p.96). He proposes to utilize the same type of structuring that he had introduced for timbre (selection of modules, partitions, focus, etc.).[72]

Boulez's approach to the idea of spatialization is more general than Stockhausen's; however, he shares the German composer's penchant for speculation. For instance, his differentiation between conjunct and disjunct intervals, as well as his discussion of the various types of symmetry and asymmetry, are not supported with any experimental data.

Nevertheless, Boulez realizes his spatial concerns in the music. As he does not share Stockhausen's preoccupation with motion (cf. his explicit contempt for "the abuse of *space-glissandi*" quoted above), he explores other, more subtle spatial effects. Thus, he focuses on enriching the spatial texture of the music by changing the location of the instrumentalists within the orchestra on the stage. In *Figures, Doubles, Prismes*, the orchestra is divided into 14 groups (six groups of strings, three of woodwinds, four of brass, and one of unpitched percussion) which are all placed on the platform, with several pitched percussion instruments interspersed among them (3 harps, celesta, vibraphone, xylophone, timpani).[73] This novel stage set-up of the orchestra has the purpose of transforming its sonorities, from separate sound blocks of different timbres (string, woodwind, brass, percussion) into more homogeneous textures woven from these various timbres. As Boulez stated in conversation with

---

[72]"The module will be the conjunction of a periodic distance with the periodicity of the elements or groups of elements, inscribed within it. Partition will be the division of this distance corresponding to an element or group of elements of the period, the focus will be defined as a point or surface, coupled with a specific family of phenomena." (Boulez 1963/1971: 96-97). These terms (module, partition, focus) are originally introduced in Boulez's enumeration of possible abstract spaces, applicable primarily to pitch and rhythm (cf. Chapter II, section 2.3).

[73]The first version of this piece was titled *Doubles* (1957). It was extended into the larger work, *Figures, Doubles, Prismes* in 1963 and revised in 1968. There is no score available for study, only recordings and the manuscript material deposited at the Paul Sacher Foundation in Basel (Edwards 1989: 6-7).

Celestin Deliège, in the traditional setting contrasting timbral groups are located at a "series of screens, as it were, or of different planes;" this arrangement is "fairly logical in that it corresponds to the instruments' volume" (Boulez 1975/1976: 100). However, by splitting the homogeneous ensembles, by scattering woodwinds, etc., the orchestra acquires a new, spatial quality. Boulez believes that "when you hear the work live, the sonorities are extremely homogeneous yet at the same time scattered, so that it is not a homogeneity of neighbouring groups but a homogeneity of fusion." (Boulez 1975/1976: 100).

In two instrumental compositions with spatial organization of sound, *Domaines* for clarinet and six instrumental groups (1961-1968) and *Rituel in memoriam Maderna* for eight orchestral groups (1974-1975) Boulez's interest in symmetry comes to the fore. In *Domaines*, the groups consist of from one to six instruments, mostly of different timbres.[74] These groups are presented individually, as they, one by one, respond to the solo clarinet; each exchange has a different musical material. After a series of such dialogues initiated by the soloist, another one follows in which the randomly chosen ensembles are "mirrored" by the clarinet. This piece, demonstrating Boulez's ideal of "the permutability of sequences within a predetermined whole" (Jameux 1984/1991: 147) suffers from the predictability of its large-scale, sectional structure. When one group is involved in an interplay with the soloist who has approached its spatial location, others remain silent. Boulez himself has been critical of the symmetry of this piece as being "too audible" (Boulez 1975/1976: 88).

While *Domaines* is organized around the number six (with six groups, six segments of musical material within each one of the six "cahiers") *Rituel in memoriam Maderna* features eight groups of homogeneous timbres, all placed on the stage (1 oboe, 2 clarinets, 3 flutes, 4 violins, woodwind quintet, string sextet, woodwind heptet, and fourteen brass instruments). Each group is accompanied by a percussion

---

[74]The groups are: one bass clarinet, a duet of marimbaphone and double bass, a trio of oboe, horn guitar, four trombones, a quintet of flute, saxophone, bassoon, trumpet, harp, and a string sextet (Boulez 1970).

player (two for the brass) beating out the rhythm on a variety of unpitched instruments. This work is--as is *Domaines*--structured in "perpetual alternation" (Boulez 1975). However, the pattern is more complicated and consists of a sequence of 15 sections: even-numbered verses (non-synchronous heterophonies) and odd-numbered refrains (immense chords of all groups together, starting from the brass group with gongs).[75] The large scale form is articulated by the change of the number of the groups, first increasing from one (sections 1 and 2) to all eight (sections 13 and 15), then decreasing to two. Here the symmetry of the spatial location of the instruments on the stage may have a role to play (Ex. III-12).[76]

In the opening of the piece, the order of the entries seems to be spatially balanced. Group VIII (brass, Centre-Back) is followed by group I (oboe, Front-Right), and their conjunction (sections 1-3). Then, three groups play in heterophony (section 4): oboe (Front-Right), clarinets (Centre-Back), and flutes (Front-Left). The entry of the flutes from the left side of the platform creates a spatial balance in the music, which was earlier predominantly heard from the opposite direction. In addition, the three groups in section 4 outline a triangle on the stage (Left Front--Centre Back--Right Front). However, Boulez does not corroborate the importance of such geometrical symmetry in the spatial interactions of the groups in *Rituel* (Boulez 1992).[77] According to Boulez, the location of the instrumental groups on the stage is determined by their acoustical characteristics as they are placed progressively "from

---

[75]The coherence of pitch organization stems from Boulez's use of one set of seven pitches, introduced in section II of *Rituel*. This set recurs in every verse; the refrains are based on its inversion.

[76]In the interview with Jean-Jacques Nattiez, Boulez points out the connection between the concept of *Rituel* and his discovery of the potential of spatialization realized with the "halaphon." This signal processing unit, constructed by Hans-Peter Haller, allows for a flexible movement of sound between several loudspeakers (Haller 1972: 43; Boulez and Nattiez 1991: 116). Boulez used it in a New York performance of *Explosante-fixe* in 1973 (Vande Gorne 1988: 13).

[77]Boulez's spatial preoccupations in the 1990s are far removed from the concerns of *Musikdenken heute*.

the biggest and strongest at the back of the stage to the smallest ones at the front" (Boulez 1992: 5). Moreover, the placement of all groups on the stage is a compromise with practical considerations; Boulez would much prefer to "put the groups very far from each other." This would allow the listeners to hear the separated groups very clearly, with a lucid articulation of details. Each member of the audience would listen to the work from a different perspective. In this respect, adds the composer, a far-away view, made possible by the location of all the groups on the stage in front of the listeners, also has merits because it allows one to perceive the "work in its totality" (ibidem). In the first version of the published score of *Rituel* (1975), the entries of groups in the refrains are simultaneous. Boulez's recordings, however, reveal that he preferred to stagger these entries in time (Jameux 1984/1991: 356-357).[78] As he explained in an interview, the unison performance does not create the impression of space:

> If there are echoes played very quickly by groups entering each time in different order, and resounding from different points on the stage, the space is "described" each time with a new pattern of these echoes. This is much more interesting than having everybody play together.
>
> (Boulez 1992: 5)

Thus, spatialization transforms the static texture of immense orchestral chords into a lively pattern of responses. This change involves structuring in time (from complete simultaneity to partial succession) and serves to enrich the perceptual experience of the music which acquires, through spatialization, a new vividness and clarity. According to Boulez, the main function of space in music is,

> to clarify the situation, generally, the situation of polyphony. For me, it is not spectacular at all, I do not like spectacular effects. If I write polyphony which is not only dense or complex (that is not necessarily the case) but consists of different layers and different components which have to be separated by the ear, the distance certainly clarifies the situation and helps the listener to understand the various components much better.
>
> (Boulez 1992: 1)

---

[78] The revised version of the score explicitly indicates the delayed entries of the various groups.

However, the composer makes it clear that such topographical space is not the "substance" of the music. For Boulez, music is organized hierarchically with pitch or duration as the strongest elements (he reiterates the order used in the classification of musical parameters in "Musical Technique" of 1963). These elements, however, are not the most apparent in perception. The characteristics perceived immediately are tone colour and dynamics:

> That is a kind of immediate perception while pitch and duration, while more decisive, are much more difficult to perceive. Space, topography is like instrumentation: it clarifies something else. For instance, one can play a polyphonic piece on the piano without timbral contrasts and polyphony will be there, but this polyphony will be much more distinct if different groups will play different parts. Space works exactly the same way.
> (Boulez 1992: 2)

Here, Boulez considers spatialization in the context of polyphony, just as Mahler and Brant did.[79] Speculations about "conjunct and disjunct intervals" no longer interest him. However, he continues to link spatialization with orchestration, and spatial location with timbre; these are the "non-essential," though perceptually most vivid, elements of the musical language.

Boulez's "last word" on spatialization is not expressed explicitly in his writings but in his music. Through the years, his preoccupation has shifted from codifying elements of musical language towards exploring the territory that had been discovered (and, sometimes, well known in the past). He features spatialization prominently in *Répons* for six instrumental soloists, instrumental ensemble, and electroacoustic equipment (1981-1988), a piece that Boulez continued to revise and refine throughout the 1980s. This work, based on the ancient principle of antiphonal dialogue, draws the soloists, the ensemble and the electroacoustic sound projection into an immense,

---

[79]One of Brant's experiments dealt with a spatialized performance of a polyphonic composition by J. S. Bach in which each part was played from a different point in space. Here, spatial separation was detrimental to the music consisting of different lines tightly knit to form a coherent whole (Brant 1967). The perceptual differentiation of the voices in the fugue does not benefit from spatialization because it is already provided by register (and, sometimes, timbre).

musical "conversation."[80] Here, Boulez returns to the mainstream of spatialization, to music consisting of "superimposed layers which do not coincide exactly" and, therefore, create a fascinating, vivid, spatial texture (Boulez 1992).

The choice of Stockhausen and Boulez as the two most prominent and vocal representants of "Darmstadt" does not imply the absence of spatial concerns among other participants in the international avant-garde. Luciano Berio, for instance, who also belongs to the Darmstadt generation, had actually experimented with spatialization in orchestral music earlier than Boulez or Stockhausen (but not earlier than Brant). In 1955, in *Allelujah I*, he "placed five different instrumental groups on the podium" but later decided that they could not be heard separately (Berio 1981/1985: 154). He revised the piece into *Allelujah II* (1957-1958) in which he specified the location of the groups at different points in the hall. Here, Berio followed the principle of perceptual separation (advocated by Brant), linking space and timbre: "groups containing similar instruments were placed as far apart as possible, while those with different instruments were seated closer to each other" (Berio 1981/1985: 155). This was, for Berio, hardly a general rule. According to the composer, the use of space differed in each of his compositions (p. 154). For instance, in *Coro* for 40 voices and instruments (1975-76), Berio adopted Boulez's solution from *Figures, Doubles, Prismes* and subdivided the whole performing apparatus into small ensembles distributed on the stage. Similarly to Boulez, Berio tried to replace the homogeneity of large scale textures of separated groups (chorus and orchestra) with a microscopic textural differentiation. However, in *Coro*, "the role of space is determined by the relationship between the registers of the human voice and the instruments" (Berio 1981/1985: 154). High voices are coupled with high instruments, thus creating "a soprano territory, an alto territory, and so on" (p. 155). Therefore, spatial

---

[80]I discuss *Répons* in Chapter V, section 5.5.

distribution is connected to pitch.[81]

The thrust of the Darmstadt generation ensured the inclusion of spatialization as an obligatory feature of "modern" music written by composers in many countries. However, in the process of discovery and exploration, the initial fascination with structuring individual, separated "parameters" including the spatial position of sound, was gradually replaced by a concern for perceptual clarity. In other words, the emphasis shifted from considering compositional material in abstraction to "constructing" the experience of the listener in the concert hall. Spatialized compositions, while remaining "musical works" in the common sense of this term (cf. Chapter IV), have enriched the physical actuality of music through the greater involvement of the listeners, often completely surrounded by sounds, through the articulation of distinct sonorous layers and through the spatial articulation of large-scale forms.

---

[81]Recall that Stockhausen considered a case of musicians located along the line and performing a spatial scale of pitches in "Music in space" (Stockhausen 1959/1961: 79; cf. above).

3.5.

Conceptual experimentation: Cage, Lucier and Schafer

The shift in emphasis from abstract musical materials to perceptual experiences which is apparent in the evolution of the views on space of the members of the Darmstadt avant-garde, brings their ideas close to the preoccupations of the musical experimentalists.[82] Artists-philosophers, such as John Cage, sought to broaden the definition of music, restructure musical experience, and challenge the basic assumptions of the musicians and the listeners. Here, a cursory description of Cage's views on space and spatialization is followed by a review of some of Alvin Lucier's acoustic-perceptual experiments which exemplify the expansion of compositional interests into the domain of installations, site-specific music, etc. Finally, the discussion turns towards the experimental musical theatre of R. Murray Schafer, who, inspired by Ives, Cage and the theatrical experiments at Bauhaus, envisions a form of art that would change the spectators' self-awareness and, perhaps, their existential status.

John Cage

In 1939, John Cage advocated "making music with its materials, sound and rhythm, disregarding the cumbersome, top-heavy structure of musical prohibitions" (Cage 1939/1961: 87). This meant, primarily, a rejection of pitch organization as the basis for compositional thinking.[83] Music based on "sound and silence" may include any sounds conceivable "within a rhythmic structure that includes silence" (Cage

---

[82]I borrow the distinction between "avant-garde" and "experimental" music from Michael Nyman's *Experimental Music: Cage and beyond* (Nyman 1973).

[83]Cage reiterated this view in 1949: "Sound has four characteristics: pitch, timbre, loudness and duration. . . Of the four characteristics of sound only duration involves both sound and silence therefore a structure based on durations (rhythmic: phrase, time lengths) is correct (corresponds with the nature of the material) whereas harmonic structure is incorrect (derived from pitch which has no being in silence)." (Cage 1949/1961: 63)

1949/1961: 56). As Cage wrote in his "Credo," he believed "in the use of noise," in the substitution of "organized sound for music" and in the widening of musical materials to the "entire field of sound" (Cage 1961: 3).[84] The doctrine of experimental music, as envisioned by Cage, includes the disappearance of the oppositions of subject-object, art-life, etc. (1955/1961: 14). Sound is defined as a "transmission in all directions, from the field's center." Each sound is "inextricably synchronous with all other, sounds, non-sounds" (ibidem). Here, the influence of Zen philosophy is as pronounced as that of Varèse, whose definition of music as "organized sound" provided Cage with a starting point.[85] In a new, experimental music,

> nothing takes place but sounds: those that are notated and those that are not. Those that are not notated appear in the written music as silences, opening the doors of the music to the sounds that happen to be in the environment.
> (Cage 1957/1961: 7-8)

As any sound may be juxtaposed with any other, "a total sound-space is available" for compositional explorations (p. 8). Thus, the musicians are able to "transform our contemporary awareness of nature's manner of operation into art" (p. 9).[86] This "manner of operation" implies a simultaneous presence of incongruous

---

[84]The text, entitled "The future of music: Credo," was originally written in 1937, revised in 1958 and published in *Silence* in 1961.

[85]Cage criticizes Varèse because "rather than dealing with sounds as sounds, he deals with them as Varèse" (Cage 1958/1961: 84). For Cage, apparently, the virtue of compositional originality is a thing of the past, and he has words of praise only for Varèse's "acceptance of all audible phenomena as material proper to music." According to James Pritchett, Cage's notion of organized sound arose independently of Varèse (Pritchett 1993: 16).

[86]This statement is one of the many references to the theory that art should "imitate Nature in her manner of operation" borrowed by Cage from an Indian philosopher, Ananda K. Coomaraswamy (Pritchett 1993: 37). Cage's words almost literally repeat an excerpt from St. Thomas Aquinas's *In libros physicorum Aristotelis expositio* [II.4.] (quoted from Tatarkiewicz, 1960): "Ars imitatur naturam; . . . tota natura ordinatur ad finem suum, ut sic opus naturae videatur, esse opus intelligentiae, dum per determinata media ad certos fines procedit: quod etiam in operando ars imitatur."

types of material in new music, which "is more clearly heard when several loudspeakers or performers are separated in space rather than grouped closely together" (p. 12). As Cage observes,

> this music is not concerned with harmoniousness as generally understood, where the quality of harmony results from a blending of several elements. Here we are concerned with the co-existence of dissimilars, and the central points where fusion occurs are many: the ears of the listeners wherever they are.
>
> Cage 1957/1961: 12)

Cage develops this point in "Indeterminacy," the second of his three lectures at Darmstadt ("Composition as process;" 1958). In a composition which is "indeterminate with respect to its performance," every performance is unique and unrepeatable, and it cannot be "grasped as an object in time" (Cage 1958/1961: 39). Instead, it develops in the physical space of the performance and occupies a segment of the physical time. Writing in a deliberately convoluted language, Cage explains:

> Where the performance involves several players (two or more) it is advisable for several reasons to separate the performers one from the other, as much as is convenient and in accord with the action and the architectural situation. . . This separation allows the sounds to issue from their own centers and to interpenetrate in a way which is not obstructed by the conventions of European harmony and theory about relationships and interferences of sounds.
>
> (Cage 1958/1961: 39)

Cage believes that throughout the history of Western art music, a fusion of sound was essential. Therefore, the players in an ensemble were brought as close to each other as possible: together, they produced a coherent work of music, "an object in time" (p. 39). The ideal of new music, however, is "a non-obstruction of sounds;" spatial separation of musicians facilitates "the independent action of each performer." The players should be separated one from another "in order to show a musical recognition of the necessity of space" (p. 40). The placement of the performers may involve their dispersion within the audience itself. This arrangement will heighten "the independent action of each person, which will include mobility on the part of all" (p. 40). The exact temporal coordination of these actions is not necessary; new music does not need a common meter because it is based on the co-presence of dissimilarities.

This text, although echoing some of the preoccupations of the Darmstadt avant-garde, bears a closer resemblance to notions of spatialization articulated in the American tradition of Ives and Brant.[87] Cage reiterates Ives's concern for the necessity of the spatial separation of the musicians, and mirrors Brant's reasoning about the necessary dissimilarity of musical materials involved in spatialization and about the absence of exact rhythmic coordination. Nonetheless, Cage does not relate spatial organization to polyphony; he is more interested in simultaneities that cannot be reduced to any common denominator. Moreover, inspired by Eastern philosophy, he posits the need to overcome separation of music from non-music, art from life. This separation usually results in creating "a compendium of masterpieces" and obscures the necessary "interpenetration" of all through all.[88] Cage requires his listeners and followers "to accept that a sound is a sound and a man is a man, to give up illusions about ideas of order, expressions of sentiment, and all the rest of our inherited aesthetic claptrap." (Cage 1959: 82).

While realizing Cage's requirement, composers, performers, and listeners cease to fulfil their traditional roles. Musical open-mindedness means that "anything goes" (Cage 1974: 178). Musical performances, freed from the constraints of interpreting the score, are not imaginary objects, they have no stable identity which could be independent of their particular circumstances. The "work of music" disappears, replaced by processes, rituals, theatre, happenings. Music is taken beyond the concert hall into all possible (and impossible) spaces: geodesic domes, unused subway platforms, laundromats, fields and forests (Cage 1974: 185). Hence, art is not separated from life. The listeners/musicians create their own musical experiences, everyone is central. Cage considered this "democratization" of music as a

---

[87]In the texts surveyed for this dissertation, Cage does not refer to either of these composers. Rather, he includes frequent references to Satie and Varèse.

[88]These expressions come from the third lecture "at Darmstadt," entitled "Communication" and, in part, inspired by Dr. Suzuki (Cage 1958/1961: 44-46).

characteristic feature of the American avant-garde to which he belonged. It was prefigured in compositions that

> envisage each auditor as central so that the physical circumstances of a concert do not oppose audience to performers but dispose the latter around-among the former, bringing a unique acoustical experience to each pair of ears. . . Admittedly a situation of this complexity is beyond control, yet it resembles a listener's situation before and after a concert--daily experience, that is.
> (Cage 1958/1961: 53)

As the borderline between art and life evaporates, the music loses strict pitch organization, coherent temporal progression and directed motion, and gains indeterminacy of form, diversity of material and simultaneity of unrelated sound events. It moves into the domain of Being, not Becoming (to paraphrase Rochberg's expression of 1963). Thus, while the music reaches into space, it becomes increasingly static.[89]

Temporal stasis, resulting from an absence of directional motion characterizes much of Cage's music, whether spatialized or not. One of the basic characteristics of his style, from *Music of Changes* for piano (1951) to *Freeman Etudes* for violin (1977-80/1989-90), is the absence of continuity, since each sound event appears independently of the others, "floating"--as it were--in silence. In the most radical works from Cage's "indeterminate" period, these sound events are unspecified, and the composer merely delineates an open-ended procedure to be followed.[90] Here, he constructs "compositional tools" rather than fully articulated musical works.

---

[89]Cage's association with painters and visual artists, and his linking of spatialization with the renunciation of development in music have been understood by some writers, especially those with a limited expertise in the domain of contemporary music, as symptomatic of this music in general (e.g. Goehr 1992).

[90]In *Variations II* (1961), the performers have at their disposal several transparencies with points and lines. The superimposition of these transparencies creates a pattern decifered by measuring distances on the lines which define "freqency, amplitude, timbre, duration, and point of occurrence" (Pritchett 1993: 137). The measurements, providing the performer with data about sound events, may be interpreted in any manner, and the action repeated any number of times. The only certain fact about sound placement in this work is its random distribution in space.

In *Variations IV* (1964), Cage devises a way of defining the placement of randomly chosen sound events by dropping transparencies with several points and two circles onto a map of the selected performance space. If any of the lines drawn from one circle through each of the points touches the second circle, this sound should be performed inside the chosen space, if not--outside. The spaces selected for the performance of *Variations IV* could range from a concert hall, through an outdoor space, to a cave. The adherence to this compositional procedure results more often in leaving the concert hall, than in remaining within the boundaries of the traditional "musical" space.

These pieces have been conceived during the most radical phase of Cage's compositional career, in which he focused on conceptual experimentation and performance art (1962-1969). At that time, Cage created an impossible work of zero duration, entitled *0'00"* (1962). Its score consists of one sentence: "In a situation provided with maximum amplification (no feedback), perform a disciplined action" (Pritchett 1993: 138). During the first performance of *0'00"*, Cage typed letters while seated on a squeaky chair; the sounds accompanying his actions were amplified and projected from loudspeakers scattered through the perfomance space.[91] Thus, a moment from Cage's life was transformed into art, and accidental noise became--at least in his intention--music.[92] Cage's idea of music as a by-product of an action or a process was further developed by many of his associates, including the organizer of the concert at which *0'00"* was first presented, Alvin Lucier.

---

[91]Rose Art Museum at Brandeis University, May 1965.

[92]Terry Eagleton describes the dismantling of the boundaries between art and life as the objective of the revolutionary avant-garde who seek the undoing of Art. He wonders: "For if art smashes through the formal contours which demarcate and estrange it from ordinary life, will it not simply succeed in spilling and defusing its critical contents?" (Eagleton 1990: 370).

Alvin Lucier

According to Thomas DeLio 1984, Alvin Lucier was "one of the first American composers to eschew all gestural aspects of traditional composition and to replace them with the pure physical presence of sound" (DeLio 1984: 91). In other words, Lucier exemplifies what Cage has envisioned. In Lucier's music,

> materials are never used to fabricate dramatic scenarios nor to express abstract relations. Instead, they are made present to the listener in some heightened way. . . Art's most vital function is to re-create the condition of being--not the experiences of one's life but that perpetual state of transcendence which is the very substance of life.
>
> (DeLio 1984: 104)

The reduction of music to the bare bones of its sound matter, serves to increase the listeners awareness of the process of perceiving and of themselves as perceiving subjects. Simultaneously, the focus on sound as "an end in itself" implies the use of spatialization, because all sounds are primarily spatial. Lucier's own account of his compositional interests reveals a preoccupation with the acoustic peculiarities of space unprecedented among composers (Lucier 1985).

As a truly conceptual artist, Lucier is concerned with reducing the phenomena that he explores in music to their underlying principles. Then, all complexity disappears and "the work may now exist in its purest form" (Lucier 1985: 160). Here, "the work" designates a composition like, for instance, *Music for solo performer* (1965) in which brain waves (registered live and amplified) are used to control a battery of percussion instruments and loudspeakers dispersed in space.

In a series of such works, Lucier studies the acoustic characteristics of natural and architectural spaces (1968-72). A different set of compositions explores "the spatial characteristics of sound itself," such as standing waves, phantom sonic images in space, diffractive properties of sound, etc. (Lucier 1985: 145). One of these works, entitled *Outlines of Persons and Things* (1976) "makes the inaudible audible" through the exploration of acoustic shadows (changes of timbre caused by the presence of an object between the sound source and the listener). As Lucier explains, "in order to perceive the shadow vividly, one of the three components in the system--sound source, person or thing around which sounds flow, or listener--must move, so that comparisons in time may be made." (Lucier 1985: 148-149).

Thus, it is possible to "uncover aspects of sound which we seldom hear because of our concern with musical language" (p. 149). Appropriately, Lucier's work makes use of acoustic testing equipment, sine wave oscillators, etc. The latter are chosen "because of their purity. . . They enable the listener to perceive the geographical placement of sound in space" (p. 155). The process of testing and exploring by the listeners-performers actively involves them in the discovery of the acoustic properties of rooms, objects, instruments, etc. The emphasis on process, on space, on personal experience is here equivalent to a renunciation of musical structure and high-level organization, in short, to the abandonment of composing in the traditional sense of this term.

Lucier's works display a continuity that "often consists simply in letting the sound material flow according to its own laws" (p. 156). The evolution of this material depends on features of the studied system, which may, for instance, consist of a very long wire stretched across a building which resonates in an unpredictable manner. In *Music on a Long Thin Wire* (1977), variations "caused by fatigue, heating, cooling, air currents, expansion and contraction, and other physical changes in the system or the environment determine the pitch, harmonic, timbral, rhythmic and other musical parameters" of the resonating wire (p. 150). As Cage wrote in *Empty Words*, the composer just sets a process going, and observes the result (Cage 1974: 145). For Lucier, as for Cage, "language or structure interferes with the clarity of the perception of the phenomenon to be explored" (p. 159). Non-musical ideas, such as programmatic ones, also distract, directing the attention away from a sounding process--the expected focus of the listener's perception. Yet, often, there is no concert to attend, no performers to applaud. The context for "musical" explorations has been drastically revised.

R. Murray Schafer's theatre of confluence

The focus on the perceptual experience and the self-awareness of each listener, which characterizes Lucier's acoustic experiments, is also an important feature of the *theatre of confluence* proposed and realized by R. Murray Schafer (Schafer 1991a).[93] The Canadian composer has developed this form of music theatre over the course of thirty years; his monumental cycle of musical/theatrical works, *Patria*, still awaits its completion (Mackenzie 1992). Inspired by projects of Bauhaus artists, such as Andreas Weininger (whose spherical theatre predates Stockhausen's designs, cf. Section 3.4), Schafer envisioned a theatre, which would join together all the arts in a new form of "confluence" (a modern *Gesamtkunstwerk*) and, thus, imitate life itself which is "the original multi-media experience" (Schafer 1991a: 32). The privileged position of music among the arts is justified by Schafer's belief in the primacy of hearing: "If the sense of touch is the most intimate of the senses, then the sense of hearing, it appears, is the next best approximation of this intimacy. Hearing is like touching at a distance." (Schafer 1991a: 41-42).

For Schafer, "all art should lead to altered states of consciousness" (p. 33). The purpose of art is to "affect a change in our existential condition" (Schafer 1991a: 87). The role of the artist is "to assist in regaining the spirit lost in the long evolution of civilization" (p. 102). Therefore, theatre, involved in "the recovery of the sacred," should become a form of ritual. To this purpose, it requires a change of context, new performance spaces, new means of expression (p. 90). The distinction between audiences and performers should be overcome, the separation of art and life should disappear. Here, Schafer gives a new twist to Cage's idea of the dissolution of art into life (or transforming life into art). His musical/theatrical works have a lofty purpose: "What they will reveal is man subdued by reverence for nature and the cosmos. What they will reveal is human dependence on an environment consisting of all things understood, misunderstood, and mysterious." (p. 102).

Schafer expresses a profound dissatisfaction with modern theatre buildings as

---

[93] I discuss spatial aspects of Schafer's music in Chapter VIII.

"impediments to the existential changes we would like to achieve in those who attend our productions" (p. 159). Therefore, for instance, in the reenactment of the myth of Theseus and Ariadne, *Patria 5: The Crown of Ariadne*, the theatrical action should take place at the seashore, with a labyrinth set on sand and then burned in the dramatic conclusion of this work (p. 158). Ideally, of course, the composer would like to have a story presented "during a lull in a Dionysian marathon of dancing, indulged in by the whole audience" (ibidem). So far, his search for a suitable performance space on both shores of Canada has been futile. The work needs a large surface of water (theatrical reason) which should be relatively quiet (musical reason). Canadian beaches are either too populated or too noisy for this enterprise.

The next segment of the *Patria* cycle, *Ra*, goes further in the focus on the existential transformation required of the audience. Here, initiates are conducted through a mystery ritual, an all-night experience in a specially prepared setting. The ritual, appealing strongly to senses which function best in darkness (touch, hearing and smell), requires 25-30 locales, both indoors and outdoors (Schafer 1991a: 172). Participants wander through this labyrinth, encountering gods, meditating, preparing a feast, etc. As the composer writes, "the itinerary of active and passive episodes, participating, observing, walking, sitting, standing and lying down were as vital in the structure as any pacing of music and dialogue." (p. 177).

Schafer's theatre verges on creating a new religion. Music, and drama have subordinate roles in his grand project, because the composer has ambitions not just "to entertain theatre customers but to induce a radical change in their existential status" (p. 177). In other words, he is composing a work of human existence in time and space. Thus, music, having transversed a full circle, comes back to its original involvement in religious rituals (e.g. the consecration of the wall of Jerusalem discussed in section 3.1). The problem is that artistic ritual is not "real" in the way a religious ritual is to believers participating in what they consider a sacred action. Regardless of whether Schafer's theatre succeeds in its ultimate, existential goal, its musical layer has aesthetic values of its own and constitutes a significant contribution to the development of the idea of music in space.

Conclusion

Music has always been spatial, but not always spatialized. Various spatial aspects of this art have risen to prominence at different stages of its history. Before the emergence of the concept of the "musical work," the bodily-spatial experiences of the listeners and performers constituted important factors of the musical experience. Musical spatiality relating to the acoustic conditions of performance (types of enclosures, outdoor environments) influenced sound ideals of different times and places. The location of musicians or sound sources within the space of performance has become important only when composers begun to notate all the features of the "musical work." Since spatial features of sound have been its least noticeable characteristics, their full musical articulation has occurred relatively late in this development, during the 20th century.

Modern spatialization has privileged these aspects of musical spatiality which are associated with patterns of distribution of sound in space. Mahler, Ives, and Brant have linked spatialization to polyphony (i.e. the simultaneity of multiple layers separated in space). Varèse's vision of sound masses projected into space has endowed sounds with a tangibility of material objects; this tendency has been further articulated in electroacoustic music (section 3.3). In contrast to these two areas of spatialization, speculative theories proposed by Stockhausen (serialization of direction) and Boulez (spatial intervals) have not survived the test of time (section 3.4). At present, composers often attribute to space the role of clarification of dense textures and segregation of polyphonic layers. This preference implies an existence of "textures" and "layers" before their spatialization occurs; thus, it indirectly suggests a continuous hold of the "work-concept" on compositional thinking. Many contemporary composers tend to specify all details of their musical artefacts, from pitch-rhythm structure, through instrumentation, down to the level of sound location. The conceptual experiments of Cage and his followers (section 3.5), with their focus on perceptual experiences (in space, of space), have not permanently transformed the way that music is conceived of. Spatialization has become yet another feature of musical *works*, which are envisioned in the auditory reality of sound.

PART TWO

SPATIALIZATION

IN THEORY AND PRACTICE

CHAPTER IV

SPATIALIZATION AND THE MUSICAL WORK

4.1.
Introduction: Listening to "B-A-C-H"

Let us begin by imagining a musical situation: a listener seated in a concert hall witnesses a performance by a trumpet player (standing on the stage) of a sequence of four quarter-notes, with the pitches of Bflat3--A3--C4--B3. The listener ignores the immediate physical surroundings and hears one of the following: (a) four trumpet sounds equally spaced in time, (b) a sequence of intervals, minor second--minor third--minor second, (c) an instance of set 4-1, (d) a motive refering to the name of BACH. The "web of interpretants" (term from Nattiez 1990) surrounding a simple musical fact is already quite dense, even though I have only considered its aspects relating to pitch, pitch class, and pitch-notation (representation by letters). What if the performer's gestures, the facial expressions, the direction of the bell of the instrument became important? Might one say, then, that the music has become theatre?

Let us consider a different situation. Four trumpet players stand in the corners of a rectangular hall, each playing one note of the motive in succession. The listener is now surrounded by the "B-A-C-H." When the notes slightly overlap in time, one might say that the sound rotates, or meanders through space (depending on the order of entries). The motive has become "spatialized." A different effect arises when the four musicians play each note of the motive together. The identity of pitch, the timbral and temporal coherence lead to a transformation of the sound image heard by the listener in the centre, equidistant from the four musicians. The sounds appear to extend in space, covering the whole area in-between; Henry Brant calls this phenomenon "spill" (Brant 1967). Again, the spatialization of music has occurred. Is it negligible from the analytic standpoint?

What if the musicians walk around while playing repeatedly the same motive, each presenting the same pitches in a different rhythmic pattern and a different order? The listener may focus on any of the four trajectories of sound movement, she or he may notice evolving timbres, changing distances and directions. Is the music reducible to the simple "B-A-C-H"? Is it theatre? Would it be music or theatre if all the participants of the musical situation wandered through the entire hall, foyer, backstage, in a sort of a "hide-and-seek" game? Would it make a difference if the composer just gave one page of vague instructions or if the entire spatio-temporal design was specified in detail in the score?

Imagine a situation of quadrophonic sound projection created by four loudspeakers surrounding the listener. The recorded trumpet motive swirls around at a breathtaking speed in the virtual space. Imagine that while rotating it simultaneously approaches the listener and accelerates to an overwhelming, dizzying climax. Could this form of "spatialization" be ignored as inessential to the music's true identity? What if sound-processing resulted in the motive's drifting in and out of the threshold of audibility, so that the old "B-A-C-H" would be barely recognizable, like an apparition from a distant past? What if, to change the sound image completely, a huge brass chorus "blared away" from all directions at once, crushing the listener with the immensity of a quasi-Brucknerian apotheosis? And, to outline just one more option, would anything in the music change if a musician, the trumpet player from the beginning of this "what-if" game, appeared in the middle of the virtual space, and if the motive performed by the live musician was surrounded, overwhelmed and silenced by a barrage of distorted, artificial sounds (with the same sequence of pitches, though, the perennial "B-A-C-H")?

In addition to the obsessive reliance on one, short sequence of pitch-classes, all the situations outlined above have one element in common. All imply the presence of the listener. The location, orientation, attention, and, sometimes, movement of this person are crucial for the "spatialization" to occur. The listener orients him/herself toward the music, the music is directed toward the listener. Their reciprocal relationship is essential.[1]

The appraisal of the musical situation changes when the attention shifts to the spatial perspective of the performer. A solo musician deals merely with the space of the instrument, or, if walking around, of the performance setting (Merleau-Ponty 1945/1962: 146). Two or more performers may interact with each other. Louis Andriessen asks: "What is the difference between two people playing a melody and one person playing the same melody? And what about two people playing one note turn and turn around?" (Andriessen 1977). Andriessen's answer is musical--*Hoketus* for two groups of musicians (cf. Chapter V). This composition is a musical game which challenges the performers to compete with each other. The "artefacts" of the sound images, though interesting as such, are merely by-products of the musical actions.

This example notwithstanding, most concert music subordinates the aural perspective of the performers to that of the listeners, to whom the music appeals for an aesthetic judgement. Iannis Xenakis expresses this stance lucidly:

> The conductor hears the orchestra in a certain way during the performance, he has certain instruments to the right or to the left, he has the string orchestra around him, then the woodwinds and brass farther away, followed by the percussion. The listener in the auditorium does not have the same sound image as the conductor, and the conductor has to conduct for the listener, not for himself. How can he do that when he is not there? He should conduct from the auditorium and listen to the orchestra from that place.
>
> (Xenakis 1992: 11)

The emphasis on the aural perspective of the listener brings in a paradigmatic shift in the understanding of music and musical works. The traditional account draws from "the notion of a pure or disembodied sound" (Ihde 1976: 78) which deprives music of its physical spatiality. Often, musical substance is thought to consist only of structures in pitch and time which unequivocally determine the identity of a

---

[1] Here, I have considered the "spatialization" of music as perceived by a lone auditor. The presence of a larger audience complicates the situation, because each listener hears a slightly different sound image from a different spatial position.

composition (Goodman 1976). The notion of "spatialization" requires a change of perspective which, however, does not necessarily contradict and invalidate the tradition. Musical spatiality, though always present, is not always crucial for the understanding of this art in which spatial relationships may be (and have been) expendable. Heelan's horizonal epistemology posits the existence of "many-to-one and one-to-many mappings of perceptual objects contextually defined within mutually incompatible but complementary contexts" (Heelan 1983: 270). The "spatial" perspective is just one such mapping, reformulating perceptual objects of music in a new context. In order to point out the compositional potential of the various spatial aspects of sound (i.e. "the perceptual objects of music"), I include a review of the current research in the domain of spatial hearing (section 4.2).

In the final section of this chapter, I define "spatialization" and review its relationships to polychorality, music theatre, etc. The addition of spatial features of sound to the list of musical characteristics deserving compositional attention takes place within the context of the "work-concept." Therefore, I precede my discussion of spatialization with an outline of a classical account of the work of music, found in Roman Ingarden's phenomenological aesthetics (Ingarden 1958/1986; section 4.3).[2] Despite its shortcomings, due to the idealization of musical material and the identification of all music with the "work-concept," Ingarden's theory provides the basis for the inclusion of the spatiality of sound within the boundaries of the notion of the musical work. In order to embrace spatialization, the idea of the work has to be modified; this transformation is possible because "the work of music" is, as Lydia Goehr reminds us, an open concept (Goehr 1992).[3] The work-concept "sometimes

---

[2]The Polish text of Ingarden's essay bears an annotation that it had been written in: Paris 1928--Lwów 1933--Kraków 1957. A German version of this text was published in *Untersuchungen zur Ontologie der Kunst* (Tübingen 1962) and an English translation appeared in 1986. All references are to this translation, which, though criticized as "unclear and awkward" (Ferrara 1991: 168), provides a faithful rendition of Ingarden's thought.

[3]An open concept (1) does not correspond to fixed or static essences, (2) does not admit absolutely precise definitions, (3) is intensionally incomplete--unforseen situations

undergoes quite radical shifts in function and meaning, but it does not thereby lose its identity" (Goehr 1992: 93). My study of spatialization reveals the scope of conceptual changes necessary for the re-formulation of the idea of music to include its spatial characteristics. At the same time, it documents the continuing relevance of "works" in the domain of contemporary composition. The recognition of the spatial features of the musical work leads to a re-definition of music as a spatio-temporal art.

4.2.
Listening to music in space: a psychoacoustic account

Denis Smalley observes that "musical space is not empty and cannot be separated from its sounding content" (Smalley 1991: 123). This connection underlies the difficulty encountered in attempts to isolate spatiality from timbre and dynamics. In fact, according to Albert Bregman's theory of auditory scene analysis, such a separation cannot be made (Bregman 1990). Bregman explains how the auditory system segregates and integrates incoming signals into "auditory streams;" spatial cues play an important role in this process.[4] Bregman states that spatial corrrespondence is "one of the strongest scene-analysis principles;" the rule is that "acoustic components that can be localized as coming from the same position in space should be assigned to the same stream" (Bregman 1990: 293). He refutes a theory that only frequency and time are "indispensable attributes" in audition (cf. Kubovy 1981) and writes:

> It is true that a spatial difference alone cannot cause segregation of two simultaneous tones that go on and off at precisely the same time. However, as soon as the situation becomes more complex, two simultaneous frequency components differing only in place of origin can be heard as parts of two separate sounds at different spatial locations rather than uniting to form a sound heard between those locations. In addition, when a spatial difference is added

---

can lead to changes of definitions (Goehr 1992: 91). "Concepts are mutable and flexible in the light of their particular descriptive and prescriptive functions" (p. 93).

[4] The "auditory stream" is an auditory analogue to "object" in visual perception (Bregman 1990: 11).

to some other difference (say in frequency or in a match to a prior event in one ear), it greatly increases the amount of segregation.

(Bregman 1990: 293-294)

Bregman includes the tendency to segregate "sounds that come from different spatial locations" (p. 299) among the primitive, i.e. innate, principles of auditory analysis (in opposition to schema-based principles created through the mediacy of culture and learning).[5] He speculates that the spatial separation of a multiplicity of sounds prevents "the auditory system from computing certain dissonances between them" (p. 300). These observations illuminate the basic function of spatialization as described by composers: the clarification of complex textures by separating their various components. Spatial separation divides textures into distinct "streams" or layers (cf. Chapter III, section 3.2). The creation of a single stream with separated sources (e.g. virtual sound movement) is feasible, but more difficult.

Bregman points out the importance of conscious focus of attention, apparent in the so-called "cocktail party effect." Listeners immersed in complex sound fields (e.g. a noisy crowd at a cocktail party) are able to pick out sounds reaching them from one direction as more worthy of attention (e.g. words of their partner), and exclude other, simultaneous sounds (e.g. other conversations).[6] However, Bregman's praise for the usefulness of spatial cues in audition is not unqualified. He notices that reverberant environments, the presence of strong echoes, and the bending of sounds around obstacles cause a decrease in the precision of localization. He also warns about conflicting cues: if two sound events occur at the same point in space, their integration may depend on other cues (i.e. spectrum, envelope, common fate). Bregman concludes: "when the cues all agree, the outcome is a clear perceptual

---

[5]Incidentally, this distinction parallels the phenomenological separation of the two types of *Lebenswelt*, the pre-reflective ("natural") and the cultural (cf. Merleau-Ponty and Heelan discussed in Chapter I). The two types of auditory organization may be, at times, in conflict, or one may override the other.

[6]This effect is strongest for the frequency range around 1 kHz; below 400 Hz it noticeably worsens.

organization, but when they do not we can have a number of outcomes" (p. 302). Moreover, spatial cues are weaker than visual ones. In the so-called "ventriloquism effect," sounds originating as far as 30 degrees away from their apparent, visible source will be integrated with this source (p. 307). This occurrence is due to the importance of "world structure cues" in perception (p. 312): the coherence of visual and auditory stimuli, the assumption of the spatial permanency of sounds (sounds of similar spectral characteristic and close in time are probably related).

The fact that Bregman's theory of hearing embraces cognitive, not merely physiological, aspects of auditory perception determines its relevance for musicological research. However, his theory does not include a detailed account of the characteristics of spatial hearing; for this I turn to the research of Jens Blauert (1983).[7] Blauert reminds his readers that sound localization, spaciousness of the hall, etc., are features of sound images, that is percepts, not physical objects. He distinguishes two main categories of the perception of sound in space: (1) free-field perception (i.e. anechoic chamber, on a mountain-top) and (2) enclosed-space perception. In the first situation, the number of sound sources ranges from one to multiple; in enclosures, sound sources are always multiple because of the separation of the reflections off the walls of the hall from the original source (the reflections come from different directions, at different times, with transformed timbres; as such they are independent sources).

Free-field spatial hearing involves the perception of direction and distance. The acuity of directional hearing in the horizontal plane ("azimuth") is highest in the front of the listener and lowest at the sides. The acuity of directional hearing in the median plane ("elevation") is worse in all respects than in the horizontal plane. The perception of azimuth and elevation strongly depends on the familiarity with the sound

---

[7]Other studies of spatial perception include: Mills (1975), Rasch and Plomp (1982), Yost and Gourevitch (1987), Wenzel (1992). Particular issues are discussed by: Goad and Keefe (1992), Kendall (1992), Lakatos (1991), Lehnert and Blauert (1991), Meyer (1978), O'Leary and Rhodes (1984), Perrott and Musicant (1977), Rhodes (1987), Sheeline (1982), Toole and Olive (1988), Winckel (1973).

and its type.[8] Distance hearing is based on cues relating to sound intensity and delay. In the intermediate area of distances between 3 and 15 meters, the intensity decreases with increasing distance (by 20 dB when the distance is doubled). However, the perceived distance increases more slowly than the actual distance of the sound source. If a sound source is located more than 15 meters away from the listener, the attenuation of high frequencies by the air begins to be heard. This effect, depending on moisture and wind, is already audible at 10 kHz. It is possible, then, to create the impression of a greater distance by cutting high frequency components and decreasing the intensity of sounds. Composers have often used the effect of imitating distance through dynamics in instrumental music.[9] Spectral manipulations, however, are much rarer; they belong more to the domain of electroacoustics.

Free-field conditions are infrequent in musical practice.[10] Even outdoor performances often require acoustic environments with particular patterns of echoes, resonances, etc.[11] Performances of the majority of musical works take place in enclosed spaces. Here, the sounds produced by the performers are surrounded by a multitude of reflections arriving at the ears of the listener from various directions (Blauert 1983: 276).[12] Therefore, the listener is immersed in a diffuse sound field in

---

[8]Lateralization (the recognition of sound elevation and azimuth) depends on the type of sound, on the interaural differences, and other cues, e.g. the movement of the head which helps to distinguish sounds from the back and front. Blauert describes two mechanisms of lateralization based on (A) time shift below 1.6 kHz, and (B) time shift plus differences in intensity for sounds with strong components above 1.6 kHz.

[9]Cf. Mahler's *Symphony No. 2* (Chapter III).

[10]I do not know of any works designated for performance in an anechoic chamber or on a mountain top. However, the composition of "virtual spaces" for virtual reality systems may involve imitation of free-fields (Wenzel 1992).

[11]For instance, R. Murray Schafer's works designed for performances at wilderness lakes exploit the features of sound transmission over the surface of the water (cf. Chapter VIII).

[12]Early reflections are often integrated with the sound from the source; distinct, strong reflections form undesirable echoes; the sum of reflections creates reverberation.

which sound images lose their precise locatedness: "The primary auditory event merges into the reverberant auditory event in such a way that the primary event appears to disperse spatially" (p. 279). Blauert uses the term "the primary event" to denote the auditory counterpart of sounds emanating from the original sound source; the "reverberant event" arises from the summary perception of sound reflections. The perceptual appraisal of distance in enclosed spaces relies on the proportion of direct to reverberant sound as one of the most important cues. The manipulation of these proportions is accessible primarily to composers of electroacoustic music.

The perceptual evaluation of room acoustics is closely connected to the spatial, temporal and qualitative attributes of sound events. One may hear the spectral and temporal behaviour of the reverberation as well as the level and direction of incidence of early reflections. The presence of early lateral strong reflections (from the sides) creates the impression of the spaciousness of the hall (p. 282). This feature, despite its importance for acousticians and architects constructing new concert halls, has a very limited musical significance. Only composers of electroacoustic music may transform the impression of the spaciousness of the performance space. Others, however, frequently explore the *spaciousness* of auditory events; these events are perceived as being spread out in an extended region of space (either individual events of large extent, or multiple events occuring simultaneously in a segment of space). Blauert notices that the region of space occupied by auditory events is larger than that of their sources (and larger than in a free-field space); the size depends on the degree of coherence (p. 348). Weakly correlated signals give their listeners the impression of being completely enveloped by auditory events. According to Blauert, music in enclosed spaces is temporally incoherent, because of the differences of amplitude and phase between the direct signal and reflections from various directions. Therefore, in enclosed spaces, music is perceived in the form of broad, diffusely located images. Moreover, when the distance between the listener and the performers increases, the sonorities become more diffuse and spatially extended (p. 280). In addition, these features of sound images are strongly dependent on the type of primary sound sources (instruments, voices, loudspeakers); various instruments and their groupings "react" to the same physical space of the concert hall in a different manner (e.g. the sound image of the trumpet is more clearly localized than that of the organ or the orchestra).

Blauert's explanations illuminate Don Ihde's phenomenological analysis of listening in the concert hall, which he characterizes in terms of the "surroundability" of the sound field:

> If I hear Beethoven's Ninth Symphony in an acoustically excellent auditorium, I suddenly find myself immersed in sound which surrounds me. The music is even so penetrating that my whole body reverberates, and I may find myself absorbed to such a degree that the usual distinction between the sense of inner and outer is virtually obliterated.
>
> (Ihde 1976: 75)

This immersion in sound, which, for Ihde, implies forgetting about one's surroundings, is a characterstic feature of the listener's concrete spatio-temporal presence in an enclosed room filled with sounds. Blauert states that the effects he describes accompany all performances in enclosures; music-as-heard is both spatio-temporal and diffuse. The further the listener is from the orchestra, the less clear is the awareness of sound directions and localizations. Obviously, in this situation, the whole spatial reality may be bracketed out and music may be construed as "purely temporal." However, when composers consciously explore spatial aspects of music in their works (in spatialization) the human experience of space becomes a part of the artistic construct. The composers envision certain spatial experiences and notate their models, providing the performers with schemas of spatial images or the means for their realization. The actualization of these "intentional" images may or may not be possible. Therefore, the compositional intention differs from the psychoacoustic reality of performance and perception. In order to clarify the relationships between the various aspects of music (notated and performed) I turn to Roman Ingarden's phenomenology of art.

4.3.

Roman Ingarden's "work of music" revisited

Ingarden's preoccupation with the idea of the work of art is central to his phenomenological aesthetics (Rieser 1971/1986: 159). The philosopher was convinced that working out "an eidetic view of a general idea of a work of art and of the less general ideas of the works of the particular arts" should precede empirical-inductive studies of specific aesthetic issues.[13] Ingarden's work of art is an "intentional object," which requires for its existence a material basis (i.e. the score, book, canvas), and a constitution in "the minds of the creator as well as the receptive experiences of the enjoyer of art" (Rieser 1971/1986: 160). Rieser explains that "the intentionality of the work of art means that it has no independent existence like material objects, nor is it an ideal object like a triangle; it must have a material subsoil in tone, marble, ink spots, etc." (p. 163). The work of art is incomplete in itself and requires its concretization by the perceiving person (listener, reader). In addition, Ingarden sees most works of art (except the musical) as stratified. For instance, a poem consists of four strata: the sounds of the words, the meaning of the sentences, the schematized representation of objects, and the represented objects themselves.

Ingarden's definition of the musical work crowns an extensive discourse on the issue of its identity (the work is not the score, not the performance, not the perceptual experience, not the composer's idea; what is it, then?). In the philosopher's words,

> A musical work, understood as an artistic product of its composer, is first a schema designated by the score, second a determined multiplicity of possibilities designated by the areas of indeterminacy of the schematic product--each providing in realization one of the work's profiles. And each such profile may be realized within a certain class of identical, or at least similar, correct performances.
>
> (Ingarden 1958/1986: 150)

---

[13]Lecture in Amsterdam, 13 March 1970, quoted by Max Rieser (Rieser 1971/1986: 159). Ingarden borrows the term "eidetic," which is coined from the Greek "eidos" (idea, essence) from Husserl's notion of "eidetic reduction," fundamental in constituitive phenomenology (Husserl 1913).

This definition articulates the co-constitution of the work by the imprecisely notated score and concrete performances, realizing various aspects of the notated work. The "work itself remains like an ideal boundary at which the composer's intentional conjectures of creative acts and the listeners act of perception aim" (p. 119).[14] It is one and the same, "in contrast to the many concretions in specific performances." Moreover--and Ingarden is very adamant about this point--the musical work

> never attains the status of concrete sounds because these sounds are spatially and temporarily individual objects, whereas a musical work is a supraindividual and supratemporal structure, its individuality being purely qualitative.
> (Ingarden 1958/1986: 120)

The musical work may not be experienced as such, only in one of its profiles, articulated through a performance.[15] the lacunae in notation allow for the introduction of ornaments, changes in instrumentation, tempo, etc. Notice that Ingarden's definition may be applied equally well to Bach's *Kunst der Fuge* which does not have a "performing means structure," (term from Levinson 1980) and to Boulez's *Rituel* which specifies the positions of all instrumentalists on the stage (cf. Chapter III). Yet, Ingarden transcends the distinction between the work and performance; he notices that each performance may be "actualized" in many different ways by the members of the audience.[16] The individual, unrepeatable "concretion" of the performance occurs in a unique segment of lived time and depends on the listener's experience,

---

[14] Jean-Jacques Nattiez's semiology disperses the work's being "between three spheres, in the *interaction* between its symbolic components, as a total musical fact; as poietic strategies, a resultant trace, and esthesic strategies unleashed by that trace" (Nattiez 1989: 70). A scheme on p. 73 distinguishes between: poietic process--score--musical result--esthesic process. The score is interpreted in performance; the poietic and esthesic processes aim at creating or contemplating the score and its sonorous interpretation.

[15] In Ingarden's theory, the musical work "is supraparticular and supratemporal, not ideal" (p. 64).

[16] He introduces a "differentiation between the work of music, its performance, and its concretion" (p. 20).

knowledge, mood, attention, etc. (p. 66).[17] The same acoustic sequence may lead to different concretions. These perceptual images vary even if, for instance, the same person repeatably listens to the same recording. The physical sound sequence is identical in each repetition, but the perception changes.[18]

Here, Ingarden notices the importance of the acoustic perspective on the music heard; if the listener walks around the hall during a musical performance, the changes of position transform the sound image that she or he hears. The perceptual transformation also results from shifts in voluntary attention and concentration (ibidem). Nonetheless, most music implies an ideal, optimal position for the listener; it should be heard from "a certain distance" not from one kilometer away (p. 20). In the philosopher's opinion, "every work determines a certain ideal system of auditory aspects to be experienced by the listener" (p. 20). Yet, the work differs from these aspects as much as it differs from its performance.

According to Ingarden, the work and the performance belong to two distinct ontological categories; the work is an object ("a purely intentional object," p. 117), the performance a process (p. 16).[19] The work is "a model and a measure" for the performers, an unattainable ideal. The performance occurs at a determined point in space and time (p. 11). In contrast, the "work of music possesses no defined spatial localization. No such localization is specified either by the creative acts of the

---

[17]Ingarden models the idea of the "concretely experienced time" on Bergson's "duration" (Bergson 1889/1950; cf. Chapter I). He is also indebted to Husserl's phenomenology of time-consciousness (Husserl 1928).

[18]For Ingarden, a recording is a full definition of a work, a real object, not an intentional object like the work itself (p. 116-119). The recording captures one of the multitude of possible performances, in which everything is "concretized" (p. 119).

[19]"All the movements of the musical work itself exist together in a completed whole" while "each individual performance of a musical work spreads itself in time" (Ingarden 1958/1986: 16). Ingarden's ontology distinguishes three types of entities (in respect to their temporal permanence): objects subsisting in time (things), processes revealing the continuity of change and events which occur instantaneously (temporal moments).

composer or by the score" (p. 18).[20] The work can be performed anywhere, at any time, but it is "not a real event lasting during the performance" (p. 55). Here, Ingarden clearly articulates the belief that "pure or disembodied sound" (term from Ihde 1976) is the material of music. Even though "sounds, tones, and sound-constructs of a higher order . . . constitute an essential element of the work" (p. 42), sounds as "processes or objects persisting and taking place here and now in real time and constituting the elements of specific performances do not belong to the musical work itself" (p. 42-43). Ingarden also notices the "ecstatic" character of the perceptual experience of music (cf. Ihde 1979, Lippman 1952). While listening to a composition "we seem involuntarily to ignore the individual mode of existence of the currently occurring individual concrete sounds" (p. 64). Listeners "commune with something complete in itself" (p. 56).[21]

The supratemporality of the musical work does not preclude the existence of a unique, internal, temporal ordering within this work. Time in music is "structurally and qualitatively organized and the type and character of that organization depend on what sound structures fill out a particular movement or larger period of the work as a whole" (p. 76). According to Ingarden, this "quasi-temporal structure" which "does not enter into the time-continuum of the real world" (p. 77) is an essential feature of each musical work. He explains that "both its supratemporality and its quasi-temporal structure remove the musical work from the real world and give it a self-contained character" (p. 79).

The fixed temporal form of the musical work may exist because of this work's articulation in the material basis of the score, "a schematic construct with areas of indeterminateness" (p. 117). The score is a sign system, an arrangement of symbols denoting pitch and rhythm, with additional information provided in verbal expressions

---

[20]In a work of music "there are no features or elements that in any way establish its specific location in real space or constitute that location" (p. 61).

[21]Yet, the philosopher claims that we cannot hear the work in its schematic shape and we cannot even imagine it this way (p. 141).

(p. 39). The score designates the work and instructs how to actualize it in performance. Yet, for Ingarden, the score is not a part of the work, which consists of sounds and sound constructs. In addition, Ingarden purges the work of music from texts, programs, images, representations, evocation of feelings, etc. (pp. 50, 107). For him, all these elements merely *belong* to the work, they are not a part of it. Here, he reveals his allegiance to the formalist school of thought (he even cites Hanslick's *Vom Musikalisch-Schönen*; 1854/1986).[22] Since the notation is also extramusical, only the bare structure of pure sounds remains. Having stripped music of all the "inessentials," the philosopher concludes that the musical work does not have a stratified structure and differs from the works of other arts.[23]

Nevertheless, Ingarden distinguishes sonic and non-sonic components within the work of music.[24] Over and above a layer of tone constructs, that is, the sonic components,[25] the musical work includes: (1) quasi-temporal structure, (2) movement, (3) the musical space in which the movement occurs (cf. Chapter II), (4) emotional qualities, (5) aesthetically valuable qualities, (6) qualities of the values themselves (pp.

---

[22] While Ingarden silently assumes the universal validity of absolute music, this idea has had many critics. Jean-Jacques Nattiez criticizes Hanslick's position from a semiological vantage point (Nattiez 1989: 109-110). Lydia Goehr points out the existence of the "separability principle" underlying the detachment of art from life (Goehr 1992: 158) while Carl Dahlhaus dicusses "the principle of aesthetic autonomy" which frees music from its social functions and historical contexts (Dahlhaus 1977/1983: 146).

[23] He lists several conditions for a stratified structure: (1) the existence of diverse elements (in literature--sounds, meanings, objects); (2) homogeneous elements should combine into a layer of a higher order, without (3) losing distinctiveness. Finally, (4) an organic totality of style should emerge (p. 50).

[24] Adam Czerniawski translates Ingarden's "dzwiekowe i nie-dzwiekowe skladniki" (Ingarden 1958: 235) as "sounding and non-sounding elements" of the musical work. I prefer the more accurate translation of "sonic and non-sonic."

[25] The sound constructs are complex agglomerates of various features (p. 87).

88-104).[26] The list of non-sonic components contains what Ingarden has already relegated to the domain of the "extramusical," for instance the congruence between form and content, the beauty and ugliness of timbres, the qualities of lyricism or pathos, etc. This is one of Ingarden's inconsistences: he is convinced that the musical work contains just one stratum, yet he discovers a two-fold structure in this stratum.

Ingarden's theory locates music in the aesthetic domain of pure Art; this thesis has obvious socio-cultural limitations.[27] For the philosopher, neither dance, nor music of religious ceremonies (e.g. African drumming) are music in the strict sense: "The dance as ritual phenomenon or human expression should be classified with extra-artistic phenomena, birdsong and the like" (p. 46).[28] He also errs in considering improvisation and the oral repertory of folk-music in terms of works.[29] In addition, Ingarden expects the presence of certain aesthetic values in the musical work (e.g. formal coherence and unity); thus, for instance, he claims that temporal discontinuity

---

[26]The philosopher borrows the notions of *movement* and *musical space* from Ernst Kurth's *Musikpsychologie* (1931).

[27]In Poland, Zofia Lissa criticized Ingarden's theory of the musical work from the Marxist point of view and supported her own definition with a full range of examples from folk music, through improvisation, to aleatoricism and electronic music (Lissa 1966/1975, 1968/1975). Lissa points out that Ingarded ignores the cultural aspects of musical works, such as their belonging to socially defined genres, their philosophical and cultural contexts, and the conditions of their reception (Lissa 1966/1975: 173). She stresses the chronological, geographical, social and aesthetic boundaries of Ingarden's theory (Lissa 1966/1975); she also argues that an all-embracing concept of work cannot exist because of its historical groundedness and changeability (Lissa 1968/1975).

[28]According to Ingarden, dance music "arousing in dancers a certain passion for expression through movement" is particularly unmusical (p. 46). The disembodiment of music could not have a more eloquent advocate. For a critique of this position see McClary (1991). Ingarden's exclusion of African music from the domain of works is not consistent (cf. pp. 44-45, 87).

[29]According to Goehr, the disregard for conceptual differences between a work and an improvisation is a clear case of "conceptual imperialism" (Goehr 1992: 245). Here, she repeats the criticism by Zofia Lissa (1966/1975).

places a composition at the "borderline between a musical work and a sequence of uncoordinated sounds" (p. 93).[30]

Despite these shortcomings, however, Ingarden does reveal an awareness of the mutability of the work of music as it evolves in historical time.[31] He notices that the work undergoes an evolution as a result of changing opinions of the musical public. In a given country at a given time "a single intersubjective dominant aesthetic object" exists (p. 155).[32] This object, that is, one of the work's profiles, may be modified because of the intentional nature of the work itself. The awareness of the historical groundedness of the musical work anticipates Goehr's vision of the work of music as an open concept.[33]

Ingarden's two-fold definition of the musical work, requiring for its existence both the score and a multitude of performances interpreting the notation in a variety of ways (cf. the quote from p. 150 cited above) has many advantages. Ingarden does not identify the work with its notation and he does not reduce music to pitch-time relationships. He considers the "schematic" character of notation as a virtue: it allows for many different performances, which interpret and realize the same work in a multitude of ways. Even the limitation to purely instrumental, non-programmatic

---

[30]Contemporary music has seen many challenges to this belief, e.g. *Freeman Etudes* by John Cage (1977-80/1989-90) which are discontinuous in perception, but also fully notated and potentially variable in performance--as Ingarden's "works."

[31]Such awareness is absent in other "supra-temporal" theories of music and the musical work (Goodman 1976, Levinson 1980).

[32]I do not think that the existence of the work separate from the score and from its performances is "projective or fictional" (expression from Goehr 1992: 106).

[33]Yet, Goehr explicitly opposes the supratemporal existence of the "musical work" as such; she claims that such an object of music is found "through projection or hypostatization" (Goehr 1992: 174). In her book about "the imaginary museum of musical works," Goehr focuses on the central role of the work concept in Western music. The existence of this supratemporal museum has been noticed earlier, for instance by Carl Dahlhaus: "the musical repertory emerged from the idea of the 'classical' work towering above history" (Dahlhaus 1977/1983: 148).

music may be seen in a positive light. As Don Ihde writes, "wordless music, in its sonorous incarnation, when compared to language is 'opaque,' as nothing is shown through the music. The music presents itself; it is a dense embodied presence." (Ihde 1979: 158). The adoption of Ingarden's constraint makes possible a description of the "embodied presence" of music as a spatio-temporal reality without complications arising from the music's theatrical, narrative, or textual aspects.[34] These features of Ingarden's theory enable me to accomodate it to the field of contemporary music involving spatialization.

The notion of "the musical work" has a continuing relevance in this domain. The scores, that is the notational schemas of spatialized compositions, usually include spatial designs and features which should be realized in performance. Even compositions with large areas of indeterminacy (e.g. works by Lucier, Cage) often imply the presence of a certain spatio-temporal framework (e.g. the presence and actions of the performer) and reveal the composers' intention to view the products of their imagination as "works" (cf. the discussion of Lucier's ideas in Chapter III).

Here, I develop two aspects of Ingarden's concept of the musical work: the idea of *sound-construct* and the notion of *quasi-temporal structure*. Ingarden identifies the basic material of music with pure sound, not with pitch.[35] Every work of music consists of a chain of successive sound-constructs which "possess various properties of melody, rhythm, harmony, agogics, dynamics, and coloring" (p. 86).[36] These complex entities pass one into another and form the "sound base" of the work on

---

[34] I do not adhere to the "absolutist" school of thought; on the contrary, I consider pictorial and narrative aspects of music as essential. Nevertheless, the adoption of Ingarden's theory suits my purpose of describing the spatio-temporal features of sound as musical material. Here, the theory itself is seen as schematic and containing lacunae which may be completed in various ways.

[35] Nonetheless, he acknowledges the primacy of melody, rhythm and harmony in structuring the musical work (p. 87).

[36] Here, Ingarden refers to a classification of the elements of music in *Formy Muzyczne* by Józef Chominski, a Polish musicologist.

which the various non-sonic qualities and constructs are superimposed (p. 83-4). The notation designates these constructs imprecisely, while the performance realizes their concrete images by completing the notational schema in a particular way.

The sound-constructs may be described as "virtual" and may include spatial position, extent, and movement among their features. Albert Bregman describes how composers create "chimeric" or "virtual" sounds from a juxtaposition of several distinct instrumental sonorities (e.g. the fusion of a drum roll, a clash of the cymbal and a woodwind click performed simultaneously; Bregman 1990: 460). These virtual sounds possess a variety of "emergent properties" which do not belong to any of the elemental sounds. Bregman writes that

> the virtual source in music plays the same perceptual role as our perception of a real source does in natural environments. It provides a sense of an entity that endures for some period of time (perhaps only briefly) and serves as a center of description.
>
> (Bregman 1990: 460)

He comments that music often tries to "fool the auditory system" into hearing fictions (p. 457), and that the "sonic objects of music derive only in a very indirect way from the real instruments that are playing" (p. 459). These statements illuminate the virtuality of music which manifests itself in certain types of spatialization. A sound image with a virtual extent may arise when listening to spatially separated musicians simultaneously playing the same material (cf. Brant's theory and practice, Chapters III, VI). The image of a moving sound may be created by distant musicians playing sounds of identical pitch and timbre successively (cf. Stockausen and Xenakis, Chapters III, V, VII). These forms of spatialization reveal the fact that many contemporary composers do not work with pitch-class or pitch-and-time schemata: they compose virtual sound images only imperfectly approximated in notation. The composers specify seating plans for their works in order to evoke certain aural images through the position of the sound sources and their interactions. They require the performers to produce a series of sounds (i.e. physical occurrences) in the hope of achieving a series of sound images (i.e. auditory events) as a result."[37] The difficulty is to imagine what the listener would hear when a particular musical action happens.

The second aspect of Ingarden's theory that may be revised to include spatialization is the "quasi-temporal structure" of the musical work. This structure is "quasi" and not fully temporal because temporal relationships encoded in the score are approximated in a different way in each performance. By extending Ingarden's terminology, it is possible to speak of a fixed *quasi-spatial structure* in music.[38] This structure is indicated by the instrumentation which usually assumes certain acoustical conditions for the performance (e.g. a background of silence and an appropriate size and quality of performance space) as well as standards of performer placement (e.g. soloists and groups centered on the stage, facing the audience). The relational character of the quasi-temporal and quasi-spatial aspects of the musical work becomes more apparent when we think about the identity of the work in different performances. It is not the physically spatial and temporal features that are preserved from one performance to the next, but their schematic outlines fixed in the musical notation. The absence of indications about performing forces deprives the music of its quasi-spatial structure and limits it to the abstract contour of pitch and time (Bach's *Kunst der Fuge* is a classic case of this occurrence).

Music for one instrument, such as the piano, has only a weakly-manifested *latent quasi-spatial structure*. Spatially speaking, there is no difference between a prelude by Debussy and one by Chopin, if both are performed on the same instrument in the same concert hall (or, more appropriately for Chopin, an aristocratic salon) and

---

[37] In current psychoacoustic practice "sound" denotes the physical event, while "sound image," or "auditory event," or "auditory stream" describe its psychoacoustic counterpart (Blauert used the second term in 1983; Bregman the third in 1990). "Sound" in my text draws from both meanings; it refers to the idealized image envisioned by the composer and schematically notated in the score. This type of "sound" is, to use Ingarden's terminology, an "intentional object" and, as such, is not strictly perceptual.

[38] *Spatial design* is synonymous to *quasi-spatial structure*.

if the dynamic levels are similar.[39] Obviously, a standard placement of audience and performer is assumed; we should not forget, however, that in certain works for a solo instrument the performer moves around the concert hall or the audience around the instrumentalist. In these circumstances the structure of the work is *quasi-spatial*.

Chamber and orchestral music has a full *quasi-spatial structure* when the seating plan given by the composer differs from the conventional one, when the audience or the performers are required to move, and when there are several ensembles of performers dispersed in the hall or on the stage. Conversely, chamber and orchestral music has a *latent quasi-spatial structure* when the ensemble placement is standard, well-known and does not have to be specified. Most of the music composed for standard instrumental groups takes for granted certain types of spatial relationships inherent in the kind and size of the ensemble. The distinction between chamber and symphonic music, for instance, implies musical differences resulting from the various number of performers and the nature of the interactions of the instrumental sounds with the acoustic properties of the concert hall (cf. Chapter III). Spatial relationships of positions of and distances between various instruments and groups, the necessity of balancing their sonorities, the influence of the acoustic properties of concert halls on the perceived sounds of voices and instruments--all these are taken into account in the instrumentation. It is not surprising that Berlioz, author of the *Traité d'instrumentation et d'orchestration moderne* (Berlioz 1844) is also one of the important pioneers of spatialization (e.g. *Requiem Op. 5*).

---

[39]Timbre and dynamics are linked to the spatial qualities of sound (cf. Rasch and Plomp 1982; Bregman 1990).

4.4.
Towards a definition of spatialization

There are several difficulties in proposing a clear definition of spatialization. The distinction between works with quasi-spatial structure (unusual seating plans, movement, ensemble dispersion) and latent quasi-spatial structure (standard seating plans) may be a source of concern. If what is latently spatial can be termed "spatialized," the definition is too inclusive. Spatialization relates to compositions in which the orchestra is split into separate ensembles; nevertheless it suffices to have a large number of divisi parts to obtain a spatially extended sonority, varied within the confines of the stage. In this case, spatialization does not relate to the measurable aspects of the performance space (distances, angles, symmetries), but rather is expressed through internal, microscopic differentiation in the orchestral sonorities.[40] In other words, space is linked to texture, a tactile (in metaphorical sense) and--again--spatial entity. This aspect of spatialization should not be excluded from the definition.

Another difficulty in defining spatialization stems from the difference between this phenomenon and traditional polychorality. Polychoral music involves more than one choir or ensemble without specifying its spatial position in the performance space.[41] Spatial aspects of such works are limited to the division of the performers into separated ensembles; this distribution in space implies unspecified mutual distances. At the same time, the musical interactions of these separate groups can be quite sophisticated. The label of polychorality can be attached to those 20th-century

---

[40]Pierre Boulez, for example, has criticized the traditional set-up of the orchestra subdivided into a series of homogeneous groups, and proposed to split these groups in order to create a new fusion of orchestral sonorities (Boulez 1976: 100; cf. Chapter III).

[41]However, polychoral compositions for specific buildings, such as San Marco Basilica in Venice, often require the location of the performers around or above the listeners (e.g. on the balconies of the Basilica); this is one of the reasons for including polychorality in the domain of spatialization.

works that include a number of large ensembles placed separately on the stage. These groups of performers either do not have a specific placement plan or are given several (two or three) optional positions on the stage.[42] Here, important spatial features of sound direction, distance have no significance. What matters is that the distance between the various groups of performers should provide a degree of separation. Nonetheless, I consider polychorality a type of spatialization.

In addition, I would like to clarify the distinction between spatialized music and musical theatre. Reinhard J. Sacher (1985) maintains that all spatialization of music is essentially theatrical. He argues that when the performers surround the audience, visual cues tend to dominate over their aural counterparts. This is, however, a matter of the voluntary focus of attention by the listener or viewer: a conventional concert may also be perceived as a form of theatre. Spatialized music and musical theatre are distinct: all theatre is spatial but not necessarily spatialized, and not all spatialization is theatrical. However, the consideration of music in terms of the gestural aspects of performance (common in France, also in reference to electroacoustic music) implies its transformation into a form of theatre. Here, the attention shifts to the origins of the sounds in human activities; music becomes a performance art.[43]

Finally, I would like to point out that it is possible to "spatialize" compositions which do not explicitly require it in performance. This form of *spatialization* may transform real instruments into virtual ones, for instance in recording. Marco Stroppa describes the electroacoustic transformation of the sound image of the piano from a

---

[42] Henry Brant, "totally commited" to spatialization strongly criticizes such optional arrangements: "From my point of view this is like saying 'play C# and D, if not, play some other note.'" (Brant 1992: 6).

[43] I use this term in its current, North-American sense; performance artists are neither mimes, nor dancers, nor musicians, nor actors, nor poets, but play several (or all) of these roles simultaneously. In a wider sense, "performance art" denotes every art requiring live performers: theatre, dance, classical music, jazz, happening, etc.

point-like entity into a spatially extended object.[44] In the new image, each pitch has a definite spatial location on the axis from left to right (from low to high pitches), as if the keyboard has "exploded" into the two-dimensional space of stereophony.[45] Incidentally, this transformation of the spatial image reflects a change in aural perspective: instead of imitating the impression of the distant listener who hears the piano at a point "out there," such a recording presents the auditory image of the performer who faces the instrument at a close distance. In the area of electroacoustics, the term "spatialization" often appears in the sense described here, that is in reference to making spatial something that was not originally composed spatially (cf. Haller 1972). Nonetheless, I prefer to limit this term to the "poietic" aspect of music-making ("poietic" in the sense introduced by Nattiez, 1987/1990).

Spatialization of music means, then, the compositional introduction of the *quasi-spatial structure*.[46] *In this dissertation, the term spatialized music refers to music with a quasi-spatial structure defined by the composer in the score or in another medium of sound coding (digital or analog recording, specific software). This quasi-spatial structure can assume different forms, including ensemble dispersion, the movement of sounds, performers or audience, and the juxtaposition and interaction of real and virtual sound sources. The presence of spatialization can be recognized in every situation in which the spatial positions of the sound sources (separation into groups; directions and distances) and the acoustic quality of the performance space have compositional importance.*

My definitions of spatialization and quasi-spatial structure relate to the composed space of the musical work. Here, I support Ingarden's thesis that *the work is identical neither with the score nor with an individual performance. The work*

---

[44]Private communication, IRCAM, Paris, August 1992 (cf. Stroppa 1991, 1992).

[45]Here, stereophonic image is two-dimensional. However, stereophony may involve more than an imaginary plane: in Chapter V, I describe the expansion of stereo image into three dimensions by means of the spatializer.

[46] The notion of the *quasi-spatial structure* is discussed in section 4.3:

consists of a series of idealized aural images that are approximated in the score and instantiated in performance. Therefore, the spatialized composition contains quasi-- spatio-temporal sound-constructs organized in a quasi--spatio-temporal framework. For reasons of convenience, I usually omit the affix "quasi" in the text.[47] Composers of spatialized music assume that the ideal listener is blessed with a perfect location in the concert hall, and endowed with a perfect hearing ability in both the psychosomatic and cultural sense (i.e. the capability to be attentive to various aspects of music at once). The listener's experience is spatio-temporal while the music is "embodied"--not in the sense of the performers's bodily gestures, but in relation to the perceptual fullness of the listener who is located--not just literally--at the centre. The spatial orientation of the listener matters; the differences between various directions (front--back, left--right) have musical significance. The music, in Don Ihde's words, "enlivens one's own body. To listen is to be dramatically engaged in a bodily listening which 'participates' in the movement of the music" (Ihde 1976: 159). Yet, for the composer, the listener is not a real person, but an idealization necessary for the creation of virtual sound images which should be heard in space. The extent of this idealization depends on the composer's knowledge of acoustics, psychoacoustics, technology, etc. The listener might be expected to hear what is inaudible; this is a real danger in the practice of spatialization.[48]

In the third chapter, I describe three main aspects of musical spatiality: the role of the acoustic environment, the bodily experience of the performers and the listeners, and the placement of the musicians in the performance space. I also point out that the sonorous reality of music is always spatio-temporal. Ingarden's theory reveals how this reality has been removed from the realm of musical works, which he defined as supratemporal intentional objects, not spatio-temporal, real processes. Yet, his precise

---

[47]Since the temporality of music hardly needs to be argued for, I frequently use "spatial" instead of "spatio-temporal."

[48]For an analysis of the perceptual difficulties caused by spatialization in the domain of computer music see Begault (1986).

analysis of the ontological status of the work, score and performance has enabled me to add the quasi-spatial structure to the list of non-sonic components of music. Music is spatialized when its spatio-temporal reality becomes a focus of compositional attention, through the choice of room acoustics, through the location of performers and listeners within this space, through the design of their movements, and through the articulation of their experiences.

Ingarden's distinctions between the score and the performance, and his emphasis on the different ways in which the composer, the performer and the listener relate to the musical work, articulate the existential complexity of music. The three-fold relationship between people and musical artefacts reflect the divisions in Jean-Jacques Nattiez's scheme of tripartition (Nattiez 1990: 73). This scheme separates the poietic, neutral and esthesic levels of music. The poietic process results in the creation of the score, which is interpreted in performance (musical result); the listeners relate both to the score and the performance (esthesic level).

Thus, the ontological schema of musical processes and objects includes five levels, each pointing towards the "intentional" work from a different perspective: (1) the compositional process (idea), (2) the score (notational representation), (3) the performance (action), (4) the sonorous results of the performers actions (sounds), (5) the perception and cognition (auditory images and ideas).[49] Music may be spatial at all these levels, involving imaginary, symbolic, geometric, acoustic and auditory types of space. However, theories of "musical works" often limit music to non-spatial ideas and their notations (levels 1 and 2). The expanded definition of the musical work,

---

[49]I developed this schema on the basis of Ingarden's theory in my M.A. thesis in musicology (Harley 1986). Jean Jacques Nattiez uses a similar design in his discussion of "the musical work" (Nattiez 1987/1990). According to Prof. Bo Alphonce, a similar scheme has been introduced by Ingmar Bengtsson in the 1970s. Bengtsson's theory divides the process of musical communication, directed from the producer (composer), to the receiver (listener), into six stages: (1) composer, (2) notation, (3) performer, (4) instrument, (5) physical sound, (6) listener (Bengtsson 1973: 23). At each stage, Bengtsson considers the role of "feed-back," tradition, conventions, etc., so that the process becomes quite sophisticated and is not equated with a simple transmission of a musical message.

including spatialization among its features, indicates the possibility of compositional structuring of the spatio-temporal reality of the performance, sound, and perception (levels 3-5).

Compositional ideas (the poietic level in Nattiez's tripartition) may relate to different modes of musical spatiality, i.e. to notational, geometric, auditory, and symbolic spaces. The score, the result of the compositonal process, is in itself a material object of a definite spatial extent and temporal permanence.[50] Each page of the score may become a two-dimensional space, the domain of musical geometry and the spatial symbolism of notation (this type of spatiality is static, i.e. permanent in time). The performance has many spatial characteristics. First, each performer explores his or her own physical space of action while playing the instrument. Second, the musicians interact with the acoustics of the performance space (reverberation, blending). Third, they are located at specific spatial positions which determine their mutual distances and directions, as well as their distances from the audience. Finally, the performance is an interpretation of the spatial ideas of the composer (this is the most important feature for the "work-concept"). The creation and formation of the physical sounds which arise from the musicians' actions leads to the fourth level of the spatio-temporal reality of musical matter (sound). Here, the difference between the physical and the perceptual features of sound has to be kept in mind. The perception and cognition of auditory, notational, and symbolic spaces crown this schema.

Musical works, usually regarded as supratemporal objects contemplated as existing in themselves, here reveal their human orientation. They create spaces to be experienced and inhabited. As Martin Heidegger writes, "to be a work means to set up a world. . . . A work, by being a work, makes space for that spaciousness" (Heidegger 1950/1971: 44).

---

[50]Lydia Goehr avoids the difficulty of identifying the notated form of the work with a particular, physical object by talking about "score copies" rather than the scores (Goehr 1992).

CHAPTER V

SPATIAL DESIGNS IN CONTEMPORARY MUSIC

5.1.

Classification of spatial designs

As Bas van Fraassen observes in his introduction to the philosophy of time and space, "with respect to space, it is not easy even to make a plausible preliminary list of basic relations" (van Fraassen 1985: 4). The task of classifying all possible spatial designs in music is equally daunting. In this chapter, I introduce a new classification scheme for spatialized music, limiting a potential infinity of patterns to a few manageable, basic models (cf. Table V-1). This typology reconciles theoretical premises (i.e. the number of dimensions that a space may have) with practical considerations (i.e. compositional preferences of specific designs, the variety of types existing in spatialized music).

Among the theories of spatialization discussed in the third chapter, only one, by Pierre Boulez (1963), includes a rudimentary classification of spatial designs. Boulez divides spatial distribution into static and mobile types and considers realizations of various kinds of symmetry and asymmetry within the static layout of musicians. I find his categories of staticity and mobility quite inspiring, although I focus on the movement of performers and audiences, instead of the virtual motion of sounds as Boulez has done. His categories of symmetry are less useful for the purposes of classifying spatialized compositions, because symmetric designs may appear in different structural types (in virtual space, on the stage, around the audience etc.). Boulez's scheme is limited to instrumental music with a static audience in a concert hall, while a general typology should cover the whole field of spatialization as defined in Chapter IV. Finally, his perspective is that of a composer contemplating the range of possibilities, while I plan to do justice to the varied aural perspectives of the listeners.

The classification of spatial designs proposed here, is inspired by the image "from point to sphere," from music without spatial characteristics, perceived as if it resounded from a point (i.e. as if it were purely temporal, with zero spatial dimensions), to the full three-dimensionality of sounds surrounding the listeners from all sides.[1] Since the point has no volume, it is bodiless, it may easily represent the situation in which the spatiality of music is irrelevant. The sphere symbolizes the opposite. Music is perceived in the entirety of its spatio-temporal presence surrounding the listeners with a multi-directional pattern of sounds.[2] The typologies of patterns in "real sound-space" (no. 4 in Table V-1) and in "virtual sound-space" (no. 5 in Table V-1) reflect this organizational scheme.

As I point out in Chapter IV, spatialized music is really "spatio-temporal" not "spatial." The categories of spatialization may seem to belong outside of time, but their realization is always temporal. For instance, the perceptual experience of

---

[1]This typology of spatial designs in music is based on the principle of an increasing number of dimensions, from zero to three. I borrowed this idea from a mathematical theory of dimensions (Engelking 1977). Engelking's topological study reveals the multidimensionality of mathematical spaces, with the number of dimensions varying from zero (e.g. point), through one (e.g. line segment), two (e.g. square), three (e.g. cube), "n" (e.g. multidimensional form), to an infinity of dimensions (Engelking 1977: 11-14, 74). This scheme was also helpful for my analysis of ideas of "musical space" and spatial representations of music in Chapter II. However, the existence of fractal dimensions of various sizes in mathematics (e.g. a curved line that fills in a plane and has a dimension between 1 and 2; cf. Mandelbrot 1982) suggests that spatial dimensions of a similar complexity may exist also in music.

[2]Actually, the image of the sphere is an idealization implying a stationary audience located within a spherical enclosure, or a single listener limited by his or her hearing range which extends equally in all directions (Ihde 1976). The standard concert hall does not create conditions for such equidistant location of sound sources.

musical layers originating from different spatial locations involves the awareness of their succession and simultaneity. Space may be experienced only in time, and time only in space.

As the second "abstract" criterion for my typology I use the number of independent groups of musicians separated in space. At first, I tried to order the various designs according to the increasing number of ensembles or performers. While collecting examples of spatialized compositions, however, I noticed that the difference between 4 and 5 groups of instrumentalists is less important than the pattern of their location in space, e.g. on the stage or dispersed among the audience. A different number of ensembles may articulate the same structural category of surrounding the audience or interspersing the musicians and the listeners. Therefore, my classification of spatial designs reflects the divisions present in the repertory of spatialized music instead of following a rigid scheme of the number of groups of performers which are separated in space (2, 3, 4, 5, 6, etc.).

Several factors have a bearing on the classification of musical-spatial designs. Firstly, these designs are not purely geometrical as they are realized in sound.[3] "Space" in music is neither empty, nor absolute, nor homogeneous; it is revealed through the spatial attributes of sound matter. Therefore, various types of sound-sources should be included in the classification. Secondly, the human auditory perspective constitutes an essential element of spatial arrangements. If, for instance, groups of musicians are scattered in the hall, their distribution among listeners is more important perceptually than their exact balance of timbre and volume.[4] Since the performance and perception of spatialized music takes place within certain acoustic environments and the choice of these conditions may be part of a composition, the typology should include the appropriate criterion (no. 1 in Table V-1). Moreover, even the same acoustic environment may be perceived from different auditory

---

[3] For this reason I abandoned the initial plan to use the arrangement of Platonic bodies (tetrahedron, cube, etc.) as an organizing principle for musical-spatial designs.

[4] I locate all such patterns in one category (no. 4.5 in Table V-1).

perspectives which vary because of the mobility of performers and listeners (no. 3 in Table V-1).

Table V-1: Classification of spatial designs

1. Acoustic environments

E-1. Enclosed space of the concert hall
E-2. Enclosed space of any other kind
E-3. Open air (different acoustic backgrounds)
E-4. Variable space (mobile performers and audiences)
E-5. Private, virtual space (headphones)

2. Sound-space types

A. Real sound-space (with vocal-instrumental sound sources);
B. Virtual sound-space (with electroacoustic sound sources);
C. Mixed sound-space (with sound sources of both kinds).

3. Categories: static or mobile performers and/or audience

I. Static performers and audience;
II. Mobile performers with static audience;
III. Static performers with mobile audience;
IV. Mobile performers and audience.

4. Selected designs in real sound-space (type A, setting I)

4.1. Two ensembles in dialogue or antiphony.
4.2. Several ensembles placed on the stage.
4.3. Three more groups placed symmetrically around the audience.
4.4. A mixture of orchestra and public on one spatial plane (the audience is 'inside' the music).
4.5. Several groups dispersed in various patterns on the stage, around and in-between the audience and at various levels within the whole three-dimensional performance space.

> Table V-1: Classification of spatial designs, continued.
>
> 5. Selected designs in virtual sound-space (type B)
>
> 5.1. One point source;
> 5.2. Stereophony;
> 5.3. Quadrophony;
> 5.4. Multi-loudspeaker projection systems.

From the acoustic point of view, there is a difference if one listens to music in a concert hall, any other space, such as that of the home, during an open air concert, while changing one's surroundings, or via the headphones[5] (cf. the five acoustic environments in the classification).[6] If such an environment is specified by the composer who forbids the performance of the music otherwise, it belongs to the composition. Examples of this type of spatialization may be found in works by John Tavener (the requirement of at least 6 seconds of reverberation for *Ultimos Ritos*) and R. Murray Schafer (the choice of a small, wooded lake as the site of *Music for Wilderness Lake*, 1979).

Once the "where" of the music's performance has been dealt with, the question

---

[5] Headphones create virtual sound images inside the listener's head ("head space") or illusory images surrounding the listener ("virtual reality"). For "inside-the-head locatedness" of auditory images see Blauert (1983: 131-137). Only recently, experiments with compositional use of private, virtual spaces have begun (i.e. Art and Virtual Environment Project of the Banff Centre for the Arts, 1992-1994).

[6] This differentiation is unimportant from the point of view of traditional music analysis (in the wide sense of the term), which demotes performances to mere approximations of ideal musical works. Only the features of such works which are represented on paper (with the priority given to pitch and rhythm) are deemed worthy of attention, because they seem to safeguard the structure and guarantee the identity of the music (cf. Goodman 1976).

of "what" needs to be answered. In this respect, a distinction must be maintained between a real instrument played by a live musician and a recording of such a performance reproduced with electroacoustic means (i.e. via headphones or loudspeakers). Therefore, one can distinguish three types of sound-space: (A) real sound sources (voices or instruments), (B) virtual sound sources (loudspeakers), and (C) a mixture of both.[7] In all three kinds of sound-space similar spatial effects can emerge.[8]

In instrumental and vocal-instrumental music (sound-space type A) the classification of spatialized works is related to the geometrical layout of these ensembles in space and their position in respect to the audience. Thus, the main designs are: (1) two ensembles in dialogue or antiphony (on the stage, between the two sides of the hall or on its front--back axis); (2) several individual ensembles on the stage; (3) three to several groups placed symmetrically around the audience (the audience is surrounded by music); (4) a mixture of musicians and the public on one spatial plane (the audience is "inside" the music); (5) several groups dispersed in various patterns on the stage, around and in-between the audience, and at various levels within the whole three-dimensional performance space (an extension of design no. 4). The realization of new spatial configurations in music frequently requires the use of unconventional seating plans. Therefore, these arrangements may entail the abandonment of a traditional, rectangular concert hall for the sake of more variable performance spaces. In most instrumental music, the acoustic quality of the performance space, once chosen, lies beyond the control of the composer unless the audience is taken on a listening tour through various sonorous environments. Even then, the listeners are only visiting different, static "spaces."

---

[7]Examples of the three types of sound-space are discussed below in sections 5.4 (type A), 5.5 (type B) and 5.6 (type C).

[8]One important effect--which could almost be called the "emblematic" idea of spatial organization--is the imitation of continuous sound movement in space by using discrete sources, such as 4 or 6 orchestral groups or loudspeakers surrounding the audience.

The spatial character of compositions in which the musicians are placed traditionally on the stage may be easily overlooked. Obviously, works in which the orchestra is split into several separate ensembles are spatialized.[9] However, it may suffice to have a large number of parts divisi (as in Ligeti's micropolyphony) to obtain a spatial texture, extended and varied within the confines of the stage. Here, spatial organization of sound is based neither on the measurable aspects of the performance space, nor on sound distances and directions. Instead, it is connected to textural differentiations.

All spatial arrangements may be enriched by the inclusion of the movement of the musicians or the audience (see four possible categories listed in Table V-1).[10] These settings may be realized within any type of sound-space; this is to say that the two criteria of spatialization, sound-space type and the category of mobility, are independent of each other. Nonetheless, the wealth of possibilities opened up here is limited by the theatrical character of the performer's movement in music. When the importance of the musicians' actions overshadows that of the sonorous results of these actions, music is transformed into musical theatre.[11] The movement of the audience forms a category of spatialization rarely employed in the concert hall. The noisy informality of mobile listeners is more suitable for experimental music in which all conventions and limits are being contested.[12]

---

[9] Cf. Bartók's *Music for Strings, Percussion and Celeste* discussed in section 5.3.

[10] Examples of mobility are discussed in section 5.3.

[11] In my interviews of 1992, Henry Brant and Iannis Xenakis expressed a dissatisfaction with the use of performer's movement in music as too slow to be expressive and too theatrical--turning the listeners' attention away from the auditory towards the visual. Pierre Boulez and R. Murray Schafer, on the other hand, have remained unconcerned with this criticism.

[12] Works in open form, for instance, have utilized ensemble dispersion in separate rooms of a house or other spatial locations (e.g. Stockhausen's *Musik für ein Haus*; cf. Maconie 1990). Various conceptual compositions have included the idea of giving the public the task of exploring certain, specific acoustic spaces (Lucier 1985, Nyman 1973).

In the area of electroacoustic music (sound-space type B) spatiality is a condition sine qua non. Here, static and mobile distributions of sound are interrelated, because virtual sound sources are not tied to the location of their carriers (loudspeakers) and may change positions in the course of the work. In electroacoustic music, all aspects of sound have to be defined directly, including the spatial positions, extensions, and movements of sound objects, as well as the quality of simulated spaces (apparent size, reverberation time and timbre, resonances, echoes). Therefore, this method of composing is quite different from writing out a score which indicates the instruments and includes an imprecise specification of their timbres and dynamics as well as a schema of locations. The classification of spatial patterns in electroacoustic music relates to the material basis for the stationary and moving sound images, that is, to various configurations of loudspeakers.[13] The possible arrangements include: one point source (images of different depth); (b) stereophony with two loudspeakers creating a continuous, virtual two-dimensional sound image in front of the listener; (c) quadrophony with four loudspeakers at the corners of the performance space around the audience (the shape and extension of the auditory image being disputable); (d) multi-loudspeaker projection systems using point sources, or stereo pairs in various configurations.

All electroacoustic categories of spatialization can be linked to those of vocal-instrumental music (mixed sound spaces, type C of the general classification). The most common arrangement is that of a solo instrument with a stereo or quadrophonic sound projection system. This design transcends the limitations of its constituent elements, that is, the disembodied quality of the sound from the loudspeakers and the

---

[13]Despite the widespread use of headphones, electroacoustic compositions have not been designed especially for this sound projection system. Headphones project sound images into headspace or create an illusion of being in a space of performance (depending on the choice of the recording technique). "Head images" are a sub-category of stereophonic projection. Only recently, experiments with artistic use of full spatial images realized with headphones have begun in virtual reality systems (e.g. the continuing Art and Virtual Environment Project of the Banff Centre for the Arts, Banff, Alberta, 1993-).

constraints of a solo performance, especially that involving a monophonic instrument. The complexity of spatial forms of music reaches its peak in mixed sound-spaces with many performers and multi-loudspeaker sound projection systems. Here, instead of attempting to classify all possible patterns, I will describe selected aspects of one composition, Pierre Boulez's *Répons* (1981-1988) for 6 instrumental soloists (surrounding the audience), instrumental ensemble of 24 musicians (in the midst of the audience) and electroacoustic equipment to process and spatialize the sound (including two sets of 6 loudspeakers on the outskirts of the performance area; cf. Section 5.4).

5.2.
Categories of mobility: Performers and audiences

In the majority of designs introduced in spatialized music the performers and the audiences are static (cf. Section 5.4). The dispersion of musicians in the space of the concert hall provides many opportunities for varied spatial distributions and interactions of sounds. However, in the composition in which the first detailed plan of performer placement was used, Bartók's *Music for Strings, Percussion and Celeste* (1936-1937), the musicians are not dispersed throughout the auditorium. Here, all the performers are located on the stage in a symmetrical design with percussions and keyboards framed by the two groups of the strings (cf. Ex. V-1).[14] Since the audience faces the musicians, as in a traditional concert hall arrangement, the presence of spatialization in Bartók's work may remain unnoticed.

The first movement of *Music for Strings, Percussion and Celeste* explores the

---

[14] In reference to this work, Ernö Lendvai writes about the "quadrophonic stage" of music; he also describes Bartók's inner hearing as "stereo hearing" (Lendvai 1983). Lendvai's article contains speculations about the symbolism of the right and the left side (left being associated with emotions, right—with the spiritual) and focusses on Bartók's structuring of pitch. Issues of spatialization, such as the patterns of antiphonal alternation, and the identity and difference of spatially separated materials are only briefly mentioned.

central symmetry of the placement of the strings. At the beginning, two violas in unison (one from each distant group of the strings) present the theme of the fugue. The musical and timbral identity of the material resounding from two points in space causes the sound image to extend over the whole area in-between the performing instruments.[15] The image is spatially balanced around the centre of the stage, because of the symmetrical position of the violas. Due to the transparency of sound, successive entries of new voices blend in with this central image: two violins from the right, two celli from both groups, violin II from the left, two double basses from the centre, violin I from the left (mm. 1-27). Bartók organizes the entries of fugal voices in an alternating pattern of directions: Centre--Right--Centre--Left--Centre (inside and back)--Left.

The second movement of *Music for Strings, Percussion and Celeste* juxtaposes the two groups of strings in a variety of antiphonal patterns. The movement begins with a dialogue (mm. 1-18) which soon develops into a series of canons between the whole groups (m. 40-60) or individual instruments (mm. 70-86, mm. 286-293). Bartók often introduces patterns of several antiphonal exchanges leading to a section in rhythmic unison (e.g. mm. 56-66).[16] These patterns appear frequently in the work's finale. In mm. 184-203, the two groups of the strings alternatively play music with identical rhythm, articulation, and dynamics, but with melodic motion in different directions (Group II--up, Group I--down); these differences gradually disappear on the way to a full identity of musical material (cf. Ex. V-2, mm. 184-193).[17] In a

---

[15]Cf. Brant's notion of *spill* discussed in Chapter III, and issues of signal coherence mentioned in Chapter IV (Blauert 1983).

[16]This design of the gradual reconciliation of initial oppositions also underlies the conclusion of the second movement (mm. 490-520). This section begins with a dialogue of the two groups, matching spatial symmetry with a symmetry of pitch motion: an ascending passage in Group I (left) is answered by its inversion in Group II (right). At the end, the groups fully share their musical material.

[17]In another segment (mm. 114-120), all the strings are involved in an exchange with the centrally placed piano and harp (the pattern of the dialogue is: Outside-versus-Centre).

	Cb. I	Cb. II	
Vc. I	Timp.	Gr. cassa	Vc. II
Viola I	Tamb. picc.	Piatti	Viola II
Viol. II	Celesta	Xyl.	Viol. IV
Viol. I	Pianoforte	Arpa	Viol. III

Ex. V-1: Positions of the performers in Béla Bartók's *Music for Strings, Percussion and Celeste* (1937).

Copyright 1937 by Universal Edition. Copyright renewed. All Rights Reserved. Used in the territory of Canada by permission of European American Music Distributors Corporation, sole U.S. and Canadian agent for Universal Edition.

Ex. V-2: Antiphonal dialogue in Bartók's *Music for Strings, Percussion and Celeste*, movement IV, mm. 184-193.

Copyright 1937 by Universal Edition. Copyright renewed. All Rights Reserved. Used in the territory of Canada by permission of European American Music Distributors Corporation, sole U.S. and Canadian agent for Universal Edition.

Ex. V-3: Textural transformation in Bartók's *Music for Strings, Percussion and Celeste*, movement IV, mm. 224-232.

Copyright 1937 by Universal Edition. Copyright renewed. All Rights Reserved. Used in the territory of Canada by permission of European American Music Distributors Corporation, sole U.S. and Canadian agent for Universal Edition.

beautiful moment of textural transformation (mm. 224-232), a cluster of descending melodic lines entering from alternating directions converges on a single chord performed by the two groups together with the same articulation (trills, cf. Ex. V-3). The tempo changes to Adagio and an expressive violin solo emerges from the background of this shimmering chord. *Music for Strings, Percussion and Celeste* transcends the principle of antiphonal dialogue encountered in many compositions for two orchestras by connecting symmetries in pitch space with symmetries in performance space. Here, Bartók reveals the full potential of spatial designs in music composed for static performers placed in traditional concert settings.

Static musicians do not necessarily create static sound images: it is possible to articulate various patterns of sound movement by dispersing musicians in the performance space. Spatial sound movement may be *discrete*, that is, it may proceed stepwise--if a musical phrase is presented successively in one ensemble of performers after another. This technique has been known since the Venetian school of polychorality in the late renaissance (or even earlier, cf. Carver 1988). Trajectories of discrete sound movement depend on the placement of performers. The apparent motion of sound from the front to the back of the hall (and vice versa) is a basic feature of Henry Brant's *Millennium II* (1954), where it results from successive entries of the trumpets and trombones placed along the walls of the hall (cf. Chapter VI). In John Tavener's *Ultimos Ritos* (1972), the vertical direction of motion from high to low is suggested by the alternation between groups of instruments placed in a high gallery and on the ground level of the church (cf. section 5.6).

Sound movement in space may also assume a *continuous* form. An interesting method of creating continuity of motion introduced in instrumental music of the post-war avant-garde, involves ensemble dispersion, dynamic shading and temporal overlapping of sounds. Stationary instrumental groups are placed around the audience and successively play sounds of the same pitch and timbre with similar dynamic envelopes (crescendo--decrescendo). The sound seems to rotate in space, gradually shifting from one instrumental ensemble to another. This effect, first used in Karlheinz Stockhausen's *Gruppen für Drei Orchester* (1955-57; cf. Chapter III, section 3.4), appears, for instance, in Stockhausen's *Carré* for four orchestras and choirs (1959-60), Kazimierz Serocki's *Continuum* for six percussionists (1965-66), as well as in several compositions by Xenakis discussed in Chapter VII, e.g. *Terretektorh* for 88 musicians scattered among the audience (1965-66) and *Persephassa* for 6 percussionists encircling the audience (1969).

The second category of mobility (from Table V-1) involves the movement of performers in-front-of, around, and in-between a static audience. This motion, despite problems with its theatrical associations, may serve a number of musical purposes. From the audience's vantage point, two general categories may be distinguished: (a) movement within the area of the stage in the concert hall (in front of the audience); (b) movement onto and off the stage, and around the concert hall or another performance space (around and in-between the audience). In the first case, the musicians may perform axial rotations while standing in one position, thus transforming the timbre of their instruments (the brass players in Xenakis's *Eonta* for brass and piano, 1963). They may also change their locations on the stage, following pre-designed routes, from one static position to another. This form of movement is usually expected from a soloist--to require a whole orchestra to wander around would be impractical, if not downright dangerous.

Thus, in Boulez's *Domaines* for clarinet and six instrumental groups (1961-1968), the solo clarinetist approaches groups that she/he wishes to be musically involved with. The solo singer in Berio's *Circles* for female voice, harp and two percussionists (1960) has to move from one music stand to another (cf. Ex. V-4). In each location, she performs different musical material and has at her disposal a distinct set of percussion instruments (position 1--claves, finger cymbals, position 2--wood chimes, position 3--glass chimes and finger cymbals). Berio's score contains a diagram of performer/instrument placement with the route for the soloist; similar graphs with trajectories of movement of the solo performer are also included in Thea Musgrave's *Clarinet Concerto* (1969) and *Horn Concerto* (1974).

If the performers are dispersed through the entire area of the concert hall, the scope of their movements is limited by the location of the audience and the type of the hall (i.e. a traditional setup allows only for the motion along the aisles). Another limitation is purely practical: only the musicians with portable instruments may simultaneously perform and move (unless they ride on a cart).[18] In the first movement of R. Murray Schafer's *Third String Quartet* (1981), for instance, the cellist, whose instrument is too heavy to be played and carried around, is seated on the stage. The violinists walk from their initial positions at the farthest distance from each other to join the cellist on the stage (cf. Chapter VIII).

The specification of the musical material and spatial location of the performers in Schafer's *Quartet* is partly approximate: the initial and final points of the temporal/spatial motion are defined, but not the details in-between. Many experimental works in open form leave these details to the discretion of the performer. Joan La Barbara's *Space Testing* (1977), for instance, involves "an exploration of the acoustical properties of the room in which the performance takes place" (La Barbara 1979).[19] The singer uses a variety of sounds including wide-ranging glissandi and sounds of varied durations and articulations to determine the resonances of the room; the position and movement of the singer/explorer may change in order to facilitate the achievement of this goal.

The movement of the listeners (category III and IV in the Table V-1) is impossible in the standard setting of the concert hall, not only because of the fixed layout of the seats. This type of motion is excluded in principle, as a source of acoustic disturbance: the music requires a container of silence for its proper

---

[18]This idea appears in Brant's answer to my question about the virtual sound movement in music: "Movement would take place when the players would actually move. This is a problem, of course, because they cannot move fast enough for the sound movement to have any emphatic effect. If the players were on some kind of a quiet automobile which went about 15 miles an hour--this would be very difficult to do in the concert hall--then one would get the impression of movement. If they went faster you would get a more pronounced impression of motion. But if they went much faster you would lose the identity of what was moving and all you would notice would be that some sound was going by." (Brant 1992: 5).

[19]La Barbara's work belongs to the group of acoustic experiments (Lucier, Neuhaus) inspired by Cage's philosophy of music (Nyman 1974; cf. Chapter III).

appreciation. Therefore, composers of contemporary "concert music" rarely allow their audiences to wander around. In the words of Iannis Xenakis:

> The problem is that when people move around they can not listen in the same way, they do not concentrate on the music. They do not know how to pay attention while walking and they do not notice the fact that when they change position they have a different aural perspective caused by the difference in location. Besides, they are distractive, they annoy other people who are listening, when they move.
>
> (Xenakis 1992: 9-10)

The listeners enjoy such freedom, though, during performances of conceptual works or multi-media events held in unusual locations: art galleries, museums, out-of-door spaces. John Cage, who is often credited with the invention of this type of performance art, thus describes the behaviour of the audience (in "Diary: Audience 1966"):

> An audience can sit quietly or make noises. People can whisper, talk, and even shout. An audience can sit still or it can get up and move around. People are people, not plants.[20]
>
> (Cage 1967: 51)

Cage's multi-media performances not only allow for, but require the mobility of the audience witnessing simultaneous performances of independent musical, theatrical, and visual works.[21] In *Musicircus* (1967), *Reunion* (1968), or *HPSCHD* (1967-1969), the spectators are free to wander around and experience various aspects of the whole event, or perceive one of its elements from different aural and visual perspectives. Their behaviour results from the abundance of events to be attended to. The musical anarchy of *HPSCHD* and the audience's anarchic behaviour are in

---

[20]Conversely, the audience in *The Princess of the Stars* by R. Murray Schafer (1981-1984), a musical/theatrical ritual held at a wilderness lake, is supposed to be "transformed" into trees. At the beginning of the *Princess*, the Presenter addresses the spectators: "The figures you see here are not human, therefore, in order that you might witness without disturbing these actions, I shall turn you into trees. . . Watch now and listen carefully faithful trees, but of the things you witness here remain silent, for they are ancient and sacred" (Schafer 1986: 22).

[21]Cage called some of these works "circuses" (e.g. *Musicircus*); James Pritchett applies Cagean term to the whole category (Pritchett 1993: 156).

keeping with Cage's political preoccupations of the time. In this "five hour multi-media extravaganza" (Pritchett 1993: 161), created by Cage in cooperation with Lejaren Hiller, up to seven harpsichords play different music at the same time (works by Mozart, Mozart transformed by Cage, etc.). The harpsichords are accompanied by the simultaneous playback of up to 51 tapes, each presenting music in a different tuning system. The individual layers are almost inaudible in the total din of simultaneous sonorities.

A much thinner texture co-exists with an unusual form of the listeners's mobility in *Elevator Music* by Elliott Schwartz (1967). This is a work for

> twelve groups of performers arranged in the vestibules or lobbies outside the elevator doors of a tall building and an audience which is taken for rides in groups by the conductor/elevator operator among the floors.
> (Schwartz 1981: 297)

The number of 12 groups of performers allows for vertical arrangements of the 12 pitch-classes, with one pitch assigned to each level in spatial effects of rapid "*building up* from the lowest to highest floor." Twelve-note rows are used in two brief sections of this work which lasts for one hour (Stages 4 and 11). The musical material of the remaining 10 Stages of *Elevator Music* is described verbally (e.g. patterns of repeated notes, glissandi of all kinds, single notes, phrases from well-known songs and "anything you choose" to play very softly, almost inaudibly). An individual listener witnesses only 3 minutes of the music: this is the duration of the elevator ride (floors are visited in random order). Moreover, every group of the audience hears a different segment of the piece. This is, then, to adopt Cage's expression from his Darmstadt lecture on indeterminacy, "a composition indeterminate in respect to its perception" (Cage 1958/1961). *Elevator Music* is also indeterminate in respect to its performance. Neither the exact number of musicians, nor their instruments are specified by the composer who requires solely the availability of pitched and percussive sounds at each of the floors.[22]

---

[22]The music is coordinated by the conductor who rings the emergency button in the elevator every 5 minutes, thus providing cues for each of the 12 stages of the work.

The increasing significance of the mobility of performers and audiences in music (category IV) often leads to a change in the music's context: the disappearance of the traditional form of the concert. Musical performances can take place outdoors or in unusual spaces, as in Brant's *Brand(t) aan de Amstel*, a site-specific composition for 4 boatloads of flutes floating through the canals of Amsterdam and encountering multiple ensembles dispersed throughout the city (1984). The informal, outdoor performances often transform musical works into theatrical actions or acoustic explorations (e.g. Max Neuhaus's series of *Listen. Field Trips thru Found Sound Environments* of 1966-1968). Here, the division of performers and audiences disappears, the musical notation gives way to written instructions, and the supratemporal musical work is replaced with a process or an action which cannot be repeated twice in the same way. The increasing mobility of participants in such "musical" situations is associated with profound changes in the understanding of music, its artefacts, and its social contexts.

5.3.
Spatial designs in real sound-space

In "acoustic" music performed in the concert hall, the placement of the musicians may be either regular or irregular.[23] The latter is, actually, a more common option, especially if spatialized works are conceived of in musical rather than geometrical terms. If a composition consists of several layers performed simultaneously at different locations, the symmetry of the geometric pattern outlined by the placement of the musicians may not matter as much as their co-existence within the same performance space. Here, spatial separation is more important than exact direction and specific location. In other words, this type of spatial organization is topological.

---

[23]Cf. the discussion of the "circle" in section 5.1 and of "symmetry" below.

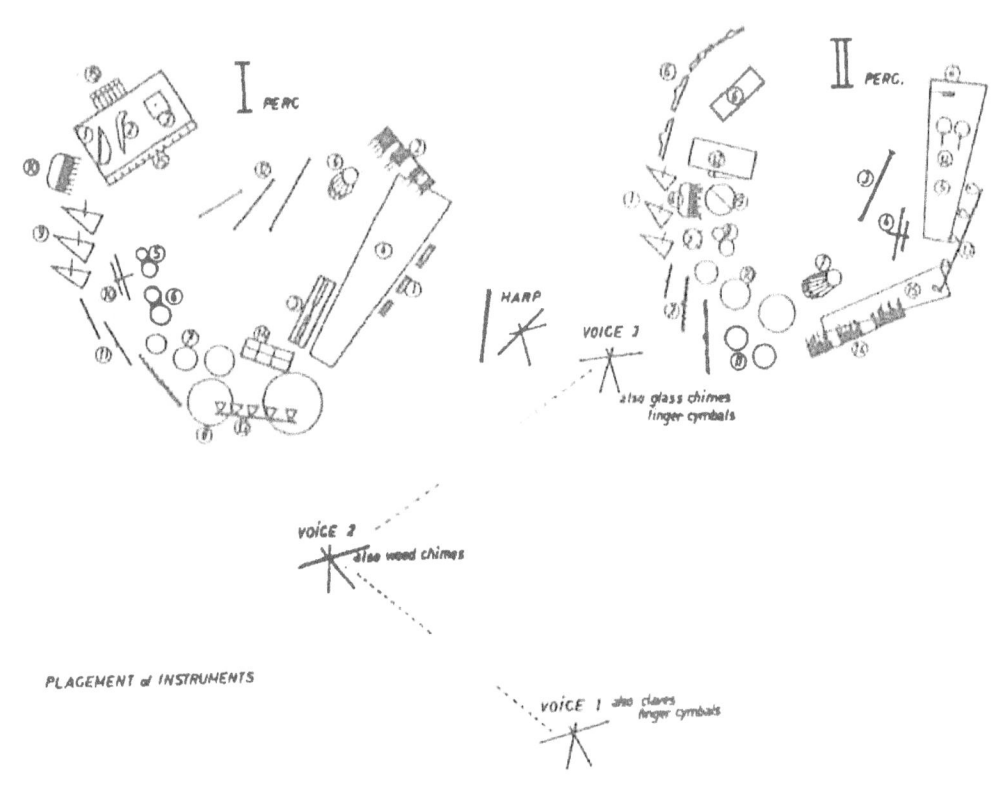

Ex. V-4: Three positions of the singer in Berio's *Circles* for female voice, harp and two percussionists (1960).

© Copyright 1961 by Universal Edition (London) Ltd., London. © Copyright renewed. All Rights Reserved. Used by permission of European American Music Distributors Corporation, sole U.S. and Canadian agent for Universal Edition (London) Ltd., London.

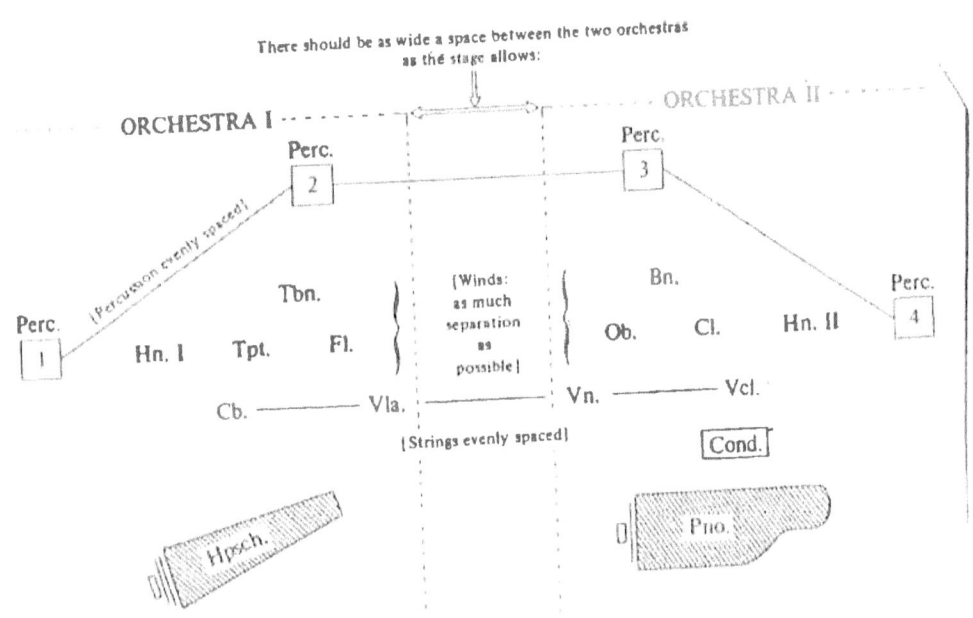

Ex. V-5: Seating plan in Elliott Carter's *Double Concerto* (1961) for harpsichord and piano with two chamber orchestras (from Schiff 1983: 208).

The spatial separation of two groups of musicians on the stage (design No. 4.1. in Table V-1, cf. Section 5.1) in conjunction with the symmetry of their sizes and timbres, amplifies textural contrasts existing, for instance, in the opposition of the soloists and the orchestra. Elliott Carter's *Piano Concerto* (1963-65) features two ensembles: the piano with a group of seven soloists (flute, English horn, bass clarinet, violin, viola, cello, double bass) and the orchestra.[24] In the score, the composer suggests three possible placements of these groups of musicians in space. Here, spatial separation heightens the sense of opposition between the lyrical concertino and the "deliberately crude, massive music" of the orchestra (Schiff 1983: 229). As Schiff comments, "the soloist and the concertino redefine virtuosity as freedom, vision and imagination, and so inevitably become locked in battle with the orchestral monster" (ibidem).

The opposition of two groups of performers is more clearly articulated in space in Carter's *Double Concerto* (1961) for harpsichord and piano with two chamber orchestras. The score includes a precise seating plan which allows for antiphonal dialogues as well as various patterns of sound movement (Ex. V-5). Two groups of wind instruments, placed as far as possible at the sides of the stage, are surrounded by four evenly spaced groups of percussion. The strings and the soloists are located at the front of the stage. This composition, inspired by Stockhausen's *Gruppen für drei Orchester* (1955-1957), includes instances of sound motion, a novelty associated with Stockhausen (cf. Chapter III, section 3.4). In m. 5, for instance, a cymbal tremolo moves from the right side of the stage (percussion 4) to the left (percussion 1). It is for the sake of such effects that the percussion and the strings are evenly spaced on the stage.

Two identical instrumental groups require a wide separation in space in order

---

[24]More recently, in his *Oboe Concerto* of 1987, Carter exploits a similar division of the performers; a concertino group supporting the soloist (one percussion and four violas), and the orchestra. According to the composer, "each of the two groups use different musical materials which they develop throughout the work" (Carter, 1988). However, the score does not contain references to the spatial locations of the two groups.

to be perceptually distinct. The groups, led by two conductors, may be involved in a musical game, as in Xenakis's *Strategie* for two orchestras (1962).[25] The idea of composing spatialized music for the musicians rather than the audience underlies Louis Andriessen's *Hoketus* (1975-1977), described by Andriessen as "one of the most radical pieces" he has ever written (Andriessen 1994: 139). The inspiration for this work came, in equal measure, from the "noisy, dirty sounds" of American minimalism and from the hocket technique of the medieval and folk music.[26]

In *Hoketus*, two groups of five instrumentalists (pan-flutes, electric pianos, pianos, bass guitars and sets of congas) produce sounds "of exactly the same sound and volume" (Andriessen 1991). The groups should be as wide apart as possible, facing each other. The musicians "alternate in playing chords that are practically identical. They are free to repeat a bar or group of bars as often as they wish" (Andriessen 1977; cf. Ex. V-6).[27] This loud, exciting music challenges the performers into a virtual contest, while the audience observes this musical game. Andriessen admits that the work, written for an ensemble of musicians bearing the same name, could not have come into being without them; "with different musicians it would have been a different composition" (Andriessen 1977). The composer cherishes the intensity of the live performance: "only in this way . . . you can hear *what music is about*, not only through the notes but through the musicians as well." (Andriessen

---

[25]This is an indeterminate piece created by means of mathematical game theory. The two ensembles of *Strategie* may be located either at the sides of the stage, or on two platforms at opposite extremes of an auditorium. Xenakis's first game piece, *Duel* for two orchestras with two conductors (1958-1959) does not specify spatial location of the musicians.

[26]The quote about minimalism comes from Andriessen's inteview (1994). Potter cites the influence of Terry Riley's *In C,* Steve Reich's *Drumming* and the music of Guillaume de Machaut (Potter 1982: 18-19).

[27]In Example V-6, the pitches of the chords (C and D) are listed at the top of the page, above the rhythmic patterns of their performance. The pan-flutes play the encircled notes, the bass guitars the lowest ones. Note that the single chord in D should be repeated a specific number of times.

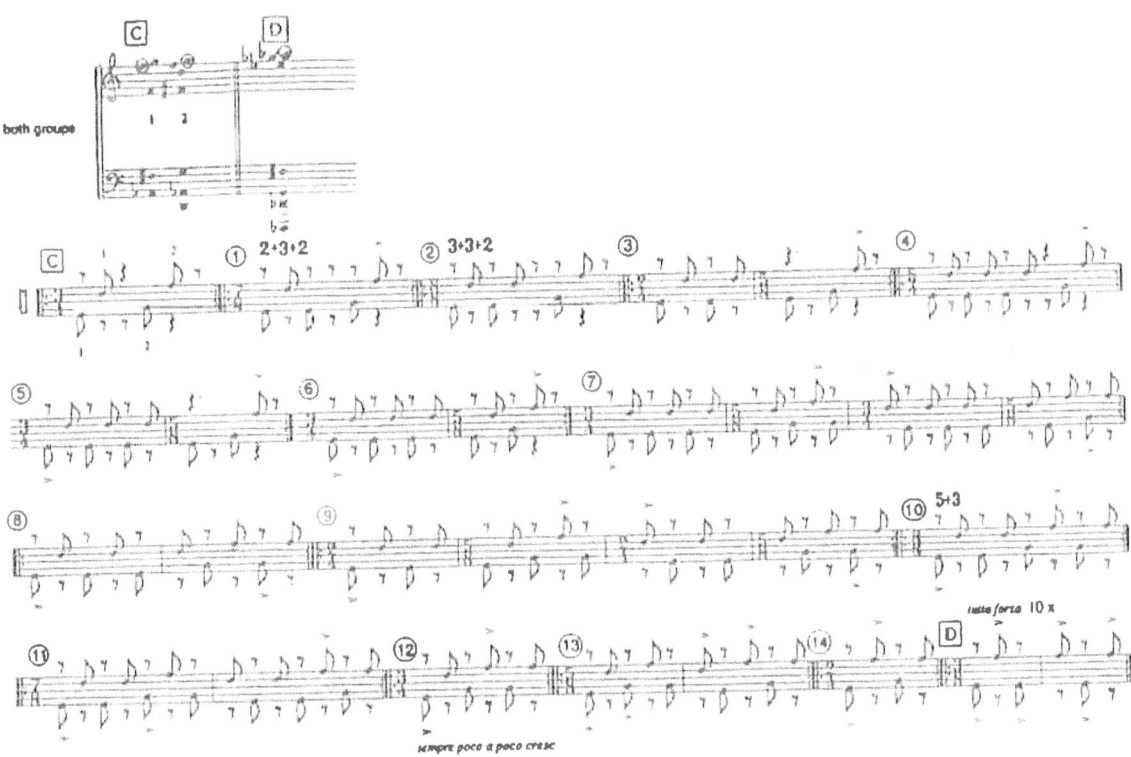

Ex. V-6: Excerpt from Louis Andriessen's *Hoketus* for two groups of five instrumentalists (1975-1977), p. 5.

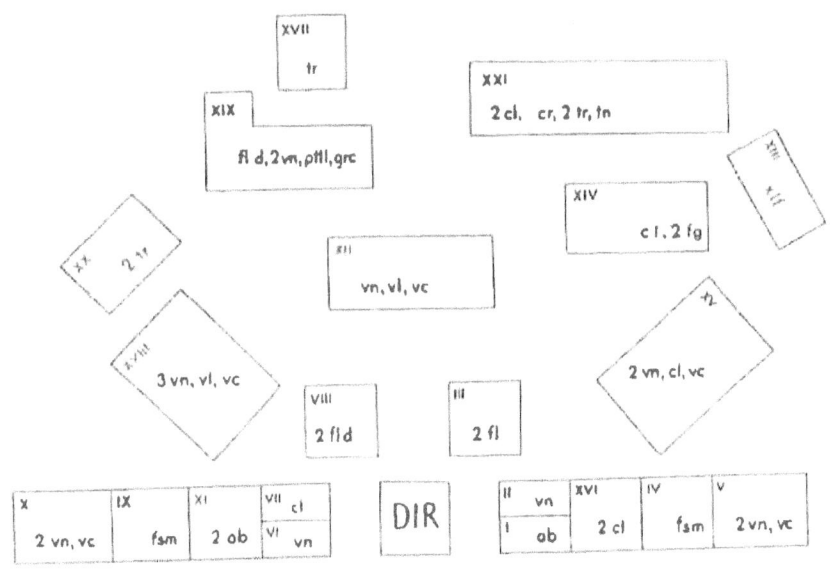

Ex. V-7: Placement of 21 instrumental groups in Zygmunt Krauze's *Folk Music* for orchestra (1972).

Ex. V-8: Excerpt from Krauze's *Folk Music* (1972), p. 7.

1977). Thus, *Hoketus* reveals inter-personal aspects of spatialized music. It consists of an interactive, spatio-temporal, musical game, rather than a series of static, "frozen" spatial shapes contemplated by the audience. This music, like Maurice Merleau-Ponty's body-subject, "inhabits space and time" (Merleau-Ponty 1945/1962: 121). If, as Merleau-Ponty put it, the spatio-temporal body "is our general medium for having a world" (p. 147), it is also our medium for experiencing music in its full gestural, personal and spatio-temporal articulation.

The audience facing the orchestra on the stage in the concert hall may perceive a spatial sound image of great plasticity and depth. If the whole area is occupied by musicians, the image is a three-dimensional spatial relief: a panorama from left to right with the added dimensions of depth (front-back of the stage) and a slight elevation (the musicians at the back are raised by platforms). The orchestral instruments are usually organized in groups of common timbre. A new subdivision of the performers on the stage into separated groups may be a substitute for their dispersion in the hall (four groups of common pitch range in Carter's *Concerto for orchestra*, 1970) or may result from the polychoral conception of the music (three choirs a cappella in Krzysztof Penderecki's *Stabat Mater* of 1962; a work included in his *St. Luke's Passion*, 1965).

By changing the position of the instruments from the conventional one and by redistributing the orchestra into a mixture of small groups on the stage the music gains a new plasticity of texture (design no. 4.2. in Table V 1; cf. section 5.1). The fragmentation of the orchestra is often associated with the technique of the collage, in which many musical layers are presented at once. In Zygmunt Krauze's *Folk Music* (1972), for example, the orchestra is subdivided into 21 small ensembles simultaneously performing authentic folk melodies (cf. Ex. V-7 the seating plan and Ex. V-8, excerpt of the music). Through the course of the piece, the conductor selects instrumental groups to be momentarily highlighted by their higher dynamic level. Thus, individual melodies (or their pairs) briefly dominate the complex, spatially extended texture of the piece. The spatial separation of instrumental groups on the stage articulates the differences in musical characteristics. Nonetheless, *Folk*

Music would not benefit from a dispersion of the musicians around the hall. In this situation, the musical layers performed by individual groups would remain distinct instead of melting into a continuous fabric of sound--a colourful, lively background from which individual melodies momentarily arise and into which they dissolve."[28]

Textural fluidity notwithstanding, more spectacular spatial effects arise when several groups of performers are placed symmetrically around the audience (design no. 4.3. in Table V-1; cf. section 5.1). Four, six, eight or twelve groups (somehow, composers have favoured even numbers) approximate the circle and allow for the creation of various patterns of sound distribution and movement. The effect of surrounding the listeners with sounds may serve a programmatic purpose (e.g. the apocalyptic trumpets of the Last Judgement in Berlioz's *Requiem op. 5*). Sound rotations may also create dramatic and expressive climaxes in "purely musical" compositions (Xenakis's *Persephassa*; cf. Chapter VII). Finally, the idea of immersing the listeners in stationary, circular sound-fields may have quasi-mystical overtones, as this design serves to evoke other-worldly stillness and to induce a state of contemplation (Schafer's *Credo*, cf. Chapter VIII).

An early example of a "continuous" sound-space approximated by a square appears in Stockhausen's *Carré* for four orchestras and choirs with four conductors (1959-60). The four groups of musicians are located at central points of the sides of a rectangular performance space (Ex. V-9). Vocal and instrumental sonorities are integrated into one static sound world, realizing the composer's wish that "this music should give a little inner stillness, breath and concentration" (Stockhausen 1964: 103). The temporal staticity of *Carré* is a consequence of the music's slow tempo, the absence of meter, and the frequent use of long, motionless chords. It also results from the work's Moment form. *Carré* consists of 101 self-sufficient Moments and nine Interludes, which, like the interludes in *Gruppen*, exploit various patterns of

---

[28]Luciano Berio uses a similar subdivision of the performers into a large number of small groups in *Coro* (1975-76) for 40 voices and orchestra. Each of the singers is placed next to an instrument of a corresponding range; these forty instrument-voice duos perform soloistic passages or unite in gigantic orchestral-vocal mixtures.

sound rotation.²⁹ The circular motion connects the four groups in a clockwise or counter-clockwise direction. In addition, *Carré* presents a variety of spatial configurations, often linking two or three of the distant ensembles in criss-crossing patterns.

The cover of the score of this work presents some of Stockhausen's sketches (Ex. V-10) which seem to have inspired the Polish composer, Andrzej Dobrowolski, to create a related series of spatial designs for his *Muzyka na smyczki i 4 grupy instrumentów detych* [Music for strings and four group of wind instruments] composed in 1964 (Ex. V-11). Stockhausen and Dobrowolski use parallel geometric forms as well as similar timbral and textural effects (e.g. trills shifting from one group to another). Thus, again, spatial organization is linked with timbre.³⁰

In the next type of spatial design the mixture of the performers and the listeners increases by scattering the orchestra and the public on one spatial plane (design no. 4.4. in Table V-1; cf. section 5.1). Here, as in circular arrangements, the audience is 'inside' the music. Each listener, however, has a unique aural perspective resulting from his/her position close to some performers and away from others. This arrangement appears in Xenakis's *Terretektorh* and *Nomos Gamma* (cf. Chapter VII). In both of these large-scale compositions, the orchestra and the public are placed within a circular performance space.

A circular or spherical shape filled with sound, although certainly favoured by composers of spatialized music, is not the essential feature of this music. Performers

---

²⁹Rotations, often in two opposing directions, appear in Moments 63x, 69x, 75x and 82x. The presence of this effect in *Carré* reflects Stockhausen's contemporaneous preoccupation with sound movement: electroacoustic experiments with rotating loudspeakers, new forms of movement (varied speed, changing directions) in *Kontakte* of 1960 (Harvey 1974: 88).

³⁰The strength of this bond in the Polish school of "sonorism" may be exemplified by the music of Kazimierz Serocki who, incidentally, was also indebted to Stockhausen (Zielinski 1985). In Serocki's *Epizody* for three percussion groups and strings (1959), all the performers are located on the stage. Here, clusters of pitches and percussive sonorities create spatial figures and configurations (e.g. fan-like shapes, travelling from the outside to the center and back).

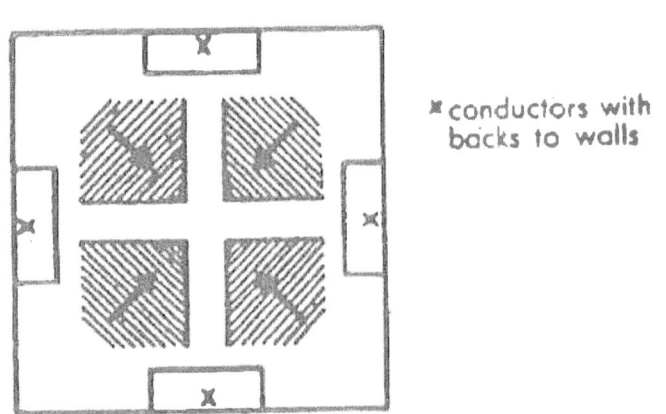

Ex. V-9: Placement of musicians and the public in Karlheinz Stockhausen's *Carré* for four orchestras and four mixed choirs with four conductors (1959-60). Arrows indicate the orientation of the listeners facing the centre.

©Copyright 1971 by Universal Edition (London) Ltd., London. All Rights Reserved. Used by permission of European American Music Distributors Corporation, sole U.S. and Canadian agent for Universal Edition (London) Ltd., London..

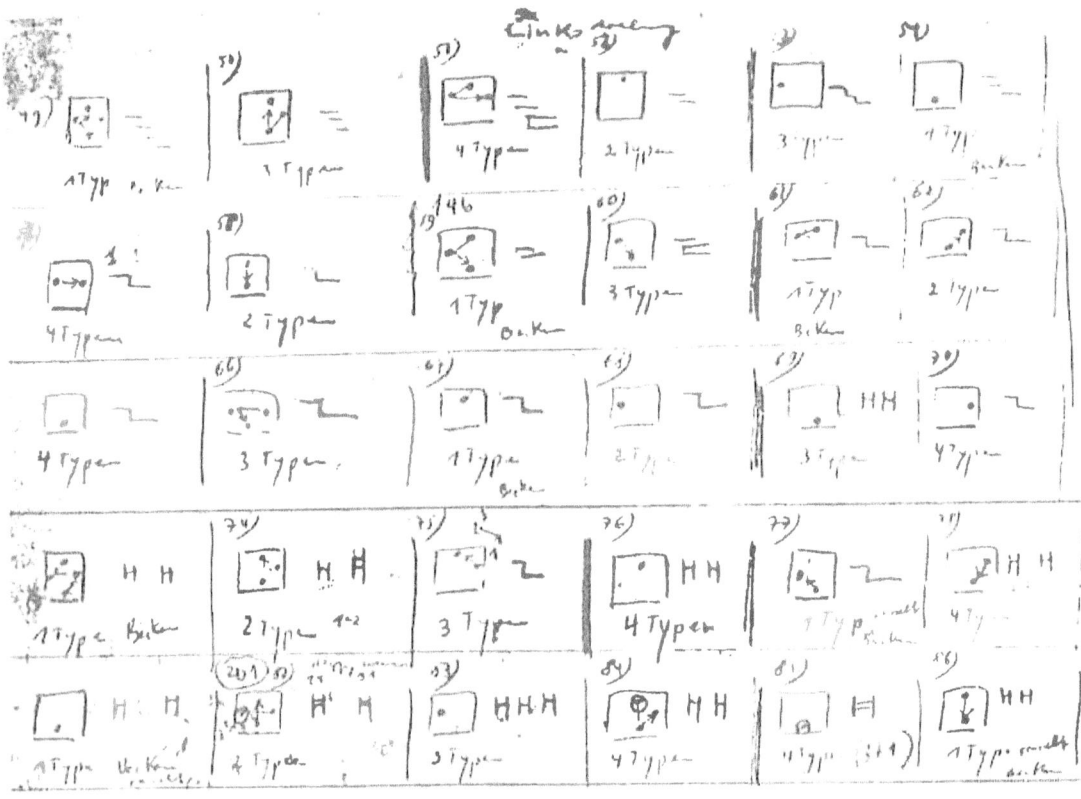

Ex. V-10: Fragment of Stockhausen's sketches for *Carré* (from the cover of the score).

©Copyright 1971 by Universal Edition (London) Ltd., London. All Rights Reserved. Used by permission of European American Music Distributors Corporation, sole U.S. and Canadian agent for Universal Edition (London) Ltd., London..

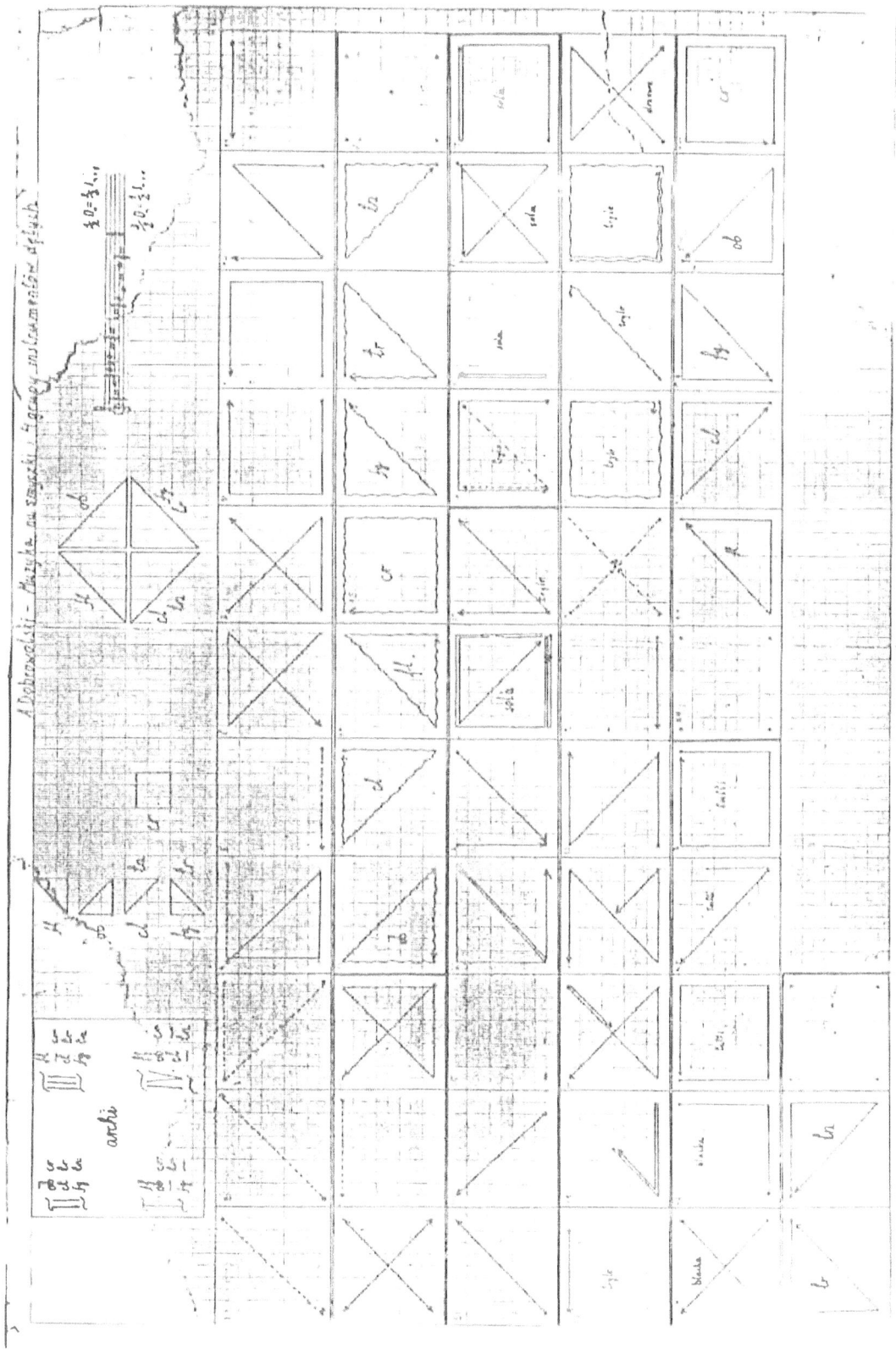

Ex. V-11: Spatial patterns in *Muzyka na smyczki i 4 grupy instrumentów detych* by Andrzej Dobrowolski (1964).

may be dispersed in various patterns within the whole three-dimensional performance area. In the concert hall they may be located on the stage, around and in-between the audience and at different levels from below the floor to the highest balcony (design 4.5. in Table V-1; cf. Section 5.1). Such "total antiphonal distribution" occurs in the music of Henry Brant (*Voyage Four*, cf. Chapter VI). Spatialized music of full multi-directionality completely fills the performance space with sounds originating in front of, beside, above, behind and below the listeners.[31]

5.4
Selected designs in virtual sound-space

In the virtual space of electroacoustic music, the positions and extensions of sounds are not unequivocally connected to the positions of the loudspeakers. The virtuality and mobility of sound images is already apparent in the early *musique concrète* experiments which Pierre Schaeffer and Pierre Henry presented at their concerts in Paris in 1951-52 (cf. Chapter III, section 3.3). An abundance of new spatial phenomena has emerged throughout the history of electroacoustic music, from synthetic, non-spatial sounds, through multi-layered, moving sonorities to variable spaces (Blaukopf 1971; Dhomont 1988, 1991).

The "internal" space of an electroacoustic work has to be "composed" (expressions quoted from Smalley 1991, and Chion 1988; cf. Chapter III, section 3.3). The plethora of patterns of sound positions, extensions, and movements reflects the scope of potential sound material and its transformations. In addition, composers may introduce variations in the size and type of acoustic space during the course of the work by changing the reverberation time, the temporal pattern of simulated

---

[31]This may not be very practical because of perceptual habits and associations: people are not used to hearing music from below, and tend to turn their heads to see the music behind them.

reflections and the resonances (Blaukopf 1971; Lehnert and Blauert 1991). According to Roger Reynolds, however, we are not used to evolving acoustic environments; the overcoming of this perceptual limitation is a condition for the "acceptability" of variable spaces and sound motion in music (Reynolds 1978).

One loudspeaker used as a point source can transmit only the depth of the sound image (the apparent distance of the sound sources) and the apparent size of the room suggested by reverberation time (Harley 1986). These limitations are too severe for musical purposes: I do not know of any electroacoustic compositions for a single loudspeaker sound projection system.[32]

A classic, stereophonic sound image is created by two loudspeakers placed at a distance (design 5.2 in Table V-1; cf. Ex. V-12). This virtual image imitates the extent and dimensions of sounds produced by an orchestra located on-stage in a concert hall. The stereo image is continuous and two-dimensional (directions Left-Right and Front-Back); a veritable wall of sound may fill in the area between the two loudspeakers. Nonetheless, the perception of stereophonic spatial images strongly depends on the positions of the listeners in relation to the loudspeakers. New inventions continuously redefine the "virtuality" of spatial images emitted by two loudspeakers. For example, sophisticated digital signal processing units, called "spatializers" allow for the placement of a sound source anywhere within the 350 degrees around the listeners--except in the 10 degrees directly behind them (cf. Ex. V-12). Spatializers create "a thick sound field emanating out from beyond the two front speakers and surrounding the listener" (Petersen 1994: 148).[33]

Quadrophony (design no. 5.3 in Table V-1) transcends the spatial limitations of stereophony by using four loudspeakers located at the corners of a rectangular space (Begault 1986). The quadrophonic image approximates the circle (continuous sound-

---

[32]However, mono compatibility is a standard requirement for sound recordings; even the most sophisticated signal processing systems have to meet this requirement (c.f. Petersen 1994).

[33]See also Bloch et al. (1992).

space around the listeners) with the square (location of the loudspeakers). The illusion of circularity works well only for listeners located in the limited area at the centre, equidistant from the four sound sources.[34] This type of sound projection, used for the first time in a concert situation in 1962 (in *Tautologos 1 et 2* by Luc Ferrari; cf. Vande Gorne 1988: 11) soon became a standard in electroacoustic music, especially music realized with computers.

The technology of digital sound synthesis and transformation has enabled composers to enrich the spatial potential of electroacoustic music with many new effects.[35] For instance, an ingenious computer program for the simulation of moving sound sources in a four channel system has been developed by John Chowning (1970). Here, the apparent position and movement of sound in a virtual, quadrophonic space is controlled by the distribution of direct and reverberant signals between the four loudspeakers to provide the angular and distance information, and by using the Doppler shift for velocity information (Ex. V-13). Chowning applied his program in *Turenas* (1972), the first composition realized with the Frequency Modulation (FM) sound-synthesis method. The paths of the sounds in *Turenas* trace outlines of Lissajous figures (resulting from variable phase relationships between a sine and cosine projection). Sounds of a stable pitch and timbre (i.e. with a clearly recognizable identity) move along these trajectories with varied velocities and changing directions. The movement occurs within the whole 360 degree sound projection space--not only around its outskirts, but anywhere above the listeners heads.[36]

---

[34]F. Richard Moore suggests that the loudspeakers are like windows, or holes in the corners of the walls, looking into an imaginary larger room in which the sounds are located (Moore 1983).

[35]See Begault's discussion of spatial manipulation and computers (1986).

[36]The possibility of realistic simulations of, say, a flying trumpet, created by Chowning's program, raises some fundamental, aesthetic questions. Why would a composer need a trumpet to fly? Perhaps to challenge and perplex the listeners. As Roger Reynolds writes, an "arresting, potentially unsettling aura" surrounds the

Ex. V-12: Extent and dimensions of virtual sound images in stereophonic sound projection systems: (a) standard image, (b) image enhanced by spatializer.

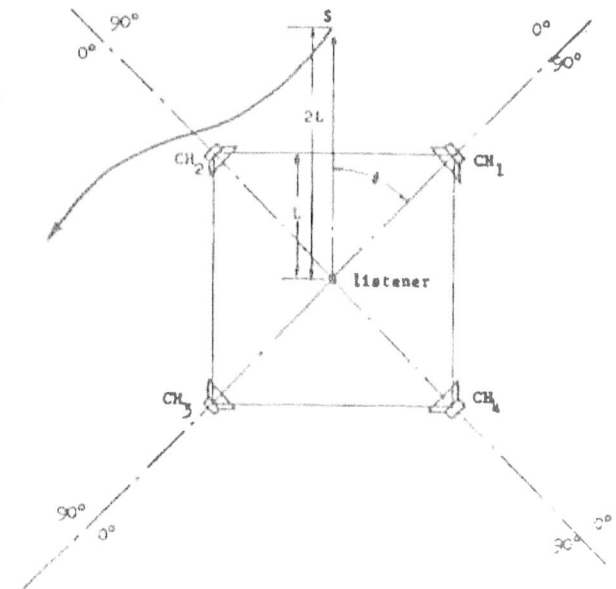

Ex. V-13: Virtual sound movement in quadrophonic space (Chowning 1970).

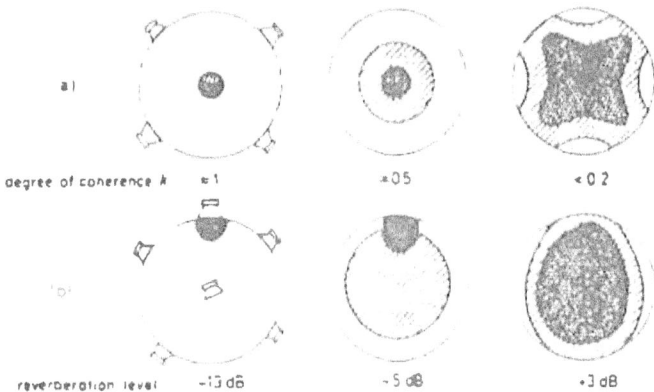

a: Directions of auditory events for 4 bandpass-filtered noise signals whose degree of coherence with each other is variable (after Damaske 1967/68; level at the position of the listener 75 dB, two experienced subjects). b: Directions of auditory events when a direct sound (level 70 dB) and five mutually incoherent reflections (reverberation, delayed by 80 ms) are presented. The signal was music at a fast tempo. More than 20 subjects (after Wagener 1971).

Ex. V-14: Dependence of the apparent size of sound images on reverberation and signal coherence (Blauert 1983: 272).

In a quadrophonic space, the apparent size and extension of the virtual sound image depends on the type of the signal. Jens Blauert describes two experiments proving that a decreased degree of signal coherence and an increased level of reverberation cause a diffusion of the perceived sound image (Blauert 1983: 272). In the first experiment, four loudspeakers projecting a coherent signal create a small, virtual image located at the center of the space. The image grows in size when the signals become less coherent (Ex. V-14). In the second experiment, if the level of reverberant sound (simulated by late reflections) increases the image becomes progressively more diffuse--finally covering the whole area between the loudspeakers (cf. Ex. V-14). Albert Bregman's theory of auditory scene analysis corroborates these findings (Bregman 1990). If two distinct sounds are heard from different directions they will be perceptually separated. If, on the other hand, we "use correlated micromodulation in the two signals to tell the auditory system that they are one and the same event it will derive only one (diffuse) spatial estimate for the whole sound" (Bregman 1990: 659).

This interrelationship of the temporal micro-form and the spatial location underlies a paradoxical effect synthesized at IRCAM by Roger Reynolds and Thierry Lancino for Reynolds's *Archipelago* (1980-1982), a composition for instrumental ensemble and computer-generated tape (Vérin 1991). In this effect, the sound of an oboe is split into even and odd harmonics located in two separate channels (stereo loudspeakers). The harmonics are modulated by tiny frequency fluctuations (FM). If the modulation is identical in the two channels, a complete oboe sound is heard at the centre. If the modulation of the two signals differs, the sound splits into two sonorities located at the sides (McAdams 1984: 55). Here, Reynolds explores a "flexible, continuously transforming source geometry" (Reynolds 1978: 185).

In multi-channel, multi-loudspeaker projection systems, the shape of the listening space delimits the possible "shapes" of sound and the trajectories of movement. Stockhausen used circular and spiral patterns in the Osaka sphere (cf. Ex.

"unfamiliar mobility" of sound images (Reynolds 1978: 184).

III-10 in Chapter III, section 3.4). Varèse's designs followed the complex outlines of the Philips Pavilion (cf. Ex. III-3 and III-4 in Chapter III, section 3.3). Both spaces were designed for performances of newly composed electroacoustic music.

In the standard shape of the concert hall, with a separation of the audience from the performers, multi-loudspeaker sound projection systems may assume the form of an orchestra of loudspeakers which replaces the standard orchestra on the stage. As the orchestra is divided into groups of instruments of the same timbre, the electroacoustic "orchestra" distributes the loudspeakers in space depending on their frequency range (low, medium, high). The *Gmebaphone* system used in Bourges and the *Acousmonium* of the GRM in Paris are both based on this principle (Clozier 1988, Vande Gorne 1988). Such multi-loudspeaker sound projection systems are often called "acousmatic." This English neologism is derived from the French term "acousmatique" meaning imaginary sounds without visible sources.

Acousmatic music "organizes morphologies and sonic spectra coming from a multiplicity of sources" which require a particularly attentive way of listening (Dhomont 1991a: 25). During an acousmatic concert, labelled "cinema for the ear" by Francis Dhomont, an electroacoustic composition acquires full spatial plasticity (Dhomont 1988: 17). The configuration of loudspeakers for this type of a concert consists of a series of stereo pairs of loudspeakers (4, 6, 8, 12 or more), each pair constituting an independent "écran de projection" for a layer of sounds (Dhomont 1988: 18). Here, the design of the sound projection system does not depend on the shape of the "composed" or "internal" space of a piece. Jacques Lejeune, for instance, presents several different layouts for the projection of the same composition, *Messe aux oiseaux* (Lejeune 1991: 80; Ex. V-15).[37]

Dhomont's composition *Espace/Escape* (1989) explores the associative and symbolic aspects of space and movement. The composer's notes about this piece are quite poetic:

---

[37]In the diagrams, Lajeune represents multi-loudspeaker sound projection systems with point sources, rather than stereo pairs.

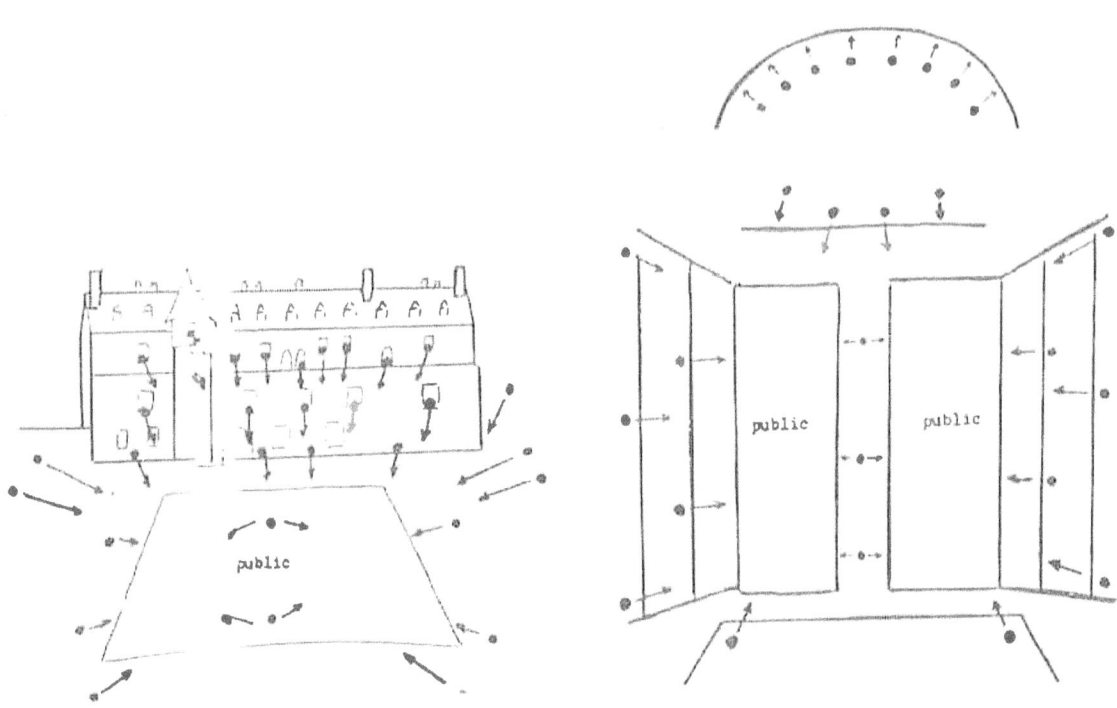

Ex. V-15: Two arrangements of multiple loudspeakers for Jacques Lejeune's *Messe aux oiseaux* (Lejeune 1991).

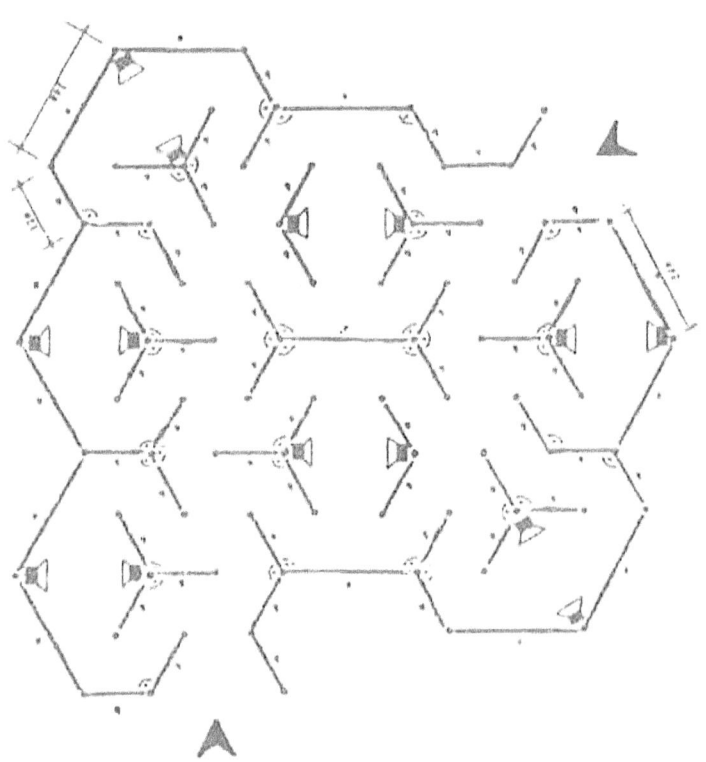

Ex. V-16: Projection space in Zygmunt Krauze's *La rivière souterraine* (1987).

Space.
Open, intimate, confused spaces. Broken spaces, whirling.
Indecisive edges of the space.
Space-refuge, enclosed, maternal, space of reminiscence and of associations.
Tumult or murmur in the space of a thousand reflections.
Escape.
The flight engenders a vertigo of multiple elsewheres.
Here... There...

(Dhomont 1991b: 32)

Espace/Escape brings together the immensity and intimacy of the human experience of space. Sounds from various acoustic environments, ranging from a bird's cage (the flutter of wings) to an airport lobby (muffled din of footsteps and conversations, noise of the planes' engines) are juxtaposed with synthetic sonorities in complex, evolving formations that defy description. This instance of contemporary *musique concrète* draws from the acoustic physicality of human life and from the exploration of spatial dimensions of sounds possible in acousmatic projection, "the dimensions of volume, of near and distance, of front and back, left and right" (Guérin 1991: 106).

The situation of the audience during an acousmatic concert resembles that of the concert of instrumental music: a series of compositions is presented to static listeners. Electroacoustic music may also involve the mobility of the listeners, free to explore sound installations--a form of spatio-musical architecture. In Zygmunt Krauze's *La rivière souterraine* (1987), the public is invited to wander around a specially designed architectural space (a series of cubicles connected in a labyrinthine pattern) and listen to music emitted from several loudspeakers placed at various points of this space (Ex. V-16).[38] According to the composer, here the architecture fulfils

---

[38] This work is known in Polish as *Rzeka Podziemna*, in English as *Underground River*. Its premiere took place at the 1987 Rencontres Internationales de la Musique Contemporaine, Metz, France. Krauze's spatial compositions include two earlier electroacoustic works, *Kompozycja Przestrzenno-Muzyczna* [Spatial Music Composition] of 1968, co-designed with architects, Teresa Kelm and Henryk Morel, and *Kompozycja Przestrzenno-Muzyczna No. 2* (1970, with Teresa Kelm). Another work in this series, *Fête galante et pastorale* (1974-75) is scored for 13 chamber ensembles and 13 tapes

"the role of an instrument" (Krauze 1987/1988). The composer describes his spatial compositions as consisting of

> simultaneous performances of live and recorded music with unlimited duration, transmitted to different cubicles or rooms connected to each other. By walking through the space each listener creates his own version of the piece.
> (Krauze 1987/1988)

In *La rivère souterraine* each of the seven pairs of loudspeakers emits music performed on a different instrument (transformed electronically); one to three of these sources may be heard at the same time. The listeners may dwell in some of the cubicles filled with music, return to the ones already visited, or stop in one of the intermediary spaces and enjoy the mixture of the neighbouring musical layers. The durations of individual segments depend on the duration of the listeners' presence in one cubicle, the dynamic proportions shift when they walk, thus depending on the direction and velocity of motion.

Krauze's spatial works have been presented in art galleries, not concert halls; in this setting it is possible to consider constellations of loudspeakers as unusual works of art (Raaijmakers et al. 1971). Here, musical sounds, without definite temporal envelopes, exist in space in a quasi-objective, reified manner, they are continuously present in the segments of space. Thus, electroacoustic installations approximate the mode of existence of Satie's *musique d'ameublement*. In addition, Krauze's spatial music shares vital characteristics of spatialized music as exemplified by Ives and Brant. This music consists of many simultaneous layers separated in timbre, pitch material and spatial location. The perceptual freedom of the static listener in, e.g. Brant's music, implies shifts of attention from one sound layer to another. Krauze externalizes these shifts into motion in performance space.

---

performing simultaneously in a series of rooms. This work was written for the Festival Steirischer Herbst, 1975 and performed in the 26 rooms of the Eggenberg Castle (Graz, Austria). The rooms were connected in a circular pattern so that the visitor could walk around the whole building and experience the music which "inhabited" the space (it was played in every second room).

5.5.

Mixed designs: *Répons* by Pierre Boulez

Since Varèse's *Déserts*, the juxtaposition of instrumental and electroacoustic sounds within one musical work has posed problems for composers. The mutual relationship of the two types of sonorities may range from total opposition (*Déserts*) to smooth blending (*Verblendungen* for orchestra and tape by Kaija Saariaho, 1982-1984). Pierre Boulez's *Répons* (1981-1988) for six instrumental soloists (two pianos--one doubling a YAMAHA DX7 keyboard set to electric organ, harp, vibraphone, cimbalom, glockenspiel doubling xylophone), instrumental ensemble of 24 musicians and live electronics creates a middle ground between these extremes.[39]

The title of *Répons* refers to a form of plainchant in which the soloist (individual) alternates with the choir (collective). Boulez's work explores various types of responsorial dialogues between the individual soloists and the ensemble, the instrumental sounds and their electronic transformations. This interplay of acoustic and electroacoustic sonorities is only partly notated in the score.[40]

The audience surrounds the central instrumental ensemble and is, in turn, encircled by six soloists and two sets of six loudspeakers--one set for the amplified

---

[39] This study of *Répons* results from my participation in the work's rehearsals at IRCAM, Paris, 3-7 August 1992. At that time, the Ensemble InterContemporain, conducted by Boulez, was preparing for concerts at the Salzburg Festival (15 and 19 August 1992). I am indebted to Pierre Boulez, Denis Lorrain and Cort Lippe for their insights into different aspects of *Répons*. I am particularly grateful to Cort Lippe, without whose assistance this part of my research would not have been possible.

[40] Although a copy of the autograph score is deposited at the Universal Edition, London (1988), a definitive edition of *Répons* does not yet exist. I consulted copies of the score and performance materials used in 1992 at IRCAM: (1) the score used for computer transformations by Denis Lorrain, containing only the music for the soloists and heavily annotated (probably by Andrew Gerzso whose stamp with address is on the first page), (2) the full score used for spatialization (with annotations), (3) fragments of the soloist's parts. I will call the first copy, which should not be mistaken for the technical documentation created by Denis Lorrain, the "computer" score; the second will be referred to as the "audio" score.

sounds of the soloists and one for the sounds processed electronically (cf. Ex. V-17). The transformation, distribution and "spatialization" of sounds is computer-controlled.[41] Only the soloists' sounds are spatialized (amplified or processed and dispersed into space by means of two sets of 6 loudspeakers surrounding the performance area).[42] Spatial distribution of instrumentalists and loudspeakers is an essential component of the work's concept. Boulez thus describes his intention: "I do not want my audience to look at music from a distance but to be involved and immersed in the music" (Boulez 1992). The composer compares listening to his work with the lived experience of architecture (ibidem). The awareness of a building as an architectural work of art entails more than seeing it from the outside. One needs to be conscious of the interior, to walk through the different rooms, see their proportions and qualities, experience the architecture from a mobile point of view. This does not mean, though, that the audience should walk around during the concert.[43] Instead, Boulez proposes listening to *Répons* several times, from different locations. Only then can the liveliness and richness of the spatial interactions between the various elements of the music be fully experienced.

In Table V-2, I describe the changing instrumentation and varied forms of

---

[41] In earlier versions of *Répons* (until 1988) signal processing was realized on the 4X computer system, controlled by Andrew Gerzso (Jameux 1991, Boulez and Gerzso 1988). For the performances of 1992, this task was transferred to the IRCAM Signal Processing Workstation. Denis Lorrain wrote the "Répons patch" in MAX (a computer language developed by Miller Puckette at IRCAM); he also, with Cort Lippe, initiated sound transformations during the 1992 performances. The spatial sound projection was realized with the Matrix 32 system by Xavier Bordelais and Daniel Raguin.

[42] Few procedures are used for sound transformation: delays, frequency shifts, ring modulation, comb filters, spatialization dependent on amplitude. This apparent limitation safeguards the music's consistency and its large-scale coherence.

[43] However, this is exactly what I did during the rehearsals of *Répons* at IRCAM—in order to hear the work from various vantage points. Many of my observations about the nature of spatialized music, scattered throughout the pages of this dissertation have originated during these rehearsals. It is my strong conviction that spatialized music has to be experienced live to be fully appreciated.

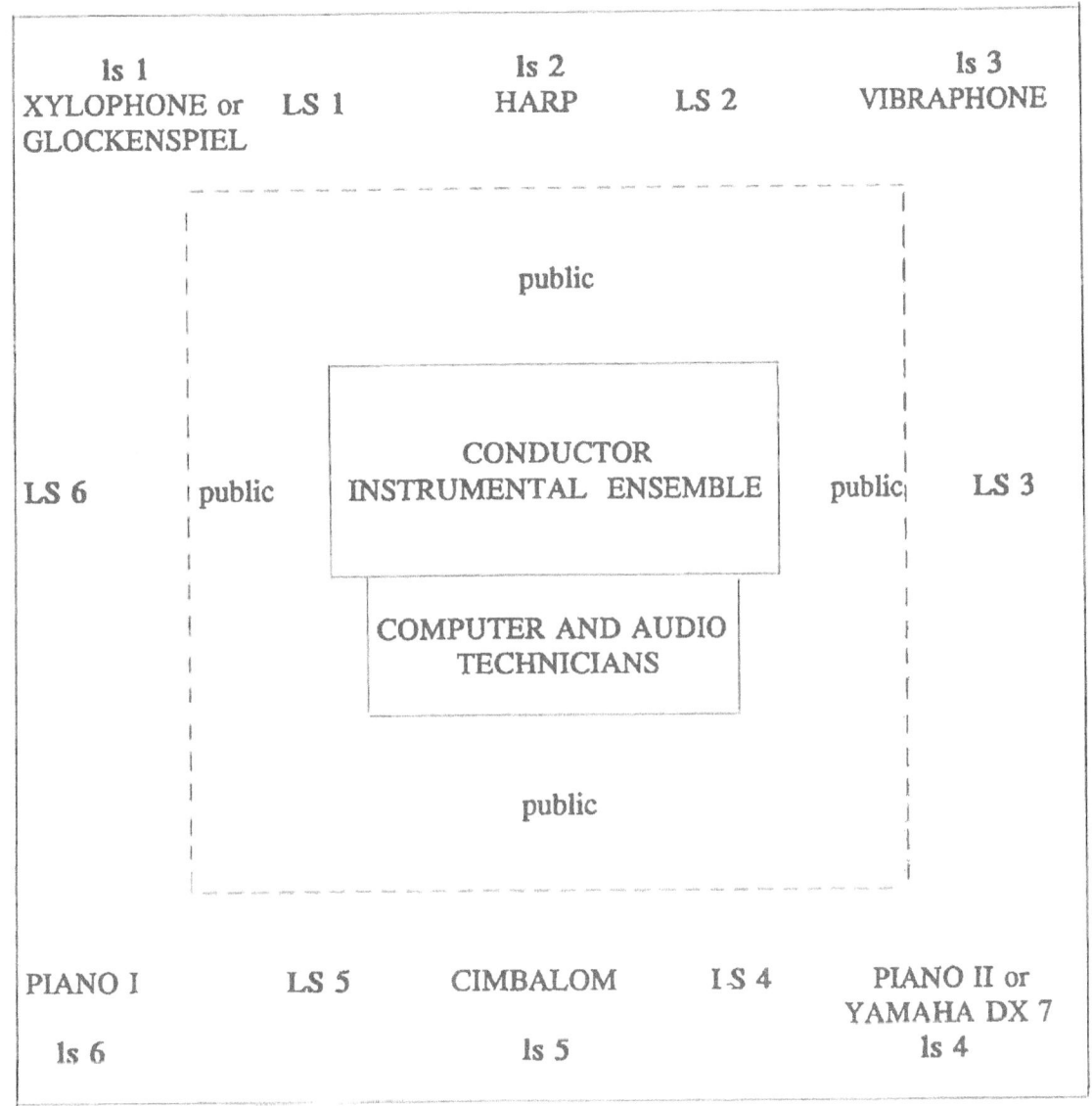

Ex. V-17: Placement of soloists, orchestra and loudspeakers in Pierre Boulez's *Répons* (1981-1988). "LS 1"--loudspeaker no. 1, for electronically transformed or synthetic sounds; "ls 1"--loudspeaker no. 1, for amplified sounds of the soloists.

spatial interactions in the main sections of *Répons*.[44]

Table V-2: Spatialization in *Répons*	
rehearsal number and name or letter	brief description of the music (instrumentation, spatial effects)
1-20	introduction by the central ensemble, no electronics
21-26 A	exposition of the soloists and electronics; alternating sections of (1) sound movement the speed of which is controlled by the amplitude of the music, the louder the faster (each soloist is assigned a different set of 4 loudspeakers controlled by flip-flop units) and (2) stationary sounds with a varied number of delays, from 7 to 15, (different in each section) and frequency shifts, from 5 to 8 (usually the same number for all soloists). Each rehearsal no. starts with the spatial movement and continues with delays-plus-frequency shifts.
27-31 B	soloists and ensemble, textural and dynamic contrasts, the soloists have different numbers of delays in each section (4-24), all delays of each instrument are heard from a single loudspeaker which varies in each section.
32-33	tutti, no electronics

[44]This description is based on *PETIT RÉPONS, dit BREVIAIRE: documentation succincte* by Denis Lorrain, a brief summary of the technical documentation for the computer signal processing (Lorrain 1992). Dominique Jameux gave a cursory description of the whole work in its 1982 and 1984 versions (Jameux 1991). Other published studies of *Répons* have concentrated on the first portion of the piece. Nattiez (1988) and Deliège (1988) analyze the introduction (no. 1-20). Boulez and Gerzso (1988) discuss the first entry of the soloists (no. 21).

\multicolumn{2}{c}{Table V-2: Spatialization in *Répons*, continued}
34-41 Bali	tutti, glockenspiel replaces xylophone, the soloists have timbral transformations with ring modulation (1 to 5 settings per soloist) and comb filters (1 to 4 settings)
42 wallpaper	xylophone, DX7 (electric organ setting) replaces piano 2; quiet music with an overall crescendo pattern; sounds of 5 soloists trigger synthetic sounds (Noise Gates and synthesis are used)
43-46	tutti, no electronics
47-52 X	tutti, the ensemble plays continuously; each soloist alternates between two settings of delays or delays with ring modulation, their placement in space is governed by flip/flop functions; the number of loudspeakers increases from 1 (or 2 with the same signal) in no. 47-50 to 5 (or 6, including 2 with the same signal) in no. 52.
53 Y1	tutti, each of the soloists with a different number of delays (piano I--9, piano II--15, cimbalom--16, vibraphone--24, harp--27) and ring modulation transforming the timbre of delayed sounds; each instrument is heard from one, always the same, loudspeaker.
54-64 Y2 girophare	"spotlight" on various soloists in turn (the highlighted musician plays louder, has soloistic passages); music is dense, loud and varied (soloistic passages in the ensemble, dialogues between various groups); frequent scales and fast arpeggios; the overall shape of is of a decreasing number of shifts of the "spotlight" and an increasing number of repeated delays.
54 Y2, cont.	fast shifts of "spotlight" (highlighting each of the soloists in turn for 1111 milliseconds)--the alternation of all soloists, with 2-4 delays.

Table V-2: Spatialization in *Répons*, continued	
55	shifts of "spotlight" (durations of 1190 ms)--independent alternations of (1) piano I with harp and (2) the remaining group of the soloists; 5 or 6 delays each.
57	shifts of "spotlight" (durations of 1667 ms)--independent alternations of (1) piano I and vibraphone and (2) three other soloists, (3) cimbalom is static; 7 or 8 delays each.
60	shifts of "spotlight" (durations of 2778 ms), (1) cimbalom and harp are constant, (2) two pianos and (3) the percussion alternate in pairs; 8-11 delays each
64	slow shifts of "spotlight" (durations of 8333 ms) on piano 1 and the xylophone, the other four soloists are static; 10-13 delays
65-90	tutti, no electronics, the main section of instrumental, responsorial dialogues between individual soloists and between soloists and orchestra, fast tempo, changing meter.
91-95 Z (A-E)	coda, return to the original material of soloists' arpeggios with delays and frequency shifts as well as rotation in space
91 Z, cont. (A)	xylophone, harp, vibraphone, piano II, cimbalom (without piano I), each soloist has 7 delays, 6 frequency shifts, and rotation between a different set of 4 loudspeakers
92 (B)	without piano I and harp, each soloist has 12 delays, 6 frequency shifts, and rotation between loudspeakers nos. 2,4,6, only piano II has a different set (loudspeakers nos. 1,3,5)
93 (C)	without piano I, harp and cimbalom; each soloist has 7 delays, 7 frequency shifts, and alternation between 2 loudspeakers, different for each soloist and near him/her

		Table V-2: Spatialization in *Répons*, continued
94	(D)	xylophone and piano II remain, each soloist has 9 delays, 7 frequency shifts, and movement between a set of different 3 widely-spaced loudspeakers
95	(E)	piano II; with 5-6 delays, 5-6 frequency shifts, and an increasing number of loudspeakers--at first used individually (from 1 to 4 loudspeakers), in the final arpeggio together (with the same signal in 1 to 3 neighbouring speakers)

One of the most notable sections of *Répons*, unique in terms of the signal processing method (used nowhere else within this work), is rehearsal no. 42, nicknamed the "wallpaper."[45] For Boulez, this name is self-evident:

> That is exactly it: the wallpaper. When you hear the instruments that are playing loud, you also hear that the loudspeakers play something else at the same time. This sound is practically inaudible. It is just a kind of a chord slightly varied in timbre: more colour, less colour, etc. Usually you do not look at the wallpaper, and you do not listen to this sound really--you listen to it at a point, then you stop. . . I could call that a cloud--you look at it and it disappears, and then you look at it again, and it is there again. It is like wallpaper, always with the same kind of structure but you look at a different point. . . At first you do not hear much, the sounds are barely there. Then the instruments make a crescendo, and the sound appears--the louder the instruments are, the more of the "wallpaper" there is. The amount of sound is controlled by the dynamics of the soloists.
>
> (Boulez 1992)

---

[45]The composer, asked for an explanation of this caption, gave two reasons, (1) it is useful to have "'code' names to recognize immediately the sections of the music," (2) these names reflect the source of inspiration (Boulez 1992).

Ex. V-18: Excerpt from the "audio" score of *Répons*, with changes of attenuation levels for different soloists, no. 42, p. 58.

© copyright 1981 by Universal Edition A.G., Vienna. All Rights Reserved. Used by permission of European American Music Distributors Corporation, sole U.S. and Canadian agent for Universal Edition A.G., Vienna.

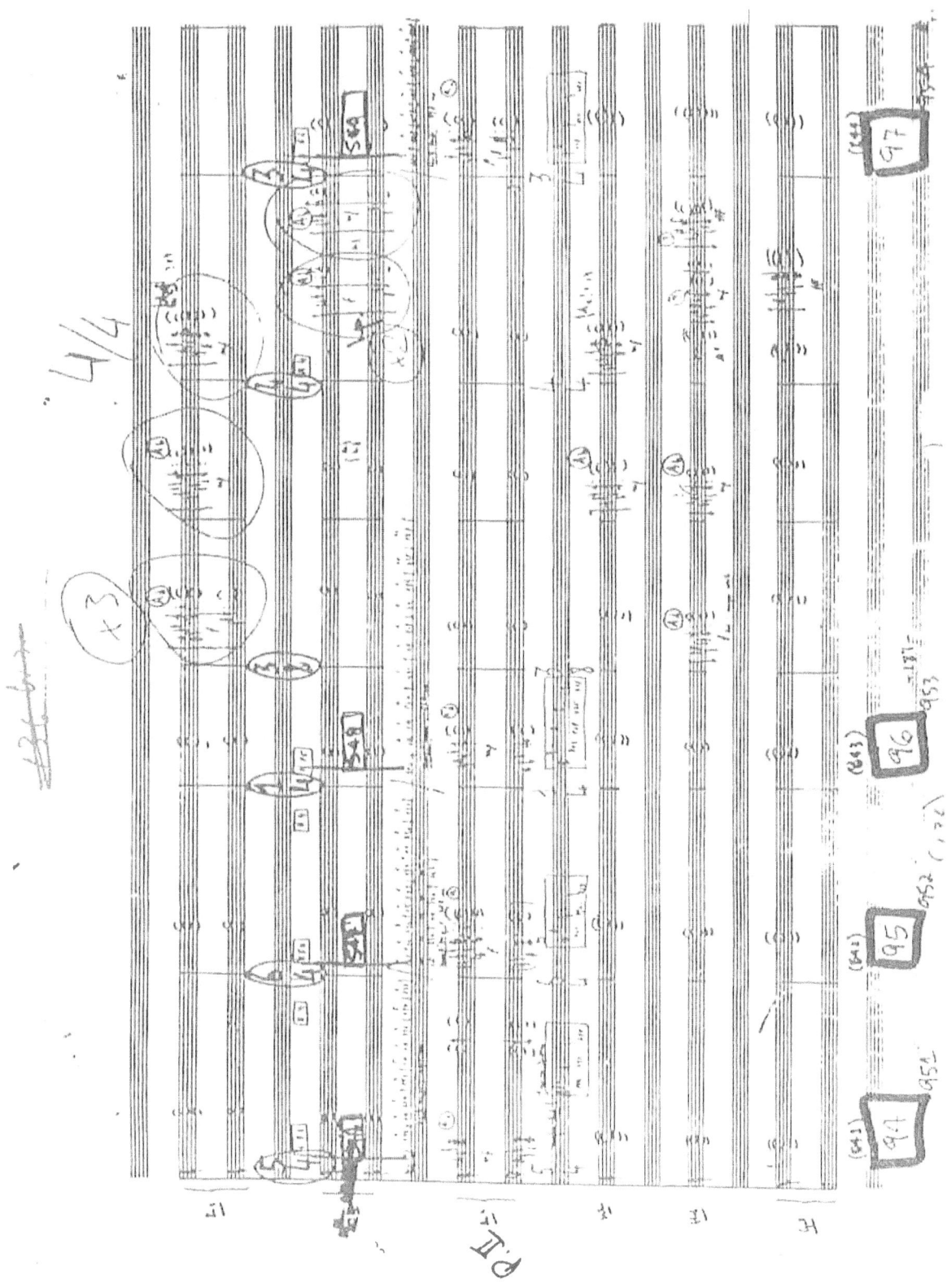

Ex. V-19: Excerpt from the "computer" score of *Répons* with hand-written annotations specifying frequency shifts and delay times, no. 95, p. 187.

© copyright 1981 by Universal Edition A.G., Vienna. All Rights Reserved. Used by permission of European American Music Distributors Corporation, sole U.S. and Canadian agent for Universal Edition A.G., Vienna.

Technically, this effect is realized by using the Noise Gate as an envelope follower.[46] Usually, the Noise Gate is open when the instrument plays and closed when it is silent in order to cut out the ambient noise or prevent the sound of the orchestra from entering the delays. Here, the amplitude of the instrument "gates" the synthesis: below a certain point there are no synthetic sounds, the louder the instrument plays the higher the level of electronic sonorities.

The mixture of electronic, amplified and instrumental sounds is an essential feature of the "wallpaper" music, a quiet interlude between two lively, bustling sections of the work. In this section, the instrumental sounds are amplified, not processed. Nonetheless, the balance between the amplification and sound synthesis is difficult to achieve. Ex. V-18, an excerpt from the full "audio" score of *Répons* (used by the audio technicians in 1992) presents the differences of attenuation levels set for the five channels of the five soloists.

The synthetic sounds surround the instrumental arpeggios and trills with a delicate aura of high, tinkling sonorities. Each of the soloists triggers a different response; the timbral and spectral variety of the electronic sounds mirrors the diversity of the instruments. A diffuse (not clearly localized) and continuous sound tapestry emerges and disappears in space with the rising and falling dynamics of the instrumental sounds. Here, Boulez creates an impression that the space itself participates in the responsorial patterns of *Répons*.

Instrumental and electronic sounds relate in a different way in the final section of the piece (no. 95). As the outline of the work reveals, the coda (no. 91-95) resembles the solo exposition in terms of texture, sound movement and type of electronic transformations.[47] In both sections, these transformations involve frequency shifts and delays. In the coda, the number of instruments which are electronically

---

[46]According to the explanation by Denis Lorrain (private communication during the rehearsals of *Répons*, 6 August 1992).

[47]The first entry of the soloists in no. 21 has been described in detail by Andrew Gerzso (Boulez and Gerzso 1988, Gerzso 1988).

processed decreases from five (no. 91, without piano I) to one at the end (No. 95, piano II). The number of delays, frequency shifts, and the pattern of movement between a set of loudspeakers differs in each segment of the music (5-12 delays, 5-7 shifts). At the end, only the transformed echoes remain, resounding in space from various directions, gradually slower and quieter, like ripples on the surface of water.

The closing gesture of *Répons* reveals the difference in the style of writing ("écriture") between the central ensemble which is conducted and the soloists who "are playing on cue, according to a very slow and regular beat, so that they do not really have to look at the beat very much while playing" (Boulez 1992). Here, the substance of the music depends on its spatial, physical aspect: the soloists placed at the outskirts of the performance area simply cannot see all the movements of the conductor.

The "computer" score of *Répons* contains numerous hand-written annotations with data about frequency shifts and delay times. An example from p. 187 (Ex. V-19) presents four series of frequencies which define the shifts of the four chords of piano II (up or down). The last series includes the following frequency shifts (in Hertz): 687 up--327 down--687 down--327 up--291 down--727 up--327 down. Four of these numbers are also written in an rectangular box with the approximate notation of the pitch of each frequency. The details of the shifts have been specified by Boulez; they are as important a part of the composition as any of the instrumental writing.

At the first entry of the soloists and at the conclusion of *Répons* Boulez uses spatialization to create spectacular, dramatic gestures. In both sections (rehearsal numbers 21-26 and 91-95) the attention of the audience is

> suddenly turned away from the center of the hall to the perimeter, where the soloists and the speakers are. The audience hears the soloists' sounds traveling around the hall without being able to distinguish the paths followed by the individual sounds.
>
> (Boulez and Gerzso 1988: 48)

This unclear awareness of the complexity of the spatial aspects of the music heightens the experience of the listeners who are fully encircled by and immersed in sound. According to Jean Jacques Nattiez, the perceptual experience of *Répons* involves listening to various levels of the music at once, the macrostructure and the microstructure, the interplay of order and entropy (Nattiez 1988). These relationships are structured in space, which articulates the contrasts between the ensemble and the soloists, between the instruments and their electronic echoes and shadows. The originality and richness of the spatial organization in Boulez's *Répons* places this work among the masterpieces of spatialized music.

5.6.
Spatial imagery and symbols

The classification of spatial designs in music proposed in this chapter does not include the musical simulation of spatial imagery. The reason for this omission is quite straightforward: composers use different types of spatialization for programmatic purposes.[48] A review of the repertory of spatialized music reveals the continuous hold of geometry on the imagination of composers.[49] The spatial geometry of music realized within the confines of the concert hall can assume the well-known regular forms of a line-segment (Ton de Leeuw's *Car nos vignes sont en fleur* for 12 voices in a linear arrangement on the stage, 1981), a triangle (three instrumental ensembles in

---

[48] However, unusual spatial images may also be transformed into pitch and time. In *Hadewijch* by Louis Andriessen (1984-1988), the temporal dimensions of the work (the length of each section) are modelled on the spatial proportions of the Rheims cathedral (the distance between the pillars; cf. Harley 1994a). John Cage uses the constellations of the stars represented in star charts as models of pitch material and attack points in *Atlas Eclipticalis* for orchestra (1961). In Cage's *Ryoanji* (1983-1985), the contours of stones of various sizes portraying a Japanese Zen garden (a garden of stones and sand) are traced onto paper to create melodic outlines.

[49] Henry Brant had little appreciation for such geometry in sound: "Ideas of that kind seem to me more an expression of hope than of reality. . . . It is hard enough to make the sounds do what you want 'in sound' without saying that the sound should be shaped like a pretzel or something like that." (Brant 1992: 3).

Iannis Xenakis's *Alax* of 1985), a square (four choirs in *Bells of Light [Sculpture II]* by James Harley, 1984), or a cube (Julio Estrada's *Canto Naciente* for eight brass instruments, 1975-1978). One of the fundamental shapes of spatialized music, the circle, appears in a variety of contexts.[50] The idea of surrounding the audience with sound underlies, for instance, Henry Brant's *Orbits* for 80 trombones (1979), Iannis Xenakis's *Persephassa* for 6 percussionists (1969), and R. Murray Schafer's *Credo* for 12 choirs (1978)--to mention only three works by the composers discussed in Part Three of this dissertation (Chapters VI--VIII).

The compositional use of spatial distribution may be inspired by geographic or architectural shapes. In Charles Hoag's *Trombonehenge* of 1980, for instance, thirty trombones surround the audience in a pattern imitating the outline of the ruins at Stonehenge. Spatial designs may also be motivated by the intent to portray or evoke mythical, ritual or imaginary spaces. The latter option appears in Gavin Bryars's *The Sinking of the Titanic*, a conceptual work-in-progress begun in 1969 (Bryars 1975). Bryars considers an impossible situation: what if the music, supposedly resounding at the bottom of the North Atlantic for over sixty years, could have been refloated? Thus, the music supposedly played by a band on board while the *Titanic* was going down (performed by an ensemble of instrumentalists) is surrounded with musical glosses associated with memories of the survivors, with the titles of hymns played by the band, etc. (transformed, pre-recorded sounds heard from various locations in space). The hymn played at the moment of the sinking undergoes timbral transformations to suggest four stages in its imaginary history: "as heard in the open air on the deck, as the ship sinks, as it remains stable on the bottom of the ocean, and

---

[50]The image of the circle may be approximated in time, as in Luciano Berio's *Circles* (1960)--through the music's return to the opening material at the conclusion of the piece (a design similar to that of James Joyce's *Finnegan's Wake*). Similar circular designs are common in earlier music, e.g. the forms of the rondo and the canon. Moreover, the musical notation of renaissance canons often includes the geometric shape of the circle (cf. Besseler and Gülke 1973: 124).

in a new state in the open air" after the ship's raising (Potter 1981: 9).[51]

Geometric patterns are frequently endowed with a symbolic function. Works with varied and unusual placements of performers are often meant to communicate something, to convey a message through the articulation of sound in space. In Brian Ferneyhough's *Transit* for six solo voices and chamber orchestra (1975), the orchestra is seated in four semicircles on the stage. This setting represents an image from the Renaissance woodcut which inspired this composition (depicting the four spheres of the Universe). As Jonathan Harvey explains:

> In the first semicircle, at the front of the stage, are the six singers and three woodwind (flute, oboe, and clarinet with various doublings), all nine amplified; these represent the 'normal' human world. In the next semicircle are piano (four hands), cimbalom, guitar, harps and light percussion; these represent the stars above the human landscape. In the next semicircle are the strings representing the intermediary darkness, and in the outermost one are the heavy brass, representing the music of the spheres itself.
> (Harvey 1979: 726)

In the woodcut (reproduced on the cover of *The Musical Times* in which Harvey's report has been published, cf. Ex. V-20), a Magus breaks through the last sphere separating the domain of the mortals from the divine. This event is portrayed in the music by delaying the brass entry to the second half of the piece; thus, the music follows the "transitio" of the Magus. In addition, the placement of the heavy brass at the furthest distance from the audience fulfils an acoustic purpose: the loud instruments are prevented from overpowering the quieter woodwinds.[52] Moreover, Ferneyhough exploits the traditional association of high pitch, bright timbre, and the percussive articulation of the cimbalom and the harps with the shimmering light of the stars--bringing in the topical spatial symbolism of pitch and timbre.

---

[51]However, Bryars explains in notes to the work's recording that "it should be a mistake to think of this sounding music as being the piece, there have been performances which use none of these elements" (Bryars n.d.). In conceptual music, the idea of the Work may exist even without a definite musical content.

[52]A similar placement plan, with the brass at the farthest end of the stage and woodwinds close to the audience, is used in Boulez's *Rituel* (cf. Chapter III, section 3.4).

Ex. V-22: Fragment of "The descent of the Eucharist" in the second movement of *Ultimos Ritos*, p. 67.

Ex. V-20: Renaissance woodcut, the inspiration for Brian Ferneyhough's *Transit* for six solo voices and chamber orchestra (1975).

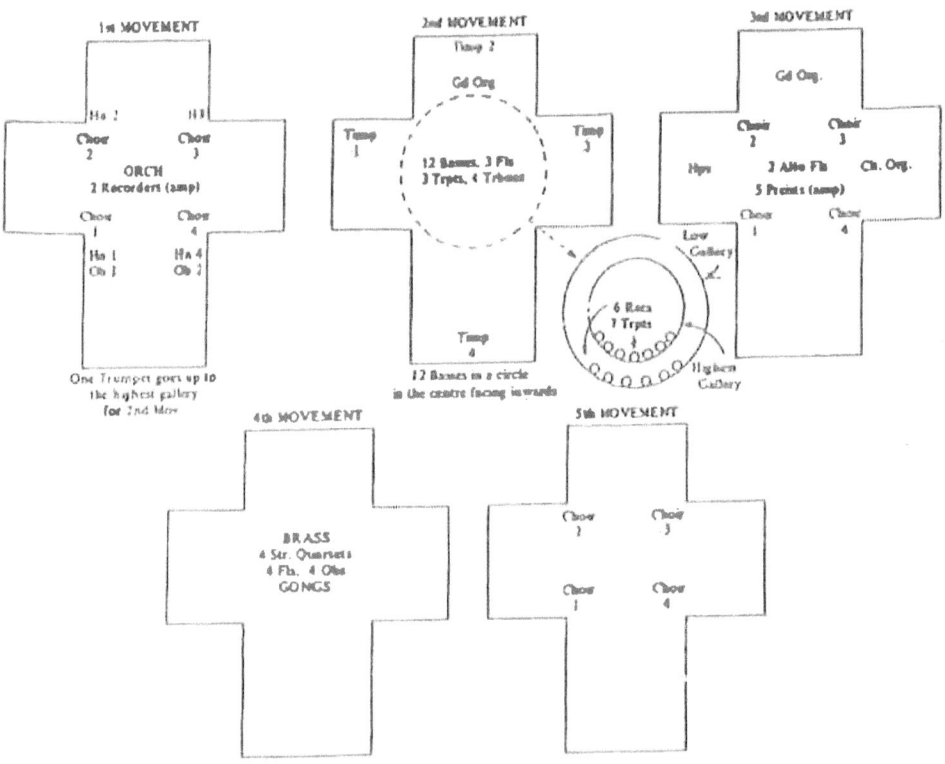

Ex. V-21: Positions of the performers in *Ultimos Ritos* by John Tavener (1972).

In the second movement of John Tavener's *Ultimos Ritos*, dedicated to St. John of the Cross (1972), the circle coexists with the shape of the cross. Both images participate in the religious symbolism of the music. The contour of the cross, a standard floor plan in many churches, provides the basic architectural design for the work (Ex. V-21). Tavener writes: "the proportions of the work are those of a cross, and so is the layout of the choirs and some of the instruments" (Tavener 1974: 1). For the composer, the size of the architectural space is also important:

> Ideally, *Ultimos Ritos* should be performed in a cathedral or large church with gallery space. If performed elsewhere, it is essential that the building has a minimum of 6 seconds reverberation.
> (Tavener 1972)

This acoustic requirement is reflected in the score by frequent indications to "clear the sound" before proceeding with a subsequent section of the music. The spatial elevation of the high-pitched and highly directional sounds of recorders and trumpets in the second movement of *Ultimos Ritos* also reflects acoustic considerations.[53] At the same time, though, Tavener associates these instruments with "royalty and love" and places them in the two high galleries to represent the heavenly elevation of Christ descending to this Earth in the Eucharist.

The Eucharist "descends" in response to an ardent prayer by 12 basses, placed in a circle and chanting a poem by St. John of the Cross.[54] The voices enter one by one with the same text, gradually "filling-in" the circle. The singers, however, do not surround the audience, who must witness the musical ritual from the outside (cf. Ex. V-21). The singers surround the instrumentalists who articulate the symbolic "descent" in the second part of the second movement, subtitled "El descenso de la

---

[53] Recall that the elevated spatial position of high-pitched sounds constitutes one of the basic premises of Henry Brant's conception of spatial music (Cf. Chapter III, section 3.2). It is realized, for instance, in *Voyage Four* with the placement of the double basses in the audience and the flutes and soprano on the highest balcony (Brant 1967; cf. Chapter VI).

[54] This movement, entitled "Cantar del alma que se huelga de conoscer a Dios por fe" (after the poem of the same title), begins with the meditative chant section.

Eucaristia." The descent takes the form of an alternation between the elevated and floor-level instruments of the same timbre. Six trumpets, located in the highest possible gallery surrounding the central cupola of the building, and six recorders placed in a lower gallery play a slow sequence of chords three times before it starts to resound from the ground, performed by trumpets and flutes located directly below the cupola. These sections are interrupted by music from the timpani, trombones and organ, instruments which outline the shape of a cross on the horizontal plane (cf. Ex. V-21). Example V-22 presents one such intervention followed by the "descent"--a dialogue of trumpets from high and low spatial locations. In *Ultimos Ritos*, Tavener creates a rare musical instance of spatial motion in the vertical direction. At the same time, the interlocking designs of a vertical descent and a horizontal cross represent a theological statement: the incarnation of Christ (i.e. the living Eucharist) was completed by His crucifixion.[55]

The auditory realization of complex geometric designs, easily conveyed in musical notation, may be quite problematic. In Tavener's piece, for instance, a listener seated near the entrance to the church--at the bottom of the cross, as it were--will recognize neither the circular arrangement of the distant singers, nor the shape of the cross outlined by the placement of the timpani. Thus, Tavener's composition illustrates the perceptual fragility of spatial designs and the dependence of their symbolic interpretation on notation (i.e. the graphic images of the cross and the circle included in the score). Simultaneously, *Ultimos Ritos* reveals the complexity of the coexistence of various aspects of spatialization in one work (e.g. the choice of the acoustic environment of the church, the realization of geometric images in music, and the location of performers in a three-dimensional space).

---

[55] In 1994, Tavener, who meanwhile has embraced Eastern Orthodoxy, renounced this work for theological reasons: "Now, looking back, I have a dislike for this concept of St. John of the Cross, this whole idea of God as a lover. I don't terrifically look forward to hearing the older pieces in the festival, I must say, because I've got into a certain mode of thinking, a certain ethos, and going back to hear myself struggling to find that ethos I don't terribly relish." (Tavener 1994: 11).

Conclusion

The variety of designs reviewed in this chapter reveals the diversity of spatial features in musical works and the richness of the spatiality of musical experience. The classification includes criteria relating to the choice of the acoustic environment for the performance, to the mobility of the musicians and audiences, to the type of sound-sources, and to their arrangements within the chosen performance space. The various types of spatial designs are illustrated with examples from works by European and North-American composers of many nationalities. Thus, spatialization is described in the context of the international avant-garde. In the following three chapters I concentrate on three distinct approaches to musical spatiality. The compositional philosophies of Henry Brant, Iannis Xenakis and R. Murray Schafer are as different as their music, but these composers share a preoccupation with a single common theme: space.

PART THREE

IMPLEMENTATIONS
(THREE COMPOSERS)

CHAPTER VI

EXPERIMENTAL TRADITION IN
THE "SPATIAL MUSIC" OF HENRY BRANT

Introduction

In 1933, Henry Cowell praised Brant as "a musician with knowledge, technique, original ideas, feeling, something to say, and courage" (Cowell 1933b: 96). An overstatement in reference to a young composer, these words acquire a new significance sixty years later; years filled with explorations of Brant's idea that space is "an essential aspect of musical composition" (this expression comes from the title of Brant's seminal essay of 1967).[1]

In this chapter, examples from seven compositions will highlight the basic features of Brant's music and help to trace the course of its development since his first spatial work of 1953, *Antiphony I* for symphony orchestra divided into five separated groups (1953/1968).[2] An analysis of this composition will be followed by studies of

---

[1] I discuss Brant's idea of musical space and his contribution to the conceptual development of spatialization in Chapter III. Here, I follow his usage of the term "spatial music" instead of "spatialized music."

[2] The 1992 *Rental Catalog* of Carl Fisher, Inc. (Carl Fischer 1992) lists 76 spatial and 57 non-spatial compositions by Brant. It does not mention works withdrawn by the composer, but already recorded (e.g. *Orbits* for 80 trombones, organ and voice, 1979), nor works published and deposited elsewhere (*Verticals Ascending* for 2 wind ensembles, 1967, MCA Music c/o Belwin Mills). A brief *Catalog of Compositions* (by C. Fisher, Inc., Circ no. 8519) lists Brant's works up to 1982 and differs from the *Rental Catalog* in regards to some details of instrumentation.

Millennium II for brass, percussion and high voice (1954) and *500: Hidden Hemisphere* for 3 concert bands and an ensemble of Caribbean steel drums (1992).[3] In addition, I will discuss *Voyage Four* for 1 singer and 83 instrumentalists in "total antiphonal distribution" (1964),[4] *Meteor Farm* for 2 sopranos, orchestra, 2 choruses, brass choir, 2 percussion groups, jazz band, Javanese gamelan orchestra, West African drumming ensemble, and South Indian trio (1982), *Western Springs* for 2 orchestras, 2 choruses and 2 jazz combos (1984), as well as *Bran(d)t aan de Amstel* (site-specific music of multiple ensembles dispersed throughout the city of Amsterdam, 1984).[5]

Brant's spatial music can be grouped into a number of recurring categories, which differ from the conventional solo, chamber and orchestral genres.[6] All spatial works require separation of groups of performers in the concert hall. Distances between the separated ensembles should be large, and the ensembles frequently placed at several levels (some scores contain schemes for the required settings and forbid performance otherwise).[7] The instrumental forces sometimes form symmetrical pairs, from the simplest antiphonal opposition of 2 wind ensembles in *Verticals Ascending*

---

[3] Dorothy Drennan's dissertation (1975) is a good source of information about *Antiphony I*, *Millennium II* and *Voyage Four*.

[4] Brant uses the term "antiphonal distribution" in his article of 1955 and in many musical scores to denote the basic spatial feature of his works. "Antiphony" or "antiphonal" appear also in his titles, e.g. *Antiphony I* (1953), *September Antiphonies* (1962), *Antiphonal Responses* (1978).

[5] In this piece, 4 boats with musicians (flutes, percussion) floating down the canals of Amsterdam encounter land-based choirs, bands, carillons, street organs, etc.

[6] Brant's hostility towards electroacoustic music and amplification explains the nearly total absence of electroacoustics from his output. The article of 1967 includes a reference to one exception, a piece for tape entitled *St. Catherine's Wheel*.

[7] In Brant's words: "From experience, I would say that no space less than 20 feet is emphatic from the point of view of the audience. The distance of 4 or 10 feet, when you are sitting in front of it, does not really cause a perception of space. . . The direction from the back of the hall to the front of the hall is the best; from ground level to the top balcony--that is also good. And, perhaps, distances half of that." (Brant 1992: 5).

(1967) to the expanded symmetry of 2 orchestras, 2 brass ensembles, 2 steel drum bands and 2 wind bands in *Prisons of the Mind* (1990). The use of widely separated and contrasting ensembles is far more common: e.g. mezzo-soprano, speaker, mixed chorus, orchestra, band and percussion group in *Atlantis* (1960) or 5 solo voices, chorus, orchestra, flute choir and jazz ensemble in *Skull and Bones* (1990). Brant reveals his preference for homogeneous instrumental choirs in works with a large number of wind instruments, e.g. *Orbits* for 80 trombones, organ and voice (1979) or *Flight Over a Global Map* for 100 trumpets, 3 percussions and piano (1990).

A separate category of works with performer movement includes *Hieroglyphics I* for viola with instrumental ensemble and voice (1957)[8] and *Windjammer* (1969) with specific walking routes for the performers of the wind quintet. Some of Brant's large-scale pieces contain much "found" musical material in the spatially separated layers (e.g. for the non-Western ensembles in *Meteor Farm*). Improvisation is frequently introduced in some strands of the music, especially when jazz groups are among the instrumental forces (e.g. *Western Springs*).

Brant's reliance on jazz is not limited to the use of jazz ensembles in the orchestration, but constitutes an important element of his compositional style which draws from "jazz idioms, the exploitation of the timbral aspects of the instrumentation, and the extensive use of counterpoint" (Drennan 1975: 47). In the creation of spatial music, Brant acknowledges his indebtedness to Gabrieli, Berlioz and Ives.[9] The influence of Ives has a special significance, and--as will be shown--extends beyond the idea of the spatial separation of instruments. Brant's spatial music is rooted in American experimental tradition,[10] a tradition initiated by Charles Ives.

---

[8]This composition predates Berio's *Circles* of 1960, which is often cited as the earliest work which requires the soloist to move from one stage position to another (cf. Vande Gorne 1988).

[9]Brant (1967, 1992); Drennan (1975: 60-61).

[10]I borrow this term from David Nicholls's book of 1990.

Ex. VI-1: Five layers in the climax of Brant's *Antiphony I* (1953/1968), p. 44.

Ex. VI-2: Polytonal imitation in *Antiphony I*, p. 31.

6.1.

Antiphony I and the American experimental tradition

Brant composed his first spatial work, *Antiphony I*,[11] in 1953 and expanded it by the addition of a 2-part chorus in 1968.[12] Here, he divided the orchestra into 5 groups: strings, woodwinds (3 piccolos, 3 oboes, and 3 clarinets), 4 horns, muted brass (3 trumpets and 3 trombones), and percussion (glockenspiel, xylophone, chimes, timpani). Each group is, according to Brant's note in the score, "situated in a different part of the hall, having its own distinct tempo, meter, and bar-line scheme." The strings are on the stage and the remaining groups in the hall. The composer warns: "On no account may all five groups be placed together on the stage, or near the stage! This would go directly counter to the specific spatial-polyphonic concept of the music." (Brant 1968: Explanatory Remarks).

The spatial separation of instrumental groups highlights the contrasts of timbre, meter, key, texture and motivic content between the five layers of the music. Example VI-1, drawn from the dramatic climax of the piece, illustrates the independence of the musical material of the five superimposed layers, distinct in all aspects, including spatial location.

Here, as often in Brant's music, the complexity of the music does not result from elaborate compositional operations, but from a juxtaposition of many distinct elements. It is because the composer believes that "a purposeful lack of relationship between the intervals, phrasing, note-values, tone-quality and sonorities of the various

---

[11] Brant (1967) names *Antiphony I* as his first spatial work. The *Rental Catalog* (1992) lists the earlier *Millenium I* (1950) as a spatial piece but its score does not indicate any separation of instrumental groups. *Antiphony I*, although preceding Berio's and Stockhausen's spatial compositions, postdates experiments in spatial sound projection by Pierre Henry and Pierre Schaeffer (1951-52, Paris).

[12] The revisions of 1968 include the option of replacing the strings with a clarinet choir and the addition of the chorus which consists of two groups of voices of different range (mixed, male or female).

lines will necessarily produce a complex result as soon as the lines are combined" (Brant 1955: 13). Spatial separation is essential because, according to Brant, the main function of space in music is "to make complexity intelligible" (Brant 1992: 1).

The frenzied culmination of *Antiphony I*, thought by Drennan to represent a summer storm, an element in the pastoral program of the work (Drennan 1975: 65-66),[13] seems closely related to an Ivesian "pandemonium"--a dramatic climax of superimposed layers of melodies in different keys and rhythms (Nicholls 1990: 24, 29). The pandemonium is one example of Ives's "layering technique" (term from Morgan 1974) based on the accumulation of independent strata of sound (c.f. Chapter III). "Total polyphony," a different term describing Ives's compositional technique, refers to the "independence of musical ideas or parts" (Nicholls 1990: 34), which may be achieved in two ways: by means of polytempi (as in *The Unanswered Question* or movements II and IV of the *Fourth Symphony*) or by "contrapuntal superimposition of dissonant, rhythmically unrelated lines" as in *Tone Roads* (Nicholls 1990: 64). Both options resurface in Brant's spatial music: the former in *Antiphony I*, the latter in *Millennium II*.[14]

In *Antiphony I*, the five instrumental groups are assigned different tempi. In the strings one quarternote equals MM45, in the muted brass--MM75, in the percussion--MM90, in the woodwinds--MM105, and in the horns--MM120. These tempi create the numerical proportion of 45:75:90:105:120 that can be reduced to the series 3:5:6:7:8. The strings are distinguished by the slowest tempo and a privileged placement on the stage. The absence of common denominators between the remaining tempi (except MM90 of the percussion and MM120 of the horns) increases the disparity between the distinct strata of the music.

---

[13]Drennan discovers images of birdsong in *Antiphony I* (Drennan 1975: 66). Indeed, the parts of the woodwinds in rehearsal numbers 7-10 (p. 19-30) bear standard features of the musical representation of birdsong: brief, repeated motives in high register (fixed pitches) with alternating staccato and legato articulation, trills and grace notes.

[14]These works provide merely two instances of common procedures, for almost all of Brant's spatial music is built from independent layers in different tempi.

The differentiation of superimposed layers through contrasting tempi is further augmented by polytonality: each group and each section of the strings play in a different key. The choice of tonalities emphasizes dissonant relationships between the layers (e.g. C--D flat--E flat--E in the strings).[15] Polytonality has Ivesian precedents (cf. Nicholls 1990: 7-11) as does the use of strings as a continuous layer of music, against which other strands of sound are heard from various points in space (as in *The Unanswered Question* of 1906).[16] In *Antiphony I*, the distant groups enter on cues, and proceed at their own speed without a strict relationship to the main stream of the music.[17]

"Polyphony" refers both to the juxtaposition of many layers and to the techniques of imitation, canon and inversion--all featured prominently in *Antiphony I*. The music of the strings, for instance (cf. Ex. VI-2), consists of a series of "points of imitation" in which a head motive is exactly repeated by successive voices (usually in ascending order) in different keys; the phrases continue independently.[18] The connection between polyphony and dissonance, made by Brant in a two-fold manner (by assigning different keys to the music of spatially separated groups and by using different keys in one group on the stage) is rooted in the American experimental tradition, including Brant's own musical past.[19] Charles Seeger introduced the idea of

---

[15]According to Drennan, Brant uses polytonality to increase the density of musical textures (Drennan 1975: 270).

[16]In Chapter III, I discuss the central role of this composition for Brant's conception of spatial music.

[17]The entries of the groups usually overlap in time: one group is still playing while another one begins in a different point in space. This formal design antecedes "chain form" introduced by Witold Lutoslawski in the 1980s (Martina Homma pointed out this similarity; private communication, November 1993).

[18]Free and strict imitation as well as the simultaneous use of a motive and its inversion are quite common throughout Brant's oeuvre.

[19]Brant's early association with the group of experimental composers inspired by Ives and led by Cowell can be seen in the inclusion of an essay by Cowell about the,

"dissonant counterpoint" in 1930 (Nicholls 1990: 90); Brant's own invention of "oblique harmony" in which a perpetual dissonance is achieved by contrapuntal means dates back to the same period (Drennan 1975: 48).[20] According to recent psychoacoustic theory, spatial separation of tonally unrelated layers of sound may actually diminish the peception of the dissonance between these layers (Bregman 1990: 521).[21] Therefore, the turmoil of Brant's "pandemonium" may not be as violent as that of Ives.

In summary, the influence of Ives, the forefather and the chief representative of the American experimental tradition, on Brant's spatial music includes the use of polytonality, polyrhythms and polytempi to enhance contrasts between the distinct, simultaneous strata of sound, presented in spatial relief. The connection of polyphony and dissonance, known to Ives, but also advocated by Seeger and Cowell (Nicholls 1990: 90, 135) and--as such--one of the main traits of the American experimental tradition, appears in many of Brant's works, including *Millennium II* (1954).

---

then, 18-year-old composer in the collection of articles *American Composers on American Music* (Cowell 1933).

[20]Brant introduced the idea of "oblique harmony" in *Variations for Four Instruments* and abandoned it soon afterwards. Here, "the resolutions of separate voices occur almost invariably at different moments, often as far apart as three bars of moderate time... in this way a perpetual dissonance is achieved, one set of 'suspensions' sliding into the next" (Brant 1931: i). The idea was favourably reviewed by Cowell in his essay on Brant (Cowell 1933: 93-96). Recently, Bo Alphonce described a similar procedure of juxtaposing rhythmic shifts with dissonances in the music of Robert Schumann, e.g. the "chordal anticipation technique" in the first movement of *Kreisleriana* (Alphonce 1994: Example 4).

[21]"Since we know that spatial separation is a basis for segregating signals we should be able to suppress the dissonance between two tones by placing their sources in quite different spatial locations" (Bregman 1990: 522).

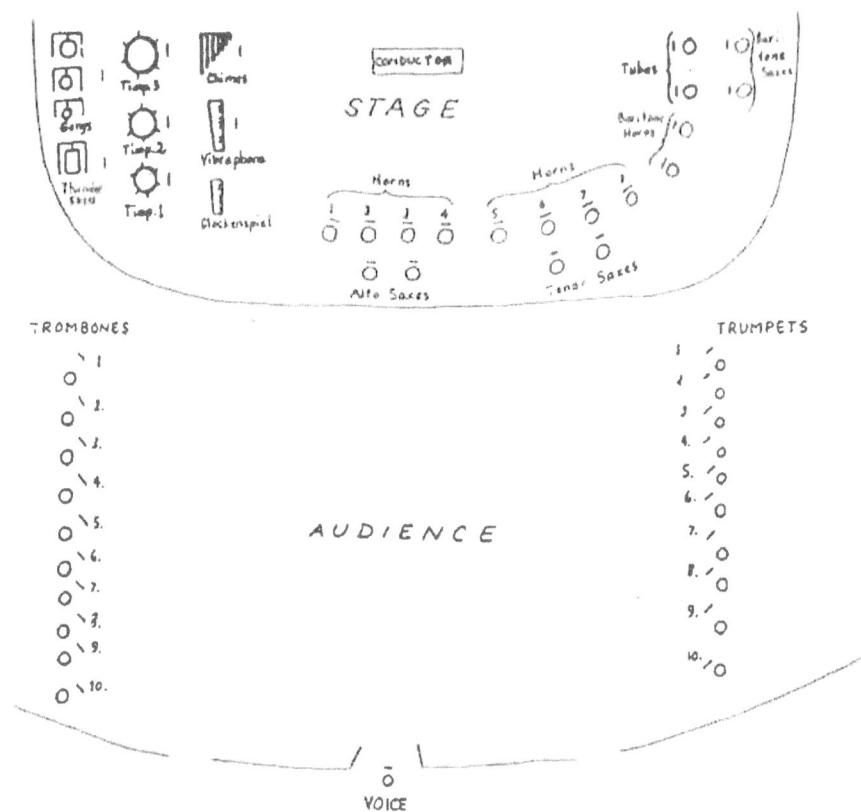

Ex. VI-3: Arrangement of the instruments in Brant's *Millennium II* (1954).

Ex. VI-4: Entries of Trumpets 1-5 in *Millennium II*, p. 1-3.

Ex. VI-5: Sound axes in *Millennium II*, p. 54.

6.2.
New spatial effects in *Millennium II*

The score of *Millennium II* contains a detailed placement plan for all the performers (cf. Ex. VI-3); here, the exact location of sounds, not just their separation, has a great compositional significance. The instrumentation of this "spatial assembly" includes 10 trumpets and 10 trombones placed along the walls of the hall, 8 horns, 2 tubas and 4 percussion players on the stage and a high voice located anywhere at a distance from the stage and the brass (preferably in a high balcony).[22]

Millennium II begins with successive entries of the trumpets and the trombones (in the order of their placement in the hall), each playing a different melody in a different key (Example VI-4). This is a clear case of dissonant polyphony. Yet, the total effect is spatial: through the accumulation of the melodies, performed continuously by an increasing number of instruments of the same timbre placed along the walls of the hall, the sound seems to move along these walls and gradually fill up the hall. Brant refers to this phenomenon simply as **travel and filling-up** and notes that the impression of sound movement is "progressively less well defined as the further entrances and accumulations occur" (Brant 1967: 238).[23]

The perception of the filling-up of the hall with sound may also result from hearing successive entries of pairs of instruments placed at the opposing sides of the auditorium (i.e. trumpet 1 and trombone 1, followed by trumpet 2 and trombone 2, etc.). Each pair of instruments creates a **sound axis**.[24] A series of such sound axes

---

[22]This instrumentation resembles that of *Millennium I*, a non-spatial composition of 1950, scored for percussion and 8 trumpets, often divided into two groups of 4. *Millennium I* contains numerous canons, frequently with pairs of voices in inversion. Athough the music includes simultaneous melodies in different rhythms, there is no polytonality.

[23]Drennan calls this effect "cumulative polyphony," to indicate the linearity of the superimposed melodies which form a dense texture (Drennan 1975: 95). A similar effect of "a sound coming from one, then successively from other loudspeakers, thus gradually filling up the hall" (Harvey 1974: 88), appears in Stockhausen's *Kontakte* (1960).

in the work's conclusion links movement in physical space with motion in pitch space. The entries of instrumental pairs begin with the highest sound of the trumpet coupled with the lowest sound of the trombone (spanning the distance from F2 to B-flat5), and end with a convergence around C4 (Ex. VI-5).[25]

Millennium II, the first composition to explore such spatial patterns, features numerous instances of "sound travel" along the walls of the hall (represented in diagrams in Ex. VI-6).[26] According to the composer,[27]

> During the various successions of accumulating entrances, the audience, situated inside the continuous walls of brass, experiences a physical sense of the sound travelling around and across the hall in various ways, and a sense of the hall as a vessel, being filled up and emptied by sound.

The instruments on the stage, especially the horns and timpani, also participate in creating spatial sound patterns, although of less refinement than the ones presented by the "wall brass." The direction of movement on the stage is back-to-front for timpani, centre-to-right for horns and tubas. The successive entries of the three timpani or the groups of horns and tubas are rhythmically coordinated, and accumulate to form three-part canons (cf. Ex. VI-7).

---

[24]**Sound axis** is "the aural axis formed when two instruments, each located in opposite areas of the hall, play simultaneously" (Drennan 1975: 15).

[25]The composition begins with the pitch class F, and ends with a dissonant, 12-note chord based on a pedal point F. The fact that the climax of the work, the entry of the solo voice, is "in C"--i.e. the dominant of F--suggests the existence of a simple tonal scheme (tonic--dominant at the climax--tonic) underlying the polytonal contrasts and dissonant sonorities of *Millennium II*.

[26]This form of sound movement differs from those used by Stockhausen and Xenakis (cf. Chapter III, VII). Unlike these composers, Brant does not attempt to create an illusion of continuity of sound motion around the hall. The *sound travel* proceeds step-wise, increasing the spatial extent of the music by the gradual addition of melodies to the texture.

[27]The composer's comments from the recording entitled *Music for Brass Choir* which includes performances by the Lehigh University Instrumental Ensemble (Lehigh 1103) are quoted by Drennan (1975: 83).

At the climactic point of the work, the effect of the "filling-up" of the hall with sound by means of superimposed sound axes in the brass (rehearsal letter M, p. 30-38), followed by percussion tremolos (on timpani and thundersheet), prepare the sudden appearance of the soprano vocalise. The successive sound axes accumulate from the front to the back of the hall. This arrangement leads the listeners' attention towards the unexpected vocal timbre and spatial elevation of the soprano singing from a distant, high balcony. Here, vertical distance and spatial location have compositional significance--they help to articulate the culmination of the work.[28]

Millennium II shares one important trait with *Antiphony I*--the rhythmic uncoordination of spatially separated layers. According to the note in the score of *Millennium II*, each trumpet and trombone "begins in the same 'medium jump tempo' and plays steadily ahead, but makes no attempt to maintain ensemble or uniform tempo with the other players" (Brant 1978: 1). Each part includes a number of phrases marked with a termination sign and, after several phrases, with a repeat sign. The phrases should be repeated until a percussion cue is heard; the current phrase should then be brought to an end. This method of creating a continuous layer of sound from definite elements superimposed in an approximate manner, finds an analogy in the "controlled aleatoricism" introduced by Witold Lutoslawski in *Jeux Venitiens* (1961). In contrast to Lutoslawski's work, in which the coordinated and uncoordinated passages are presented sequentially, Brant's composition makes simultaneous use of both types of rhythmic organization (the parts of the instruments on the stage are coordinated, in the hall--uncoordinated).

---

[28]The culmination takes place at about two-thirds of the length of this one-movement piece. Drennan (1975: 81) describes the form as A A' B, because of repetitions of directional sound-flow patterns. However, her scheme ignores the presence of the voice (she considers it optional).

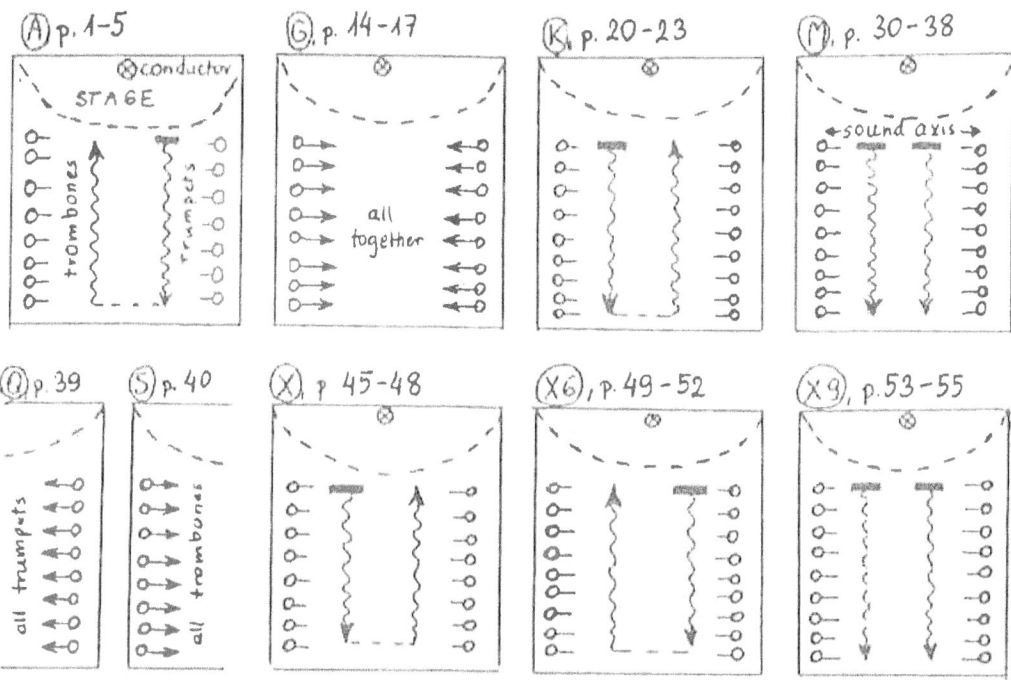

Ex. VI-6: Directional sound patterns in *Millennium II* (only in the parts of the trumpets and the trombones).

Ex. VI-7: Canons in horns and tubas, and in timpani in *Millennium II*, p. 28.

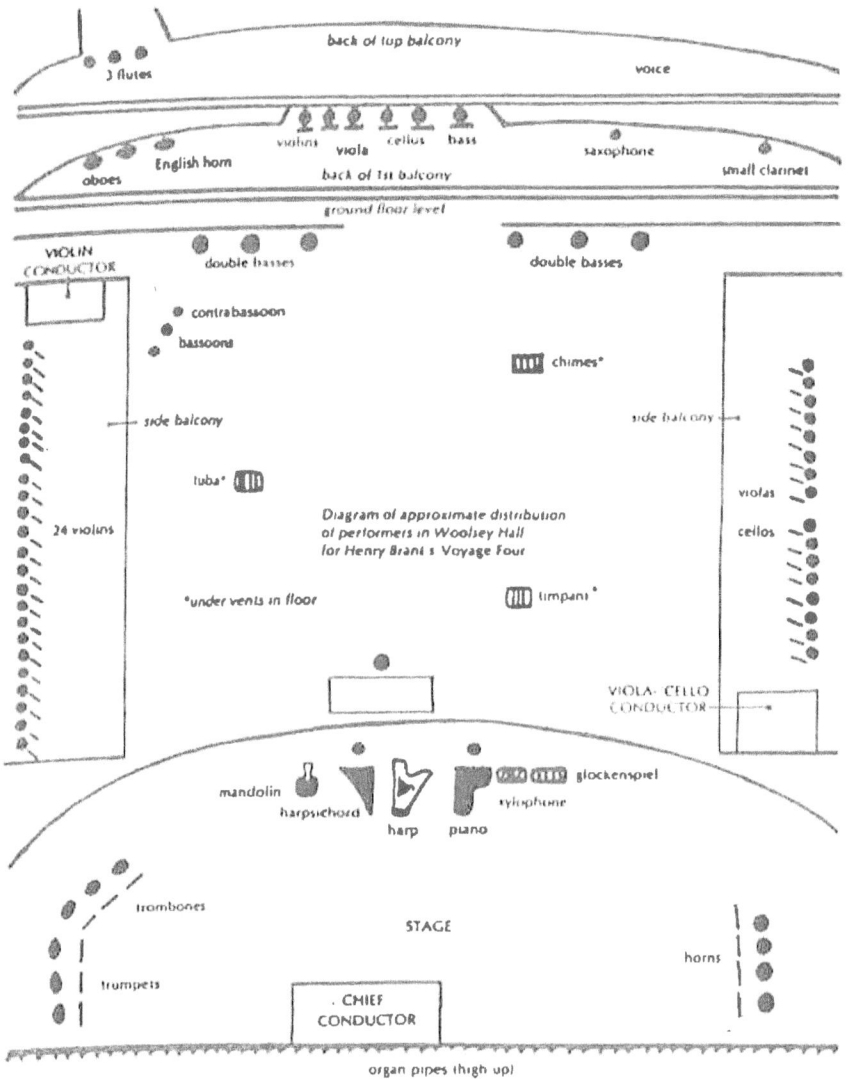

Ex. VI-8: Placement of musicians in Brant's *Voyage Four* (1964).

6.3.

Stylistic contrasts and collages:

Voyage Four, Meteor Farm, and *Bran(d)t aan de Amstel*

In 1970, Brant thus described his "*modus operandi,*" that is, the basic premises of his compositional method:

> 1. Each piece comprises at least two . . . distinct ensemble groups, each of which keeps to its own style, highly contrasted to the styles of the other groups, and retains its own rhythmic, harmonic and instrumental scheme consistently throughout. There is no interchange of style or material from group to group.
>
> 2. The ensembles must be dispersed to specific locations throughout the hall (not merely upon the stage) and must be widely separated from each other. My spatial plans are never optional or small-distanced, they are mandatory and the distance must be the maximum possible.
>
> 3. Each ensemble, although in itself rhythmically exact throughout, may, where an elaborate but natural-sounding complexity is desirable, be directed to perform in 'non-co-ordinated rhythm' (in partial or complete rhythmic independence of the other separated groups).[29]

This is an accurate description of the general features of *Antiphony I* and *Millennium II*, as well as of *Voyage Four*. The latter work is a virtual encyclopaedia of Brant's spatial experiments.

Voyage Four (1964)

In *Voyage Four*, 83 instrumentalists and one singer are dispersed on several levels in the concert hall (cf. Ex. VI-8): on two balconies at the back (flutes and voice on the higher balcony, other woodwinds and strings beneath), on two side balconies (24 violins along the wall of one balcony and 8 violas with 8 cellos along the wall of the other), under the overhang of the back balcony (low-pitched instruments: double

---

[29] Brant's remarks from a recording *Henry Brant--Music 1970*; cited by Drennan (1975: 64).

basses, contrabassoons and bassoons), on the stage (three separate groups: 3 trumpets with 3 trombones on the right, 4 horns on the left, "Gamelan 6" of keyboards and percussion in the centre), high up above the stage (the location of the organ pipes) and in 3 places under vents in the floor (tuba, chimes, timpani).[30]

This setting, called in the score "a total antiphonal distribution" allows for many spatial effects, including the ones introduced in *Antiphony I* (the simultaneity of different layers widely separated in space) and *Millennium II* (sound travel, filling-up and sound axes, possible because of the placement of the strings along the opposite sides of the hall). Novel effects, particular to *Voyage Four*, explore the association of the vertical dimension of physical space and of pitch space: the high sounds of flutes and soprano are heard from the highest point in the hall, the low sounds of double basses emanate from under the balcony. According to Brant,

> There is no mistaking the compelling naturalness of effect when high pitches originate in a high location (e.g. a piccolo in a top balcony), or low pitches from a low position--the latter effect being *enhanced*, not detracted from, if the sounds originate from under a projecting level (e.g. tympani placed in back of the ground floor level, which in many halls is under a balcony).
> (Brant 1967: 232)

The association of the vertical dimension in the performance space and pitch height also underlies the effect created by the woodwinds. Since the bassoons are placed at the ground floor, the oboes above them on the first balcony and the flutes on the second balcony (cf. Ex. VI-8), the music may emanates from a vertical segment of the back wall.[31] The only exception to the one-to-one mapping of physical height and pitch, is the placement of instruments under the grilled openings in the floor of the hall. In this case, the sounds--instead of being 'subterreanean'--seem to emanate from "points in midair above the audience's heads" (Brant 1967: 231). The tuba solo in Ex. VI-9 illustrates this phenomenon; the instrument plays solo so that the unusual

---

[30]The diagram of this setting comes from Brant's article (Brant 1967: 225). Drennan's dissertation presents a slightly different placement plan (p. 240-273).

[31]Brant is quite fond of this "extremely vivid and concentrated directional effect" in which "the entire wall space seems to be sounding at once" (Brant 1967: 231).

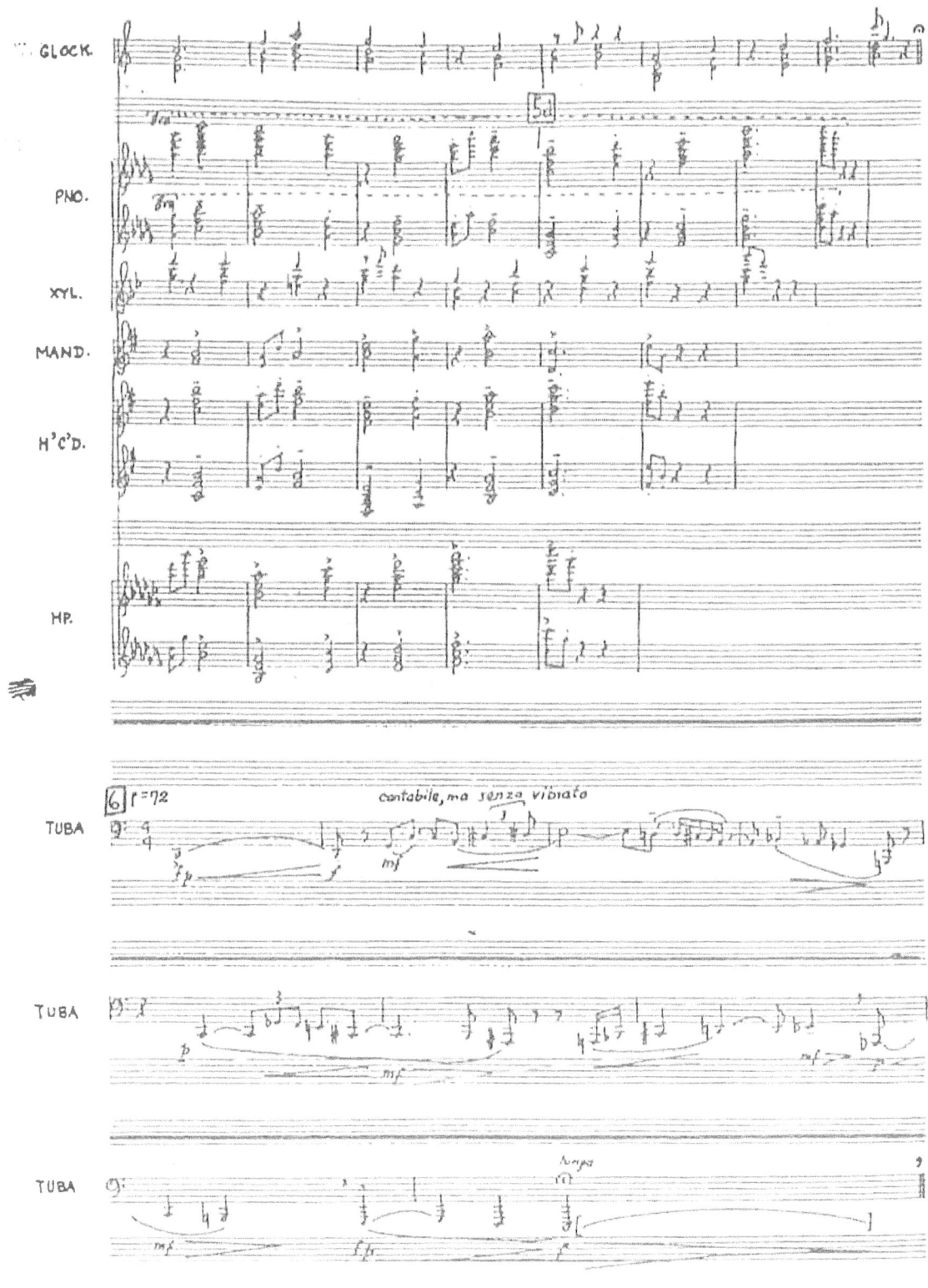

Ex. VI-9: "Gamelan 6" and tuba solo in Brant's *Voyage Four* (1964), p. 10.

localization of its sound would be clearly perceptible.

Here, Brant explores the difference between physical and perceptual features of sound (i.e. actual location of the instrument and virtual localization of the music). In *Voyage Four*, he also experiments with virtuality of spatial extents of sounds. The two groups of brass separated on the stage (trumpets with trombones and, on the opposite side, horns) perform what the composer calls the **spill**. Brant ascribes the introduction of this effect to Berlioz's *Requiem* (the "Tuba Mirum" with four separated groups of brass) and describes it in the following way:

> The four brass ensembles, placed in the corners of a continuous balcony . . . present a common tone-quality participating in a common texture. They seem to reach out to each other when all are sounding, to extend the brass-harmonic texture continuously over the *entire* balcony area, not merely confining it to the corners of the balcony where the sounds originate.
> (Brant 1967: 232)

In addition to these unusual spatial gestures, *Voyage Four* exemplifies the overall influence of spatial separation on the perception of texture, volume and dynamic balance of a large instrumental ensemble. During the rehearsals of the piece, Brant compared the aural result of the placement of all the performers on the stage (in a conventional arrangement of the symphony orchestra), with the setting created by ensemble dispersion according to his design (Brant 1967: 228). He concluded that, in the first case, the resonance was limited, the balances poor and textures unclear, with an "irritating effect of meaningless non-relationship." After the separation,

> there was an immediate and startling increase in volume and resonance from all sections; heights and depths of pitch became immediately vivid; balances in volume between the superimposed but now separated textures immediately righted themselves; contrapuntal amalgams, even in the most complex places, became easily clear, and individual parts easily identifiable by direction.
> (Brant 1967: 228)

In *Voyage Four*, a variety of strands of the music, differing in style, timbre and spatial location, appear simultaneously or in antiphonal alternation. Since this composition is "a set of twenty-four descriptive pieces relating to the composer's trip to Spain and North Africa" (Drennan 1975: 272)[32] its stylistic diversity extends to include Spanish and Arabic features of melodic ornamentation, as well as an imitation of a gamelan. The Indonesian gamelan--an ensemble of gongs and other metallophones--is simulated by piano, harp, harpsichord, mandoline, xylophone and glockenspiel playing simultaneously in different keys (cf. Ex. VI-9). In his later pieces (e.g. *Meteor Farm*) Brant replaces such attempts at representing non-Western timbres with Western instruments by the inclusion of real Asian or African groups performing "authentic" non-Western music.

Meteor Farm (1982)

Among the vast array of instrumental forces in *Meteor Farm* there are three non-Western ensembles: Javanese gamelan orchestra, West African drumming ensemble and South Indian trio (a singer accompanied by sitar and tabla). The Western portion of the instrumentation includes 2 sopranos, 2 choruses, orchestra, brass choir, 2 percussion groups and jazz band. All the ensembles are placed as far as possible in the various areas of the hall. Here, the idea of juxtaposing layers of music of distinct timbre and style is taken to its extremes, yet the plurality of musical styles has a programmatic justification: "the work unfolds as an image of a culture in which the most diverse elements remain unassimilated."[33] These extreme stylistic contrasts resemble the disparities envisioned by Charles Seeger in "total heterophony" in which a non-Western ensemble would play along a symphony orchestra.[34]

---

[32]A pause after the 19th section subdivides *Voyage Four* into two parts, relating to the two large geographic areas visited by the composer, Spain and North Africa (the itinerary of the trip is given at the end of the score). In this way, the form of the spatialized composition portrays (in time) the spatio-temporal outline of the composer's travel.

[33]From the program notes for the premiere of *Meteor Farm* by the Wesleyan University Orchestra and Chorus, cited by Gilbert Mott in a review of the concert (Mott 1982: 36).

[34]I discussed this issue with David Nicholls, who suggested that "total heterophony" may be an appropriate label for Brant's polystylistic and multicultural

This lack of unity results from the fact that the non-Western strands of the music are not composed but quoted from the repertories of the non-Western musicians.[35] The score gives only general indications about the order of entries and the duration of the sections in which individual groups perform (cf. Ex. VI-10). While juxtaposing different strata in the music, the composer attempts to balance the textures and dynamics of the disparate elements, so as, for example, to not overpower the delicate sonorities of the Indian music. Nevertheless, he is not concerned with the "unity" or "coherence" of the work as a whole:

> I try to avoid relationships between the elements. I not only have them contrasted in tone colour and position, but I try to avoid any musical relationship as much as I can. I think that this is what kills all music: there are so many things that are related that people are not listening to anything past the first minute because it all sounds the same and there are so many repetitions that it is not possible to keep track of it. I try to counter that in every way possible.
>
> (Brant 1992: 9)

This way of designing music (structuring would be too strong a word) leaves much room for indeterminacy. The two choruses in section 17, for instance, are provided with an assortment of two-part "songs" to be chosen from and repeated ad libitum, for as long as necessary. Chorus I has sixteen songs (No. 12 is presented in Ex. VI-11), Chorus II--ten, slightly longer songs, all of which begin with a formulaic exclamation ("Meteor farm") and continue with descriptions and impressions of meteors (texts by the composer) set in a simple, quasi-declamatory manner.

---

collages (private communication; letter of 27 April 1994).

[35]The *Notes on Performance* in the score of *Meteor Farm* include the following statement: "It is central to the conception of the piece that these non-Western ensembles perform in their own styles and traditions, and no attempt should be made to dilute or Westernize their music" (Brant 1982: C). During the interview, Brant, asked about borrowing musical material, responded: "I seldom quote anything. I make examples of my own in that genre, I prefer to do that. Except when I have the participation of groups from other cultures, such as the gamelan group or a group of Indian soloists. In that case I listen to their music alone, I pick up what I want and decide where it should go. They use actual examples from their repertory which I never change." (Brant 1992: 9).

Ex. VI-10: Order of events in Section 17 of Brant's *Meteor Farm* (1982), p. 88.

Ex. VI-11: Song No. 12 of Chorus I in *Meteor Farm*.

In *Meteor Farm*, the score is not a definite representation of the music, but a plan for performance. It indicates entries of sonorities (some of which are specified in detail in appendices). In spite of his reliance on indeterminacy, Brant distances himself from the idea of aleatoricism; he also opposes calling his assemblages of sonorities "collages" (Brant 1992). He understands musical collage as a somewhat unordered juxtaposition of short fragments of existing musical material, a phenomenon analogous to collage in the fine arts. When "collage" is defined more broadly, as a simultaneous juxtaposition of unrelated musical material (of unspecified degree of completeness and duration), it becomes an appropriate label for Brant's technique of polystylistic juxtaposition--especially if the musical material is borrowed and not composed.

Bran(d)t aan de Amstel (1984)

The idea of a collage of layers of pre-existing musical material finds its ultimate realization in *Bran(d)t aan de Amstel* [Fire on the Amstel], a spatio-musical spectacle encompassing almost the whole city of Amsterdam. Elliott Schwartz thus describes the work's first, and only, performance:[36]

> Four boatloads of performers (25 flutists and one percussionist per boat) followed one another along a pre-designated route, traversing many canals and passing by a number of landmark churches and bridges along the way. At each of these intermediate checkpoints, other prearranged musical levels (land based) would be added to the overall texture.
> (Schwartz 1984: 35)

The added layers of the music include "the carillons of the four big churches, the bands in the public squares and the choruses along the boat routes" (Brant 1992: 10). The massive performing forces of the finale include "a youth jazz band, two choruses, two civic brass bands . . . and four of the colorfully decorated street organs . . . all spread out over a large outdoor space separated by canals" (Schwartz 1984:

---

[36]Schwartz lists 25 flutists per boat; according to Fischer's Catalog there are 20 flutes per boat, but the parts call for only 17 flutists on each boat. They are divided into two groups of (A) 8 and (B) 9 flutes.

36). Only the parts of the flutes have been written down and are available for study; other music was borrowed. The composer explains:

> I wanted as many things from the various Dutch repertoires as possible. . . If you are in a country where there is a certain kind of music or many different kinds of music, one way would be to use what is there, but combined in a way in which they have never heard it before. The other way would be to introduce foreign elements. In *Fire on the Amstel* I tried to use what was there, but combined and constructed in ways that would be original.
> (Brant 1992: 11)

Brant's work consists of a continuous layer of sounds (the "floating music" of the flutes) juxtaposed with fragments of musics scattered through the city. Thus, in principle, it resembles a typical, visual collage (a canvas plus a plentitude of objects).[37] The music for the procession of boats, the analogue to canvas, is not entirely static. It evolves with the changing acoustic environment. According to the composer, "in the narrow, quiet canals we could have had slow and quiet music safely, but going into the big broad canals we could not, we had to have a different kind of music, just for it to be heard at all." (Brant 1992: 11).

The "slow and quiet" music makes use of nuances of timbre and articulation, e.g. trills, tremolos, dynamic pulsation, glissandi. The contrasting faster and louder music features piccolos, the sound of which carries well at long distances. Example VI-12 illustrates the two different types of music for the flutes. The music for each boat differs from that of the remaining ones by the particular timbre of its percussion instruments (the first boat has 4 small tom-toms, and snare drum, the second--woodblock, maracas and gongs, etc.). In addition, each boat carries two groups of flutists performing music in keys a semitone apart (e.g. C/B on boat I, C/D-flat on

---

[37]According to J. Peter Burkholder, in Ivesian collages, "borrowed tunes are added to an already existing musical structure in the same way assembled objects are fixed on a painted or prepared surface to create a collage in the visual arts." (Burkholder 1993: 2). Burkholder points out that the musical elements of Ivesian collages, unlike those of Brant, are closely related (private letter of 20 December 1993). Because of Brant's reluctance to accept the label of "collage" for his music, I searched for a better term; David Nicholls suggested the use of "total heterophony" (cf. note 34). Yet, this is not an unproblematic choice; besides, "collage" is shorter.

Ex VI-12:
Flute parts of Brant's *Bran(d)t aan de Amstel*:
a: part for boat IV, p. 1;
b: part for boat I, p. 20.

boat II, A-flat/A on boat III and E-flat/E on boat IV).

Despite the ample duration of the whole performance (4 hours) the composed "boat music" lasts only for 3 minutes, requiring extensive repetitions of this material during the performance. *Bran(d)t aan de Amstel* has no score, only plans of the temporal outline of the whole spectacle. Brant's excursus through the space of Amsterdam leads away from the idea of a musical work in closed form, defined by the notation in the score. The orientation is towards a vision of music as an artistic, spatial and social event, the temporal contours of which have been designed by the composer and filled in with pre-existing musical material. The focus on space, Brant's main preoccupation, allows for a large dose of indeterminacy of details regarding the elements dispersed within this space.

6.4.

Symmetry and improvisation in *Western Springs*

The symmetrical instrumentation of *Western Springs* (2 orchestras, 2 choruses and 2 jazz combos) provides a framework for symmetries of musical design, relentlessly explored by the composer who, in this piece, abandons his principle of total musical independence of spatially isolated groups. Firstly, the placement of ensembles in the hall is symmetric: "Each chorus/jazz aggregate is situated in a back corner of the hall and each orchestra at the extreme of the stage, grouped in such a way that there is a space of at least 60 feet between them." (Brant 1985).[38] Secondly, the music follows one pattern of ensemble interaction throughout: two identical groups play or sing simultaneously, one of them starting or ending after a brief delay. Both groups perform music of the same texture and similar or identical material, though in

---

[38]Brant's notes for the recording of *Western Springs* by La Jolla Civic/University Symphony and Chorus. Composers Recordings Incorporated, CRI SD 512, (Brant 1985).

different tempi and, partly, meter.³⁹ Thirdly, the symmetry extends to the work's large-scale form which consists of five sections, all following the same outline (these sections are further grouped into two parts). This scheme of five units reflects the textual division of the descriptions of hot springs and geysers in five Western states: Oregon and California in Part I, Nevada, Idaho and Wyoming in Part II of the piece. The texts, written by the composer, present "such data as the locations of the springs, their temperatures, flow rates and chemical contents, identification of underlying geological strata, and measurements of the heights and frequencies of the geysers." (Brant 1985).⁴⁰

Each section of the music accompanies a "report" on the springs in one state, and each consists of 6 segments. In all of these segments the music resounds from both sides of the hall. During one complete section the music is heard: from the back of the hall (segment 1), from the front (segment 2), from the back (segments 3-5), from the front and, later, again from the back (segment 6). Table VI-1 contains a brief description of the segments.

---

³⁹Orchestra I plays in 3/4, MM72; orchestra II in 4/4, MM88; chorus/jazz I in 2/2, MM80 and chorus/jazz II in 2/2, MM66. Because of their different tempi, each group needs a separate conductor. All tempi must be adhered to closely, without coinciding with the tempi of other groups.

⁴⁰Brant comments on his choice of texts: "I usually, or very often, use texts like that, which are not poetry and not prose but simply factual descriptions. The moment you sing something it begins to sound like poetry. I rely on the text to supply the verbal imagery that is there." (Brant 1992: 10).

Ex. VI-13: Tutti in Brant's *Western Springs* (1984), p. 96.

Table VI-1: Formal units in *Western Springs*

1. <u>Choral introduction</u> in two-part polyphony [41] accompanied by the percussion which, with its regular beat, establishes the tempo and meter for the chorus; trumpets and trombones improvise on pitches of major ninth chords (on F in jazz band I, and D in band II).

2. <u>Orchestral episode</u> of 2-4 different layers contrasting in timbre and in musical material, with frequent canonic imitations within one of the layers, and percussion signals at the end.

3. <u>Choral description of the springs</u>: each chorus has 2 different texts set to two independent melodies of definite rhythm and approximate pitch contours; choral entries are preceded by 1-2 measures of percussion which continues playing a regular beat to stabilize the tempo; brief phrases in the saxophones punctuate the end of each statement of the text.

4. <u>Jazz band interlude</u> with free improvisation in the percussion, and improvisation of trumpets and trombones in a prescribed "jagged style" using limited sets of 7 pitches.

5. <u>Choral description of the springs</u>, continued.

6. <u>Orchestral conclusion</u> of several layers (in different keys, registers, rhythms); the use of controlled improvisation in some layers; the orchestral music is repeated and during the repetition various types of improvised or notated material in the chorus/jazz group are added to enrich the texture.

Both main parts of *Western Springs* follow the same outline in each subsection; this design is modified only through the addition of an introduction to each part and a "tutti finale" at the end.

The orchestral segments contain some ingeniously detailed writing, e.g. the

---

[41] The 2 choruses sing textual variants, e.g.: "First we present some of the world renowned hot springs of Oregon, North and South" (chorus I) and "First we offer some of the famous hot springs of Oregon from South to North" (chorus II).

layered texture of the portrayal of geyser eruptions (cf. Ex. VI-13),[42] but the overall effect seems too repetitive.[43] *Western Springs* makes use of improvisation but the composer limits the scope of variation by assigning specific sets of pitches, registers, and ways of playing to most of the improvised segments. For instance, he instructs the pianist in Orchestra II to "improvise: highest 2 octaves only, fast descending figures, sparse" (*Western Springs*: 25). This controlled improvisation serves to enrich the textural density of the work. The music is neither "minimal" (despite its limitations, for minimalism is process-oriented) nor truly "modernist" (for it lacks formal complexity, development and coherence). The example of *Western Springs*, an experiment in similarity, symmetry and repetition, suggests that static spatial designs benefit from a diversity of the material.

6.5.
Tradition and innovation in *500: Hidden Hemisphere*

One of Brant's most recent works, *500: Hidden Hemisphere* (1992) reveals the continuity and change in Brant's approach to spatial music. This piece was commissioned by the Lincoln Center Out-Of-Doors to celebrate the 500th anniversary of Columbus's voyage to America.[44] The commission specified the conditions of

---

[42]In Ex. VI-13 the note "TRUMPET ascents, TROMBONE ascents" refers to improvised passages described on p. 85 of the score as "very short, ascending figures and 'rips' during orchestra passages."

[43]Parts I and II are not differentiated in style, texture or timbre. Moreover, the music contains many exact recurrences of accompanying or subordinate material, unjustified by the context of the remaining strands in the texture.

[44]Brant's attitude to this celebration is clearly "Western" or "Eurocentric," which is apparent in the title of his composition: before Columbus's time the Western Hemisphere was "hidden" for the Europeans, not for its native inhabitants.

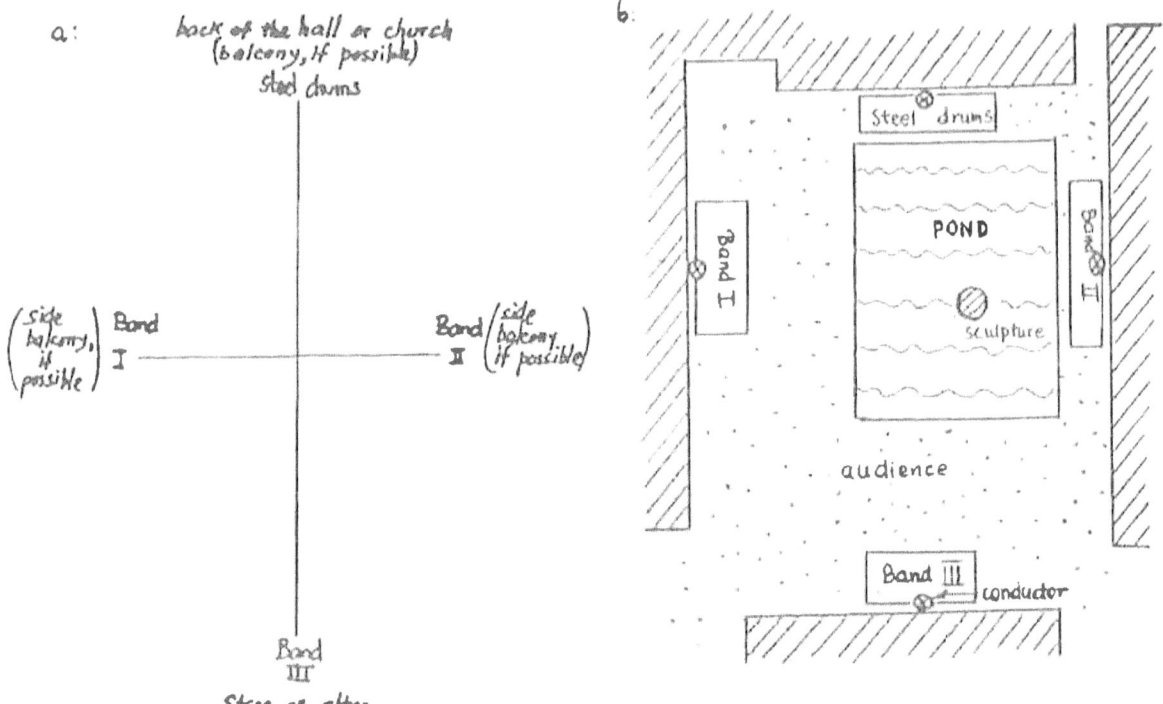

Ex. VI-14: The placement of the bands in Brant's *500: Hidden Hemisphere* (1992);
a: according to the score; b: during the first performance at Lincoln Center.

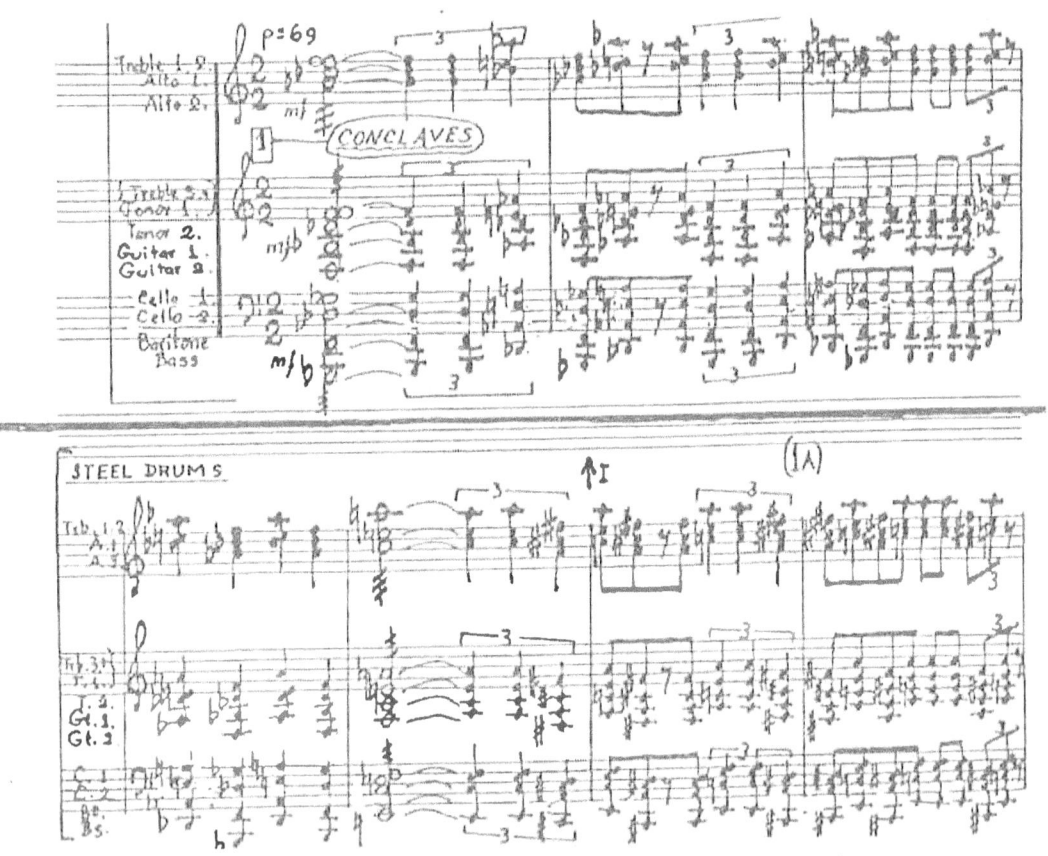

Ex: VI-15: Steel drums in *500: Hidden Hemisphere*, p. 1.

performance (out-of-doors at the North Plaza of the Lincoln Center)[45] as well as the instrumental forces of 3 concert bands and an ensemble of Caribbean steel drums. For the composer,

> One of the disadvantages of the setting was that the three wind bands had the same instrumentation, so it was very difficult to achieve contrast. That is why I had to try out some unusual things. I wanted the three bands to sound as different as possible and it seemed to me that that was so. But this is a difficult kind of composing to do. I would much prefer to have all the trombones, and all the trumpets and all the clarinets and to make the groups that way.
>
> (Brant 1992: 8)

According to the score, the bands should be "widely separated in a 'points-of-the-compass' arrangement . . . using the front, back and sides of the hall or church" (cf. Ex. VI-14a). At the Lincoln Center, the deployment of forces followed a version of this scheme, limited by the shape of performance space with a pond in the middle (Ex. VI-14b). The bands were placed rather far apart, by the walls of the buildings bordering the plaza, partly to strenghthen the sonorities of the individual ensembles by sound reflections off the walls, and partly to leave some space for the audience.

The composition is divided into 16 distinct, though overlapping units, the titles of which reflect their musical character and their programmatic intention. *500: Hidden Hemisphere* consists of the following sections:[46]

1. *Conclaves* (p. 1-6): two chordal phrases (repeated) in SD; distinct material for each band; the order of SD, BI, BIII, BII, SD, BI, BIII, BII (anticlockwise motion); each band has different percussion instruments to provide timbral contrasts (BI chimes, BII timpani, BIII glockenspiel).

---

[45]The composer's opinion of performances out-of-doors is not favourable: "Performing out of doors is a risk. I do not like to do it, but sometimes it is feasible. Even under ideal conditions, you do not get a 100 percent of the sound, 80 percent is good. And sometimes it is less than that. . . . If there are people who say that they welcome the addition of low flying planes and fountains and traffic noise to the music I am not one of them." (Brant 1992: 7).

[46]In this cursory description of the music, I abbreviate the names of the bands: "Steel Drums" to SD, Band I to BI, Band II to BII, Band III to BIII.

2. *Citadels* (p. 6-13): ostinato of parallel minor chords with added sixths in SD; each band has at least 2 different layers of music; canons in percussion, longer themes in the brass, increasing density and variety of layers at the end.

3. *Incantations* (p. 14-35): ostinato of parallel minor chords in SD continued throughout; BI-III enter one by one (with themes in clarinets in BIII, in Flügelhorns in BII and in euphonium and tuba in BI); then canons and quasi-canons (staggered entries) of the various instrumental groups of the bands in the order of BI, BII, BIII; the section is complicated spatially and musically.

4. *Trinities I* (p. 35-42): no SD; canon at the unison between the three bands (not strictly co-ordinated); theme in trombones and tubas, counterpoint in horns, saxophones and euphonium, figuration in percussion and woodwinds; the instrumentation is identical in the three bands, except for the percussion; the order of entries--BII, BIII, BI (clockwise motion).

5. *Relays* (p. 43-54): ostinato of 14 diminished-seventh chords (each played tremolo with a fermata) in SD, repeated throughout; "relays" of melodies from one band to another (at the end of a melody in one band a long held note waits for the start of the melody in the following band); the melodies, performed by several instruments in unison, are juxtaposed with brief "interventions" from the remaining two bands; each melody is in a different key; the order of bands is BI, BII, BIII, BI, BII, BIII, BI, BII.

6. *Bazaar I* (p. 55-67): juxtaposition of four different 'musics' first presented one by one (SD, BII, BIII, BI), then superimposed; SD--tango in C minor, 4/4, MM 72; BII--polka in E-flat major, 2/4, MM 96; BIII--quiet, sentimental music in D major, 2/2, MM 56; BI--march in G minor, 6/8, MM 108.

7. *Fanfaronade* (p. 68-86): no SD; 4 segments of the same outline; beginning with brass glissandi in BI, followed with layered patterns in BII and low-pitched melodies in BIII (in each segment in a different key); spatial scheme and musical gestures are repetitive, musical material--developmental.

8. *Dirges* (p. 86-102): no SD; 6 segments, each based on a sustained minor chord and a timpani ostinato in BII (successively on the pitches of A-flat, B, B-flat, G, D, F-sharp); the same order of bands (BII, BIII, BI) in each segment, with gong or glockenspiel signals at the end; mournful themes in the brass of BIII, counterpoints in BI; the conclusion of superimposed minor--major seventh chords (G in BI, F in BII and G-flat in BIII, p. 102).

9. *Bazaar II* (p. 102-120): juxtaposition of four different musical layers, simultaneous or alternating in various combinations; SD-- chordal ostinato in A minor, 2/2, MM 56; BI--waltz in B-flat major ("mechanical, without Viennese lilt"), 3/4, MM 144; BII--"military" march (with snare drum) in D-flat major, 4/4, MM 112; BIII--tango in C major, 4/4/, MM 120.

10. *Riots* (p. 121-135): no SD; all bands in different tempi and the same meter (4/4) supported by a regular rhythm in the drum sets; besides the percussion, each band has two layers (e.g. a canon at the unison in trumpets and trombones plus two melodies in tubas in BII); the order of BII, BI, BIII, then all 3 bands together; polyrhythmic and dissonant.

11. *Lamentations* (p. 135-143): no SD, slow mournful themes in the three bands, each preceded by slow percussion strokes (gongs in BIII, timpani in BII, chimes in BI); slower tempo and thinner texture than before (the maximum of two bands)

12. *Trinities II* (p. 144-160): no SD; canon at the minor third between the three bands; long, chromatic theme presented in all winds unison; the bands are not strictly co-ordinated, but in the same meter and tempo; the order of BIII, BI, BII; followed by entries of trumpets and trombones playing simultaneously several melodic lines in different keys and rhythms, the same order of entries as the continuing canonic voices (BIII--12 lines, BI--9 lines, BII--10 lines); finally, the brass melodies replaced with percussion entering in the same order (BIII--glockenspiels, BI--chimes, BII--timpani) with angular, rhythmic themes.

13. *Proclamations* (p. 161-175): no SD; long passages of each band playing by itself: two-layered texture based on chromatic tetrachords (presented as chords, figurations, fanfares or melodic phrases in the different bands); the same texture accompanies themes differing in timbre and range (BI--piccolos and clarinets, BIII--trumpets and trombones, BII--horns, euphoniums, tubas, saxophones in unison).

14. *Collisions* (p. 176-189): no SD; "marcatissimo sempre"--the predominance of rhythm; series of repeated or parallel chords (built from perfect fourths); the texture is enriched by special timbral effects, i.e. "horse whinny" in the trumpets of the three bands; BII and BI continue throughout, BIII has shorter sections.

15. *Solar Fountains* (p. 189-194): no SD; BIII is the main ensemble with a canon in 3 slide trumpets, followed by canons (on the same theme) in 3 slide clarinets, in 3 trombones and, finally, in 3 mouth sirens (the theme contains numerous glissandi); this canonic section is repeated once with added figuration in the piccolos; BI and BII enter later with ascending scales, figurations and glissandi--short segments repeated as required until a percussion signal.

16. *Dispersions* (p. 194-210): a series of tremolo chords in SD (tonal) provides the basic, continuous layer of the music; a variety of different tempi and meters (SD--4/4, MM 66; BI--3/2, MM 60; BIII--5/4, MM 88; BII--3/2, MM 60); BI-III are added separately to SD; each band has 3-4 distinct layers (trills, glissandi, chordal patterns, brief melodies, scale fragments); tutti at the end features four coordinated, 12-tone chords with percussion tremolos.

The distinct timbre of the steel drums sets this band apart from the remaining groups in *500: Hidden Hemisphere*. The musical importance of the "Caribbean" ensemble stems from the programmatic concept of the work, for--as the composer explains--"the steel band is an obvious association to Columbus's first contact with the New World in the Caribbean" (Brant's words quoted in Reich 1992). Actually, this association is quite distant: steel bands did not exist in Columbus's time, they have emerged in the 20th century as a result of the interaction between the European and the Caribbean cultures.[47] The music of the steel band, featured in sections 1-3, 5-6, 9 and 16 of the piece, is there at the beginning (cf. Ex. VI-15, after p. 270) lasts through the arrival of the "European" music, takes over some of its material (section 6) and returns to the original style at the end (repeated chordal passages or ostinati).

Brant's favourite idea of stylistic contrast finds its most vivid realization in the *Bazaar* sections, in the clashes of four different musical styles assigned to the four bands (Ex. VI-16, an excerpt from *Bazaar II*). Despite Brant's resistance to the term "collage" this is the best label for such polystylistic juxtaposition. The presence of canonic techniques in *500: Hidden Hemisphere* constitutes another link with Brant's musical past. The use of canons within one ensemble or one spatial layer of the work is quite pervasive throughout all of Brant's music. Canons between the distant groups are much rarer. Incidentally, Brant describes the introduction of canons between the three wind bands in two sections of *500: Hidden Hemisphere*, *Trinities I* and *II*, as a

---

[47]Steel drums are made from oil drums, pitched and tuned to particular scales and intervals (not standarized). Steel bands, first developed in Trinidad in the 1930-1940s, supplanted other bands for the Carnival and include both Caribbean and European items in their repertory (Rimmer 1980).

Ex. VI-16: Clash of different styles in *Bazaar II* from 500: *Hidden Hemisphere* p. 117 (SD--ostinato, BI--waltz, BII--march, BIII--tango).

Ex. VI-17: Spatial canon between 3 bands in *Trinities I*, from *500: Hidden Hemisphere*, p. 35-36 (canonic voices only, counterpoints are omitted).

consequence of the conditions of the work's commission:

> Because I had bands of the same instrumentation, I decided to do one or two pieces where we could explore possible identities between them. . . . What I created was a spatial canon--the spaces were in canon with each other, not just musical lines. . . . [However] the co-ordination was not exact. The three conductors were not keeping very closely together, but every band was playing as precisely as possible within itself.
>
> (Brant 1992: 8)

Ex. VI-17 presents the entries of the three voices in the first of the two spatial canons in *Trinities I*.[48] The timbral similarity and spatial separation of the three wind bands gives rise to an interesting effect in *Relays* (section 5). Here, a melody, played by several wind instruments in unison (clarinets, English horns, bassoons, horns, tenor saxophones and euphoniums in the three bands) ends on a long-held note, awaiting to be taken over and carried on into a melody in another band (a literal "relay").

Parallels to Brant's earlier music include also dissonant polyphony (i.e. the polytonal collection of melodies in trumpets and trombones in *Trinities II*, resembling that of *Millennium II*), the accumulation of ascending scales and glissandi in various instruments in *Solar Fountains* (as in *Western Springs*), and the polystylistic juxtapositions or collages in *Bazaar I* and *II* (as in *Meteor Farm*, albeit in the *Bazaars* all material is composed by Brant, without recourse to literal quotation). *500: Hidden Hemisphere* does not contain much spatial experimentation and unusual effects à la *Voyage Four*, but the separation of groups is essential in this composition. The use of space embraces also the manipulation of sound direction by ordering the entries of individual groups. Brant uses all possible patterns; the piece begins with the anticlockwise direction of the successive entries in *Conclaves* (SD-BI-BIII-BII) and ends with an angular pattern of Back-Right-Left-Front (SD-BI-BII-BIII) in the final chords in *Dispersions* (the zig-zagging pattern of BI-BII-BIII is also used in *Incantations*, *Relays*, and *Fanfaronade*).

In *500: Hidden Hemisphere*, Brant explores the spatial contrasts, canons and

---

[48] I discuss spatial canons in Xenakis's *Alax* for three identical ensembles (1985) in Chapter VII.

collages that have preoccupied him throughout his career. The four instrumental groups, widely separated in space, play in different--and changing--tempi and meters. The music encompasses a variety of styles and textures, contrasting the material within the individual sections (e.g. four different types of music in *Bazaar I* and *II*) as well as from one section to another (e.g. the predominance of chords of perfect fourths in section 14, chromatic clusters in section 13, or glissandi in section 15). One may say, as does the author of the program note for the premiere of the work (Lincoln Center Out-Of-Doors, 22-23 August 1992) that "the whole effect is one of cultures in collision."

Conclusion

In Brant's spatial music ensemble dispersion is linked to a variety of acoustic designs and compositional purposes, beginning with the basic function of clarifying complex, multi-layered textures (from *Antiphony I* onwards). Often, Brant juxtaposes simultaneous layers in distinct styles (e.g. *Meteor Farm*, *Bran(d)t aan de Amstel*, and the *Bazaar* sections of *500: Hidden Hemisphere*). The music for these superimposed strata may be newly composed (stylizations of jazz, popular and dance music) or borrowed from traditional repertories (e.g. carillons, non-Western ensembles). Brant often places the ensembles at various levels, in between and around the audience in order to (1) allow the identification of separate strands in the texture and (2) create unusual sound effects (*Millennium II*, *Voyage Four*). Exceptions to the general principle of contrast arise from the use of canonic techniques (*500: Hidden Hemisphere*) and symmetrical designs (*Western Springs*)

Brant's spatial music calls for a special mode of listening, in which the listeners' attention may shift, at will, from one layer to another, one point in space to another.[49] For this purpose the strands of the music have to be kept perceptually

---

[49]Ives toyed with a similar idea of "trying out a parallel way of listening to music" in a piece built from two independent layers; this work would have to be played twice, the listener first focussing on one layer, then on another (*Memos*: 106; cf. Chapter III).

distinct. Albert Bregman notices, that "the further apart performers are in space (horizontal angle), relative to ourselves, the more independent we will hear their lines to be" (Bregman 1990: 500). Yet, this perceptual clarity does not come without cost, because it is

> hard to hear the harmonic properties of a chord when its componenets are originating at widely different places. . . Similarly, it is hard to hear any connection between the rhythmic patterns coming from widely separated players. One solution to this musical problem is to have several players in each location and to compose the music in such a way that the harmonic and rhythmic relations are important only between the instruments that are at the same place.
> (Bregman 1990: 501-502)

This is the solution adopted by Henry Brant. The composer explores the co-existence of distinct 'musics' in many of his works. However, his undogmatic approach to the plurality of style, an approach resembling that of Charles Ives or Harry Partch, may cause perceptual difficulties. As J. Peter Burkholder notices,

> listeners schooled in European art music experience Ives's frequent incorporation of existing music into his own works as a kind of formal dissonance, an extraordinary and deliberate violation of the customary integrity of compositions in the cultivated tradition, which are normally individual, self-contained, and derived from unique, newly invented musical ideas.
> (Burkholder 1985: 1)

Brant ignores typical modernist ideas such as structural coherence, serialization and the analytical segregation of the various characteristics of sound. His spatial music has little in common with that of the radical avant-garde composers such as Xenakis, Carter or Boulez. Neither does Brant's idea of musical spatiality resemble that of Edgard Varèse, in which sonorities are reified into quasi-tangible musical objects, seemingly endowed with a mass and a volume and projected in imaginary space (Varèse 1967). Brant's compositions, influenced by American vernacular styles (jazz, dance music) and American experimental tradition (Ives) contain an abundance of ideas, relating mostly to space, but also to form, rhythm, and perceptual experience (e.g. selective listening to one of the many strands of music).

Brant's music built with simultaneous sound layers, contrasted in many aspects including spatial location, continues the line of development which I associated with Mahler and Ives (cf. Chapter III). These composers have explored the simultaneity of various musical processes taking place at different points of space. Their ideas of the co-existence of several distinct strands within a composition are rooted in polyphony. As Mahler expressed it, only music of many layers projected from different directions is really polyphonic, "everything else is merely many-voiced writing, homophony in disguise" (Mitchell 1975: 342). In Brant's case, distant groups of musicians perform strands of music which co-exist without a common, tonal denominator and, therefore, belong to separate "auditory streams" (term from Bregman 1990). The discovery of this type of musical spatiality in the 20th century is not synonymous with forsaking the music's temporal nature and transforming it into a static analogue to painting. Rather, through the exploration of the co-presence of different, evolving musical strata a full articulation of time and space becomes possible.

CHAPTER VII

SPATIAL SOUND MOVEMENT IN THE INSTRUMENTAL MUSIC OF IANNIS XENAKIS

Introduction

> For a human being it is difficult to understand space. According to relativity theory, space is linked to time through the speed of light; this theory also says that space has a curvature, but the theory does not explain the meaning of the space itself. On the other hand, from the point of view of everyday life, space is something limiting: if you are in one place you cannot be in another place at the same time.
>
> (Xenakis 1992: 1)

These words reveal the scope of Xenakis's reflection on space, embracing paradigms of modern science along with spatial features of human experience. A similar range of interests underlies Xenakis's music, from compositional implementations of mathematical concepts of space to explorations of the physical spatiality of sound.[1] This chapter presents the evolution of Xenakis's approach to spatialization as realized in his instrumental music, from *Pithoprakta* (1956) to *Alax* (1985).[2] The discussion also includes analytical examples from *Eonta* (1963), *Terretektorh* (1965-66), *Nomos Gamma* (1967-68) and *Persephassa* (1969). The study

---

[1] I discuss notions of space in Xenakis's compositional theory in Chapter III, 3.3.

[2] The first draft of this chapter has been presented in a paper entitled "The technique of spatial sound movement in the instrumental music of Iannis Xenakis" (Fall Meeting of the New York State--St. Lawrence Chapter of the AMS, at the State University of New York at Albany, October 1992). A revised version of this paper is forthcoming in *Interface. Journal of New Music Research* 23 no. 3 (August 1994).

of *Terretektorh* and *Nomos Gamma* is based, in part, on compositional sketches that had not been available before.[3] In addition, the review of Xenakis's music and ideas benefits from his insights expressed in an interview of 1992.[4]

Xenakis's continuing interest in the technique of spatialization is not limited to the works discussed in this dissertation. Different aspects of spatial sound are explored in *Polytope de Montréal* for 4 identical orchestras (1967), the musical component of Xenakis's audiovisual installation at EXPO 67 in Montreal.[5] Multi-channel sound projection is required in a variety of Xenakis's electroacoustic compositions, from *Concrete PH*, an incandescent prelude to Varèse's *Poème eléctronique* for the Philips Pavilion (1958), through *Bohor* with its monumental sound masses (1962), to *La Legende d'Er* (1977) with its complex patterns of sound movement in time, space, pitch and timbre.[6] Xenakis's experience with electroacoustics has not been without consequences for his role in the development of the technique of spatial sound movement in instrumental music.[7]

---

[3] Xenakis graciously supplied me with copies of his compositional sketches in August 1992 (7 pages in total).

[4] I interviewed Xenakis in Paris on 25 May 1992. References to the typescript of this conversation will be labelled (Xenakis 1992). The French translation is forthcoming in *Circuit* in 1994.

[5] This work is the first in Xenakis's Polytope series, multi-media presentations which explore space (and time) by means of sound and light in movement. The earlier Polytopes (Montreal, *Persepolis* of 1971 and *Polytope de Cluny* of 1972) are discussed in a book edited by Olivier Revault d'Allonnes (1975); other works in this genre include *Polytope de Mycenae* (1978), *Le Diatope* (1978) and *Taurhiphanie* (1987).

[6] *La Legende d'Er* for seven track tape was composed for *Le Diatope*, designed for the opening of the Centre Georges Pompidou in Paris and premiered in 1978 (Matossian 1986). References to the chronology of Xenakis's compositions are based on the catalogue compiled by Lohner (1987) and the *List of Works* issued by Xenakis's publishers, Editions Salabert of Paris (1992).

[7] This experience dates back to 1956, when Xenakis began working with Le Corbusier on the Philips Pavilion for EXPO 1958 (cf. Chapter III, section 3.3). References to this work are included in *Formalized Music* (1971), in Matossian (1986) and other sources.

7.1.

Real and virtual motion of sound in *Pithoprakta* and *Eonta*

In 1955-56 Xenakis composed *Pithoprakta*, the first instance of "stochastic music," a music in which the number of individual sonic particles is so large that their behaviour is regulated by the laws of probability.[8] In this work, scored for an orchestra of 50 instruments (i.e. a string orchestra with two tenor trombones, xylophone and woodblock), all the instruments are placed on the stage according to the traditional seating plan. Nevertheless, spatially extended sonorities result from the use of a large number of divisi parts. Here, spatialization does not relate to the measurable aspects of the performance space (distances, angles, symmetries), but rather is expressed through internal, microscopic differentiation in the orchestral sonorities.

In *Pithoprakta* various categories of sound create stationary or moving clouds of sonorous material. The movement occurs in pitch and time, but may lead to a rudimentary form of spatial motion--motion confined to the expanse of the stage. The sketch for measures 239-250 of *Pithoprakta* (Ex. VII-1) displays the evolution of a stochastic sound mass in pitch space, with the divisi strings playing irregular glissandi sul ponticello from the low to the high registers. This transformation is mirrored by a shift of the sound mass from the right to the left side of the stage. However, it does so only if the traditional seating plan is preserved. In *Pithoprakta*, according to Xenakis:

> If the instruments are seated in the conventional order of the first violins followed by the second violins, violas, and cellos--all placed in a semicircle on the stage--the movement in pitch also becomes a spatial movement. But if the first violins are placed to the left and the second violins to the right, this effect is lost.
>
> (Xenakis 1992: 9)

---

[8]Xenakis introduced the term "stochastic music" in 1956 in reference to the results of his compositional use of the laws and calculus of probability (Xenakis 1956, cf. *Formalized Music* 1971: 8).

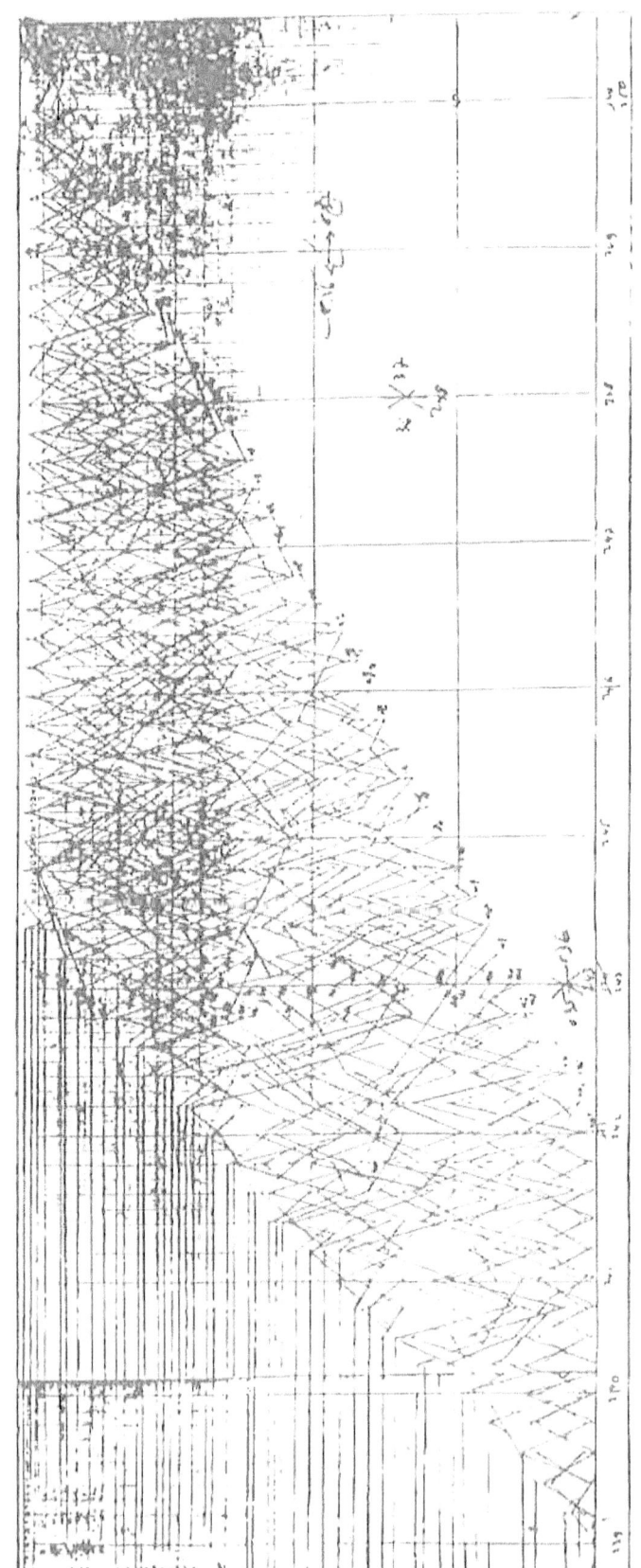

Ex. VII-1: Xenakis's sketch for mm. 239-250 of *Pithoprakta*.

Ex. VII-2: Mm. 238-247 of *Pithoprakta* by Iannis Xenakis (1955-56).

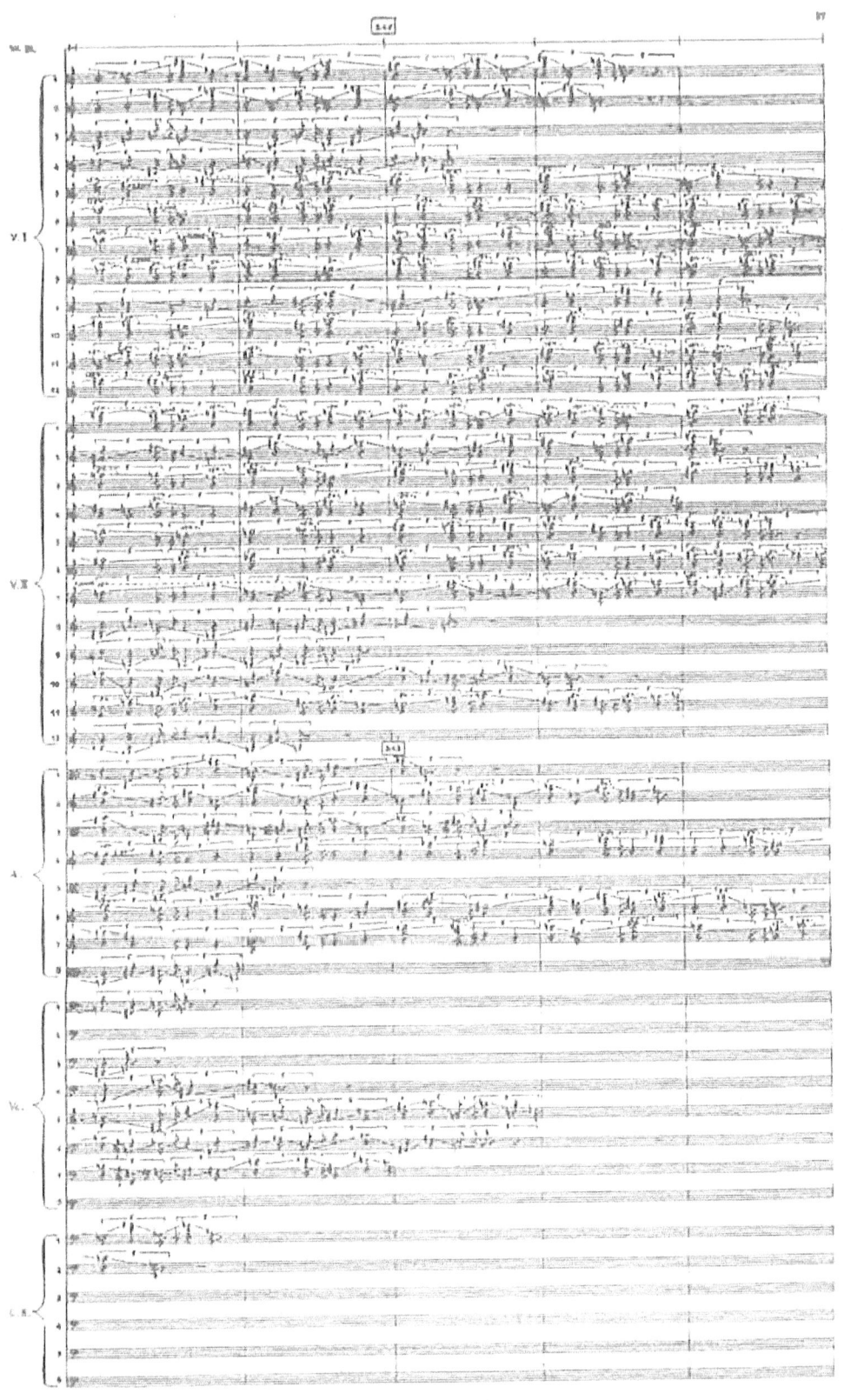

Ex. VII-2: *Pithoprakta*, continued.

The broad movement across the pitch space filled with a mass of irregular glissandi is realized by individual instruments, not complete groups. The score shows that the movement is conceived more in terms of the evolution of pitch content than of spatial position (Ex. VII-2). The transformation is achieved by a gradual dropping out of the lower string instruments, starting with the double basses and ending with the violas, second and first violins, some of which play together at the end.

The virtual movement of sound masses is realized in *Pithoprakta* by a stationary orchestra placed on the stage, in front of the listeners. By contrast, in *Eonta* (1963-64), a work for piano, two trumpets and three trombones, the movement is a consequence of the physical motion of the instrumentalists.[9] Brass players have to change their placements on the stage six times during the course of the work (see Ex. VII-3). Moreover, on three occasions they are required to simultaneously play and move: (a) altering the timbre of their instruments by slow axial rotations in mm. 55-79, (b) walking towards the piano in mm. 82-85, (c) wandering around the "promenade" area in mm. 335-375.

That *Eonta* is an exploration of the directional qualities of sound is already apparent in the first entry of the brass instruments--the players begin with the bells pointing to the ground (mm. 40-43) and raise them to normal position during a slow crescendo (mm. 44-48). The following fragment of the music (mm. 55-79) reflects Xenakis's idea, jotted down in a notebook in 1963: "the brass concentrated with little

---

[9] The spatiality of *Eonta* is just one of the many aspects of this work, which, according to the composer's note in the score, "makes use of stochastic music (based on the theory of probabilities) and of symbolic music (based on logistics)." Sections of free stochastic music, such as the piano solo in mm. 1-40, have been calculated with Xenakis's computer program developed for his 'ST' works (*ST-4*, *ST-10*, cf. chapter V of *Formalized Music* 1971). Symbolic music, composed with pitch sets structured by means of operations from Boolean algebra (union, intersection and negation), had been introduced in *Herma* (cf. chapter VI of *Formalized Music*). *Eonta* makes use of operations on two basic sets (Ψ and Θ; e.g. $\Psi\Theta + \overline{\Psi\Theta}$) as well as of set Σ, the universal set appearing in all stochastic sections.

internal movements, slow and fast (alteration of timbre) and chords."[10] Here, the alteration of timbre is achieved by means of changing sound direction and fluctuating dynamics. The brass players turn slowly to the right (↻) or to the left (↺) while performing a continuous chord (G#3-D4-E4-A4-G5) which varies in timbre depending on the direction and loudness of the individual sounds (Ex. VII-4). As the score calls for rotations spanning an indeterminate "obtuse angle" (between 90 and 180 degrees) it is difficult to foresee the exact positions of the instruments at a specific moment. However, the players usually move in the same direction (the second trumpet and the second trombone to the left, the rest to the right) which means that, at times, they are turned with their backs to the audience. Example VII-5 presents two hypothetical positions for the brass at the end of m. 74: (a) assuming that each motion spans $90°$, (b) assuming that the angles vary between $90°$ and $180°$ and the players finish their motions by facing forward (in m. 79).[11]

The movements of the performers in *Eonta*, however interesting visually, have an acoustic purpose. Brass players vary the timbre of their instruments by pointing the bells in various directions (up, down, to the sides). Brass instruments are known to be highly directional, i.e. their timbre depends on the direction from which the sound is heard (Meyer 1978). Pointing the bells to the floor or to the side of the stage changes the timbre of the sounds heard by the audience (by a reduction of the loudness of the highest partials). Playing towards the back of the stage further transforms the brass sonority; the sounds have a darker timbre (a further reduction of the high partials) and the loudness decreases (because of the directional characteristics of the instruments and the acoustic shadow of the performers). Consequently, the instruments sound more distant (the perception of sound distance depends on dynamic

---

[10] Xenakis's remark, notated after an afternoon boating in Tanglewood in the summer of 1963, is quoted in the biography by Matossian (1986: 177), presumably in her translation.

[11] Neither of these conditions are explicitly required by the composer; following this section the instrumentalists walk to the piano, so their direction at the beginning may not be important.

and timbral cues, cf. Sheeline 1982, Blauert 1983). In addition, the varied direction of instrumental sounds triggers different room responses. The pattern of reflections and its result--the reverberant sounds which influence the timbre--depend on the position and direction of the sound sources in the room.[12]

In mm. 144-168 of *Eonta* brass instruments are pointed at the ceiling so that their sounds are changed by the varied resonance of the hall (Ex. VII-6a). Simultaneously, the brass sonorities resonate in the silent chord of the piano (F-A in two octaves, 3rd pedal)--as the third and fourth partial of the pitch A3 in the piano part (pitches E5 and A5 respectively, mm. 144-147 in Ex. VII-6a).[13] To increase the resonance, the brass notes are doubled at a higher octave in another chord played by the piano.

This moment of sound 'reflection' brings to mind Xenakis's original inspiration for the piece: "Reflection in water. Water is the piano. . ." For the composer, "the piano is the centre, the others in circumference, they approach to resonate the piano" (Matossian 1986: 177). The realization of this idea may be found in mm. 86-92 and mm. 317-321 of *Eonta* where the brass players stand beside the piano and direct the bells of their instruments toward its strings. The resonance is either clearly heard in a moment of silence (general pause in mm. 92-94) or becomes a part of the overall sonority, colouring the timbre of all the instruments which continue to play without pauses (mm. 317-321, cf. Example VII-6b).[14]

The effects of resonance and timbral transformation are not the only instances

---

[12] Rasch and Plomp (1982) as well as Bräm (1986) review the role of acoustic space for music perception. For a study of the dependance of timbre on resonances, see Toole and Olive (1988); for a study of room acoustics and artificial reverberation, see Schroeder (1984). A recent study of source placement and room response (Goad and Keefe 1992) indicates that differences in early reflection response contribute to timbre discrimination.

[13] A5 is also the fifth partial of F3 and the tenth partial of F2.

[14] In example VII-6b, all the pitches of the brass chord are contained in the two chords played by the piano, which amplifies the resonance.

of sound spatialization in *Eonta*. A spectacular moment of spatial sound movement is presented in the "promenade" section of the work (mm. 335-375), in which the brass players are asked to wander freely around a T-shaped area of the stage while performing soloistic passages (Ex. VII-7).[15] The changing direction of the sounds, aided by fluctuating dynamics, creates a rich and 'mobile' texture--an effect which later became a standard element of the 'contemporary-music' style adapted by many other composers. Paradoxically, Xenakis himself has come to dislike performer movement as a compositional device:

> The problem is that the movement of performers is theatrical. Besides, when the sound moves along with the speed of a walking human it is not interesting enough. If you could ask the players to run and play at the same time, that would be more interesting, but I have not seen such a thing anywhere. Sound movement is very difficult to obtain also because most performers do not like to walk, even slowly, and play at the same time.
>
> (Xenakis 1992: 10)

These words result from years of compositional experience acquired while working on a series of musical essays in spatialization (from *Eonta* to *Alax*). In the sixties, after experimenting with the performers' movements on the stage and using spatial effects to enrich the timbral aspects of the music in *Eonta*, Xenakis turned to the exploration of the space itself.

7.2.
Spirals and circles in *Terretektorh*

In *Terretektorh*[16] for large orchestra (1965-66), the 88 players are scattered

---

[15]Greek letters in m. 356 and 357 of Ex. VIII-7 refer to sets from which the pitches (not pitch classes) of the brass have been chosen. These sets are constructed through intersection, union and negation from two basic sets, Ψ and Θ.

[16]Here, the most common spelling of the title is used (as in the score, the revised version of *Formalized Music* and the *Catalogue General*). Other options include: *Terrêtektorh* (Xenakis 1971: 236-237), *Terretêktorh* (Xenakis 1971: 273) and *Terretéktorh* (Matossian 1986: 271). Matossian uses also *Terretektorh* (p. 182-3) and *Terretéktorh* (p.

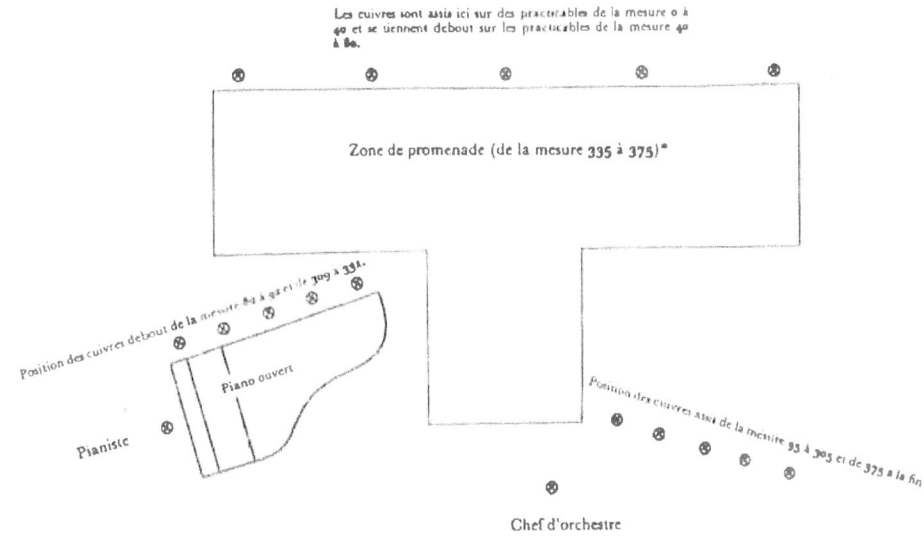

Ex. VII-3: Placement of performers in Xenakis's *Eonta* (1963-64).

Ex. VII-4: Alteration of brass timbre by movement and dynamics in mm. 72-74 of *Eonta*.

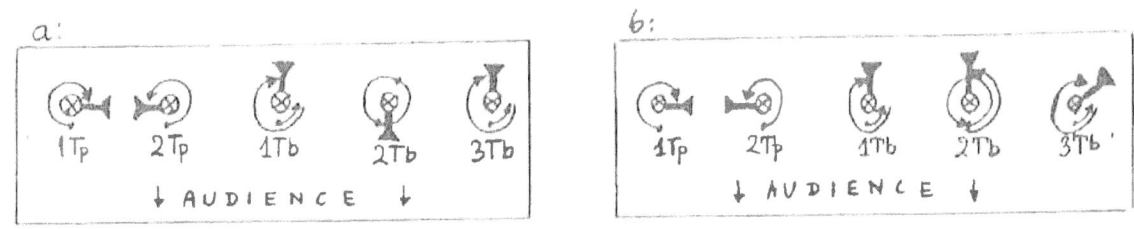

Ex. VII-5: Hypothetical positions of brass instruments in m. 74 of *Eonta*;
(a) if each motion spans 90°; (b) if II and III Trombone move by 120° to 180°.

Ex. VII-6: Resonances of brass sounds in the piano in *Eonta*: (a) Brass players seated at the right, bells directed at the ceiling, piano with 3rd pedal, mm. 143-153; (b) Brass players standing next to the piano, bells in the piano, mm. 317-318.

Ex. VII-7: Excerpt from the "promenade" in *Eonta* (mm. 356-359).

Ex. VII-8a: Xenakis's sketch of the seating plan for *Terretektorh* (1965).

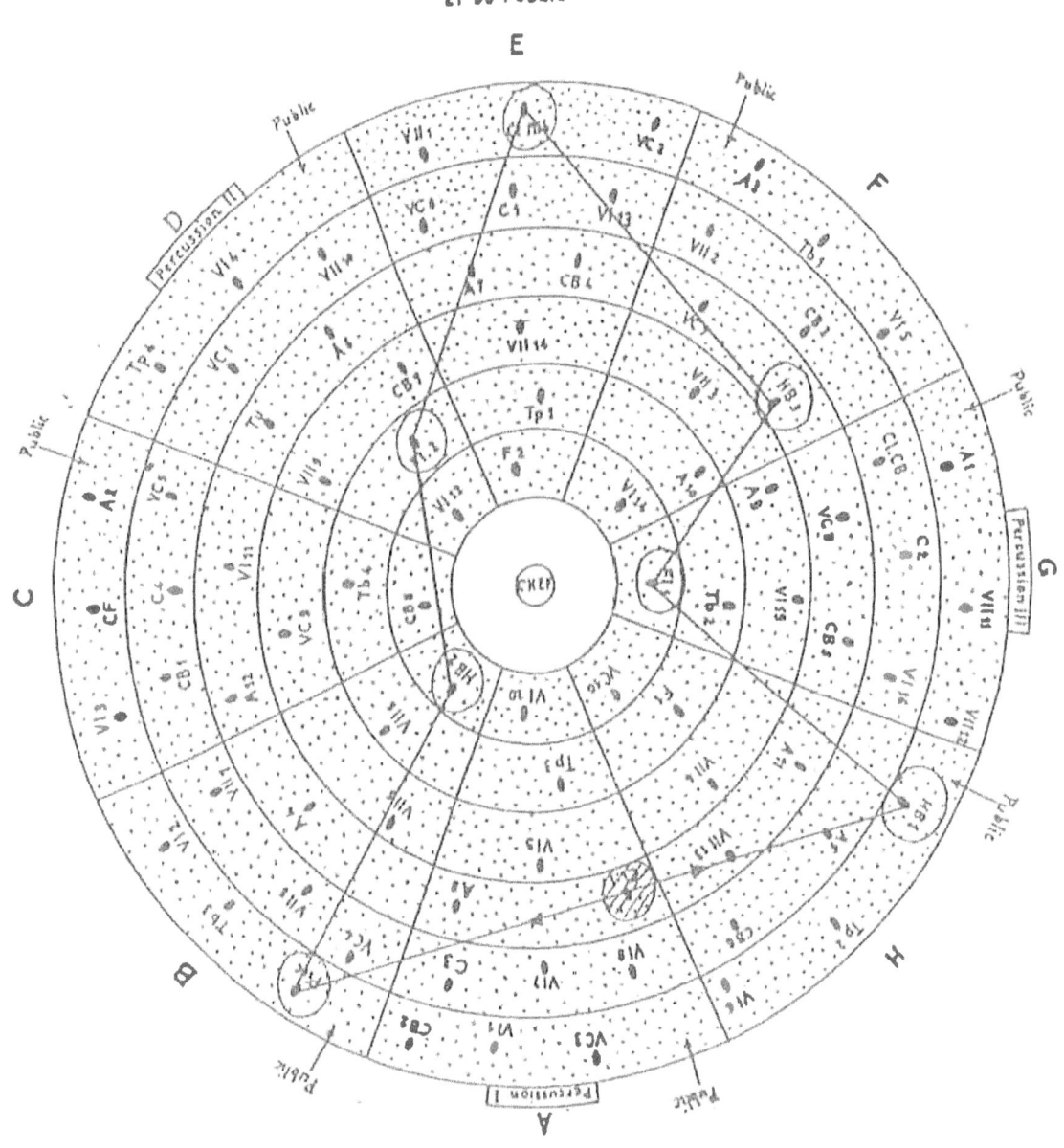

Ex. VII-8b: Final version of the seating plan of *Terretektorh* in the score (1969), with the indication of the placement of high woodwinds participating in sound rotations in mm. 125-195 (cf. Ex. VII-11).

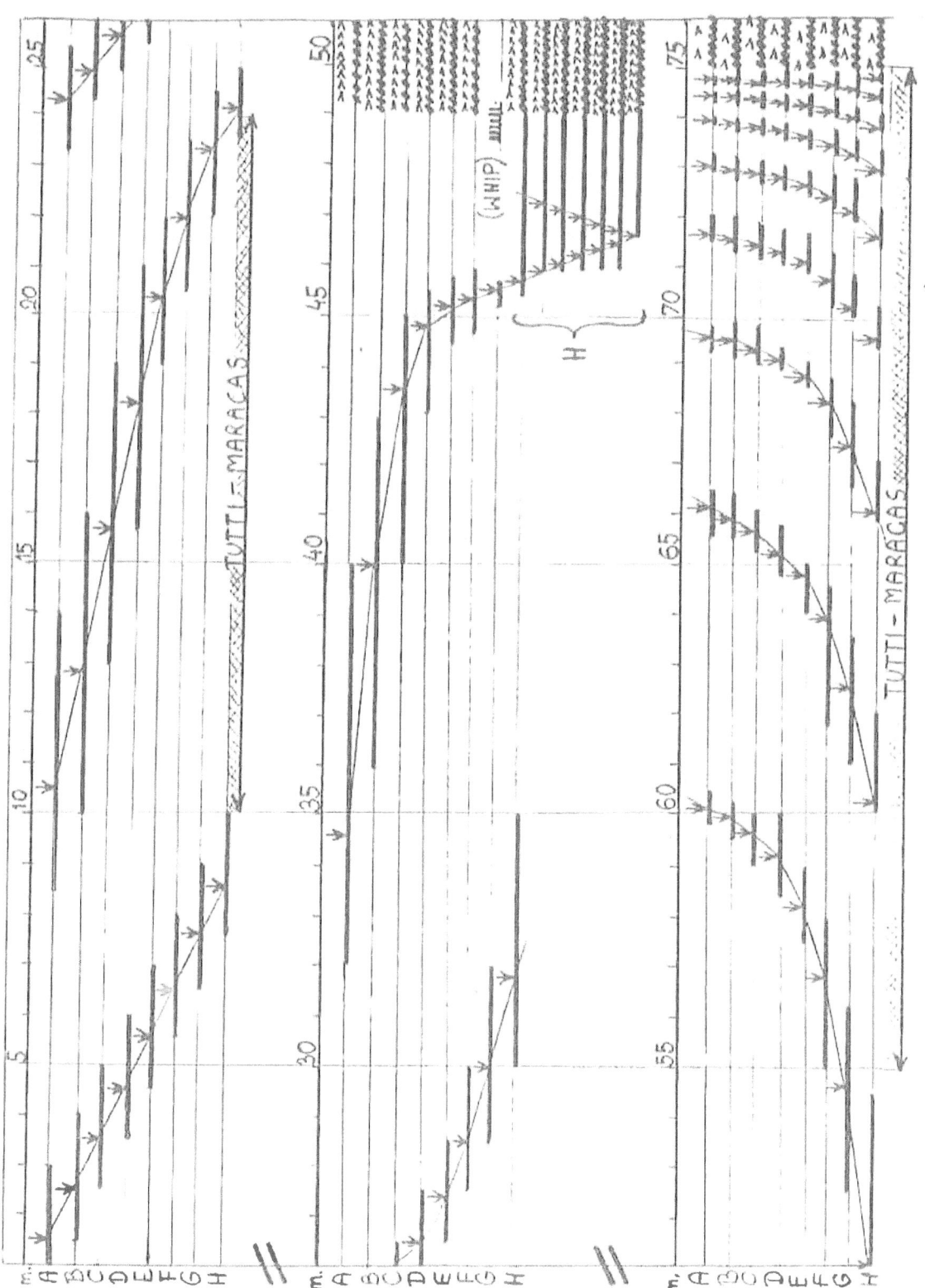

Ex. VII-9: Diagram of rotations of one pitch (E4) in mm. 1-75 of *Terretektorh*.

among the audience (an early sketch of the seating plan without percussionists is shown in Ex. VII-8a). The instrumentalists are divided into eight groups, A to H, filling out a circular performance space framed by three percussionists placed in a triangle (Ex. VII-8b).[17]

In this arrangement, the psychological and auditive curtain which separates the listener from the performers seated on stage is removed. The proximity of the sound creates a new aural experience strengthened by the movement of sound masses in space and enhanced by the novelty of the sounds themselves. Each musician is required to play, besides his normal instrument, four percussion instruments: woodblock, siren-whistle, maracas and whip. Here, according to the composer:

> The orchestra is in the audience and the audience in the orchestra. ... The scattering of the musicians brings in a radically new kinetic conception of music. . . The composition will thereby be entirely enriched . . . both in spatial dimension and in movement. The speeds and accelerations of the movement of the sounds will be realized, including logarithmic or Archimedean spirals in time and geometrically . . . [as well as] ordered or disordered sonorous masses, rolling one against the other like waves.
> (Xenakis 1971: 237)

At the beginning of the work, one pitch, E4, played by the strings in contiguous groups starting with group A, revolves around the circumference of the orchestra. A renotation of the score in graphic form brings out the various patterns of this movement (Ex. VII-9). As can be seen, each rotation displays a particular outline of dynamic accents (represented in the diagram by tiny, vertical arrows) superimposed on its scheme of durations (the duration of each note is depicted with a thick, black line). The instruments play overlapping sounds with similar dynamic envelopes (crescendo followed by decrescendo; these envelopes are not marked on the diagram)

---

203).

[17]Example VII-8b shows also the location of high woodwinds participating in the rotations in mm. 125-195 (clarinet 1, oboe 1, flute 1, oboe 3, E-flat clarinet, flute 2, oboe 2, piccolo); cf. Ex. VII-11.

thus creating the illusion of sound movement.[18] The idea of using superimposed dynamic envelopes and temporal shifts to cause continuous changes in the apparent position of instrumental sounds was modeled on an electroacoustic technique, that is, on stereo sound projection. In stereophony, differences of intensity between identical signals from two separate channels (loudspeakers) are used to suggest changes in the location of virtual sound sources. Xenakis describes this in the following way:

> Let us say that we have a monophonic recording of one sound and we want to make this sound move from loudspeaker A to loudspeaker B when the two are separated spatially. In order to do so we need to use two potentiometers, one for each channel, opening potentiometer A then closing it while slowly increasing the level in channel B. The balance is very sensitive; the most difficult thing is to have the sound coming from the center between the loudspeakers. This is just a simple example; in reality, sound movements are usually more complex and depend on the architecture of the performance space, the position of the speakers and many other things. When you want to reproduce such a complicated phenomenon with live musicians playing one after another with amplitude changing in the same way that you change the levels in a stereo sound projection, sometimes it will work and sometimes it will not. It depends on the speed of the sound as well as on the angle of two loudspeakers or musicians, that is on the relative position of the listener. These two considerations are equally important.
>
> (Xenakis 1992: 6-7)

According to Xenakis, "in the case of circular motion one can establish a uniform progression resembling the movement of the second hand on a clock: the same amount of time--the same distance" (Xenakis 1992: 7). This is how *Terretektorh* begins. At first, the motion is circular both in space (because of the position of the instruments) and in time (because of the temporal structure of the movement with constant velocity).[19] Soon, the temporal pattern of dynamic accents changes, bringing in sound acceleration and deceleration, while the spatial form of the movement

---

[18] The perception of this effect is very fragile; it depends on the position of the listener and the quality of performance, that is the placement of the groups, the exact matching of pitch, timbre, dynamics and so forth.

[19] In Xenakis's geometric representation of time, linear progressions (successive, equal durations) are represented by circles, while non-linear patterns (increasing or decreasing durations) are modelled with spirals.

remains circular. Following a change of direction in mm. 45-48 the movement gradually increases in velocity until the single sonic particle, E4, splits into an unstable microtonal cluster. At the moment of the change of direction, the spatial pattern of sound movement is also momentarily disturbed. Now, the motion is constrained to group H, highlighting its wedge shape from the tip outwards and back again. This disturbance, followed by an equally rapid motion of whip sounds in group G leads to a brief moment of 'turbulence' in mm. 49-50.

The increased speed of movement in mm. 51-74 is noticeable right away. What is not obvious, though, is the construction of this spatio-temporal motion. Describing *Terretektorh* in *Formalized Music*, Xenakis wrote about realizing accelerations with logarithimic and Archimedean spirals (in an excerpt quoted above). Before proceeding to search for these patterns in the opening of the work, let us turn our attention to a different fragment of *Terretektorh*, a fragment in which the identification of spirals is made possible by Xenakis's sketch (Ex. VII-10).

Xenakis's sketch does not contain information about all the layers of this section of the music; it reveals only the structure of the movement in the woodwind instruments. The pattern of durations and accents shown on the sketch is rendered in the score as a pattern of dynamic changes of a sustained eight-note chord in the flutes, oboes and clarinets (Ex. VII-11). Each of the instruments, placed at a different point in space (cf. Ex. VII-8b), plays one pitch continuously, ranging from D#6 to Bb7.

The spatial sound movement realized by the high woodwinds in mm. 125-195 of *Terretektorh* constitutes only one of the layers of the music. The complex, multilayered texture also includes (1) a steady rhythm on low drums from the three percussionists placed outside the circle, (2) irregular clouds of percussive sounds (that is whips, wood blocks, maracas) scattered throughout the orchestra, and (3) sporadic glissandi in the strings at various points in the space. In fact, when listening to a recording of the work, one may notice least the sustained chord in the high woodwinds. Here, the idea of spatial sound movement is raised to a new level of abstraction: continuous motion involving different elements of a chord instead of a single pitch.

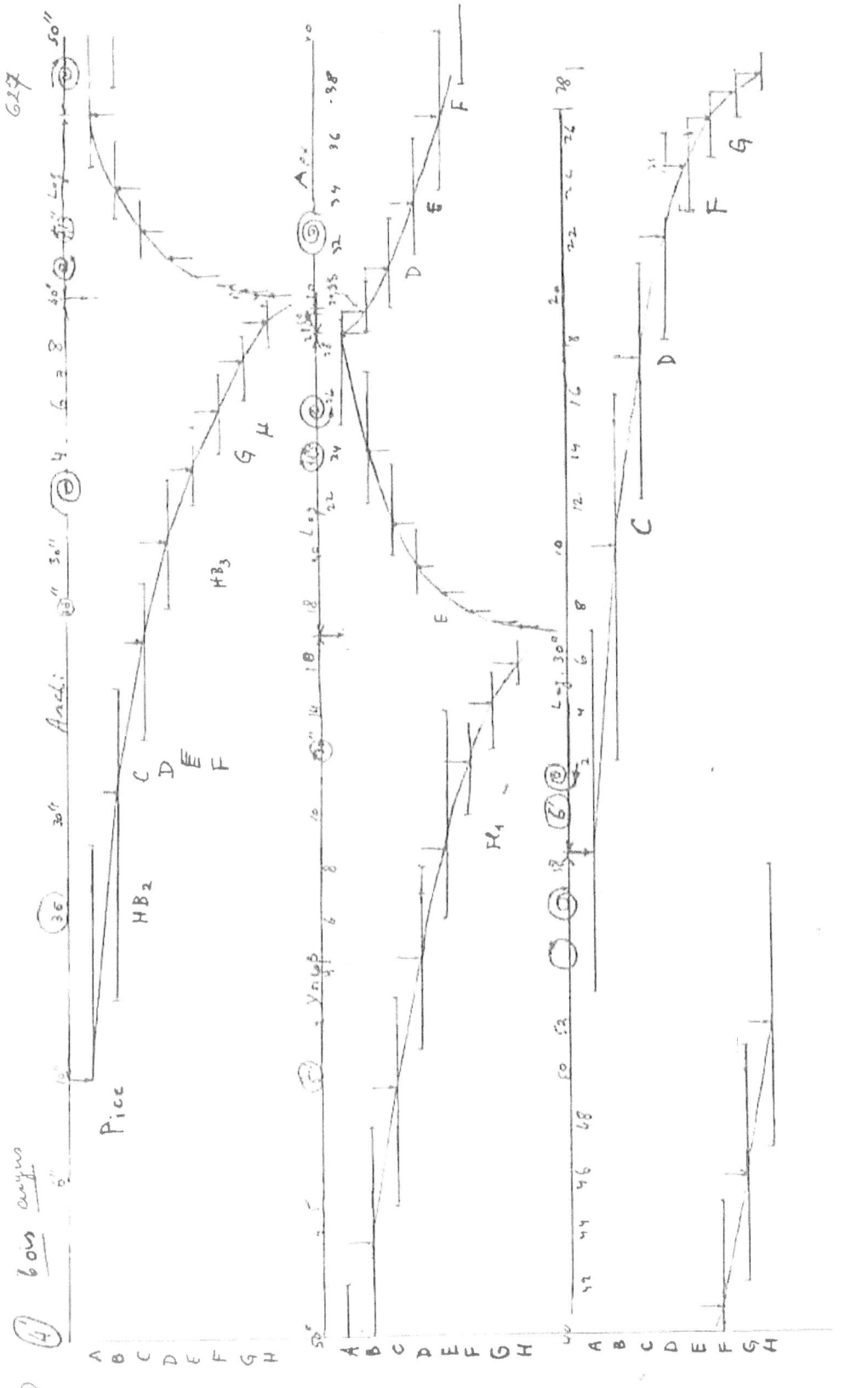

Ex. VII-10: Xenakis's sketch of rotations in mm. 125-195.

Ex. VII-11: The woodwind parts of mm. 125-146 of *Terretektorh*.

What is the temporal pattern of this motion? The composer's sketch contains the answer (cf. Ex. VII-10). There are 6 spirals outlined on the graph paper and identified by abbreviations of their names in Greek. The direction of the movement is also specified, together with the basics of the instrumentation (details were changed later: there are two high woodwinds in group B, and group C is missing). Among the six spirals presented in this sketch, two are Archimedean, three logarithmic and one hyperbolical. They do not look like spirals; in fact, they are not complete spirals but only segments. Spirals, described by the appropriate mathematical functions, are infinite (for the mathematical functions and diagrams of three types of spirals used by Xenakis see Ex. VII-12, after p. 290). Xenakis uses segments of spirals, represented graphically as curves (in this representation a circle, denoting motion with constant speed, would be a straight line). To obtain different patterns of velocity the composer places dynamic accents at the points of intersection of various spirals with eight straight lines assigned to the eight instrumental groups, A to H. In the score, each spiral segment is, then, represented by a temporal outline of eight successive accents suggesting an accelerating or decelerating sound motion. Thus, mathematical functions structure the patterns of spatial sound movement.

A comparison of the diagram of mm. 1-75 (Ex. VII-9), made on graph paper similar to that of Xenakis's sketch, with the sketch itself allows for the identification of the velocity patterns presented at the beginning of the work as various types of spirals. In particular, spirals No. 4 and 5 of the diagram (mm. 51-65) are very similar to spirals No. 2 and No. 4 of the sketch, that is, to logarithmic spirals. The spirals differ in their curvature and their musical realizations follow different temporal patterns: deceleration in the woodwinds (sketch), and acceleration in the strings (diagram). The underlying mathematical structure remains the same. The full list of patterns presented in mm. 1-74 of *Terretektorh* includes eleven spirals (acceleration or deceleration), one circle (rotation with constant velocity) and one instance of non-revolving motion:

    mm. 1-9: circle,
    mm. 8-24: Archimedean spiral, acceleration,

mm. 23-34: Archimedean spiral, deceleration,
mm. 32-45: hyperbolical spiral, acceleration,
mm. 45-47: angular, linear motion in group H,
mm. 51-60: logarithmic spiral, acceleration, new direction,
mm. 60-65: similar logarithimic spiral with steeper curvature,
mm. 65-74: six logarithmic spirals with increasing curvature (increasing acceleration of movement).

The predominantly circular (in space) and spiral (in time) movement of a single pitch in the opening of *Terretektorh*, first developed in the form of spiralling woodwind chords (mm. 125-195), finds continuation in rotations of chords and clouds of percussive sounds (maracas, sirens and wood blocks) throughout the piece (for example, two types of sonorities moving in opposite directions in mm. 313-330). Huge masses of sound inter-react and crash together to produce new sonorities; a state of equilibrium is reached only in the final chord, a sustained mass of quarter-tones which covers the whole range of the orchestra (mm. 435-447). The incessant dynamism of sound matter in *Terretektorh* is well captured by the composer's metaphoric description of this work as "an accelerator of sonorous particles, a disintegrator of sonorous masses, a synthesizer" (Bois, 1967: 35).

7.3.
Spatialization and group theory in *Nomos Gamma*

The similarity of the seating plans of *Terretektorh* and *Nomos Gamma* (1967-68), for a larger orchestra of 98 musicians scattered among the audience (Ex. VII-13), does not imply a total identity of compositional concerns in both works. In fact, *Nomos Gamma* resembles *Nomos Alpha* for cello solo (1965) in this respect, for it is also based on the principle of mathematical group structure.[20] Xenakis explains:

---

[20]Unlike *Nomos Alpha*, a favoured topic for analysts of Xenakis's music, who have been assisted by the composer's detailed discussion of the work in *Formalized Music* (e.g. Vandenbogaerde 1968, Naud 1975, DeLio 1980, Vriend 1981), *Nomos Gamma* has not

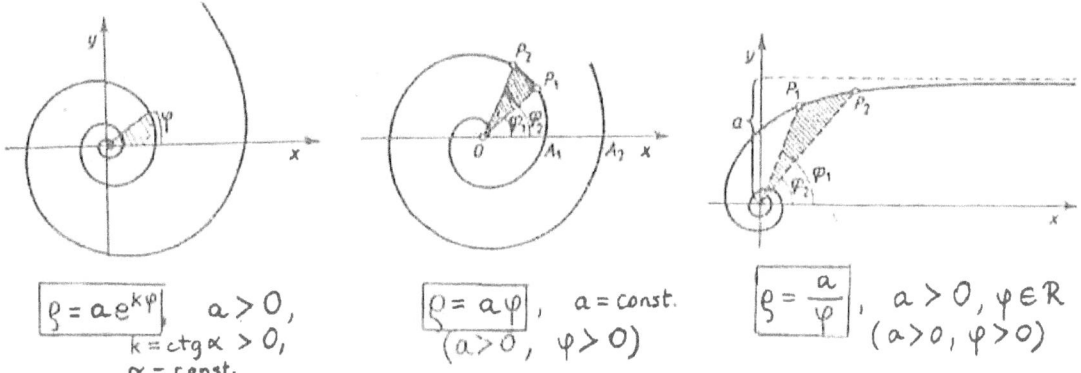

Ex. VII-12: Mathematical functions for logarithmic, Archimedean and hyperbolical spirals.

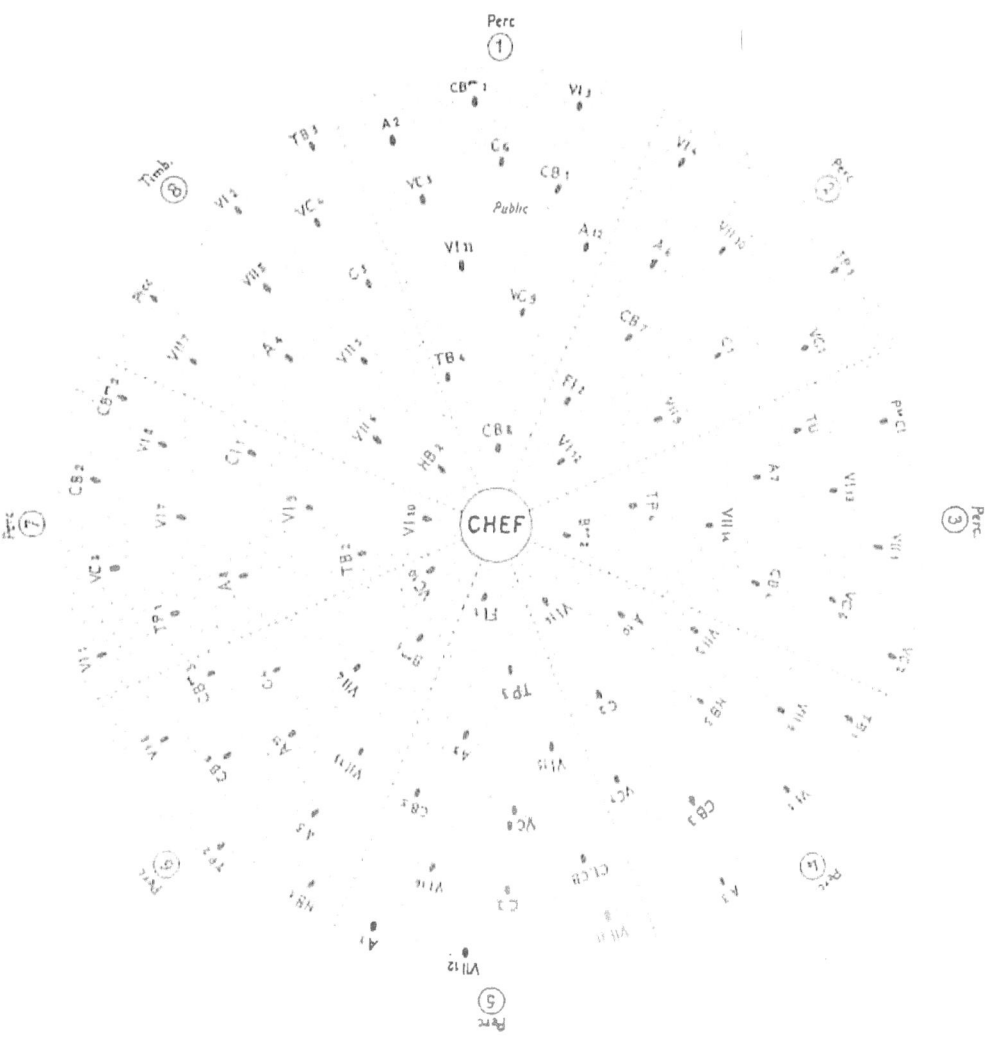

Ex. VII-13: Seating plan of Xenakis's *Nomos Gamma* (1967-68).

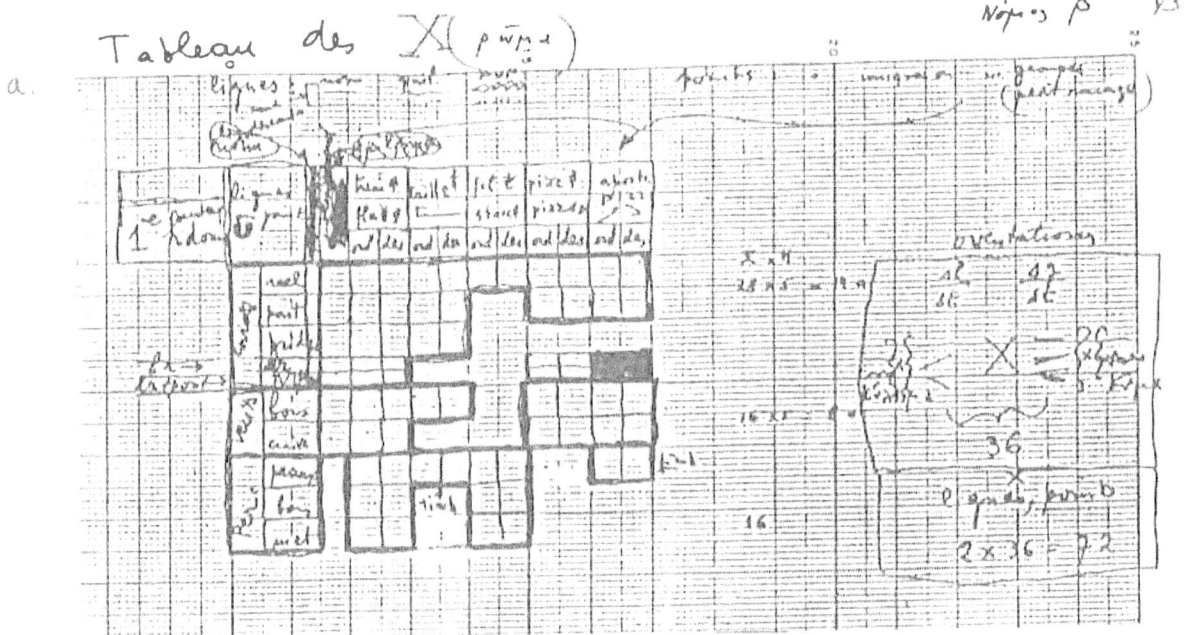

Ex. VII-14: Xenakis's sketches for *Nomos Gamma*.

a: A table of sound material (set X);
b: Sketch of alternating spatial textures in the strings.

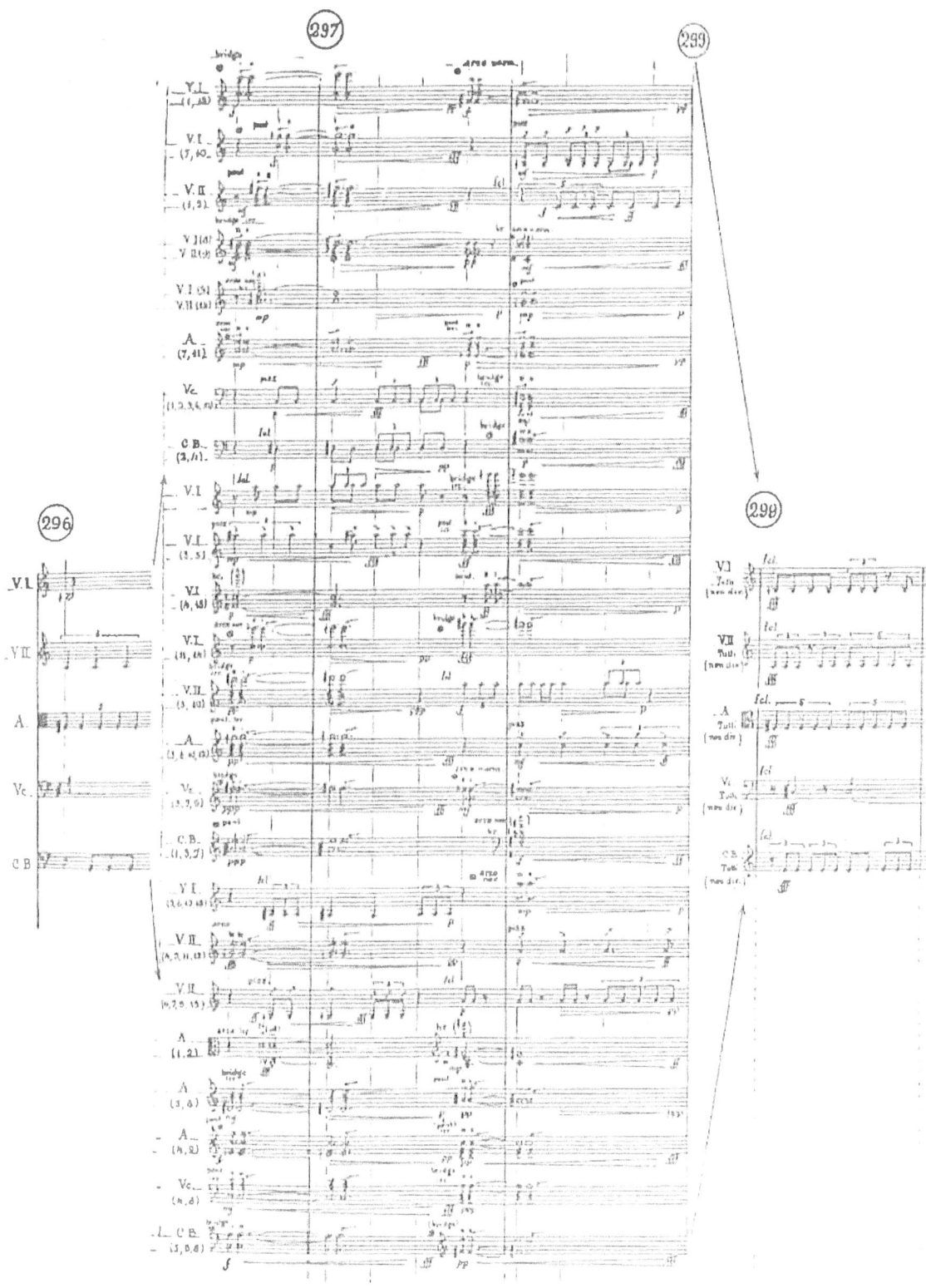

Ex. VII-15: Shifting textures in the strings in mm. 296-299 of *Nomos Gamma*.

> Group structure means that there are elements which are connected in some way: two elements combined together create another element which belongs to the same set, or group. Suppose that you have a melodic pattern. You can create the retrograde of this pattern thus obtaining two elements, one normal and one backwards. Now, if you take the inversion of the intervals of the normal sequence of notes, you create a third pattern, and if you take the retrograde of the inversion you get a fourth pattern: there are four forms here, no more. . . . These four forms can be combined with each other: the retrograde of the retrograde creates the first pattern, the retrograde of the retrograde inversion brings back one of the four forms again. So the system is closed, it is a set of four elements that can be combined by coupling them. The same isomorphic group (iso means equal) appears in the geometric pattern of the rectangle. If you study the symmetries of the rectangle you may notice that it can be inverted around the middle axis plotted both vertically and horizontally. There are four transformations of the rectangle onto itself, exactly like in the melodic pattern. This kind of group structure can be found in *Nomos Gamma*.
>
> (Xenakis 1992: 10)

According to the composer, spatial sound placement is included among the elements of mathematical group structure. If, for instance, the number of positions of instruments is limited to four and if in each of these positions a different melodic pattern is performed, a systematic exchange of spatial placements of the patterns is made possible by rotations of the rectangle on which these patterns and positions are plotted. In addition to the rectangle, *Nomos Gamma* exploits group tranformations mapped onto "the triangle, the square, the pentagon, the hexagon, the tetrahedron and the hexahedron" (*Formalized Music* 1971: 237). Here, compositional thinking involves a high level of abstraction in manipulating the elements of the music. Nevertheless, the elemental building blocks are quite simple--as can be seen in Xenakis's sketch for *Nomos Gamma* (still titled *Nomos Beta'* in Ex. VII-14a). This sketch contains a table of types of musical material (set X) attainable from the strings,

---

been well studied yet. The difficulties of approaching this enormous work are increased by the lack of information about its compositional procedures. While discussing *Nomos Gamma* in *Formalized Music* (chapter 8), Xenakis states that this work "is not entirely defined by group transformations. Arbitrary ranges of decisions are disseminated into the piece, as in all my works." (Xenakis 1971: 238).

wind instruments and percussion, such as, for instance, ordered or disordered tremolos, trills, and various types of pizziccati.[21] These basic types of ordered or disordered materials may be used to create straight, curved or broken lines, as well as various groupings of points--elements for an outside-time musical architecture. By assigning these elements (lines, points) to definite spatio-temporal locations, Xenakis constructs dense sound masses which extend throughout the performance space. These masses of complex texture either slowly evolve in time or rapidly alternate with contrasting spatial and textural patterns.

The second type of spatio-temporal distribution, involving rapid shifts of texture, appears in the strings (cf. Xenakis's outline of material for the strings in Ex. VII-14b). Here, the basic ideas of order and disorder govern the temporal succession of musical sections. The sketch indicates the type of group transformations applied to the material (double tetrahedron, cube) as well as the number of sectors of the orchestra involved (4 or all 8). The alternating sections of unison and of chaotic turbulences plotted in this sketch are realized, for instance, in mm. 296-300 of *Nomos Gamma* (Ex. VII-15). Here, the texture alternates between 5 parts (each section of the strings in unison) to 24 parts (2 to 5 instruments from the same section in each part).

Formalized Music (1971: 236-241) contains two analytical examples from *Nomos Gamma*, that of the work's beginning (mm. 1-22) and of the "sound tapestry" in mm. 404-442. The latter example is more interesting from the spatial point of view: the music has a very complex, evolving and spatially extended texture built from a multitude of sound-elements performed by divisi strings. In addition, this

---

[21]Not all instruments are capable of performing all such effects, yet the score of *Nomos Gamma* requires, for example, the winds to imitate pizziccato by means of a special type of articulated attack. In Ex. VII-14a instrumental sonorities are plotted on the vertical axis: strings (playing normally, sul ponticello, sul tasto, harmonics and harmonics sul ponticello), winds (woodwinds and brass), and percussion (skins, wood, metal). The horizontal axis enumerates various articulations: normal, tremolos, trills, col legno or staccato, pizziccato and pizziccato glissando. These ways of playing are subdivided into two categories of lines or points and of order or disorder.

"tapestry" of sound is structured by means of what Xenakis terms "tapisserie du cube" (in the sketches), indicating that group theory provides a detailed organization for the intricate and seemingly unordered texture.

Spatialization in *Nomos Gamma* is not limited to transformations of complex sound-masses. The work concludes with an interesting spatial effect which makes use of percussion instruments (tuned tom-toms and kettle drums) assigned to each of the eight groups of the orchestra (cf. Ex. VII-13). In mm. 445-559, the percussion performs a series of 198 rotations.[22] The velocity of this circular sound movement is stable (at a quarternote = 150 MM) and each rotation, constructed from overlapping tremolos, lasts for just 0.8 seconds. To avoid monotony, the timbre changes, usually in an descending pattern; the beginning of each circle is marked by the sonority of the kettle drum in Group 8 (Ex. VII-16).

7.4.

Sound rotations in *Persephassa*

The elaborate construction of velocity patterns in *Terretektorh* utilizes individual segments of spirals; the conclusion of *Nomos Gamma* presents a repeated circular motion of stable velocity. The idea of continuous sound movement is further developed in *Persephassa* (1969) for six percussionists encircling the audience.[23] The percussionists are placed at equal distances on the circle, so that they outline a hexagon (Ex. VII-17). Unpitched instruments of skin, metal and wood are used, some with identical timbre in all locations (e.g. metal or wooden simantras, Xenakis's invention) and some differing slightly (e.g. cymbals or gongs of various sizes).

---

[22]The rotations are subdivided into seven segments consisting of 26, 98, 5, 18, 12, 15 and 24 revolutions.

[23]According to the composer, *Persephassa* "exploits in a new manner the Screen Theory of the logical functions of residue classes modulo m, together with space-sound kinematics, as in *Terretektorh*, *Polytope* and *Nomos Gamma*" (liner notes for the recording by *Les Percussions de Strasbourg*, Philips PG 310, stereo 6718040, no date).

Ex. VII-16: Sound rotations in *Nomos Gamma*, mm. 511-513 (percussion parts).

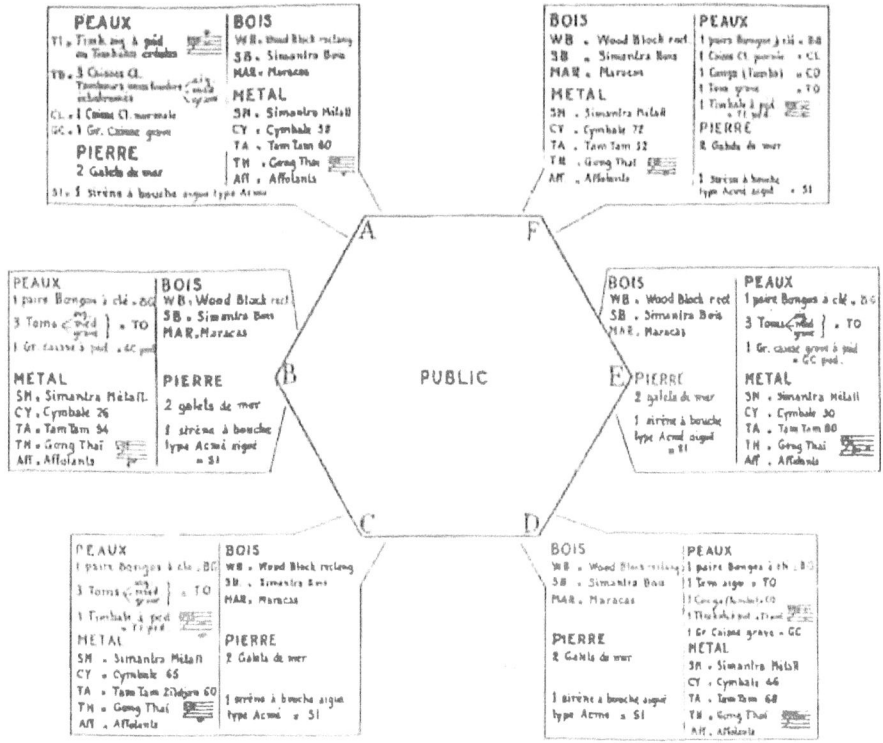

Ex. VII-17: Placement of instruments in *Persephassa* (1969).

Ex. VII-18: Semicircular movement in mm. 38-41 of *Persephassa*.

Ex. VII-19: Mm. 1-5 of *Persephassa*, percussions A-F in unison.

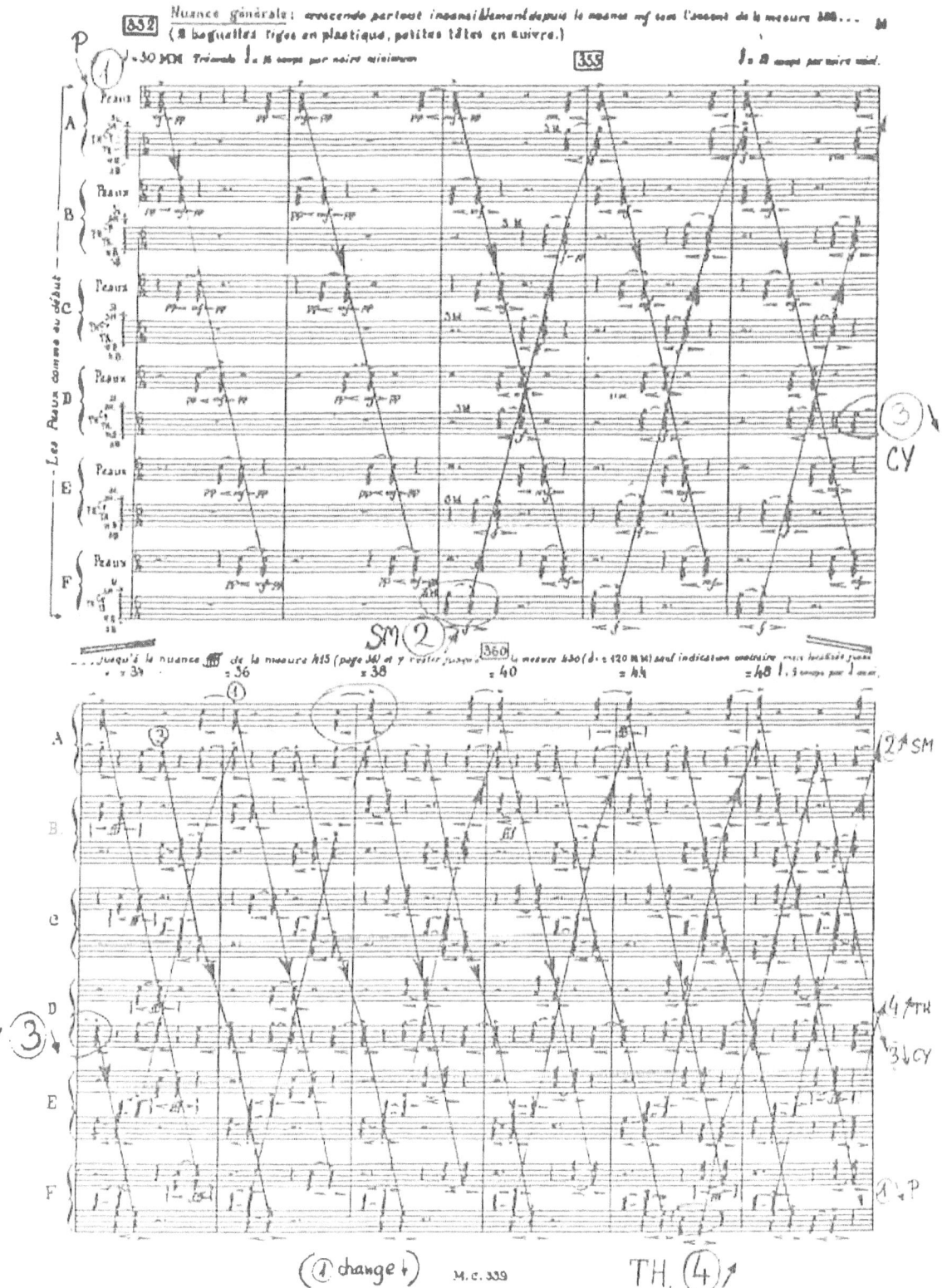

Ex. VII-20: Entries of 4 layers of rotations in mm. 352-362.

Ex. VII-21: Diagram of all rotations, mm. 352-420.

Spatial sound movement is usually created by means of overlapping dynamic envelopes; the dynamic peaks mark the shift of sound from one spatial location to another. The first instance of such movement in *Persephassa* provides a semicircular background for a more prominent rhythmic pattern in percussion A (m. 38-41; Ex. VII-18). This is only a hint of what will follow in the dramatic climax and finale of the work. Other allusions to a full scale dynamic sound movement are scattered throughout *Persephassa*: brief moments of rotation, patterns shifting in a circle, dynamically shaped tremolos. Even the opening of the piece, with tremolos on the tom-toms (mm. 1-5; Ex. VII-19) brings associations, in retrospect, with the climactic "space-sound kinematics" by following the familiar dynamic pattern of pp--crescendo--ff--decrescendo--pp.

The climax of *Persephassa* (mm. 352-455) begins with a slowly rotating tremolo on the drums (4 tom-toms and 2 snare drums) to which other timbrally distinct layers are gradually added, thus increasing the density of the texture (Ex. VII-20). The superimposed cycles of rotations are performed on metal simantras (from m. 354), cymbals (from m. 357), Thai gongs (from m. 361), wooden simantras (from m. 369), tam-tams (from m. 381), and wood blocks (from m. 395). The seven layers alternate in direction and differ in their starting points. The whole section is characterized by a gradual increase of speed and an overall crescendo, culminating in the eruption of sirens in all the groups in m. 410.

This construction consists of an impressive number of rotations varying from 69 revolutions of the drum layer to 25.5 rotations of the wood block tremolos (Ex. VII-21). Each single rotation is circular rather than spiral, i.e. each one is in a constant tempo. These tempi, however, increase rapidly, from that of one quarternote = 30 MM in m. 352 to 240 MM in m. 420, and to 360 MM at the end of the piece. At this point, (from m. 430 to the end), the complex multilayered texture of the music is reduced to one layer of rotating drum tremolos of varied timbre and erratically changing direction. The rotations, lasting only 1 second each, are interspersed with silences and fortissimo sound clouds. Thus, the accelerating motion ends in a vortex of sound, moving so fast that it seems to become stationary. As the duration of one complete rotation decreases from 12 seconds to 1.5 seconds during the continuous cycle of rotations (in m. 420), and to 1 second at the end of the work, it is easy to calculate the total increase of velocity. The seven layers of tremolos move 8 times faster at the end of their cycle of rotations than at the beginning, while the following solitary cycle of drum tremolos revolves 12 times faster than the same drums at the beginning. In *Terretektorh*, accelerations are constructed as segments of spirals, here, a large-scale temporal spiral is built from many individual circles of increasing tempi.

The timbral features of the distinct layers are also noteworthy. There are two types of timbral groupings: instruments of exactly the same timbre perform cycles 2, 5, and 7 (metal and wooden simantras, wood blocks), while instruments of the same quality but different pitch are used in cycles 3, 4, and 6 (cymbals, Thai gongs and tam-tams). All these metal instruments differ in size; their dimensions and relative pitch change irregularly from group to group. But it is the timbre of the first layer of drum tremolos that is the most varied: all available skin instruments are ordered in 6 groups according to their relative pitch (higher bongos, lower bongos, high, medium and low tom toms with timpani, low bass drums). The rotating sound gradually descends, with each level presented during at least one complete revolution. Moreover, regardless of the pitch, drums of percussion A always differ in timbre from the remaining ones, in order to articulate the beginning of each rotation. There are, then, two types of spatial motion: (1) of one timbral entity, resembling the motion of a single pitch in *Terretektorh* and (2) of varied colour, analogous to the randomly presented ingredients of the woodwind chord, the second instance of spirals in *Terretektorh*.

It is known from psychoacoustics that the fusion of distinct sound images (here: overlapping tremolos) into one auditory stream (here: the image of continuously moving sound) is possible when the sounds are sufficiently similar (Bregman 1990). The perception of the continuity of movement requires timbral identity of the sound supposed to be moving and Xenakis fulfills this condition, at least in approximation. The difference between various layers in the climax of *Persephassa* is greater than the difference between the elements belonging to the same layer. Naturally, proper dynamic balance and mutual distances between the instruments are imperative for the perception of the spatial movement to take place.[24]

7.5.
Spatial canons and sound planes in *Alax*

Following *Persephassa*, the 'tour de force' of rotations, Xenakis's compositional interests turned elsewhere, but the technique of 'spatial movement by dynamics' remained his and he used it again, to a different purpose, in *Alax* of 1985. This work for three identical instrumental ensembles placed at the summits of an equilateral triangle explores timbral and spatial interactions of various instruments and their groupings. According to Xenakis, the title means "transformations of planes, disorders, orders, sonorities, structures (inside or outside time)." It also denotes "interchange between the positions of the sound sources . . . and the sound planes."[25]

The familiar overlapping dynamic envelopes reappear to highlight spatially extended sound planes of different timbres in mm. 94-96 (Ex. VII-22). These planes, composed of all the woodwinds, the brass, the strings with harps and all the instruments in turn, intersect or transform into each other. There is no movement from one point in space to another, for all the sound planes are performed by instruments from the three ensembles in unison. In these circumstances, according to Henry Brant, the pioneer of spatialization, a "spill" phenomenon takes place (Brant 1967). Instead of hearing what one might expect, that is, isolated sounds localized

---

[24] The preservation of the equidistant placement of the percussionists seems particularly important. This was very evident during one disastrous rendering of *Persephassa* by the Warsaw Percussion Group in the 1980s. The performance took place in the concert hall of the Academy of Music in Warsaw, which allowed neither for a symmetrical placement of the players nor for their sufficient distance from the audience. On another occasion, in a more suitable performance space, the same group presented *Persephassa* in a very convincing manner.

[25] From Xenakis's note in the score of *Alax* (1987).

exactly at their points of origin at the summits of the triangle, we hear diffuse, spatially extended sonorities, aptly named sound planes by the composer.[26]

In *Alax*, timbral similarity is also explored in spatial canons which involve instruments from the three groups (for example all horns, or three solo celli sul ponticello). The structure of a 12-part canon in mm. 44-48 (Ex. VII-23) with voices entering successively in different ensembles at the interval of one thirty-second note leads to an effect of spatial sound movement: each entry of a sustained note is presented in a cascade of dynamic accents around the audience. The instrumentation balances solo horns and trombones with three other instruments playing together (flute, clarinet, harp). The overall dynamic scheme is that of a large-scale crescendo; the movement has a stable background of one "sound plane" of violins and cellos from the three ensembles performing a sustained octave (G5-6).

Obviously, sound movement realized by means of only three ensembles is quite rudimentary, and spatial effects in *Alax* lack the complexity of those introduced in the earlier compositions. This compromise is a consequence of Xenakis's experience with the realities of the concert hall; as the composer confesses with resignation,

> I have changed the conventional location of the musicians in the orchestra by placing brass and woodwinds in different places, the percussion in several spots, etc. I have tried to do that but the musicians hate it. The reason is that they do not have the same acoustic environment as usual, an environment that helps them to play correctly. . . . Even if you have fantastic ideas if you write something that is unusual it will not be played, or maybe just once. And that is not good enough.
>
> (Xenakis 1992: 12)

In *Alax*, orchestral musicians are not exposed to the public as in *Terretektorh* or *Nomos Gamma*, for they are grouped into three separate ensembles. In addition, the score allows for the placement of these ensembles "in a line on stage from left to right." Obviously, the directional quality of the sound does not constitute the most crucial aspect of the music. Nevertheless, Xenakis makes use of a number of spatial

---

[26]Here, Xenakis uses the same perceptual effect that Brant termed *spill* (Brant 1967; cf. chapter III, 3.2 and chapter VI).

patterns: from complete temporal unison (e.g. all horns and celli playing a series of chords in mm. 88-90), through numerous spatial canons between groups of identical instruments performing similar--but not identical--musical material, such as the brass in mm. 17-22 (Ex. VII-24), three sets of bongos (mm. 25-26) or three solo cellos (mm. 31-33), to complex multilayered textures of the three ensembles playing simultaneously (the conclusion of *Alax*, especially mm. 160-186).

The realization of these effects requires timbral identity and spatial separation of the three groups. Instruments of the same timbre from the three ensembles may have staggered entries, as in the many canons, or may play simultaneously when layers of different timbres are superimposed on each other. In a particularly delicate effect of this kind, in m. 52 (Ex. VII-25) the three violins, clarinets and flutes perform an ascending scale ending at F#6. The scale is slightly asynchronous in the three timbral groups, so that the colour of the music evolves simultaneously with its rising pitch.

Even though the limited number of instrumental ensembles of *Alax* seems to invite comparison with sixteenth-century polychorality, also heavily indebted to canonic techniques, Xenakis vehemently denies the existence of this connection (Xenakis 1992: 11). There may be two reasons for his outspokeness on this subject: his distrust of organized religions (polychoral music was mostly composed for the Church) and his commitment to total creative originality--which precludes conscious links to the musical past, other than Xenakis's own. The composer believes that

> In musical composition, construction must stem from originality which can be defined in extreme (perhaps inhuman) cases as the creation of new rules or laws, as far as that is possible; as far as possible meaning original, not yet known or even foreseeable.
>
> (Xenakis 1971/1991: 258)

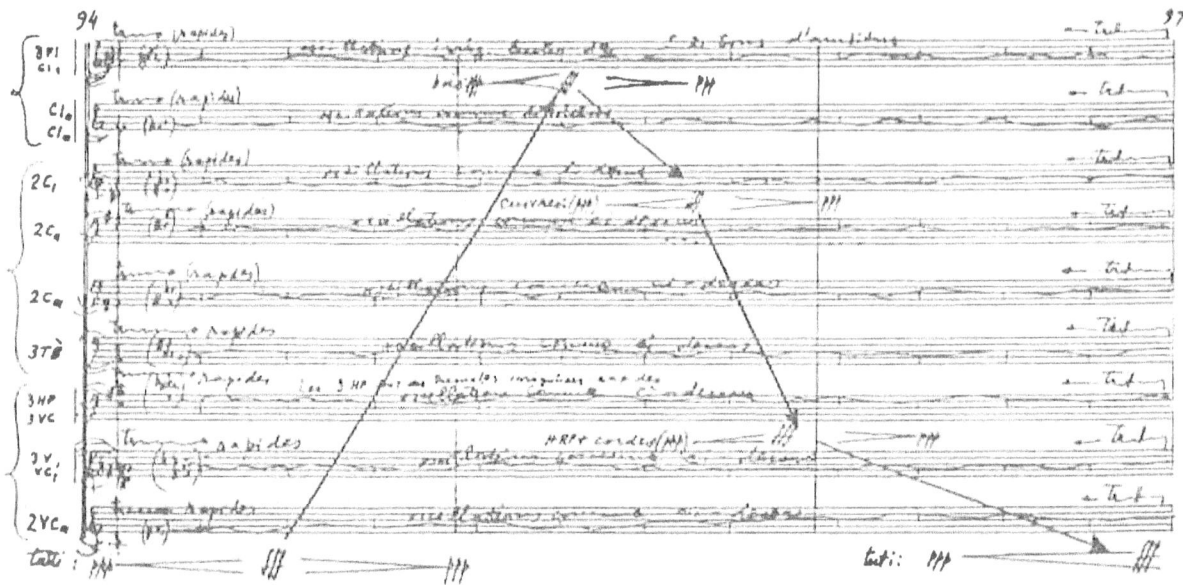

Ex. VII-22: Sound planes in mm. 94-96 of *Alax* (1985).

Ex. VII-23: 12-part spatial canon in *Alax*, mm. 44-46.

Conclusion

Xenakis's original contribution to the development of spatialization comprises a variety of techniques, from performer movement, through the use of spatial canons and superimposed cycles of rotations, to carefully structured velocity patterns. From *Pithoprakta* to *Alax*, Xenakis's spatialized music juxtaposes technical sophistication with an overwhelming forcefulness of expression. Evolution of stochastic sound masses in *Pithoprakta* (1955-56) is linked to a rudimentary form of spatial motion of sound on the stage. *Eonta* (1963-64) explores acoustic resonances, movement of the performers on the stage and the directional quality of brass instruments. The conquest of performance space goes one step further in two compositions for large orchestra, *Terretektorh* (1965-66) and *Nomos Gamma* (1967-68). In both works, the orchestral musicians are interspersed amongst the audience and the patterns of sound placement and motion are structured with mathematical means. *Nomos Gamma* concludes with a series of sound rotations around the audience; a similar effect crowns *Persephassa* (1969) for six percussionists. In the climax of this composition, seven distinct layers of sound revolve simultaneously in opposing directions (the technique of 'spatial movement by dynamics'). Spatial design is simpler in *Alax* (1985) for three identical ensembles which articulate spatial canons, interpenetration of sound planes, etc.

In his spatialized compositions, Xenakis does not consciously refer to any tradition, including that of polychorality. Neither is he indebted to his contemporaries, such as Brant (cf. Chapter VII of this dissertation), Stockhausen or Berio (cf. Chapter VI). Although Stockhausen was the first to compose the effect of virtual spatial sound movement in instrumental music (*Gruppen* of 1955-1957), Xenakis's ideas developed independently.[27] The technique of sound movement used by both composers owes its origin to their experience with electroacoustics, i.e. with stereophonic sound projection. However, Xenakis's music benefits from his mathematical and architectural background including his cooperation with Le Corbusier and Varèse on the Philips Pavilion (1957-1958). In addition, the Greek

---

[27]Cf. the discussion of virtual sound movement in chapter V.

Ex. VII-24: 3-part canon of brass glissandi in *Alax*, mm. 17-18.

Ex. VII-25:
Evolution of pitch and timbre,
(violins, clarinets and flutes)
in m. 52 of *Alax*.

composer develops Varèse's notions of "sound mass" and "sound trajectory" in instrumental music. Despite his insistence on total artistic originality and the uniqueness of his style, Xenakis's music does not exist in a vacuum. It belongs to the context of musical objects projected in space (the second large conceptual area within the domain of spatialization; cf. Chapter III, section 3.3). When Edgar Varèse postulated the idea of "the liberation of sound" he envisioned that in the music of the future

> the movement of sound masses, of shifting planes, will be clearly perceived . . . There will no longer be the old conception of melody or interplay of melodies. . . The entire work will flow as a river flows.
> (Varèse 1936/1966: 11)

This bold vision has, perhaps, found its true realization in the spatialized music of Iannis Xenakis.

CHAPTER VIII

SOUNDSCAPES AND RITUALS
IN THE MUSIC OF R. MURRAY SCHAFER

Introduction

> The big revolutions in music history are those with the power to change performance contexts. It is these which govern performance rituals and legislate musical forms and instrumentation.
>
> (Schafer 1981a: i)

These words by R. Murray Schafer give expression to one of his main preoccupations: to transform music by placing it in new concert situations. Schafer has brought music outside of the concert hall into art galleries and warehouses, into the streets and town squares, into the Canadian wilderness, into the urban or forest soundscape.[1] This great revision was, as in Cage's case, motivated by the wish to remove boundaries separating art from life, music from the environment. Here, the listeners' existential experience is at the focus, not their contemplation of self-contained, perfect works of the musical art. This approach underlies Schafer's theory of the theatre of confluence (Schafer 1991a; cf. Chapter III, section 3.5).

---

[1] Examples of different performance settings used for Schafer's works: (1) *Patria 3: The Greatest Show* in a large urban park; (2) *Situational music for brass quintet* at the Stratford city hall square; (3) *Patria 4: The Black Theatre of Hermes Trismegistos* at Toronto's Union Station; (3) *The Princess of the Stars* at a lake in Banff National Park; (4) *Musique pour le Parc Lafontaine* in Montreal's Parc Lafontaine (site-specific music).

As a consequence of Schafer's growing reliance on this theory, his use of space in music has been increasingly theatrical and ritualistic, from musical compositions for the concert hall, to music designated for the performance outdoors (urban and natural environments) and to works transcending traditional musical genres. Schafer's main preoccupation during the past two decades, his musical/theatrical cycle *Patria* includes works of unusual spatiality.[2] The 12-part cycle concludes with an as-yet-uncompleted environmental ritual, *And the Wolf Shall Inherit the Moon* (1984-). This week-long event needs to be performed in the woods near a lake; groups of participants prepare and 'live through' the various aspects of the musical/theatrical ritual without the presence of the audience.

In this chapter, however, a different segment of Schafer's musical/theatrical cycle will be discussed--*Patria: The Prologue. The Princess of the Stars* which is designed for performance at dawn at the centre of a lake (1981-1984). This work, as well as *Music for Wilderness Lake* for 12 trombones placed around a small lake (1979), transplants music into an outdoor environment characterized by acoustic conditions far removed from that of a concert hall. Schafer believes that "we are made by the environment in which we live" (Schafer 1992: 2). His environment of choice is that of the Canadian wilderness, hence the setting and conditions for these two compositions. The interest in the Canadian soundscape is also reflected in *North/White* for orchestra (1979).[3] This composition belongs to the group of pieces

---

[2] Cf. Chapter III, section 3.5. Various aspects of the *Patria* cycle, including its compositional history, are discussed in a doctoral dissertation by Kirk L. Mackenzie, entitled "A Twentieth-Century Musical/Theatrical Cycle: R. Murray Schafer's *Patria* (1966-)" (Mackenzie 1991). The work on *Patria* was begun in 1966 and has become Schafer's main concern since 1979 (Mackenzie 1991: 167).

[3] Canadian topics are common in Schafer's works. For instance, in Train for youth orchestra (1976) time and pitch are modeled on features of the geography of Canada. The distance from Vancouver to Montreal is translated into time and the altitudes of the stations into pitch so that the pitches of the string parts "rise and fall with the terrain of the land" (Adams 1983: 128). The only aspect of "spatialization" in this work is the placement of the brass and woodwind instruments off stage (they imitate the sound of the train whistle by playing an E-flat minor triad).

using spatialization within the concert hall. The *Third String Quartet* (1981), another example from this group, features structural use of performer movement. As musical theatre is Schafer's favourite genre, one more large-scale work of this type will be discussed here: *Apocalypsis*, a two-part monumental music drama (*John's Vision* and *Credo*, 1976-1977).[4]

8.1.
Canadian soundscape in *North/White*

R. Murray Schafer's orchestral composition, *North/White* (1979), an ecological protest against the destruction of the silence and solitude of the Canadian North by man-made noise pollution, features among its instruments a real snowmobile, a machine designed to conquer the icy expanses of the sub-polar regions.[5] *North/White* begins with the sound of two off-stage trumpets, placed far to the left, behind the last desk of the first violins, and performing one pitch, B-flat5, crescendo. The violins gradually take the music over, lowering the pitch to F5 and bringing the sound onto the stage, from the left towards the centre. As the composer writes in the score, the instruments should be added "from back to front of section . . . the sound must appear to rush across the stage" (Ex. VIII-1). From the violins, the sound moves successively to the clarinets with piccolo (centre-left), to the trumpets on-stage and to the oboes (centre). This movement is created by overlapping sounds of the same pitch and of superimposed dynamic envelopes (crescendo and decrescendo). Here, as Schafer writes, "the real space of the concert hall is extended in the virtual space of dynamics--by which effects may be brought into the foreground (forte) or allowed to

---

[4]For this dissertation, I interviewed Schafer on 19 October 1992, in Toronto, after a performance of *North/White* by the Esprit Orchestra conducted by Alex Pauk.

[5]The snowmobile, though presented as evil, paradoxically becomes the piece's main attraction.

drift back towards the acoustic horizon (piano)" (Schafer 1977a: 117).

The virtual space of *North/White* is extended by dynamics and by the actual placement of sounds at a distance, off-stage. The music emerges from a distant pianissimo at the acoustic horizon of audibility and moves into the fully articulated presence of the sounds played fortissimo on the stage.[6] The spatial motion is both physical and symbolic: as the music emerges from the silence beyond, the 'North' enters into the concert hall.

In a poetic essay of 1977, entitled *Music in the cold*, Schafer writes: "The art of the North is the art of restraint. . . The art of the North is composed of tiny events magnified" (Schafer 1977b). Accordingly, the score of *North/White* is filled with strange and subtle sonorous events, all alluding to the subtlety of a Northern soundscape: soft whirring sounds (produced by sections of rubber hose spun in the air), whistling by the musicians, multiphonics in the woodwinds, quarter-tone clusters in the strings. The most unusual sound effect is produced by the bending back and forth of 3 large sheets of Masonite or thick cardboard (Ex. VIII-2; p. 11 of the score). The deep, "flapping" sonority recalls Schafer's description from *Music in the cold*: "Our snowshoes paw through the powdered snow--thwoom, thwoom, thwoom. . ." This sound is accompanied by a high, sustained pitch B-flat5 in the solo violin which evokes the silence of the Arctic heard at the beginning of the piece. The strange, flapping sounds return in the conclusion of *North/White*, after the silencing of the aggressively noisy snowmobile.

In *North/White*, Schafer uses numerous chromatic and quarter-tonal clusters to portray the whiteness of the snow, the predominant colour of the Arctic. The composer explains this choice by a simple physical analogy between a full pitch range and "white light, which is composed of all visible frequencies" (the note to the score; Schafer 1980). The quiet, refined sound-world of the Arctic, with subtle effects and delicate clusters, is disturbed by man-made noises, embodied by the roaring engine of

---

[6]Schafer writes that "a soft sound is constantly dissolving, fleeing like mist, escaping from itself. It longs to fly over the horizon into the silence" (Schafer 1973: 13).

the snowmobile, as well as loud and ugly sounds made by an array of metal objects.[7] The purpose of this accumulation of noise is to represent the auditory "rape of the Canadian North." As the composer writes in the introduction to the score:[8]

> The instruments of destruction are pipelines and airstrips, highways and snowmobiles. But more than the environment is being destroyed by these actions, for . . . Canadians are about to be deprived of the 'idea of the North' which is at the core of the Canadian identity. The North is a place of austerity, of spaciousness and loneliness, the North is pure; the North is temptationless. . . The idea of North is a Canadian myth. Without a myth a nation dies.
>
> (Schafer 1979/1980)

These are strong words, indeed, words that express a sentiment not uncommon among ecology activists defending the Canadian wilderness from senseless destruction in the name of unlimited, economic progress. *North/White* has a straightforward political message, bringing the Canadian soundscape into the concert hall in order to sensitize the audience to vital issues of acoustic ecology. The use of spatialization in this work, however, is not very extensive; it is limited to the placement of the trumpets off-stage and one instance of virtual sound movement across the stage.[9]

---

[7] The sounds are made with 3 anvils, a large chain, 2 metal drums (e.g. oil cans with good resonance), 2 suspended metal sheets, 2 suspended metal pipes, and a corrugated metal surface. This barrage of unusual percussion instruments requires 6 players.

[8] The utopian radicalism of Schafer's *Programme Note* in the score extends to include intimations of "true Canadians" living only in the country and a diatribe against technocrats without imagination. The language is toned down in a program note for a performance of *North/White* by the Esprit Orchestra (Toronto, October 17, 1992) in which the composer does not mention "rape" and writes: "*North/White* is inspired by man's careless treatment of the ecology in the Canadian North--a destruction which is carried out through the introduction of airstrips, highways, and snowmobiles.

[9] During performances of *North/White* by the Esprit Orchestra (Toronto, 17 and 19 October 1992) the work was "spatialized" beyond the requirements of the score. The woodwinds were placed in the auditorium, the brass on the balcony above the stage.

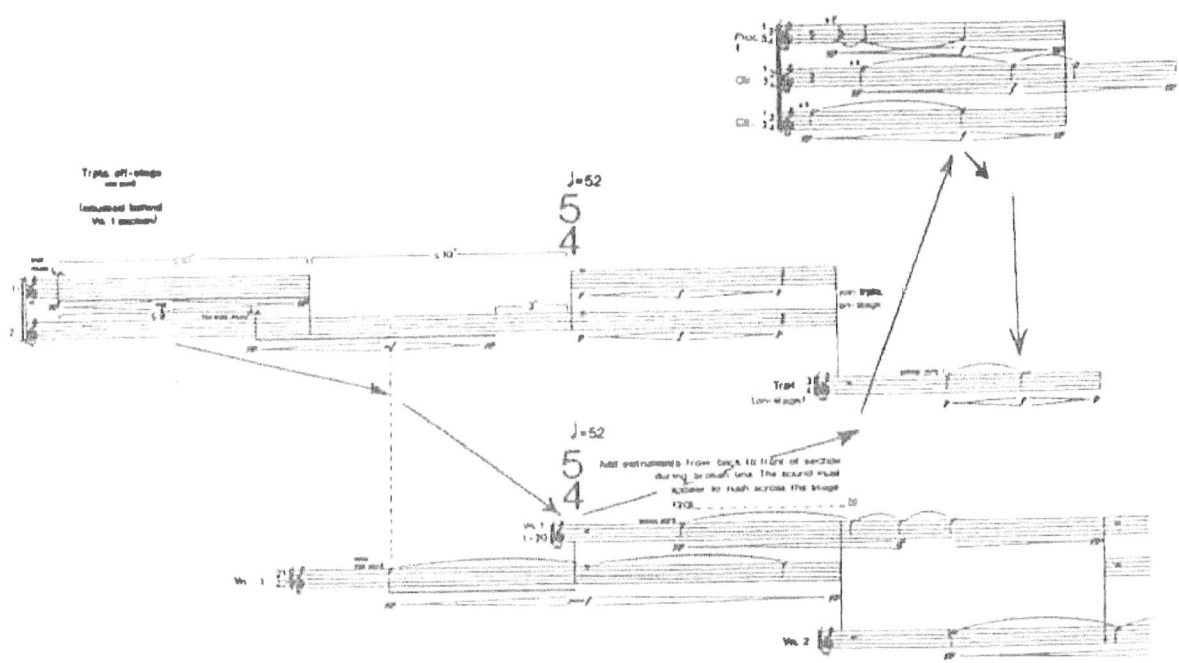

Ex. VIII-1: Spatial sound movement in *North/White* by R. Murray Schafer (1979), p. 1.

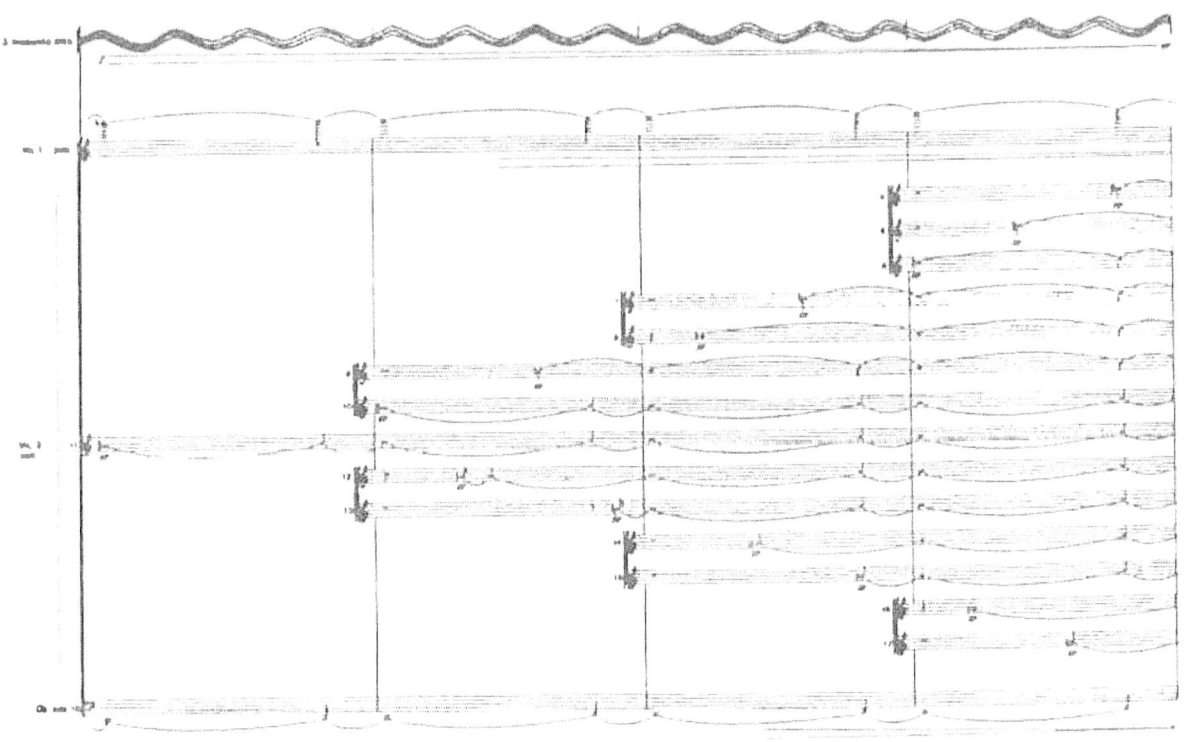

Ex. VIII-2: Sounds of Masonite sheets and a quarter-tone cluster in *North/White*, p. 11.

Ex. VIII-3: Performer movement in Schafer's *Third String Quartet* (1981), I, p. 9.

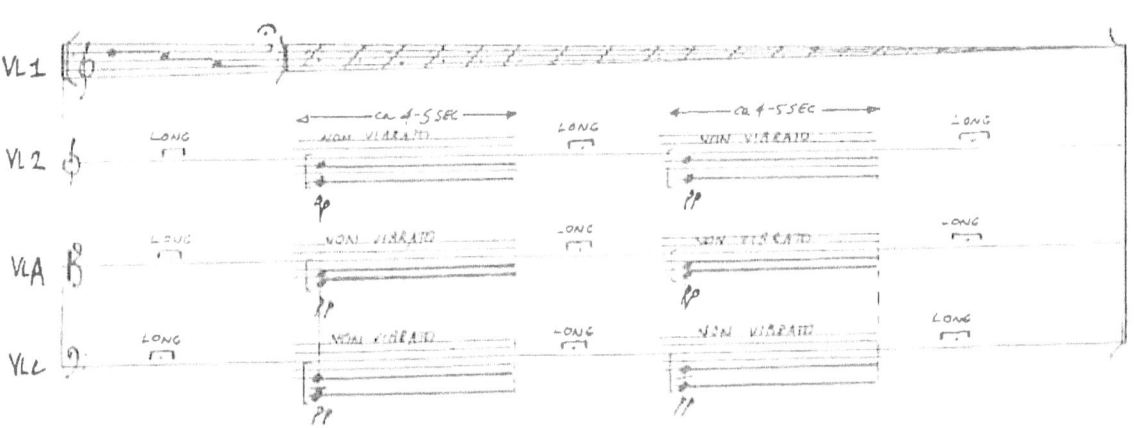

Ex. VIII-4: Conclusion of Schafer's *Third String Quartet* (1981), III, p. 26.

8.2.

Movement to unity: *Third String Quartet*

Spatial dispersion and motion of the performers are far more impressive in Schafer's *Third String Quartet* (1981). In the first movement of this work, the musicians, placed at various points in space and performing unrelated material, gradually converge on the stage, carrying contrasting layers of the music from different spatial locations. The piece begins with a long cello solo (from the stage); the cello is joined by the viola from backstage, the first violin from the back of the hall and the second violin from the opposite side at the back. As if reversing the finale of Haydn's *Farewell Symphony*, Schafer brings the players one by one onto the stage. The first movement concludes when the last performer (violin II) walks towards the chair and sits down (Ex. VIII-3). This theatrical gesture is a part of the musical design.

In the second movement of the *Quartet*, the physical effort of becoming one entity, a "quartet" playing together, results in the performers' intense vocalizations accompanying each instrumental gesture. In the note in the score, Schafer explains that these vocalizations

> should be uttered as if the gestures to which they are attached are calling them forth--like the vocal shouts of gymnastic exercises. . . so that they do not stand out as a separate set of sounds but appear born of the identical physical gesture that has produced the string tone.
>
> (Schafer 1983: 1)

The third movement celebrates a complete unity "not only with the notes played, but also with all physical gestures (bowing, body swaying, etc.)." When a brief motive is carried away at the end of the *Quartet*, it becomes a token of this unity, taken far beyond (cf. Ex. VIII-4, p. 26).[10] Here, the composer writes:

---

[10]Schafer introduced the gesture of carrying the music off the stage at the conclusion of *String Quartet No. 2* (1976). Here, the performers leave the stage one by one while playing (the cellist remains). This *Quartet* also uses a representation in pitch-time space of a spatio-temporal phenomenon--the lapping of ocean waves on the shore.

At this point the first violinist slowly rises and moves off-stage, continuing to play. He (she) should move to a very distant point so that the playing continues to be heard for a long time even though it may be unheard.

The violinist carries the music, as it were, into an infinite distance; yet the violin continues to be heard, or imagined to be heard, in "the mind's ear" for a long time after the physical sound has became silent. Thus, while moving very far, the music moves inwards, into the mental space of the listener's imagination.[11]

In the interview of 1992, Schafer explains that sound movement in this work, as well as in the *Second String Quartet*,

> is both symbolic and also very real. You can definitely hear when the instruments at the end of the *Second String Quartet* leave gradually; you can hear how the sound changes, how it passes by. The same phenomenon occurs in the *Third Quartet*, so it is more than symbolic, it is really using the adjacent spaces of the building--the foyer and the back stage--and incorporating them in the piece.
>
> (Schafer 1992: 1)

It is the particular balance between the acoustic and the symbolic features of spatialization that make Schafer's *Third String Quartet*, with its spatially-articulated form and content, a work of exceptional merit. Simultaneously, this piece articulates one of Schafer's main concerns--the mystique of oneness. The theme of unity returns in various guises throughout his oeuvre. Recently, it relates to the ecological union of humans with their environment, reenacted in the final work from the *Patria* cycle (*And the Wolf shall Inherit the Moon*). In his works from the 1970s, the theme of a spiritual oneness was rooted in religious mysticism of the East (*East*, *Lustro*), or of the Christian Europe (*Credo* from *Apocalypsis*).[12]

The composer believes that this slow, slightly irregular rhythm induces contemplation (Schafer 1977).

[11]This disappearance of music into the silence is also suggested by the graphic image of the lines of the stave converging to one point.

[12]*East* (1973) is a contemplative work for orchestra with two separated groups (one backstage and one at the rear of the auditorium). *Lustro* (1969-1972) consists of three movements: *Divan i Shams i Tabriz*, *Music for the Morning of the World*, *Beyond*

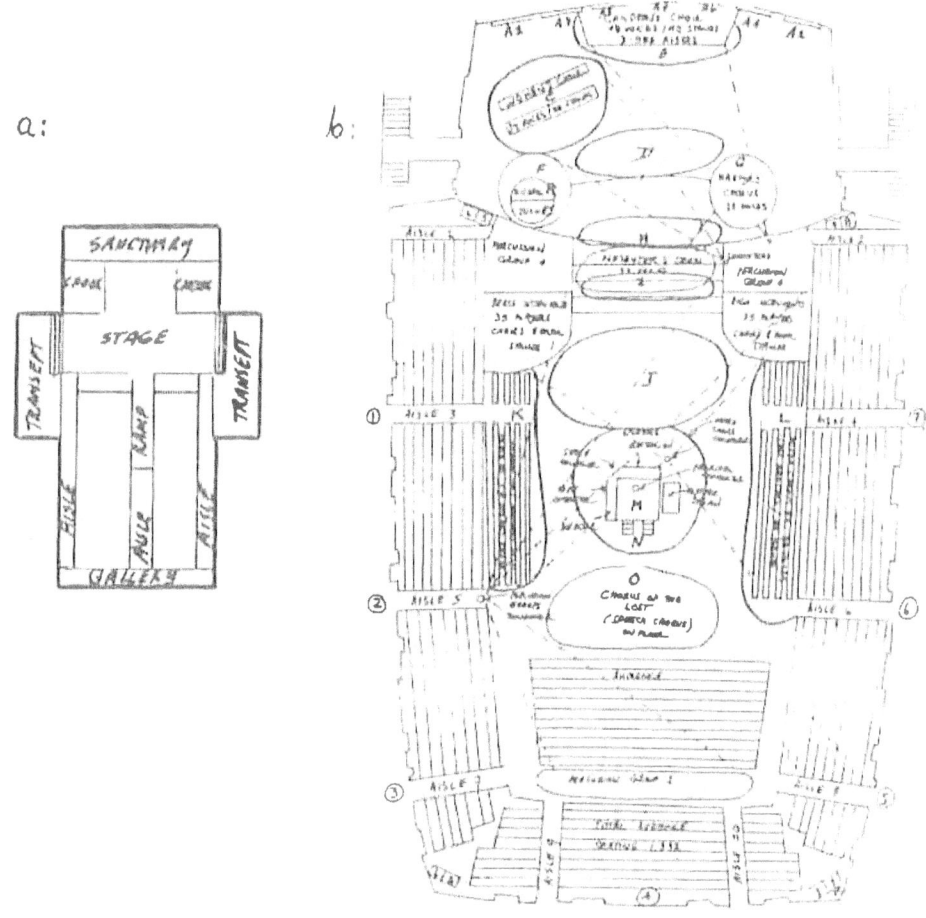

Ex. VIII-5: Ideal and actual performance space for Schafer's *Apocalypsis Part One: John's Vision* (1977), (a) ideal, p. ii; (b) actual, p. B.

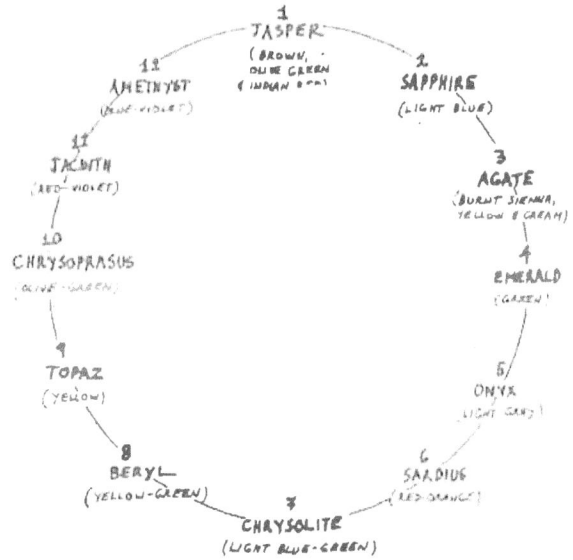

Ex. VIII-6: 12 choirs in Schafer's *Apocalypsis Part Two: Credo* (1976), p. 3.

8.3.

Mysticism and virtual space in *Apocalypsis Part Two: Credo*

Apocalypsis (1976-1977), one of Schafer's larger works crossing the border between music and theatre, "is intended to be performed in a large church or cathedral, or failing this a large hall with a minimum of four seconds of reverberation" (Schafer 1981b: ii). The score of the first part of *Apocalypsis, John's Vision*, calls for extensive forces, including 12 solo voices, 5 choruses, 4 groups of instruments and 7 conductors (over 500 performers). The location of the musicians, distributed throughout the performance space, varies in each section of this dramatic representation of the end of the world (cf. Ex. VIII-5; comparing the ideal and the actual performance space of *John's Vision*, p. ii and p. B from "Post-production Notes"). The composer thus describes the use of space in *Apocalypsis*:

> In the first part, portraying the turbulence of the last days of the Earth there is a lot of motion, the musicians are moving in various directions throughout the hall. The second part is very slow-moving and almost trance-like to suggest a new world. This piece does use space to some extent: I wanted the musicians to surround the audience, they also describe patterns--like the cross or the star--in the music. There is, then, a suggestion of Christian symbolism; the numbers are symbolic as well. In the whole *Apocalypsis* two numbers, 7 and 12, are particularly important and they are used all the way through.
> (Schafer 1992: 2)

The contrast between the two parts of this piece is not limited to the scope of activity within the performance space. *John's Vision* is described in the score as a music-theatre work. It involves the use of costumes, lighting, films, and large performing forces. The chaotic, loud and frantic activity of this colourful, yet naive portrayal of the Last Judgement, gives way in *Credo*, the second part of *Apocalypsis* (1976), to the stasis of vocal sonorities from 12 mixed choirs surrounding the audience

---

the Great Gate of Light. This "evocation of mystical experience" (Adams 1983: 100) is based on writings by Jalal al-Din Rumi, a 13th-century Persian poet. In the first movement, the scattering of the musicians in space (the orchestra is divided into 13 groups, each with a different musical material) evokes the primordial chaos, disappearing when the music gradually converges toward a unison.

(*Credo* may be performed as a concert piece).

All through the *Apocalypsis Part Two: Credo* the voices blend with pre-recorded bell sounds.[13] In order to create an illusion of the immateriality and omnipresence of these sounds the loudspeakers are hidden behind the performers around the auditorium (the four-channel tape may be projected from more than four loudspeakers). The composer intends to create a continuous, "uniform, wrap-around sound" which would support and enrich the static sonorities of the choirs, but not compete with them. The sound material of the tape part consists of "filtered bells from Salzburg Cathedral, recorded in 1975 by the World Soundscape Project" (Schafer 1986a: 58).[14] The filtering is gradually released and, at the conclusion of this 46 minute piece, the bells are heard in their natural form and "surge forward to overwhelm the choir."

The presence of recorded sounds in the two parts of *Apocalypsis* as well as many of Schafer's other large-scale spatialized works may seem like a contradiction of his views.[15] The composer has been quite critical of the "schizophonia: split between an original sound and its electroacoustical transmission or reproduction" underlying the dependence of musical culture on electricity (Schafer 1973: 15).[16] Yet, he has

---

[13]The recording may be replaced by a synthesizer simulation of bell sounds. The presence of bells is essential to the conception of the piece; Schafer also permits other, optional instruments.

[14]*John's Vision* concludes with the tolling of the bells--this sonority provides a link between the two parts of *Apocalypsis*.

[15]The four-channel tape is used profusely in *Lustro* (1969-1972), especially in the central movement scored for a soprano and quadrophonic tape. Here, pre-recorded sounds often rotate around the hall (creating a "whirlpool" effect).

[16]In the interview of 1992, Schafer cites ecological reasons for his objection to loudspeakers: "I object to amplification of sound, often to overpowering degrees that are threatening us all with deafness. It also bothers me a great deal when I think of the way that the whole Western European tradition is plugging itself into electricity, because the assumption that is being made is that there is always going to be a constant supply of electricity. . . I think that if there was a real energy crisis so that there was no more electricity our whole Western musical tradition would disappear. It would be vaporized

used recorded sounds in order to realize his programmatic goals and to expand the virtual space of music. In Schafer's opinion,

> the introduction of dynamics, echo effects, the splitting of resources, the separation of soloist from the ensemble, are all attempts to create virtual spaces which are larger or different from natural room acoustics.
>
> (Schafer 1973: 16)

In *Credo*, the sounds of bells recorded at the Salvator Mundi cathedral in Austria have the same function: to take the listeners beyond the concert hall into the spiritual domain of Christianity. The use of 12 choirs in *Credo* also stems from Christian symbolism. St. John's Revelation (i.e. *Apocalypsis*) describes the heavenly New Jerusalem as a square city with 12 foundations and 12 gates (analogous to the 12 generations of Israel and the 12 Apostles; cf. Revelation 21: 19-20). In this miraculous vision of the city for the saved, each foundation is made of a precious stone of a different colour. By analogy, each choir in Schafer's work is supposed to wear robes of a distinct hue, identified by the name of a different jewel (cf. Ex. VIII-6; the placement of choirs and colour scheme for *Credo*).

In *Credo*, however, Schafer replaces the Biblical design of the square with a large circle; he also rejects St. John's metaphor of the city for the sake of a pantheistic creed by Giordano Bruno. The text is divided into 12 Invocations ("Lord God is Universe") and 12 Responses which complete the repeated, opening statement in a number of ways. The universe is "all that exists" (No. 1), it is "infinite in extent, immobile in time" (no.2), it "has no parts yet it contains all parts. . . It is formed yet it is formless. It is end yet unending" (no. 9). The universe "has no before, after or present. It has no up, down or position" (no. 10). In the universe, "point does not differ from circumference, finite from infinite, maximum from minimum. Therefore, the universe is all centre yet nowhere centre, and all circumference yet nowhere circumference" (no. 11). The universe is one: "one act, one form, one soul, one body, one being, the maximum and only" (no. 12). This

---

like a whiff. There would not be any music left apart from what we still could play on acoustic instruments, which is less, and less, and less all the time." (Schafer 1992: 9).

image of unity and perfection is, perhaps, best approximated by a circle, which does not privilege any of the points at its circumference.

The music of *Credo* aims at portraying the calmness of heavenly bliss following the turmoil of the last moments of existence of this world. Accordingly, it presents "motion within tranquility" and follows a simple overall dynamic pattern: all the invocations are sung forte, while the responses show a gradual dynamic increase. In addition, as Schafer writes, "within each response the dynamics should be exaggerated to create the impression of the sound shifting from choir to choir; this is a structural feature of the work" (Schafer 1986a: 3).

The Invocations resound from a semi-circle, their positions gradually shift around (cf. Table VIII-1).[17] The texted portions are accompanied and followed by humming or slow glissandi resounding from various sectors of the circle and leading into the following Responses.

Table VIII-1: Invocations in *Credo*

no.	voice + choir no.	accompanying voices (transitions)
I.	soprano 1-6	humming in all basses
II.	soprano 2-7	glissando in altos and tenors 2-7
III.	tenor 3-8	humming in altos and basses 3-8
IV.	alto, bass 4-9	humming in all sopranos
V.	tenor, soprano 5-10	humming in all basses
VI.	bass 6-11	humming in sopranos 6-11
VII.	soprano 7-12	humming in altos and basses 7-12
VIII.	soprano and alto 8-12,1,	glissando in tenors 8-1
IX.	soprano 1 2 9 10 11 12	glissando in altos, then with basses
X.	altos 1-3 10-12	slow glissando in tenors
XI.	basses 1 2 3 4 11 12	glissando in sopranos 1 3 5 7 9 11 followed by a slow glissando in all
XII.	S, A, T all choirs unison	

[17]Adams summarizes *Apocalypsis* on p. 217-220 (1983).

Ex. VIII-7: Sound rotation and spatial texture in Response VI from *Credo*, (p. 22-23).

The invocations are rather brief, and apart from the gradual shift in location on the circle, do not contain many of the spatial effects which Schafer included in the Responses (see Table VIII-2). Here, minute dynamic fluctuations result from the use of a set of dynamic envelopes (patterns of crescendo and decrescendo) which depend on the order and type of the consonants and vowels in each syllable of the text. This dynamic variability enriches the texture of dense sound masses but is detrimental to the perception of sound movement around the hall--requiring a specific type of overlapping crescendi (cf. *North/White* and the discussion of this technique in Chapter VII). In *Credo*, this effect is possible if the successive voices sing the same syllable, preferably with a crescendo (e.g. "u" in the tenors in Response 6, p. 22; Ex. VIII-7). The same example presents a typical static texture of sustained pitches enlivened by dynamic fluctuations.

\multicolumn{3}{c}{Table VIII-2: Spatial patterns in Responses from Schafer's *Credo*}		
no.	voice	description
I.	A	movement from choir no. 12 along both sides at the same time (the right hand side is delayed by a quarter-note) ending at no. 6; followed by fluctuations and movement along both sides simultaneously in the opposite direction (from no.7 to no. 12); at the end a slow return to no.7.
II.	S, A	S from no. 12 (1) to 6 once; 7 complete, circular rotations in A (no. 1-12), followed by a more chaotic pattern; successive entries of voices on each syllable of the text; two cycles of movement in the same direction--choirs 1,3,5,7,9,11 are followed by choirs of even nos. after the delay of 6 quarternotes.

		Table VIII-2: Spatial patterns in Responses, continued.
III.	T, B	from no. 6 to 12, at both sides simultaneously, six complete, circular rotations, from no. 12 to 1 in the basses.
IV.	B	response simultaneously all together, then patterns of the cross in no. 3,6,9,12 singing simultaneously the same pitch (m. 70) and no. 2,4,8,10 (another pitch on a different syllable of the text); followed by the completion to the whole circle; another cross with no. 1,5,7,11 (m. 74) followed by symmetrical patterns: 3 and 9 together (a diameter of the circle, m. 76) then the cross of no. 2,4,8,10 (m. 77), then a diagonal cross superimposed with another diameter, no. 1,5,7,11, with 6 and 12; then completion to the whole circle.
	A	begin rotation from no. 7 through 1 to 8, a full circle in the anticlockwise direction (m. 70-71); followed by a semicircle in no. 2 to 8 and irregular dynamic fluctuations (patterns are superimposed on those of B).
V.	S, T	all voices begin simultaneously with complex fluctuations (a gap of no. 6-7 at the beginning is completed immediately); a fluctuating mass of sounds, without divisions into distinct patterns.
VI.	SATB	S, A, T, simultaneously start with one rotation, clockwise 1-12; followed by imitation in S (three pitches BC#D#): 6,5,8,4,3,9,2,1,10,11,12; similar successive entries in T, A add up to a fluctuating mass of sounds; at times repeated brief phrases (scale-wise), max. 3 times in succession; B enter in the middle of section.
VII.	all	choirs no. 4,5,6,7,8,9, are treated as separate entities in free imitation; melody in S supported with sustained, dissonant chords in ATB (two-part texture in each choir); choral entries after 3 quarternotes, with melodic variants and fragmentation.

		Table VIII-2: Spatial patterns in Responses, continued.
VIII.	all	choirs no. 10,11,12,1,2,3, (completion) with free imitation between whole choirs, each in two-part texture, similar to no. VII.
IX.	all	choirs, with free imitation of ascending themes, (order of 6-12-7); circular motion previously realized by individual voices on one pitch, here with choirs and melodies with slightly varying rhythmic motives and identical pitch content; accompanied by parallel fifths (allusion to parallel organum).
X.	all	choirs no. 5,7,3,9,11,1 (entries in this order, pattern of the star) have a theme of ascending contour in T and, later, A; the remaining voices hold a perfect fifth bourdon.
XI.	all	similar to X.; choirs no. 10,8,6,4,2,12, have the theme in B first, then in T, A and S. All voices successively outline the same pattern of the star.
XII.	all	tutti; successive entries of S with the theme and sustained other voices, imitation at unison; four rotations in clockwise direction (1-12) followed by a tutti repetition of "Lord God;" meanwhile the tape level increases and the voices fade into the sounds of bells; the final acclamation fff, is sung tutti and followed by "Amen" circulating from no. 12 to 1 in an anticlockwise direction.

According to John Adams, "Schafer's Jerusalem is surely a heaven for the faithful only, for others would find it intolerable--a 46 minute expanse of nearly featureless, inwoven choral sound" (Adams 1983: 170). This motionless music also "touches the outer limits of the possible" in the domain of spatialization. Schafer intends to create patterns of crosses, stars, etc. by means of using voices from certain

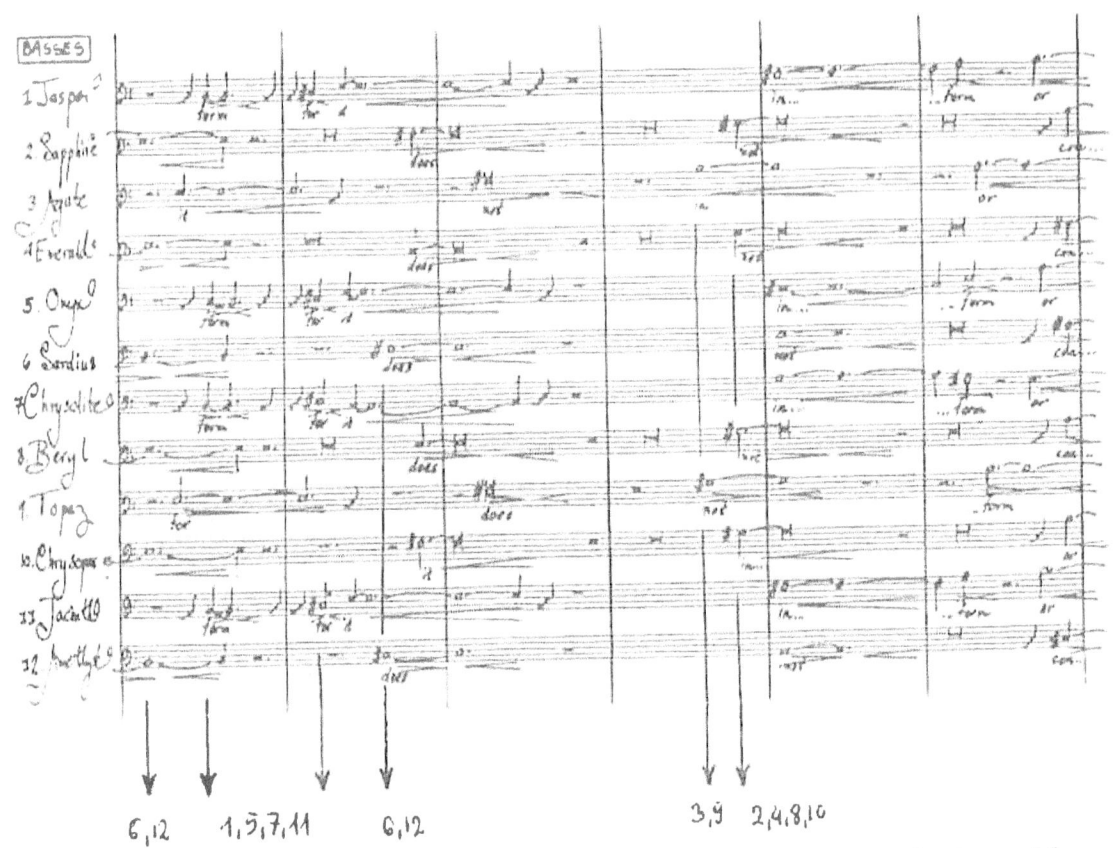

Ex. VIII-8: Spatial patterns in Bass parts in Response IV from *Credo*, p. 16.

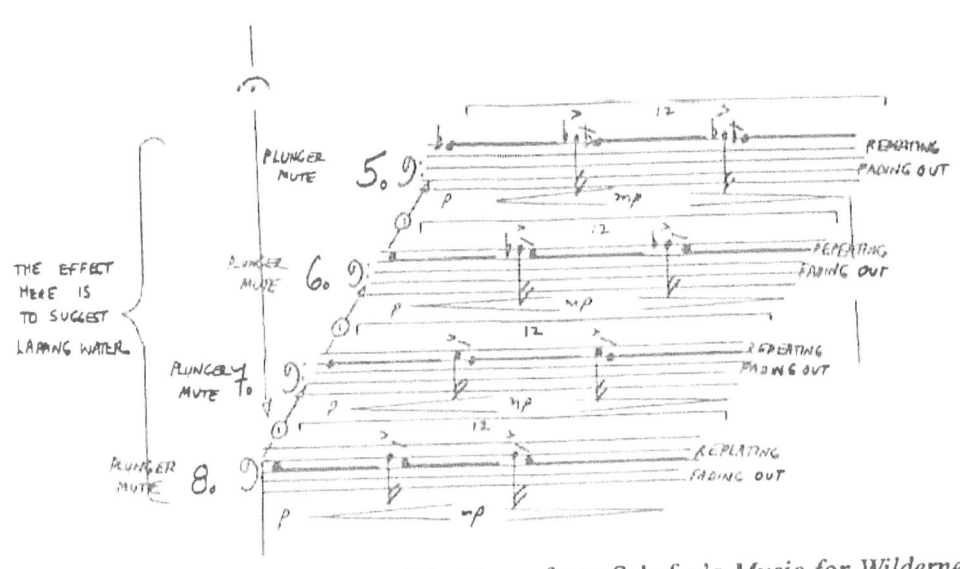

Ex. VIII-9: Image of "lapping water" in *Dawn* from Schafer's *Music for Wilderness Lake* (1979), p. 16-17.

choirs only; the audibility of these patterns, perceivable on paper, is doubtful. In Ex. VIII-8, presenting the Bass parts from Response 4 (p. 16 of the score, Altos are omitted) reveal the intricacy of Schafer's spatial designs. The patterns of the cross and the star are articulated by the simultaneous entries of voices from various directions.

8.4.
Music for Wilderness Lake and its soundscape

While in *North/White* Schafer brought Canadian soundscape into the concert hall, and in *Apocalypsis* transformed the auditorium into the scene of an eschatological ritual, in *Music for Wilderness Lake* he brought music into the soundscape, away from human civilization. This work abandons the very idea of the audience and requires the musicians (12 trombonists) to make a pilgrimage into the depths of the Canadian wilderness, to a secluded, distant lake. The two parts of the composition are to be performed at dusk and dawn, in late spring, when the woods around the lake are filled with birdsong. In the composer's words, "the location, the climate and time of day are as essential here as the musical notes" (Schafer 1981a: i). The lake should not be too small (the one that inspired the work is nearly a kilometre long). Moreover,

> it is important that the soundscape around the lake consists of natural rather than man-made sounds--totally without traffic and aircraft noises---for the performers need to interact with the environment, relaxing at the places indicated to allow it to sing back to them.
> (Schafer 1981a: ii)

And, as the composer writes,

> *Music for Wilderness Lake* returns to a more remote era, to an era when music took its bearings from the natural environment, a time when musicians played to the water and to the trees and then listened for them to play back to them . . . This interplay requires a spiritual attitude. . .
> (Schafer 1981a: i)

This utopian goal of recovering a mythological, ancient harmony between humans and nature may never be completely achieved. Yet, Schafer's work, by taking the music into the environment and subjecting it to the influence of the elements transforms the idea of music as art. Again, to quote the composer:

> I am not trying to absolutely dictate how the music should sound in the environment. I am very much aware of the things that might happen in the environment to affect that sound. Therefore, I compose the music in such a way that it will be enhanced by the things that change it.
>
> (Schafer 1992: 4)

The consideration of the acoustics of the environment results in a certain indeterminacy in the music. For instance, the duration of the work and the temporal co-ordination of the parts are flexible. This is appropriate in a situation when the performers are very far apart and the wind may carry the sound away. Moreover, there is no meter and no exact, specific tempo. The music consists of a series of overlapping episodes, each with a different texture, density and content. A full repertoire of avant-garde timbral and articulation effects is explored. Some of the effects are programmatic and evoke the location of the performance, e.g. a vocal 'wolf howl' (*Dusk*, p. 9) and a suggestion of lapping water by muted trombones (*Dawn*, p. 16-17; Ex. VIII-9). Other sections of the music contain acoustic interactions with the environment (e.g. timbral transformations introduced by axial rotations by the performers and by raising and lowering the bells of the instruments; Ex. VIII-10, *Dusk*, p. 14).[18]

At rehearsal letters F, G, and H, the performers play brief chords and wait for echoes from the mountains and forests surrounding the lake (Ex. VIII-11, *Dawn*, p. 20). The chords are played successively by Trombones 2-8 (letter F), 7-12 (letter G), and 1-4 with 6-8 and 11-12 (letter H) in response to a single pitch from Trombone 5. These chords should sound as soon as the cue is heard (rehearsal letters F, H) or after

---

[18]These effects are also used in Schafer's *Musique pour le Parc Lafontaine* for four symphonic bands in movement (1992). In this piece the bands are dispersed through the Montreal park and the players are required to march, rotate and raise and lower their instruments while playing.

a delay of one second (letter G). In the score, the temporal alignment of simultaneous pitches is exact; this may not be so during the actual performance. Due to large distances across the lake and the physical limitation of the speed of sound (about 330 meters per second) some pitches will be delayed; this delay will depend on the relative positions of the trombonists around the lake (cf. Ex. VIII-12). Therefore, Trombone 4, by being the closest to Trombone 5, will be the first one to respond, while Trombones 11 and 12 will lag behind. If the diameter of the lake is 660 meters, these two trombonists will hear the cue from Trombone 5 two seconds after its beginning (and 1-2 seconds later than the other trombonists). Thus, the entries of pitches in each chord will be staggered, rather than simultaneous. This may not matter; for Schafer, as for Lutoslawski (1976/1986) and Brant (1967), a degree of rhythmic non-coordination does not destroy the identity of the music. Nonetheless, there are moments in *Music for Wilderness Lake* when a stricter correlation is required.

In the concluding section of the piece, ensemble coordination is aided by visual signals: a series of coloured flags raised from a raft in the centre of the lake (cf. Ex. VIII-12). A visual cue of that kind allows for a nearly simultaneous response from all trombonists; hence, these segments of the music will sound together. They will, that is, if they are heard at the centre of the lake.[19] For a listener placed on the shore, near one of the trombonists, the sound from that particular instrument will precede other sounds which emerge from more distant locations, e.g. from the opposite side of the lake. Since, in principle, there are no listeners in this piece, the temporal coherence perceived at the centre of the lake should be of no importance. Each trombonist will hear the music from his/her unique aural perspective. Thus, a piece for 12 trombones will split, in perception, into a cluster of 12 works for one trombone accompanied by 11 trombones from a distance.

Does this perceptual relativity affect the identity of the music? This is a perplexing question. However, Schafer's answer seems to be negative. According to

---

[19]The central location of the hypothetical listener, equidistant from all performers, resembles the privileged position of the conductor in Xenakis's *Terretektorh* (1965-66).

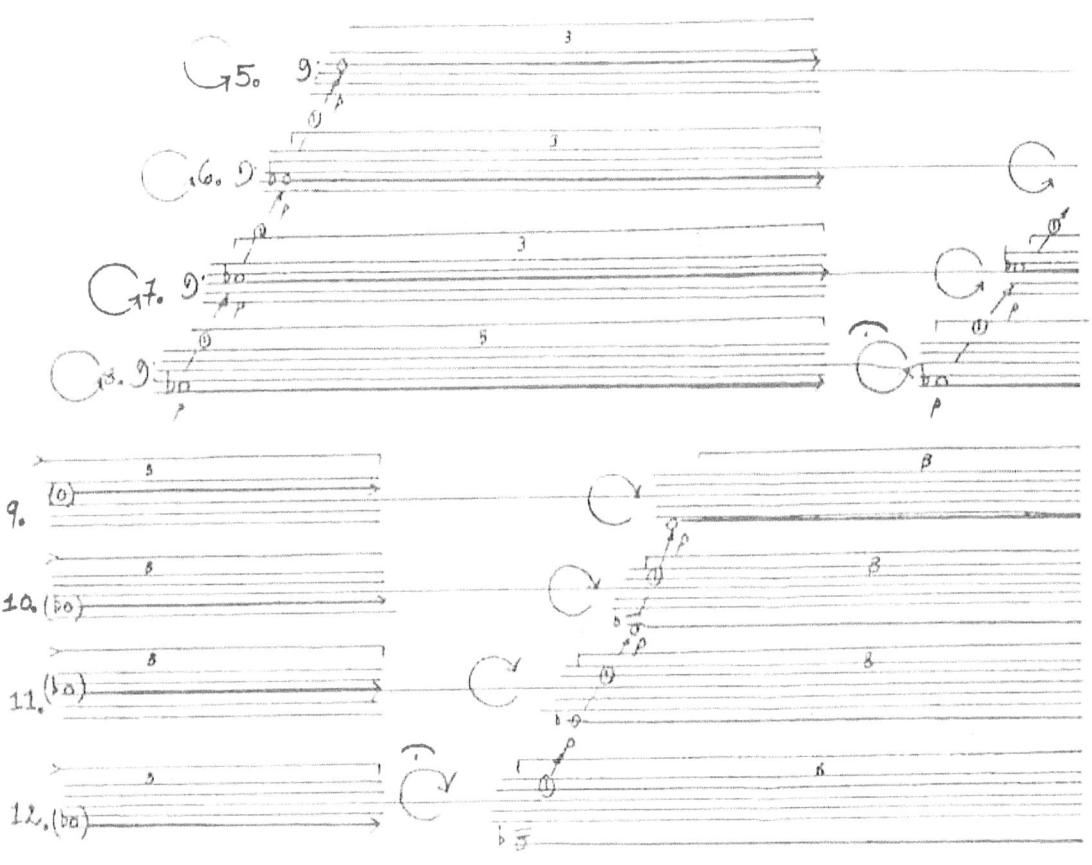

Ex. VIII-10: Axial rotations of performers in *Dusk, Music for Wilderness Lake*, p. 14.

his remarks in the score (Schafer 1981a: i-iv), in the overall conception of the piece its highly unusual performance context is more important than rhythmic and interpretative details.[20] The choice of this context includes a concern for the proper acoustic conditions of the performance. This is one of the reasons for the incorporation of the temporal framework of dusk and dawn into the work's structure (imagine a requirement that a Beethoven Symphony only be performed at sunrise!). At dawn and dusk "the wind is slightest and refraction is the most apparent . . . making for clear listening across wide distances" (Schafer 1981a: iii). Refraction of sound waves over water, that is, bending caused by differences in air temperature (close to the surface and higher up), helps to hear distant sounds. Schafer uses this effect to compensate for the loss of indirect sound waves (early reflections and reverberation) which reinforce sonorities heard in the concert hall.

Acoustics, however, is not the only consideration. In order to arrive at the performance site before dawn (during the work's premiere in 1979), the trombonists had to walk through the forest in darkness. Their solitude and closeness to nature affected their manner of playing and provoked, at times, "pantheistic" sensations, giving rise to an unforgettable existential experience (Schafer 1981a: ii). Not surprisingly so, because for Schafer this is the main purpose of art: "to affect a change in our existential condition. . . To change us. It is a noble aim, a divine aim" (Schafer 1991a: 87).[21] In order to facilitate the realization of this goal, the listeners and spectactors should be transformed into active participants of the musical actions. As the composer explains, it is easy to create an art form without spectators: "all one has to do is to remove the chairs" (Schafer 1991a: 36). Without chairs, without the concert hall--the whole experience of music is bound to be different.

---

[20]Why, then, one might ask, was *Music for Wilderness Lake* performed in Amsterdam during the Holland Festival of 1984? (That is the same festival that included Henry Brant's *Bran(d)t aan de Amstel*.) If spatio-temporal requirements may be abandoned, what is the source of identity of this site-specific music?

[21]The form of art designed to realize this lofty objective is Schafer's theatre of confluence, i.e. his 12-part cycle, *Patria* (cf. Chapter III, section 3.5).

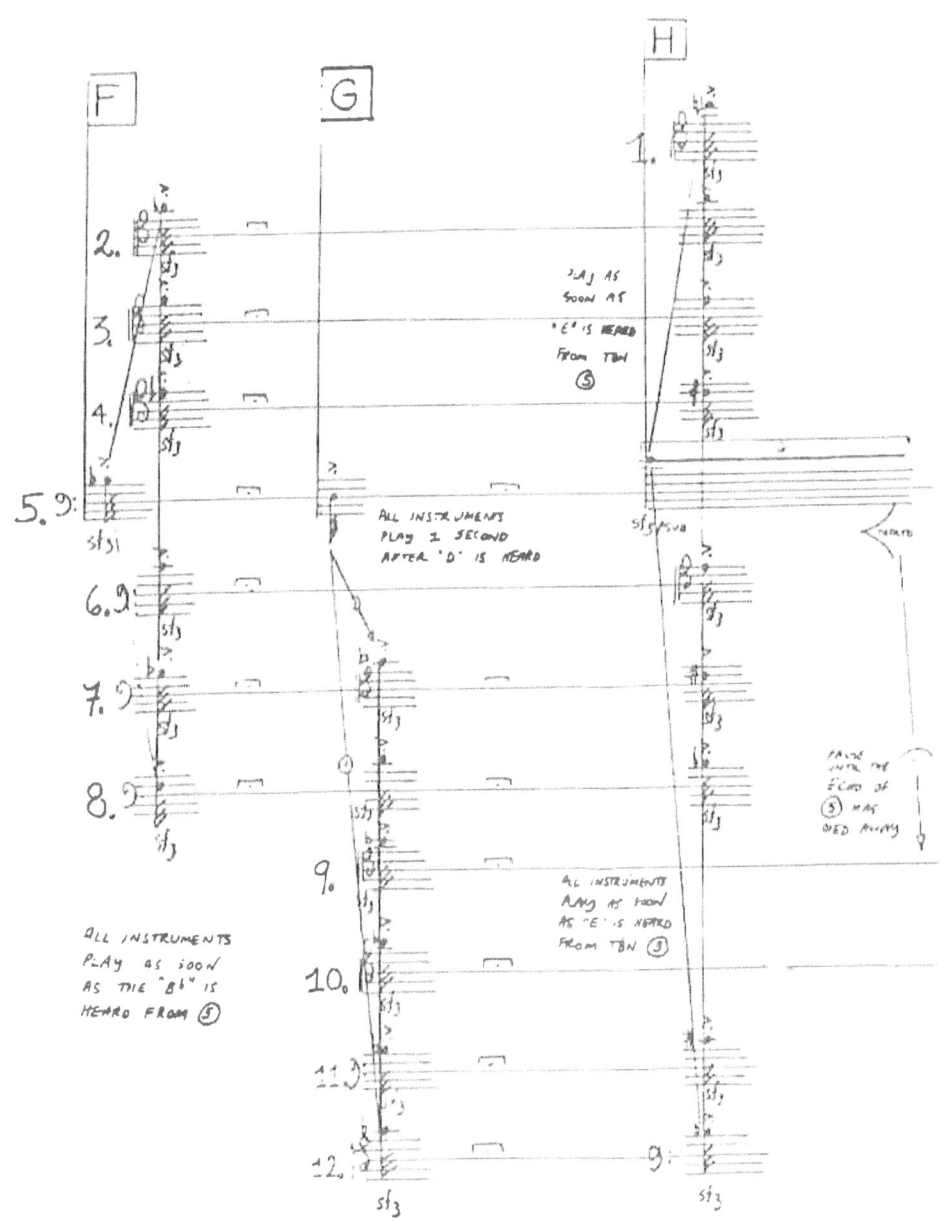

Ex. VIII-11: Chords and echoes in *Dawn, Music for Wilderness Lake*, p. 20

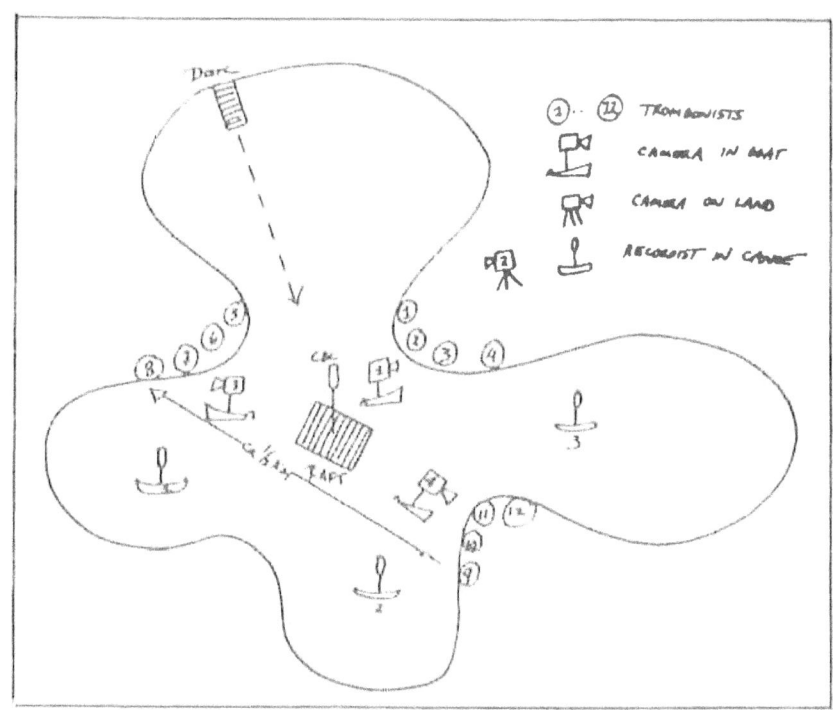

Ex. VIII-12: Position of performers and recording crew during the first performance of *Music for Wilderness Lake*.

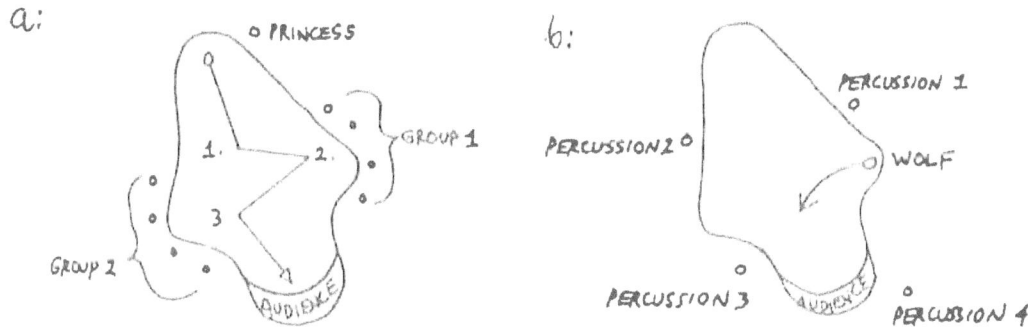

Ex. VIII-13: Placement of the audience and peformers in *Patria: The Prologue. The Princess of the Stars* (1981-1984); (a) Editing Unit 2: "The Dawn Light Breaks;" (b) Editing Unit 4: "Wolf's Arrival."

Ex. VIII-14: Editing Unit 8: "Arrival of Dawn Birds," *The Princess of the Stars*, p. 34.

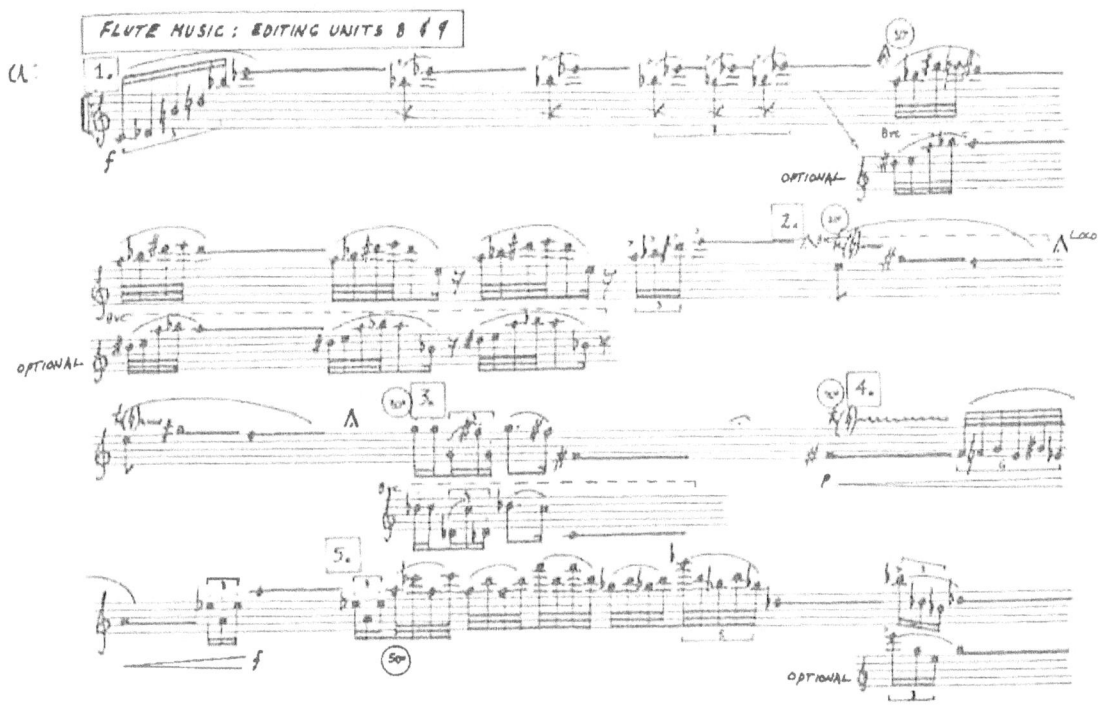

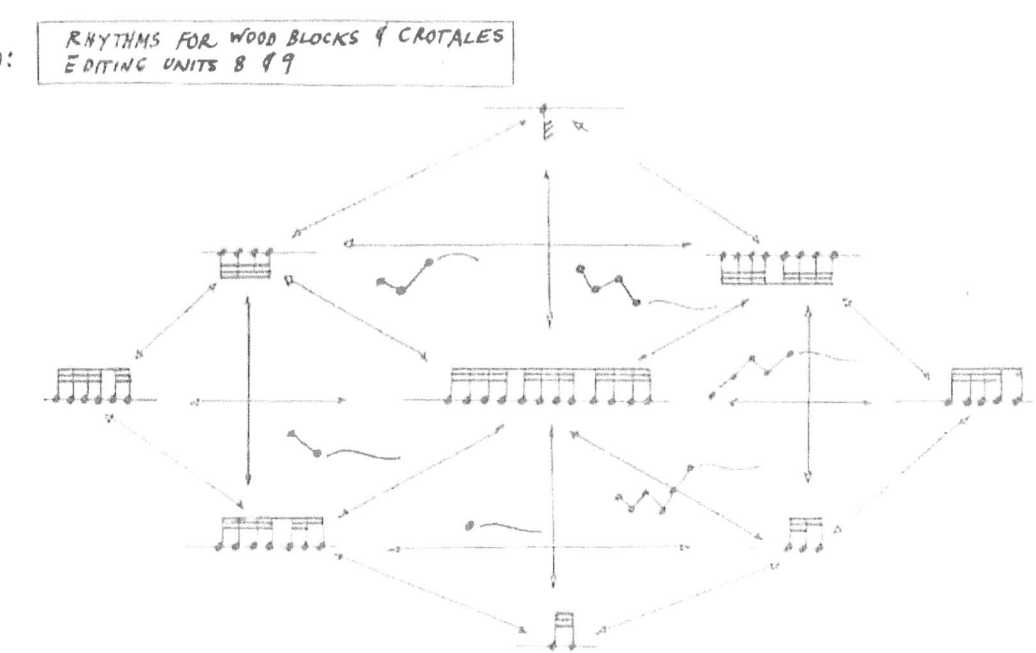

Ex. VIII-15: Excerpts from instrumental parts for the "Dawn Birds" section of *The Princess of the Stars* (Editing Units 8 and 9); (a) flute, p. 37; (b) percussion, p. 42.

8.5.

An outdoor ritual: *The Princess of the Stars*

In contrast to *Music for Wilderness Lake*, *The Princess of the Stars* (the *Prologue* to *Patria*, 1981-1984) is directed towards an audience who are located at the shore of a mountain lake (cf. Ex. VIII-13: the placement of the audience and the performers in Editing Units 2 and 4). The musicians are dispersed around the lake, some as far as a kilometre away (the voice of the Princess); the protagonists are in canoes paddled along prescribed routes. In the performer's notes in the score, Schafer writes:

> The two choral groups should be on opposite shores and the four percussionists should be positioned like the points of a star. The other instrumentalists should be situated to provide an ensemble balance, but also to take advantage of geographical features producing unusual echoes or resonance. Only experiment on the site will provide the optimum solution.
>
> (Schafer 1986b: 5)

Nonetheless, the composer is quite specific about his general spatio-temporal requirements: the performance should take place at dawn on an autumn morning and the lake "should be about half a kilometre wide and a kilometre long with an irregular shoreline to allow the principal characters to enter in their canoes from 'off-stage'" (Schafer 1986b: 4). Thus, the mountains, the water, the sunrise, the birds, become elements in a gigantic theatre of Nature. The success or failure of *The Princess of the Stars* depends on Nature as much as on human efforts, "and knowledge of this must touch the performers, filling them with a kind of humility before the grander forces of the work's setting" (Schafer 1986b: 4). The spectacle is, indeed, grand.[22] Dramatic

---

[22]The composer's summary of the plot: "*The Princess of the Stars* tells the story of how the Princess fell from the sky into the lake at which the presentation takes place. Wolf comes to find her and enlists the help of the Dawn Birds, but is prevented from rescuing her by the Three-Horned Enemy, who is keeping her captive beneath the lake. A battle develops but is interrupted by the arrival of the Sun Disk (sunrise) who comes to demand what has happened to the stars. The Sun Disk drives the Three-Horned Enemy away, sets tasks for Wolf before he can release the Princess, and exhorts the

events are closely coordinated with natural occurrences--the chorus of birds at dawn, the sunrise.[23] This is more than a work of art, it is a sacred ceremony, a revelation of

> Dawn itself, the most neglected masterpiece of the modern world... And like all true ceremonies it cannot be adequately transported elsewhere. You can't poke it into a television screen, you can't make postcards of it... Like the art of ancient times it is wedded to its time and place by indissoluble links...
> (Schafer 1986b: 5)

In a natural soundscape, the sunrise is announced by a morning chorus of birds, greeting the new day with their song. The Dawn Birds are also the protagonists of *The Princess of the Stars*--represented by dancers in fantastic bird-costumes placed on canoes in the middle of the lake. According to the score, "the Dawn Birds appear at precisely the time the real dawn birds are waking up, and singers and instrumentalists around the lake coax them into song by imitating their calls" (Schafer 1991a: 111).

In Ex. VIII-14 (p. 34 of the score) the arrival of the Dawn Birds is accompanied by the flute, clarinet, trumpet and percussion performing "birdsong" motives (Ex. VIII-15a, the flute, p. 37; Ex. VIII-15b, the percussion, p. 42). The flute part is written out, and should be repeated for as long as necessary; the percussionists create their own music by combining a small number of predetermined rhythmic motives. The chorus enters at the beginning of the Dawn Birds Dance with musical material resembling that of the percussionists: six phrases with different onomatopoeic syllables, approximate pitch contours and precise rhythmic patterns. One of the phrases of the sopranos, for instance, bears the annotation: "very fast arpeggios in descending cascades, repeated 6-8 times. Listen to the Hermit Thrush" (Schafer 1986b: 40). Thus, the musicians have to learn from the birds in order to communicate with them during this ritual of Art and Nature.

Another link between the music of *The Princess of the Stars* and Nature is

---

Dawn Birds to sing there no longer until the Wolf succeeds." (Schafer 1986b: 4).

[23]The work should start exactly 52 minutes before sunrise; the entry of the Sun Disc into the dramatic action on the lake should coincide with the natural event.

provided by the musical exploration of the echoes off the mountains around the lake. This is possible, as in *Music for Wilderness Lake*, "because of the way that the music is composed, with many written-out silences, certain climaxes and sudden pauses" (Schafer 1992: 6). When the dawn light breaks, (Editing Unit 2, see Ex. VIII-16), the aria of the distant Princess awakens echoes from the woods and mountains, and responses from other voices:

> Thus, a very complex form of heterophony is created, in which one singer is echoed by the natural environment, then she is echoed by other singers in different positions, and then there are the echoes of their voices.
> (Schafer 1992: 6)

While the Princess's aria is textless, the vocal echoes repeat her phrases with words meaning "princess, wolf, star, moon, or lake" in various Indian languages. These are the main protagonists of the plot; here the lake awakens with a voice, telling the story of an ancient, mythical drama.[24] In Ex. VIII-16 (p. 13 of the score) a soprano repeats a phrase of the Princess, with an added text ("tumeoni" means "wolf"). This sonority triggers a response of extended tremolos on crotales on two sides of the lake (percussion 1 and 4). These percussive sounds are delicate and may be easily destroyed by the wind carrying them off in unintended directions. However, the effect of the wind may also be considered beneficial: it enhances the distant, subdued and mysterious sound quality of the music in which the concert-hall ideal of "sound presence" needs to be abandoned.

As Schafer maintains, the same effect of mysterious, distant sound was created by Wagner who placed the orchestra in the pit, and separated the audience from the stage with this "mystical abyss" (Schafer 1991a: 113). At Bayreuth, the performance became a ritual and the spectators were transformed into pilgrims visiting the temple of a sacred art. The audience of *The Princess of the Stars* is also on a pilgrimage; the spectators have to arrive at the site before dawn in order to witness the musical, theatrical and environmental ritual--come rain or shine. Schafer's ecological art,

---

[24] Actually, this "ancient" drama has been written by Schafer himself and based on elements from many Indian legends.

P2 P4 P2 P4
A — NA — SU-TÚ — QUA —
O — THAI-Ó — NI —
ME-TU-MÉ — U —
REPEAT ONCE AD LIB.
ECSTATICALLY
REPEAT 4 OR 5 TIMES CRESCENDO.
TU-ME-Ó-NI
TREMOLO 13 SECONDS
TREMOLO 10 SEC.
A — A — TU-ME-O-NI
CROTALES
L.V.
REPEAT
REPEAT 4 TIMES
TU-ME-Ó-NI
WA-YA
PERHAPS SING ONCE TOGETHER; THEN EACH SINGER REPEATS IT INDEPEND-ENTLY, FADING.
O — THAI — Ó — NI —
RELAXING...
SLOWING AND FADING..
REPEAT 4 TIMES RELAXING...
NÍ — O — TA
REPEAT 4 TIMES SLOWING AND FADING
GÉ -- SHUSH

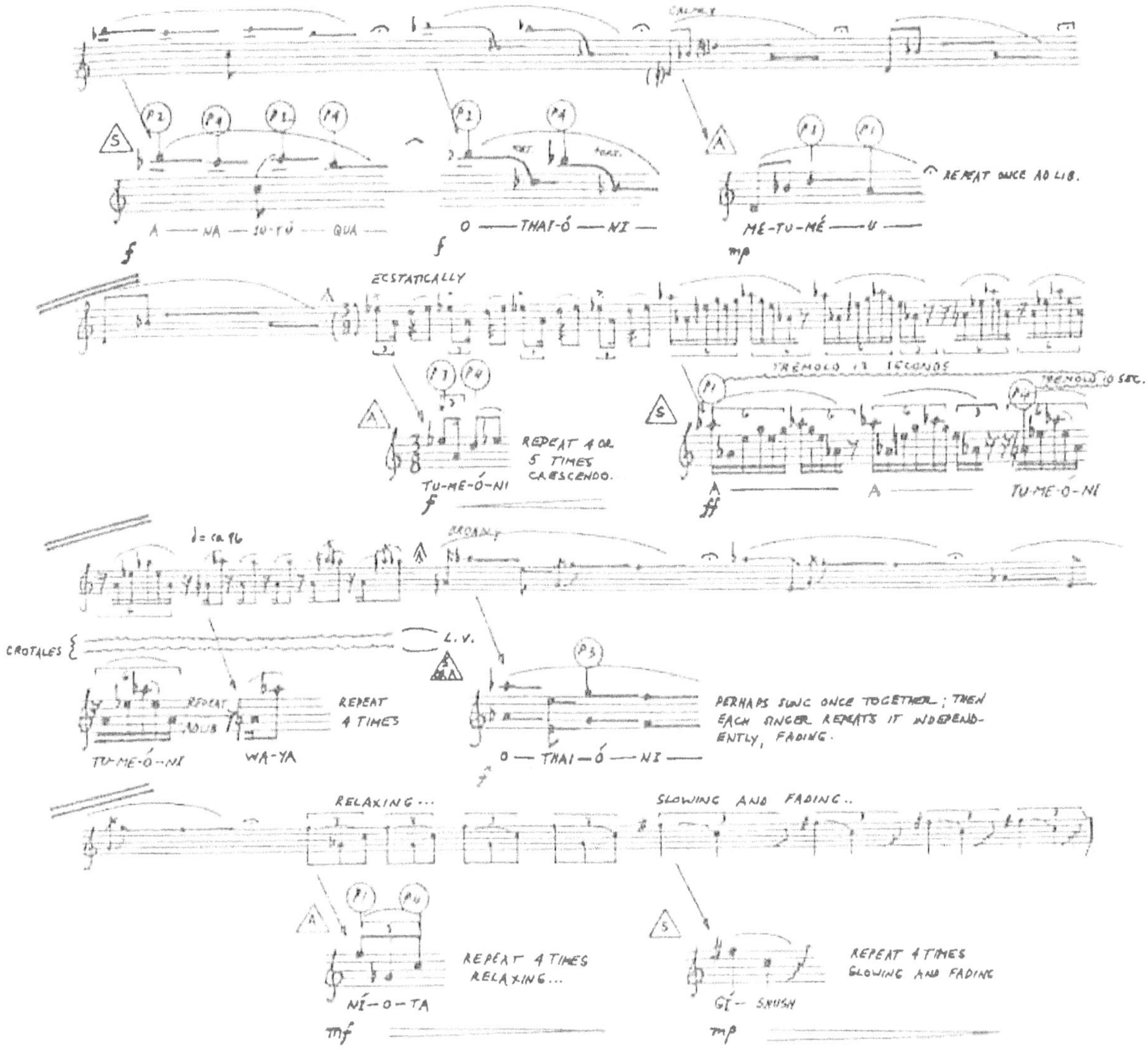

Ex. VIII 16: Vocal echoes in Editing Unit 2 from *The Princess of the Stars*, p. 13.

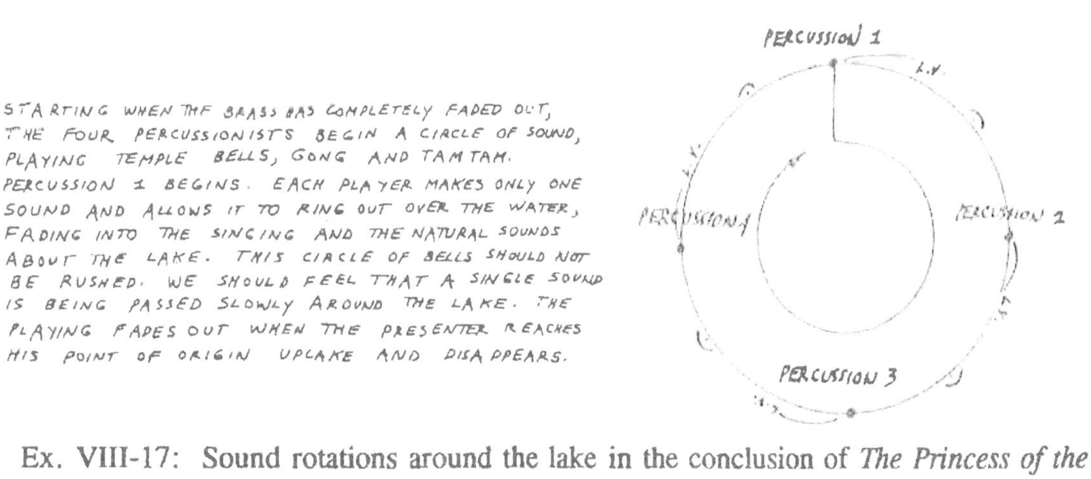

STARTING WHEN THE BRASS HAS COMPLETELY FADED OUT, THE FOUR PERCUSSIONISTS BEGIN A CIRCLE OF SOUND, PLAYING TEMPLE BELLS, GONG AND TAM TAM. PERCUSSION 1 BEGINS. EACH PLAYER MAKES ONLY ONE SOUND AND ALLOWS IT TO RING OUT OVER THE WATER, FADING INTO THE SINGING AND THE NATURAL SOUNDS ABOUT THE LAKE. THIS CIRCLE OF BELLS SHOULD NOT BE RUSHED. WE SHOULD FEEL THAT A SINGLE SOUND IS BEING PASSED SLOWLY AROUND THE LAKE. THE PLAYING FADES OUT WHEN THE PRESENTER REACHES HIS POINT OF ORIGIN UPLAKE AND DISAPPEARS.
PERCUSSION 1
L.V.
PERCUSSION 4
PERCUSSION 2
PERCUSSION 3

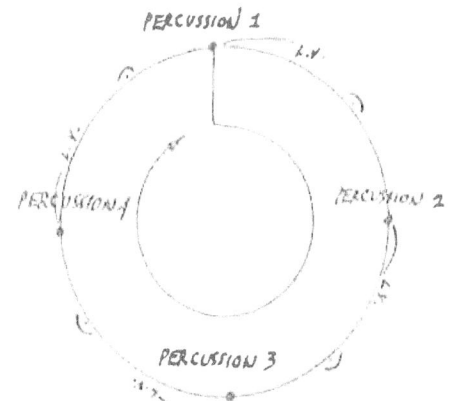

Ex. VIII-17: Sound rotations around the lake in the conclusion of *The Princess of the Stars*, p. 83.

transcending traditional musical and theatrical genres, contains overtones of non-Christian mysticism, in its closeness to nature and in its elevated purpose of initiating a spiritual, existential change in the audience. The empathy with the natural environment experienced in outdoor performance is one of the premises of Schafer's theatre of confluence:

> Why not a concert under a waterfall or a dramatic presentation in a blizzard? And why should we not feel the rain on our faces when we sing or a distant mountain throw back to us the voice we have just sent out to it? . . . These are the miraculous arenas of living drama inviting us to interaction.
> (Schafer 1991a: 97)

In *The Princess of the Stars*, this interaction takes the form of dialogues with the birds, echoes off the mountains and the use of log drums, which should be built from the wood found on site. The sounds of the log drums greet the arrival of Wolf in Editing Unit 4. Four percussionists placed at the square around the lake (cf. Ex. VIII-13) play the log drums in alternation with tom-toms, gradually building up a texture of increasing density, enriched with echoes. Schafer believes that the sonority of the log drum, the instrument of the Indians, is eminently suitable for outdoor performance:

> If you take a log drum into a concert hall it has no special quality to it and you do not hear it as far as you can hear timpani or the strings. However, if you take it out into the woods, you can hear its sound from further away, for there the log drum is in its own environment.
> (Schafer 1992: 6)

Nonetheless, it is not these "natural" instruments but the more traditional, concert percussion instruments that are given the task of concluding the work. While the protagonists of the drama disappear, the distant voice of the Princess echoes around the lake (echoes of the women's voices from the two choirs), percussive sounds of temple bells, gongs and tam-tams "slowly continue to circle around the lake, gradually fading to stillness" (Schafer 1986b: 86; cf. Ex. VII-17, p. 83 of the score).

For Schafer, the images of the circle and the stillness have mystical overtones (cf. Credo discussed earlier); the emergence of these symbolic entities at the conclusion of *The Princess of the Stars* reminds us that this is a ritual, not just a musical-theatrical performance. With its modern sound vocabulary and ecological friendliness (incorporating birdsong and echoes into the music, excluding technological noises) Schafer's composition is idealistic and demanding. It requires the performers and the audience to subordinate themselves to the artistic vision of the composer: to undertake a pilgrimage, to undergo a powerful experience with consequences lasting a lifetime.

Conclusion

The music of R. Murray Schafer is usually vividly "pictorial" and often constitutes an element in a musical/theatrical drama--the composer's main preoccupation. However, Schafer's original approach to musical spatialization deserves fuller recognition. Schafer's music reveals his involvement in various pursuits of the contemporary avant-garde: the co-presence of electroacoustic and acoustic sound sources creating a virtual sound world, the creation of geometric patterns by the spatial placement of sounds. Effects of his awareness of, and participation in, the avant-garde experiments may be found in the *Third String Quartet* (performer movement) and *Credo* (geometric patterns, spatial texture, sound movement by dynamics). Schafer's interest in contemplation, silence and stillness, at first linked to religious mysticism (*Apocalypsis*), has survived through the change in his outlook. In 1991, he described himself as "neither Christian nor a humanist" (Schafer 1991a: 91). For Schafer, Christian humanism, asserting man's domination over nature, is responsible for the destruction of the Earth's resources, including the natural soundscape. Hence the ecological protest of *North/White*; hence environmental rituals (*The Princess of the Stars*, *Music for Wilderness Lake*) bringing music to carefully chosen Canadian sites. Yet, there is a pragmatic aspect to his "environmentalist" gospel, stemming from his belief that human identity is greatly influenced by geographic context:

> My environment is very different from the environment of a European composer. A lot of things that I have done, even the fact that the *Patria* pieces

are composed for outdoor performances, have been done because I have not had resources here that existed, for instance, in Poland or in Germany, or somewhere else.

(Schafer 1992: 2)

The mystique of the Canadian North, of the purity of natural soundscape, filled with birdsong, sounds of wind and water, but not the noise of the airplanes, is as utopian as any other form of belief. Schafer's music, whether integrated with wildlife sounds, dispersed through an urban park, or found within the concert hall, as all art, transcends everyday reality. It creates its own realm and changes the pre-existing human world in the process.

SUMMARY AND CONCLUSIONS

In the *Foundations of Music History*, Carl Dahlhaus writes that

there is, strictly speaking, no such thing as 'time' in the singular--a homogeneous medium binding events of various durations and rates of change--but only 'times' in the plural, the times of overlapping structures in conflicting rhythms.

(Dahlhaus 1977/1989: 142)

Dahlhaus points out the "non-contemporaneity of the contemporaneous" (p. 141) which characterizes the simultaneous co-presence of divergent compositional trends and artistic ideologies. This dissertation presents a similar plurality of the ideas of space in music, from constructs of pitch space to spatiality of performance and perception. Thus, it suggests that *the* "musical space" does not exist; this term may have many different senses which often reflect the meanings of space outside the musical domain. In **Chapter I**, I distinguish two large denotation areas of "space"--as a synonym and complement to time (section 1.1). The temporal senses of "space" associate this term with "measurement" and "distance," e.g. the Bergsonian "spatialization of time" (cf. section 1.5). When "space" relates to "area or extension" it denotes that which co-exists simultaneously. It may mean "an interval or distance," or "an empty place," or "the dimensional extent occupied by a body," or "the cosmic void," etc. Often, the various meanings of "space" are intertwined.

Classical philosophy and science (chapter I, section 1.2) separate time from space. Descartes and Newton envisioned an "absolute," three-dimensional, infinite and empty space, existing independently of time and matter. This image of space, accepted as a depiction of what space *really is*, has become a paradigm of Western culture. The development of mathematics (non-Euclidean geometry, topology; section 1.3) created conditions for the relativisation of the notion of space in modern philosophy of science. Since Einstein, it is possible to speak of a four-dimensional "spacetime" instead of separated space and time (section 1.4). However, scientists and philosophers of science agree neither about spacetime's existential status nor about its structure. Some authors are convinced that spacetime is absolute, so that it may exist without any content; others regard spacetime as an attribute of matter (i.e. there is no spacetime, only spatio-temporal relations). The awareness of the historical evolution of the notion of space and of the current lack of scientific consensus about its nature provides the conceptual foundation for an analysis of the theories of space in music. Space cannot be separated from time neither in modern physics nor in "lived" experience--described by the phenomenology of Husserl, Merleau-Ponty and Heelan. The interconnection of space and time implies a change of the human self-image, from a supratemporal and disembodied consciousness into "body-subject" (term from Merleau-Ponty) living in a "Life-world" (term from Husserl and Heelan). This phenomenological "embodiment" has vital consequences for my critique of various concepts of musical space (Chapter II) and my presentation of different aspects of musical spatialization (Chapters III--VIII).

Chapter II outlines the history of the idea of "musical space" in the 20th-century and clarifies the relationships of the various theories of musical spatiality. I divide these theories into four large thematic areas. In the first area (section 2.1), the concept of musical space presupposes the "notion of a pure or disembodied sound" (term from Ihde 1976). This "space," perceived while listening to music without noticing the location of sounds in auditory space, includes pitch as one of its dimensions. I trace the history of this notion back to the writings of the German theoreticians of the 1920-30s followed by various European and North American authors (up to the 1980s).

Hans Mersmann (1926) introduces geometric terminology for the two dimensions of music (the vertical and the horizontal) and posits the opposition of "space" and "force" (equated with the dichotomy of feminine--masculine, passive--dynamic).[1] Ernst Kurth (1931) considers musical spatial impression as an aspect of

---

[1] Other definitions of spatiality (Nadel, Riezler) were proposed at the *Raum-Zeit-Kongress* of the *Gesellschaft für Ästhetik* (organized in 1930 by Ernst Cassirer).

inner, psychic processes. For him, music possesses three dimensions: pitch (height), time (width), and an ambiguous dimension of depth which has nothing in common with the physical dimension of distance. Albert Wellek (1934/1963) also distinguishes a three-dimensional sonic space from the auditory space of sound localization. He reserves the term "musical space" for the total perceptual experience in which all spatial aspects of music interact. Other authors continue to emphasize the "auditory-versus-musical" opposition. Langer (1953) considers space as "a secondary illusion," Ingarden (1958/1986) includes the "peculiar musical space" among the non-sonic components of the musical work, Lippman (1952) explains that the abstraction from spatio-temporal reality is a characteristic feature of romantic music which attempts to transport the listeners into realms beyond. Zuckerkandl (1957) construes musical space as a "place-less" and dynamic entity; he raises tonal relationships of the Western art tradition to the level of metaphysics. Finally, Clifton argues for the distinction "between being physically located in acoustical space and phenomenally located in musical space" (Clifton 1983: 142). He describes various spatial textures: lines, surfaces, surfaces with varying degrees of relief, and masses with different degrees of solidity. Clifton, Kurth, Langer, and others, perceive musical space as "heard" in temporal motion. This is a manifestation of the interrelationship of space and time, known from modern physics ("spacetimes" of relativity theory) and human experience. However, the image of a phenomenal musical space, including aspects of "lived" time but not "lived" space, ignores the spatio-temporality of music heard during its actual performance.

The second section of Chapter II presents views of those theoreticians and composers who consider space as the epitome of stasis and claim that the "spatialization of time" is an important feature of contemporary music. These ideas relate to Schoenberg's concept of "the two-or-more-dimensional space" (1941/1975) as well as to Adorno's critique of Stravinsky's music as "pseudomorphosis to painting" (1948/1973). Eimert and Ligeti (1960/1965) connect the spatialization of time to serialism. Others (Kagel, Cage) equate the two-dimensional plane of a page of notation with the two-dimensional space of pitch and time. Space also means "temporal stasis" for Rochberg (1963) and McDermott (1966) who propose the "spatial image" as a paradigm of modern music. Bayer (1987) assumes that the notion of sonic space is a key to explaining the evolution of contemporary music as a whole, while Morgan (1980) deplores the ubiquity of static spatiality in new music.[2] Despite these claims that the existence of a "spatial image" is an exclusive characteristic of modern music, spatial representation of musical structures is possible regardless of musical style.

In section 2.3 of Chapter II, I discuss the identification of space with pitch, frequent in compositional and analytical theories. Pitch is spatial either as a set (mathematical space) or as an analogue to the spatial dimension of height.[3] According to Duchez (1979), the ubiquity of the cognitive model of pitch-height caused the emergence of a "conceptual perception" in music. The vertical representation of pitch has become an attribute of pitch itself and a condition for the creation and perception of music as well as theoretical reflection about both. The parallel between pitch height and the vertical dimension of height is used in musical notation, in which the direction towards the top of the staff means an ascent in pitch and the direction towards the right side of the page denotes a progression in time. This concept of a two-dimensional spatiality is deeply rooted in Western art music; the notation of pitch and time provides music with an unchangeable skeleton which ensures its survival beyond one, unique performance. The existence of the pitch/time space allows for the visualization of music as well as for the introduction of graphic analytical methods (e.g. McDermott, Bernard, Brinkman and Mesiti).[4]

However, the graphic representation of music on the two-dimensional plane of pitch and time has many limitations. One problem is with the one-dimensional,

---

[2]Morgan also introduces a notion of space related to Schenker's theory.

[3]Similarly, the musical framework of pitch and time may be spatial in a geometric sense (on a plane) and in a mathematical sense (as the realm of sets).

[4]The use of two-dimensional spatial images is current in music analysis, cf. the "wedge-shaped linear motion" discussed by Bo Alphonce (Alphonce 1994).

vertical image of pitch. As has been said, pitch and pitch-class coexist in music as two co-dependent dimensions. Another difficulty arises from the fact that musical time may also be regarded as a multidimensional phenomenon (Kramer 1988, Pressing 1993). Nonetheless, the two-dimensional image of music has important advantages, such as simplicity, (otherwise it would not have persisted). The representation of music in pitch/time space allows for the visualization of the temporal relationships of simultaneity and succession. Such a geometric image of music on one spatial plane is useful if all the elements of music belong to one "stream" (e.g. parts in tonal polyphony). If not--as often occurs in spatialized compositions--the two-dimensional representation of simultaneous musical layers falsifies (instead of clarifying) their relationships.

Mathematical notions of space (space as a set of points with some specified structure) appear in theory and composition of serial or atonal music (Boulez, Morris, Xenakis). These generalized or formalized theories of space have emerged simultaneously with the "spatialization of time" in new music. Boulez (1963) creates a taxonomy of potential pitch-spaces of a very high degree of generality while Xenakis (1963/1971) introduces two-, three- and multidimensional spaces into his compositional theory. The introduction of abstract, multidimensional sound-spaces isolating various "parameters" of sound (frequency, time, duration, spectrum, etc.; e.g. Cage 1957, Carapezza 1961) occur in the context of the avant-garde's efforts to rupture the continuity of musical tradition and create a new objectivity in music.

Finally, a conceptual transformation of "musical space" leads to the association of this term with the space in which music is performed and heard (section 2.4 of Chapter II). Here, "musical space" relates either to the enclosed space providing the acoustic environment for music (Brant 1967, Bräm 1986, Hoffman-Axthelm 1986), or to the space delimited by the presence of the performers and listeners (Bielawski 1976). The meaning of "musical space" as the space of sound localization is current in the domain of electroacoustic music (Smalley 1991).

Chapter III opens the second part of the dissertation and presents the historical development of the idea of "spatialization" in the theory and practice of contemporary music. In section 3.1, I precede this review with a consideration of three general aspects of the relationship of music and the performance space: (1) the link between the acoustic environment and the instrumentation (sound quality), (2) the dispersion of sound sources within performance space (polychorality), and (3) the "lived" bodily-spatial experience of the listeners and performers (religious rituals).

I subdivide 20th-century theories of spatialization into four domains: (a) spatialization as an extension of polyphony, i.e. music of simultaneous, spatially separated layers (Mahler, Ives, Brant; section 3.2); (b) spatialization as the "reification" of musical material, i.e. music built from sound objects projected into space (Satie, Stravinsky, Varèse, *musique concrète* and electroacoustics; section 3.3); (c) spatialization as a new "parameter" manipulated compositionally, in Darmstadt and beyond (Stockhausen and Boulez, section 3.4); (d) spatialization as conceptual experimentation with performance rituals and their contexts (Cage, Lucier, and Schafer; section 3.5).[5]

The separation of performers into groups has preceded other notions of musical spatialization, especially those advocated by the Darmstadt avant-garde. I begin its 20th-century history with Gustav Mahler, who stated that true polyphony arises from the total spatial distribution of contrasted material. An example from the finale of Mahler's *Second Symphony* (1894) illustrates his ingenious use of off-stage groups, the association of different musical layers with spatial locations, and the illusion of sound movement (changing distance) created through dynamics. Charles Ives explored the musical independence of simultaneous layers with two orchestras which perform musical material differing in its harmonic, melodic and rhythmic features (e.g. the second movement of the *Fourth Symphony*). He imagined, but never realized a *Universe Symphony* with contrasts in pitch space, the type of material and spatial locations. He considered spatial separation of performers as a means of clarifying textures and realizing the inner content of the music (Ives 1933). He was particularly

---

[5]All four domains include manipulations of the physical and perceptual aspects of space; however, the specific techniques and philosophies differ in each area.

interested in enriching music with aspects of perspective and distance. Finally, he described the active type of perception in which the listener's attention shifts from one musical layer to another.

Ives's reflections about musical spatiality influenced Brant, Schafer and Cage. Henry Brant (1967, 1992) is convinced that Ives's *The Unanswered Question* presented "the entire twentieth-century spatial spectrum in music" (Brant 1967: 225). His spatial music shares this work's features: contrasts of widely separated layers of sound and the absence of rhythmic coordination between these layers. Brant's writings on "the use of antiphonal distribution in composing" (1955) and the "essential role of space in music" (1967) outline the principles of his approach to musical spatiality. In particular, Brant points out that separation in space allows for the differentiation of musical strands in a complex texture. In descriptions of his spatial experiments, Brant claims that vertical height creates an impression of higher pitch. He notices the effects of *a wall of sound*, *spill* and *filling up* in which musical sounds tangibly occupy segments of physical space. He discusses positive aspects of the absence of strict rhythmic coordination and reveals an interest in a total perceptual experience, rather than a preoccupation with the detailed planning of isolated features of musical sounds.

The second conceptual area of spatialization involves a "reification" of musical material (section 3.3). I identify the origins of this approach (fully articulated by Edgard Varèse) in Satie's *musique d'ameublement* (1920) and Stravinsky's concept of the *musical object* (1924). Satie's "furniture or furnishing" music fills in a space for a time; it should not be consciously listened to, it is not Art. It belongs with other physical objects endowed with concrete physical dimensions and a definite spatial location. Stravinsky's notion of musical objects possessing a solidity of material things expresses his anti-romanticism, not an interest in spatialization; however, this notion influenced Edgard Varèse (Mattis 1993). The projection of sound-masses (i.e. musical objects) into space is a fundamental feature of Varèse's vision of spatial music (1936/1967). Since in this music sound-masses are in motion, time is not static; in this respect Varèse differs from younger avant-garde composers who proclaim the staticity of time.⁶ Musical objects (*sound-masses* or *zones of intensities*) evolve, expand and contract, yet they have clearly defined boundaries which are articulated by differences in tone colours and dynamic levels. Thus, Varèse relates spatiality to timbre and dynamics. He also envisions the spatio-temporal movement of sound objects in *spatial projection* (Varèse 1936/1967). The notion of *projection* is quite ambiguous; one of its definitions (i.e. the distribution of sound sources into various locations in space) has been accepted in the domain of electroacoustic music. Varèse's realization of spatial music in *Poème électronique* (1957-1958) includes the design of *sonic trajectories* of sound movement. He borrowed this notion (as well as the term *spatial relief*) from Pierre Schaeffer, the founder of *musique concrète* which involved composing with pre-recorded sound objects and the use of electroacoustic sound projection.⁷ During the early concerts of *musique concrète*, multi-loudspeaker systems allowed for the creation of effects of *static relief* (dispersion of sound sources in space) and *kinematic relief* (sound movement in three-dimensional space).⁸ Recently, the notion of "space" has become the paradigm of electroacoustic music.

However, the terminological framework of electroacoustic "spaces" is not clearly defined. Chion (1988) distinguishes *internal space* (compositionally predetermined) and *external space* (articulated during the work's performance). Risset (1988) notices the fragility of the *illusory space* designed by the composer and presented in the *real space* of performance. Smalley (1991) enumerates different types of space in electroacoustic music, e.g. the *composed space*, the *listening space*, and a *superimposed space*. He points out the inseparability of space and sound, of virtual environments and their contents.

---

⁶Cf. Chapter II, section 2.2 and Chapter III, section 3.3.

⁷Schaeffer, Henry and Poullin formed the Groupe de Recherches de Musique Concrète in Paris in 1951.

⁸Perceptual experiences at these concerts of *musique concrète* played a formative role in the development of Stockhausen's and Boulez's interest in spatialization.

Theories of the Darmstadt composers, Stockhausen and Boulez, exemplify a speculative approach to spatialization (section 3.4). In "Music in space" of 1959, Karlheinz Stockhausen links the dispersion of music into space with the spatialization of time and musical material; he also argues for the *serialization of direction* as the best compositional option. In his hierarchy of the tone-characteristics in Western art music, *location (topography)* occupies the final, lowest place. Stockhausen composed his first spatialized works in the mid-1950s, after Brant, Schaeffer and Berio. In *Gruppen für drei Orchester* (1955-57), he introduced the effect of virtual sound motion (successive entries of orchestras with the same sustained pitches and overlapping dynamic patterns of crescendo--decrescendo). Stockhausen's approach to spatialization evolved through the years of his experience with electroacoustics; he moved towards the "mainstream" of spatialization involving the co-existence of distinct layers (1971/1989).

Pierre Boulez followed a similar trajectory away from the speculative theory of spatialization that he formulated in 1963. In *Musikdenken heute*, he distinguishes two types of *spatial distribution*, static and mobile (also called *static relief* and *dynamic relief*--as in *musique concrète*). Mobile distribution can be realized by *conjunct and disjunct movements*. Boulez expresses a preference for a fixed spatial lay-out in which he could explore various types of symmetry and asymmetry (relating spatialization to timbre and volume). The composer realized this interest in symmetry in *Rituel in memoriam Maderna* for eight orchestral groups (1974-1975). Recently, Boulez expressed a conviction that the main function of space in music is to clarify polyphonic textures (Boulez 1992).

Due to the strength and persuasiveness of the Darmstadt generation, spatialization became an important characteristic of new music in different countries. Gradually, though, the emphasis shifted from considering spatial location as an additional "parameter" of an abstract design to constructing the experience of the listener in the concert hall or elsewhere. This shift of focus to a social or "ritualistic" use of space originated with John Cage who challenged the assumptions of both the musicians and the listeners. From 1939 he advocated "making music with its materials" and rejecting the primacy of pitch (Cage 1939/1961). He claims that indeterminate music develops in the physical space of the performance and occupies a segment of the physical time (Cage 1958/1961). Cage proposes to "juxtapose the dissimilars" and separate musicians in space in order to ensure their full musical independence. He takes music beyond the concert hall and allows the listeners to cherish an autonomy that they seldom enjoyed elsewhere. Cage's music includes indeterminate forms, diverse materials and simultaneous presentation of unrelated sound events. *Variations IV* (1964) illustrates how spatial location becomes an element in a randomly controlled network of relationships. *0'00"* (1962) allows for a transformation of everyday life into art.

One of Cage's associates and followers, Alvin Lucier, reduces music to sound matter, and reveals a preoccupation with the acoustic peculiarities of space unprecedented among composers (Lucier 1985). He involves the listeners-performers in processes of discovery of the acoustic properties of rooms, objects, instruments, etc. Lucier abandons "composing" in the traditional sense of this term without parting with the notion of the "work." R. Murray Schafer's theatre of confluence connects all the arts in a new form of "confluence" and, thus, imitates life itself (Schafer 1966, 1991). The Canadian composer shares Cage's concern with the perceptual experiences of the listeners and has attempted to affect their lives with his art.[9] Thus, he gives a new twist to Cage's idea of uniting art with life. Schafer's theatre is a form of artistic ritual which requires unconventional performance spaces and the involvement of the total spatio-temporal corporeality of the listeners-participants.

This review of compositional writings about spatialization (illustrated with musical examples) demonstrates the lasting importance of the notion of "musical work" in contemporary music. In **Chapter IV**, I present a phenomenological interpretation of this concept (Ingarden 1958/1986) and point out ways in which spatial features of sound may be incorporated into "the work." A description of a

---

[9] Schafer's cycle of musical/theatrical works, *Patria*, is still unfinished (Mackenzie 1992).

series of imaginary perceptual situations (listening to the motive "B-A-C-H" in various spatial arrangements) alerts the reader to the multiplicity of ways of perceiving music. When the physical spatiality of sound is taken into account, the presence of the listeners, as well as their spatial locations and orientations becomes essential. Spatialized music presupposes an idealization of the listeners, who should be endowed with perfect hearing abilities and located in optimal positions in space. The extent of this idealization varies, but the listeners may be required to hear what is inaudible. In order to present the musical potential of spatiality of sound I briefly review Blauert's study of spatial hearing (1983) and Bregman's theory of auditory perception (1990).

Blauert suggests that sound localization, spaciousness of the hall, etc., characterize sound images not physical sounds. This separation of "the perceptual" from "the physical" is important for my notion of spatialization. Blauert contrasts free-field perception (i.e. in anechoic chamber) with perception in enclosed spaces (i.e. the concert hall) and describes a number of specific features and effects, including directional and distance hearing, the loss of locatedness in diffuse sound fields, and the *spaciousness* of auditory events in enclosures (the apparent extent of sounds in space). Spatial location plays an important role in the current psychoacoustic theory of "auditory scene analysis" (Bregman 1990). For Bregman, position in space is one of the main criteria for the segregation of incoming stimuli into "auditory streams." He argues that it is difficult to isolate spatiality from timbre and dynamics, and that the "what" and "where" are interrelated.

In section 4.3 of Chapter IV, I turn towards Ingarden's definition of the musical work which divides the work's ontological basis into the score and the performance. The work is schematically defined in notation and imperfectly realized in real sonorities--it is an "ideal boundary" of both the score and performance, an object of compositional and interpretative intentions. Moreover, Ingarden notices that each performance splits into a number of unique "concretions" heard by individual listeners. While the work is an intentional object, the performance is a process occurring at a determined spatial and temporal location. Ingarden believes that musical works consist of pure sounds (sound-constructs), yet he claims that these works include sonic and non-sonic components (the latter group comprises quasi-temporal structure, movement, aesthetic values, etc.). His theory reveals how music has lost its spatio-temporal reality in order to gain a supratemporal existence in the form of intentional objects, musical works.

Regardless of its historical and social limitations (pointed out by Lissa and Goehr), Ingarden's theory may serve as a basis for the inclusion of spatialization among the features of the musical work. I expand his concepts of "sound-construct" and "quasi-spatial structure." The first notion resembles the concept of virtual sound image discussed by Bregman (1990). I argue that many composers intend to create complex sound images ("sound-constructs") and imperfectly approximate these images in notation by analytically isolating their features. Ingarden's notion of the "quasi-spatial structure" serves as a model for my definition of a fixed *quasi-spatial structure in music*.[10] Weak, *latent quasi-spatial structure* exists in most music for solo performers and in compositions for larger, standard ensembles without any spatial specifications. Chamber and orchestral music may have a full *quasi-spatial structure* when the composer requires a certain acoustic environment for the performance, includes a seating plan in the score, divides the musicians into groups dispersed in space, etc. *Spatialization* of music means, precisely, this introduction of the *quasi-spatial structure*. The term *spatialized music* refers to music with a quasi-spatial structure defined by the composer in the score or in another medium of sound coding (digital or analog recording, specific software).[11] This quasi-spatial structure can assume different forms, including ensemble dispersion, the movement of sounds, performers or audience, and the juxtaposition and interaction of real and virtual sound sources. This definition relates to the composed space of the musical work. "Spatialization" may also refer to the addition of spatial characteristics to music during performance; thus, any work of music may be "spatialized."

---

[10]*Spatial design* and *spatial organization of sound* are synonyms to *quasi-spatial structure*.

[11]Here, I repeat the definition from chapter IV verbatim.

Here, I support Ingarden's thesis that the work is identical neither with the score nor with a performance. I claim, however, that the work consists of a series of idealized aural images that are approximated in the score and instantiated in performance. Therefore, the spatialized work contains quasi--spatio-temporal sound-constructs organized within a quasi--spatio-temporal framework. (The sonorous, i.e. psychoacoustic, reality of music is always spatio-temporal, not quasi-spatio-temporal).

The ontological schema of "musical works" includes five stages: (1) the compositional process (idea), (2) the score (notational representation), (3) the performance (action), (4) the results of these actions (physical sounds), (5) the perception and cognition (auditory images and ideas). Music may be spatial at all these levels, involving imaginary, symbolic, geometric, acoustic and auditory types of space. Theories of "musical works" often limit music to non-spatial ideas and their notations (levels 1-2). The expanded definition of the spatialized work indicates structuring of the spatio-temporal reality of performance, sound, and perception by the composers (levels 3-5).

In the analytical portion of the dissertation (Chapters V--VIII) I attempt to stress the unity of time and space by focusing on the perceptual and temporal aspects of musical spatiality. This has not always been possible, because many composers and theoreticians consider "space" as a synonym of "stasis." Therefore, I document the composers' interests in the geometric and mathematical spaces, e.g. various non-temporal designs (circles, sets).

Chapter V contains a survey of spatial designs in contemporary music and a new classification scheme for spatialized works illustrated with many musical examples. The classification of spatial designs includes three aspects of music in space: (1) acoustic environments, (2) types of sound-space (real with vocal-instrumental sources, virtual with electroacoustic sources, and mixed), (3) categories of mobility (static and mobile performers and audiences). In addition, I list a number of (4) selected designs in real sound-space (from two ensembles in dialogue to total dispersion) and (5) selected designs in virtual sound-space (from one to many loudspeakers).

The analytical examples range from Bartók's *Music for Strings, Percussion and Celeste* (1937) to Boulez's *Répons* (1981-88) and illustrate several aspects of spatialization: (a) the spatiality of the orchestra on the stage, (b) the compositional use of apparent sound movement through dynamics, (c) the varied approaches to the movement of performers and audiences, (d) the spatial characteristics and effects of electroacoustic music, (e) the composing of perceptual experiences rather than detailed "works." The spatially extended textures on the stage are exemplified with Bartók's work and Krauze's *Folk Music* (1972) for 21 orchestral groups. In addition to exploring various patterns of movement of performers and audiences, composers create effects of virtual sound movement with stationary sources surrounding the listeners (Stockhausen's *Gruppen für drei Orchester*; works by Xenakis discussed in Chapter VII). The movement of performers in front of a static audience occurs, for instance, in Boulez's *Domaines* for clarinet and six instrumental groups (1961-1968), and Berio's *Circles* for female voice, harp and two percussionists (1960). The listeners are invited to wander around in Cage's *HPSCHD* (1967-69), and are taken for a musical elevator ride in Schwartz's *Elevator Music* (1967). Both works are indeterminate in many respects, which is characteristic of conceptual experimentation.

In more traditional types of instrumental music, the simplest form of spatialization involves the interaction of two groups of performers on the stage (e.g. Carter's *Piano Concerto* of 1963-65 and *Double Concerto* of 1961). The spatial dialogue may also be composed for the performers, rather than for the audience who witness a musical contest (Andriessen's *Hoketus* of 1975-1977). The idea of surrounding the audience with sound has been realized with symmetric patterns of 4, 6, 8, or 12 groups. Spatial designs from Stockhausen's *Carré* for four orchestras and choirs with four conductors (1959-60) inspired Dobrowolski's *Muzyka na smyczki i 4 grupy instrumentów detych* (1964). Here, spatial organization is linked to timbre; this seems to be an important characteristic of the Polish school of "sonorism" (e.g. Serocki's *Epizody* of 1959).

In the virtual space of electroacoustic music, spatial features of sound are only partly articulated through loudspeaker arrangements. Nonetheless, the classification follows the plan from one to multi-loudspeakers systems. The abundance of electroacoustic designs reflects the vastness of available sound material; each plan of loudspeaker placement involves a different set of possibilities. New technological developments continue to transform the spatial potential of basic sound projection systems (e.g. spatializers expanding the two-dimensional stereo image into sounds surrounding the listeners; or Chowning's program for virtual sound movement in a quadrophonic space, 1970). I mention just a few examples from the rich repertory of electroacoustic music: Chowning's *Turenas* (1972), Reynolds's *Archipelago* (1980-1982), Dhomont's *Espace/Escape* (1989) and Krauze's *La rivière souterraine* (1987).

Boulez's *Répons* (1981-1988) for six instrumental soloists, an instrumental ensemble of 24 musicians and live electronics provides an example of mixed sound-space (section 5.5 of Chapter V). This work includes responsorial dialogues between the individual soloists and the ensemble, between the instrumental sounds and their electronic transformations. The sounds of the soloists are amplified or processed and projected from two sets of 6 loudspeakers surrounding the performance area. The audience, located in-between the soloists and the central ensemble, is immersed in the music--this is an essential feature of the concept of this work. I discuss the role of technology in *Répons* and focus on two sections presenting the interaction of instrumental and electronic sounds. In rehearsal no. 42 (the "wallpaper") the soloists' sounds trigger a response of synthetic sonorities. In the coda (rehearsal no. 91-95), the soloists' arpeggios rotate in space and shift in frequency at the same time.

The compositional use of spatial distribution is often inspired by geometric, geographic or architectural shapes, or an intent to portray or evoke mythical, ritual or imaginary spaces. I conclude the review of spatial designs in Chapter V with three such examples. Gavin Bryars's *The Sinking of the Titanic* (1969-1975) recreates an impossible situation of the ship's refloating. It surrounds the music, which supposedly had been played on board while the *Titanic* was going down (live musicians), with a halo of musical glosses and associations (pre-recorded sounds). In Brian Ferneyhough's *Transit* for six solo voices and chamber orchestra (1975), the seating of the orchestra on the stage (four semicircles) represents the four spheres of the

Universe (an image from the Renaissance woodcut, the inspiration for this composition). In John Tavener's *Ultimos Ritos*, dedicated to St. John of the Cross (1972), the location of musicians within the space of a cross-shaped church as well as spatial sound movement participate in the religious symbolism of the music.

The third part of the dissertation (Implementations) presents three different approaches to spatialization. Here, I include brief analyses of many compositions which have not been studied before; in this research I use compositional sketches and other unpublished material, as well as my interviews with the composers.

In **Chapter VI**, I discuss Henry Brant's spatial music, from *Antiphony I* for five orchestral groups, through *Western Springs* (1984) for 2 orchestras, 2 choruses and 2 jazz combos, to *500: Hidden Hemisphere* (1992) for 3 concert bands and an ensemble of Caribbean steel drums. Brant's music has close ties to American vernacular styles and experimental tradition (Ives), not to the European avant-garde. *Antiphony I* (1953) consists of five independent layers with different timbres, motivic materials, rhythms, tempi, and keys. Here (and in all his later works), the spatial distribution of musicians serves to reinforce the musical contrasts and clarify the work's complex texture. *Millennium II* (1954) has a detailed plan of the positions of musicians; this plan is necessary for the realization of spatial effects such as sound travel along the walls of the hall. In *Voyage Four* (1964), eighty-four musicians are dispersed in a "total antiphonal distribution" throughout the auditorium, from below the floor to the highest balcony. The music presents a number of unusual spatial effects (spill, sound travel, wall of sound, etc.). Brant often juxtaposes simultaneous layers in distinct styles, e.g. jazz band, Javanese gamelan and West African drumming group in *Meteor Farm* (1982) or bands, choruses, carillons, street organs and four boatloads of flutes floating down the canals of Amsterdam in *Bran(d)t aan de Amstel* (1984). The latter piece of site-specific music involves the whole city in a grand-scale outdoor celebration. Brant's spatial music calls for active listening, in which the listeners choose what they want to pay attention to. The composer creates the conditions for this choice through the simultaneity of various musical processes taking place at different points in space.

Chapter VII presents the technique of spatial sound movement in the instrumental music of Iannis Xenakis, from *Pithoprakta* (1955-56) to *Alax* (1985). The evolution of stochastic sound masses in *Pithoprakta* is linked to a rudimentary form of motion of sound on the stage. *Eonta* (1963-64) explores performer movement and the directional quality of brass instruments (e.g. change of timbre through axial rotations of the players). In *Terretektorh* (1965-66) for orchestra scattered among the audience, apparent sound motion is constructed by means of Archimedean, logarithmic and hyperbolical spirals. The musicians are interspersed among the public also in *Nomos Gamma* (1967-68) where sound placements and movements are structured by means of mathematical group theory. The climax of *Persephassa* (1969) consists of several superimposed layers of sound, rotating simultaneously in different directions. *Alax* (1985) for three identical ensembles, presents spatial canons, sound planes, etc. Xenakis's original use of spatial sound movement in music juxtaposes technical sophistication with an overwhelming forcefulness of expression. The adoption of "space" as a compositional tool enables Xenakis to structure spatial sound locations and motions with mathematical means. His music is spatial on many levels at once.

Finally, in **Chapter VIII**, I turn towards the Canadian composer R. Murray Schafer and his explorations of spatial soundscapes and rituals, in compositions ranging from *North/White* (1979) to *The Princess of the Stars* (1981-84). In *North/White* for orchestra with a large array of percussion instruments, including a snowmobile, Schafer brings the soundscape of the Arctic into the concert hall in an ecological protest against its destruction. The *Princess of the Stars*, prologue to his musical/theatrical cycle, *Patria*, takes the performers and the audience outdoors, into the soundscape of a mountain lake. This environmental ritual is synchronized with the sunrise and includes close interactions with the natural soundscape (echoes, birdsong). Here, and in *Music for Wilderness Lake* (1979) for 12 trombones placed around a small lake, Schafer uses the acoustic properties of the surface of water (carrying sounds at large distances). Schafer's works for more conventional performance spaces, such as the *Third String Quartet* (1981) and *Apocalypsis*, a two-part monumental music drama (*John's Vision* and *Credo*, 1976-1977) reveal his involvement in various pursuits of the contemporary avant-garde. In *Apocalypsis Part Two: Credo*, Schafer juxtaposes electroacoustic and acoustic sound sources in a virtual sound world. He also articulates geometric patterns by the spatial placement of sounds and enlivens static textures with sound movement and dynamics. The formal design of the *Third String Quartet* includes detailed plans of performer location and movement so that the spatial position and musical material are closely coordinated. Schafer's music, whether integrated with wildlife sounds, or found within the concert hall, as all art, transcends the reality of ordinary human existence.

Selected topics for future research

In conclusion, I would like to point out some areas for future studies, areas which are merely outlined in this dissertation. The history of space and spatialization lays out the conceptual framework by identifying the principal denotations of these terms, and describing their evolution in the theory and practice of spatialized music. However, this account encompasses over 50 years of the Western music tradition in one narrative. Little attention is paid, for instance, to regional differences or to the subtleties of temporal evolution. These lacunae should be filled before a comprehensive history of spatialized music is written. The basic research should widen the geographical base of the study of spatialization to include compositions from Asia and countries outside the Northern hemisphere (this dissertation contains only examples from North America and Europe). The collection of precise chronological data about works and performances could reveal the waxing and waning of the interest in spatialization in different countries. The realization of this project requires the international cooperation of a team of scholars (perhaps under the aegis of UNESCO). Since this may not be easy to accomplish, research should concentrate on what is feasible: the study of repertories within smaller spatio-temporal limits.

Particular socio-cultural conditions may influence different visions of spatialization so that composers from one country may have more in common with each other than with their contemporaries abroad. My postdoctoral research will concentrate on contemporary Polish music in the study of "Spatiality, 'sonorism' and the Polish avant-garde (1956-1976)."[12] In this project, I will attempt to discover links between the compositional concerns for space and for sonority, and to delineate differences between, and similarities to, the ideas of the avant-garde in Western Europe (e.g. Xenakis, Boulez, Stockhausen). The institutionalization of "contemporary" music in the Polish People's Republic (e.g. obligatory membership in Composers' Union; relatively few, large state-funded festivals such as the *Warsaw Autumn*) allows for an unequivocal demarcation of the field of study. Similar projects could be undertaken for other East European countries and major centres such as the Darmstadt New Music Courses in Germany. I have pointed out the speculative character of two theories presented at Darmstadt; it would be interesting, for instance, to write a fuller history of the role of space in the ideology of the "modernist" avant-garde, and to trace the dissemination of theories of spatialization in various countries.

The dissertation presents a glipse of the current state of new music by including studies of recent works (e.g. Brant's *500: Hidden Hemisphere* of 1992) and excerpts from interviews with composers (conversations with Boulez, Brant, Xenakis, and Schafer, all from 1992). Various aspects of the music by the three composers discussed in the third part of the dissertation (Brant, Xenakis, Schafer) merit further study. Henry Brant's oeuvre could be re-examined with more attention paid to his use of musical borrowing, and to the relations to his predecessors, contemporaries, and students (i.e. Seeger, Cage, Linda Bouchard). Studies of Xenakis's music could concentrate on the spatio-temporal architecture of his large-scale, complex compositions such as *Terretektorh* and *Nomos Gamma*. In Chapter VII, I investigate Xenakis's use of sound movement; his designs of static distributions in instrumental

---

[12]This study constitutes the first part of my Postdoctoral Fellowship from the Social Sciences and Humanities Research Council of Canada. The second year of my Fellowship will be devoted to a study of the music and social position of Polish women composers (who, albeit not less active compositionally, have not become as famous as their male colleagues). I will work on these two projects at McGill University in cooperation with the University of Warsaw (in the years 1994-1996).

music and the spatiality of his electroacoustic works are equally fascinating. Schafer's theory and practice of the theatre of confluence "asks" for ideology critique; in addition, more of his spatialized compositions for the concert hall merit a detailed examination. Many other compositions mentioned or described in this dissertation could become topics for further research. For instance, published studies of Boulez's *Répons* (Nattiez, Deliège) indicate the existence of a sophisticated pitch design in the work's instrumental introduction. A detailed analysis of pitch coherence in the whole composition should include an examination of relationships between instrumental and electronic sounds (e.g. frequency shifts in rotating arpeggios).[13]

The history of the concepts of "space" in music (outlined in Chapter II) could also be perfected, perhaps by the addition of a comprehensive classification of notions of space: e.g. physical, acoustic space, perceptual space (with visual, tactile, and aural modes of perception), abstract space, imaginary/visionary space, cognitive space, etc. However, the introduction of such an all-embracing classificatory scheme causes difficulties of a philosophical nature.[14] Which spaces are real, which are ideal or intentional? Is it possible to separate the notions of musical, sonic and auditory spaces into well-defined categories? The answer depends on the researcher's epistemological stance, scholarly methodology and personal belief system. A plethora of intentional, "musical" spaces may emerge, spaces that are neither real nor ideal, but intersubjectively shared by communities of musicians, composers, and musicologists. Scholars of phenomenological orientation would focus on different types of musical spatiality (e.g. intentional, phenomenal spaces of experience) than researchers who embrace the mindset of logical positivism (e.g. abstract spaces of pitch, pitch-class, geometric spaces). The musical *Lebenswelt* of Western culture is far from being uniform and coherent.

---

[13]This study requires the knowledge of technical data, such as details of frequency shifts, delays, etc. Therefore, it could be realized only in collaboration with the composer and his technical staff at IRCAM.

[14]For this reason, the dissertation does not contain such a generalized scheme, but a review and a description of various *existing* theories and conceptions of space.

In this dissertation, I have limited the area of research into issues of musical spatiality to "contemporary music." It would be advisable to transcend these limitations historically and stylistically, and to re-consider the role of spatial features of music in different periods and repertories. For instance, spatiality of sound is an important element in the American tradition of Sacred Harp singing:

> Sacred Harp music is traditionally sung in a 'hollow square' with each voice part taking one of the four sides and facing the center. The song leader stands in the center, beating out the rhythm and delighting in the surge of voices and blending of sound from all four sides. Newcomers are often encouraged to 'stand in the middle' to experience the full power and exaltation of the music.
> (Grayson 1994)

Finally, musicological research into issues of space and spatiality may benefit from closer ties to acoustics and psychoacoustics. Assuming that the human hearing system has not been radically transformed during the past millennium, current psychoacoustic knowledge might illuminate studies of music from different historical periods (e.g. Bregman's theory of auditory stream segregation might explain many aspects of polychorality).

As the composition and performance of music continues, all studies proclaiming that they deal with what is "contemporary," invariably concentrate on music of the recent past. To paraphrase John Cage: "How can we possibly tell what contemporary music is, since now we're not listening to it, *we're reading a book about it*, and that isn't it." (adopted from Cage 1958/61: 44). By knowing and interpreting the past we predict and shape the future. This dissertation, examining a full range of topics relating to musical spatiality, creates a space for space.

BIBLIOGRAPHY

This bibliography contains selected entries on "space" in general (writings about concepts of space in philosophy, science, literature and the arts, discussed in Part I of the dissertation) and a comprehensive list of entries relating to sound and music (especially, but not exclusively, writings about space and spatialization in music and spatialized compositions discussed in Parts I-II of the dissertation). These entries are presented in Bibliographies A and B respectively. Bibliography B (SOUND AND MUSIC) contains also entries relating to three composers dicussed in Part III of the dissertation (i.e. their works and writings, as well as secondary literature about their music and ideas). The bibliography is written in the style of "reference list" because of the use of parenthetical references in the text of the dissertation and in the footnotes. Multiple entries by one author are listed in chronological order. Double dates in some entries, e.g. 1889/1950, indicate the date of the original publication (1889) and the date of the translation or edition used as citation (1950).

BIBLIOGRAPHY A: SPACE

Bachelard, Gaston. 1967/1969. *The poetics of space*. Transl. from the French by Maria Jolas. Boston: Beacon Press, 1969. [*La Poetique de l'Espace*. Paris, 1967].

Becker, Oskar. 1923/1970. "Contributions toward the phenomenological foundation of geometry and its physical applications." Excerpts from "Beiträge zur phänomenologischen Begründung der Geometrie und ihrer physikalischen Anwendungen" [1923] transl. and edited by T.J. Kisiel, in J. J. Kockelmans and T.J. Kisiel eds., *Phenomenology and the natural sciences. Essays and translations*. Evanston: Northwestern University Press, 1970: 119-146.

Bergson, Henri. 1889/1950. *Time and free will: An essay on the immediate data of consciousness*. Transl. from the French by Frank L. Pogson. London: G. Allen & Unwin, 1950. Muirhead Library of Philosophy. 6th ed., 1st ed. 1910. [*Essai sur les données immédiates de la conscience* 1883-1887, published in 1889].

———. 1922/1965. *Duration and simultaneity. With reference to Einstein's theory*. Transl. from the French by Leon Jacobson. Indianapolis: the Bobbs-Merrill Company, Inc., 1965. [*Durée et Simultanéité*, Paris: 1922].

Braun, Kazimierz. 1982. *Przestrzeń teatralna* [Theatrical space], in Polish. Warsaw: Państwowe Wydawnictwo Naukowe.

Cassirer, Ernst. 1921/1953. *Substance and function. Einstein's theory of relativity*. Transl. from the German by W. C. Swabey, M. C. Swabey. New York: Dover Publications, Inc., 1953 [1st. ed. 1921].

———. 1953-1957. *The philosophy of symbolic forms*. Transl. from the German by Ralph Manheim. New Haven: Yale University Press, [*Philosophie der symbolischen Formen*]. Vol. 3 "The Phenomenology of Knowledge."

Einstein, Albert. 1921/1976. "Geometry and experience" Lecture before the Prussian Academy of Sciences, January 27 1921, in *Ideas and opinions*. Transl. from the German by Sonja Bargmann. New York: Dell Publishing Co., 1976, 227-239.

———. 1934/1976. "The problem of space, ether, and the field in physics," in *Ideas and opinions*. Transl. from the German by Sonja Bargmann. New York: Dell Publishing Co., 1976, 270-278, [first published in *Mein Weltbild*, Amsterdam: Querigo Verlag, 1934].

———. 1954/1976. "Relativity and the problem of space," in *Relativity, the special and the general theory: A popular exposition*. Transl. from the German by Robert W. Lawson. London: Methuen, 1954. Reprint, *Ideas and Opinions*. New York: Dell Publishing Co., 1976, 350-366.

Eliot, John. 1987. *Models of psychological space. Psychometric, developmental and experimental approaches*. New York, Berlin, Heidelberg: Springer Verlag.

Field, Hartry. 1989. *Realism, mathematics and modality*. Oxford: Basil Blackwell.

Fraassen, van, Bas C. 1985. *An introduction to the philosophy of time and space*. New York: Columbia University Press.

Friedman, Michael. 1983. *Foundations of space-time theories. Relativistic physics and philosophy of science*. Princeton: Princeton University Press.

Frye, Northrop. 1982. *The great code. The Bible and literature*. Toronto: Academic Press Canada.

Genette, Gerard. 1966-69. "Espace et langage," in *Figures, Essais*. Paris: Éditions du Seuil.

Głowiński, Michał and Aleksandra Okopień-Sławińska, eds. 1978. *Przestrzeń i literatura. Z dziejów form artystycznych w literaturze polskiej*. [Space and literature. From the history of artistic forms in Polish literature]. Wrocław: Ossolineum.

Gosztonyi, Alexander. 1976. *Der Raum. Gesichte seiner Probleme in Philosophie und Wissenschaften*. 2 vol. Freiburg-Munich: Verlag Karl Alber GmbH.

Gray, Jeremy. 1979. *Ideas of space: Euclidean, non-Euclidean, and relativistic*. Oxford: Clarendon Press.

Grünbaum, Adolf. 1973. *Philosophical problems of space and time*. New York: Knopf, 1963, 2nd. ed. enlarged, Dordrecht, Boston: Reidel.

_____. 1977. "Absolute and Relational Theories of Space and Space-Time," in Earman J., Glymour, C. and Stachel, J., eds., *Foundations of space-time theories: Minnesota studies in the philosophy of science*. Vol. VIII. Minneapolis: University of Minnesota Press.

Heelan, Patrick A. 1983. *Space perception and the philosophy of science*. Berkeley: University of California Press.

Heidegger, Martin. 1929/1967. *Being and time*. Transl. from the 7th German edition by John Macquarrie and Edward Robinson. Oxford: Blackwell, 1967. [*Sein und Zeit*. 1929, repr. Frankfurt an Main: Klosterman, 1977].

_____. 1950\1971. "On the origin of the work of art," in *Poetry, language, thought*. Transl. from the German by Albert Hofstadter, New York: Harper and Row, 1971: 17-87. ["Der Ursprung des Kunstwerks" in *Holzwege*, 1950].

Husserl, Edmund. 1913-37/1980-82. *Ideas pertaining to a pure phenomenology and to a phenomenological philosophy*. Transl. from the German Ted E. Klein and William E. Pohl, The Hague: Martinus Nijhoff Publishers, vol. 1 *General introduction to pure phenomenology*, 1980; vol. 2 *Studies in the phenomenology of constitution*, 1982. [*Ideen zu einer reinen Phänomenologie und phänomenologischen Philosophie*, vol. I, Halle: Max Niemeyer Verlag, 1913; vol. II, 1937].

_____. 1935/1970. "The Vienna Lecture. Philosophy and the crisis of European humanity" 1935, Appendix I to in *The crisis of European sciences and transcendental phenomenology. An introduction to phenomenological philosophy*. Transl. from the German and with an Introduction by David Carr. Evanston: Northwestern University Press, 1970: 269-299.

_____. 1928/1964. *The phenomenology of internal time-consciousness*. Bloomington, London: Indiana University Press, 1964. Transl. from the German by Calvin Schrag [*Vorlesungen zur Phänomenologie des inneren Zeitbewusstseins*, 1928].

_____. 1954/1970. *The crisis of European sciences and transcendental phenomenology. An introduction to phenomenological philosophy*. Transl. from the German and with an introduction by David Carr. Evanston: Northwestern University Press, 1970. [*Die Krisis der europäischen Wissenschaften und die transcendental Phänomenologie: Eine einleitung in die phänomenologische Philosophie 1934-1937*, ed. by Walter Biemel, The Hague: Martinus Nijhoff, 1954].

Jammer, Max. 1954. *Concepts of space. The history of theories of space in physics.* Cambridge: Harvard University Press, 1954.

Julesz, B. and Hirsh I. J. 1972. "Visual and auditory perception--An essay of comparison," in E. E. David, Jr., and P. B. Denes eds., *Human communication: A unified view.* New York: McGraw Hill.

Kesting, Marianne. 1962. "Antonin Artaud und das Theater der Grausamkeit." *Akzente. Zeitschrift für Dichtung.*

Kockelmans, Joseph, J. 1970. "Merleau-Ponty on space perception and space," in J. J. Kockelmans and T.J. Kisiel eds., *Phenomenology and the natural sciences. Essays and translations.* Evanston: Northwestern University Press, 274-311.

Kockelmans, Joseph, J. and Theodore J. Kisiel, eds. 1970. *Phenomenology and the natural sciences. Essays and translations.* Evanston: Northwestern University Press.

Kuhn, Thomas S. 1962. *The structure of scientific revolutions.* Chicago: The University of Chicago Press.

Langer, Monika M. 1989. *Merleau-Ponty's Phenomenology of perception. A guide and commentary.* Tallahassee: Florida State University Press.

Mandelbrot, Benoit. 1982. *The fractal geometry of nature.* New York: W.H. Freeman and Company. A revised version of *Fractals*, 1977.

Merleau-Ponty, Maurice. 1945/1981. *Phenomenology of perception.* Transl. Colin Smith. London: Routledge and Kegan Paul, 1981 [*Phenomenologie de la perception*, Paris, 1945].

_____. 1964/1972. "Eye and mind." Transl. Carleton Dallery. In *Aesthetics* ed. by Harold Osborne. Oxford: Oxford University Press, 1972, 55-85. [*L'Oeil et l'esprit.* Paris: Gallimard, 1964].

Mitchell W. J. T. 1980. "Spatial form in literature: toward a general theory." *Critical Inquiry* 6 (Spring): 539-567.

Norberg-Schultz, Christian. 1971. *Existence, space and architecture.* London: Studio Vista.

Piaget, Jean and Inhelder, Barbel. 1956. *The child's conception of space*. Transl. from the French by F. J. Langdon and J. L. Lunzer. London: Routlege and Kegan Paul. [*La Representation de l'Espace chez l'Enfant*].

Porebski, Mieczyslaw. 1978. "O wielosci przestrzeni" [On plurality of space], in *Przestrzen i literatura* eds. M. Glowinski and A. Okopien-Slawinska. Wroclaw: Ossolineum, 24-32.

Reichenbach, Hans. 1928/1957. *Philosophy of space and time*. Transl. M. Reichenbach and J. Freund. New York: Dover Publications Inc., 1957 [originally published in German in 1928].

Rieser, Max. 1971/1986. "Roman Ingarden and his time." *The Journal of Aesthetics and Art Criticism* 39 no. 4 (summer 1971). Reprint in R. Ingarden, *The Work of Music and the Problem of its Identity*. Berkeley: University of California Press, 1986, 159-173.

Schmitz, Hermann. 1967. *System der Philosophie*. Vol. 5. *Der Raum*. Bonn: H. Bouvier und Co. Verlag.

Simpson, J. A. and E. S. C. Weiner, eds. 1989. *The Oxford English Dictionary*. Oxford: Clarendon Press; Oxford, New York: Oxford University Press.

Sklar, Lawrence. 1974. *Space, time and spacetime*. Berkeley: University of California Press.

———. 1985. *Philosophy and spacetime physics*. Berkeley: University of California Press.

Slawinski, Janusz. 1978. "Przestrzen w literaturze: elementarne rozroznienia i wstepne oczywistosci" [Space and literature: elementary distinctions and introductory manifestations], in *Przestrzen i literatura* ed. M. Glowinski and A. Okopien-Slawinska. Wroclaw: Ossolineum, 9-22.

Solomon, Robert C. ed. 1972. *Phenomenology and existentialism*. New York: Harper and Row.

Soreth, Marion. 1991. *Kritische Untersuchung von Elisabeth Ströker's Dissertation über Zahl und Raum nebst einem Anhang zu ihrer Habilitationsschrift*. 2nd ed. Cologne: P & P Verlag.

Ströker, Elisabeth. 1965/1987. *Investigations in philosophy of space*. Transl. Algis Mickunas. Athens, Ohio: Ohio State University Press, 1987 [*Philosophische Untersuchungen zum Raum*, Frankfurt am Main: Vittorio

Klosterman, 1965].

Tatarkiewicz, Wladyslaw. 1960. *Historia Estetyki*. Warszawa: PWN.

Teilhard de Chardin, Pierre. 1955/1977. *The phenomenon of man*. Transl. from the French by Bernard Wall. London: William Collins Sons & Co., 1959. Reprint, 1977 [1st ed. *Le Phoméne Humain*, Paris: Editions du Seuil, 1955].

Weyl, Hermann. 1918/1952. *Space--time--matter*. Transl. from the German by Henry L. Brose. New York: Dover Publications Inc., 1952 [*Raum--Zeit--Materie*, 1918].

─────. 1918/1970. "On time, space, and matter." English transl. by J. J. Kockelmans of Weyl's essay from *Raum, Zeit, Materie: Vorlesungen über Allgemeine Relativitätstheorie* [1st ed. 1918, 5th rev. ed., Berlin: Springer, 1923], in J. J. Kockelmans and T.J. Kisiel eds., *Phenomenology and the Natural Sciences. Essays and Translations*. Evanston: Northwestern University Press, 1970: 93-99.

Whiteman, Michael. 1967. *Philosophy of space and time and the inner constitution of nature. A phenomenological study*. London: George Allen and Unwin Ltd.

Wittgenstein, Ludwig. 1922/1988. *Tractatus Logico-Philosophicus*. Transl. from the German by C. K. Ogden, with an Introduction by Bertrand Russell. London and New York: Rutledge & Kegan Paul Ltd., 1st ed. 1922. Reprint, 1988 (page references are to reprint edition).

PART B: SOUND AND MUSIC

Adams, Stephen. 1983. *R. Murray Schafer.* Toronto: University of Toronto Press.

Adorno, Theodor W. 1948/1973. *Philosophie der Neuen Musik.* Tübingen: J.C.B. Mohr, 1948. [English transl. by Anne G. Mitchell and Wesley V. Blomster. *Philosophy of modern music.* New York: The Seabury Press, 1973.]

_____. 1966. "Über einige Relationen zwischen Musik und Malerei," in *Festschrift für Daniel Henry Kahnweiler*, Stuttgart: Verlag Gerd Hatje.

_____. 1967/1990. "Arnold Schoenberg 1874-1951," in *Prisms*. Transl. from the German by Samuel M. Weber. Cambridge, Mass.: The MIT Press, 1990, 5th ed. [1st. MIT Press edition 1981; original title *Prismen*, 1967].

Albersheim, Gerhard. 1939. *Zur Psychologie der Ton- und Klangeingenschaft. Sammlung Musik-Wissenschaftlicher Abhandlungen.* Strassburg: Heitz & Co.

_____. 1980. "On some new ideas in the psychology and theory of music." *Journal of the Indian Musicological Society* 11 no. 3-4 September--December, 1980: 29-42.

Alphonce, Bo. 1974. *The invariance matrix.* Ph. D. Diss, Yale University.

_____. 1994. "Dissonance and Schumann's reckless counterpoint." *Music Theory Online* 0 no. 7 March 1994.

Amy, Gilbert. 1960. "Orchestre et Espace Sonore." *Esprit*, No. 1.

Andriessen, Louis. 1991. *Hoketus* for two groups of five instruments (composed in 1975-77). Amsterdam: Donemus.

_____. 1977. "Notes to a recording of *Hoketus, De Staat, Il principe, Il Duce*" Set of 2 LP records, Amsterdam: Donemus, Composer's Voice CV 7702.

_____. 1994. "Down these mean streets: Life downtown. Louis Andriessen talks to Gavin Thomas." *The Musical Times* 135 no. 1813 (March): 138-142.

Angermann, Klaus and Barbara Barthelmes. 1984. "Die idee des klingenden Raumes seit Satie," in *Musik zwischen E und U: Ein Prolog und sieben Kongressbeitrage*. Veroffentilichungen des Instituts für Neue Musik und Musikerziehung Darmstadt, ed. Ekkehard Jost. Mainz: Schott, 1984, 107-126.

Bachem, A. 1950. "Tone height and tone chroma as two different pitch qualities." *Acta Psychologica* 7: 80-88.

Bacic, Marcel. 1980. "Klangraum--Raumklang." *International Review of the Aesthetics and Sociology of Music* 11 no. 2: 197-217.

Bagenal, H. 1930. "Bach's music and church acoustics." *Music and Letters* 11.

Barrière, Jean-Baptiste, ed. 1991. *Le Timbre: Métaphore pour la composition*. Paris: I.R.C.A.M. and Christian Bourgois Editeur.

Barthelmes, Barbara. 1986. "Musik und Raum--ein Konzept der Avantgarde," in *Musik und Raum. Eine Sammlung von Beiträgen aus historischer und künstlerischer Sicht zur Bedeutung des Begriffes <Raum> als Klangträger für die Musik*, ed. Thüring Bräm. Basel: GS Verlag, 75-90.

Bartók, Béla. 1937. *Music for Strings, Percussion and Celeste*. Budapest: Editio Musica, n.d. [1st. ed. Vienna: Universal Edition, 1937].

Bass, E. C. 1969. "Musical time and space in Berlioz." *The Music Review* 30 no. 3: 211-24.

Bayer, Francis. 1987. *De Schönberg à Cage. Essai sur la notion d'espace sonore dans la musique contemporaine*. Paris: Editions Klincksieck.

Begault, Durand R. 1986. "Spatial manipulation and computers: A tutorial for composers." *Ex Tempore: A Journal of Compositional and Theoretical Research in Music* 4 no. 1 (Spring-Summer): 56-88.

Beiche, Michael. 1981. "Serielles Denken in *Rituel* von Pierre Boulez." *Archiv für Musikwissenschaft* 38 no. 1: 24-56.

Benary, P. 1964. "Raum und Zeit im heutigen musikalischen Denken." *Schweizerische Musik* no. 6: 338-346.

_____. 1981. "Tonalität als Klang-Raum. Ein Phanomen im Stilwandel der Musik." *Neue Zuricher Zeitung* 271 (November): 67-68.

Bengtsson, Ingmar. 1973. *Musikvetenskap. En översikt.* [Musicology. An overview]. In Swedish. Stockholm: Esselte Studium (Scandinavian University Books).

Bennett, Gerald. 1986. "Imaginäre Räume," in *Musik und Raum. Eine Sammlung von Beiträgen aus historischer und künstlerischer Sicht zur Bedeutung des Begriffes <Raum> als Klangträger für die Musik*, ed. Thüring Bräm. Basel: GS Verlag, 91-94.

Berger, Karol. 1984. "O integracji muzycznej" [On musical integration], in *Dzielo muzyczne, teoria, historia, interpretacja*, ed. Irena Poniatowska. Kraków: PWM Edition.

Bergmann, W. 1938. "Raumgefühl und Raumstrukturen in der Musik und in den bildenden Künsten." *Schweizerische Musikpädagogische Blätter*.

Berio, Luciano. 1958. *Allelujah II* for five instrumental groups (composed in 1957-58). Milan: Suvini Zerboni.

―――. 1961. *Circles* for female voice, harp, two percussion players, (composed in 1960). London: Universal Edition.

―――. 1963. *Passaggio*. Messa in scena with text by Sanguineti, for soprano, chorus A in the pit, chorus B in the auditorium and orchestra. London: Universal Edition.

―――. 1977. *Coro* for 40 voices and instruments 1975-76. London: Universal Edition, 1977.

―――. 1985. *Two interviews, with Rossana Dalmonte and Bálintas András Varga*. Transl. by David Osmond-Smith. New York, London: Marion Boyars. [Dalmonte's interviews originally published by Gius. Laterza I Figli Spa, Rome-Bari, as *Intervista sulla musica*, 1981; Varga's interviews originally published by Editio Musica, Budapest, as *Beszélgetések Luciano Berióval*, 1981].

Berkhout, A. J. 1988. "A Holographic approach to acoustic control." *Journal of the Audio Engineering Society* 36 no. 12: 977-995.

Berlioz, Hector. 1844. *Traité d'instrumentation et d'orchestration moderne*. Paris.

Bernard, Jonathan W. 1983. "Spatial sets in recent music of Elliot Carter." *Music Analysis* no. 2: 5-34.

_____. 1986. "Space and symmetry in Bartók." *Journal of Music Theory* no. 30.

_____. 1987a. *The music of Edgard Varèse*. New Haven and London: Yale University Press.

_____. 1987b. "Inaudible structures, audible music: Ligeti's problem and his solution." *Music Analysis* 6 no. 3: 207-36.

Bertola, Elena, de. 1972. "On space and time in music and the visual arts." *Leonardo* 5 no. 1: 27-30.

Besseler, Heinrich and Peter Gülke. 1973. *Schriftbild der Mehrstimmigen Musik*. [Notation of polyphonic music]. Leipzig: VEB Deutscher Verlag für Musik.

Bielawski, Ludwik. 1976. *Strefowa teoria czasu i jej znaczenie dla antropologii muzycznej*. [A zonal theory of time and its importance for musical anthropology]. Kraków: PWM.

Binkley, Thomas, E. 1986. "Der scenische Raum in mittelalterlichen Musikdrama," in *Musik und Raum. Eine Sammlung von Beiträgen aus historischer und künstlerischer Sicht zur Bedeutung des Begriffes <Raum> als Klangträger für die Musik*, ed. Thüring Bräm. Basel: GS Verlag, 47-59.

Birch, Deborah. 1979. *Time in new music*. M.A. thesis, Brigham Young University.

Birtwistle, Harrison. 1969. *Verses for Ensembles* for woodwind quintet. London: Universal Edition.

Blauert, Jens. 1983. *Spatial hearing. The psychophysics of human sound localization*. Transl. from the German by John S. Allen. Cambridge: The MIT Press, [*Räumliches Hören*. Stuttgart: S. Hirzel Verlag, 1974].

Blaukopf, Kurt. 1971. "Space in Electronic Music," in *Music and Technology. Papers from UNESCO conference held in Stockholm, June 1970. La Revue Musicale*, Paris, 157-72.

Bloch, Georges, and Gérard Assayang, Olivier Warusfel, Jean-Pascal Julien. 1992. "Spatializer: from room acoustics to virtual acoustics." *Proceedings of the 1992 International Computer Music Conference*, San Diego, 253-256.

Bogucki, Janusz. 1969. "O kompozycji przestrzenno-muzycznej i jej społecznym odbiorze" [A 'space-and-music' composition and its reception by the public]. *Projekt* no. 3: 6-13.

Boulez, Pierre. 1963/1971. *Boulez on music today*. Transl. from the French by Susan Bradshaw and Richard Rodney Bennett. London: Faber and Faber, 1971 [*Musikdenken Heute*, Mainz: B. Schott's Sohne, 1963; *Penser la musique aujourd'hui*. Paris: Denoel-Gonthier, 1963].

_____. 1968. *Figures-Doubles-Prismes* for large orchestra. London: Universal Edition.

_____. 1970. *Domaines* for clarinet and six instrumental groups, (composed in 1961-1968). London: Universal Edition.

_____. 1975. *Rituel in memoriam Maderna* for eight orchestral groups (composed in 1974-1975). London: Universal Edition.

_____. 1975/1976. *Conversations with Célestin Deliège*. English transl. London: Ernst Eulenburg Ltd, 1976 [*Par Volonté et par Hasard: Entretiens avec Célestin Deliège*, Paris: Éditions du Seuil, 1975].

_____. 1985. *Dialogue de l'ombre double* for clarinet and electroacoustic equipment. London: Universal Edition.

_____. 1988. *Répons* for six instrumental soloists, instrumental ensemble and electroacoustic equipment 1981-. London: Universal Edition.

_____. 1992. *Interview with Maria Anna Harley, Paris, 6 August 1992*. Transcribed from a tape recording, selected and edited by M.A. Harley, unpublished typescript.

Boulez, Pierre and Andrew Gerzso. 1988. "Computers in music." *Scientific American* 258 no. 4 (April): 44-50.

Boulez, Pierre and Jean-Jacques Nattiez. 1991. "Musique/Espace." *L'Espace du Son II*, ed. F. Dhomont, 115-116.

Bräm, Thüring. 1986. "Der Raum als Klangträger. Gedanken zur Entstehung und zum Inhalt dieses Buches" in *Musik und Raum. Eine Sammlung von Beiträgen aus historischer und künstlerischer Sicht zur Bedeutung des Begriffes <Raum> als Klangträger für die Musik*, ed. Thüring Bräm. Basel: GS Verlag, 7-14.

_____. ed. 1986. *Musik und Raum. Eine Sammlung von Beiträgen aus historischer und künstlerischer Sicht zur Bedeutung des Begriffes <Raum> als Klangträger für die Musik*. Basel: GS- Verlag. Contents: Thüring Bräm--"Der Raum als Klangträger. Gedanken zur Entstehung und zum Inhalt dieses Buches," Dagmar Hoffmann-Axthelm--"Die innere

Kathedrale. Zur Metamorphose musikalischen Raumes am Beispiel von Kirche und Kammer," Jürgen Meyer--"Gedanken zu den originalen Konzertsälen Joseph Haydns," Sylvia Eichenwald--"'Wir wandeln durch des Tones Macht . . .' Zur komponierten Räumlichkeit in Mozarts 'Zauberflöte'," Thomas E. Binkley--"Der szenische Raum im mittelalterlichen Musikdrama," Sharon Neumann Solow--"Musik ohne Klang," Armin Brunner--"Musikvermittlung durch den 'zweidimensionalen' Raum des Bildschirms," Barbara Barthelmes--"Musik und Raum - ein Konzept der Avantgarde," Gerald Bennett--"Imaginäre Räume," Walter Fähndrich--"Serenaden in Luftschlössern," Andreas Gutzwiller--"Musik ohne Raum und Zeit."

Brant, Henry. 1931. *Variations for Four Instruments*. New Music 4 no. 4 (July): 1-17.

⎯⎯⎯⎯. 1955. "The uses of antiphonal distribution and polyphony of tempi in composing." *American Composer's Alliance Bulletin* 4 no. 3: 13-15.

⎯⎯⎯⎯. 1964. *Voyage Four*. A spatial concert piece for 83 instrumentalists and one singer in total antiphonal distribution led by one chief conductor and 2 assisting conductors. New York: Carl Fischer, rental score.

⎯⎯⎯⎯. 1967. "Space as an essential aspect of musical composition," in *Contemporary composers on contemporary music*, Elliott Schwartz and Barney Childs, eds. New York: Holt, Rinehart and Winston, 221-242.

⎯⎯⎯⎯. 1970. Notes to a LP recording *Henry Brant--Music 1970*, performed by the Oakland Symphony Orchestra, cond. by Gerhard Samuel. Desto DC-7108.

⎯⎯⎯⎯. 1977. *Antiphony I* for symphony orchestra (composed in 1953, revised in 1968). New York: Carl Fischer.

⎯⎯⎯⎯. 1978. *Millennium II*. Spatial Assembly for Separated Brass and Percussion Ensembles and High Voice (composed in 1954). New York: Carl Fischer.

⎯⎯⎯⎯. 1982a. *Meteor Farm* for 2 sopranos, orchestra, 2 choruses, brass choir, 2 percussion groups, jazz band, Javanese gamelan orchestra, West African drumming ensemble, South Indian trio. New York: Carl Fischer, rental score.

⎯⎯⎯⎯. 1982b. *Horizontals Extending* for wind instruments and percussion. New York: Carl Fischer, rental score.

⎯⎯⎯⎯. 1984a. *Western Springs* for 2 mixed choruses, 2 orchestras and 2 jazz combos. New York: Carl Fischer, rental score.

_____. 1984b. *Brandt aan de Amstel* for 80 flutes and percussion. New York: Carl Fischer, rental parts.

_____. 1985. Notes to a LP recording of *Western Springs,* performed by La Jolla Civic/University Symphony and Chorus, orchestral conductors Henry Brant and Thomas Nee, choral conductors David Chase, and Amy Snyder. Composers Recordings Incorporated, CRI SD 512.

_____. 1992. *On space, spatial music and other topics. Henry Brant in conversation with Maria Anna Harley. New York, 22 August 1992.* Excerpts transcribed from a tape recording, selected and edited by Maria Anna Harley; unpublished typescript.

_____. 1992b. *500: Hidden Hemisphere*. A Spatial Quadruplum for 3 symphonic bands and steel drums. New York: Carl Fischer, rental score.

_____. [n.d.] *Recorded comments. Music for Brass Choir,* performed by the *Lehigh University Instrumental Ensemble,* cond. by Henry Brant. Lehigh, RINC 1103.

Bregman, Albert S. 1990. *Auditory scene analysis: The perceptual organization of sound.* Cambridge, Mass.: Bradford Books, MIT Press.

Bregman, Albert S., and Steiger H. 1980. "Auditory streaming and vertical localization: Interdependence of 'what' and 'where' decisions in audition." *Perception and Psychophysics* 28: 539-546.

Brelet, Gisèle. 1949. *Le temps musical. Essai d'une esthetique nouvelle de la musique.* Paris: Presses Universitaires de France.

_____. 1967. "Musicalisation de l'espace dans la musique contemporaine," in *Festschrift für Walter Wiora,* L. Finscher and Ch-H. Mahling, eds. Kassel: Bärenreiter.

Brinkman, Alexander R. and Martha R. Mesiti. 1993. "Graphic display of musical data." Presented at the Special Session, "New Resources in Computational Musicology," at the Annual Meeting of The Society for Music Theory, Montreal, (November).

Brion, K., and Brown, J. E. 1976. "The spatial wind music of Henry Brant." *Instrument* 30 (January): 36-39.

Brockett, Clyde W. 1980. "The role of the office antiphon in tenth-century liturgical drama" in *Musica disciplina* Int. 34: 5-27.

Bryars, Gavin. [n.d.] "*The Sinking of the Titanic*," Liner notes from LP recording. London: Polydor Records Limited.

_____. 1975. "*The Sinking of the Titanic.* Composer's Notes." *Soundings* no. 9.

Bush, Regina. 1985-1986. "On the horizontal and vertical presentation of musical ideas and on musical space." *Tempo. A Quarterly Review of Modern Music* no. 154 (September 1985): 2-10; no. 156 (March 1986): 7-15; no. 157 (June 1986): 21-26.

Burkholder, J. Peter. 1985. "'Quotation' and emulation: Charles Ives's uses of his models." *The Musical Quarterly* 71: 1-26.

_____. 1992. Handout for Special Session "Musical borrowing as a field" at the Annual Meeting of the AMS, Pittsburgh.

_____. [1993]. *All made of tunes: Charles Ives and the uses of musical borrowing*, forthcoming.

Cage, John. 1961. *Silence: Lectures and writings*. Middletown, Conn.: Wesleyan University Press. Includes articles cited: "The future of music: credo" (1937, rev. 1958), 3-6; "Percussion music" (1939); "Forerunners of modern music" (1949), 62-66; "Experimental music: doctrine" (1955) 13-17; "Experimental music" (1957), 7-12; "Edgard Varèse" (1958), 83-88; "Composition as process," three lectures given at Darmstadt in September 1958, [I. Changes; II. Indeterminacy, III. Communication], 18-56.

_____. 1967. "Diary: Audience 1966," in *A year from Monday*. Middetown, Conn.: Wesleyan University Press, 50-51.

Cadoz, Claude. 1991. "Timbre et causalité," in *Le Timbre: Métaphore pour la composition*. Ed. by Jean-Baptiste Barrière. Paris: I.R.C.A.M. and Christian Bourgois Editeur, 17-46.

Carapezza, Paolo E. 1961/1971. "Konstytucja nowej muzyki." [The Constitution of new music]. Transl. from the Italian into the Polish by Antoni Buchner. *Res Facta* No. 6, Kraków: PWM Edition [Palermo, 1961].

_____. 1974. *Le Constituzioni della Musica: Disegno Storico*. Palermo: S. F. Flaccovio.

Carl Fischer, Inc. [n.d.]. *Henry Brant. Spatial Music. Catalog of Compositions*. Leaflet, New York. Circ. No. 8519.

_____. 1992. *Rental Catalog of Orchestral and Instrumental Music*. New York.

Carter, Elliott. 1964. *Double Concerto* for harpsichord and piano with two chamber orchestras (composed in 1961). New York: Associated Music Publishers.

_____. 1991. *Piano Concerto 1963-1965*. Milwaukee: Associated Music Publishers.

_____. 1978. *A Symphony of Three Orchestras 1976*. New York: Associated Music Publishers.

_____. 1988. *Oboe Concerto* (composed in 1987). N.p.: Hendon Music, Inc. a Boosey & Hawkes Company.

Carver, Anthony F. 1988. *Cori Spezzati*. Vol.I [*The development of sacred polychoral music to the time of Schütz*], Vol. II [An anthology of sacred polychoral music]. Cambridge: Cambridge University Press.

Charbonnier, Georges. 1970. *Entretiens avec Edgard Varèse*. Paris: Pierre Belfond.

Chiarucci, Henri. 1973. "Essai d'une analyse structurale d'oeuvres musicales." *Musique en Jeu* No. 12 (October): 11-44.

Chion, Michel. 1988. "Les deux espaces de la *musique concrète*." *L'Espace du Son I*, ed. Francis Dhomont, 31-33.

Chomyszyn, Jan. 1992. "Loudness as a cue in distance perception." *Proceedings of the 1992 International Computer Music Conference*, San Diego, 257-260.

Chowning, John. 1970. "The simulation of moving sound sources." Presented at the 38th Convention of The Audio-Engineering Society (May 4-7), Preprint No. 726. Reprint, *Computer Music Journal* 1 no. 3 (June 1977): 48-52.

Clifton, Thomas. 1983. *Music as heard: A study in applied phenomenology*. New Haven, Conn.: Yale University Press.

Clozier, Chrisian. 1988. *Un instrument de diffusion: Le Gmebaphone*. *L'Espace du son I*, ed. Francis Dhomont, 88.

Cogan, Robert. 1984. *New images of musical sound*. Cambridge, Mass.: Harvard University Press.

Cogan, Robert and Pozzi Escot. 1976. *Sonic design. The nature of sound and music*. Englewood Cliffs, N. J.: Prentice-Hall.

_____. 1981. *Sonic design. Practice and problems.* Englewood Cliffs, N. J.: Prentice-Hall.

Cone, Edward T. 1980. "Berlioz's Divine Comedy: The *Grande messe des morts*." *19th-century music* 4 no. 1: 3-16.

Conrad, Leopold. 1958. *Musica Panhumana. Sinn und Gestaltung in der Musik.* Berlin.

Cowell, Henry. 1933a. "Charles E. Ives," in *American composers on American music*. A Symposium. Ed. Henry Cowell. Stanford, California: Stanford University Press, 128-145.

_____. 1933b. "Henry Brant," in *American composers on American music: A symposium*, ed. H. Cowell. Stanford: Stanford University Press, 93-96.

Dadelsen, Hans-Christian, von. 1976. "Über die musikalischen Konturen der Entfernung. Entfernung als räumliche, historische und aesthetische Perspektive in Ligeti's *Lontano.*" *Melos* 2 no. 3: 187-190.

Dahlhaus, Carl. 1978/1989. *The idea of absolute music.* Transl. from the German by Roger Lustig. Chicago and London: The University of Chicago Press, 1989. [*Die Idee der absoluten Musik.* Kassel: Bärenreiter Verlag, 1978].

_____. 1977/1985. *Foundations of music history.* Transl. from the German by J. B. Robinson. Cambridge, London, New York: Cambridge University Press, 1983, reprint 1985. [*Grundlagen der Musikgeschichte.* Cologne: Musikverlag Hans Gerig, 1977].

Davies, L. 1983. "Serocki's spatial sonoristics." *Tempo* no. 145 (June): 28-32.

Deliège, Célestin. 1988. "Moment de Pierre Boulez: Sur l'introduction orchestrale de *Répons,*" in *Répons. Boulez.* Paris: Fondation Louis Vuitton pour l'Opéra et la Musique, 45-69.

_____. 1989. "On form as actually experienced." Transl. from the French by Deke Dusinberre. In Stephen McAdams and Irène Deliège, eds., *Music and the cognitive sciences.* Proceedings from the 'Symposium on Music and the Cognitive Sciences' 14-18 March 1988, Paris. *Contemporary Music Review* no 4. London: Harwood Academic Publishers, 101-116.

Deliège, Irène. 1989. "A perceptual approach to contemporary musical forms" in Stephen McAdams and Irène Deliège, eds., *Music and the cognitive sciences*. Proceedings from the 'Symposium on Music and the Cognitive Sciences' 14-18 March 1988, Centre National d'Art et de Culture 'Georges Pompidou,' Paris. *Contemporary Music Review* no 4. London: Harwood Academic Publishers, 213-230.

DeLio, Thomas. 1980. "Iannis Xenakis's *Nomos Alpha*: the dialectics of structure and materials." *Journal of Music Theory* 24 no. 1: 63-96.

_____. 1984. "The shape of sound--Alvin Lucier: *Music for Pure Waves, Bass Drums and Acoustic Pendulums*," in *Circumscribing the open universe*, Lanham, New York: University Press of America, 91-105. Reprint from *Percussive Notes* 21 no. 4 (1980).

De Poli, Giovanni, Aldo Piccialli, and Curtis Roads, eds. 1991. *Representations of musical signals*. Cambridge, Mass.: The MIT Press.

Deutsch, Diana, ed. 1982. *The psychology of music*. New York: Academic Press.

Dhomont, Francis. 1988. "Navigation a l'ouie: la projection acousmatique." *L'Espace du Son I*, 16-18.

_____. 1988. "Parlez moi d'espace." *L'Espace du Son I*, 37-39.

_____. 1991a. "Acousmatic, What is it?" In *Dhomont: Mouvances--metaphores*. Program book for a set of CD recordings of Dhomont's music. Montreal: Diffusion i Média, 25-26.

_____. 1991b. "*Espace/Escape*. Program notes." In *Dhomont: Mouvances--metaphores*. Program book for a set of CD recordings of Dhomont's music. Montreal: Diffusion i Média, 31-32.

_____. ed. 1988. *L'Espace du Son I*. Special issue of *Lien. Revue d'Esthétique Musicale*. Ohain, Belgium: Musiques et Recherches. Contents: Francis Dhomont--"Editorial," Annette Vande Gorne--"Espace/Temps: Historique," Francis Dhomont--"Navigation à l'ouïe: la projection acousmatique," Jean Claude Risset--"Quelques observations sur l'espace et la musique aujourd'hui," François Bayle--"L"Odyssée de l'espace," Michel Chion--"Les deux espaces de la musique concrète," Denis Lorrain--"L'espace, oui," Eric Mulard--"Pour une dramaturgie du sonore," Francis Dhomont--"Parlez moi d'espace," Xavier Garcia--Géomètrie de l'image acoustique," Christian Calon--"Occuper le temps," Nicolas Verin--"Spatialisation: interprétation, composition, improvisation?," Christian Clozier--"Un instrument de diffusion: le Gmebaphone," Léo Kupper--"Space perception in the computer age," Serge De Laubier--"Le processeur spatial multiphonique," Jonty Harrison--"Space and the BEAST concert diffusion system," Pierre Alain Jaffrennou--"Quelques considérations sur l'apport de l'informatique à la musique envisagée comme art d'interprétation," Patrick Ascione--"Pour une écriture de l'espace," Jacques Lejeune--"La forme dans le paysage," Jacques Diennet--"La paisibilité des détournements," Greet Ramael--"Baudouin Oosterlynck: La musique du corps à l'espace," Cécile Le Prado and Bruno Billaudeau--"Théorie et pratique de la composition bimodale," Michel Chion--"Un espace éclaté," Patrice Bouqueniaux--"L'espace lumière," Luc Coeckelberghs--"Espace réel, espace virtuel."

_____. ed. 1991. *L'Espace du Son II*. Special issue of *Lien. Revue d'Esthétique Musicale*. Ohain, Belgium: Musiques et Recherches, 1991. Contents: Francis Dhomont--"Editorial," Pierre Louet--"Espace de la musique et musique de l'espace," R. Murray Schafer--"Acoustic space," Claude Schryer--"L'espace écologique," Robin Minard--"La musique environnementale," Gabriel Poulard--"Quels espaces d'écoute pour l'électroacoustique?," Cécile Le Prado--"Deux espaces sonores urbains," Charles de Mestral--"La composition de l'espace public sonore," Lucien Bertolina--"Comme un trou de mémoire . . .," Michel Redolfi--"Ecouter sous l'eau," Daniel Charles--"Michel Redolfi: Musique et profondeur," Philippe Menard--"Le projet de Vancouver," Nicolas Frize--"La musique: une histoire de cadres!," Bernard Parmegiani--"L's-pace vide de sens," Pierre Schaeffer--"March of time," Catherine Portevin--"L'espace radiophonique: le son en plus," Michel Chion--"Une dramaturgie de la retransmission," René Farabet--"Au commencement était l'oreille,' Patrick Ascione--"La polyphonie spatiale," Jean-François Minjard--"Stéréo ou multipiste?," Arsène Souffriau--"Espace-support/Espace-Acousmatique," Jacques Lejeune--"La forme dans le paysage II," Jean Marc Duchenne--"Habiter l'espace acousmatique," Daniel Teruggi--"Un espace pour la réflection," Philippe Jubard--"Un monde de simulacres," Daniel Habault--"SYSDIFF, un système de diffusion," Léo Kupper--"The well-tempered space sound instrument. A new musical instrument," Justice Olsson--"L'espace, la chair, la pluie," Christian Zanesi--"L'espace des deux sons," Alain Savouret--". . . Des illusions," Robert Normandeau--"L'espace en soi," Pierre Boulez and Jean-Jacques Nattiez--"Musique/Espace," Horacio Vaggione--"Jeux d'espace: Conjonctions et disjonctions," Denis Smalley--""Spatial experience in elecro-acoustic music," Annete Vande Gorne--"Espace et structure," François Guerin--"Un espace mental à favoriser," François Bayle--"Mi-lieu," Denis Dufour--"Les espaces de l'extase," Jean-Christophe Thomas--"Quelques propositions pour étudier l'espace imaginaire dans les musiques acousmatiques."

Doblhoff, Raimund. 1959. "Der Zuschauer fährt im Theater heraum." *Melos*, 207-15.

Dobrowolski, Andrzej. 1969. *Muzyka na smyczki i 4 grupy instrumentów dętych* [Music for strings and four groups of wind instruments], composed in 1964. Kraków: PWM Edition.

———. 1976. *A-la Muzyka na orkiestre No. 4*. Kraków: PWM Edition.

Dominick, Lisa. 1983. "Mode and movement in recent works of Ton de Leeuw." *Key Notes* no. 17: 15-23.

Dowling, W. J. and D. L. Harwood. 1986. *Music cognition*. New York: Academic Press.

Drennan, Dorothy, Carter. 1975. *Relationship of ensemble dispersion to structure in the music of Henry Brant*. Ph. D. Diss.,, University of Miami.

———. 1977. "Henry Brant's use of ensemble dispersion." *The Music Review* 38, 1 (February): 65-68.

———. 1977b. "Henry Brant's choral music." *Choral Journal* 17 no. 5: 27-29.

Drew, James, M. 1968. "Information, space and a new time--dialectic." *Journal of Music Theory* 12 no. 1.

———. 1986. *Conceptual relationships in twentieth century music and art and the subsequent development of visual coordinates in musical composition*. Ph. D. Diss.,, Washington University, 1986.

Duchez, Marie-Elisabeth. 1979. "La représentation spatio-verticale du caractère musical grave-aigu et l'élaboration de la notion de hauteur de son dans la conscience musicale occidentale." *Acta Musicologica*, no. 1: 54-73.

———. 1989. "An historical and epistemological approach to the musical notion of 'form-bearing' element," in *Music and the Cognitive Sciences*. Proceedings from the 'Symposium on Music and the Cognitive Sciences' 14-18 March 1988, Paris. Eds. Stephen McAdams and Irène Deliège. *Contemporary Music Review* 4. Chur, London: Harwood Academic Publishers, 1989, 199-212.

Dufour, Hughes. 1991. "Timbre et espace," in *Le timbre, métaphore pour la composition*. Paris: IRCAM and Edition Christian Boourgeois.

Dziubinski, I. and T. Swiatkowski eds.. 1982. *Poradnik Matematyczny*, 3rd. ed. Warsaw: Panstwowe Wydawnictwo Naukowe.

Eagleton, Terry. 1990. *The ideology of the aesthetic*. Oxford: Basil Blackwell.

Ebbeke, Klaus. 1984. "Musik und Raum, " in *Musik der Zukunft. Musik auf dem 49ten Karlsruhe 1984, 16. November--9. Dezember*. Ed. Manfred Reichert. Weingarten: Druckatelier Gerbing GmbH, 36-38.

Edwards, Allen. 1989. "Unpublished Bouleziana at the Paul Sacher Foundation." *Tempo* no. 169 (June): 4-15.

Eggebrecht, Hans Heinrich. *Studien zur Terminologie der Musik*. Wiesbaden 1955.

_____. 1975. "Opusmusik." *Revue musical de Suisse romande* 115 no. 1 (January): 2-11.

_____. ed. 1974. *Zur Terminologie der Musik des 20. Jahrhunderts*. Stuttgart. Musikwissenschaftliche Verlags-Gesellschaft mbH.

Eichenwald, Sylvia. 1986. "'Wir wandeln durch des Tones Macht...'Zur komponierten Räumlichkeit in Mozarts Zauberflöte," in *Musik und Raum. Eine Sammlung von Beiträgen aus historischer und künstlerischer Sicht zur Bedeutung des Begriffes <Raum> als Klangträger für die Musik*, ed. Thüring Bräm. Basel: GS Verlag, 39-46.

Eimert, Herbert. 1955/1958. "A change of focus." *Die Reihe* no. 2, *Anton Webern*. Bryn Mawr, Pennsylvania: Theodore Presser, 1958 [in German, Vienna: Universal Edition, 1955].

Epperson, Gordon. 1967. *The musical symbol*. Ames, Iowa: Iowa State University Press.

Fearn, Raymond. 1990. *Bruno Maderna*. Contemporary Music Studies, vol. 3. Chur, London, Paris, New York: Harwood Academic Publishers.

_____. 1992. "I dreamed a theatre: The musical theatre of Luciano Berio." Presented at the AMS Annual Meeting, Pittsburgh, November 1992, unpublished typescript.

Federkov, Guy, William Buxton, and K. C. Smith. 1978. "A computer-controlled sound-distribution system for the performance of electroacoustic music." *Computer Music Journal* no. 3: 33-42.

Ferneyhough, Brian. 1974. *Time and Motion Study III* for 16 solo voices with percussion and electronic amplification. London and New York: Edition Peters.

Ferrara, Lawrence. 1991. *Philosophy and the analysis of music: Bridges to musical sound, form and reference*. New York and Westport, Conn.: Greenwood Press.

Forte, Allen. 1973. *The structure of atonal music.* New Haven: Yale University Press.

Francès, Robert. 1972/1988. *The perception of music.* Transl. from the French by W.J. Dowling. Hillsdale, N.J.: Lawrence Erlbaum Associates, 1988, [*La perception de la musique,* 2nd ed. Paris: Vrin, 1972].

Gelhaar, Roberto. 1991. "SOUND=SPACE: an interactive musical environment," in *Live Electronics. Contemporary Music Review* 6 part 1, ed. Stephen Montague. London, Paris: Harwood Academic Publishers.

Gerzso, Andrew. 1984. "Reflections on Répons," in *Musical Thought at IRCAM*, ed. Tod Machover. *Contemporary Music Review* 1, part 1. London, Paris: Harwood Academic Publishers, 23-34.

_____. 1988. "L'ordinateur et l'ecriture musicale" in *Répons. Boulez.* Paris: Fondation Louis Vuitton pour l'Opéra et la Musique, 71-81.

_____. 1992. "IRCAM: Current research and compositions" Guest Lecture at Electronic Music Studio, Faculty of Music, McGill University (23 January).

Gilbert, Anthony. 1981. "Critical response I. Musical space: a composer's view." *Critical Inquiry* 7 no. 3: 605-611.

Gillmor, Alan, M. 1992. *Erik Satie.* New York, London: W. W. Norton & Co., 1992. [1st ed. New York: G. K. Hall & Co, 1988].

Giuliani, R. 1988. "Festival Spaziomusica 1987 Cagliari 29 X--28 XI 1987." *Rivista di Musicologia Italiana* 22: 118-120.

Coad, Pamela, J. and Douglas H. Keefe. 1992. "Timbre discrimination of musical instruments in a concert hall." *Music Perception* 10 no. 1: 43-62.

Goehr, Lydia. 1992. *The imaginary museum of musical works. An essay in the philosophy of music.* Oxford: Clarendon Press.

Goldring, Elisabeth and Piene, Otto. 1982. "Sky art." *Parnass, Österreichische Kunst und Kulturzeitschrift* 2 no. 5: 52-57 [account of 1982 Ars Electronica Festival, Linz].

Goodman, Nelson. 1976. *Languages of art. An approach to a theory of symbols.* Indianapolis, Indiana: Hackett Publishing Company, Inc.

Gottwald, Clytus and Györgi Ligeti. 1974. "Gustav Mahler und die musikalische Utopie. I. Musik und Raum. II: Collage." *Neue Zeitschrift für Musik* 135 no. 1, 5 (January, May): 7-11, 288-91.

Graham, Dan. 1983. *Pavilions. Catalogue of the exhibition 12 March-17 April at the Kunsthalle, Bern.* Bern: Kunsthalle [three installations 1975-81: Public space/Two audiences; Two viewing rooms; Pavilion/Sculpture for Argonne].

Grayson, Lisa. 1994. "Sacred Harp: Basics for new singers." Handout at the 1994 Meeting of the Sonneck Society for American Music Worcester, Mass. (6-10 April).

Griesinger, David. 1989. "Equalization and spatial equalization of dummy head recordings for loudspeaker reproduction." *Journal of the Audio Engineering Society* 37 no. 1/2 (January-February): 20-29.

Gryc, Stephen. M. 1976. "Musical space and music in space: a twentieth century history." *In Theory Only* 2 (June/July): 23-26.

_____. "More space for space." 1976b. *In Theory Only* 2 (August): 27-28. A rejoinder to C. J. Smith's comment on Gryc's "Musical space" [*In Theory Only* (June-July 1976): 27].

Guérin, François. 1991. "Between departure and arrival: A look at Francis Dhomont." Transl. from the French by Laurie Radford and Claude Schryer. In *Dhomont: Mouvances--Métaphores*. Program book for a set of CD recordings of Dhomont's music. Montreal: Diffusion e Média, 81-112.

Haftmann, Werner. 1959. "Musik und moderne Malerei," in *Musica Viva*, ed. I. Bachmann. Munich, 173-220.

Haller, Hans-Peter. 1972. "Mutations et spatialisation du son." *Musique en Jeu* no. 8: 43.

Hanslick, Eduard. 1854/1986. *On the musically beautiful.* [Vom Musikalish-Schönen]. Transl. from the German by Gregory Payzant. Indianapolis, Indiana: Hackett Publishing Company.

Harley, James. 1993. "A proposal for a new analytical approach to the music of Iannis Xenakis." Forthcoming in *Canadian University Music Review*, 1995. First version read at the 1993 Annual Meeting of the Canadian University Music Society, Ottawa, May 1993.

Harley, Maria Anna. 1986. *O problemach estetycznych muzyki na tasme.* [On aesthetic problems of music for tape]. M.A. thesis in musicology. Warsaw: University of Warsaw.

_____. 1987. *O naturalnosci sztucznego poglosu.* [On the naturalness of artificial reverberation]. M.A. thesis in sound recording. Warsaw: F. Chopin Academy of Music.

_____. 1992. "The concept of 'musical space' in music theory and aesthetics 1930s-1980s." Paper read at the 12th Congress of the International Association for Empirical Aesthetics, Berlin, July 1992.

_____. 1993. "From point to sphere: spatial organization of sound in contemporary music (after 1950)." *Canadian University Music Review* 13 1993: 123-144.

_____. 1994a. "'To be God with God': Catholic composers and the mystical experience." Forthcoming in *Contemporary Music Review*, vol. "Contemporary Music and Religion," ed. Ivan Moody.

_____. 1994b. "Spatial sound movement in the instrumental music of Iannis Xenakis." *Interface. Journal of New Music Research* 23 no. 3 (August). First version read at the Fall Meeting of the New York State--St. Lawrence Chapter of AMS, SUNY--University at Albany, October 1992.

Harvey, Jonathan. 1975. *The music of Stockhausen.* Berkeley and Los Angeles: University of California Press.

_____. 1979. "*Transit* by Brian Ferneyghough." *The Musical Times* 120 no. 1639 (September): 723-728.

Hasty, Christopher, F. 1986. "On the problem of succession and continuity in twentieth century music." *Music Theory Spectrum* 8: 59-60.

Helm, Everett. 1979. "The music of Ton de Leuw." *Key Notes* no. 9: 3-12.

Helmholz, Hermann, von. 1863/1954. *On the sensations of tone as a psychological basis for the theory of music.* Transl. from the 3rd German edition 1877 by A. J. Ellis. New York: Dover Publications Inc., 1954 [reprint of the second edition of 1885; *Die Lehre von den Tonempfindungen as physiologische Grundlage für die Teorie der Musik,* published in 1863].

Hodeir, Andre. 1973. "L'espace tonal," [Tonal space]. *Panorama instrumental* 47 (June-July): 13-16; 48 (September): 19-25.

Hoffmann-Axthelm, Dagmar. 1986. "Die innere Kathedrale," in *Musik und Raum. Eine Sammlung von Beiträgen aus historischer und künstlerischer Sicht zur Bedeutung des Begriffes <Raum> als Klangträger für die Musik*, ed. Thüring Bräm. Basel: GS Verlag, 1986, 75-90.

Honing, Henkjan. 1984. "Über das CASA-Project," in *Musik der Zukunft. Musik auf dem 49ten Karlsruhe 1984, 16. November--9. Dezember*. Ed. Manfred Reichert. Weingarten: Druckatelier Gerbing GmbH, 34-35.

Hunstiger, Susan C. 1982. "L'exploration de l'espace-temps a partir de la composition musicale assiste par ordinateur." *Musique presente. Revue d'esthetique*.

Ihde, Don. 1976. *Listening and voice: A phenomenology of sound*. Athens, Ohio: Ohio University Press.

Ingarden, Roman. 1958/1986. *The work of music and the problem of its identity*. Transl. from the Polish by Adam Czerniawski. Berkeley: University of California Press, 1986. Orig. "Utwór muzyczny i sprawa jego tozsamosci" in *Studia z Estetyki*, vol. 2, Warszawa: PWN, 1958, 163-299. 1st. version of the text, "O tozsamisci dziela muzycznego," in *Przeglad Filozoficzny* 26 (1933). German version of the full text, "Das Musikwerk," in *Untersuchungen zur Ontologie der Kunst, Musik, Architektur, Film*. Tübingen: Niemeyer, 1962. English transl. from the German by R. Meyer and J. T. Goldthwait. Athens: Ohio University Press, 1989.

———. 1970. "Bemerkungen zu den Bemerkungen von Professor Zofia Lissa." *Studia Filozoficzne* 4: 351-361.

Ives, Charles. 1906/1985. *The Unanswered Question* for trumpet, flute quartet and strings (composed in 1906). Critical edition by Paul C. Echols and Noel Zahler. New York: Peer International, 1984-1985.

———. 1916/1965. *Symphony No. 4* (composed in 1909-1916). Fascimile edition of the performance score of 1965. Preface by John Kirkpatrick. New York: Associated Music Publishers, Inc.

———. 1933. "Music and its future," in *American composers on American music*. Ed. Henry Cowell. Stanford: Stanford University Press, 191-198.

———. 1972. *Memos*. Ed. John Kirkpatrick. New York: W.W. Norton.

Jackson, Roland. 1980. "Polarities, sound masses and intermodulations: A view of the recent music." *The Music Review* 41 no. 2 (May).

Jacobs, Jo Ellen. 1977. *Toward an ontology of musical works of art.* Ph.D. Diss, Washington University, St. Louis.

Jakobik, Albert. 1983. *Arnold Schoenberg. Die verräumlichte Zeit.* Regensburg: Bosse Verlag. Vol. 6 of *Perspektiven zur Musikpädagogik und Musikwissenschaft.*

Jameux, Dominique. 1984/1991. *Pierre Boulez.* English transl. by Susan Bradshaw. London: Faber & Faber. [*Pierre Boulez,* Paris: Fayard/Sacem, 1984].

_____. 1984. "Boulez and the 'machine': Some thoughts on the composer's use of various electro-acoustic media," in *Musical thought at IRCAM,* ed. Tod Machover. *Contemporary Music Review* 1, part 1. London, Paris: Harwood Academic Publishers, 11-22.

_____. 1988. "Pierre Boulez. L'oeuvre singulière," in *Répons. Boulez.* Paris: Fondation Louis Vuitton pour l'Opéra el la Musique, 1988, 15-21.

Jerusalem Bible. Popular Edition. 1974. London: Darton, Longman & Todd.

Jost, Ekkehard, ed. 1984. *Musik zwischen E und U: Ein Prolog und sieben Kongressbeitrage Verffentlichungen des Instituts für Neue Musik und Musikerziehung Darmstadt.* Mainz: Schott.

Judkins, Judith. 1988. *The Aesthetics of musical silence, virtual time, virtual space, and the role of the performer.* Ph. D. Diss.,

Kaegi, Werner. 1967. *Was ist elektronische Musik.* Zurich: Orell Fussli.

Kagel, Mauricio. 1960/1965. "Translation--Rotation." *Die Reihe* no. 7, *Form-Raum.* Original German edition, Vienna: Universal Edition, 1960; English edition, Bryn Mawr, Pennnsylvania; Theodore Presser Co., 1965.

Kazem-Bek, Jan. 1978. "Über die Nachahmung räumlicher Erscheinungen in der Musik." *International Review of the Aesthetics and Sociology of Music* 9 no. 1 (June).

Keane, David. 1984. "The Bourges International Festival of Experimental Music. A retrospective." *Computer Music Journal* 8 no. 3.

Kendall, Gary S. 1992. "Directional sound processing in stereo reproduction." *Proceedings of the 1992 International Computer Music Conference,* San Diego, 1992, 261-264.

Korte, A. 1915. "Kinematoskopische Untersuchungen." *Zeitschrift für Psychologie* 72: 193-206.

Korsyn, Kevin. 1993. "Review of Leonard B. Meyer's *Style and Music: Theory, History, and Ideology*." *Journal of the American Musicological Society* 46 no. 3: 469-475.

Kramer, Jonathan D. 1988. *The time of music: New meanings, new temporalities, new listening strategies*. New York: Schirmer Books; London: Collier Macmillan Publishers.

Krauze, Zygmunt. 1974. *Folk Music* for orchestra (composed in 1972). Kraków: PWM Edition.

_____. 1987/1988. *La Rivière souterraine. Architecture sonore* [The Underground River. A Spatial Music Composition]. Program notes in French from the work's premiere during the 16th Rencontres Internationales de Musique Contemporaine in Metz France, November 1987. Program notes in English from the presentation of the work at the 31st Festival of Contemporary Music, "Warsaw Autumn," Warsaw, Poland, September 1988.

Krauze, Zygmunt, Teresa Kelm and Henryk Morel. 1968. *Kompozycja Przestrzenno-Muzyczna* [Spatial Music Composition]. Program of the musical/architectural installation in Galeria Wspólczesna, Warsaw, Poland (September).

_____. and Teresa Kelm. 1970. *Kompozycja Przestrzenno-Muzyczna No. 2* [Spatial Music Composition Number 2]. Program of the musical/architectural installation in Galeria Wspólczesna, Warsaw, Poland (October).

Krellmann, H. 1970. "Verunsicherung der traditionellen Künste-Anmerkungen zu Raummusik und Interaktionen." *Neue Musikalische Zeitung* 18 no. 6.

Kubovy, M. 1981. "Concurrent-pitch segregation and the theory of indispensable attributes," in *Perceptual Organization*, eds. M. Kubovy and J.R. Pomerantz. Hillsdale: Erlbaum.

Kunze, Stefan. 1974. "Raumvorstellungen in der Musik--zur Geschichte des Kompositionsbegriffs." *Archiv für Musikwissenschaft* 31 no. 1: 1-21.

_____. 1981. "Rhythmus, Sprache, musikalische Raumvorstellung. Zur Mehrchorigkeit Giovanni Gabrielis" in *Schutz-Jahrbuch* 3, 12-23.

Kupper, Léo. 1986. "Musikprojektion in Elektro-Akustischen Raum. Von der Monophonie zum Raumklang Kinephonie." *Österreichische Musik Zeitschrift* 41 no. 6 (June): 293-297.

_____. 1988. "Space perception in the computer age." *L'Espace du Son I*. Special issue of *Lien. Revue d'Esthétique Musicale*. Ed. Francis Dhomont. Ohain, Belgium: Musiques et Recherches, 58-61.

_____. 1991. "The well-tempered space sound instrument. A new musical instrument." In *L'Espace du Son II*, special issue of *Lien. Revue d'Esthétique Musicale*. Ed. Francis Dhomont. Ohain, Belgium: Musiques et Recherches, 92-98.

Kurth, Ernst. 1931. *Musikpsychologie*. Berlin. Reprint, Hildesheim-New York: Georg Olms Verlag, 1969.

La Barbara, Joan. 1979. *Space Testing* (composed in 1977), notes in *Program Book of the Festival d'Automne à Paris*, Paris, October 5-6.

Lakatos, Stephen. 1991. *Temporal constraints on apparent motion in auditory space*. Center for Computer Research in Music and Acoustic. Report No. STAN-M-74. Stanford: CCRMA, Department of Music, Stanford University.

Landy, Leigh. 1991. *What's the matter with today's experimental music? Organized sound too rarely heard*. Contemporary Music Studies: Volume 4. Chur Switzerland: Harwood Academic Publishers.

Langer, Susanne K. 1953. *Feeling and form: A theory of art developed from "Philosophy in a New Key."* New York: Charles Scribner's Sons.

Le Blanc, Hubert. 1740/1984. *Defense of the viola da gamba against the designs of the violin and the pretensions of the cello* ["Défense de la basse de viole contre les enterprises du violon et les prétensions du violoncel"], 1740. Transl. Barbara Garvey Jackson, *Journal of the Viola da Gamba Society of America* 10 1973: 24-27. Reprint, in Piero Weiss and Richard Taruskin, eds., *Music in the Western World: A History in Documents*, New York: Schirmer Books, Macmillan, Inc., 1984, 206-207.

Lehnert, Heimar, and Jens Blauert. 1991. "Virtual Auditory Environment." Presented at the 5th International Conference on Advanced Robotics IEEE/ICAR, Pisa, Italy.

Lehrdahl, Fred. 1988. "Tonal pitch space." *Music Perception* 5 no. 3: 315-349.

Leitner, Bernhard. 1986. "Ton--Räume." *Österreichische Musik Zeitschrift* 41 no. 6 (June): 289-292.

Lejeune, Jacques. 1991. "La forme dans le paysage II." *L'Espace du Son II*, special issue of *Lien. Revue d'Esthétique Musicale*. Ed. Francis Dhomont. Ohain, Belgium: Musiques et Recherches, 77-81.

Lendvai, Ernö. 1983. "The quadrophonic stage of Bartók's *Music for Strings, Percussion and Celesta*," in *The workshop of Bartók and Kodály*. Budapest: Edition Musica, 71-91.

Leppert, Richard, D. and Susan McClary. 1987. *Music and society: the politics of composition, performance, and reception*. Cambridge, New York: Cambridge University Press.

Levarie, Siegmund and Levy, Ernst. 1983. *Musical morphology. A discourse and a dictionary*. Kent, Ohio: The Kent State University Press.

Lewin, David. 1987. *Generalized musical intervals and transformations*. New Haven and London: Yale University Press.

Ligeti, György. 1960/1965. "Metamorphoses of musical form." *Die Reihe* no. 7 1965 [originally published in German, as "Wandlungen der musikalischen Form," *Die Reihe* no. 7, 1960].

_____. 1971. "Fragen und Antworten von Mir Selbst." *Melos* no. 12: 509-516.

Ligeti, György, and Willnauer Franz. 1960. "Die Funktion des Raumes in der Musik." *Forum* no. 76.

Lippe, Cort. 1979/1984. *Music for 12 Brass Instruments* for 4 trumpets, 4 horns and 4 trombones. Cort Lippe. (composed in 1979, revised in 1984).

Lippman, Edward, A. 1952. *Music and space. A study in the philosophy of music*. Ph. D. Diss.,, Columbia University.

_____. 1963. "Spatial perception and physical location as factors in music." *Acta Musicologica* 35: 24-34.

_____. 1992. *A history of Western musical aesthetics*. Lincoln and London: University of Nebraska Press.

Lissa, Zofia. 1965. "O procesualnym charakterze dziela muzycznego," [On the nature of the musical work as a process]. In *Studia Estetyczne*, 1965, 91-105. Reprinted in *Szkice z Estetyki Muzycznej*, Kraków, 1965, 316-331. German transl. "Die Prozessualität der Musik" in *Hegel-Jahrbuch*, 1965, 27-38.

———. 1968/1975. "Über das Wesen des Musikwerkes." *Musikforschung* no. 2 (1968): 157-182. Reprinted in Zofia Lissa, *Neue Aufsätze zur Musikästhetik*, Wilhemshaven: Heinrichshofen's Verlag, 1975, 1-54. German translation of "O istocie dziela muzycznego" [On the essence of the musical work"]. *Polish Musicological Quarterly. Muzyka* 13 no. 1 (1968): 3-30.

———. 1966/1975. "Einige kritische Bemerkungen zur Ingardenschen Theorie des musikalischen Werkes," in *Neue Aufsätze zur Musikästhetik*, Wilhemshaven: Heinrichshofen's Verlag, 1975, 172-207. Reprint from *International Review of the Aesthetics and Sociology of Music* 1 (1972): 75-95. Revision and German transl. of "Uwagi o Ingardenowskiej teorii dziela muzycznego, " *Studia Estetyczne* (1966): 95-113. Earlier transl. into German, "Zur Ingardenschen Theorie des Musikalischen Werkes," *Studia Filozoficzne* 4 (1970): 331-350. Also published in English as "Some remarks on the Ingardenian theory of the musical work," in P. Graf and S. Krzemien-Ojak eds. and trsl., *Roman Ingarden and contemporary Polish aesthetics*, Warsaw, 1975, 129-144.

Lohner, Henning. 1987a. "Auswahlbibliographie." *Musik-Konzepte. No. 54/55: Iannis Xenakis,* ed. Heinz-Klaus Metzger and Rainer Riehn.

———. 1987b. "Chronologisches Werkverzeichnis 1952-1986." *Musik-Konzepte. No. 54/55: Iannis Xenakis*, ed. Heinz-Klaus Metzger and Rainer Riehn.

Louet, Pierre. 1991. "Espace de la musique et musique de l'espace," in *L'Espace du Son II*. Ed. Francis Dhomont. Special issue of *Lien. Revue d'Esthétique Musicale*. Ohain, Belgium: Musiques et Recherches, 7-11.

Lowinsky, Edward, E. 1941. "The concept of physical and musical space in the Renaissance." *Papers of the American Musicological Society*, 57 84.

Lucier, Alvin. 1985. "The tools of my trade," in *Contiguous Lines: Issues and Ideas in the Music of the '60's and '70's*, ed. Thomas DeLio. Lanham, New York: University Press of America, 143-160.

Lucier, Alvin, Elie Siegmeister and Mindy Lee. 1979. "Three points of view." *The Musical Quarterly* 65 no. 2 (April): 281-95.

Mackenzie, Kirk. 1991. *A Twentieth-Century Musical/Theatrical Cycle: R. Murray Schafer's "Patria" 1966-*. Ph.D. diss., University of Cincinnati.

Maconie, Robin. 1976. *The works of Karlheinz Stockhausen*. With a foreword by K. Stockhausen. London: Oxford University Press. 2nd. ed. 1990.

_____. 1990. *The concept of music*. Oxford: Clarendon Press.

_____., ed. 1989. *Stockhausen on music. Lectures and interviews*. London: Marion Boyars.

Maderna, Bruno. 1969. *Quadrivium per 4 esecutori di percussione e 4 gruppi d'orchestra*. Milan: Ricordi.

Mahler, Gustav. 1894/1971. *Symphony No. 2* (composed in 1894). Revised version. Vienna--London: Universal Edition, 1971.

Malinowski, Wladyslaw. 1981. *Polifonia Mikolaja Zielenskiego* [Polyphony of Mikolaj Zielenski]. Muzyka polska w dokumentach i interpretacjach. Kraków: PWM Edition.

Matossian, Nouritza. 1986. *Xenakis*. London: Kahn & Averill.

Mattis, Olivia. 1993. "Stravinsky: a surprising source for Varèse's spatial ideas." Presented at the 1993 Annual Meeting of the American Musicological Society, Montreal, (November).

_____. 1992. "Varèse's multimedia conception of Déserts." *The Musical Quarterly* 76 no. 4 (Winter): 557-583.

McAdams, Stephen. 1984. *Spectral fusion, spectral parsing and the formation of auditory images*. Ph. D. diss., Stanford: Stanford University.

_____. 1989. "Psychological constraints on form-bearing dimensions in music," in *Music and the cognitive sciences*, Stephen McAdams and Irène Deliège, eds. Proceedings from the 'Symposium on Music and the Cognitive Sciences' 14-18 March 1988, Paris. *Contemporary Music Review* 4. London: Harwood Academic Publishers, 181-198.

McAdams, Stephen and Irène Deliège, eds. 1989. *Music and the cognitive sciences*. Proceedings from the 'Symposium on Music and the Cognitive Sciences' 14-18 March 1988, Centre National d'Art et de Culture 'Georges Pompidou,' Paris. *Contemporary Music Review* 4. London: Harwood Academic Publishers.

McCallum, Peter. 1989. "An interview with Pierre Boulez." *The Musical Times* 80 no. 1752 (January): 8-10.

McClary, Susan. 1991. *Feminine endings: Music, gender, and sexuality.* Minneapolis, University of Minnesota Press.

McCoy, Marilyn, L. 1993. "'Wie aus der Fern': The aesthetic metamorphosis expressed in Gustav Mahler's exploration of the otherworld." Unpublished paper presented at the 11th International Congress of Gesellschaft für Musikforschung, Musik als Text, Freiburg im Breisgau, (27 September--1 October).

McDermott, Joseph, Vincent. 1966. *The articulation of musical space in the twentieth century.* Ph. D. diss., University of Pennsylvania.

_____. 1972. "A conceptual musical space." *Journal of Aesthetics and Art Criticism* 30 no. 4 (Summer): 489-494.

Ménard, Philippe. 1991. "Space at performer's fingertips." Presented at the 1991 Internation Computer Music Conference, Montreal.

Mersmann, Hans. 1926. *Angewandte Musikästhetik* [Applied musical aesthetics]. Berlin: M. Hesse.

Meyer-Eppler, Werner. 1955a. *Musik, Raumgestaltung, Elektroakustik.* Mayence: Ars Viva.

_____. 1955b. "Elektronische Musik," in *Klangstruktur der Music. Neue Erkentnisse musik-elektronischer Forschung*, ed. F. Winckel, Berlin-Borigswalde: Verlag für Radio-Foto-Kinotechnik GMBH, 133-157.

Meyer, Jürgen. 1978. *Acoustics and the performance of music.* Transl. J.W. Bowsher. Frankfurt am Main.

_____. 1986. "Gedanken zu den originalen Konzertsälen Joseph Haydns," in *Musik und Raum. Eine Sammlung von Beiträgen aus historischer und künstlerischer Sicht zur Bedeutung des Begriffes <Raum> als Klangträger für die Musik*, ed. Thüring Bräm. Basel: GS Verlag, 1986, 27-38.

Milhaud, Darius. 1953. *Notes without music.* Transl. Donald Evans. New York: Alfred A. Knopf.

Miller, G. A. 1956. "The magical number seven, plus or minus two: Some limits on our capacity for processing information." *Psychological Review*, 63, 81-97.

Mills, A. W. 1975. "Auditory localization," in *Foundations of Modern Auditory Theory*, ed. J.V. Tobias. New York: Academic Press.

Mitchell, Donald. 1975. *Gustav Mahler: the Wunderhorn years. Chronicles and commentaries*. London: Faber & Faber.

Moldenhauer, Hans. 1978. *Anton von Webern: A chronicle of his life and work*. London: Gollancz.

Moles, Abraham A. 1960. *Les musiques experimentales: Revue d'une tendance importante de la musique contemporaine*. Transl. Daniel Charles. Paris: Editions du Cercle d'Art Contemporain.

Monahan, Caroline Benson. 1984. *Parallels between pitch and time: The determinants of musical space*. Ph. D. diss., in experimental psychology. Los Angeles: University of California.

Montague, Stephen, ed. 1991. *Live Electronics. Contemporary Music Review* 6 part 1. Harwood Academic Publishers.

Moore, Richard F. 1983. "A General Model for Spatial Processing of Sounds." *Computer Music Journal* 7 no. 3 (Fall): 6-15.

Morgan, Robert P. 1974. "Spatial form in Ives," in *An Ives Celebration. Papers and Panels of the Charles Ives Centennial Fastival-Conference*. Chicago: University of Illinois Press, 145-158.

_____. 1978. "Ives and Mahler: mutual responses at the end of an era." *19th-century music* 2 no. 1 (July): 72-81.

_____. 1979. "Notes on Varèse's rhythm," in *The New Worlds of Edgar Varèse: A Symposium*, ed. Sherman Van Solkema. New York: Institute for Studies in American Music, Department of Music, School of Performing Arts, Brooklyn College of the City University of New York, 9-25.

_____. 1980. "Musical time/musical space." *Critical Inquiry* 6 no. 3 (Spring), 527-538.

Morrill, Dexter. 1981. "Loudspeakers and performers." *Computer Music Journal* 5 no. 4 (Winter): 25-29.

Morris, Robert D. 1987. *Composition with pitch classes: A theory of compositional design*. New Haven: Yale University Press.

Moser, Hans Joachim. 1953. *Musikästhetik*. Berlin.

Mott, Gilbert. 1982. "Wesleyan University Orchestra and Wesleyan Singers: Brant 'Meteor Farm' [premiere]." *High Fidelity/Musical America* 32 no. 7 (July): 36-37.

Motte-Haber, de la, Helga. 1986. "Zum Raum wird hier die Zeit." *Österreichische Musik Zeitschrift* (June): 282-288.

Nadel, Siegfrid F. 1931. "Zum Begriff des musikalischen Raumes." *Zeitschrift für Musikwissenschaft*, Leipzig, 329-331.

Nattiez, Jean-Jacques. 1988. "*Répons* et la crise de la "communication" musicale contemporaine." *Inharmoniques* no. 2. Paris, 1987. Reprinted in *Répons. Boulez*. Paris: Fondation Louis Vuitton pour l'Opéra et la Musique, 23-43.

_____. 1987/1990. *Music and discourse. Toward a semiology of music*. Transl. from the French by Carolyn Abbate. Princeton, New Jersey: Princeton University Press, 1990 [*Musicologie génerale et sémiologie*, Paris, 1987].

Naud, Gilles. 1975. "Aperçus d'une analyse sémiologique de *Nomos Alpha*." *Musique en Jeu* no. 17: 63-71.

Nicholls, David. 1990. *American experimental music, 1890-1940*. Cambridge: Cambridge University Press.

Nyman, Michael. 1974. *Experimental music. Cage and beyond*. London: Studio Vista.

O'Connell, Walter. 1962/1968. "Tone Spaces." *Die Reihe* No. 8, *A Retrospective*, 1968; [in German, *Die Reihe* no. 8, 1962].

O'Leary, A. and G. Rhodes. 1984. "Cross-modal effects on visual and auditory object perception." *Perception and Psychophysics* 35: 565-569.

Palombini, Carlos. 1993. "Machine Songs V: Pierre Schaeffer-from research into noises to experimental music." *Computer Music Journal* 17 no. 3 (Fall): 14-19.

Pasler, Jann Corinne. 1981. *Debussy, Stravinsky, and the Ballets Russes: The emergence of a new musical logic*. Ph.D. diss., University of Chicago.

Patterson, Roy, D. 1990. "The tone height of multiharmonic sounds." *Music Perception* 8, no. 2 (Winter): 203-214.

Penderecki, Krzysztof. 1972. *Utrenja. The Entombment of Christ* for 2 choirs, solo voices and symphony orchestra. Kraków: PWM Edition.

_____. 1974a. *Magnificat* for bass solo, 7-part male vocal ensemble, 2 mixed choruses, boy's chorus and symphony orchestra. Kraków: PWM Edition.

_____. 1974b. *Passio et mors Domini nostri Iesu Christi secundum Lucam.* Kraków: PWM Edition.

Perrott, D.R. and A. D. Musicant. 1977. "Minimum auditory movement angle: Binaural localization of moving sound sources." *Journal of Acoustic Society of America* 62: 1463-1466.

Petersen, George. 1994. "Field test: Desper Spatializer." *Mix* 18 no. 3 (March): 142-148.

Peyser, Joan. 1976. *Boulez.* New York: Schirmer Books.

Potter, Keith. 1981. "Just the tip of the iceberg: some aspects of Gavin Bryars' music." *Contact*, 4-15.

_____. 1982. "The music of Louis Andriessen: Dialectical double-Dutch?" *Contact*, 16-22.

Poullin, Jacques. 1954. "Son et Espace." *La Revue Musicale*, special issue devoted to the Décade de la Musique Expérimentale. Paris: Editions Richard Masse; reprinted as no. 236, 1957.

_____. 1955. "Musique Concrète," in *Klangstruktur der Musik. Neue Erkentnisse Musik-elektronischer Forschung*, ed. Fritz Winckel. Berlin: Verlag für Radio-Foto-Kinotechnik GMBH, 109-132.

Pratt, C. C. 1930. "The spatial character of high and low notes." *Journal of Experimental Psychology* 13, 278-285.

Pressing, Jeff. 1993. "Relations between musical and scientific properties of time." *Contemporary Music Review* vol. 7: 105-122.

Pritchett, James. 1993. *The music of John Cage.* Cambridge: Cambridge University Press.

Przybylski, Bronislaw Kazimierz. 1984. *Muzyka przestrzenna. Wybrane zagadnienia z projektowania przestrzennego w kompozycji wspolczesnej.* [Spatial music. Selected problems of spatial projection in modern compositions]. Prace specjalne 34, Gdansk: Akademia Muzyczna im St. Moniuszki.

Purce, Jill. 1974. "La Spirale dans la Musique de Stockhausen." *Musique en Jeu* no. 15 (September): 7-23.

Raaijmakers, Dick, Ton Bruynèl, and Peter Struycken. 1971. *Sound< = >Sight. Three Audiovisual Projects.* Includes: Bruynèl--"Cubes project 1969-1971," Raaijmakers--"Ideophone I, II and III, 1970-1971," Struycken--"Image and Sound programme 1, 1970." Stedelijk Museum, Amsterdam, 5 March--18 April 1971. Catalogue no. 498.

Ramaut, Béatrice. 1992. "Dialogue de l'ombre double de Pierre Boulez: analyse d'un processus citationnel." *Analyse Musicale* no. 3: 69-75.

Rasch, R. A. and R. Plomp. 1982. "The Listener and the Acoustic Environment," in *The Psychology of Music*, ed. Diana Deutsch. New York: Academic Press, 135-148.

Reich, Deborah, Ziskind. 1992. "Penetrating space and sound." *The Upper West Side Resident* 3 no. 20 (24 August): 15.

Reihe, die, no. 7, *Form--Raum.* 1960/1965. Original German edition, Vienna: Universal Edition, 1960; English edition, Bryn Mawr, Pennnsylvania; Theodore Presser Co., 1965. Contents: György Ligeti: "Metamorphoses of musical form," Ursula Burghardt-Kagel: "Amancio Williams' space theatre," Christian Wolff: "On form," Mauricio Kagel: "Translation--Rotation," John Whitney: "Moving pictures and electronic music," Jörn Janssen: "Initial project. Designed for Gottfried Michel Koenig."

Revault d'Allones, Olivier, ed. 1975. *Les Polytopes.* Paris.

Révész, Geza. 1937. "Gibt es ein Hörraum?" *Acta Psychologica* 3.

──────. 1946. *Einführung in die Musikpsychologie.* Bern.

Reynolds, Roger. 1978. "Thoughts on sound-movement and meaning." *Perspectives of New Music* 16 no. 2 (Spring/Summer): 181-190.

──────. 1983. *Archipelago* for instrumental ensemble and 4-channel tape (composed in 1980-1982). New York: C.F. Peters Corporation, 1983.

Rhodes, G. 1987. "Auditory attention and the representation of spatial information." *Perception & Psychophysics* 42: 1-14.

Rieser, Max. 1971/1986. "Roman Ingarden and his time." *The Journal of Aesthetics and Art Criticism* 39 no. 4 Summer 1971. Reprint, R. Ingarden, *The Work of*

Music and the Problem of its Identity. Berkeley: University of California Press, 1986, 159-173 (page references are to reprint edition).

Riezler, Walter. 1930. "Das neue Raumgefühl in Bildender Kunst und Musik," in *Kongress für Ästhetik*, Bericht 4.

Rimmer, Joan. 1980. "Steel band," entry in *The New Grove Dictionary of Music and Musicians*, vol 18. Ed. Stanley Sadie, London: McMillan.

Rissett, Jean-Claude. 1988. "Quelques observations sur l'espace et la musique ajourd'hui." *L'Espace du Son I*, ed. F. Dhomont: 21-22.

_____. 1991. "Musique, recherche, théorie, espace, chaos." *Inharmoniques* no. 8/9. Paris, 273-316.

Rochberg, George. 1963. "The new image of music." *Perspectives of New Music* 2 no. 1: 1-10.

Romano, Anthony. 1987. "Three-dimensional image reconstruction in audio." *Journal of the Audio Engineering Society* 35 no. 10 (October): 749-759.

Rzewski, Frederic. 1967. "A photoresistor mixer for live performance." *Electronic Music Review* no. 4 (October): 433-434.

_____. 1967. "Plan for 'Spacecraft'." *Source* 2 no. 1: 66-68.

Sacher, Reinhard Josef. 1985. *Musik als Theater. Zur Entstehungsgeschichte des Instrumentalen Theaters*. Ph. D. diss., Cologne.

_____. 1985. "Musik als Theater. Tendenzen zur Grenzüberschreitung in der Musik von 1958 bis 1968." *Kölner Beitrage zur Musikforschung*. Regensburg: Klaus Wolfgang Niemöller.

Sachs, Curt. 1918-1919. "Kunstgeschichtliche Wege zur Musikwissenschaft" in *Archiv für Musikwissenschaft* 1: 451-464.

Sandroff, Howard. 1992. "Realizing the spatialization processing of *Dialogue des l'ombre Double* by Pierre Boulez." *Proceedings of the 1992 International Computer Music Conference*, San Diego.

Schaeffer, Pierre. 1952. *A la recherche d'une musique concrète*. Paris: Édition du Seuil.

_____. 1966. *Traité des objects musicaux*. Paris: Éditions du Seuil.

———. 1967. *La musique concrète*. Paris: Presses Universitaires de France.

———. 1991. "March of Time." *L'Espace du Son II*, ed. F. Dhomont, 51-52.

Schafer, Murray, R. 1967. "The Philosophy of Stereophony." *West Coast Review* no. 1 (Winter): 4-19.

———. 1977a. *The Tuning of the World*. New York: Knopf.

———. 1977b. *Music in the Cold*. Toronto: The Coach House Press.

———. 1980. *North/White* for orchestra (composed in 1979). Toronto: Universal Edition (Canada) Ltd.

———. 1981a. *Music for Wilderness Lake* (composed in 1979). Bancroft, Ontario: Arcana Editions.

———. 1981b. *Apocalypsis. Part 1: John's Vision* (composed in 1977). Bancroft, Ont.: Arcana Editions.

———. 1983. *Third String Quartet* (composed in 1981). Bancroft, Ont.: Arcana Editions.

———. 1984. *On Canadian Music*. Bancroft, Ont.: Arcana Editions.

———. 1986a. *Apocalypsis. Part Two: Credo* (composed in 1976). Bancroft, Ont.: Arcana Editions.

———. 1986b. *Patria. The Prologue: The Princess of the Stars*. A ritual for performance at dawn on an autumn morning on a lake (composed in 1981-1984). Toronto: Arcana Editions.

———. 1987. *The Greatest Show*. Toronto: Arcana Editions.

———. 1991a. *Patria and the Theatre of Confluence*. Special issue of *Descant* 22 no. 2 (Summer): 11-215.

———. 1991b. "Acoustic space." *L'Espace du Son II*, ed. F. Dhomont, 1991, 15-20.

———. 1992. *Interview with Maria Anna Harley, Toronto, 19 October 1992*. Excerpts transcribed from a tape recording, selected and edited by M. A. Harley; unpublished typescript.

_____, ed. 1973. *The Music of the Environment*. No. 1 of an Occasional Journal devoted to Soundscape Studies. Vienna: Universal Edition.

Schaffer, Boguslaw. 1969. *Dzwieki i znaki* [Sounds and Signs]. Kraków: PWM Edition.

Schiff, David. 1983. *The Music of Elliott Carter*. London: Eulenburg Books.

Schlemm, W. 1972. "Raum und Musik in der elektroakustischen Übertragung: Ein Beitrag zur Frage der Hörsamkeit" ["Space and music in electroacoustical transmission. A contribution to the problem of acoustics"]. *Neue Zeitschrift für Musik* 130 no. 4, 5 (April, May): 195-200, 251-57.

Schmidt, Christian Martin. 1977. *Brennpunkte der Neuen Musik. Historisch-Systematisches zu wesentlichen Aspekten*. Series Musik-Taschen-Bücher Theoretica 16. Cologne: Gerig.

Schnebel, Dieter. 1958/1960. "Karlheinz Stockhausen." *Die Reihe* no. 4, *Young Composers*. Vienna: Universal Edition, 1958 [German]. Bryn Mawr, Penn.: Theodore Presser, 1960, 121-135 [English].

_____. 1972. "Sichtbare Musik," in *Denkbare Musik. Schriften 1952-1972*. Cologne.

_____. 1974. "Raumkompositionen, Lichtspiele, Bewegung der Personen bei Wagner." *Neue Zeitschrift für Musik* 135: 90-93.

_____. 1976. "Composition de l'espace." *Musique en Jeu* no. 22 (January): 57-63.

_____. 1976. "Über experimentelle Musik und ihre Vermittlung." *Melos/Neue Zeitschrift für Musik* 2 no. 6: 461-467.

Schneider, Max. 1930. "Raumtiefenhören in der Musik," presented at IV Kongress für Ästhetik und allgemeine Kunstwissenschaft, Hamburg, 1930, in *Kongress für Ästhetik*, Bericht 4.

Schoenberg, Arnold. 1975. "Composition with Twelve Tones," 1941 in *Style and idea. Selected writings of Arnold Schoenberg*, ed. Leonard Stein, transl. Leo Black. London: Faber & Faber.

Schroeder, Manfred. 1984. "Progress in Architectural Acoustics and Artificial Reverberation: Concert Hall Acoustics and Number Theory." *Journal of the Audio-Engineering Society* 32, 194-203.

Schwartz, Elliott. 1970. "Elevator Music." *Composer US* no. 2: 245-54.

_____. 1984. "Henry Brant embraces Amsterdam. The Holland Festival sets his music afloat." *High Fidelity/Musical America* 34 no. 12 (December): 35-36.

Schwartz, Elliott and Daniel Godfrey. 1993. *Music since 1945. issues, materials, and literature.* New York: Schirmer Books.

Semal, Catherine and Laurent Demany. 1990. "The upper limit of 'musical' pitch." *Music Perception* 8 no. 2 (Winter): 165-176.

Serocki, Kazimierz. 1957. *Sinfonietta per due orchestre d'archi.* Kraków: PWM Edition, 1957, 3rd ed. 1976.

_____. 1961. *Epizody* for strings and 3 groups of percussion. Kraków: PWM Edition.

_____. 1969. *Continuum* for 6 percussionists. Kraków: PWM Edition.

Sheeline, Christopher. 1982. *An investigation of the effects of direct and reverberant signal interaction on auditory distance perception.* Ph.D. diss., Stanford University/CCRMA.

Shepard, Roger N. 1982. "Structural representations of musical pitch," in *The psychology of music*, ed. Diana Deutsch. New York: Academic Press, 344-390.

_____. 1984. "Ecological constraints of internal representation: Resonant kinematics of perceiving, imagining, thinking and dreaming." *Psychological Review* 91, 417-447.

Shepard, Roger N., and Lynn A. Cooper. 1982. *Mental images and their transformations.* Cambridge: The MIT Press.

Sine, Nadine. 1983. *The evolution of symphonic worlds: Tonality in the symphonies of Gustav Mahler, with emphasis on the First, Third, and Fifth.* Ph. D. diss., New York University.

Slonimsky, Nicolas. 1971. *Music since 1900.* New York: Charles Scribner's Sons, 4th ed.

Smalley, Denis. 1991. "Spatial experience in electro-acoustic music." *L'Espace du Son II*, ed. F. Dhomont.

Smith Joseph F. 1979. *The experiencing of musical sound. Prelude to a phenomenology of music.* New York, London: Gordon and Breach.

Stautner, John and Miller Puckette. 1982. "Designing multichannel reverberators." *Computer Music Journal* Vol. 6 No. 1: 52-65.

Stockhausen, Karlheinz. 1959/1961. "Musik im Raum." *Die Reihe* no. 5, 1959. Also published in Stockhausen, *Texte zur elektronische und instrumental musik.* Bd. I. 1952-1962. Aufsätze zur Theorie des Komponierens. Cologne: Verlag M. DuMont Schanberg, 1963. [English transl. by Ruth Koenig: "Music in Space." *Die Reihe* No. 5 (1961): 67-82].

_____. 1963. *Gruppen für drei Orchester* (composed in 1955-1957). London: Universal Edition.

_____. 1964. *Carré* for 4 choirs and 4 orchestras (composed in 1959-1960). London: Universal Edition.

_____. 1964. *Texte. Bd. 2. Aufsätze zur Musikalische Praxis, 1952-1962.* Cologne: Verlag M. DuMont Schauberg.

_____. 1973. *Spiral* for one soloist (composed in 1970). London: Universal Edition.

_____. 1977. *Sternklang. Park Music for 5 Groups.* Werk Nr. 34. Stockhausen.

_____. 1989. *Texte zur Musik. Band 5. 1972-1984. Komposition.* Selected and edited by Christoph von Blumröder. Cologne: DuMont BuchVerlag, 1989.

Stofft, Paul William. 1975. *A Structuralist Approach to Music and Painting Emphasizing Space and Time.* Ph. D. diss., University of Southern California.

Stowpiec, Mariusz. 1980. *Poglady estetyczne Edgara Varèse'a - Ich zródla, kontekst i rozwój.* [Aesthetic views of Edgar Varèse: Their sources, context and development]. M.A. thesis in musicology. Warsaw: University of Warsaw.

Stravinsky, Igor. 1936/1963. *An Autobiography.* New York: W. W. Norton & Co, [1st ed. 1936].

_____. 1924/1979. "Some ideas about my *Octuor.*" *The Arts* 5 no.1 (January 1924): 5-6. Reprint in Eric Walter White, *Stravinsky. The composer and his works.* London: Faber and Faber, 574-577.

Strawn, John. 1978. "The *Integrales* of Edgard Varèse: space, mass, element, and form." *Perspectives of New Music* 17 no. 1 (Fall/Winter): 138-160.

Stroppa, Marco. 1991a. "Les enjeux musicaux," typescript, Paris. Published in German transl. in *Motiv: Musik in Gesellschaft andere Künste*, Berlin: Verlag Constructiv (October).

_____. 1991b. "Espace et Figure," typescript, Paris. Published in translation by Rudolf Kimmig in *Motiv. Musik in Gesellschaft anderer Künste*. Berlin: Verlag Constructiv, (February 1992).

Strybel, T. Z., Manligas, C. L., and Perrott, D. R. 1989. "Auditory apparent motion under binaural and monaural listening conditions." *Perception & Psychophysics* 45: 371-377.

Szwajgier, Krzysztof. 1973. "Muzyka Przestrzenna," [Spatial Music]. *Forum Musicum* 15: 36-48.

Tavener, John. 1972. *Ultimos Ritos. En Honor de San Juan de la Cruz*. London: J. & W. Chester Ltd.

_____. 1974. *Notes about 'Ultimos Ritos,'* unpublished typescript. London.

_____. 1994. "A fish out of water: All at sea? John Tavener talks to Malcolm Crowthers." *The Musical Times* 135 no. 1811 (January): 9-14.

Texier, Marc. 1977. *Manifeste de musique architecturale. Pour une ecriture spatiale et atemporelle de la musique*. Boulogne: Editions du GMA.

Toole, Floyd E. and Sean E. Olive. 1988. "The modification of timbre by resonances: perception and measurement." *Journal of the Audio Engineering Society* 36 no. 3 (March): 122-142.

Ueda, K. and K. Ohgushi. 1987. "Perceptual components of pitch: spatial representation using a multidimensional scaling technique." *Journal of the Acoustical Society of America* 82, no. 4: 1193-1200.

Vande Gorne, Annette. 1988. "Espace/Temps: Historique," in *L'Espace du Son II*. Ed. Francis Dhomont. Special issue of *Lien. Revue d'Esthétique Musicale*. Ohain, Belgium: Musiques et Recherches, 8-15.

_____. 1991. "Espace et structure," in *L'Espace du Son II*. Ed. Francis Dhomont. Special issue of *Lien. Revue d'Esthétique Musicale*. Ohain, Belgium: Musiques et Recherches, 125-127.

Varèse, Edgard. 1967. "The liberation of sound," ed. Chou Wen-chung, in *Contemporary composers on contemporary music,* Elliott Schwartz and Barney Childs eds. New York: Holt, Rinehart, and Winston, 1967, 195-208. The collection of lectures includes, among others: "New Instruments and New Music" Santa Fe, 1936, "Music as an Art-Science" University of Southern California, 1939, and "Spatial Music" Sarah Lawrence College, 1959. Also published in *Perspectives of New Music* 5 No. 1 (1966): 11-19 (an abridged version, without "Spatial Music").

Vandebogaerde, F. 1968. "Analyse de *Nomos Alpha* de Iannis Xenakis." *Sonda V* (April): 19-34.

Vérin, Nicolas. 1991. "*Archipelago* de Roger Reynolds." *Inharmoniques* no. 8/9: 179-206.

Vogt, Hans. 1972. *Neue Musik seit 1945.* Stuttgart: Reclam.

Vriend, Jan. 1981. "*Nomos Alpha* for violoncello solo Xenakis 1966: analysis and comments." *Interface* 10: 15-82.

Waiswisz, Michel. 1992a. "Interactive music systems," Guest Lecture at Electronic Music Studio, Faculty of Music, McGill University (3 March).

_____. 1992b. *Songs from the Hands,* interactive electroacoustic music without notation and/or recordings. Concert "Jeux de Mains." 4-5 March 1992, Maison de la Culture Frontenac, Montreal.

Walker, Alan. 1987. *Franz Liszt: the Virtuoso Years, 1811-1847.* Ithaca.

Watkins, Glenn. 1988. *Soundings. Music in the Twentieth Century.* New York: Schirmer Books.

Watanabe, Memoru. 1967. "Ongaku ni okeru kukan" ["Space in music"] in *Bigaku* 17 no. 2 (Fall): 1-13.

Wehmeyer, Grete. 1977. *Edgar Varèse.* Regensburg: Gustav Bosse Verlag.

Wellek, Albert. 1931. "Der Raum-Zeit-Kongress der Gesellschaft für Ästhetik." *Zeitschrift für Musikwissenschaft.* Leipzig.

_____. 1934/1963. "Der Raum in der Musik." Appendix to *Musikpsychologie und Musikästhetik. Grundriss der Systematischen Musikwissenschaft.* Frankfurt am Main: Akademische Verlagsgesellschaft, 1963 [1st ed. *Archiv für die Gesamte Psychologie* 91 (1934): 395-443].

Wenzel, Elisabeth M. 1992. "Localization in Virtual Acoustic Displays." *Presence* 1 no. 1: 80-107.

Wessel, David L. 1979. "Timbre space as a musical control structure." *Computer Music Journal* 3 no. 2: 45-52.

White, Eric Walter. 1979. *Stravinsky. The composer and his works*. London: Faber & Faber, 574-577.

Winckel, Fritz. 1960/1967. *Music, sound and sensation. A modern exposition.* Transl. from the German by Thomas Binkley. New York: Dover Publications, Inc, 1967. [a revised version of *Phänomene des musikalishen Hörens*, Berlin: Max Hesses Verlag, 1960].

───────. 1969. "Elektroakustische Musik--Raummusik--Kybernetische Musik," in *Beiträge*, ed. K. Roschitz. Kassel, 72-79.

───────. 1971. "Musique dans l'espace et musique spatiale sur les rapports entre la musique et l'architecture." Transl. J. Mortier. *Musique en Jeu* no. 2: 44-51.

───────. 1973. "Akustischer und visueller Raum als Mitgestalter in der experimentellen Musik" [Acoustical and visual space as components in experimental music], in *Experimentelle Musik*, ed. F. Winckel, 7-23.

───────, ed. 1955. *Klangstruktur der Musik. Neue Erkenntnisse Musik-elektronischer Forschung*. Berlin: Verlag für Radio-Foto-Kinotechnik.

───────, ed. 1970. *Experimentelle Musik: Raum Musik, visuelle Musik, Medien Musik, Wort Musik, elektronik Musik, Computer Musik*. [Internationale Woche für Experimentelle Musik, Berlin 1968] Berlin: Mann.

Wörner, Karl H. 1963/1973. *Stockhausen: Life and work*. Transl. from the German by Bill Hopkins. Berkeley: University of California Press. ["Karlheinz Stockhausen. Werk und Wollen," in *Kontrapunkte* No. 6. Rodenkirchen/Rhein: P. J. Tonger Musikverlag, 1963].

Wright, James, K. and Bregman, Albert, S. 1987. "Auditory stream segregation and the control of dissonance in polyphonic music," in *Music and psychology: a mutual regard*, ed. Stephen McAdams. *Contemporary Music Review* 2, part 1. London, Paris: Harwood Academic Publishers, 63-92.

Wyttenbach, Jürg. 1986. "Serenaden in Luftschlössern," in *Musik und Raum. Eine Sammlung von Beiträgen aus historischer und künstlerischer Sicht zur Bedeutung des Begriffes <Raum> als Klangträger für die Musik*, ed. Thüring Bräm. Basel: GS Verlag, 99-106.

Xenakis, Iannis. 1956. "Wahrscheinlichkeitstheorie und Musik." *Gravesaner Blätter* no. 6: 28-34.

_____. 1958. "Architecture", in *Le Poème électronique Le Corbusier*, ed. Jean Petit. Paris: Editions de Minuit.

_____. 1967a. *Pithoprakta* for orchestra (composed in 1955-56). London, Paris: Boosey and Hawkes.

_____. 1967b. *Eonta* for 2 trumpets, 3 trombones and piano (composed in 1963-64). London: Boosey and Hawkes.

_____. 1968. *Nomos Gamma* for 98 musicians scattered among the audience (composed in 1967-68). Paris: Editions Salabert.

_____. [1969?]. Sketches for *Pithoprakta* and other works, reproduced in liner notes for a set of recordings 5 LPs, Xenakis, ERATO STU 70526-70530, n.d.

_____. 1969. *Terretektorh* for a large orchestra of 88 musicians scattered among the audience (composed in 1965-66). Paris: Editions Salabert.

_____. 1970. *Persephassa* pour six percussionistes (composed in 1969). Paris: Editions Salabert.

_____. [n.d.]. "Persephassa"--Liner notes from LP recording, Les Percussions de Strasbourg Pilips PG 310, Stereo 6718040.

_____. 1963/1971. *Formalized music. Thought and mathematics in composition*. Bloomington and London: Indiana University Press, 1971. [Chapters I-VI appeared in French as *Musiques Formelles*. Paris: Editions Richard Masse, 1963].

_____. 1987. *Alax* pour trois ensembles identiques d'instruments (composed in 1985). Paris: Editions Salabert.

_____. 1991. *Formalized music. Thought and mathematics in composition*. Revised and enlarged edition. Stuyvesant, New York: Pendragon Press.

———. 1992. *Music, space and spatialization: Iannis Xenakis in conversation with Maria Anna Harley.* Paris, 25 May 1992, transcribed from a tape recording, selected and edited by Maria Anna Harley; unpublished typescript. French transl. by Marc Hyland forthcoming in *Circuit. Revue Nord-Americaine de Musique du XXe Siècle*, special issue about Iannis Xenakis, 1994.

Yost, William, A. and George Gourevitch, eds. 1987. *Directional Hearing.* New York, Berlin: Springer Verlag.

Zuckerkandl, Victor. 1956. *Sound and symbol: Music and the external world.* Transl. from the German by W. R. Trask. New York: Pantheon Books.

Zielinski, Tadeusz. 1985. *O twórczosci Kazimierza Serockiego.* Kraków: PWM Editions.

Zipp, F. 1985. *Vom Urklang zur Weltharmonie: Werden und Wirken der Idee der Sphaerenmusik.* Kassel: Mersburger.

www.ingramcontent.com/pod-product-compliance
Lightning Source LLC
Chambersburg PA
CBHW080721300426
44114CB00019B/2448